Discovery and Commitment

A Guide for College Writers

Leonard J. Rosen

Harvard University
Expository Writing Program

Allyn and Bacon

Boston   London   Toronto   Sydney   Tokyo   Singapore

Vice President, Humanities: Joseph Opiela
Developmental Editor: Allen Workman
Marketing Manager: Lisa Kimball
Production Administrator: Susan McIntyre
Copyeditor: Kathy Smith
Editorial-Production Service: Ruttle, Shaw, & Wetherill, Inc.
Text Designer: Deborah Schneck
Cover Administrator: Linda Knowles
Cover Designer: Susan Paradise
Composition Buyer: Linda Cox
Manufacturing Buyer: Louise Richardson

 Allyn & Bacon
A Simon & Schuster Company
Needham Heights, Mass. 02194

Library of Congress Cataloging-in-Publication Data
Rosen, Leonard J.
    Discovery and commitment : a guide for college writers / Leonard
J. Rosen.
       p.   cm.
    Includes bibliographical references and index.
    ISBN 0-205-14249-4
    1. English language—Rhetoric. 2. English language—Grammar—
Handbooks, manuals, etc. 3. College readers. I. Title.
PE1408.R678   1995
808'.042—dc20   94-39162
                                       CIP

Printed in the United States of America
10 9 8 7 6 5 4 3 2 1   99 98 97 96 95 94

Overview of Contents

Contents

Preface

Discovery and Commitment: A Guide for College Writers is a rhetoric intended for first- and second-semester composition courses. Two principles distinguish this text from the many rhetorics currently available: first, that good writing, produced by students or by professionals, is nearly always motivated by a personal commitment to an essay's idea; and second, that writing at the college level nearly always involves the use of source materials. I did not presume to write a new book without first searching for an existing one that satisfied my teaching needs. Specifically, I looked for a rhetoric that did not drive a wedge between a student's personal interests and experience and topics suitable for academic writing. As it happened, I did not find such a book.

In Search of Motivated College Writing

Like so many of my colleagues, I have struggled over the years with too many flat, uninteresting essays, and I have been buoyed by (admittedly fewer) essays in which the real voice of a real person emerges and works hard to communicate something important. I learn from virtually every essay I read; but I *enjoy* reading the essays of those who clearly care about their own work and who want me and others to care. These are the writers hungry to learn and use time-tested rhetorical strategies, including the judicious use of sources. Because I assume that all students have their interests and loyalties, and because I assume that the best writing is motivated by the personal, I put two questions to myself continually: How can I change my practice to better help students discover in themselves and in their materials a personal link to the writing task at hand? How can I then help students broker this discovery into the commitment needed to sustain them from an essay's conception, through the messy process of drafting and revision, and forward to a finished product?

Answers for me come slowly, for I am always testing and adjusting through practice in the classroom. Over the years, I have designed and redesigned individual assignments and whole courses; hatched and tinkered with strategies that prompt ownership of ideas; juxtaposed readings to highlight shadings of difference; read the work of and conversed with colleagues; and discussed with students, particularly those who have produced both flat and committed essays in the same semester, what motivates them to write. *Discovery and Commitment* is the product of this work, of two decades of thinking about how to help students find ideas worth writing about both in their own experience and in their course-related reading.

This Book's Organization and Features

The text opens with an exercise/introduction intended to make a point: A writer's job is to discover a personally meaningful or useful idea and then to make it public. To have an idea is *not* to have an essay, however. The move from personal to public is a move from monologue to discussion, in some respects a move from solipsism to a recognition that others, who may hold different ideas, exist and must be addressed. The brute fact that there *is* an audience out there changes everything for a writer; still, insights for an essay begin with the individual. A bridge must be built from the personal to the public, from writer to audience. This tension between the private and public is the springboard from which I develop materials in the first two parts of the book. The language introduced in Part I is used throughout Part II, where students will find twelve source-based "Occasions for Discussion and Writing."

Part I of *Discovery and Commitment* follows directly from the principles laid out in the opening exercise. Students are shown a process of writing, and are shown what an idea is (my students, anyway, have never been quite sure what an idea looks like in the context of college-level writing). Then they are shown techniques for discovering ideas in their own experience and in their course materials. Finally, they are shown techniques for taking personal ideas and making them public.

The Personal *with* the Academic in College Writing

Chapter 1 is devoted to discovery. I urge students *not* to separate the personal from the academic, as so many guides to writing seem to do, but rather to infuse the personal *with* the academic, *with* course materials, so that a strong commitment to writing may arise. In chapter 2, students learn how to gauge and control the level of their commitment to an idea by writing and rigorously examining a working thesis. A passage from Justice Holmes provides a playful but powerful metaphor for thinking of writers as having a one-, two-, or three-story commitment to an essay. Chapter 3 is devoted to strategies for creating *in* an essay the points of reference, or common ground, necessary to ensure a reader's full understanding. Anticipating what readers know and need to know is the first step writers take in making their ideas public. Chapter 4 presents specific strategies for incorporating source materials in an essay through "cycles of development." The chapter introduces the idea of synthesis and provides a technique for "quizzing" a working thesis in order to project the structure of an essay. Chapter 5 presents techniques for reading to understand and evaluate and for preparing two related forms of writing, summary and critique, that students will draw on repeatedly in their college careers.

Throughout Part I, students have ample opportunity to practice the strategies discussed by working through numerous exercises in each chapter. One of the threads binding these chapters is the recurring example of a single student essay: "Technology, History, and Jazz" appears in its entirety in the book's "Opening Exercise"; parts reappear, with the author's commentary, in the final section of chapters 1–5, "A Student Writer at Work."

Part II of the text consists of six chapters that introduce students to the most common occasions for writing at the college level: the familiar essay (chapter 6) and essays of explanation (chapter 7), analysis (chapter 8), problem/solution (chapter 9), literary interpretation (chapter 10), and argument (chapter 11). Each chapter takes the following form:

- Definitions and examples, with questions for critical thinking.
- Structures and strategies—advice on the processes of writing in each form.
- Occasions for Discussion and Writing—assignment occasions, with source readings to spark ideas on two related topics.

Writing Occasions That Spring from Evidence and Reading

The example essays in "Definitions and Examples" are followed with questions to prompt student thinking about the ideas and structure of the piece. Two example essays are accompanied by "Commitment Statements" from the authors, discussing the personal motivations underlying their writing of a public document.

"Structures and Strategies" uses the language and the concepts from Part I to present how writers discover ideas for and then construct a particular form of writing. The Part II chapters present *particular* strategies—a fine tuning of the broader principles introduced in Part I—for each form of writing. Throughout, explanations are grounded in examples, usually from the example essays that open each chapter.

Each chapter in Part II concludes with a pair of casebooks to provide "Occasions for Writing." The first of these is suitable for discussion and the second, longer one provides a good occasion for writing. Each gathers source materials on a tightly defined topic—for instance, student dress codes or the race riots at Crown Heights. These readings provide the occasion for discussion and writing, just as readings typically do for students in their courses beyond the composition classroom. *Discovery and Commitment* is the only comprehensive rhetoric that prepares students for writing beyond freshman composition by asking them to write essays that spring from evidence found in written materials.

Instructional Flexibility in Parts III, IV, and V

A major goal for this text is to offer flexible approaches to the teaching of writing. After introducing the process of discovery and development of ideas in Part I, instructors can choose to direct students toward "Writing Occasions" to develop ideas and assignments from readings in Part II, or they can show students how the discovery processes are integrated with the other recursive aspects of the writing and rewriting process, as demonstrated in Part III. The three chapters in Part III cover specific elements of the writing process that grow out of the processes shown in Part I. Chapter 12 covers "Drafting, Paragraph Development, and Early Revision"; chapter 13 demonstrates "Rewriting, Paragraph Structure, and Final Revision"; chapter 14 gives guidance on collaborative efforts in "Writing and Rewriting in Groups."

Part IV offers an extension of the process of advancing writing ideas with sources; its four chapters present extensive material on the research process and documentation, using detailed models to demonstrate what students need to launch their own independent research projects. Part V provides guidance on specialized strategies, with unique support in chapter 19 for writing and rewriting with a computer, often as part of a collaborative effort. Chapter 20 gives concrete help for writers taking essay exams or writing under pressure.

Handbook

Part VI provides a brief handbook of grammar and usage with several distinctive features: a "spotlight" guide for troubleshooting common errors, a reference guide for standard topics of usage and style, and a special reference for students needing help with ESL topics, as well as a glossary of usage.

The Instructor's Resource Manual

Each section, assignment, and reading selection in *Discovery and Commitment* is closely supported with instructional background material in *The Instructor's Resource Manual*, a 350-page teaching companion to the text compiled by Deanne Harper of Northeastern University and myself. Here instructors will find chapter overviews, question and exercise discussions, and extensive suggestions to amplify discussion and writing assignments. The Manual offers a wide range of short writing or critical thinking exercises and activities for students to work on individually, in small groups, or in combination. Assignment suggestions present varied opportunites to write—for background to writing, for critical thinking or note taking about evidence, for clarifying writing ideas, or for drafts and revisions of sections or essays. Numerous cross-references among different parts of the book show a wealth of options and potential connections between rhetorical elements as well as between themes or issues raised in the readings.

My Commitment to This Book

I have written this text to help students produce the sort of writing that engages a reader's interest. Before readers—outside of college or inside, across disciplines—can make their own commitment to a piece, they need to see the writer make a commitment. And they need to see a recognition on the writer's part that his or her own ideas exist in relationship with those of others. They also need to see that sophisticated writing acknowledges and makes productive use of others' ideas. Whatever the merits of the many rhetorics I examined, I did not find any that placed at the center of every writing occasion the robust combination of strategies for discovery, commitment, and use of sources that has so enlivened my students' writing. The pedagogical initiatives I have developed and presented in this text have worked in my classroom and in others. My earnest intention is that they will work for you in yours.

Discovery and Commitment is a book in process. After twenty years in the profession, I have presumed to take a snapshot of one stage in my evolution as a teacher and writer and to present my thinking. Preparing a comprehensive guide to college writing has been a daunting and humbling experience; and while I am confident that the ideas and strategies presented here will prove useful, I am certain that they are evolving still through my own classroom practice and through contacts I continue to make with interested colleagues across the country. Write with your comments and suggestions, and pass along student essays sparked by any of the materials in the pages that follow. I invite and welcome your contributions.

Acknowledgments

My thanks go to two colleagues who contributed directly, and to one who contributed indirectly, to the preparation of this text. Derek Owens, formerly of the Expository Writing Program at Harvard and now of St. John's University, wrote chapter 19 on working with computers and chapter 14 on writing collaboratively. Deanne Harper of Northeastern University wrote a fine and useful Instructor's Resource Manual, which I will refer to often when teaching from this text. Larry Behrens' influence has been everywhere felt in my work. Our fruitful and most happy collaboration has lasted since I was his student in graduate school a dozen years ago. While *Discovery and Commitment* is a solo effort, Larry's insistence on pedagogical rigor and his view that college-level writing is based on reading are steady presences in this book—or at least I have attempted to make them so. To Larry Behrens of the University of California, Santa Barbara, I owe a continuing debt of thanks.

During my own writing process I have had the benefit of constructive comments in each of my drafts from many forthright reviewers, whose directness I particularly value. Thanks to each of the following: Bruce Appleby, Southern Illinois University–Carbondale; Richard Batteiger, Oklahoma State University; Kathleen Bell, University of Central Florida; Kathleen Shine Cain, Merrimack College; Peter Carino, Indiana State University; Carol K. Cyganowski, DePaul University; Carol David, Iowa State University; Irene Gale, University of South Florida; Christopher

Gould, University of North Carolina–Wilmington; Douglas Hesse, Illinois State University; Eric Hibbison, J. Sargeant Reynolds Community College; Christine Hult, Utah State University; Maurice Hunt, Baylor University; David Joliffe, University of Illinois, Chicago; William Lalicker, Murray State University; Elizabeth Larson, West Chester State College; Twyla Yates Papay, Rollins College; James Porter, Purdue University; Joseph Powell, Central Washington University; Duane Roen, Syracuse University; Lucy Shultz, University of Cincinnati; Irwin Weiser, Purdue University; Michael Williamson, Indiana University of Pennsylvania; Randy Woodland, University of Michigan–Dearborn; and Richard Zbaracki, Iowa State University.

My thanks also go to many people without whose help I could not have written *Discovery and Commitment*. Joe Opiela, Vice President and Editor-in-Chief, Humanities, at Allyn and Bacon, has been a loyal advocate through the years. His early interest in and commitment to the project helped sustain me through the long months of writing. Allen Workman once again demonstrated why he is of the elite among development editors. He always pushed me for clarity and, during the writing of this text, proved himself a teacher's teacher with his patience, skepticism, and support. Seminal help in bringing coherence to the project came from participants in a workshop at the 1994 meeting of the Southeastern Conference on English in the Two-Year Colleges. In the final stages of my writing, copy editor Kathy Smith peppered me with many helpful queries.

Books made by Allyn and Bacon are always gorgeous, and for this book's design and its coherent implementation I have to thank designer Deborah Schneck and production editor Susan McIntyre. I also thank cover coordinator Linda Dickinson, and the management team in Production, Elaine Ober and Judy Fiske. For publishing support I thank Bill Barke, President of Allyn and Bacon, and Sandi Kirshner, Vice President for Marketing, as well as John Gilman, Vice President for Sales and an unstinting supporter of my work. For marketing support I thank Lisa Kimball, Marketing Manager, and Doug Day, Marketing Specialist in English.

Final words of appreciation and dedication are reserved for Linda Rosen and for our sons, Jonathan and Matthew. My work all these years has been about helping writers to make meaning and to speak with conviction about things that matter. For me what matters most is the love of family, from whom my blessings flow.

Leonard Rosen
September 12, 1994

Credits

Preparations for Thinking, Reading, and Writing

Opening Exercise

Making Your Personal Idea Public

So much about writing *can* be taught: strategies for convincing readers, techniques for crafting effective sentences, tips for correcting grammar and punctuation, and more. Yet what is most important about the writing of an essay is impossible to teach: caring about your own idea. Real interest in an essay topic *must* come from you, the writer. When this happens, a reason for writing is born and an essay can take shape. This book has two goals: first, to present you with numerous occasions for writing—for having and expressing ideas; and second, to help you move from personal statements of ideas to *public* statements—to essays.

Here is a personal statement by a student writer, Mike Bergom, explaining his interest in "The Technology of Jazz," an essay he wrote for his composition course.

> Jazz has always been an intense interest of mine. I play the saxophone, I'm in a band, I talk jazz with friends, and I read articles about jazz constantly. When I began reading about the influence of technology in my expository writing class, many questions related to jazz music came to mind. Several jazz publications told of prominent young musicians who refused to use technologies like synthesizers. Why? This refusal contradicted my common-sense notion that people will accept technologies designed to help them. I was drawn to the idea that some musicians might avoid technology in order to pursue jazz in its "purer" historical (that is, acoustic) form. This was an idea I could write about and get excited about.

Mike Bergom has a clear idea in mind and a clear reason to write. But let's not fool anyone: Bergom began writing because his composition teacher handed him an assignment. He had an obligation to submit something—but notice that his topic was of great personal interest. And this is the key: if you are going to write, find a topic that matters to you. Everything else about producing an essay can be taught, and your teacher will work closely with you to transform your private ideas into public statements. Your job is to have an idea. If your ideas excite you, the chances are good that essays built on them will excite readers.

Still, an exciting idea—no matter how firmly you believe in it and no matter how crucial it is to the outcome of an essay—is *not* itself an essay. Mike Bergom could not have submitted the preceding paragraph to his teacher and called it a finished product. Why not? Why is the naked statement of an idea *not* an essay? Consider this question as you read the document that Bergom actually submitted.

STUDENT PAPER

Technology, Jazz, and History
Mike Bergom

Dixieland, the Swing Era, Bebop, Cool Jazz—these are some of the 1 many stages that define the jazz music of different times. Jazz continues to progress even to this day. What started as a simple drum rhythm in the heart of Africa has exploded into thousands of performers in nightclubs playing thousands of melodies. Jazz evolves with us and is a reflection of the world we live in—which, increasingly, is a technological world.

Machines today are being integrated with all aspects of life, music 2 included. For instance, we have seen the development of the synthesizer, the electric bass, and the electronic wind instrument (a flute-like instrument connected to a computer). These new instruments have slowly begun to infiltrate jazz clubs around the world. Recording techniques have also progressed to technologies such as multitrack digital recording and digital tone modulation and amplification. Jazz has definitely not gone untouched by the pervasive force of technology.

And yet several young jazz musicians are saying "No!" to technology 3 and are pursuing, with acoustic instruments, what might be called the "roots" of jazz. Trumpeter and jazz historian Wynton Marsalis, saxophonist and former *Tonight Show* band leader Branford Marsalis, and acoustic guitarist Mark Whitfield—these musicians, all under 35 years old, refuse to use the latest technologies in their music. They instead employ traditional instrumentation and jazz formats. On the face of it, this rejection is odd: as a culture, we are quick to demand and accept new technologies. We scramble for faster computers, we insist on cars with dual airbags, we debate which electric toothbrush will keep our smiles brightest. Why, then, do these young musicians, who have grown up in a technological age, refuse what has been designed to help them?

One way to get at an answer is to examine the career of a musician 4 who *did* embrace technology, Miles Davis. A jazz trumpeter since the 1940s, Davis was a guiding light for jazz musicians for many years. From the 1940s to the 1970s, he single-handedly changed the direction of jazz several times with recordings such as "Kind of Blue" and "Birth of the Cool." Davis helped jazz music to evolve, but one of his experiments proved too radical: when he began using electric instruments, he was accused of turning his back on a history he had helped to create. His playing ability was not at question—that had been established in his many years of performance. The issue was his reliance on technology and his apparent rejection of the acoustic tradition.

Tradition is a fundamentally important element—a defining element—of jazz, and the jazz community was willing to follow Davis wherever he ventured, as long as he remained true to the music's acoustic roots. Davis believed that new electric instruments should be incorporated into jazz, but many of his fellow artists refused to follow his lead. A historian, Melvin Kranzberg, helps us understand why. Kranzberg is a specialist on the role of technology in society and claims that "[a]lthough technology might be a prime element in many public issues, nontechnical factors take precedence in technology-policy decisions" (249). Stated another way, a new technology's existence does not guarantee its use or value. Other factors such as emotional or artistic response and resistance to change will decide how extensively the technology is used. 5

History proves Kranzberg's point. In early nineteenth century England, cloth makers were being displaced by machines that outperformed them. These workers, known as Luddites, rose up and destroyed the frames (the new machines) that had caused their unemployment. The Luddites destroyed frames not only because of their displacement but also because they judged the quality of the goods produced by these machines to be inferior. A contemporary newspaper made the point this way: 6

> The machines . . . are not broken for being upon any new construction . . . but in consequence of goods being wrought upon them which are of little worth, are deceptive to the eye, are disreputable to the trade, and therefore pregnant with the seeds of its destruction. (qtd. in Thompson 532)

The Luddites did not embrace a technology merely because it existed. They could not agree that so-called "improvements in mechanism" (qtd. in Peel 71) led to improvements in product. The cloth produced by the new weaving machines was judged according to ancient standards of the weaver's craft and found to have "little worth." Nontechnical factors, in this case artistic ones, contributed to the Luddites' rejection of technology. 7

Today, several influential jazz musicians have applied the standards of their craft to electronically boosted music and have reached a similar conclusion: the product has little worth. Beyond question, recent "improvements in mechanism" have provided many benefits for the aspiring musician. Synthesizers create totally unique new sounds. Improved recording techniques open a new world of special effects. Computers print, transpose, and perform music with the touch of a button. Yet there are jazz purists who regard the new technology, in effect, as a frame to be smashed. This was largely the reaction that many had to the electronic experiments of Miles Davis. 8

Branford Marsalis redesigned the *Tonight Show* band, creating a traditional jazz format of acoustical instruments. When asked about this transformation, he said, "I was interested in doing what we did—having people remember us for being musicians. Not for the last joke or the flashy suit" (qtd. in Heckman 25). Marsalis believes technology is a musical gim- 9 mick—a diversion from the essence of jazz. He feels technology has not only *not* added anything worthwhile to jazz music but has actually obscured its roots. For Marsalis, the mere existence of technologically advanced instruments has in no way guaranteed their use and value.

Marsalis's brother, Wynton, takes a stronger stand against technology   10
in jazz. Wynton Marsalis is a jazz educator, performer, and clinician who travels the world promoting jazz. He regards jazz as a history of performance, not just an art form played in clubs around the country every night. Any intrusion on the history is an intrusion on jazz music. Technology, he contends, attempts to change a history that has existed for over a hundred years. Again, we see Kranzberg's "nontechnical factors" influencing people's decisions on whether to accept or reject a technology. Guitarist Mark Whitfield provides a final example. Whitfield started in the jazz idiom as an electric guitarist but switched to the acoustic guitar after he gained popularity. Whitfield gives many reasons for the change—one being the acoustic guitar's relatively long history, dating back to pre-World War I Dixieland bands. The electric guitar, a latecomer, was introduced in the 1950s.

For these three young musicians—Branford Marsalis, Wynton Mar-   11
salis, and Mark Whitfield—nontechnical factors have prevented the acceptance of emerging technologies. For them, as for the Luddites, improvements in mechanism have not translated into artistically improved products. This is not to say that electronic instruments do not have a place. They obviously do in *many* kinds of contemporary music, but not in jazz according to the purists. Technology may one day find a place in jazz history, as jazz evolves to accommodate new inventions and discoveries. No technology can be uninvented, and synthesizers are here to stay. Eventually, jazz musicians may turn to these new technologies, but then again they may not: in the world of jazz, history and the beauty of acoustic instrumentation matter deeply, and technology may continue to be resisted.

Of this much we can be sure: if the Marsalis brothers and others ever   12
do incorporate the new technologies into their music, they will do so on their own terms, working *with* history—not against it.

Works Cited

Heckman, Don. "To Live and Play in L.A." *Jazz Times.* June 1993: 25.

Kranzberg, Melvin. "One Last Word—Technology and History: 'Kranzberg's Laws.' " *Technology and Culture.* July 1986: 544–560.

Peel, Frank. *The Rising of the Luddites.* 4th ed. n.p.: Frank Cass, 1968.

Thompson, E. P. *The Making of the English Working Class.* London: Victor Gollancz, Ltd., 1965.

Discussion   What qualities distinguish this essay from Mike Bergom's earlier personal statement on page 2? Perhaps the key point to consider is Bergom's awareness of an audience for his essay. Bergom realizes that people who know little about jazz may be reading his work, and he is careful to help readers follow him. First, he sets a context, giving background information so that readers can understand a discussion of jazz musicians who have rejected technology. Bergom also provides a structure: the essay has a beginning, middle, and end that help readers follow the point he is making. And he uses source materials to help make his point. Bergom does none of this in his personal statement, which is *not* an essay but more of a review of his intentions at the beginning of the writing process.

That process led eventually to the finished product you have just read. Bergom needed a first draft and several revisions before he fully discovered and expressed his idea. Revision, in fact, helped him to understand his own thinking about jazz and technology. As you will see when reading portions of his rough drafts in chapters 2 through 5 (see the end of each chapter, "A Student Writer at Work"), Bergom began the process of writing with no more than a hunch about the reasons certain musicians avoided synthesizers. In the beginning, his writing was quite rough, but by the time he finished his final draft, he was sure of both his idea and the quality of his writing. Mike Bergom had a reason to revise: he had something to learn and something to say about what he had learned, and he wanted to say it well.

Exercise

1. What is the central idea of this essay?
2. How can you tell that Mike Bergom cares about his idea? In answering, refer to specific lines in the essay.
3. Reread Mike Bergom's personal statement (see page 2). Why is this statement *not* an essay?
4. In what ways are the personal statement and the essay closely related? In what ways do they differ?

1

Discovering Ideas

The best writing in any discipline often springs from a writer's desire to communicate a *personally* important idea. Committed writers motivate themselves to work through the writing and revising process until they have made their ideas accessible to others. Your goal should be to find this commitment and give your essays the spark of personal insight that only you can provide.

Personal motivation for writing can be as valuable for your professors when they write as it can be for you. Recently two researchers at the University of California, Santa Barbara—Judith Kirscht and John Reiff, of the Writing Program—interviewed some of their colleagues from other disciplines to learn what motivates them as researchers and as writers. For example, they asked Diane Mackie, a professor of psychology, about how her research projects begin. Professor Mackie replied:

> I guess most of the ideas really come out of interacting with other people. When colleagues are talking, or when you're talking with students about something, and somebody just says, "I don't follow how these people came to that conclusion," or "Didn't somebody do something else that was inconsistent with that?" And we're sitting there thinking . . . yes that seems inconsistent and . . . what could we do to see which one is right, or which one is wrong . . . or is one right under different circumstances? And it seems to me that's where the majority of our ideas come from.

Kirscht and Reiff interviewed other professors who spoke about levels of personal commitment to their work. Julia C. Allen, who has published extensively in the field of geography and environmental studies, spoke of how she grew interested in the subject of forest management. On a trip to Tanzania, she was "so struck by the deforestation in the country that [she] decided . . . to do a Ph.D. . . . on the problem of managing forests and the environmental effects of that process." In an interview, Professor "R," an historian, explained his personal commitment to research projects this way:

> Basically, I think I've always chosen research topics that respond to something I personally am looking for. I've always tried to construct a coherent, philosophical world view for myself, and I'm always interested in topics that help me better understand basic questions I'm asking.

The common thread among these writers is the deep personal interest they take in their work. That interest may be sparked by talking with friends, by traveling (near or far) and observing conditions in the world, by reflecting on personal experience, and by reading. Whatever the spark, the result is the same: an idea worth committing oneself to and worth, eventually, a reader's attention. In this chapter you will find advice on generating ideas both on the basis of your personal experience and on the basis of what you read. The approaches are complementary, though they need not occur together.

Discover Ideas by Reflecting on Your Experience

Personal Reflection and the Writing Occasion

Personal experience can give you much to think about, including questions that can provide a powerful, motivating force for your writing. You will seldom be invited to "choose any topic at all" and roam freely through your experience in preparing for an essay. More likely, your occasions for writing will narrow possible topics for you. This is just as well, for narrowing your focus gives you specific topics to think about and actually helps you to generate ideas. For instance, if you were writing an opinion piece for your former high-school newspaper on the wisdom of instituting a dress code, you could begin to reflect on personal experiences in particular ways. Your initial focus would be narrowed considerably.

If you were writing because your sociology professor had given you an assignment to explain why so many youths turn to violence, your occasion for writing would prompt you to reflect on very different personal experiences. Everything about these two occasions for writing would differ: your topic, your readers, your likely purpose, and your experience. Yet for both occasions you would do well to begin thinking about your topic in very personal terms, by asking these questions:

- How have I (or has someone I know) addressed this or a similar issue?
- What do *I* know that could help me to write?

Pose these questions once you have a particular occasion to write. And then reflect on your experience, searching for a personal connection to your general topic. Your goal at this stage is to find in your experience a solid motivation to begin the writing process. Much later, after you have pursued various discovery strategies and, perhaps, have done research on your topic, you will generate and commit yourself to a *specific* idea that can launch an essay.

Six strategies for prompting you to reflect on your experience follow. These strategies mark a beginning to the writing process, and at this very early stage your goal should be to *discover* what is of particular interest about your topic. No one method of discovery will prompt satisfying results for all topics. Some methods may not suit your style of discovery, and some will work well when combined. If one method seems unproductive, move quickly to another.

Following a general discussion of each strategy, the work of a single student will be presented that illustrates how the strategy might be used. Jim Walker's occasion for writing was the one described earlier: to explain (for his sociology course) the reasons many youths turn to violence.

Brainstorming

The object of **brainstorming** is to write quickly and, once finished, to return to your work with a critical eye. Place your topic at the top of a page, and then list any related phrase or word that comes to mind. Set a time limit of five or ten minutes, and list items as quickly as you can. All items are legitimate for your list, since even an allegedly bad idea can spark a good one. To brainstorm in a small group, a technique that allows the ideas of one person to build on those of another, write your topic on a board or sheet of easel paper. Sit in a circle and ask each member of the group to offer two or three words or phrases for your list. Work about the circle a second time, asking each member to add another one or two ideas, based on an item already mentioned. Finally, open the floor to anyone who can add more ideas. As a ground rule, urge each group member to understand that all ideas are equally useful.

After you have generated your list, group related items and set aside items that do not fit into a grouping. Groupings with the greatest number of items indicate areas that should prove fertile in developing your essay.

Jim Walker divided his topic into two parts and brainstormed separately about each part (school violence and street violence). The illustration shows one part—school violence—being explored.

Illustration: Jim Walker's Paper
Brainstorming

School Violence: My Experience
anger—using weapons is lethal
fear—anybody can get hurt
respect—earned by being tough, without fear
disrespect—paybacks for getting "dissed"
rumors—real and imagined weapons, fights
safety—weapons for self-defense, power, equalizer

(Brainstorming continued)

weapons—guns, knives, X-Acto knives, boxcutters, screwdrivers
violence—TV version, somebody getting blown away, popped, smoked
violence—reality, Emergency Room, medical bills, legal problems
lost generation—no hope for the future
peer mediation—talking through differences

My Experience

Negatives	*Positives*
rumors	respect
safety ≠ weapons	peer mediation
weapons	anger: at weapons
disrespect	violence: realizing reality
anger = payback	
media violence	
lost generation	

Freewriting and Focused Freewriting

Freewriting is a technique to try when you are asked to write but have no topic. Think for a moment about the subject area in which you have been asked to write. Recall lectures or chapters read in textbooks. Choose a broad area of interest and then start writing for some predetermined amount of time—say, five or ten minutes. Alternately, you can write until you have filled a certain number of pages (typically one or two). As you write, do not stop to puzzle over a word choice or punctuation. Do not stop to cross words out because they do not capture your meaning. Push on to the next sentence. Freely change thoughts from one sentence to the next, if this is where your thinking takes you. Once you have reached your time limit or page allotment, read over what you have done. Circle ideas that lend themselves to possible paper topics. To generate ideas about these specific topics, you may then try a more focused strategy for invention: brainstorming, focused freewriting, or any of the other strategies that will be discussed in this section.

Focused freewriting gives you the benefits of freewriting, but on a *specific* topic. The end result of this strategy is the same as brainstorming, and so the choice of invention strategies is one of style: do you prefer making lists or writing sentences? Begin with a definite topic. Write for five or ten minutes; reread your work; and circle any words, phrases, or sentences that look potentially useful. Draw lines that link circled words, and make notes to explain the linkage. Then clarify these linkages on a separate sheet of paper. The result will be a grouping of items, some in sentence form, that looks a great deal like the result of brainstorming. Save your work for the next step in the planning process: selecting, organizing, and expanding information.

Following is a portion of Walker's focused freewrite around the second part of his topic: street violence.

Illustration: Jim Walker's Paper
Focused Freewriting

Not just gangbangers or drug dealers but a lot more. Kids have access to weapons and more of them are bringing them to school. The streets are still more dangerous than schools but they would find knives, boxcutters, screwdrivers at my old high school, sometimes even a gun. Why were there so many weapons? Were they for getting a reputation? Or were they for self-defense, for survival? There were a lot of fights—mostly over someone thinking they had been disrespected or over expensive sneakers or girlfriends or boyfriends—not as much over gang rivalry or sour drug deals. That was usually kept out of the school. Fights led to more fights and that led to more anger and fear and so weapons became a natural part of the cycle of violence. Choosing to arm yourself in school could be lethal if your weapon was answered with a knife or a gun. I saw my friend get cut because he pushed too far and flashed a weapon at the wrong person.

Walker organized his freewriting into these notes:

Cycle of Violence	*Why?*
—weapons are lethal	—weapons raise the ante
—anger and fear	—reputation
—rumors	—self-defense, survival
—fights lead to more fights	—disrespect
	—payback
	—variety of reasons for fights

The "Many Parts" Strategy[1]

Another method for generating ideas about a topic is to list its parts. Number the items on your list. Then ask: "What are the uses of Number 1? Number 2? Number 3?" and so on. If *uses of* does not seem to work for the parts in question, try *consequences of:* "What are the consequences of Number 1?" The *many parts* strategy lets you be far more specific and imaginative in thinking about the topic as a whole than you might be ordinarily. Once you have responded to your questions about the uses or consequences of some part, you might pursue the one or two most promising responses in a focused freewrite.

Following is Walker's use of this strategy to explore the topic of school violence.

---

[1]This strategy is adapted from John C. Bean and John D. Ramage, *Form and Surprise in Composition: Writing and Thinking Across the Curriculum* (New York: Macmillan, 1986) 170–71.

The Many Parts Strategy

What are the parts of "school violence"?

1. weapons	7. rumors
2. fights	8. self-defense
3. fear	9. students are injured
4. anger	10. disrespect
5. settling differences	11. respect
6. arguments	12. reputation

One Part Explored

What are the uses of weapons?

—to hurt	—to feel powerful
—to intimidate	—for protection

What are the consequences of weapons?

—serious injuries	—rumors buzz the school
—arguments can become lethal	—students are afraid, angry
—medical bills	—more weapons show up, risk increases
—legal problems	

Mapping

If you enjoy thinking visually, try **mapping** your ideas. Begin by writing your topic as briefly as possible (a single word is best). Circle the topic and draw three, four, or five short spokes from the circle. At the end of each spoke place one of the journalist's questions, making a major branch off the spoke for every answer to a question. Now, working with each answer individually, pose one of the six journalist's questions once again. After you have completed the exercise, you will have a page that places ideas in relation to one another. Notice how the "map" distinguishes between major points and supporting information.

The Journalist's Questions

You have read or heard of the journalist's questions: *who, what, when, where, why,* and *how.* In answering the questions, you can define, compare, contrast, or investigate cause and effect. Again, the assumption is that by thinking about parts you will have more to write about than if you focused on a topic as a whole. The journalist's questions can help you to narrow a topic, giving you the option to concentrate, say, on any three parts of the whole: perhaps the *who, what,* and *why* of the topic. Under the topic of mapping, you will find Jim Walker's notes made in response to five of the journalist's questions.

Mapping the Journalist's Questions

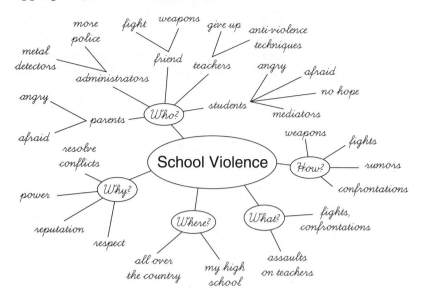

Journal Writing

You might keep a journal in conjunction with your writing course. A *journal* is a set of private, reflective notes that you keep, in which you describe your reactions to lectures, readings, discussions, films, current events—any topic touching on your course work. A journal borrows from both diary writing and course notebooks. As in a diary, your journal entries are private, reflective, and "safe" in the sense that you know no one is looking over your shoulder; thus, you are free to experiment with ideas and to express your thoughts honestly without fear of consequences. Unlike a diary, a journal focuses on matters relating to your course work and not on matters of your private life, unless such observations tie in with your course work. Journal writing gives you an opportunity to converse with yourself in your own language about what you have been studying. You pose questions, develop ideas, reflect on readings, speculate and explore, and try to pinpoint confusions. The more you write, the more you clarify what you know and, equally important, what you do not know. The language of your journal entries should reflect your voice: use the words, expressions, and rhythms of vocabulary that you use when you chat with friends. Punctuation is not important as long as you can reread your journal entries. Periodically review journal entries, looking for ideas in which you seemed particularly interested. As with freewriting, use these ideas as the basis for a more focused strategy of invention.[2]

---

[2]Discussion of journal writing here is based on Toby Fulwiler, ed., *The Journal Book* (Portsmouth, NH: Boynton/Cook-Heinemann, 1987) 1–7.

Discover Ideas by Reading Critically

If you have found that reflecting on your experience has generated strong interest in a topic, then go to the library. Pursue what fascinates you by seeking further information. Interested as he now is in his topic on youth violence, Jim Walker might want to locate source materials on what he termed "cycles" of violence. We can see an essay developing here: Walker was given an assignment concerning a specific topic; he considered this topic in light of his experience and generated what he thought was an original insight; and now he begins to read, not only because he was assigned a topic but also because he is interested for his *own* reasons. Every bit as much as the professors (pages 7–8) who began their writing projects with real intellectual commitments, Walker launches into his project with real commitment. His writing is used to illustrate the process of drafting and revising an essay in chapter 12.

In the best of cases, your reading will result from a strongly felt desire to learn and explore. In less-than-optimal cases, you will read and write only because you have been required to do so. In either event, you do well to think critically about your reading. Critical reading, quite independently from reflections on your personal experience, can help you to generate ideas for an essay and to discover a personal motivation for writing. The discussion here will provide strategies for doing both.

First, a note: your first task in critical reading is reading to understand. This (and the writing that follows from it) is so important that the topic receives special treatment in the first part of chapter 5, "Focus on Summary and Evaluation." Readers can do little with a source until they understand its content. See chapter 5 for specific advice, should you need it, on strategies for reading. For instructional purposes, four other approaches to critical reading are discussed individually. In fact, your individual responses as a reader will be rich and complex, and will not occur in the neat "layers" presented here. Still, you should find it useful to separate these layers as you remind yourself to be alert to differences, to challenge sources, to broaden contexts, and to form opinions.

Active, Critical Thinkers Are Alert to Differences and Discrepancies

As an active, critical thinker, you are alert to differences and discrepancies. Think of a difference as a disagreement between what you expect to see and what you see, or as a discrepancy between what two or more people say about a single subject, issue, or problem. You will have many occasions to notice such differences, both in college and later on. Assume that in a government class, your professor gave you this assignment: to read two newspapers daily, a local paper and a national one. If you lived in Cleveland and were working on this assignment for November 19, 1992, you might have noticed a difference or discrepancy in the way two newspapers treated a single story:

Cleveland's *Plain Dealer*

Bishops leave door open for women

Washington

Catholic bishops yesterday chose dialogue over dogma, rejecting a controversial proposal on women's roles in the church.

The National Conference of Catholic Bishops, convening here this week, failed to muster the two-thirds vote needed to adopt the proposal, which would have firmly prohibited women's ordination, as a formal church statement. Instead, members accepted the committee report for further study and discussion.

"This does as much as we can do right now," said Cardinal Joseph Bernardin, who proposed keeping the document a committee report only.

USA Today

U.S. bishops reject wider women's role

U.S. Catholic bishops voted down a long-planned policy statement on women after a fractious debate over whether women can ever be priests.

After nine years of work and four separate drafts, the pastoral letter received 137 "yes" votes, 53 short of the two-thirds needed to make it the policy of the National Conference of Catholic Bishops.

Voting no: 110 bishops.

Auxilary Bishop Austin Vaughn of New York said he considered the papal rule against ordaining women "infallible and unchangeable. Women priests are impossible as me having a baby."

Differences Lead to Questions

These articles present a difference: contrasting accounts of a national conference of Catholic bishops, called to discuss the roles of women and men in the church. Of the tens of thousands of people who glanced at both newspapers that day, how many noticed the contradictory headlines? How many noticed that two authoritative sources provided vastly different coverage of a single event? *You* would have noticed, if you had trained yourself to be alert to differences and discrepancies. And beyond noticing, you would have posed a question or two, because questions—primarily the question *why*—follow from observing such a difference. When you spot a difference, you naturally say: "What explains this?" Such a question can lead to fruitful lines of research. Here is a set of techniques for being alert to differences.

Be Alert to Differences

Before Reading:

- Skim a text and identify its topic.
- Make a note, mental or written, on what you know about the topic or what you can remember that others have written about it.

During Reading:

- Compare what the author has written with your notes.
- Identify differences.
- Complete your reading by returning to each point of difference and using it to generate questions.

After Reading:

- Option: Begin an investigation or create an action plan for doing so, guided by your questions.

Pose Questions Based on a Difference between Sources

Having read and noticed differences or discrepancies between two accounts of a single subject, issue, or problem, you are in a position to pose some questions—the answers to which could help you to understand the difference. In the case of the bishops' conference, the following questions seem useful:

- What happened at the conference?
- What were the key elements of the debate?
- What does the pastoral letter on women's roles actually say?
- Why were the bishops meeting on this issue?
- What did a "yes" or a "no" vote represent?
- How have women's groups responded to the vote?

Focused freewriting in response to any of these questions can help you generate ideas for an essay.

Pose Questions Based on a Difference between a Text and Your Experience

Not only can you pose questions on differences you've observed between two or more sources, but you can pose questions based on differences between what an author presents and what you know to be true or likely, based on your experience. Return to the bishops' conference: perhaps on reading one of these articles you noticed a difference between what the Catholic bishops had decided concerning women in the priesthood and what you knew about the gender of priests in other denominations. Perhaps you knew that in the Jewish religion there are women rabbis and that, only one week before the bishops' conference and after a heated debate, the Anglican church voted to ordain women as priests. Such knowledge of a difference between the views of Catholics and the views of some Jews and Anglicans could prompt questions such as these:

- What are the relevant differences among Anglican, Catholic, and Jewish religious traditions?
- What is the role of the priest or rabbi in these religions?
- What is the role of women and men in these religions?
- How will women priests change the Anglican church? Have they changed the Episcopal churches in America, or have women rabbis changed Jewish congregations?
- What will be the effect of men continuing to dominate the priesthood in the Catholic church?
- What were the key issues in the Catholic and Anglican debates, and how can these be compared and contrasted?

Focused freewriting in response to any of these questions can help you generate ideas for an essay.

Option: Generate an Action Plan

Questions that you pose suggest activity on your part. The preceding questions, for instance might lead to an investigation of the roles of men and women in the Catholic church and in other denominations. With a more limited focus, you might decide to learn what happened at the bishops' conference by obtaining a draft of the bishops' policy statement on the role of women. Once you notice and develop questions based on a difference, you can undertake a research project. Indeed, in many disciplines, researchers begin their investigations by noticing a difference and speculating on causes. Of course, not every question you pose will lead to full-blown research. Be aware, though, that your questions can direct you to further work.

Active, Critical Thinkers Challenge, and Are Challenged by, Sources

Spotting a difference or discrepancy based on your reading gives you an entrance into a source. The word *entrance* suggests that reading selections and buildings share a certain quality: both have interiors. To know what's inside a building you open the door and step inside. What are the "doors" to a text? *Questions.* When carefully posed, questions can lead you deep into a reading selection. The more questions you ask and the more times you turn to the text (or to others) seeking answers, the deeper and more informed your reading will be.

Asking Questions of the Text

Every reading invites specific questions, but the following basic questions can get you started in your effort to read any text critically:

- What central problem, issue, or subject does the text explore? What are the reasons for this problem? What are the effects of this problem?
- What is the most important, or the most striking, statement the author makes? Why is it important or striking?
- Who is the author, and what are the author's credentials for writing on this topic? What is the author's stake in writing this? What does the author have to gain?
- How can I use this selection? What can I learn from it?

Focused freewriting in response to any of these questions can help you generate ideas for an essay.

Illustration: Responses to General Questions about the Newspaper Articles on the Bishops' Conference

Central issue: Should women be priests in the Catholic church?

Reasons for the controversy: Over the last twenty years, women have demanded more control over institutions that affect their lives. The Catholic church is one such institution. In this conference, the debate in the larger culture was brought into the Catholic church for formal consideration.

Most striking statement: No single statement stands out; however, the sharply different coverage in the two newspaper accounts is startling.

The authors' stakes: The authors' personal biases seem to have entered the news reporting; for example, the first quotations that the authors use represent very different points of view, which happen to be consistent with the tone and information of the rest of each piece—including the differing headlines.

Using the selections: These pieces suggest that further research is needed to understand what happened at the bishops' conference. A research paper on the topic could begin with the two differing accounts of what happened.

Asking Questions of Yourself, Based on the Text

A critical reading points in two directions: to the text(s) you are reading, and to *you*. The questions you ask about what you read can prompt you to investigate your experience, values, and opinions. As part of any critical reading, allow the issues that are important to the text to *challenge* you. Question yourself and respond until you know your views about a topic. Pose the following questions to yourself:

- What can I learn from this text? Will this knowledge change me?
- What is my background on this topic? How will my experience affect my reading?
- What is the origin of my views on the topic?
- What new interest, or what new question or observation, does this text spark in me?
- If I turned the topic of this selection into a question on which people voted, how would I vote—and why?

Focused freewriting in response to any of these questions can help you generate ideas for an essay.

Illustration: Responses to Personal Questions Raised by the Articles on the Bishops' Conference

My background: I'm not Catholic, so I view the debate from the outside. I'm Anglican Episcopal, and the Anglican church in England just finished a fierce debate and voted to allow women to be priests.

My vote: The debate among Catholics and Anglicans is obviously intense. As an Anglican, it's easy for me to say that I'd vote as most of the Anglicans have. But rather than vote just yet, I'd want to find out more about the disagreement among Catholics.

New interests: I want to learn more about the roles of men and women in the Jewish and Muslim religions. How do these roles compare with those of Catholics and Anglicans? Why have gender roles been assigned as they have in various religions?

Active, Critical Thinkers Set Issues in a Broader Context

To the extent that you can, identify issues and questions important to a single text and then think large: assume that every particular issue, concern, or problem that you read about exists in a larger context—in a larger cluster of related issues, concerns, or problems. (In the example that follows, you will see how the debate over women in the priesthood can be seen in the larger context of the history of debates in the Catholic church and in other organized religions.) Do not expect that this larger context will be obvious. Usually, you will have to work to discover it. Here is a set of techniques for setting issues in their broader context:

- Begin by identifying one or more issues you feel are important to a text.
- Assume that each issue is an instance, or example, of something larger. Your job is to speculate on this larger something.
- Write the name of the issue at the top of a page, or on the computer screen. Below this, write a question: "What's this a part of?" Then write a one-paragraph response.
- Reread your response, and briefly state the broader context.
- Use this broader context to stimulate more thought on the reading selection and to generate questions about the issues of interest.
- Option: Begin an investigation or create an action plan for doing so, guided by your questions (optional).

Illustration: The Debate over Women as Priests

What's This a Part of?

Following the advice given previously, you might write a paragraph that looks like this:

The debate about the role of women in the church is part of the larger debate about gender relations and power sharing in our society. The feminist revolution of the past three decades has made its way to the most conservative of our institutions: our religions. The "fractious debate" reported in *USA Today* is an instance in the Catholic church of the same debate in the larger culture: to what extent do women share power in institutions that affect their lives? This debate has probably taken place in other religious traditions as well. It is also an example of how the church responds to pressure from the outside. Over the centuries, the Catholic church has changed—but very slowly. How do social issues of the day become a subject of debate within the church? And what's the process by which the church changes as the result of such debate?

Broader context: the feminist revolution
the history of debate in the Catholic church
the roles of women and men in the Jewish, Muslim, Catholic, and Protestant traditions

In your search for broader contexts, you may find in a single text more than one key issue on which to write. In the case of the bishops' conference, at least two issues are important: the one just illustrated (the debate over the roles of men and women in organized religion) and the fact of conflicting news accounts. Both issues can be a source of questions, and both can be set in a larger context.

Option: Generate an Action Plan

Every broader context that you define gives you opportunities for generating new questions about a source and, potentially, for launching a broader-scale investigation.

Active, Critical Thinkers Will Form and Support Opinions

Know what you think about what you see and read. Have an opinion and be able to support it. Opinions generally follow from responses to questions such as these:

- Has the author explained things clearly?
- In what ways does this topic confuse me?
- Has the author convinced me of his or her main argument?
- What is my view on this topic?
- Would I recommend this source to others?

Focused freewriting in response to any of these questions can help you generate ideas for an essay. Whatever your opinion, be prepared to support it with comments that are based on details about what you have seen or read. Later, in chapter 5, you will learn techniques for reading to evaluate a source and for writing an evaluation—a type of writing in which you formally present your opinions and give reasons for holding them. It is not practical or necessary that you develop a formal response (oral or written) to every source you read. Still, as a critical and active thinker you should be able to offer reasons for believing as you do. Here's an illustration of an opinion based on the differing news accounts of the bishops' conference:

Illustration: Opinion and Support Concerning the Differing Articles on the Bishops' Conference

One or both of these authors are biased in their reporting. In support of this view, see the contrasting headlines: "Bishops leave door open for women" vs. "U.S. bishops reject wider women's roles." Here's a case of a glass being half empty or half full, depending on the point of view of the person who's making the judgment. Obviously, points of view in these two accounts differ.

You and your classmates may agree or disagree about particular ideas, as they are expressed in a source. In either case, you should be able to have an informed discussion about these ideas. For an extensive discussion on stating and supporting opinions, see chapter 11 on argumentation.

Summary

Generating ideas that are personally important is a key to effective, engaging writing. One way to generate ideas is to reflect on your experience. Once you have identified an occasion for writing and have narrowed your topic, ask: How have I addressed this or a similar issue? What do *I* know that could help me to write? Try to discover something in your experience that connects you personally with your topic. A second way to generate a topic of interest is by reading either as a follow-up to personal reflection or as a strategy in itself. You will want to read critically because critical reading helps you to pose questions, and questions, in turn, help you to generate ideas. As you read, try to remain alert to differences, to challenge an author and yourself, to broaden contexts, and to form opinions. By reading critically and reflecting on experience, you are very likely to identify at least one topic of interest that will motivate you through the writing process.

For Discussion and Writing

Exercise 1

Work with an idea suggested in this chapter. Would your former high school be doing the right thing, in your opinion, to institute a dress code? Use one or more strategies to generate ideas for this topic by reflecting on your own experience.

Exercise 2

Work with a second idea suggested in this chapter: should women be priests? Use one or more strategies to generate ideas for this topic by reflecting on your own experience. You might want to begin a focused freewrite with any of the questions on this topic that you find in the chapter.

Exercise 3

a. Every day, for a week, read two or more newspapers—your town's local paper(s) and one or more of the following: the *New York Times*, the *Wall*

Street Journal, and *USA Today.* Pay special attention to each paper's coverage of a single news event. Read the accounts and observe differences among the papers or between what any of the pieces report and your own experience. Pose questions based on these differences. Finally, outline a plan for potential research based on your questions.

b. Reread the newspaper pieces you selected. Based on suggestions in the preceding section, pose questions that challenge each piece. Also, use one or two of the pieces as a basis on which to pose questions that challenge you.

c. Explore the larger context suggested by the differing news accounts of the two articles. Create a phrase that summarizes one issue, subject, or problem that you think is important to these accounts. Place that phrase at the top of a page and the question "What's this a part of?" below it. Then write an answer in order to identify a broader context. Based on this broader context, generate an action plan: identify some research activity that could follow from your writing.

d. Use the suggestions in the preceding section to develop an opinion based on one or more of the articles you selected. In writing, state your opinion in a sentence or two. Then, in a brief paragraph, support your opinion by pointing to particular paragraphs or sentences in the news accounts.

Exercise 4

Complete the activities for Exercise 3, based on the following readings:

The Boston *Globe,* March 5, 1993 (page A3)

White House rebuffs AMA bid for role

By Elizabeth Neuffer
GLOBE STAFF

WASHINGTON – The White House yesterday rebuffed an appeal from the American Medical Association for a direct role in revamping national health care, but the powerful medical lobby said it will nonetheless assemble hundreds of doctors here this month to make their views heard.

The 290,000-member AMA had sent a letter to White House officials asking for more hands-on participation in shaping legislation revamping the nation's health care system, due before Congress in May.

"Bring us into the process and we can help make it work," wrote AMA executive director James S. Todd to Clinton health adviser Ira Magaziner.

Signaling a shift in the stance of the physicians' organization, Todd wrote in the letter that the group would for the first time be willing to accept working within state or national health-spending targets to control costs.

But White House spokeswoman Dee Dee Myers yesterday said the AMA's direct participation would be a "conflict of interest," as would that of other interest groups. "The AMA has a significant voice in the process already," Myers said.

President Clinton, in remarks made at a photo session, ruled out participation by interest groups, saying: "Nobody does that. You can't get anything done."

The AMA's plea comes as the National Task Force on Health Care Reform, led by Hillary Rodham Clin-

ton, works to find a solution for overhauling health care and as much of the nation's medical community struggles with how to make their voices heard on the subject.

Hillary Clinton also visited New Orleans yesterday to promote health care reform and heard horror stories from steel workers who could not afford medical insurance. She promised them that no matter what plan the administration chooses, "What happens to you or your family when one person is already ill will not keep happening."

Many interest groups have paraded before the task force and its 300 advisers to make their case on the best course for reform. But none have been allowed a seat at the drafting table. A few have filed suit in an effort to make the meetings public.

Such exclusion has prompted cries of dismay, particularly from the AMA, which complains that the task force has no practicing doctors on its staff. "We thought it would be helpful if people on the front line of delivering care to patients were involved," said AMA spokesman Jim Stacy.

The AMA, in fact, has planned its first-ever "grass-roots" session, in which doctors from around the country will come to Washington and lobby members of Congress and the administration. The meeting is planned for March 24–25, not long after the first rough draft of the Clinton plan is due.

This week's letter from the AMA underscores the medical lobby's difficulty in defining a role for itself in the current health care debate. In the past, the group blocked efforts to revamp health care.

But the AMA, like other health groups here, has repeatedly acknowledged that changes are needed and even suggested its own plan. The group, however, has been rent with dissent over that plan.

Most of the AMA's members are more conservative than Todd, who has reportedly had to cajole the group into accepting the reforms it has proposed.

In December, the group embraced a version of "managed competition," the system backed by Clinton, but only if it did not force doctors to work on a salaried rather than fee-for-service basis.

Under managed competition, doctors, hospitals, and other medical providers would band together to offer services.

The *Wall Street Journal*, March 5, 1993 (Editorial page)

AMA Gets Stiffed

"We know the status quo must change," said another suppliant to the Clinton White House health-reform task force. Get lost, replied the Clintonites, perhaps giving the American Medical Association about as much respect as it deserves for its game plan of strategic surrender. The White House's Dee Dee Myers said letting the AMA participate would be a "conflict of interest." And health czar Hillary R. Clinton spoke Wednesday of the need to "beat back the powerful lobbies and special interests that are already lining up to defeat any plan we develop."

The *New York Times*, March 5, 1993 (page A1+)

DOCTORS SOFTENING STAND ON CHANGES IN HEALTH SYSTEM

MEDICAL GROUP ASKS ROLE

Association Drops Opposition to Some Clinton Proposals, Seeking More Influence

By PHILIP J. HILTS
Special to The New York Times

WASHINGTON, March 3 — Fearful of being left out of the debate on reshaping the nation's health-care system, the American Medical Association has told the White House that it will drop its long-held and formidable opposition to some proposals favored by President Clinton.

In return, A.M.A. officials said, they are asking for a seat at the table as the policy group led by Hillary Rodham Clinton works out what promise to be sweeping changes in medicine.

In a letter sent today to Ira Magaziner, Mrs. Clinton's righthand man on health care, the group signaled its willingness to support the idea of "spending limits" on health care, to accept a National Health Board to review prices and practices in medicine and to accept that large "managed care" organizations like preferred-provider groups or health-maintenance organizations may be a large part of the health-care system in the future.

Some Caveats

The A.M.A. put caveats on some of these items and repeated its opposition to other items under discussion by the White House, like the proposal for a "global budget" that would set a strict limit on the amount the nation spends on health care.

But the A.M.A. did offer to support a cap plan, probably less restrictive than the global-budget approach, under which doctors would accept ational or regional health-care spending limits if they can help set them.

Medical Group Will Back Some of Clinton's Plans

Robert Boorstin, a White House spokesman on health care, said today that the White House "welcomes the participation of the A.M.A., as we always have." He said the A.M.A.'s shift showed that a "consensus is being formed that there has to be immediate change, and that it is coalescing around the principles that the President's plan is being built on."

An A.M.A. spokesman today said that it is a "reasonable reading of the proposal" to say that the overall spending limits would be at the level of inflation in the rest of the economy. Last year, that was 2.9 percent, while inflation for doctors' fees and other medical costs was 6.6 percent.

Requested in Return

In return for its concessions, the A.M.A. is asking that practicing doctors be represented on the White House health-care group and that a number of proposals be considered, including curbs on malpractice suits, assurance that some patients will still be able to choose doctors freely and some antitrust relief so doctors can negotiate fees with any government board setting budgets.

The letter to Mr. Magaziner marks a "major change, a quite different approach for the A.M.A.," said one association spokesman.

It was an especially significant shift for an organization that has been viewed as responsible for killing a number of health-care proposals in the past. The medical association, with its more than 290,000 members and its lobbying budget of tens of millions of dollars, could have posed a substantial obstacle to a Clinton package, and its support could add momentum to attempts to press the package both before the public and in Congress.

In the past, the association and allied doctors have been credited with killing health-insurance proposals in the Administration of Franklin D. Roosevelt, defeating President Harry S. Truman's national health program and halting President Jimmy Carter's hospital cost-containment measures.

New Climate in Capital

But in the new climate in Washington, according to various A.M.A. officials, the group worried that it was being left behind as Democrats on Capitol Hill, other medical organizations and such health-industry stalwarts as the Pharmaceutical Manufacturers Association have embraced "managed competition" and some limits on price increases.

The A.M.A. proposal was delivered to the White House today, after last-minute changes were made last night to back away from some more specific proposals, like expressing a willingness to freeze fees for a short time if asked by the Administration.

The letter offered to join in the "shared sacrifice" by others in health care when the final proposals for change are made in May. It said that the A.M.A. proposes a "new partnership" with the Government.

"We know that status quo must go," wrote the A.M.A. executive vice president, Dr. James S. Todd, but he also warned the White House that doctors have so far been excluded from shaping the new package, and that "any reform system will fail without the support of the profession."

What Clinton Wants

The main elements of the Administration package include keeping costs down, reforming insurance rules, letting people choose their doctors and keeping the quality of health care high, Mr. Boorstin said.

The A.M.A.'s offer is widely seen as an attempt to try to regain leadership among the medical groups. Others have been quicker to support some of the Clinton proposals, most notably the American College of Physicians last fall.

In addition, the American Academy of Family Physicians and the Ameri-can Nurses Association have led the way with offers to support a ceiling on medical spending imposed by the Government or a national health board.

'Share Our Knowledge'

Many doctors have been the beneficiaries of huge pay increases and realize that they are likely to be targets for anger and budget-cutting if they do not offer to make sacrifices now. Between 1983 and 1991, the mean income of doctors has gone from $88,000 to $170,000 per year, according to the A.M.A.'s own figures. The lowest-paid doctors are family physicians, making $111,000 per year; the highest are surgeons, at $234,000 per year.

"These are times such as we have never seen before," Dr. Todd said in a telephone interview, adding that extraordinary measures are called for.

He said the doctors' group "wants to be part of the center of the picture, a significant player. We want to share our knowledge." Until now, he said, "we have not had what you would call significant input."

The group, along with many other, much smaller medical groups, has been invited to make presentations to the White House, but has not been privy to any of the work of fashioning a health-care plan, which is due by May.

The offer to the White House goes beyond the positions the group has been willing to take in the past on several counts. The group has come around to the view that managed care—in the form of preferred-provider organizations or health-maintenance organizations, in which doctors are on staff, rather than acting as self-employed free agents paid on a fee-for-service basis—is an acceptable model for health care as long as it is possible for some doctors to continue to operate on a fee-for-service basis.

A Student Writer at Work: Mike Bergom

The opening exercise to this book presents an essay by student writer Mike Bergom: "Technology, Jazz, and History." Bergom began thinking about his essay with this question: Why were recent jazz musicians turning away from technological innovations? Bergom plays the saxophone, is in a jazz band, and was intensely interested in knowing why musicians like Branford Marsalis insisted on playing only acoustic instruments. In one of his course readings, Bergom encountered a reference he had never seen, to "Luddites." Here's an excerpt from that source:

> An unwritten law of human nature says that change, to be accepted, must come incrementally. Creeping mechanization—a better mousetrap here, a more efficient whirlgig there—disturbs only the true technophobes. The rest of us just buy the machines we think we'll need, learn the basics and try not to lose the warranties. But whenever a barrage of machines swiftly shoves a society from agriculture toward industry or from industry toward information, the forces of opposition rally.
>
> In the late 20th century a sea of troubling technology sweeps through the workplaces and marketplaces. All at once, it seems, everything that used to have a dial becomes digital, and everything once done face-to-face is "interfaced." Fax machines, computers, laser printers, voice mail, E-mail, cordless phones, cellular phones, camcorders, CD players, and extended families of compact, portable and personal devices raise questions about the uses of technology and make doubters out of dutiful workers.
>
> Political theorist Landgon Winner writes: "Rapidly evolving technologies would seem to provide us an occasion to pause and take stock, to ask . . . which factors ought to guide our choices about technology?" Writer Wendell Berry raises a dilemma implicit in the Luddite uprising: "Is the obsolescence of human beings now our social goal? One would conclude so from our attitude toward work, especially the manual work necessary to the long-term preservation of the land, and from our rush toward mechanization, automation, and computerization."
>
> Watson, Bruce. "For a While, the Luddites Had a
Smashing Success." *Smithsonian* Apr. 1993: 151–52.

what's this?

What, Bergom asked, was the "Luddite uprising"? He pursued the reference, found several readings on the Luddites, and eventually included that material in his essay on jazz and technology. Originally, the "history" portion of his essay (and his title) did not exist, but Bergom found a direct connection between his idea and the Luddites. After reading these paragraphs from the final draft of his essay, answer this question: To what extent has Bergom used reading materials to generate an important idea?

> . . . In early nineteenth century England, cloth makers were being displaced by machines that outperformed them. These workers, known as Luddites, rose up and destroyed the frames (the new machines) that had caused their unemployment. The Luddites destroyed frames not only because of their displacement but also because they judged the quality of the goods produced by these machines to be inferior. A contemporary newspaper made the point this way:
>
>> The machines . . . are not broken for being upon any new construction . . . but in consequence of goods being wrought upon them which are of little worth, are deceptive to the eye, are disreputable to the trade, and therefore pregnant with the seeds of its destruction. (qtd. in Thompson 532)

The Luddites did not embrace a technology merely because it existed. They could not agree that so-called "improvements in mechanism" (qtd. in Peel 71) led to improvements in product. The cloth produced by the new weaving machines was judged according to ancient standards of the weaver's craft and found to have "little worth." Nontechnical factors, in this case artistic ones, contributed to the Luddites' rejection of technology.

Today, several influential jazz musicians have applied the standards of their craft to electronically boosted music and have reached a similar conclusion: the product has little worth. Beyond question, recent "improvements in mechanism" have provided many benefits for the aspiring musician. Synthesizers create totally unique new sounds. Improved recording techniques open a new world of special effects. Computers print, transpose, and perform music with the touch of a button. Yet there are jazz purists who regard the new technology, in effect, as a frame to be smashed. . . .

2

Committing Yourself to an Idea

If you have worked to generate ideas and have discovered a personal insight that you think is worth pursuing, you have taken a crucial first step in writing an essay: you have discovered a *reason* to write. The next step takes you from notes that you have made to yourself to a statement that you will make to prospective readers: a *thesis*—a general statement about your topic, usually in the form of a single sentence, that summarizes what you expect will be the controlling idea of an essay.

You cannot know, before writing the first draft of your essay, what your final thesis will be. The best you can do at this early stage in the writing process is to write a *working thesis,* a statement that you think will prove reasonably accurate, based on everything you know about your topic. But the only way to be sure is to write.

Like any sentence, a thesis consists of a subject and a predicate—that is, a verb and its associated words. The *subject* of a thesis statement identifies the *subject* of your essay. The *predicate* represents the claim or assertion you will make about that subject.

Realize that your ideas for an essay and, consequently, for your thesis develop and change as your essay develops. Don't be bound by a single sentence at the beginning of your draft. Your working thesis *will* change. Nonetheless, you must depend on it to get you started.

As much as possible, you want the subject of your thesis statement to name something that is relatively narrowly defined; you want to name something you can discuss thoroughly within the allotted number of pages. How will you narrow your subject? One useful way to narrow the subject of your thesis is to pose a journalist's questions: *who, what, when, where,* and *which aspects.*

Subject (too broad): wilderness
Limiting questions: which aspects?
Narrowed subject: wilderness camping

Basing Your Thesis on a Relationship You Want to Clarify

Once you have narrowed your subject, you must make an assertion about it; that is, you must complete the predicate part of your thesis. If you have ever written an essay before, you recognize this as the moment of chaos coalescing into order. If you have generated ideas on your own, you have several pages of notes; if you have conducted research, you have filled out perhaps fifty file cards. You cannot write until you have begun to make relationships among the ideas and information that you have generated. It is only *in the process* of making relationships—trying to make logical connections one way, seeing that a certain tactic does not work, trying other tactics, and constantly making adjustments—that sense emerges and you come to know what you think about your material. In examining the notes you have generated, ask yourself: What new statement can I make that helps to explain this material or to explain my reactions to this material? Think of a relationship that ties all—or part—of your material together. You will express this relationship in the predicate part of your thesis.

The Thesis and Your Ambitions for an Essay

The legal scholar and Supreme Court Justice Oliver Wendell Holmes (1841–1935) once made an analogy between intellectual commitment and the numbers of stories, or levels, in a building. His description captures perfectly the qualities that distinguish an inadequate commitment to a writing project from adequate and superior ones:

There are one-story intellects, two-story intellects, and three-story intellects with skylights. All fact collectors who have no aim beyond their facts are one-story men. Two-story men compare, reason, generalize, using the labor of fact collectors as their own. Three-story men idealize, imagine, predict—their best illumination comes from above the sky-light.[1]

What distinguishes one-story thinkers from their two- and three-story counterparts is *not* ability. Mere fact collectors could do more than shuffle facts, but they choose not to. *Commitment* is the issue here—what the thinker is willing to do with the material at hand. You can choose a one-, two-, or three-story commitment to a writing project.

One-Story Commitment

A one-story commitment to a writing project will usually lead to a product that is unacceptable at the college level. The one-story writer does little more than assemble facts and figures and say: "Here they are. You decide what they mean." In college and in the world of business, readers need to see more than a one-story commitment. They will most often be reading to see how the writer brings facts and figures together in a meaningful way. The writer who makes a one-story commitment makes no attempt to create meaning. Consider the following assignment:

> The Board of Trustees at your school has just voted to ban overnight guests in campus dormitory rooms. Write an essay responding to the decision. If you disagree with the new policy, propose a course of action. Assume that you will submit your work to the college newspaper for publication.

A writer making a one-story commitment to this project might produce a thesis something like this:

> The recent curfew ruling has generated a great deal of debate.

This thesis does not adequately meet the expectations set out in the assignment, which has clearly asked for a response; in this thesis there is no hint of the writer's response to the ban on overnight guests. The assignment also clearly indicates a student audience, but in the thesis there is no indication that the writer will shape the essay based on an analysis of student readers. With his one-story commitment, this writer is not yet meeting the basic requirements of the assignment.

Two-Story Commitment

Holmes suggests that a thinker is someone who compares facts, generalizes from them, or reasons with them: that is, a thinker *argues* and *informs* with some degree of sophistication. Someone who reasons will define, order, classify, delineate a process, or establish cause and effect—all types of thinking and writing discussed in this book. When writers reason with

---

[1] Oliver Wendell Holmes, cited in Esther Fusco, "Cognitive Levels Matching and Curriculum Analysis," *Developing Minds: A Resource Book for Teaching Thinking,* ed. Arthur L. Costa (Alexandria, VA: ASCD, 1985) 81.

the facts and make observations about them or based on them, they are making a two-story commitment to their projects. Someone making a two-story commitment to the dormitory assignment might produce a thesis like this:

> What most alarms and angers students about the administration's recent curfew ruling is the patronizing view that students are children who cannot be trusted to act in their own best interests.

This thesis signals a level of commitment sufficient for meeting the basic requirements of the assignment. The writer clearly intends to both *respond* to the assignment and find a point of personal interest. Notice the word *patronizing* in the thesis. We can be sure that the writer will be personally involved with the essay and that she has strong, likely negative, views on the administration's attitudes.

Three-Story Commitment

In addition to addressing all the expectations set out in an assignment, the writer who makes a three-story commitment to a project shows himself willing to take intellectual risks by expanding the scope of the paper, broadening its context in order to take up a more complex and important discussion. A three-story commitment shows a writer who is thinking with enough complexity to introduce *tension* into the paper by setting elements in opposition to each other. In a thesis with tension, the writer explores opposites that are part of the topic but that may not be obvious on first inspection. The reader is delighted both by the identification of the opposites (where none were thought to exist) and by the tension that naturally arises from a contrast. Sensing tension, the reader wants to know what happens—and why.[2]

A three-story commitment signals the most ambitious commitment the writer can make, and it can be enormously satisfying as the writer sets out to "idealize, imagine, [or] predict." Holmes remarks that illumination for these thinkers comes "from above the skylight." The metaphor does not suggest someone waiting to be inspired by mysterious forces; rather, the skylight suggests a mind that is open to a world outside itself, ready to question and to hold opposites together in order to follow the play of competing ideas. The very best papers are written based on a three-story commitment. The writer making such a commitment to the dormitory assignment might produce a thesis like this:

> By instituting a curfew and by acting on what it believed was the students' behalf, the administration undermined the moral and educational principles it was duty-bound to uphold.

---

[2]The term *tension,* as it relates to the thesis statement, is borrowed from John C. Bean and John D. Ramage, *Form and Surprise in Composition: Writing and Thinking Across the Curriculum* (New York: Macmillan, 1986) 168–69.

An essay following from this thesis not only would address the specific requirements of the assignment but would go considerably beyond them. The thesis introduces a tension built on opposing elements that are not apparent on a first reading of the assignment: the educational and moral principles that the administration is obliged to uphold on the one hand versus the curfew decision on the other. Notice that the assignment does not openly raise the issue of educational and moral principles. Still, the writer recognizes that these issues are involved and thereby broadens the discussion. Clearly, of the three example theses offered in response to the curfew assignment, this is the most ambitious and shows the highest level of commitment to the writing occasion.

Is a Three-Story Commitment Necessary for Every Project?

By no means should you feel obligated to make a three-story commitment to every writing project. Given the crush of competing deadlines and given your natural interests, you will be doing well if you can meet the basic requirements of every assignment *and* be personally committed to all your assignments. This much, in itself, will entail quite a bit of work. Going beyond the basic requirements with a three-story commitment is something you want to do when you have or think you might develop the interest and when you *know* you have the time.

Making an Assignment Your Own

When the occasion for your writing is a specific assignment, read with care so that you understand your professor's expectations. Very often, these expectations will be made explicit in the assignment's key verb. The following list presents key verbs you will frequently encounter in assignments. These key verbs define the various purposes for writing discussed in Part II of this text.

Discuss: Take an idea and examine its meaning or implications.

Explain: Answer the questions *what, how,* and *why* about an object or process, keeping the reader's focus primarily on the object or process, not on your or anyone else's views about it.

Analyze: Select an analytical tool—a *principle* or *definition* offered by a writer you respect—and to systematically investigate some object or activity by applying that tool.

Resolve: Commit to a problem/solution essay in which you explain a problem or argue that one exists and then attempt a resolution—or at least suggest one. With the problem defined, you move to an argument about action, about what people *should* and *can* do.

Interpret: Discuss patterns of meaning in a text—a poem, story, novel, drama, film, painting, sculpture, or musical work. As a careful reader or viewer or listener, you find patterns in the text, bring these to the reader's attention, and argue why these patterns make the text understandable.

Argue: Attempt, through appeals to reason, emotion, and authority, to change a reader's mind or to present a debatable idea as reasonable and worthy of serious consideration. An argument consists of three parts: claim, support, and reasoning.

Evaluate: Determine the worth of something—perhaps an object, process, or work of art. The writer makes clear his or her standards of judgment and then applies them systematically, in the end giving the reader an overall sense of the object's worth.

You should be clear about and plan to meet your professor's expectations. Realize, however, that you can have expectations as well. You can respond to virtually any assignment in ways that are personally meaningful. In writing your essays, adopt these attitudes:

- I write for myself *and* for my audience.
- I will find some approach to the assignment that lets me discover something personally important.

By adopting these attitudes, you can find some way to become personally engaged with an assignment. When the idea of your essay closely corresponds with your interests, commitment comes easily; when circumstances require you to work with material that is unfamiliar or not immediately appealing, commitment must be constructed—but you *can* construct it. Two strategies for doing this are: applying the assignment directly to your experience and stretching the assignment to fit your interests.

Apply the Assignment Directly to Your Experience

Often, you will have the opportunity to use a personal experience in an assignment. Carefully choose an experience that troubles or confuses you, so that you give yourself a personal reason to write and discover. Student writer Edward Peselman did exactly this for an assignment from his sociology professor when he wrote an essay analyzing power relationships in his dormitory. Here, in the first paragraph of that essay (see pages 239–242), you can glimpse his private reasons for writing:

> During my first year of college, I lived in a dormitory, like most freshmen on campus. We inhabitants of the dorm came from different cultural and economic backgrounds. Not surprisingly, we brought with us many of the traits found in people outside of college. Like many on the outside, we in the dorm sought personal power at the expense of others. The gaining and maintaining of power can be an ugly business, and I saw people hurt and in turn hurt others all for the sake of securing a place in the dorm's prized social order. Not until one of us challenged that order did I realize how fragile it was.

Stretch the Assignment to Fit Your Interests

Before you pursue this option, check with your professor, who may for very legitimate reasons insist that you complete an assignment exactly as it was given. But if you have your professor's permission, attempt to modify the assignment, if only slightly, to fit your interests and simultaneous-ly meet the professor's requirements. For example, assume you are taking a general psychology course and are given this essay assignment:

> Write an essay in which you apply Irving Janis's theory of "Groupthink" to some event in recent American history. In your essay, provide back-ground for this event and describe the people who made faulty deci-sions. Use Janis's vocabulary to explain the breakdown of group decision making.

When you receive the assignment, you realize that you have recently read a short story, Shirley Jackson's "The Lottery," to which you could apply the theories of Irving Janis. But you see that the assignment requires you to write on an event in recent American history. You know that writ-ing on the story would interest you, but before you go ahead and do this, you should ask your professor. Write a memo, submit it for consideration, and make an appointment to discuss it. Your memo might look like this:

> TO: Professor _____
> FROM: Student
> RE: Assignment #____
>
> I am interested in applying the theories of Irving Janis not to a recent historical event but to a short story by Shirley Jackson, "The Lottery." If you don't know the story, it is about a town that practices an old and savage custom of stoning someone to death every year. The victim is chosen by lottery, and the whole town participates in the murder. No one wants to kill a neighbor, but together the group can-not break out of its savage ritual. I think that the ideas of Irving Janis can help me examine the "psychopathology" of the story.
>
> May I write on the story in place of a recent historical event? I can meet with you during office hours this week. Thanks for your con-sideration.

Write the proposal in good faith and you can assume your professor will consider it seriously. As mentioned, the professor may have clear reasons for wanting you to complete the assignment as distributed, in which case your substitution would be rejected. But as long as you show yourself willing to meet the spirit of an assignment, many professors will give you room to stretch and meet your interests. Again, be sure to ask permission before taking it on yourself to redefine an assignment.

Personal Commitment Statements

In each chapter of Part II in this text, the authors of two different essays write a "Personal Commitment Statement" that provides background on their private motivations for writing. Read these statements to gain a glimpse into the varied reasons writers can decide to make a private idea public. Following are two statements. Like Linda Hasselstrom and Michael Behrens, you too should be able to explain, if asked, your *personal* motivations for writing an essay.

Linda Hasselstrom

(See "A Peaceful Woman Explains Why She Carries a Gun," pages 412–415)

Three ideas guided me through more than ten years of writing and revising this essay before it was published:

First, I believe that humans must accept some responsibility for their safety and well-being, rather than expecting government, society, law enforcement, or other entities to furnish protection on demand.

Second, media attention often focuses on dramatic incidents involving weapons, in an atmosphere where discussion becomes emotional. I thought a calm, reasoned discussion of the options, without drama or hyperbole, might be useful to individuals who had not yet made such decisions.

Third, my decision to protect myself with a gun was made carefully, calmly, after considerable thought, to fit specific circumstances; I take full responsibility for the consequences of the decision. I hope my method might help other people find their own solution to the problem of safety in an increasingly violent world.

Michael Behrens

(See "Building Fly Rods and Living a Life," pages 36–38)

The "art" that I mention at the conclusion of this essay does not literally mean literature or painting. I actually meant "art" to connote something more like "meaning." Meaning, I suppose, is the art of human endeavor—we all hope that our lives *mean* something. In times past, only the elite intellectual caste of one kind or another wrestled with such doubts—only they had the leisure and the access to ideas. But in the second half of this century, America's sweeping middle class, educated in her huge universities, has democratized learning.

We had jobs for the engineers. But what of those who inherited a humanities education originally designed for either classics scholars or rich English dilettantes? We are brimming with ideas about meaningful things, we humanities majors; we are expected to become professionals; but few jobs are out there, and we find ourselves adrift, negotiating our way financially and spiritually. Is it any wonder that we vacillate, that we wander, that we're dubbed "slackers"? This essay is about fly rods and about finding meaning. It's set against an ongoing, generation-wide search for the good life.

Summary

Do not write an essay until you can commit yourself *personally* to an idea. Personal commitment will ensure that you write to discover something for yourself, as well as to present material to others. At times, you will need to *stretch* assignments in order to find a personal commitment that can launch a successful essay. You can be more or less committed to any idea and can signal commitment to readers through your essay's thesis. Your thesis can be characterized as having a one-, two-, or three-story commitment.

For Discussion and Writing

Exercise 1

Based on the definitions presented in this chapter, characterize the following sets of theses as having a one-, two-, or three-story commitment. Explain your reasons for labeling these statements as you do.

- Wilderness camping poses many challenges.
- Wilderness camping teaches that we must preserve what is brutal in Nature, even at the expense of public safety.
- Like holding a mirror to your personality, wilderness camping shows you to yourself—for better and worse.

- School violence affects and changes students.
- Public schools are not safe.
- Students can confront aggression in themselves and in their schools and can implement ways of breaking the cycle of violence.

- Even though voter registration drives were more successful in 1991 than in previous elections, many urban poor have given up on the American political system—for good reason.
- In the 1991 elections, there were three reasons why voter registration drives among the urban poor succeeded where earlier drives had not.
- There were many voter registration drives among the urban poor in the 1991 elections.

Exercise 2

In response to the following assignment, write three theses, showing a one-, two-, and three-story commitment:

You applied and were admitted to college. Reflecting on the experience, what advice would you give to high-school juniors about to embark on the journey that you recently and successfully completed?

Exercise 3

In response to the following question, write three theses, showing a one-, two-, and three-story commitment:

In your view, would it be a good idea for your former high school to institute a dress code? Answer this question in an opinion piece for the school newspaper.

Exercise 4

Read the following essay by Michael Behrens, "Building Fly Rods and Living a Life." As you read, characterize the level of commitment he makes to his essay. On finishing the selection, **list** all the ways in which Behrens communicates to you that he takes his ideas seriously and wants you to do the same.

STUDENT PAPER

Building Fly Rods and Living a Life
Michael Behrens

Recently I spoke to a young man about my work, which is building 1
fly rods. A good-natured, healthy Northern Californian was he: vegetarian, anti-caffeine, three triathalons finished last summer—and out of work for months. "Isn't it a sign of the affluence of our society that people can be employed full time making things like fly rods?" he asked me.

Ironically we were talking because his father had harbored hopes that 2
his boy might cotton to fly rods. "It's just the sort of thing that could blossom into a career for him." Unfortunately for dad's plans, the son, who possessed the dreamy and sometimes petulant manner of a varsity athlete whose fields of glory are now only oft-recalled memories, chose to continue his wanderings through the maze of careerdom. "I can think of a lot of things I don't want to do," he confessed to me. "I just can't come up with anything I *do* want to do."

It is a great dilemma of our generation. Our conversation did prompt 3
me to think of my own choices, but only long enough to recognize that my vegetarian friend, in his attitudes, embodied the malaise hanging about our collective twentysomething heads. This bewilderment, this overabundance of options, this jadedness—I was laboring under it all. That was before fly rods.

To appreciate their appeal it helps to understand their duties. Like jet 4
fighters or any other human endeavor that flies in the face of Newton's first law, the ideal fly rod is strong, flexible, and as light as possible. It's the rapier of fishing poles.

The rods of African lemonwood and British Guinean greenheart and 5
lancewood used by the English until the late nineteen hundreds recalled the simplicity and strength of their famed longbows, but, at lengths of up to eighteen feet, proved too unwieldy. Thus, from the 1860s on, rodmaking belongs to Americans and their slimmer split cane rods—chief among them the Maine cabinetmaker and engineer named Hiram Leonard, whose work in the years following the Civil War anointed him as the grandfather of split-cane rods.

The "cane" of split cane was Tonkin bamboo. (Actually harvested 6
from the hillsides of the Kwangtung province of China, over the centuries a thousand monsoons have whipped it into the most pliant wood in the world.) After importation and up to twenty years of aging, the cane was

split, glued into a hexagonal wand of six cane strips, and then painstakingly planed down to a tip (still containing all six strips of cane) often slimmer than a matchstick. Consuming hundreds of hours, the process contained about one hundred and fifty separate operations.

Cane rodmakers left legacies of a life's work of split cane rods scattered about the country. Like antique furniture or violins, these fly rods are distinguished by artisan. A fly fishing historian remembers his first glimpse, as an eight-year-old, of a fly rod made by the rodmaker Edward Payne, and now owned by the family doctor: "I found it strange that the doctor loved his gleaming four-ounce Payne so much that he utterly refused to fish with it. The old men laid it reverently on his red felt desktop in the lamplight and looked at the exquisite rod for hours. It obviously had the overtones of some religious relic" (Schwiebert 1). 7

Most crucial was a rod's "action"—its ability to throw a pinpoint cast with a twitch of the caster's wrist. Therein lay the engineering complexities of the rodmaking craft. In 1865 a man wrote of a meeting with a talented but now obscure rodmaker named Charles Murphy: "I listened with wonder to the talk of angles, tapers, gluing, and other details, until I thought that the building up of a split-cane bamboo rod required more careful attention than the grinding of a lens for a great telescope" (Schwiebert 20). 8

Now, instead of bamboo from the Kmangtung province we have carbon graphite, which, in engineering qualities, has it all over cane. (Cane rods are still made. Fabulously expensive, they possess the appeal of a 1969 Mercedes sports coupe—a high-performance anachronism.) The American aerospace industry concocted graphite for use in thin-skinned high-performance jet fighters, but post–Berlin wall it forms mountain bike frames, golf club shafts, ski poles, and fly rods. Just as the English harvested the tropical woods of their Empire for their fishing rods, America's technological expeditions in the name of the Cold War have enriched the leisure sports industry. 9

The company I work for began twenty years ago in the garage of an engineer and tinkerer much like Charles Murphy. Now we are twenty people working in a large warehouse. We sell fly rods in shops across the country, and we export to Spain, England, France, Italy, and Norway. 10

But the craft remains the same. It's the craft that attracts me. Not just *craft* in the sense of the actual trade, but the fact that my work claims a history. 11

I work with a twenty-year-old machinist full of squirrelly energy and as uncompromising in his craft as a curmudgeonly New England cabinetmaker. Does the fact that he labors daily upon an instrument designed to catch trout, while others chase the cure for cancer, give him pause? In 1893, did Hiram Leonard similarly pause? If so, it was probably at the proper time to ponder such matters—late at night after a few beers, and secure in the knowledge that in the morning, one will rise and go back to work. 12

I'm not anti-thought, you see, just dubious of the wisdom of always 13
analyzing, analyzing. My vegetarian friend, for example, possessed too
many opinions, and not enough passions. He reminded me of my studies
upon a university campus where, we were given to understand, everything was relative. In my field—literature—there was no right and wrong,
only opinions, and differences of opinion. Grades came down upon our
presentations of opinion like judgments from the Old Testament God—
that is to say, in unpredictable manner. Talent and hard work were usually rewarded. But was our work right? Not *right* in the moral sense—I
mean, had it at all approached *truth?*

A craftsman labors within realms of undisputable right and wrong. 14
There is, for instance, only one way to properly file a fly rod's ferrule, and
it takes months to learn. "This ferrule," I was told once early in my
apprenticeship, "has been *improperly* filed." This rejection of my work
braced me like a spray of icy water. Now I am imparting the same painful
lesson in ferrule-filing to another apprentice. We work at it late every
afternoon, painstakingly fine-tuning his skills. And then, our work done,
we'll take one of our rods outside and cast it for a few minutes. We'll
watch the line flick forward and unfurl in a tight, graceful loop. Its
rhythms will remind us that only at the farthest reaches of craftsmanship
will we find art.

A Student Writer at Work: Mike Bergom

In the opening exercise to this book, Mike Bergom's essay is paired with
his personal commitment statement. Reread the essay "Technology, Jazz,
and History" (pages 3–5) and the statement (page 2) and characterize the
level of commitment he makes to his essay. On finishing the selection, **list**
all the ways in which Bergom communicates to you that he takes his ideas
seriously and wants you to do the same.

CHAPTER 3

Creating Common Ground with Readers

Defining *Common Ground*

The following passages were written by an emergency-care physician in California. Watch as this writer, Steven Sainsbury, moves in stages from a personal idea, meant for him alone, to a public statement of his idea. With each successive move from the private to the public, the writer's awareness of you, the reader, grows:

Journal Entry

Illness, trauma, and death—not just everyday occurrences. Essence of my caregiving. Tragedies accepted. But preventable afflictions, they frustrate, cry for action. Spread of venereal diseases on rise, now AIDS. Public thinks condoms will solve problem. No!

Thesis

The only safe sex is no sex until one is ready to commit to a monogamous relationship with an uninfected person.

Essay

My 15-year-old patient with pelvic pain lay quietly on the gurney, as I asked her the standard questions.

"Are you sexually active?"

"Yes."

"Are you using any form of birth control?"

"No."

"What about condoms?"

"No."

Her answers didn't surprise me. Nor was it surprising that her pain was due to a rip-roaring gonorrheal infection, although it just as easily could have been due to some other venereal disease, a tubal pregnancy or even AIDS. As a specialist in emergency medicine, I treat teenagers like this one every day. Most are sexually active. Condoms are used rarely and sporadically.

Yet in the midst of the AIDS epidemic, I continue to hear condoms touted as the solution to HIV transmission. As part of a "safe sex" campaign, condoms are passed out in high schools, sold in college restroom dispensers and routinely discussed.

The message? Condoms equal safe sex.

As a physician, I wish that this were true. Yet, to imply that the use of condoms will safeguard both sex partners from venereal disease, including AIDS, is not only a lie, it is a dangerous lie.

If you were asked for a single word to describe how these passages differ, you would do well to say **audience.** For it is Steven Sainsbury's growing awareness of readers that largely explains why his first statement is not suitable for public view while his second and third statements are (they form parts of an essay published by the *Los Angeles Times*). Sainsbury begins with a note to himself—something like a journal entry meant to record an idea as it occurred to him. In fact, this idea is not fully formed— he has *suggested* it more than stated it openly. Sainsbury is not yet thinking of readers. But in the second passage he is. Here we find that what had been suggested privately is now stated clearly enough for anyone to follow: *The only safe sex is no sex until one is ready to commit to a monogamous relationship with an uninfected person.*

This is the main idea, the thesis, of Sainsbury's essay.[1] While fully formed and a crucial first step toward writing an essay, this idea is not itself an essay. Not yet. To communicate an idea, a writer must imagine readers and the information they need to gain full understanding. Sainsbury does this in the third of the three selections, where he provides carefully selected, albeit uncomfortable, information: we groan at his account of a 15-year-old patient with a "rip-roaring gonorrheal infection." And we wonder why, in light of preventable venereal diseases, this patient seems indifferent to birth control. A particular person's pelvic pain and carelessness about condom use are details that make Sainsbury's idea very real and create a context in which an argument about abstaining from sex has meaning. *Without* these details, Sainsbury's idea is abstract and sounds like the moralizing of a parent who wants kids to remain pure. *With* details, his idea takes on force: here is a physician who counsels abstinence not because he is a moralist but because he wants to see fewer patients with "rip-roaring gonorrheal infection[s]."

---

[1]The complete essay appears in Exercise 1 at the end of this chapter.

An idea expressed and explored through the right details gives us full understanding. Whether or not we accept an idea is a different matter altogether, and we are always entitled to evaluate. But first we must understand, and to do this we need a writer who in *every* paragraph gives us details through which we can see ideas being prepared for, explored, and expressed. *The carefully selected details of an essay, presented paragraph by paragraph, create a base of shared knowledge that we can call the essay's common ground.* As this chapter will show, writers have the best possible chance of communicating when they present common-ground details that both connect with the reader's experience *and* are well suited to developing and exploring the essay's idea. Common ground is created in response to two questions:

- What details from my own experience and reading will help me fully express my idea?
- What connections can I make to my readers' experience that will help them to understand?

Common Ground and the Writing Occasion

Every new writing project presents you with a distinct occasion for writing and requires that you start anew in creating common ground. Once you know the likely idea of your essay and your purpose for writing, your goal is to find the right details that allow you to explore your idea and encourage understanding. The diagram below suggests the close relationship among basic elements of the writing occasion: writer, topic, purpose, and audience.

Of the interrelated elements of the writing occasion, **audience** is of greatest concern in selecting details to create common ground. Unless you are writing a journal entry, you write in order to communicate *with*

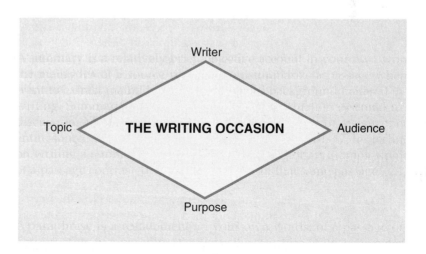

someone, and who that someone is will have a dramatic effect on your essay. If you were preparing to write on gene splicing for an audience of nonbiologists, you would need to define terms and provide examples that would help the audience understand, if only minimally, a complex technology. Your goal might be to present the barest introduction. In preparing an essay on the same topic for fellow biology majors, you would bring to the essay more sophisticated and specialized details, such as information on laboratory techniques. Determining your audience's needs and the limits of their understanding plays a significant role in the common-ground details you create in an essay. The following categories of questions will help you define your audience's experience and needs.

Pose these general questions, regardless of your purpose:

- Who is the reader? What is the reader's age, sex, religious background, educational background, and ethnic heritage?
- What is my relationship with the reader?
- What impact on my presentation—on choice of words, level of complexity, and choice of examples—will the reader have?
- Why will the reader be interested in my paper? How can I best spark the reader's interest?

If you are writing to inform, pose these questions as well:

- What does the reader know about the topic's history?
- How well does the reader understand the topic's technical details?
- What does the reader need to know? want to know?
- What level of language and content will I use in discussing the topic, given the reader's understanding?

If you are writing to persuade, pose both sets of questions above as well as the following:

- What are the reader's views on the topic? Given what I know about the reader (from the preceding questions), is the reader likely to agree with my view on the topic? to disagree? to be neutral?
- What factors are likely to affect the reader's beliefs about the topic? What special circumstances (work, religious conviction, political views, etc.) should I be aware of that will affect the reader's views?
- How can I shape my argument to encourage the reader's support, given his or her present level of interest, level of understanding, and beliefs?

Techniques for Creating Common Ground

Once you have formulated a working thesis (see chapter 1), you are ready to think about readers and strategies for creating a base of shared experience and knowledge in every paragraph of your essay. The process of creating common ground is illustrated in the following diagram.

Stage 1: Begin with Separate Experiences

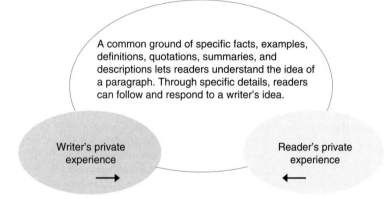

Each paragraph is about an idea. Readers have no access to the writer's experience, on which this idea is based.

Writer's private experience

Reader's private experience

Stage 2: Plan for Common Ground of Experience in the Paragraph

A common ground of specific facts, examples, definitions, quotations, summaries, and descriptions lets readers understand the idea of a paragraph. Through specific details, readers can follow and respond to a writer's idea.

Writer's private experience

Reader's private experience

Stage 3: Create a Successful Paragraph: Link Separate Experiences

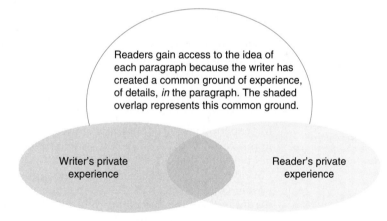

Readers gain access to the idea of each paragraph because the writer has created a common ground of experience, of details, *in* the paragraph. The shaded overlap represents this common ground.

Writer's private experience

Reader's private experience

Creating Common Ground Based on Your Experience and Reading

As you contemplate writing an essay, ask: What details from my experience and reading will I need in order to develop my idea? The possibility of answering depends, of course, on your having a clear idea. Assuming you do, the techniques of narration, quotation, summary, and description will help you to think about creating a common ground in the first draft of an essay.

Narrate an Event from Personal Experience

Let a story that you tell become an occasion to develop and explore an idea, especially when an event has strongly influenced this idea. A story told well is in itself pleasurable; but when a story also gives readers access to the important background of your thinking, it creates in a paragraph a base of shared knowledge from which both you and readers can draw conclusions. Michael Behrens creates a shared experience with the following story:

> Recently I spoke to a young man about my work, which is building fly rods. A good-natured, healthy Northern Californian was he: vegetarian, anti-caffeine, three triathalons finished last summer—and out of work for months. "Isn't it a sign of the affluence of our society that people can be employed full time making things like fly rods?" he asked me.
>
> Ironically we were talking because his father had harbored hopes that his boy might cotton to fly rods. "It's just the sort of thing that could blossom into a career for him." Unfortunately for dad's plans, the son, who possessed the dreamy and sometimes petulant manner of a varsity athlete whose fields of glory are now only oft-recalled memories, chose to continue his wanderings through the maze of careerdom. "I can think of a lot of things I don't want to do," he confessed to me. "I just can't come up with anything I *do* want to do."
>
> It is a great dilemma of our generation. . . .
>
> —Michael Behrens

Quote a Source

You will read a great deal (in chapter 4) on how to use techniques like quotation to advance your idea in a paragraph. A well-chosen quotation creates an immediate common ground with readers: the quotation gives both you and your readers precisely the same words on which to reflect. In this next example, the writer quotes a passage from Plato and then uses the passage to explore an idea important to her essay:

> In the period just after the Vietnam war, the draft was not at all popular in this country and was viewed, as one commentator put it, "as a form of involuntary servitude" (Kelley 11). Little wonder, then, that the compulsory draft was abolished. Still some argued then and argue now a position that has much merit: that the state, which nurtures and protects the individual, has the moral right to ask that individual for service. Balancing the needs of the state against the rights of the individual is an ancient concern, dating at least to the times of classical Greece. In one of Plato's dialogues, *Crito*, Socrates explains the State's position. (The "we" in this passage refers to the collective voice and authority of Athens.)
>
>> For, having brought you into the world, and nurtured and educated you, and given you and every other citizen a share in every good which we had to give, we further proclaim to any Athenian by the liberty which we allow him, that if he does not like us when he has become of age and has seen

> the ways of the city, and made our acquaintance, he may go where he
> pleases and take his goods with him. None of us laws will forbid him or
> interfere with him. . . . But he who has experience of the manner in which
> we order justice and administer the State, and still remains, has entered
> into an implied contract that he will do as we command him. (102)

In this passage, Socrates argues that a citizen who enjoys the privileges and securities of living under State protection owes that State obedience. If the authority decides that, for the good of the State, young
men should be drafted, then it is the duty of young men so called to obey
and to serve. It is true: we owe the society that nurtures us a debt. But
how best that debt is paid and to what extent the citizens who "owe" are
entitled to participate in deciding on payment—these are difficult questions that have been debated through the centuries. . . .

—Michele Pelletier

Summarize a Source

A summary is your brief and neutral restatement of a source that you have
read and found useful. (See chapter 5 for techniques on writing a summary.) The logic of creating common ground in a paragraph through summary is identical to the logic in using quotation: you want to give both
your readers and yourself the same knowledge base from which to develop an idea. If your summary accurately reflects the content of a passage,
then for your purposes, at least, your audience has read that passage; it
now becomes shared knowledge on the basis of which you can develop
an idea, as in this example:

> In "The Merits of Advertising," Wood argues that advertising is honest
> because it openly announces its intentions and because advertisers wish
> to avoid government penalties for dishonesty. According to Wood, an
> advertisement is in its very presence a warning to consumers, saying in
> effect: I am going to separate you from your money. Wood believes that
> consumers enjoy flirting with the danger implied by such a statement,
> and that consumers are flattered by the advertiser's lavish attentions.
> Advertising is honest for a second reason, as well: if it were dishonest,
> advertisers would find themselves in trouble. Wood claims that various
> laws (such as the Wiley Law and the Wheeler-Lea Act, for foods and
> drugs) along with various agencies (such as the Federal Trade Com-
> mission) set standards for the work of advertisers, who face prosecution
> if they violate these standards. But even with stringent regulations gov-
> erning their actions, advertisers remain their own strictest regulators,
> says Wood—not out of altruism but out of self-interest.
>
> Wood is correct to observe that advertisements announce that they
> are going to persuade us to spend money. Wood assumes, however, that
> this announcement alone qualifies advertisements as honest and ren-
> ders the advertiser's efforts to "entice," "soothe or excite," "frighten," or
> "order or coax" consumers likewise honest. . . .

—Alison Tschopp

Observe and Describe

Description is another technique for creating common ground. With
descriptions, you try to let readers see and feel what you have seen and

felt. "Seeing" in this sense has two meanings. You can describe what you "see" or understand—perhaps a problem, a puzzle, or a condition. "Seeing" can also be literal, as you describe for readers the appearance of some person, place, or thing. Your goal in either case is, as before, to create a base of shared experience through which to develop and explore an idea. You need not write like a novelist to describe well. Here, for instance, is a student writing a very business-like description of a problem she has observed:

> One major problem with the commercialization of college sports is the exploitation of student-athletes, many of whom come to school on athletic scholarships. Frequently, student-athletes don't deserve to be admitted to a school. Many colleges routinely lower admission requirements for their ball players, and some schools will even waive requirements for that exceptional athlete who, without his sports abilities, might not have had a place on a college campus. Most kids not interested in academics would normally shun a college education. But for gifted athletes, college appears to be a road that leads to the pros. Or so they think. . . .
>
> —Jenafer Trahar

Of course, descriptions can also be artful and can create common ground through vivid, memorable detail. Written with care, descriptions can paint visual or emotional pictures so clearly that readers come to feel that they have shared a moment with the writer—and thus common ground is created. The following opening paragraphs to Bruce Chatwin's *In Patagonia* recreate for us a child's first fascination in hearing the exotic name of a distant place. We can imagine why Chatwin would one day travel to Patagonia:

> In my grandmother's dining-room there was a glass-fronted cabinet and in the cabinet a piece of skin. It was a small piece only, but thick and leathery, with strands of coarse, reddish hair. It was stuck to a card with a rusty pin. On the card was some writing in faded black ink, but I was too young then to read.
> "What's that?"
> "A piece of brontosaurus."
> My mother knew the names of two prehistoric animals, the brontosaurus and the mammoth. She knew it was not a mamoth. Mammoths came from Siberia.
> The brontosaurus, I learned, was an animal that had drowned in the Flood, being too big for Noah to ship aboard the Ark. I pictured a shaggy lumbering creature with claws and fangs and a malicious green light in its eyes. Sometimes the brontosaurus would crash through the bedroom wall and wake me from my sleep.
> This particular brontosaurus had lived in Patagonia, a country in South America, at the far end of the world. Thousands of years before, it had fallen into a glacier, travelled down a mountain in a prison of blue ice, and arrived in perfect condition at the bottom. Here my grandmother's cousin, Charley Milward the Sailor, found it.
>
> —Bruce Chatwin

Creating Common Ground by Appealing to
Your Readers' Experiences

The techniques just presented for creating common ground—narration, quotation, summary, and description—require you to make public some aspect of your private experience in such a way that readers can share in and understand the idea that emerges from your experience. Readers, in fact, exercise enormous control over the ways in which you refer to your experience in an essay. Consider two example paragraphs taken from the work of paleontologist and evolutionary biologist Stephen Jay Gould. Gould is well known in scientific circles for his technical writings and is equally well known in other circles for books written to *non*scientists. Observe the differences in two passages when he is writing for one of these audiences and not the other. Note especially his choice of information, sentence structures, and vocabulary. Reporting in the journal *Evolution,* he and coauthor David Woodruff describe the shell of the snail *Cerion,* found in the Florida Keys:

> *Cerion* possesses an ideal shell for biometrical work. . . . It reaches a definitive adult size with a change in direction of coiling and secretion of a thickened apertural lip; hence, ontogenic and static variation are not confounded.

Now observe Gould writing for a lay audience, readers of his *Hen's Teeth and Horse's Toes: Further Reflections in Natural History.* The writing is lively and direct. Realizing that he is addressing primarily nonscientists, Gould is careful to avoid technical terms:

> In personal research on the West Indian land snail *Cerion,* my colleague David Woodruff and I find the same two morphologies again and again in all the northern islands of the Bahamas. Ribby, white, or solid-colored, thick and roughly rectangular shells inhabit rocky coasts at the edges of banks where islands drop abruptly into deep seas. Smooth, mottled, thinner, and barrel-shaped shells inhabit calmer and lower coasts at the interior edges of banks, where islands cede to miles of shallow water.

When writing for fellow scientists, Gould uses expressions like "thickened apertural lip." For nonscientists he chooses less technical words that are more conventionally descriptive, even artistic, as in "[s]mooth, mottled, thinner, and barrel-shaped shells." You can see that Gould's choice of language, the technical level of his explanations, and his sentence structures change radically when he changes audience. One type of writing is not better than the other: each is appropriate to its writing occasion and its audience. A writer can present any topic to any reader, but the common-ground details through which the writer refers to and develops ideas about the topic will change according to the needs of a particular audience. If readers and writers share a technical background, then technical references with specialized terms are likely. If readers do not share this technical background, writers must find some *other* basis on which to achieve common ground, as Gould does.

It is essential, therefore, when thinking about the details you will include in particular paragraphs, that you think of readers and of their needs and expertise. (The questions on page 42 will help you do so.) Three more techniques for creating common ground include referring to the readers' experiences, referring to public knowledge, and creating an analogy. These techniques involve going beyond personal experience to either the readers' experience or public experience shared equally by both of you. As you use these techniques, ask: What references will best help readers to understand my idea?

Refer to What You Assume Are the Readers' Experiences

If you are exploring a general condition, trend, or widespread attitude, you might try creating common ground with direct references to your readers' experiences. The trick is to guess wisely about what these might be. If you *can* name and describe an experience, you will succeed in creating common ground—this time originating with your readers. Your goal is to get readers to reflect on their lives in the context of your writing. Here is a passage from a popular guide on applying to colleges. Observe that the writer makes an assumption about his readers and their concerns. He understands, correctly, that most of his readers will be nervous 17-year-olds who buy college guides in the hope of being admitted to the best possible school.

> **Nervousness** [in an interview] is absolutely and entirely normal. The best way to handle it is to admit it, out loud, to the interviewer. Miles Uhrig, director of admission at Tufts University, sometimes relates this true story to his apprehensive applicants: One extremely agitated young applicant sat opposite him for her interview with her legs crossed, wearing loafers on her feet. She swung her top leg back and forth to some inaudible rhythm. The loafer on her top foot flew off her foot, hit him in the head, ricocheted to the desk lamp and broke it. She looked at him in terror, but when their glances met, they both dissolved in laughter. The moral of the story—the person on the other side of the desk is also a human being and wants to put you at ease. So admit to your anxiety and don't swing your foot if you're wearing loafers! (By the way, she was admitted.)
>
> —Anthony Capraro, III, *Barron's Profiles of American Colleges*, 19th ed. (1992)

Refer to Public Knowledge

One sure way to create common ground in a paragraph is to develop and explore an idea through information residing outside of *both* your experience and your readers'. Specifically, try developing an idea based on the details of some recent news event. Assuming that readers also know about this event, you will have created in your paragraph a dependable common ground. You take a gamble, of course, in making any assumptions about what the reader knows. If you were writing for your classmates, would it be reasonable to expect that they all read a daily newspaper? Your answer would determine how much detail of a news event you would need to recreate in a paragraph before using that material to develop an idea.

Some events might be called "cultural" property, including films, novels, movies, and myths. Again, depending on what you estimate to be your readers' experience, you will recreate in your paragraph more or fewer details before developing and exploring an idea. This next example is written by a forensic scientist. You will find two types of common ground at work—references to an historical event and to a myth:

> Much of the best physical evidence in crime investigation comes from the examination of distinctive marks left at the scene of the crime. The comparison of these marks with something known to be associated with a suspect can often yield unique evidence. The instinctive knowledge that such marks can be unique seems to be an integral part of human nature.
>
> Sisyphus, a figure in Ancient Greek mythology, knew it well when he marked the hooves of his cattle with notches. Because of this, when the master thief Autolycus denied stealing the cattle, Sisyphus was able to prove that he was lying.
>
> In more recent times accounts of such "shape" evidence become more frequent. One such account relates to the murder of Edward Culshaw in Lancashire, England in 1784. Culshaw was shot in the head by a muzzle-loading gun. The surgeon who carried out the post-mortem examination recovered a piece of paper, used as a wad, from the wound.
>
> This wad had been used to retain the powder and shot in the barrel of the gun and to provide a gas-tight seal in front of the expanding hot gases that pushed the shot out of the barrel. The wad was found to have been torn from a larger sheet of paper. The remainder of this sheet of paper was found in the possession of a suspect, who was convicted and hanged on the evidence.
>
> —Stuart S. Kind

Create an Analogy

An analogy is a comparison that you think provides insight into an idea. When you compare an idea that you are developing to information or an experience that you *and* the reader both know about, you again create a context in which readers gain access to your idea through information that is familiar to them. Each time you refer readers to the shared, known object in the comparison, you further clarify the idea of your essay. In this final example, an extended analogy is made between television viewing and alcohol addiction:

> Not unlike drugs or alcohol, the television experience allows the participant to blot out the real world and enter into a pleasurable and passive mental state. The worries and anxieties of reality are as effectively deferred by becoming absorbed in a television program as by going on a "trip" induced by drugs or alcohol. And just as alcoholics are only inchoately aware of their addiction, feeling that they control their drinking more than they really do ("I can cut it out any time I want—I just like to have three or four drinks before dinner"), people similarly over-

estimate their control over television watching. Even as they put off other activities to spend hour after hour watching television, they feel they could easily resume living in a different, less passive style. But somehow or other while the television set is present in their homes, the click doesn't sound. With television pleasures available, those other experiences seem less attractive, more difficult somehow.

—Marie Winn

Tone and the Writing Occasion

In addition to creating common ground through the details you select for paragraphs, you create common ground more subtly and pervasively with every word you use. **Tone,** a writer's general attitude toward the reader and the subject, is always evident in the choice of words. Every essay will have a characteristic tone, whether or not the writer intends it, because English offers numerous ways of saying the same thing. For example, the most simple request can be worded to reflect a variety of tones.

May I have the salt?	Give me that salt!	Salt!
Pass the salt.	Pass the salt, please.	

To phrase a sentence one way and not another is to make a decision about tone. Options for phrasing are always available, and when you choose one phrasing over another you implicitly project a certain attitude about your topic and your readers, even if you are unaware of doing so. For every writing occasion, then, choose a tone that you think is appropriate to your topic and that, in your view, helps to create a common ground.

Mismatching tone and topic can ruin communication. Imagine, for instance, Steven Sainsbury's discussing the AIDS epidemic with a devil-may-care attitude. Readers would surely turn away, and he would have failed in his effort to persuade us that abstinence is a sensible policy to follow in avoiding AIDS. Many writing occasions will present you with a choice of tones: formal or informal, humorous or serious, depending on your approach to a topic and your sense of what might work with a particular audience. Once you choose a tone for an essay, use it consistently.

How would you describe the tone of this brief essay?

On Knitting

Carolyn Kott Washburne

Over the years I've felt that knitting was not something I should even admit to 1 doing, much less loving. It's too staid, too frumpy—certainly not consistent with my self-image as a vibrant, worldly, with-it woman at mid-life.

So my passion was a private one until recently when, with the help of writer 2 May Sarton, I decided to come out of the closet. In her book *Journal of a Solitude,* Sarton points out that because machines do things very quickly and outside the natural rhythm of life, we've become corrupted by them. We expect instant results, instant success. "The few things that we still do, such as cooking (though there are TV dinners!), knitting, gardening, anything at all that cannot be hurried," Sarton says, "have a very particular value."

The natural rhythm of my life, even on a good day, has a beat more like a   3
tarantella than a waltz. Like that of many overscheduled women, my time is filled with coordinating family schedules, meeting work deadlines, and fighting back the tide of leaky faucets and overgrown grass.

For years knitting has provided me with low-cost psychotherapy to cope   4
with all of this. I love to caress the smooth, round needles and rub the textured yarns between my fingers. I am soothed by the reassuring clicks as the needles touch one another. When I am anxious, knitting calms me down. When I am depressed, knitting cheers me. Some people achieve these altered states through yoga or marijuana. I get there by knitting.

Over the years I have produced a few handsome items and an equal num-   5
ber of disasters—a too-short sweater, several pairs of misshapen mittens, a cardigan vest with a right front noticeably longer than the left. (My dad, bless him, wore it anyway. Mostly when he walked the dog.)

The worst items I keep for myself and the less atrocious ones get passed on   6
as gifts, most of which probably stay buried in bureau drawers. Whatever its quality, each item proudly bears the label "Hand Made for You by Carolyn." I ordered 200 of these labels in 1967 and still have 153 left.

Knitting has become a welcome antidote to the pressures of my life, a tri-   7
umph of process over outcome. And, I remind myself, if I choose to knit rather than vacuum or wash dishes, I know I'm not procrastinating—I'm developing the virtue of patience.

Washburne's idea in this essay is that knitting is "a welcome antidote to the pressures of [her] life." Maintaining psychological and spiritual calm in a high-stress world is certainly a topic for serious-minded essays and books. But Washburne's tone is not *entirely* serious: she creates a light-hearted, gently self-mocking tone that nonetheless shows real commitment to her idea. She communicates this tone through word choice:

> Over the years, I've felt that knitting was not something I should even admit to doing, much less loving.

> Over the years I have produced a few handsome items and an equal number of disasters. . . .

> My dad, bless him, wore it anyway. Mostly when he walked the dog.

> The worst items I keep for myself and the less atrocious ones get passed on as gifts, most of which probably stay buried in bureau drawers.

Here is a writer who is capable of poking fun at her experience while at the same time being committed to the significance of that experience. Has Washburne matched her tone well to the writing occasion? Yes. Had she decided to be completely earnest in this piece, readers might have complained: "Lady, lighten up. You're talking about knitting!" Washburne realizes that her topic cannot sustain an unwavering serious tone. And yet she wants to make a serious, legitimate point that in a mechanized world where efficiency is measured in nanoseconds, we do well to slow down and remember "the natural rhythm of life." The writer's task was to make a serious point with a topic that does not lend itself to high seriousness. Washburne succeeds by creating a light-hearted tone that steers the reader gently to the point. Through careful word choice, she creates common ground and makes the essay a place where readers can join in her investigation.

Washburne also creates common ground with details that build a base of shared knowledge and experience in the essay. Through carefully chosen details, readers gain background enough to her life, and are given reference enough to *their* lives, to understand Washburne's idea. Her techniques for creating common ground include narration, summary, quotation, and reference to readers' experiences.

Narration: Washburne offers stories that let us see into her experience.

> Over the years I have produced a few handsome items . . .

Summary and quotation: Washburne puts someone else's ideas and words before the reader, creating a point of common reference.

> In her book *Journal of a Solitude,* [May] Sarton points out that because machines do things very quickly and outside the natural rhythm of life, we've become corrupted by them. We expect instant results, instant success. "The few things that we still do, . . ."

Reference to readers' experiences: Washburne understands that she is not the only woman in America who is heavily burdened.

> Like that of many overscheduled women, my time is filled with coordinating family schedules, meeting work deadlines, . . .

Washburne also refers to strategies readers may have used to achieve calm:

> When I am anxious, knitting calms me down. When I am depressed, knitting cheers me. Some people achieve these altered states through yoga or marijuana. I get there by knitting.

And Washburne refers to the generosity of loved ones who accept our lopsided, homemade gifts. Very likely, readers have either given or received such gifts:

> Over the years I have produced a few handsome items and an equal number of disasters. . . . My dad, bless him, wore [a misshapen cardigan vest] anyway. Mostly when he walked the dog.

Carolyn Washburne has worked hard to create a base of shared experience in her essay—a common ground on which readers can meet her and understand her idea. She has communicated not by accident but by design. Through careful word choice, she controls her essay's tone; and through carefully chosen details from her readers' and her own experience, she creates a base of shared knowledge in the essay through which an idea can be communicated. Washburne has created a common ground.

Summary

Readers understand ideas made vivid by and explained through details. The common ground that you create in your essay lets readers stand beside you as you as prepare for, express, and explore your ideas. Draw on your own experience, on your readers' experiences, and on shared public experiences to create a common ground for every paragraph of your essay. As you write and rewrite paragraphs, ask: What are the details, here, through which I can develop an idea and help readers to understand?

For Discussion and Writing

Exercise 1

Identify the various strategies by which Steven Sainsbury achieves common ground in "Condoms: Safer, But Not 'Safe,' Sex." Work through the essay paragraph by paragraph, using the strategies for creating common ground discussed in this chapter as a guide. (Don't feel limited by these strategies; you may discover others.) On finishing, respond to these questions: How successful is Sainsbury in helping you to understand his idea? And, having understood, do you agree with him?

Condoms: Safer, But Not "Safe," Sex

Steven Sainsbury

My 15-year-old patient with pelvic pain lay quietly on the gurney, as I asked 1 her the standard questions.

"Are you sexually active?" 2

"Yes." 3

"Are you using any form of birth control?" 4

"No." 5

"What about condoms?" 6

"No." 7

Her answers didn't surprise me. Nor was it surprising that her pain was due 8 to a rip-roaring gonorrheal infection, although it just as easily could have been due to some other venereal disease, a tubal pregnancy or even AIDS. As a specialist in emergency medicine, I treat teenagers like this one every day. Most are sexually active. Condoms are used rarely and sporadically.

Yet in the midst of the AIDS epidemic, I continue to hear condoms touted 9 as the solution to HIV transmission. As part of a "safe sex" campaign, condoms are passed out in high schools, sold in college restroom dispensers and routinely discussed.

The message? Condoms equal safe sex. 10

As a physician, I wish that this were true. Yet, to imply that the use of con- 11 doms will safeguard both sex partners from venereal disease, including AIDS, is not only a lie, it is a dangerous lie.

Consider the following two vital facts. 12

Fact No. 1: Condoms are not being used. Many studies confirm this, includ- 13 ing one survey among college women—a group we might presume to be as well-informed as any on the risks of herpes, genital warts, cervical cancer and AIDS. In 1989, only 41 percent insisted on condom use during sexual intercourse! If educated women cannot remember to use condoms, how can we expect teen-agers or the uninformed to do so?

Fact No. 2: Condoms fail, and fail frequently. Because of improper storage, 14 handling and usage by consumers, the condom breakage rate during vaginal intercourse is 14 percent. Other high-risk behaviors, particularly anal intercourse, increase this rate significantly. For the person who averages sex three times a week, a 14 percent breakage rate equates to a condom failure every two weeks.

AIDS is a killer disease, and any measures taken to prevent its transmission 15 must be 100 percent effective. For condoms to be the answer to AIDS, they must be used *every* time and can *never* break or leak. Neither criterion is ever likely to be met. Condoms may mean "safer" sex, but is "safer" acceptable for this deadly epidemic?

Suppose that, for unknown reasons, automobiles suddenly began to ex- 16 plode *every* time someone turned the ignition. Motorists were getting blown up all over the country. Finally, the government comes out with a solution. Just put this additive in the fuel, they say, and the risk of explosion will go down 90 per-cent. Would you consider the problem solved? Would you still keep driving your car? I doubt it. Then why do we accept condoms as the solution for AIDS?

There is one recommendation, and only one, that is guaranteed to prevent 17 the transmission of the AIDS virus and most other sexually transmitted diseases. A recommendation that lies buried in government reports but has always resided in common sense: that the only safe sex is no sex until one is ready to commit to a monogamous relationship with an uninfected person. The key words are *abstinence* and *monogamy.*

I can hear the moans already. Condom fans begin to reflexively murmur 18 words like *unrealistic, naive,* and *old-fashioned.* Well, perhaps a return to a few old-fashioned concepts is what's needed to stem the surging tide of AIDS, unwanted pregnancies and venereal disease. Just as we try to teach our children to be honest, kind and gentle, perhaps we can also teach them to be chaste.

American families are bombarded by continual images of unprincipled sex- 19 ual activity in movies, television and print media. Planned Parenthood found that there are roughly 20,000 sexual scenes *every* year on American television. Isn't it time to lend balance to the distorted and dangerous lifestyles portrayed as the norm for our society?

The French noblewoman Madame de Sevigne, writing in 1671, described 20 the condom as a "spider web against danger." Three centuries later, little has changed.

Exercise 2

Choose a single topic about which you are an expert: playing an instrument, playing a sport, building, collecting, hiking—whatever. Select a particular part of this expertise (if you are a swimmer you might choose the flip turn). Consider how you would explain this one part of your expertise to three dif-ferent audiences: an audience of fellow experts, an audience of beginners who are not yet experts but have the spirit and talent to be, and an audience of those who know little if anything of your expertise (and may not be interest-ed). Assume that you are presenting your explanations orally. Write the *first* page of your opening remarks to these three groups. Your key challenge is this: How will these different audience situations affect your presentation?

Exercise 3

Write a series of three brief letters to a mail-order business asking why you have not received the computer software you ordered and paid for. The letters should show a change in tone and purpose, moving from a neutral inquiry in the first letter to annoyed concern in the second to controlled anger in the third.

A Student Writer at Work: Mike Bergom

In the opening exercise to this book, you will find the final-draft version of an essay by a student writer, Mike Bergom: "Technology, Jazz, and History." Below, Bergom comments on how his sense of the essay's common ground changed as he moved from his first draft to his second draft. Read his comments and then respond to the follow-up question.

Common ground proved to be one of the most difficult aspects of my essay. I planned to address two fairly difficult topics, technology and jazz, and I needed to a establish common ground in both so that readers could follow my discussions. For jazz, I had to be careful not to assume a reader knowledgeable of jazz history. Because of this, I chose prominent jazz musicians as part of my common ground. Miles Davis is known throughout the world and most people have at least heard of the "Tonight Show" band with Branford Marsalis. Hopefully, the reader would key in to these familiar musicians and would understand and take interest in my thesis. To create a common ground with readers for my points about technology, I used a theory of Melvin Kranzberg. This theory, I figured, would give the reader an insight into why people might choose or reject a specific technology. I returned to Kranzberg throughout the paper.

Common ground in my first draft was disjointed and sporadic. Instead of relying on aspects of the same common ground to guide whole paragraphs, I used several different types of common ground details in individual paragraphs—with not-so-successful results:

First Draft

So jazz has seen many transformations by technology: the electric guitar, the electric bass, synthesizers, digital multi-track recording, and digital amplification. Yet the late 1980s and early 1990s have exemplified an aversion to technology in jazz. Groups are changing from the electric bands of the 70s and early 80s to the all acoustic bands of the 40s and 50s. Examples of this include such influential young musicians as saxophonist Branford Marsalis (former director of Jay Leno's *Tonight Show* band), jazz educator and trumpeter Wynton Marsalis, acoustic guitarist Mark Whitfield, and upright bassist Robert Hurst . . . they refuse to accept the "new" ways of doing things, and instead opt to return to the roots of jazz.

In this paragraph from the first draft, my common ground is the instruments I mention in the first sentence and earlier in the essay: the electric guitar, electric bass, and so on. This produced a paragraph that summarized two pages of my essay. This summary throws the reader out of the paragraph, when details should be focusing readers' attention on the idea *in* the paragraph. As for the organization of the whole essay, this didn't work either. I organized entire paragraphs by instrument, and the essay simply jolted the reader from one example to the next. The first draft had this structure: Here's the synthesizer and why people don't like it; here's the electric sax and why people don't like it; and so on. The result was eight mini-essays, not a single, integrated whole. To remedy the problem, I abandoned the old approach and refocused on my main idea: to explain why young jazz musicians were abandoning technology. The common ground that evolved for this particular paragraph helped me to create a consistent common ground for the entire essay. Here's my second-draft version of the paragraph, with the new emphasis:

Second Draft

In spite of the hi-tech world of today, and the tendency of jazz to reflect that world, several young jazz musicians are deciding to say no to technology, and instead pursue the "roots" of jazz. Trumpeter and jazz historian Wynton Marsalis, saxophonist and former *Tonight Show* band leader Branford Marsalis, acoustic guitarist Mark Whitfield—these musicians, all under 35 years old, refuse to utilize in their music the technology offered to them. They instead employ the traditional instrumentation and format of jazz music. They regard the use of current technology in jazz as impure, almost sacrilegious, and denounce those musicians who do take advantage of technology.

For this paragraph in my second draft I created a different common ground. Instead of opening with the instruments of jazz music (which readers may or may not have cared about), I concentrated on the several well-known jazz musicians who had either experimented with technology or refused to use it. Choosing this common ground gave me a set of details about jazz music, the role of technology in jazz music, and the willingness of musicians to accept or deny technology. The new common-ground focus on individual musicians, as opposed to instruments, exactly matched the idea of my essay.

Read Bergom's final-draft paragraph that follows and comment on the ways in which he has continued to address issues of common ground. In what ways is Bergom trying even harder in this final-draft paragraph to provide details that give readers full access to his thinking?

Final Draft

And yet several young jazz musicians are saying "No!" to technology and are pursuing, with acoustic instruments, what might be called the "roots" of jazz. Trumpeter and jazz historian Wynton Marsalis, saxophonist and former *Tonight Show* band leader Branford Marsalis, and acoustic guitarist Mark Whitfield—these musicians, all under 35 years old, refuse to use the latest technologies in their music. They instead employ traditional instrumentation and jazz formats. On the face of it, this rejection is odd: as a culture, we are quick to demand and accept new technologies. We scramble for faster computers, we insist on cars with dual airbags, we debate which electric tooth brush will keep our smiles brightest. Why, then, do these young musicians, who have grown up in a technological age, refuse what has been designed to help them?

Advancing Your Idea with Sources

The purpose of an essay is to communicate an idea to a specific group of readers. You may want to persuade readers to accept your idea; you may want to explain, explore, resolve, analyze, or interpret. Whatever your purpose, your goal for every line that you write should be to advance the idea of your essay—to help readers further understand the point you wish to make. One of the most effective ways to advance an idea is to draw on the work of others who have written on that same idea. As these brief passages will show, source materials can provide you with facts, examples, and authoritative opinions, and can help to put the idea of your essay in a broader context.

Sources Can Provide You with Facts

Controversy surrounding the portrayal of racial and ethnic minorities on television is almost as old as the medium itself. Peoples of color have historically been both underrepresented and misrepresented on television. During the early years, nonwhites comprised fewer than 3% of all character portrayals (Smythe, 1953). By the early 1970s, however, this figure had increased to approximately 11% (U.S. Commission on Civil Rights, 1977), and there it remained throughout most of this decade (Greenberg, 1982). Although Blacks have always been television's most visible minority group, parity with the U.S. census data has yet to be achieved. Furthermore, minority characters, be they Blacks, Asians, Native Americans, or Latinos, have traditionally been less diverse, less dignified, and less positive than either white characters or real life minorities.

Marsha E. Williams and John C. Condry, *from* "Living Color: Minority Portrayals and Cross-racial Interactions on Television."

We know that advertisers are persuasive, and we know that the power of advertisements over children is directly related to the amount of television that children watch. According to a survey cited in a recent article by American Federation of Teachers President Albert Shanker, one-quarter of nine year olds in this country watch 42 hours of television each week (7)—approximately eight hours of which is devoted to advertisements. The most obvious way to eliminate the exposure to so much advertising is to limit television viewing. Still, we are not about to eliminate television from the American household. In a best-case scenario, we might reduce viewing time by half. If we could return our children to viewing a modest 25 hours of weekly television (the 1977 level), they would still be seeing nearly 260 hours of advertisements each year. Is this acceptable?

Alison Tschopp, *from* "Advertising to Children Should Not Be Banned"

Sources Can Provide You with Examples

Scientists have discovered the benefits and uses of genetically engineered organisms in agriculture. One important example is the ice-minus bacterium created by Steve Lindow and Nicholas Panopoulos. Realizing a bacterium commonly found in plants produces a protein that helps ice to form, these scientists removed the unfavorable gene and thereby prevented ice from forming on greenhouse plants (Carey 18). Others have manipulated genetic materials to create tobacco that kills attacking insects and to produce plants that resist herbicides. Geneticists hope in 20 to 40 years to produce plants such as corn and other grains that "fix" their own nitrogen—that will be able to extract nitrogen from the atmosphere without relying on nitrifying bacteria. If such plants could be created, U.S. farmers would save $3 to $4 billion annually in fertilizer costs and could save one third of all crops lost each year to pests. Ultimately, geneticists hope to use the same amounts of land, fertilizer, and pesticide while producing greater yields; this method of increasing productivity could be most beneficial to countries with limited usable land (Pimentel 25).

Josefa Pinto, *from* "Genetically Engineered Organisms and the Environment"

Sources Can Provide You with Authoritative Opinions

Many educated people confuse the Arab world with the Moslem world. Geographically, Arab countries stretch along Northern Africa and into the Middle East. But the Moslem world overlaps the Arab world and stretches far beyond to most of Africa continuing eastward through India, Indonesia and the Philippines. Not all of the Arab world's 150 million people are Moslem, though many, of course, are both.

Former news correspondent, radio announcer and author, Edward J. Byng, writes in his book *The World of the Arabs*, "Our Western picture of Islam and of the Arabs is a pitiful caricature of the reality. It is the result of thirteen hundred years of religious propaganda." In Arabic, "Islam" means submission to God. A religion that celebrated its 1400th anniversary in 1981, Islam provides an all-inclusive system for social and religious conduct based upon the Koran (divine revelations) and the teachings of the prophet Mohammed. It is monotheistic and shares values and traditions with Christianity and Judaism. For example, Abraham (Ibrahim, in Arabic) is considered by Moslems as the father of all monotheistic people and is thus revered in Islam. Mohammed is the *last* prophet, following the footsteps of Abraham, Moses and Jesus. Islam's most basic acts of faith are usually called "The Five Pillars of Islam"—Profession of Faith, Prayer, Almsgiving, Fasting and Pilgrimage.

But on TV entertainment programs, when performers refer to "Allah" or Islam, viewers do not see devout worshippers. TV often shows Islam as a religion that permits a man to have many wives and concubines and condones beheadings and stoning people to death. Although "Allah" means God, when performers say "Allah" on TV it is usually with the intent of evoking laughter, cynicism, or the image of some vaguely pagan deity.

Jack Shaheen, *from* "The TV Arab"

Sources Can Help Situate the Idea of Your Essay in a Broader Context

Much of the best physical evidence in crime investigation comes from the examination of distinctive marks left at the scene of the crime. The comparison of these marks with something known to be associated with a suspect can often yield unique evidence. The instinctive knowledge that such marks can be unique seems to be an integral part of human nature.

Sisyphus, a figure in Ancient Greek mythology, knew it well when he marked the hooves of his cattle with notches. Because of this, when the master thief Autolycus denied stealing the cattle, Sisyphus was able to prove that he was lying.

In more recent times accounts of such "shape" evidence become more frequent. One such account relates to the murder of Edward Culshaw in Lancashire, England in 1784. Culshaw was shot in the head by a muzzle-loading gun. The surgeon who carried out the post-mortem examination recovered a piece of paper, used as a wad, from the wound.

This wad had been used to retain the powder and shot in the barrel of the gun and to provide a gas-tight seal in front of the expanding hot gases that pushed the shot out of the barrel. The wad was found to have been torn from a larger sheet of paper. The remainder of this sheet of paper was found in the possession of a suspect, who was convicted and hanged on the evidence.

Nowadays, firearm evidence is much more complex than in the eighteenth century, although a case is recorded in the USA where, almost two hundred years after the case described above, a similar set of circumstances arose. In this case a home-loaded shotgun cartridge was used in the commission of a murder and the piece of newspaper which was used as a wad was discharged into the fatal wound, just as it had been in the eighteenth century English murder. A similar piece of newspaper, with a matching torn edge, was found in possession of the suspect.

Modern firearm evidence, much of it developed in the USA, deals with the same principles in a more sophisticated way. . . .

Stuart S. Kind, *from* "Science and the Hunt for the Criminal"

Regardless of the course for which you are writing, you can strengthen your essay by referring to the work of others. In doing so, you become a member of a larger community of thinkers and writers who refer to these same materials in their work; for example, in a physics course, you and your professors will make use of articles in specialized journals. In a literature course, you and your professors will refer to poems, plays, short stories, and novels and to the essays of literary critics. To be a member of an academic community means, in part, to value similar kinds of sources. This chapter presents you with strategies for incorporating sources into your essays in any discipline.

Sources and Cycles of Development

Organize an essay according to a single idea and its related parts, not according to source materials. Here is how you might put this first principle to use in individual paragraphs:

- Introduce your idea into a paragraph before you introduce a source.
- Working with your paragraph's idea, create a context into which you can fit a source.
- Having created a context, steer the reader directly to your source.
- Quote, summarize, or paraphrase the source.
- *Use* the source by responding to it, commenting on it, and explaining its significance.

When you apply this principle to individual paragraphs, you create what can be called a "cycle of development" for using source materials. A full cycle ensures that your reference to a source will advance your idea without dominating the paragraph in which it appears. A full cycle also ensures that you will have created a context in which readers can understand your references to a source.

Quiz Your Thesis

One idea—*your* idea—should dominate an essay. Source materials exist to support your idea. When overused, sources can undermine your authority by giving the reader the impression that you are not thinking for yourself. The key to avoiding this problem is to organize your paragraphs by ideas, not by sources. Here is one strategy you can follow: in planning a first draft, write your working thesis on a blank page. At this early stage of the writing process, your working thesis represents the clearest expression of what you *expect* your essay's idea to be. Now *quiz* this thesis in order to identify all its significant parts: circle words and phrases you think are important, and direct a clarifying question or comment to each. Here are some generic questions and comments about a thesis that you can adapt for your specific purposes:

Questions

how does/will it happen?	what has happened/will prevent
how can I describe it?	it from happening?
what are some examples?	who is involved?
what are the reasons for it?	what are the key features?
what is my view?	what are the reasons against it?
compared to what?	how often?
what is the cause?	is it possible to classify types
are there any stories to tell?	or parts?
how?	what is the effect of this?
when?	which ones?

Comments

define	review the reasoning
review the facts	explain the contrast or paradox

Directing questions and comments at your working thesis will help you identify your essay's significant parts: the subordinate ideas, stated directly and indirectly, that will make up the interconnecting sections of your essay. Using these subordinate ideas, organize a sketch, as in the following examples:

Thesis #1:   *What are the facts?*   *Review the reasons.*

Define in 2 ways. (By instituting a curfew for dormitory visitors) and acting on what it believed was in the students' best interests, the (administration undermined the moral and educational principles it wanted to uphold.

How?

Define.

Sketch #1:
What are the facts?
    Provide a history of the curfew debate.
What are the reasons for the curfew?
    In setting a curfew for dormitory visitors, the college administration said it was acting in the best interests of students.
What are the "students' best interests"?
    Define from the students' and the administration's perspectives.
What are the moral issues and educational principles at stake?
    Values, autonomy, and status as adults are at stake.
A paradox: the administration undermined its own goals.
    By denying students a chance to grapple with moral issues and reach mature decisions on their own, the administration failed in its educational role.

Thesis #2:   *Define: compared*
                   to what?   *How so?*

(The volunteer army) has succeeded in defending the security interests of
the United States and (we should not, therefore, reinstitute a draft.)

Sketch #2:   *What are the*   *What are the*
                                        reasons for?   *reasons against?*
    The volunteer army: compared to what?
        Mercenaries vs. militias (history)
    What are the reasons against?
        Moral reasons
        Racial reasons
    What are the reasons for?
        Military reasons
        Monetary reasons

Adding sources to your sketch: As you think about each section of
your prospective essay, ask: What source materials can I draw on to help
me advance my idea? This strategy of placing sources into an essay *after*
you have conceived many of the essay's ideas will ensure that sources
play an important, but supporting, role. Observe the addition of sources
in this sketch:

A Sketch *with* Sources:
    The volunteer army: compared to what?
        Mercenaries vs. militias

    What are the reasons against?
        Moral reasons: responsibilities of individual to the State
            Source: Plato's dialogue, *Crito*

        Racial reasons: army composed of disproportionately high number of
            minorities
            Source: Barone and Gergen
            Source: Gary Becker
            Source: David Kelley

    What are the reasons for?
        Military reasons:
            Highly trained soldiers needed to operate sophisticated technology
            Source: Michael Novak
            Source: David Kelley
            Source: Former Secretary of Defense, Dick Cheney

        Monetary reasons: volunteer army saves money
            Source: Deputy Assistant Secretary for Defense, David Armor

The goal is to quiz your thesis aggressively, to identify parts of your
essay's idea, and to prepare an outline based on these ideas. *Then* introduce sources. When you draw on source materials in this way, you can be
certain that they will not dominate the essay.

Principle 1: Introduce Your Idea into a Paragraph before You Introduce a Source

This is a direct application of the earlier principle, that an essay should be organized by a set of related ideas, not by sources. Each paragraph of an essay gives you the opportunity to discuss one of the related ideas that forms a part of the larger whole. If you plan on referring to a source in a paragraph, plan as well to begin with a statement of your idea.

A cycle of development begins.

> In these days of sophisticated weaponry, we need a military made up of intelligent individuals who have the ability to learn the technical aspects of warfare.

#1 The writer's idea comes first: we need a technically sophisticated military.

Principle 2: Working with Your Paragraph's Idea, Create a Context into Which You Can Fit a Source

Sources that appear without preparation strike readers as abrupt and confusing. Your goal for every paragraph in which a source appears should be to create a context in which your reference to a source fits easily. After beginning the paragraph with your idea, introduce an example or otherwise provide background information that is directly related to the source you want to summarize, paraphrase, or quote. For the moment, simply provide background; don't mention the source. Your goal is to create a *setting* for this source.

A cycle of development begins.

#2 A context is created into which the source can fit.

> In these days of sophisticated weaponry, we need a military made up of intelligent individuals who have the ability to learn the technical aspects of warfare. **The Persian Gulf War provides a good example. Shortly after the 100-hour war, nightly news programs, weekly magazines, and daily newspapers heralded the use of "smart bombs," night vision equipment, and advanced communications gear that helped U.S. soldiers gain a speedy and decisive victory. The technical sophistication of today's weapons requires that soldiers be well trained and experienced.**

#1 The writer's idea comes first: we need a technically sophisticated military.

Principle 3: Having Created a Context, Steer the Reader Directly to Your Source

You have prepared the reader for your reference to a source by opening the paragraph with a clearly stated idea and by creating a context into which the source fits. Now steer the reader directly to your source. Sometimes you can do this with a phrase or a transitional remark.

Occasionally, as in the example below, you will need a sentence or two.

A cycle of development begins.

In these days of sophisticated weaponry, we need a military made up of intelligent individuals who have the ability to learn the technical aspects of warfare. The Persian Gulf War provides a good example. Shortly after the 100-hour war, nightly news programs, weekly magazines, and daily newspapers heralded the use of "smart bombs," night vision equipment, and advanced communications gear that helped U.S. soldiers gain a speedy and decisive victory. The technical sophistication of today's weapons requires that soldiers be well trained and experienced. **During the draft era, the military was forced to take high-school dropouts. College students were able to avoid the draft because of schooling and the result, according to columnist Michael Novak, was troubling:**

#1 The writer's idea comes first: we need a technically sophisticated military.

#2 A context is created into which the source can fit.

#3 The author steers us directly to the source: the speaker is identified and the source is characterized (as "troubling").

Prepare your readers in two ways when you steer them to a source:

1. If it is useful, provide information about *who* is speaking in order to establish the authority of a source.
2. Offer some summarizing or characterizing remark as a final introduction.

In the example above, we learn (1) that Michael Novak is a columnist and (2) that the quotation we are about to read involves a "troubling" situation. Novak's remark is given a certain stature because he is a columnist and columnists are paid to be thoughtful about current events. Acknowledging a reference to a columnist who was writing about the army during the draft era is useful and very much pertinent to the essay. The following example from the same essay demonstrates two cases—one in which directly identifying the author of a source is important and one in which identifying the author is *not* important:

Today, 92% of recruits hold high-school diplomas (Kelley 11). Pay, maintenance, and morale has increased to the point that the forces are, according to former Secretary of Defense Cheney, "the highest-quality force in the nation's history" (qtd. in Barone and Gergen 45).

The source of the statistic about 92 percent of recruits is not important enough to state it directly in this sentence; a parenthetical note is sufficient. If we need to know the origin of this statistic, we can check the reference. If you can make your reference to a source more emphatic by naming a person or organization, do so. Knowing that a former Secretary of Defense was the one who called our present-day volunteer army "the highest-quality force in the nation's history" *is* significant. Cheney, an authority, lends credibility to the essay.

Principle 4: Quote, Summarize, or Paraphrase the Source

You are ready to quote, summarize, or paraphrase the source. Having prepared as you have, you can be confident that readers are in the best possible position to understand.

A cycle of development begins.

#1 The writer's idea comes first: we need a technically sophisticated military.

In these days of sophisticated weaponry, we need a military made up of intelligent individuals who have the ability to learn the technical aspects of warfare. The Persian Gulf War provides a good example. Shortly after the 100-hour war, nightly news programs, weekly magazines, and daily newspapers heralded the use of "smart bombs," night vision equipment, and advanced communications gear that helped U.S. soldiers gain a speedy and decisive victory. The technical sophistication of today's weapons requires that soldiers be well trained and experienced. During the draft era, the military was forced to take high-school dropouts. College students were able to avoid the draft because of schooling and the result, according to columnist Michael Novak, was troubling: an army **"composed disproportionately of the poor, the less intellectually able, and the less idealistic"** which **"is not healthy for our democracy" (847).**

#2 A context is created into which the source can fit.

#3 The author steers us directly to the source: the speaker is identified and the source is characterized (as "troubling").

#4 The source is quoted, summarized, or paraphrased.

Principle 5: Use the Source. Let It Help You to Begin a New Cycle of Development

You have located a source, created a context for it, and incorporated it into your essay. Now take full advantage of the opportunity you have created by *using* the source: respond to it, comment on it, and explain its significance. Complete the cycle of development by directly stating for the reader how this source advances the idea of your paragraph. In your responses and comments, you can address questions like these:

- Do I agree with this author? Disagree? How can I use my agreement or disagreement to advance the idea of this paragraph?
- How is the source significant?
- How does this source relate to my paragraph?
- What is my emotional response to the source?

Recall that an essay consists of a series of related paragraphs; the idea of one paragraph is related to the idea of the paragraph that precedes and follows it. At the end of one cycle of development in an essay, you have a very real interest in making a transition to the next idea you are going to develop. Often, you can use the source that you have just introduced to help you make this transition.

A cycle of development begins.

#1 The writer's idea comes first: we need a technically sophisticated military.

In these days of sophisticated weaponry, we need a military made up of intelligent individuals who have the ability to learn the technical aspects of warfare. The Persian Gulf War provides a good example. Shortly after the 100-hour war, nightly news programs, weekly magazines, and daily newspapers heralded the use of "smart bombs," night vision equipment, and advanced communications gear that helped U.S. soldiers gain a speedy and decisive victory. The technical sophistication of today's weapons requires that soldiers be well trained and experienced. During the draft era, the military was forced to take high-school dropouts. College students were able to avoid the draft because of schooling and the result, according to columnist Michael Novak, was troubling: an army "composed disproportionately of the poor, the less intellectually able, and the less idealistic" which "is not healthy for our democracy" (847). **Nor does such an army make for an effective fighting force.**

Novak was writing in 1980, in response to an all volunteer army that was in disarray after the Vietnam war. Given the state of military affairs, Novak was arguing to reinstitute the draft. But in the 13 years since his essay appeared in *National Review,* his objections to the volunteer army have been met *without* resorting to a draft. In 1980, only 54% of recruits had high-school diplomas. Pay was bad and maintenance of weapons and aircraft was low. Today, 92% of recruits hold high-school diplomas (Kelley 11). Pay, maintenance, and morale has increased to the point that the forces are, according to former Secretary of Defense Cheney, "the highest-quality force in the nation's history" (qtd. in Barone and Gergen 45). . . .

—Michele Pelletier, "The Volunteer Army: A Good Idea"

#2 A context is created into which the source can fit.

#4 The source is quoted, summarized, or paraphrased.

A new cycle of development begins.

#3 The author steers us directly to the source: the speaker is identified and the source is characterized (as "troubling").

#5 The writer comments on or responds to the source. The writer points to a new cycle of development.

By creating a cycle of development in your essays, you put to work a strategy for setting up, presenting, and discussing references to source materials that advances the specific idea of a paragraph. The other way to advance an idea is by discussing it on your own terms, without reference to sources. And, in fact, the majority of most essays is given to *your* discussion. Source materials support your ideas, and the strategies presented here help you to use them effectively.

Note that Michele Pelletier was careful to cite her use of sources, so that readers could consult them if needed. Whether she quoted, summarized, or paraphrased, she provided clear references in a style conforming to the subject area in which she worked. [She used Modern Language Association (MLA) parenthetical style—see pages 614–621.] Here is the passage that Pelletier quoted from Michael Novak's "Reflections on the Draft." The quoted words are highlighted:

> Much depends, then, on the willingness, generosity, and spirit of self-sacrifice of the nation's youth. It is urgent to improve the quality of the U.S. armed forces, in personnel and in equipment, as rapidly as possible. Time is very short. In this perspective, it is a Christian duty for those who see it so, to rise to the defense of the nation. It would be wonderful if intelligent, idealistic, and able young Americans volunteered for service to their nation. But it would be far more fair if selective service called upon members of every class to serve the nation.
>
> An army composed disproportionately of the poor, the less intellectually able, and the less idealistic is not healthy for our democracy. Nor is it a sufficient deterrent to the ambitious, bold, younger leaders who may emerge during the next crisis in Soviet leadership.
>
> —*National Review* July 11, 1980

Pelletier was selective in quoting Novak and putting his words to her own uses. The paragraphs in which she referred to Novak formed one part of one section of her essay. She completed the other parts and sections with similarly constructed cycles of development, as you will see.

Synthesis: Linking Cycles of Development and Multiple Sources in an Essay

A **synthesis** is an essay in which you draw together ideas and information from a variety of sources according to your own guiding purpose. Michele Pelletier's paragraphs, part of a research paper, are a synthesis. You will be asked to synthesize and forge meaningful relationships among sources in virtually every course that you take. When you refer to multiple sources in an essay, use the strategy just described and illustrated in the work of Michele Pelletier: create a cycle of development for each source.

In her essay, "The Volunteer Army: A Good Idea," Pelletier synthesizes sources to provide facts, examples, and opinions and to set her idea in a broader context. Her use of sources is highlighted so that you can make two important observations at a glance: references to sources are distributed *throughout* the essay, and Pelletier's source materials do *not* overwhelm the essay. Notes in the margin indicate where she connects one cycle of development to another. Once again, there is no doubt who *owns* this essay: Pelletier's idea dominates, and sources play an important, but supporting, role.

The Volunteer Army: A Good Idea
Michele Pelletier

Since the abolition of compulsory draft laws in 1973, the United States 1
has had an all volunteer army. As recently as 1990, in anticipation of and
then in the wake of the Persian Gulf War, powerful voices in Congress
were calling for hearings to examine reinstituting the military draft.
Senator Nunn of Georgia and others have argued that young men and
women should give something back to the country that has nurtured and
protected them, and one such means of giving would be national military
service. If the draft is reinstituted, we young men and women of college
age, along with our younger siblings, would be the ones who served. We
who will be affected must take a hard look at this debate in order to decide
which type of army is most effective and offers America the best possible
value morally, militarily, and economically.

Armies of volunteers and conscripts are today's versions of the mili- 2
tias and mercenary forces that existed in the 15th and 16th centuries.
Militias were armies made up of citizens who were fighting for their home
country. Mercenaries were professional soldiers who, better trained than
militia men (they were always men), were hired by foreign countries to
fight wars. Mercenaries had no cause other than a paycheck: if the
country that hired them did not pay, they would quit the battlefield.
Mercenaries may have been fickle, but technically they were good fighters. Militia men may not have been as technically proficient as mercenaries, but they had the will to fight. Both of these traditions—fighting for a
cause and fighting for money—have found their way into American military history of the past thirty years.

A cycle of development
begins

In the period just after the Vietnam war, the draft was not at all pop- 3
ular in this country and was viewed, as one commentator put it, "as a
form of involuntary servitude" (Kelley 11). Little wonder, then, that the

A new cycle of develop-
ment begins

compulsory draft was abolished. Still some argued then and argue now a
position that has much merit: that the state, which nurtures and protects
the individual, has the moral right to ask that individual for service.
Balancing the needs of the state against the rights of the individual is an
ancient concern, dating at least to the times of classical Greece. In one of
Plato's dialogues, *Crito,* Socrates explains the State's position. (The "we"
in this passage refers to the collective voice and authority of Athens.)

> For, having brought you into the world, and nurtured and educated
> you, and given you and every other citizen a share in every good which
> we had to give, we further proclaim to any Athenian by the liberty
> which we allow him, that if he does not like us when he has become of
> age and has seen the ways of the city, and made our acquaintance, he
> may go where he pleases and take his goods with him. None of us laws
> will forbid him or interfere with him. . . . But he who has experience of
> the manner in which we order justice and administer the State, and still

remains, has entered into an implied contract that he will do as we command him. (102)

In this passage, Socrates argues that a citizen who enjoys the privileges and securities of living under State protection owes that State obedience. If the authority decides that, for the good of the State, young men should be drafted, then it is the duty of young men so called to obey and to serve. It is true: we owe the society that nurtures us a debt. But how best that debt is paid and to what extent the citizens who "owe" are entitled to participate in deciding on payment—these are difficult questions that have been debated through the centuries. The position of Socrates, as applied to military service, leads directly to an army of draftees: The State has a need for protection. Citizens owe the State a debt. The State calls young men, and they come.

If the State institutes a draft for the purposes of protection, then we are within our rights to ask: Does an army of draftees, necessarily, offer the best possible protection? If we can demonstrate that an all volunteer force *better* serves the security interests of the State, then it should follow that we do not need a draft. If the State wants to claim its moral debt from citizens, fine: let that debt be paid with some other, non-military service. In what ways can an all volunteer army be shown to be superior to an army of draftees?

A new cycle of development begins.

First, in these days of sophisticated weaponry, we need a military made up of intelligent individuals who have the ability to learn the technical aspects of warfare. The Persian Gulf War provides a good example. Shortly after the 100-hour war, nightly news programs, weekly magazines, and daily newspapers heralded the use of "smart bombs," night vision equipment, and advanced communications gear that helped U.S. soldiers gain a speedy and decisive victory. The technical sophistication of today's weapons requires that soldiers be well trained and experienced. During the draft era, the military was forced to take high-school dropouts. College students were able to avoid the draft because of schooling and the result, according to columnist Michael Novak, was troubling: an army "composed disproportionately of the poor, the less intellectually able, and the less idealistic" which "is not healthy for our democracy" (847). Nor does such an army make for an effective fighting force.

A new cycle of development begins.

Novak was writing in 1980, in response to an all volunteer army that was in disarray after the Vietnam war. Given the state of military affairs, Novak was arguing to reinstitute the draft. But in the 13 years since his essay appeared in *National Review,* his objections to the volunteer army have been met *without* resorting to a draft. In 1980, only 54% of recruits had high-school diplomas. Pay was bad and maintenance of weapons and aircraft was low. Today, 92% of recruits hold high-school diplomas (Kelley 11). Pay, maintenance, and morale has increased to the point that the forces are, according to former Secretary of Defense Cheney, "the highest-quality force in the nation's history" (qtd. in Barone and Gergen 45). With a conscientious Congress, changes were instituted that created a volunteer force composed of educated, motivated, and loyal soldiers. No country could ask for, or want, a better fighting force. As a society we have met our obligation to the State: we are protecting our country and its interests more ably than at any other time. This being so, the State has no legitimate claim to make that we should reinstitute a draft to maintain military preparedness. We are prepared, and we got that way *through* a volunteer army.

A new cycle of development begins.

A cycle *within* a cycle begins.

With the moral and military arguments for the draft gone, some have 8 objected to the volunteer army on political grounds, claiming that the "nation's volunteer Army concentrates the burden of military service and the risk of death on poor and working-class men" (Barone and Gergen 45). Gary Becker, University Professor of Economics and Sociology at the University of Chicago, ably counters this view:

> It is true that blacks constitute over 20% of the armed forces compared with only 12% of the civilian work force. But the Army is not staffed mainly by the lower classes, as demonstrated by the preponderance of high-school graduates and by the fact that almost half of all recruits come from families with above-average incomes. (14)

A cycle *within* a cycle begins.

Not only does Becker reject the criticism that an all volunteer military 9 draws on the poor and working class, he praises the military for offering minorities a chance for advancement not found in the private sector. Writing for *Barron's,* David Kelley reports that blacks find in military life a chance for education and an environment "remarkably free of racial enmity." For every five whites who re-enlist at the end of a tour, eight blacks re-enlist (11). If the military were inhospitable to blacks, blacks themselves would be making complaints against it. But clearly, they are not. The former Chairman of the Joint Chiefs of the military services was black. So is a tenth of the army's officers. These highly visible positions of status send the strongest possible signal that blacks are welcome and participate throughout the military system, both in the infantry and in the Pentagon.

A new cycle of development begins.

The Persian Gulf war demonstrated that the security needs of the 10 United States can be met with an all volunteer force. The war also demonstrated the need for soldiers who are motivated and intelligent. The outstanding performance of American troops in the Gulf would be justification enough to maintain an all volunteer force and to resist any attempts to reinstitute the draft. What has also become apparent is that the volunteer force, in addition to being more efficient and better prepared than a drafted force, is also *less* expensive to maintain. David Armor, Deputy Assistant Secretary of Defense for Force Management and Personnel, claims that a draft would lead to shorter service for recruits, which in turn would raise training costs for new recruits. Armor estimates that the volunteer forces save the country one billion dollars annually (Becker 14).

There are no compelling reasons that we should return to a draft. An 11 all volunteer army gives us a far better value: a better value morally—

individuals who serve willingly satisfy the State's need for protection and their own need to earn a living; a better value militarily—better prepared, better trained, longer-serving soldiers increase military effectiveness; and a better value economically—the volunteer army saves money. Even though a prayer for peace is said by millions every day, wars occur and our country is best protected with a force of well-educated, highly trained, motivated volunteers. Through careful planning and a long-standing commitment, we have managed to bring together in one volunteer force the best of two traditions in military service: the commitment of a national militia and the fighting savviness of mercenaries. The volunteer army works. We should not return to a draft.

Works Cited

Barone, Michael, and David Gergen. "The Case Against Reinstituting the Draft." *U.S. News & World Report* 24 Dec. 1990: 45.

Becker, Gary S. "Leave the Draft Where It Belongs: On History's Junk Heap." *Business Week* 25 Mar. 1991: 14.

Kelley, David. "Arms and the Man: In Terms of Quality, Morality, A Volunteer Military Beats the Draft." *Barron's* 30 Mar. 1987: 11+.

Novak, Michael. "Reflections on the Draft." *National Review* 11 July 1980: 847.

Plato, "Crito." *The Works of Plato.* New York: Modern Library, 1928.

Getting a Conversation Started among Your Sources

Much of the time when you draw on source materials to support an idea in an essay, you will refer to *single* sources, as, for example, Michele Pelletier does when referring to one of Plato's dialogues (see ¶s 3–4). You will also have opportunities for working with multiple sources in support of a single idea, as Pelletier does in ¶s 8–9.

Pelletier had read a number of sources on the idea of these particular paragraphs: the racial argument against the all volunteer army. She saw and seized an opportunity to use one source (Gary Becker) to respond to a difficult criticism for her essay posed in another source (Barone and Gergen). Pelletier found a third source (David Kelley) to help counter the criticism. Watch as she introduces one source and then another, managing effective transitions all the while. Pelletier is orchestrating a conversation. Once again, notice that her idea organizes the discussion. Sources play a supporting role.

The writer's idea organizes the conversation.

1st source

With the moral and military arguments for the draft gone, some have objected to the volunteer army on political grounds, claiming that the "nation's volunteer Army concentrates the burden of military service and the risk of death on poor and working-class men" (Barone and Gergen 45). Gary Becker, University Professor of Economics and Sociology at the University of Chicago, ably counters this view:

2nd source

> It is true that blacks constitute over 20% of the armed forces compared with only 12% of the civilian work force. But the Army is not staffed mainly by the lower classes, as demonstrated by the preponderance of high-

school graduates and by the fact that almost half of all recruits come from families with above-average incomes. (14)

Not only does Becker reject the criticism that an all volunteer military draws on the poor and working class, he praises the military for offering minorities a chance for advancement not found in the private sector.

3rd source ⟶ Writing for *Barron's,* David Kelley reports that blacks find in military life a chance for education and an environment "remarkably free of racial enmity." For every five whites who re-enlist at the end of a tour, eight blacks re-enlist (11). If the military were inhospitable to blacks, blacks themselves would be making complaints against it. But clearly, they are not. The former Chairman of the Joint Chiefs of the military services was black. So is a tenth of the army's officers. These highly visible positions of status send the strongest possible signal that blacks are welcome and participate throughout the military system, both in the infantry and in the Pentagon.

Just as in a conversation taking place orally, a conversation that you orchestrate in writing can have participants agreeing with one another, disagreeing, amplifying one another's observations, and more. In Pelletier's example, Becker disagrees with the views expressed in Barone and Gergen, and Kelley agrees with and amplifies Becker. When you organize an essay by idea, as opposed to by source, you create opportunities for conversations among multiple sources. In every case, *you* control the conversation.

Referring to Sources through Summary, Paraphrase, and Quotation

You will read about specific techniques for quoting, summarizing, and paraphrasing source materials in other sections of this book. The discussion here is confined to reasons you would choose one of these strategies as opposed to the others when you refer to a source.

Summary

A summary is a relatively brief, objective account in your own words of the main idea of a source passage. You summarize a passage when you want to extract main ideas and use them as background material in your writing. Summaries help you to condense information essential to your discussion. Most often you will summarize sections of a source, not an entire source. See the discussion in chapter 5, pages 81–87, for techniques on writing a summary; and see pages 577–579 for an example summary of a passage contrasted with a paraphrase of that same passage.

Paraphrase

A paraphrase is a restatement, in your own words, of a passage of text. The structure of a paraphrase reflects the structure of the source passage.

Paraphrases are sometimes the same length as a source passage, sometimes briefer, and occasionally—if the source passage is written in especially dense language—longer. You paraphrase a passage when you want to retain all of the points in the original, both major and minor; when you want to clarify complex ideas in a brief passage; and when you want to clarify difficult language in a brief passage. See chapter 5 for techniques on writing paraphrases and for an example paraphrase contrasted with a summary of the same passage.

Quotation

When you quote, you recreate the language of a source passage *exactly*. Knowing when and how much to quote, and how to incorporate quotations into your writing, is something of an art. See chapter 16, pages 580–583, for an extended discussion that will provide you with specific techniques for quoting. Also consult a handbook on the mechanics of quoting. Several distinctions can be made briefly, here. First, read the passage that follows; this will be a source for several examples. The author is noted anthropologist Richard Marks (*The New American Bazaar*):

> When they are successful, shopping malls in American cities fulfill the same function as *bazaars* did in the cities of antiquity. The bazaars of the ancient and medieval worlds were social organisms—if we mean by this term self-contained, self-regulating systems in which individual human lives are less important (and less interesting) than the interaction of hundreds, and sometimes thousands, of lives.

How Much to Quote

Quote when you find the discussions of other writers to be particularly lively, dramatic, or incisive or especially helpful in supporting a point you wish to make. In general, quote as little as possible so that you keep readers focused on *your* ideas.

- Quote a word or a phrase, if this will do.

Anthropologist Richard Marks refers to American shopping malls as "social organisms."

- Quote a sentence, if needed.

Marks sees in shopping malls a modern version of an ancient institution: "When they are successful, shopping malls in American cities fulfill the same function as *bazaars* did in the cities of antiquity."

- Infrequently quote long passages as a "block."

Long quotations of five or more lines are set off as a block. Limit your use of block quotations, which tempt writers to avoid the hard work of selecting for quotation *only* the words or sentences especially pertinent to the discussion at hand. If you decide to use a long quotation, introduce it with a full sentence that ends with a colon. The following might introduce the full passage, above, quoted from *The New American Bazaar*:

Various commentators have claimed that shopping malls serve a social function. Anthropologist Richard Marks, for instance, compares the mall to the bazaar in cities of old:

> When they are successful, shopping malls . . .

Using Attributive Phrases

- Use attributive phrases to link a quotation to the content of your paper.

  By using attributive phrases like *Jones argues, Smith says,* or *According to Marks,* you alert readers to your use of someone else's words. (See the list of attributive verbs on page 583.) Tie these attributive phrases to the logic of your own sentences, thereby linking the quotation with the content of your paper.

  > Every American city now has its shopping malls. According to anthropologist Richard Marks, successful malls "fulfill the same function as *bazaars* did in the cities of antiquity."

- Interrupt a quotation with an attributive phrase.

  To vary the structure of sentences in which you are quoting sources, try placing your attributive comment between a quotation's subject and verb or after an introductory phrase or clause. The effect will be to emphasize a key word that comes just before or after the interruption:

  > "When they are successful," says Richard Marks, "shopping malls in American cities fulfill the same function as *bazaars* did in the cities of antiquity." [The interruption focuses attention on *shopping malls.*]

  Split a quotation with an attributive remark to maintain the rhythm or continuity of your own paragraph. Compare these two versions of a quoted sentence:

  Acceptable: Every American city has its shopping malls, its equivalents of the ancient bazaar. As anthropologist Richard Marks points out, "The bazaars of the ancient and medieval worlds were social organisms . . ."

  Preferable: Every American city has its shopping malls, its equivalents of the ancient bazaar. "The bazaars of the ancient and medieval worlds," says anthropologist Richard Marks, "were social organisms . . ." [This version maintains paragraph coherence by keeping the reader's focus on the word *bazaar.*]

- Make attributions in a parenthetical reference.

  When you decide that information to be quoted is important but that neither you nor the reader benefits by a direct reference to the author of that source, then attribute your source in a parenthetical citation (following the MLA format) or in a footnote.

  > American shopping malls can be understood as "social organisms" (Marks 24) in which we can observe complex cultural interactions of race, class, and gender.

*For Discussion
and Writing*

Exercise 1

Read "To Light the Fire of Science," by *Boston Globe* columnist, novelist, and professor of science Chet Raymo. Examine the ways in which Raymo prepares for, presents, and then uses source materials. Questions for discussion and writing follow the essay.

To Light the Fire of Science, Start with Some Fantasy and Wonder

Chet Raymo

Every year about this time I am asked by friends and colleagues to recommend   1
good science books for kids, to fill the remaining hollows in Santa's pack.

There are lots of terrific science books out there, and a good place to find   2
them is the children's book section of the Museum of Science shop. But my
advice to parents is: Don't be overly worried about providing science books for
your kids. Expose them to good children's literature, and the science will take
care of itself.

Over the years I have often referred to children's books in this column,   3
including the nonsense books of Dr. Seuss, Antoine de Saint-Exupery's "The
Little Prince," Lewis Carroll's "Alice in Wonderland" and "Through the
Looking-glass," L. Frank Baum's "Wizard of Oz," Kenneth Grahame's "The
Wind in the Willows" and Felix Salten's "Bambi."

All of these in essays about science.   4

What's the connection?   5

Children's books capture the curious, willing-to-be-surprised, "let's pretend"   6
quality of good science. Children's books are full of the playfulness that is part
of all first-rate science. And, like science, children's books insist upon the reality of the unseen.

Science books for children are packed full of interesting information. What   7
most of these books do not convey is the story of how the information was
obtained, why we understand it to be ture, and how it might embellish the landscape of the mind. For many children—and adults, too—science *is* information,
a mass of facts. But facts are not science any more than a table is carpentry.

Science is an attitude toward the world—curious, skeptical, undogmatic and   8
sensitive to beauty and mystery. The best science books for children are the ones
that convey these attitudes. They are not necessarily the books labeled "science."

From a "science" book we might learn that a flying bat might snap up 15   9
insects per minute, or that the frequency of its squeal can range as high as
50,000 cycles per second. Useful information, yes.

But consider the information in this poem from Randall Jarrell's "The Bat-   10
Poet":

> *A bat is born*
> *Naked and blind and pale.*
> *His mother makes a pocket of her tail*
> *And catches him. He clings to her long fur*
> *By his thumbs and toes and teeth.*

> *And then the mother dances through the night*
> *Doubling and looping, soaring, somersaulting—*
> *Her baby hangs on underneath.*

Oh what wondrous information! Even the rhythm of the poem ("naked and   11
blind and pale"; "thumbs and toes and teeth") mimics the flight of mother and
child, doubling and looping in the night.

More: 12

> *The mother eats the moths and gnats she catches*
> *In full flight; in full flight*
> *The mother drinks the water of the pond*
> *She skims across. Her baby hangs on tight.*

That wonderful line—"In full flight; in full flight"—conveys the single most   13
important fact about bats: their extraordinary aviator skills. Jarrell's repeated
phrase conveys useful facts about chiropteran dining; it also lets the child feel in
her bones what it is to be a bat.

In Jarrell's book, the Bat-Poet recites his poem about bats to a chipmunk.   14
Afterwards, he asks, "Did you like the poem?"

The chipmunk replies, "Oh, of course. Except I forgot it was a poem. I just   15
kept thinking how queer it must be to be a bat."

The Bat-Poet says, "No, it's not queer. It's wonderful."   16

That's what good children's literature does—makes us feel the queerness   17
and wonderfulness of nature. It's the best possible introduction to science.

Albert Einstein wrote: "When I examine myself and my methods of thought,   18
I come to the conclusion that the gift of fantasy has meant more to me than any
talent for abstract, positive thinking." The best time—perhaps the only time—
to acquire the gift of fantasy is childhood. We live in an age of information. Too
much information can swamp the boat of wonder, especially for a child. What
children need is not more information, but fantasy.

Einstein also wrote: "The most beautiful experience we can have is the mys-   19
terious. It is the fundamental emotion which stands at the cradle of all true art
and true science." At first, this might seem a strange thought. We are frequently
asked to believe that science is the antithesis of mystery. Nothing could be further from the truth. Mystery invites the attention of the curious mind. Unless we
perceive the world as mysterious—queer and wonderful—we will never be curious about what makes it tick.

Questions for Discussion and Writing

1. How would Raymo's essay have differed had he used *no* sources and based
   all discussion on his personal experience?
2. What are the different purposes for which Raymo refers to sources? (To
   present facts, examples, authoritative opinions? To set his discussion in a
   broader context?) In developing an answer, discuss specific instances in
   which Raymo quotes, summarizes, or paraphrases a source.
3. What is Raymo's thesis in this essay? Discuss how he uses sources to advance this idea. Again, refer to specific instances in developing an answer.

4. Identify two specific instances in which Raymo refers to sources. Use the language of this chapter to describe *how* Raymo introduces and comments on these sources.

Exercise 2

Create a paragraph in which you use a quotation from the following excerpt from the American Association of University Women's (AAUW's) report *How Schools Shortchange Girls.* [A full chapter from this report appears in the Occasions section of chapter 6 (pages 136–137); it is devoted to the ways in which we learn about gender identity in our culture.] To prepare your paragraph here, follow the principles discussed in this chapter:

- Introduce your idea into a paragraph before you introduce a source.
- Working with your paragraph's idea, create a context into which you can fit a source.
- Having created a context, steer the reader directly to your source.
- Quote, summarize, or paraphrase.
- *Use* the source.

Research studies reveal a tendency beginning at the preschool level for schools to choose classroom activities that will appeal to boys' interests and to select presentation formats in which boys excel or are encouraged more than are girls. For example, when researchers looked at lecture versus laboratory classes, they found that in lecture classes teachers asked males academically related questions about 80 percent more often than they questioned females; the patterns were mixed in laboratory classes. However, in science courses, lecture classes remain more common than laboratory classes.

   Research indicates that if pupils begin working on an activity with little introduction from the teacher, everyone has access to the same experience. Discussion that follows after all students have completed an activity encourages more participation by girls. In an extensive multistate study, researchers found that in geometry classes where the structure was changed so that students read the book and did problems *first* and *then* had classroom discussion of the topic, girls outperformed boys in two of five tests and scored equally in the other three. Girls in the experimental class reversed the general trend of boys' dominance on applications, coordinates, and proof taking, while they remained on par with boys on visualizations in three dimensions and transformations. In traditional classes where topics were introduced by lecture first and then students read the book and did the problems, small gender differences favoring boys remained. [Reference notes deleted in this extract.]

A Student Writer at Work: Mike Bergom

Read the following paragraphs from Mike Bergom's essay, the full, final draft of which appears in the opening exercise to this book, pages 3–5. Identify Bergom's cycles of development in these paragraphs.

From "Technology, Jazz, and History"

. . . [Miles] Davis helped jazz music to evolve, but one of his experiments proved too radical: when he began using electric instruments, he was accused of turning his back on a history he had helped to create. His playing ability was not at question—that had been established in his many years of performance. The issue was his reliance on technology and his apparent rejection of the acoustic tradition.

Tradition is a fundamentally important element—a defining element—of jazz, and the jazz community was willing to follow Davis wherever he ventured, as long as he remained true to the music's acoustic roots. Davis believed that new electric instruments should be incorporated into jazz, but many of his fellow artists refused to follow his lead. A historian, Melvin Kranzberg, helps us understand why. Kranzberg is a specialist on the role of technology in society and claims that "[a]lthough technology might be a prime element in many public issues, nontechnical factors take precedence in technology-policy decisions" (249). Stated another way, a new technology's existence does not guarantee its use or value. Other factors such as emotional or artistic response and resistance to change will decide how extensively the technology is used.

History proves Kranzberg's point. In early nineteenth century England, cloth makers were being displaced by machines that outperformed them. These workers, known as Luddites, rose up and destroyed the frames (the new machines) that had caused their unemployment. The Luddites destroyed frames not only because of their displacement but also because they judged the quality of the goods produced by these machines to be inferior. A contemporary newspaper made the point this way:

> The machines . . . are not broken for being upon any new construction . . . but in consequence of goods being wrought upon them which are of little worth, are deceptive to the eye, are disreputable to the trade, and therefore pregnant with the seeds of its destruction. (qtd. in Thompson 532)

The Luddites did not embrace a technology merely because it existed. They could not agree that so-called "improvements in mechanism" (qtd. in Peel 71) led to improvements in product. The cloth produced by the new weaving machines was judged according to ancient standards of the weaver's craft and found to have "little worth." Nontechnical factors, in this case artistic ones, contributed to the Luddites' rejection of technology.

Focus on Summary and Evaluation

When using source materials to advance an idea in your essay, there are two skills you will draw on regularly: summary and evaluation. In a **summary,** you briefly and neutrally restate the main ideas in a source; in an **evaluation,** you determine how effective and reliable an author has been. While they can be ends in themselves (you *will* be asked to write summaries and evaluations), both types of writing often form parts of larger essays. For instance, if you wanted to analyze the relationship among family members on the television series *The Simpsons,* at some point you would need to summarize specific episodes so that readers could follow your discussion. In the same essay, you might refer to a review written by a syndicated columnist who finds the Simpson family dysfunctional and a poor model for young viewers. Whether you agreed or disagreed with this reviewer, you would want to understand and evaluate the standards by which she reached her judgments. Your larger purpose in writing—to analyze the relationships among characters—would be broader than this. To achieve your purpose you would summarize and evaluate at different points in the essay.

In Part II of this text, the following terms appear in the chapter titles: explain, analyze, resolve, interpret, and argue. These chapters will help you to achieve different purposes in your writing, and in each essay you write you should be prepared to summarize and evaluate sources as necessary. To summarize and evaluate effectively, you will need to read with specific strategies. This chapter is intended to help you develop important skills that you can use in writing a wide variety of essays. There are two sections, each with two parts: (1) reading to understand/writing a summary, and (2) reading to evaluate/writing an evaluation.

Reading to Understand/Writing a Summary

Reading to Understand

Every use to which you can put a source is based on your ability to understand it. Without understanding you can do nothing, so understanding must be your very first goal as a critical reader.

Setting Goals for Reading to Understand

The steps in reading to understand can be summarized as follows:

- *Identify the author's purpose.* This will likely be to inform or to argue.
- *Identify the author's intended audience.* The text will be written with particular readers in mind. Determine if you are the intended audience.
- *Locate the author's main point.* Every competently written text has a main point that you should be able to express in your own words.
- *Understand the structure of the text.* If the author is arguing, locate the main point and supporting points; if the author is presenting information, locate the main point and identify the stages into which the presentation has been divided.
- *Identify as carefully as possible what you do not understand.*

Read the following example, which is typical of what you might encounter in one of your courses—say, in media studies. The passage is a defense of advertising written by James Playsted Wood for a text entitled *This is Advertising,* published in 1968. We will add "layers" of highlighting and notes to this passage in order to demonstrate strategies for reading to understand, respond, evaluate, and synthesize. The underlining and notes you see on the passage here illustrate how you might read to understand. Techniques for highlighting in this way follow the passage itself.

From **The Merits of Advertising**

Part 1: Account of what ad is

1 In its open declaration of intent [advertising] is perhaps the most honest form of major present-day journalism.

Thesis

2 On the face of it, an advertisement says what it is. It says: I am an advertisement. I have been bought and paid for. I make no pretense to objectivity. I am not a disinterested and impartial observer. I am a deeply interested and wholly partial pleader. My object is gain. I want to sell

Ads are honest

you something. I will persuade you by every means I can devise to buy what I have for sale.

What an advertisement has to sell may be a jet 3 airplane, a pen, an automobile, a lipstick, a new food, an old food, a fad, or a trip from wherever you are to wherever you can be persuaded to spend your money to go. It may try to sell you an idea, a dream, a fact, an opinion, or a prejudice. The advertisement may entice. It may soothe or excite. It may try to frighten you. It may order or coax. Whatever it does and in whatever way it tries to do it, it is directed at you.

Ads will sell by any means necessary

The advertisement wants to affect your mind 4 or your emotions. It wants to separate you from your money. It offers delights for hard cash or the promise of hard cash. Come buy! Come buy! Always you are the target. You are the concern of giant corporations, big department stores, and little neighborhood shops—everybody who has something to sell. There is flattery in this. It is pleasant to be offered goodies, even when you know you have to pay. It is pleasant to be tempted. It is wonderful to be the center of attention, and you are the center of attention when you enjoy or detest a television commercial or look at a page of glamorous advertising in a slick magazine.

Psychological & emotional tactics

This is an advertisement. You have been 5 warned. It may have the dignity of the Declaration of Independence or the winsomeness of a small child telling Mummy he loves her, but it is an advertisement. You know you are flirting with danger when you stop, look, or listen. There is excitement in that. Be self-indulgent and buy yourself a diamond, an almost-Paris frock, a garden tractor, or a double-edged, triple-plated, 496 hp, all-weather guarantee of attractiveness to the other sex.

Advertising in reputable media is honest in its 6 declaration of intent. It is almost always honest in the claims it makes for the product or service it brings to what it hopes will be your favorable attention. Generally the nationally advertised item is all that it claims to be. Usually it is better and less expensive than a comparable product or service not advertised. Advertising is not masquerading propaganda or disguised publicity. It blazons its intent, and it offers sound value for your approval and purchase.

Ads honest in intent: they want to separate you and your $.

Part 2: Argument that ads are honest in own self-interest

Why all this virtue? Advertising is not created 7 and used just to provide a smug example of public morality. Advertising is honest because it has to be.

Advertising is subject to all of the laws against fraud. Advertisers can be found guilty and prosecuted if they are proven to have defrauded or attempted to defraud. Advertising is scrutinized continually by Better Business Bureaus, and it comes under the jurisdiction of the Federal Trade Commission, which was set up in 1915 to enforce prohibition of unfair methods of competition in interstate commerce. The Food and Drug Administration, the Federal Communications Commission, the Alcohol and Tobacco Tax Division of the Internal Revenue Service, and the United States Post Office also have some regulatory power over advertising.   **8**   Review of laws & agencies ads subject to

In 1906, with the strong backing of reputable advertisers and advertising media, the Food and Drug Act—the "Wiley Law"—was passed. This law made it a misdemeanor to make or sell misbranded or adulterated foods, drugs, medicines, or liquors. Control was greatly extended by the passage of the Pure Food and Drug Act of 1938, known as the Wheeler-Lea Act. This forbade dissemination of false advertising about foods, drugs, related products, and cosmetics.   **9**

Advertising is policed by government, but the strongest controls are exerted by advertisers and advertising media themselves. Like most other successful activities, advertising is largely self-regulatory. It has to be. Advertising is basically honest in its own self-interest. There is no satisfactory alternative.   **10**   Self-interest, not altruism, motivates ad companies.

Applying Techniques for Reading to Understand

When you know that you must base later writing on a source you are reading, you should consciously adopt a system for reading to understand. There are many systems you can follow, but each commonly entails reading in three stages: previewing, reading, and reviewing.

The following techniques illustrate how to highlight information important to understanding a source. These techniques were used to make notes on the passage by James Playsted Wood, above.

Preview the Text

- *Read titles, openings, and closings in full.* This preview will give you a sense of topic, audience, purpose, and main point. Read the title and guess the relationship between the title and text. If you are reading an article or a chapter of a book, read the opening and closing paragraphs in full. If you are reading a book, read the preface and the first and last chapters.

- *Skim the rest of the text.* A brief look at the text will help you to understand the structure, or layout, of the source. When skimming an article, read all headings along with a few sentences from every second or third paragraph. When skimming a book, review the table of contents and then read the opening and closing paragraphs of each chapter.

- *Recall what you know about the topic.* A review of your previous exposure to a topic will prepare you to be interested and ready with questions as you begin reading. After skimming a text, think about the topic: reflect on your personal history with it.

- *Predict what you will learn from reading.* Based on your quick review of the text and on your knowledge of the topic, predict what you will learn. Predictions form an important part of a close, critical reading by keeping you focused on the content and alert to potential difficulties.

Read the Text

Read with a pen or pencil in hand and make notes that will help you understand.

- *Identify the author's purpose.* The author's purpose will likely be to inform or to argue. Locate passages that illustrate this purpose.

- *Underline important phrases and sentences.* Your underlining or highlighting of important information should work with your notes (see below) so that you can return to the text and spot the author's main topic at a glance.

- *Write notes that summarize your underlining.* You can summarize important points of an explanation or an argument by writing brief phrases in the margins; this will help you to understand as you read and to recall important information as you reread.

- *Identify sections.* A section of a text is a grouping of related paragraphs. Sometimes, an author will provide section headings; at other times, you will need to write them. In either case, your awareness of sections will help you understand the structure of a text.

- *Identify difficult passages.* You can use a question mark to identify passages that confuse you, and you should circle unfamiliar words. Unless a particular word is repeated often and seems central to the meaning of a text, postpone using a dictionary until you complete your reading. Frequent interruptions to check the meaning of words will fragment your reading and disrupt your understanding.

- *Periodically ask: Am I understanding?* You should stop at least once during your reading to ask yourself this question. If you are having trouble, change your plan for reading. For especially difficult selections, try dividing the text into small sections and reading one section at a sitting. Read until you understand each section, or until you can identify what you do not understand.

Review the Text

After reading and making notes, you should spend a few minutes consolidating what you have learned. Focus on the content of the passage and its structure. Understand the pattern by which the author has presented ideas and information. The additional minutes of review that you devote now will crystallize what you have learned and be a real help later on, when you are asked to refer to and *use* the selection, perhaps for an exam or paper.

- *Consolidate information.* Skim the passage and reread your notes. Clarify them, if necessary, so that they accurately represent the selection. Reread and highlight (with boxes or stars) what you consider to be the author's significant sentences or paragraphs.
- *Organize your questions.* Review the various terms and concepts you have had trouble understanding. Organize your questions concerning vocabulary and content. Use dictionaries; seek out fellow students or a professor to clarify especially difficult points. Even if you do not pursue these questions immediately, you should clarify what you do not understand. Your questions, gathered into one place, such as a journal, will be an excellent place to begin reviewing for an exam.

Writing a Summary

When you have read and understood a source, you are in a position to summarize it: to restate its main points briefly and neutrally. Summaries are extremely useful, whatever your purpose in an essay. When you want to comment on a source, first summarize it—create a context in which readers can follow your discussion. If you want simply to draw someone else's information into your essay, summarize a section of that source. On occasion, you will be asked to prepare a summary of an entire selection; more often, you will summarize *parts* as you need them for use in your own essays. Like any piece of writing, summary calls for you to make decisions and to plan, draft, and revise.

Setting Goals for Writing a Summary

The focus of a summary is on a specific text, *not* on your reactions to it. Your purpose is to restate the text as briefly as possible in your own words. More specifically, you should aim to meet these goals:

- Understand the author's purpose for writing—for instance, to inform, explain, argue, justify, defend, compare, contrast, or illustrate. Most often, the author will have a single purpose; sometimes an author may have two closely related purposes, such as to explain and justify.
- State the author's thesis in relation to this purpose.
- Identify the sections of the text and understand the ways in which they work together to support, or explain, the thesis.
- Distinguish information needed to explain the author's thesis from examples and less important information.
- Write the summary using your own words; avoid phrase-by-phrase "translations" from the original.

Applying Techniques for Writing Summaries

The techniques for writing a summary can now be applied to "The Merits of Advertising" by James Playsted Wood. You may want to reread the selection so that you understand the following preparations for summary.

Prepare: Make Notes for a Summary

The notes below are based on the advice offered in the preceding section. Notice that the writer begins by observing the purpose of the selection—to argue—and then incorporates that purpose into a one-sentence summary of Wood's thesis. Notice, as well, that the writer prepares one-sentence summaries for each paragraph in sections 1 and 2.

> **Purpose:**   to argue
>
> **Thesis:**   In "The Merits of Advertising," James Playsted Wood argues that advertising is an honest form of communication because it openly announces its intentions and because advertisers wish to avoid government penalties for dishonesty.

Identify Sections

Section 1 (¶s 1–6): Advertising, an honest form of communication

¶1: Advertising is an honest form of communication.

¶2: Advertising states its intentions openly—to persuade consumers to buy, by any means necessary.

¶3: Advertisers will sell anything, and they will use psychological tactics: they will "entice," "soothe or excite," "frighten," or "order or coax."

¶4: Advertising makes each consumer the object of attention, which is flattering.

¶5: Advertisements carry their own warning—beware, I'm trying to separate you from your money. Consumers enjoy the danger of ads.

¶6: Advertisements are generally honest in their claims for a product's superiority.

Section 2 (¶s 7–10): Regulations and agencies keep advertiser honest

¶7: Advertisers stay honest, not to provide an example of moral behavior but to avoid stiff penalties for illegal conduct.

¶8: Various agencies, including the Federal Trade Commission, set rigorous standards for advertisers, who face prosecution if they violate these standards.

¶9: Two laws—the Wiley Law and the Wheeler-Lea Act—extended federal oversight to advertisers' claims about food, drugs, and cosmetics.

¶10: Even with stringent standards governing their behavior, advertisers remain their own strictest regulators—not out of altruism but out of self-interest.

Guidelines for Writing a Summary

These guidelines will help you as you prepare to write your summary:

- Read your source with care, putting into practice strategies discussed in this section, reading to understand.
- Determine the purpose of the source—for instance, to inform, explain, argue, justify, defend, compare, contrast, or illustrate.
- Summarize the thesis. Based on the notes you have made and the phrases or sentences you have highlighted while reading, restate the author's main point in your own words. In this statement, refer to the author by name; indicate the author's purpose (e.g., to argue or inform); and refer to the title.
- Summarize the body of the text. STRATEGY 1: Write a one- or two-sentence summary of every paragraph. Summarize points important to supporting the author's thesis. Omit minor points and omit illustrations. Avoid the temptation to translate phrase for phrase from sentences in the text. STRATEGY 2: Identify sections (groupings of related paragraphs) and write a two- or three-sentence summary of each section.
- Study your paragraph or section summaries. Determine the ways in which the paragraphs or sections work together to support the thesis.
- Write the summary. Join your paragraph or section summaries with your summary of the thesis, emphasizing the relationship between the parts of the text and the thesis.
- Revise for clarity and for style. Quote sparingly. Provide transitions where needed.

Writing the Summary

When writing the summary, you should join paragraph- or section-summaries to the thesis and emphasize the relationship of parts. The following example presents a summary of "The Merits of Advertising."

> In "The Merits of Advertising," James P. Wood argues that advertising is honest because it openly announces its intentions and because advertisers wish to avoid government penalties for dishonesty. According to Wood, an advertisement is in its very presence a warning to consumers, saying in effect: I am going to separate you from your money. Wood believes that consumers enjoy flirting with the danger implied by such a statement, and that consumers are flattered by the advertiser's lavish attentions. Advertising is honest for a second reason, as well: if it were dishonest, advertisers would find themselves in trouble. Wood claims that various laws (such as the Wiley Law and the Wheeler-Lea Act, for foods and drugs) along with various agencies (such as the Federal Trade Commission) set standards for the work of advertisers, who face prosecution if they violate these standards. But even with stringent regulations governing their actions, advertisers remain their own strictest regulators, says Wood—not out of altruism but out of self-interest.

Reading to Evaluate/Writing an Evaluation

Reading to Evaluate

When you introduce a source into your essay to advance an idea, you make an *implicit* judgment, saying (in effect) to readers: this particular source is dependable and valuable. Whether or not you do so consciously, you evaluate the sources you use, and readers count on you to judge well. The goal of the discussion here is to make this ongoing, natural process of evaluation *explicit* and *systematic* so that you can clearly assess the worth of the material you read. As a critical reader, you should determine the extent to which an author has succeeded in a presentation. If asked, you should be able to explain why you feel the author has done a good job—or why not; and you should be able to explain why you and an author agree or disagree. In other words, you should know your standards for what makes a reading selection a success and, therefore, potentially useful to you and *your* readers.

Setting Goals for Reading to Evaluate

Your goals in reading to evaluate should include the following:

- Distinguish between an author's use of facts and opinions.
- Distinguish between an author's assumptions (fundamental beliefs about the world) and your own.
- Judge the effectiveness of an explanation.
- Judge the effectiveness of an argument.

Here is a shortened version of the passage by James Playsted Wood, which you read with summary notes earlier. Reread the passage, this time observing a second layer of notes, which represents one reader's evaluation of the passage. Recommended techniques for reading to evaluate follow.

From **The Merits of Advertising**

This is an advertisement. You have been warned. It may have the dignity of the Declaration of Independence or the winsomeness of a small child telling Mummy he loves her, but it is an advertisement. You know you are flirting with danger when you stop, look, or listen. There is excitement in that. Be self-indulgent and buy yourself a diamond, an almost-Paris frock, a garden tractor, or a double-edged, triple-plated, 496 hp, all-weather guarantee of attractiveness to the other sex.

> Ads honest in intent: they want to separate you and your $.

> And what if you don't need these? Isn't that a problem?

Advertising in reputable media is honest in its declaration of intent. It is almost always honest in the claims it makes for the product or service it brings to what it hopes will be your favorable attention. Generally the nationally advertised item is all that it claims to be. . . .

> How is he defining honesty?

> Faulty, either/or logic: I'm sure many advertisers—as well as businesses—cheat until they get caught. Also faulty cause & effect logic.

Advertising is policed by government, but the strongest controls are exerted by advertisers and advertising media themselves. Like most other successful activities, advertising is largely self-regulatory. It has to be. Advertising is basically honest in its own self-interest. There is no satisfactory alternative.

> Self-interest, not altru-im, motivates ad companies.

Applying Techniques for Reading to Evaluate

When you are reading to evaluate, you want to be alert to an author's use of *facts, opinions,* and *definitions,* and his or her *assumed views of the world.* You will also want to know if an author's purpose is primarily to inform or to argue, so that you can pose specific questions accordingly.

Distinguish Facts from Opinions

Before you can evaluate a statement, you should know whether it is being presented to you as a fact or an opinion. A **fact** is any statement that can be verified.

> Nationwide, the cost of college tuition is rising.
> New York lies at a more southerly latitude than Paris.
> Andrew Johnson was the seventeenth President of the United States.
> The construction of the Suez Canal was completed in 1869.

These statements, if challenged, can be established as true or false through appropriate research. As a reader evaluating a selection, you might question the accuracy of a fact or how the fact was shown to be true. You might doubt, for instance, that Paris is a more northerly city than New York. The argument is quickly settled by reference to an agreed-upon source—in the case of Paris, a map.

An **opinion** is a statement of interpretation and judgment. Opinions are not true or false in the way that statements of fact will be. Opinions are more or less well supported. If a friend says, "That movie was terrible," this is an opinion. If you ask why and your friend responds, "Because I didn't like it," you are faced with a statement that is unsupported and that makes no claim on you for a response. Someone who writes that the majority of U.S. space missions should not have human crews is stating an opinion. Someone who refers to the *Challenger* disaster is referring to a fact, a matter of historical record. Opinions are judgments. If an opinion is supported by an entire essay, then the author is, in effect, demanding a response from you.

Identify the strongly stated opinions in what you read, and then write a **comment note:** in the margin, jot down a brief note summarizing your response to the opinion. Agree or disagree. Later, your note will help you crystallize your reactions to the selection.

Distinguish Your Assumptions from Those of an Author

An **assumption** is a fundamental belief that shapes the way people see. If your friend says that a painting is "beautiful," she is basing that statement, which is an opinion, on another, more fundamental opinion—an assumed view of beauty. Whether or not your friend directly states to you what qualities make a painting beautiful, she is *assuming* these qualities and is basing her judgment on them. If the basis of her judgment is that the painting is "lifelike," this is an assumption. Perhaps she dislikes abstract paintings and you like them. If you challenged each other on the point or asked *why,* you both might answer: "I don't know why I think this way. I just do." Sometimes you will find that assumptions are based on clearly defined reasons, and other times (as in the painting example) you will find that they are based on ill-defined feelings. Either way, the opinions that people have (if they are not direct expressions of assumptions themselves) can be better understood by identifying the assumptions that guide them.

Consider two sets of assumptions.   When you read a source, two sets of assumed views about the world come into play: yours and the author's. The extent of your agreement with an author depends largely on the extent to which your assumptions coincide. Therefore, in evaluating a source, you want to understand the author's assumptions concerning the topic at hand as well as your own. To do so, you must perform two related tasks: identify an author's opinions, and determine whether or not each opinion is based on some other opinion or assumed view.

Identify direct and indirect assumptions.   Assumptions may be stated directly or indirectly. In either case, your job as a critical reader is to identify and determine the extent to which you agree with them.

Assumption Stated Directly

#1 A nation is justified in going to war only when hostile forces threaten its borders.

#2 A nation is justified in going to war when hostile forces threaten its interests anywhere in the world.

At times an author hints at, but does not directly state, an assumed view, as in this example:

Assumption Not Stated

#3 A conflict 7,000 miles from our border does not in any way threaten this nation, and we are therefore not justified in fighting a war that far from home.

Sentence #3 is based on the assumption expressed in sentence #1. Suppose you were reading an editorial and came across sentence #3. In a close, critical reading you would see in this statement an unexpressed assumption about the reasons nations *should* go to war. If you can show that an author's assumed views (whether directly or indirectly expressed) are flawed, then you can argue that all opinions based on them are flawed and should be rejected, or at least challenged.

Distinguish Your Definitions of Terms from Those of an Author

Consider this statement: *Machines can explore space as well as and in some cases better than humans.* What do the words *as well as* and *better than* mean? If an author defines these words one way and you define them another way, you and the author are sure to disagree. In evaluating a source, identify the words important to the author's presentation. If the author does not define these words directly, then state what you believe the author's definitions to be. At times you will need to make educated guesses based on your close reading of the source.

Match Questions for Evaluation to the Selection You Are Reading

The overall purpose of evaluation remains the same for any selection you read: to determine a presentation's effectiveness and reliability. The particular questions that you will use when evaluating a source will change, depending on the purpose of that source. One set of questions, or criteria for evaluation, should be used for sources that explain and another set should be used for sources that argue. As you move to more specialized purposes (to interpret, to resolve, to analyze), you will address more specific questions.

Sources that explain.   When a selection asks you to accept an explanation, a description, or a procedure as accurate, pose and respond to these questions:

- For whom has the author intended the description, explanation, or procedure? The general public—nonexperts? Someone involved in the same business or process? An observer, such as an evaluator or a supervisor?
- What does the text define and explain? How successful is the presentation, given its intended audience?
- How trustworthy is the author's information? How current is it? If it is not current, are the points being made still applicable, assuming more recent information could be obtained?
- If the author presents a procedure, what is its purpose or outcome? Who would carry out this procedure? When? For what reasons? Does the author present the stages of the procedure?

Sources that argue.   When a selection asks you to accept an argument, pose and respond to these questions:

- What conclusion am I being asked to accept?
- What reasons and evidence has the author offered for me to accept this conclusion? Are the reasons logical? Is the evidence fair? Has the author acknowledged and responded to other points of view?
- To what extent is the author appealing to logic? to my emotions? to my respect for authorities?

Sources that analyze, resolve, or interpret.   At the end of the Structures and Strategies discussion of each chapter in Part II you will find a "Critical Points" section devoted to criteria for evaluating sources depending on their specific purpose. Two chapters in Part II are devoted to writing essays that explain and argue, and in those "Critical Points" sections you will find specialized criteria to use in evaluating essays that explain or argue, whether these essays are yours (in an early draft version) or someone else's.

In Part II you will find other purposes for writing essays: writing based on personal experience (the "familiar" essay); writing to resolve a problem or to make a proposal; writing to analyze; and writing to interpret. Each of these essays, with its specific purpose, can also be evaluated in specialized ways, and you will find criteria for doing so in each chapter's "Critical Points" section. If you need to write a formal evaluation of familiar essays or essays intended to explain, analyze, resolve, interpret, or argue, add the criteria presented in those "Critical Points" discussions to the criteria and the strategies presented here.

Writing an Evaluation

In an **evaluation,** you judge the effectiveness and reliability of a text and discuss the extent to which you agree with the text's author. Writing an evaluation formalizes the process of reading to evaluate. Evaluation will always entail summary writing, since before you can reasonably agree or disagree with an author's work you must show that you understand and can restate its main points.

Setting Goals for Writing an Evaluation

You have two primary goals when writing to evaluate, and both depend on a critical, comprehensive reading:

- Judge the effectiveness of the author's presentation. Your concern here is on the quality of the presentation.
- Agree and/or disagree with the author, and explain your responses.

Understanding Techniques for Writing an Evaluation

The basic pattern of evaluation is: (1) offer a judgment about the text; (2) refer to a specific passage—summarize, quote, or paraphrase; and (3) explain your judgment in light of that passage. If you remember these components of evaluation, you will help to establish your authority as someone whose insights a reader can trust.

Prepare: Make Notes on the Effectiveness of the Presentation

You will evaluate the effectiveness and reliability of a presentation according to the author's purpose for writing. If the author is arguing a position, you bring one set of criteria, or standards of judgment, to bear on the text; if the author is informing—providing explanations or presenting procedures or descriptions—you bring to bear another set of criteria. You can use certain criteria for evaluating any text.

Criteria for texts that inform or persuade. The following criteria should be used to judge the effectiveness of any text. Remember: when using criteria to evaluate a text, support your evaluation by referring to and discussing a specific passage.

Accuracy: Are the author's facts accurate?

Definitions: Have terms important to the discussion been clearly defined—and if not, has lack of definition confused matters?

Development: Does each part of the presentation seem well developed, satisfying to you in the extent of its treatment? Is each main point adequately illustrated and supported with evidence?

Criteria for texts that inform.   When an author writes to inform, you can evaluate the presentation based on any of the preceding criteria as well as on the ones discussed in this section. Remember: when using criteria to evaluate a text, support your evaluation by referring to and discussing a specific passage.

Audience: Is the author writing for a clearly defined audience who will know what to do with the information presented? Is the author consistent in presenting information to one audience?

Clarity: How clear has the author been in defining and explaining? Is information presented in a way that is useful? Will readers be able to understand an explanation or follow a procedure?

Procedure: Has the author presented the stages of a process? Is the reader clear about the purpose of the process, about who does it and why?

Criteria for texts that persuade.   When an author writes to persuade, you can evaluate the presentation based on any of the preceding criteria as well as on the ones that follow. Remember: when using the following (or any) criteria to evaluate a text, support your evaluation by referring to and discussing specific passages.

Fairness: If the issue being discussed is controversial, has the author presented opposing points of view? Has the author seriously considered and responded to these points?

Logic: Has the author adhered to standards of logic? Has the author avoided, for instance, fallacies such as personal attacks and faulty generalization?

Evidence: Do facts and examples fairly represent the available data on the topic? Are the author's facts and examples current? Has the author included negative examples?

Authority: Are the experts that the author refers to qualified to speak on the topic? Are the experts neutral?

Prepare: Make Notes on Your Agreement and Disagreement with the Author

By applying the criteria above, you may decide that a selection is well written. Just the same, you may disagree with the author in part or in whole, or you may agree. In either case, you should examine the reasons for your reactions. For instance, in the upcoming example evaluation of James Playsted Wood's piece, the student writer will on the one hand admire and agree with Wood's statement that an advertisement "blazons its intent" by saying, "Come buy! Come buy!" On the other hand, the writer will disagree with Wood's argument that advertising is honest.

Whatever your reaction to a text, you should (1) identify an author's views, pointing out particular passages where these views are apparent; (2) identify your own views; and (3) examine the basis on which you and the author agree or disagree. For the most part, you can explain agreements and disagreements by examining both your assumptions and the author's. Recall that an assumption is a fundamental belief that shapes the opinions people develop. Here is a format for distinguishing your views from an author's.

Author's view on topic X:

My view:

Author's assumption:

My assumption:

Prepare: Organize Your Notes and Gain a General Impression

Once you have prepared for writing an evaluation by making notes, review your material and try to develop an overall impression of the reading. In writing an evaluation, you will have enough space to review at least two, but probably not more than four or five, aspects of an author's work. Therefore, be selective in the points you choose to evaluate. Review your notes concerning quality of the presentation and extent of your agreement with the author; select the points that will best support your overall impression of the reading. As with any piece of formal writing, plan your evaluation with care. If you are going to discuss three points concerning a selection, do so in a particular order, for good reasons. Readers will expect a logical, well-developed discussion.

Applying Techniques for Writing Evaluations

James Playsted Wood's "Merits of Advertising" provides an opportunity to practice evaluating a text. The first step of evaluation, writing a summary, was completed early in this chapter. Two questions will help to organize your thinking for an evaluation: (1) How effective and reliable is the author's presentation? (2) Do I agree with the author? Answers to one or both of these questions can provide the basis for writing an evaluation.

How Effective and Reliable Is the Author's Presentation?

Above you found ten criteria, or standards of judgment, on which to determine the effectiveness and reliability of a text: accuracy, definitions, development, audience, clarity, procedure, fairness, logic, evidence, and authority. What follows is an example of how one of these criteria— logic—applies to Wood's discussion. This evaluation assumes that Wood is arguing, trying to convince readers that advertising is honest for two reasons: because ads openly declare their intentions and because advertisers must follow government regulations.

Definitions

Wood argues that "advertising is honest." And inasmuch as advertisements openly declare their intention to separate our money from us, ads *are* honest. But Wood broadens his definition and wants to suggest that ads are honest in all respects. This simply isn't so: many ads consist of claims that are not supported with verifiable facts, and many aim at the subconscious mind, not directly—and openly—at the conscious mind. Wood twists the meaning of *honesty* in this selection.

Do I Agree with the Author?

In your response you should point to specific passages that demonstrate the author's view; summarize that view and your response to it; and then explain the assumptions underlying both your view and the author's. Here's an example:

Wood's View ¶s 1–6:	Advertisements are an honest form of communication.
My View:	Even though Wood is right that ads scream at you, "I'm going to make you buy," ads are not necessarily honest.
Wood's Assumption:	An act that is honest in its intentions is honest, generally.
My Assumption:	A person's warning to harm someone does not make the act of inflicting harm honest or admirable.

Guidelines for Writing an Evaluation

These guidelines will help you as you prepare to write your evaluation:

- Introduce the topic and author: one paragraph.

  One sentence in the introduction should hint at your general impression of the piece.

- Summarize the author's work: one to three paragraphs.

  If brief, the summary can be joined to the introduction.

- Briefly review the key points in the author's work that you will evaluate: one paragraph.*
- Identify key points in the author's presentation; discuss each in detail: three to six paragraphs.

  If you are evaluating the quality of the author's presentation, state your criteria for evaluation explicitly; if you are agreeing or disagreeing with opinions, try to identify assumptions (yours and the author's) underlying these.

- Conclude with your overall assessment of the author's work.

Writing an Evaluation

The following example presents an evaluation of "The Merits of Advertising."

STUDENT PAPER

Evaluation of James Wood's "Merits of Advertising"

Walk into a store or down a street, open a newspaper or a magazine, turn on the television: everywhere we look, we are overwhelmed by advertisements. Our consumer economy is based on selling, and in such an economy both producers and consumers depend on advertising as a medium that transmits information, along with an obvious message: BUY! Unless ads are blatantly false in the claims they make for a product, people expect a certain amount of overstatement. People also expect advertisers to sidestep discussions of a product's weaknesses.

Two-paragraph introduction: 1st ¶—ads in our society

We all understand the game: "You'll get mostly the truth here," an ad seems to say, "but perhaps not the whole truth." Magazines such as *Consumer Reports* have gained wide circulation, in part, because people value an independent ("honest") judgment of the worth and durability of various consumer goods. No one expects to find particularly honest claims in advertisements. It comes as something of a surprise, therefore, when James P. Wood calls advertisements "perhaps the most honest form of major present-day journalism."

Introduction of "honesty" as an element in the upcoming evaluation

Hint of criticism to come

In "The Merits of Advertising," Wood argues that advertising is honest because it openly announces its intentions and because advertisers wish to avoid government penalties for dishonesty. According to Wood, an advertisement is in its very presence a warning to consumers, saying in effect: I am going to separate you from your money. Wood believes that consumers enjoy flirting with the danger implied by such a statement, and

1

2

3

---

*The order of parts in the written evaluation may not match the actual order of writing. You may be unable to write this third section of the evaluation without first having evaluated the author's key points—the next section. The evaluation will take shape over multiple drafts.

that consumers are flattered by the advertiser's lavish attentions. Advertising is honest for a second reason, as well: if it were dishonest, advertisers would find themselves in trouble. Wood claims that various laws (such as the Wiley Law and the Wheeler-Lea Act, for foods and drugs) along with various agencies (such as the Federal Trade Commission) set standards for the work of advertisers, who face prosecution if they violate these standards. But even with stringent regulations governing their actions, advertisers remain their own strictest regulators, says Wood—not out of altruism but out of self-interest.

Wood is correct to observe that advertisements announce that they are 4 going to persuade us to spend money. Wood assumes, however, that this announcement alone qualifies advertisements as honest and renders the advertiser's efforts to "entice," "soothe or excite," "frighten," or "order or coax" consumers likewise honest. Advertisers must be careful to break no laws—they cannot make fraudulent claims, or they risk legal action. But this side of outright lying, is all the information that advertisers load into their ads (as well as the information they withhold) a demonstration of honesty? Based on the view that a consumer who is forewarned is forearmed, Wood seems to think so.

But this view is flawed. An ad that announces that it is going to take 5 someone's money—and then succeeds through devious psychological means—is *not* honest. So much depends on how the money is gotten. Recently, some advertisers have begun appealing to male consumers with photos of five-year-old girls, posed suggestively. Is this honest? Apparently it's legal, but the appeal is vulgar and arguably damaging to the children being posed as well as being destructive to important social values. The appeal is also based on a subconscious need that advertisers feel some men have for seeing women as young girls. Such ads do not state these needs directly, but they nonetheless suggest them. Tactics like these seek to bury a message rather than deliver it directly. Tactics like these are *dis*honest.

Wood claims too much for his definition of honesty. He is right to say 6 that advertisements are honest when it comes to announcing their motive. Yes—ads want to separate us from our money. But Wood tries to broaden this one use of the word *honesty* to include others: for instance, that honest communication is *direct* communication; or that an honest claim should be supported by verifiable facts. Very often, advertisements ignore both types of honesty. For instance, take two claims common to advertising: can all gasolines advertised as "best" be best? Does an aspirin manufacturer's claim that "we give you more for your money" count as honest when consumers are not told that "more" refers to the starch in the aspirin pill, not to the active ingredient? These are not big lies, but they are lies and they are representative. Misleading words and phrases such as these are commonplace in the world of advertising.

Much as I enjoy and agree with Wood's spirited description of advertising's bold intentions and agree with his claim that advertisements scream "Come buy!" I do not accept his calling advertisements *honest*. A

Summary

Preview of keypoint in evaluation

Author's assumption noted

The evaluator's competing assumption is provided

Agreement—but mostly disagreement—with the author over the definition of *honesty*

Conclusion

consumer culture such as ours depends on advertising to function. We are so used to advertisers stretching the truth to promote their products that we no longer see the stretching as an offense to honesty. But for Wood to claim that advertisements are *honest* is to ask too much of that word. Advertisements are not honest. They are "more or less" *honest* or, as Wood himself writes, they are "basically" honest. Let's not make advertising into a virtue. Advertising is necessary, and it is no evil. But neither is it particularly honest.

For Discussion and Writing

Exercise 1

Read "A Defense of Advertising," by Charles A. O'Neil, to examine the ways in which he uses both summary and evaluation in his essay. As you read, try to be aware of O'Neil's purpose for writing. Questions for discussion and writing follow the selection.

A Defense of Advertising
Charles A. O'Neil

Some critics view the entire advertising business as a cranky, unwelcomed child 1 of the free enterprise system, a noisy, whining, brash kid who must somehow be kept in line, but can't just yet be thrown out of the house. Because advertising mirrors the fears, quirks, and aspirations of the society that creates it (and is, in turn, sold by it), it is wide open to parody and ridicule.

Perhaps the strongest, most authoritative critic of advertising language in 2 recent years is journalist Edwin Newman. In his book *Strictly Speaking,* he poses the question, "Will America be the death of English?" Newman's "mature, well thought out judgement" is that it will. As evidence, he cites a number of examples of fuzzy thinking and careless use of language, not just by advertisers, but by many people in public life, including politicians and journalists:

> The federal government has adopted the comic strip character Snoopy as a symbol and showed us Snoopy on top of his doghouse, flat on his back, with a balloon coming out of his mouth, containing the words, "I believe in conserving energy," while below there was this exhortation: savEnergy.

> savEnergy. An entire letter e at the end was savd. In addition, an entire space was savd. Perhaps the government should say onlYou can prevent forest fires. . . . Spelling has been assaulted by Duz, E-Z Off, Fantastik, Kool, Kleen . . . and by products that make you briter, so that you will not be left hi and dri at a parti, but made welkom. . . . Under this pressure, adjectives become adverbs; nouns become adjectives; prepositions disappear; compounds abound.[1]

In this passage, Newman presents three of the charges most often levied against advertising:

1. Advertising debases English.
2. Advertising downgrades the intelligence of the public.

3. Advertising warps our vision of reality, implanting in us groundless fears and insecurities. (He cites, as examples of these groundless fears, "tattletale grey," "denture breath," "morning mouth," "unsightly bulge," "ring around the collar.")

Other charges have been made from time to time. They include:

1. Advertising sells daydreams; distracting, purposeless visions of lifestyles beyond the reach of most of the people who are most exposed to advertising.
2. Advertising feeds on human weaknesses and exaggerates the importance of material things, encouraging "impure" emotions and vanities.
3. Advertising encourages bad, even unhealthy habits like smoking.
4. Advertising perpetuates racial and sexual stereotypes.

What can be said in advertising's defense? Advertising is only a reflection 3 of society; slaying the messenger (and just one of the messengers, at that) would not alter the fact—if it is a fact—that "America will be the death of English." A case can be made for the concept that advertising language is an acceptable stimulus for the natural evolution of language. (At the very least, advertising may stimulate debate about what current trends in language are "good" and "bad.") Another point: is "proper English" the language most Americans actually speak and write, or is it the language we are told we should speak and write, the language of *The Elements of Style* and *The Oxford English Dictionary?*

What about the charge that advertising debases the intelligence of the pub- 4 lic? Those who support this particular criticism would do well to ask themselves another question: Exactly how intelligent is the public? How many people know the difference between adverbs and adjectives? How many people *want* to know? The fact is that advertisements are effective, not because agencies say they are effective, but because they sell products.

Advertising attempts to convince us to buy products; we are not forced to 5 buy something because it is heavily advertised. Who, for example, is to be blamed for the success, in the mid-70s, of a nonsensical, nonfunctional product—"Pet Rocks"? The people who designed the packaging, those who created the idea of selling ordinary rocks as pets, or those who bought the product?

Perhaps much of the fault lies with the public, for accepting advertising so 6 readily. S. I. Hayakawa finds "the uncritical response to the incantations of advertising . . . a serious symptom of a widespread evaluational disorder." He does not find it "beyond the bounds of possibility" that today's suckers for national advertising will be tomorrow's suckers for the master political propagandist who will, by playing up the "Jewish menace," in the same way as national advertisers play up the "pink toothbrush menace," and by promising us national glory and prosperity, sell fascism in America.[2]

Fascism in America is fortunately a far cry from Pet Rocks, but the point is 7 well taken. In the end, advertising simply attempts to change behavior. It is a neutral tool, just as a gun is a neutral tool, but advertising at least has not been known to cause accidental deaths. Like any form of communication, it can be used for positive social purposes, neutral commercial purposes, or for the most pernicious kind of paranoid propaganda. Accepting, for the purpose of this discussion, that propaganda is, at heart, an extension of politics and therefore is materially different from commercial advertising as practiced in the United States of America, circa 1990, *do* advertisements sell distracting, purposeless visions? Occasionally. But perhaps such visions are necessary components of the process through which our society changes and improves.

And recognize this: advertising is a mirror. It is not perfect; sometimes it 8 distorts. When we view ourselves in it, we're not always pleased with what we see. Perhaps, all things considered, that's the way it should be.

Source Notes for "A Defense of Advertising"

1. Edwin Newman, *Strictly Speaking* (Indianapolis: Bobbs-Merrill, 1974) 13.
2. S. I. Hayakawa, *Language in Action* (New York: Harcourt Brace, 1941) 235.

Questions for Discussion and Writing

1. What is the main idea of O'Neil's essay?
2. What is O'Neil's purpose for writing?
3. O'Neil's purpose in writing is *not* to summarize or evaluate the work of Edwin Newman. What is O'Neil's larger purpose? What is his thesis?
4. Why does O'Neil present a summary, when he has just quoted Newman?
5. Identify the specific sentences in which O'Neil evaluates each of Newman's arguments against advertising.
6. How does both summarizing and evaluating Newman's criticisms of advertising help O'Neil to advance his own idea?

Exercise 2

Using the techniques discussed in this chapter, read to understand and then summarize O'Neil's "Defense of Advertising."

Exercise 3

Using the techniques discussed in this chapter, read to evaluate and then prepare an *outline* for an evaluation of O'Neil's "Defense of Advertising."

1. State your overall impression of the essay in a thesis that would be appropriate for a formal evaluation.
2. Create an outline of your evaluation, and specifically note where you would place your summary of O'Neil.
3. What are your standards for judging the effectiveness and reliability of O'Neil's essay? Specifically state the two or three key points on the basis of which you have formed your overall judgment.
4. Choose *one* of these key points. Using it, write a paragraph of evaluation that you would include in a formal evaluation of O'Neil.

A Student Writer at Work: Mike Bergom

The final draft of Mike Bergom's essay, "Technology, History, and Jazz," appears in the opening exercise to this book, pages 3–5. Bergom writes that he relied "heavily" on sources in this essay. A writer in his position must evaluate the reliability of sources before putting them to use. Here is Bergom's evaluation of the most important source in his essay:

For this essay I relied heavily on sources about technology. I had to convince the reader of certain truths about technology before I could address my main point, that the mere presence of technically advanced musical instruments did not guarantee that jazz musicians, in particular, would find them desirable. Obviously, I couldn't be the authority since I haven't spent much time studying about technology. But Melvin Kranzberg has. He helped to found a national organization devoted to the history of technology. He provided the authority I needed in the essay and, more important, a special insight into technology that directly related to my thesis.

Unlike O'Neil, who in his essay on advertising makes an open and negative evaluation of Edwin Newman, Bergom suggests but does not state directly his *positive* evaluation of Kranzberg. Positive uses of a source to advance an essay automatically imply the writer's evaluation and agreement. Certainly we see Bergom's evaluation of Kranzberg implied in his essay. Reread the following paragraphs from the essay; highlight Bergom's direct and indirect use of the idea he borrowed from Kranzberg:

From "Technology, Jazz, and History"

Tradition is a fundamentally important element—a defining element—of jazz, and the jazz community was willing to follow Davis wherever he ventured, as long as he remained true to the music's acoustic roots. Davis believed that new electric instruments should be incorporated into jazz, but many of his fellow artists refused to follow his lead. A historian, Melvin Kranzberg, helps us understand why. Kranzberg is a specialist on the role of technology in society and claims that "[a]lthough technology might be a prime element in many public issues, nontechnical factors take precedence in technology-policy decisions" (249). Stated another way, a new technology's existence does not guarantee its use or value. Other factors such as emotional or artistic response and resistance to change will decide how extensively the technology is used.

History proves Kranzberg's point. In early nineteenth century England, cloth makers were being displaced by machines that outperformed them. These workers, known as Luddites, rose up and destroyed the frames (the new machines) that had caused their unemployment. The Luddites destroyed frames not only because of their displacement but also because they judged the quality of the goods produced by these machines to be inferior. A contemporary newspaper made the point this way:

> The machines . . . are not broken for being upon any new construction . . . but in consequence of goods being wrought upon them which are of little worth, are deceptive to the eye, are disreputable to the trade, and therefore pregnant with the seeds of its destruction. (qtd. in Thompson 532)

The Luddites did not embrace a technology merely because it existed. They could not agree that so-called "improvements in mechanism" (qtd. in Peel 71) led to improvements in product. The cloth produced by the new weaving machines was judged according to ancient standards of the weaver's craft and found to have "little worth." Nontechnical factors, in this case artistic ones, contributed to the Luddites' rejection of technology.

Today, several influential jazz musicians have applied the standards of their craft to electronically boosted music and have reached a similar conclusion: the product has little worth. Beyond question, recent "improvements in mechanism" have provided many benefits for the aspiring musician. Synthesizers create totally unique new sounds. Improved recording techniques open a new world of special effects. Computers print, transpose, and perform music with the touch of a button. Yet there are jazz purists who regard the new technology, in effect, as a frame to be smashed. This was largely the reaction that many had to the electronic experiments of Miles Davis.

Branford Marsalis redesigned the *Tonight Show* band, creating a traditional jazz format of acoustical instruments. When asked about this transformation, he said, "I was interested in doing what we did—having people remember us for being musicians. Not for the last joke or the flashy suit" (qtd. in Heckman 25). Marsalis believes technology is a musical gimmick—a diversion from the essence of jazz. He feels technology has not only *not* added anything worthwhile to jazz music but has actually obscured its roots. For Marsalis, the mere existence of technologically advanced instruments has in no way guaranteed their use and value.

Occasions for Thinking, Reading, and Writing

CHAPTER 6

The Familiar Essay

Definitions and Examples

> [I turn now] to the title of this essay, "In Search of Our Mothers' Gardens," which is a personal account that is yet shared, in its theme and its meaning, by all of us.
>
> —Alice Walker

This line from Alice Walker's "In Search of Our Mothers' Gardens" (see pages 111–118) provides as accurate and direct a definition of the familiar essay as can be found. A *familiar* essay, in sharp contrast to the writing you will do for most of your academic courses, is writing that concerns your personal life, presented in a way that (you presume) will have meaning for a reader. In a familiar essay you can draw on personal, private experience—in addition to public documents such as essays, articles, and books—to make your point.

The writing you submit to professors will be heavily influenced by the discipline in which you work: you will be asked, for instance, to think and write like a sociologist or a biologist, and your assignments will introduce you to the intellectual activities of academic disciplines. The familiar essay exists for a different reason, which is to create a "personal account that is yet shared." To be sure, sociologists and biologists write for personal reasons; yet their disciplines require a presentation of *public* evidence—of experiments, case studies, and the like. By contrast, the familiar essay draws heavily (though not exclusively) on personal experience, which the writer hopes to make universally significant. Being personal and universal simultaneously might seem like a paradox, but in the familiar essay these apparent opposites are joined. Consider these brief passages:

From a Journal Entry

Four years in college, studying lit. & I did fine, good grades, enjoyed the courses. Prepared for law or MBA or who knows what, anything but what I'm doing now. Maybe I should be guilty but I'm not. The fact is that I enjoy building fly rods. But I didn't have to go to college to build fly rods. Why did I go to college? Waste my money? I was an English major and now I'm an ex-English major fly rod builder paying off $15,000 in loans.

From an Essay Based on This Journal Entry

The company I work for began twenty years ago in the garage of an engineer and tinkerer. Now we are twenty people working in a large warehouse. We sell fly rods in shops across the country, and we export to Spain, England, France, Italy, and Norway.... It's the craft that attracts me. Not just *craft* in the sense of the actual trade, but the fact that my work claims a history.

The first passage is private and is meant only for the writer, who is a recent college graduate; the second passage, by the same writer (see pages 119–121), pursues an idea sparked by the journal entry and is written for public view, for an audience. This single shift in purpose, from the strictly personal to the public, accounts for the differences we see: background information, understood and not shared by the writer in the first excerpt, is presented in the second; and in the second excerpt we find full sentences directed outward to a reading public, whereas in the first excerpt we see clipped sentences written by the writer to himself. Still, we find an important similarity: the question that sparks the journal entry has become the subject of the essay.

In his *public* expression, the writer tries to make his personal experience meaningful to others. He shows pride in the fact that fly rod building has a history. Readers, who presumably also work, might ask themselves: Do *I* feel pride in my work? Does *my* work claim a history? The moment we reflect on our lives in response to the private experience of an essay writer, that writer has made a leap from the personal to the universal. Ideas that are expressed simply as ideas do not make the universal connection. Compare two more passages:

Grief is universal among higher animals.

Mark Jerome Walters reports in his study of animal sexuality, *Courtship in the Animal Kingdom,* that the ornithologist George Archibald watched a sandhill crane spend an entire summer lingering near a section of road outside Baraboo, Wisconsin. "It stood there like a gray ghost," Archibald said, "from dawn to dusk, every day from June till October. A state trooper told me its mate had been struck and killed by a car as the pair crossed the road. But their bond was so strong that when the female died, her mate returned to the same place every day, hoping that if he just waited long enough she would eventually come back to life."

—Jerry Dennis

To say that "Grief is universal among higher animals" is to express an idea, only. The idea may or may not be true, but in either event we don't understand the idea, we don't feel it, until we see *particular* grief in a particular time and place. A familiar essay gives readers access to this idea *through* one person's (or bird's!) particular experiences. If these experiences are presented well, then readers will begin to reflect on their own lives, and the leap from the private to the universal is made. What moves us in the paragraph by Jerry Dennis is not only, or even mainly, the loss felt by one sandhill crane, but the grief *we* recollect on having lost someone dear to us, or the grief we suffer in imagining the loss of a loved one. Whether or not we accept the idea that animals feel grief (after all, the sandhill crane has been anthropomorphized—given human qualities) is another matter. By relating a particular experience, the writer of this paragraph has given us an opportunity to reflect on our lives. Or, in Alice Walker's terms, the writer has given us "a personal account that is yet shared, in its theme and its meaning, by all of us." The personal becomes universal.

Your goal in writing a familiar essay is to express an idea important to you *through* particular experiences. Do this well, and you will give your private insights universal appeal.

Examples of Familiar Essays

Four successful essays follow. Watch how each writer transforms particular, personal experiences into public statements that prompt readers to reflect on their lives. Three of these writers draw on public sources as well as on private experience to make their points. Often, essay writers introduce references to articles, poems, books, and other essays both to provide occasions for them to reflect in the essay and to provide common ground for readers: if we have read these same articles or poems or books (and we will read them at least to the extent they have been quoted or summarized in the essays themselves), we too can respond and compare our responses to those of the essay writer. The first three examples are written by professional writers. The fourth is written by the builder of fly rods, a recent college graduate who found passion and meaning in a job altogether unrelated to his undergraduate major. Questions for discussion follow each essay.

A City's Needy

Anna Quindlen

Anna Quindlen, writer and editor for the New York Times *and author of numerous articles and essays that have appeared in national magazines, wrote the following essay as part of a holiday charity drive. Quindlen's purpose in this essay is to argue, though you will not find a direct statement of her thesis. As you read, consider why this might be so. Also, observe how she develops each of her points in the context of vivid details.*

The formica counter was so white, the apples so red, the veins in her hand as 1
she touched one so blue, that it might have been some modern still life: three
apples, one elderly woman, the 27th of the month.

"I have always loved apples," she said in her slightly accented English, look- 2
ing at them lined up on the kitchen counter, shiny as trophies, the only thing
left in the apartment to eat until the next Social Security check arrived on the
first day of the next month.

The most singular thing about need in New York City is not how much of 3
it there is, for in a city as large as this one, in times as hard as these, it is inevitable and, sadly, somehow accepted that pain will be legion. It is that need here
is often so private, and so proud. Behind the brick walls of thousands of apartment buildings, beneath the shingled roofs of thousands of homes, people live
with hunger and deprivation just a wall away from those who have plenty.

Need is also so various there. The woman of the apples lived in a lovely 4
senior citizens housing project on the Lower East Side, only a few blocks from
an abandoned building in which a teen-age couple had camped out with their
infant son, rigging complicated systems of electrical wires from the street to the
ceiling for lights, tucking the baby into a box, beating off the rats with a folded
newspaper. The old woman had come from Germany at the beginning of the
century, the young couple from Puerto Rico 10 years ago. Only the baby had
been born in the United States, but like the rest, he was hungry.

There are whole neighborhoods of the needy in New York, areas where the 5
buildings with sheet metal where the windows used to be tell you that there are
people in trouble there. But they are proud neighborhoods as well as poor ones,
and inside apartments with very little in the way of furniture mothers will stand
over old stoves and tell you how far you can stretch rice and dried beans and a
paper envelope of soup mix. And when it is on the table the children will dig in
as though there were really meat in it.

And there are neighborhoods that are obviously a source of pride to their 6
citizens where the unlikeliest residents eke out an existence day by day just this
side of desperation. I spent a day once in a kind of stage set of turn-of-the-
century plenty on the West Side, in an apartment large enough for a family of
10 inhabited by one very old lady. The armoires, the mirrors, the prints, the
china, the silver—the contents of the apartment at auction would have garnered
hundreds of thousands of dollars, but, like most memories, they were not for
sale. I was the first visitor my hostess had had in three years. She was living on
instant oatmeal and tea; her one extravagance was aspirin, which she took
almost every hour to relieve the pain of her arthritis.

There are more-visible people in need. There are the legions of the home- 7
less, lying on the benches in Grand Central Terminal, huddled in doorways
against the cold, carrying their lives on their backs, trading subsistence for life.
In soup kitchens they lean over their meals as though in prayer and use the broth
to warm as well as feed them, and use their dinnertime to stoke their beaten
souls as well as their empty innards.

And there are more-helpless people in need, too: the children. There are 8
the ones who come into the world with heroin or cocaine in their frail bodies,
who flail in their cribs with the poison in their veins. There are the ones who
are born with acquired immune deficiency syndrome, born to die because their
parents used dirty needles. There are the ones who are left in hospitals to lie in
the metal cribs, their only stimulation the occasional visit from a nurse. There
are those who are freezing, and starving, and those who are beaten and bruised.

A doctor in the neonatal intensive care unit at one city hospital looked 9
around at the incubators one afternoon and wondered aloud about the tubes,
the medicines, the machines needed to make the premature thrive and the sickly ones bloom. It was not at all uncommon, she said, to find that an infant who
had been coaxed from near death to life in the confines of that overly warm
room, in one of those little plastic wombs, had turned up two or three years later
in the emergency room with cigarette burns, broken bones, or malnutrition.

It is all horrible to contemplate until the day you first see someone, in some 10
small way, doing something about it: finding a meal ticket at a senior citizens
center for the lady of the apples; getting the teenagers into a sweat equity project that will end with a new apartment; sending a neighborhood college student
to fix meals and listen to old anecdotes amid the faded splendors of the Upper
West Side apartment.

There are good people in this city, people who peel the vegetables in soup 11
kitchens and cuddle the babies who are diseased and discarded, who see, not
still lifes or half lives, but lives in search of sustenance, and who give it.

For Discussion and Writing

Reading and Thinking Critically

1. *Personal response:* What is significant about Quindlen's claim that need in New York City is "private and proud"?
2. *Be alert to differences:* Have you witnessed poverty similar to that which Quindlen is describing? Quindlen studies the impoverished carefully enough to distinguish one type of neediness from another. What distinctions does she make? Do these distinctions seem meaningful to you?
3. *Challenge the reading:* Quindlen makes no effort to lay blame, to look for reasons, to explain: her goal is to set the reader in a direct relationship with the needy. Has she succeeded in her task? Are you comfortable with this relationship?

Examining "The City's Needy" as an Essay

1. Quindlen prepares for the structure of her essay with a sentence in ¶3 and another in ¶4. But she does *not* openly state her purpose for writing. What is her purpose, the central idea pervading the essay? Why do you think Quindlen has withheld it?
2. Outline the structure of this brief essay, and list all the points at which Quindlen develops her ideas through stories, descriptions, and examples.
3. How do Quindlen's vivid descriptions create a common ground for read-ers? How do these descriptions help us to understand the idea of her essay?

Mates for Life

Jerry Dennis

Jerry Dennis's "Mates for Life" appeared in his regular column for Wildlife Conservation. *Dennis is the author of five collections of essays, most recently* A Place on the Water: An Angler's Reflections on Home *(1993). Observe how he builds interest immediately through a personal anecdote about fathers who are worried about young men courting their daughters. Dennis is adept at maintaining this interest throughout the essay. In the sidebar to this piece, he explains his personal motivation for writing "Mates for Life."*

In spring a young man's fancy turns to love, and those friends of mine who are 1 fathers of teenaged daughters are not at all happy about it. They are vigilant, those nervous dads, peeking around their living-room drapes and complaining about the boys idling in cars at the curb and riding past on bicycles, one wheel in the air and one eye on the house, and calling, calling, calling on the telephone. I remind my friends that humans sometimes mate for life, and that such long-term investments demand elaborate courtship rituals. They say I, the father of boys, don't understand. Perhaps. But I know from my own memories of courtship what a wonderful and terrible business it is. I suspect, in fact, that it is the pain of courtship itself that makes us want to mate for life.

It's curious that people in our 2 society, who claim to be champions of marriage, are so bad at it. The latest news from the marriage wars is dire: 50 percent or more of the weddings performed in the United States in the next year are likely to end in divorce. Some sociologists predict the number will be closer to 60 percent, because the generation now reaching marrying age was raised in the divorce-racked sixties and seventies, and countless studies have demonstrated that children of divorced parents tend to become divorced themselves. Decades before the biggest surge in divorces in our nation's history (from 400,000 in 1960 to 1,175,000 in 1990), the curmudgeonly British philosopher Bertrand Russell declared, "Even in civilized mankind faint traces of monogamous instinct can be perceived."

Jerry Dennis: My Commitment to This Essay

Jerry Dennis writes engagingly on the sociology of mating among humans and among animals. As it turns out, the idea for this essay was sparked by a very specific event in his personal life. This statement, describing the event and his commitment to the essay that followed, is *not* itself an essay. Why not? What are the differences between this and the essay? What are the similarities?

"Mates for Life" originated from a conversation with my wife, Gail, during a weekend we spent on Michigan's Mackinac Island celebrating our 17th wedding anniversary. On the beach one evening, while we talked about the good luck that had kept us together so many years, Gail said she found it odd that some animals have a biological tendency to mate for life while others do not, and that humans seem to be losing the tendency. It's the kind of idea I like to pursue in a personal essay because the broad freedoms of the form make it possible to probe and test from many angles, to mess around with facts and whimsies, and to have some fun. I started working on the fun parts that same weekend.

Those of us determined to keep those faint traces of instinct from getting 3 fainter are in both smaller and larger company than we might imagine: smaller because one survey of human cultures found that out of 849 societies only 141 were truly monogamous; and larger because in the rest of the animal kingdom a surprising number of species have found it an advantage to maintain sexual relationships with one individual.

About 90 percent of the world's 8,800 or so bird species practice one form 4 or another of monogamy. Most, like the eastern bluebird, are seasonally monogamous, courting a new mate each breeding season and staying together until their offspring are fledged. Other species change mates several times in a season, raising a brood with each. Still others are fairly faithful, the male establishing a monogamous relationship but occasionally indulging in extra-pair copulations.

A few birds are permanently monogamous, forming the kind of long-term 5 attachments we humans seem to long for. Canada geese sometimes become "engaged" up to a year before they reach breeding age, creating a pair bond that may last their entire lives. Cranes are so diligent in their monogamy that in Japan the red-crowned crane is considered a symbol of a happy marriage. Most ravens and other corvids, storks, swans, and some owls likewise form long monogamous relationships.

There is a simple reason so many birds remain with one mate: the kids. The 6 demands of raising young often take the full attention of two adults. Biologists like to discuss the behavior in economic terms, speaking of parental "investment," and pointing out that it is more profitable for a male bird intent on propagating his own genes to stick with one mate and ensure the survival of a brood than to impregnate many females haphazardly. Once committed to monogamy, a male bird takes the job seriously. He may help build nests, take turns brooding the eggs, gather food, and stand watch. In studies where the male has been removed, the percentages of eggs that hatch and fledglings that survive decline dramatically.

Species that stay together season after season may do so because it is ener- 7 gy efficient. Large birds exert so much energy in flight, especially during migration to summer nesting areas, that they have little to spare for the flashy and frivolous courtship games of smaller birds. A pair of Canada geese get right to the business of mating, nesting, and laying eggs, taking every advantage of good weather and abundant food while they last, and giving their offspring the chance to fledge and mature in time for the fall migration.

But what if you find you can't live with your mate? Not all gulls mate for 8 life, but among those that do there can be a biological mandate for divorce. Biologist William Jordan reports in his book *Divorce Among the Gulls* that more than 25 percent of newly paired gulls separate after their first attempt to raise young. They break up for some of the same reasons humans do, primarily good old-fashioned incompatibility. When a male and female gull are incompatible—say they both insist on doing all the brooding—they can spend so much time squabbling over who gets to sit on the nest that the eggs are forgotten. Gulls that fail to nest successfully usually divorce and return to the nesting area the following year with a different mate. Those that get along—and reproduce successfully—stay together.

Monogamy is much less common among mammals than birds. Some 97 9 percent of mammal species are polygamous, the males mating with numerous females in an effort to maximize their genetic investments. Where bonding is more permanent, it is because it is more efficient genetically to stay with a female and help protect and feed the offspring. Foxes, wolves, and other canids stay together because they must cover a lot of territory to find food, and because a lactating female alone would have little hope of feeding and defending her young. Jackals in the Serengeti live in close-knit families composed of a monogamous male and female along with various young, including one or more adult offspring that assist in caring for their younger siblings. The klipspringer, a small African antelope, forms permanent pair bonds so that one mate can constantly watch for predators while the other grazes. Another African mammal, the tiny elephant-shrew, apparently bonds for life, but the male plays little part in rearing offspring and the bond is probably more useful in guarding the home range than in rearing young. Beavers expend a great deal of effort maintaining a lodge and cutting and storing a winter's supply of food. It is more efficient for them to stay together than to wander promiscuously from mate to mate.

My unmarried friends (who *do* wander promiscuously from mate to mate) report that the singles scene in this pheromone-laced season is only slightly less desperate than usual. Everybody is a little frisky and more inclined to be pleasant after the first date. There is an aura of impending urgency, like when the participants in a game of musical chairs sense the music will soon and abruptly end. No one wants to be left standing alone. But neither does anyone want to plop down in an ill-fitting chair.   10

We ought to know a thing or two about the courtship rituals of humans, but we don't. I've been married to the same fine woman nearly 18 years and I'm still not sure why our marriage works while so many in our generation have failed. We're planning to celebrate our next anniversary at the aptly named Grand Hotel on Mackinac Island, Michigan. We'll bicycle, walk the beaches, watch birds, and enjoy fancy meals served by gracious waiters. It's a magical place. At some point we'll probably discuss the mystery of successful long-term pair bonding. But we won't talk about it much. You can analyze the magic right out of some things.   11

For Discussion and Writing

Reading and Thinking Critically

1. *Personal response:* Are you at all heartened by Dennis's report that some 97 percent of the world's mammals are polygamous and that only 141 of some 849 human societies are monogamous? Are you discouraged? Indifferent?
2. *Broaden the context:* Dennis does an excellent job of broadening our discussions of monogamy and divorce. Does your understanding of human bonding change at all, based on this essay?
3. *Challenge the reading:* Dennis concludes: "You can analyze the magic right out of some things." What is your reaction to this conclusion? Do you feel it is an appropriate ending to the essay?

Examining "Mates for Life" as an Essay

1. Dennis begins his essay with an anecdote about male friends who are worried about their daughters and ends with an anecdote about his thus-far stable marriage. How is the opening of the essay related to its closing, and how are both related to the main business of the essay?
2. Dennis implies in ¶3 that studying courtship and mating in the animal world can teach us something about these rituals in human society. What can we learn, according to Dennis?
3. How does Dennis create a common ground for his readers? What are his techniques?

In Search of Our Mothers' Gardens
Alice Walker

Alice Walker, prolific African-American essayist, novelist, and poet, is the award-winning author of The Color Purple *(1982) and* The Temple of My Familiar *(1989). The present piece is the title essay in her collection* In Search of Our Mothers'

Gardens (1974). References to "gardens" do not appear until the end of the essay; by the time we have reached that point, Walker has prepared us to understand. She has created a common ground for readers through stories of black "grandmothers and mothers . . . driven to a numb and bleeding madness by the springs of creativity in them for which there was no release." We see the creative "seeds" these women have handed to their daughters and, more particularly, the seeds that Walker's own mother handed to her.

I described her own nature and temperament. Told how they needed a larger life for their expression. . . . I pointed out that in lieu of proper channels, her emotions had overflowed into paths that dissipated them. I talked, beautifully I thought, about an art that would be born, an art that would open the way for women the likes of her. I asked her to hope, and build up an inner life against the coming of that day. . . . I sang, with a strange quiver in my voice, a promise song.

Jean Toomer, "Avey," CANE

The poet speaking to a prostitute who falls asleep while he's talking— 1

When the poet Jean Toomer walked through the South in the early twenties, 2 he discovered a curious thing: black women whose spirituality was so intense, so deep, so *unconscious,* that they were themselves unaware of the richness they held. They stumbled blindly through their lives: creatures so abused and mutilated in body, so dimmed and confused by pain, that they considered themselves unworthy even of hope. In the selfless abstractions their bodies became to the men who used them, they became more than "sexual objects," more even than mere women: they became "Saints." Instead of being perceived as whole persons, their bodies became shrines: what was thought to be their minds became temples suitable for worship. These crazy Saints stared out at the world, wildly, like lunatics—or quietly, like suicides; and the "God" that was in their gaze was as mute as a great stone.

Who were these Saints? These crazy, loony, pitiful women? 3

Some of them, without a doubt, were our mothers and grandmothers. 4

In the still heat of the post-Reconstruction South, this is how they seemed 5 to Jean Toomer: exquisite butterflies trapped in an evil honey, toiling away their lives in an era, a century, that did not acknowledge them, except as "the *mule of the world.*" They dreamed dreams that no one knew—not even themselves, in any coherent fashion—and saw visions no one could understand. They wandered or sat about the countryside crooning lullabies to ghosts, and drawing the mother of Christ in charcoal on courthouse walls.

They forced their minds to desert their bodies and their striving spirits 6 sought to rise, like frail whirlwinds from the hard red clay. And when those frail whirlwinds fell, in scattered particles, upon the ground, no one mourned. Instead, men lit candles to celebrate the emptiness that remained, as people do who enter a beautiful but vacant space to resurrect a God.

Our mothers and grandmothers, some of them: moving to music not yet 7 written. And they waited.

They waited for a day when the unknown thing that was in them would be 8 made known; but guessed, somehow in their darkness, that on the day of their revelation they would be long dead. Therefore to Toomer they walked, and even ran, in slow motion. For they were going nowhere immediate, and the future was not yet within their grasp. And men took our mothers and grandmothers, "but got no pleasure from it." So complex was their passion and their calm.

To Toomer, they lay vacant and fallow as autumn fields, with harvest time 9 never in sight: and he saw them enter loveless marriages, without joy; and become prostitutes, without resistance; and become mothers of children, without fulfillment.

For these grandmothers and mothers of ours were not Saints, but Artists; 10 driven to a numb and bleeding madness by the springs of creativity in them for which there was no release. They were Creators, who lived lives of spiritual waste, because they were so rich in spirituality—which is the basis of Art—that the strain of enduring their unused and unwanted talent drove them insane. Throwing away this spirituality was their pathetic attempt to lighten the soul to a weight their work-worn, sexually abused bodies could bear.

What did it mean for a black woman to be an artist in our grandmothers' 11 time? In our great-grandmothers' day? It is a question with an answer cruel enough to stop the blood.

Did you have a genius of a great-great-grandmother who died under some 12 ignorant and depraved white overseer's lash? Or was she required to bake biscuits for a lazy backwater tramp, when she cried out in her soul to paint watercolors of sunsets, or the rain falling on the green and peaceful pasturelands? Or was her body broken and forced to bear children (who were more often than not sold away from her)—eight, ten, fifteen, twenty children—when her one joy was the thought of modeling heroic figures of rebellion, in stone or clay?

How was the creativity of the black woman kept alive, year after year and 13 century after century, when for most of the years black people have been in America it was a punishable crime for a black person to read or write? And the freedom to paint, to sculpt, to expand the mind with action did not exist. Consider, if you can bear to imagine it, what might have been the result if singing, too, had been forbidden by law. Listen to the voices of Bessie Smith, Billie Holiday, Nina Simone, Roberta Flack, and Aretha Franklin, among others, and imagine those voices muzzled for life. Then you may begin to comprehend the lives of our "crazy," "Sainted" mothers and grandmothers. The agony of the lives of women who might have been Poets, Novelists, Essayists, and Short-Story Writers (over a period of centuries), who died with their real gifts stifled within them.

And, if this were the end of the story, we would have cause to cry out in 14 my paraphrase of Okot p'Bitek's great poem:

> O, my clanswomen
> Let us all cry together!
> Come,
> Let us mourn the death of our mother,
> The death of a Queen
> The ash that was produced
> By a great fire!
> O, this homestead is utterly dead
> Close the gates
> With *lacari* thorns,
> For our mother
> The creator of the Stool is lost!
> And all the young women
> Have perished in the wilderness!

But this is not the end of the story, for all the young women—our mothers 15 and grandmothers, *ourselves*—have not perished in the wilderness. And if we ask ourselves why, and search for and find the answer, we will know beyond all efforts to erase it from our minds, just exactly who, and of what, we black American women are.

One example, perhaps the most pathetic, most misunderstood one, can 16 provide a backdrop for our mothers' work: Phillis Wheatley, a slave in the 1700s.

Virginia Woolf, in her book *A Room of One's Own,* wrote that in order for 17 a woman to write fiction she must have two things, certainly: a room of her own (with key and lock) and enough money to support herself.

What then are we to make of Phillis Wheatley, a slave, who owned not even 18 herself? This sickly, frail black girl who required a servant of her own at times— her health was so precarious—and who, had she been white, would have been easily considered the intellectual superior of all the women and most of the men in the society of her day.

Virginia Woolf wrote further, speaking of course not of our Phillis, that "any 19 woman born with a great gift in the sixteenth century [insert "eighteenth century," insert "black woman," insert "born or made a slave"] would certainly have gone crazed, shot herself, or ended her days in some lonely cottage outside the village, half witch, half wizard [insert "Saint"], feared and mocked at. For it needs little skill and psychology to be sure that a highly gifted girl who had tried to use her gift for poetry would have been so thwarted and hindered by contrary instincts [add "chains, guns, the lash, the ownership of one's body by someone else, submission to an alien religion"], that she must have lost her health and sanity to a certainty."

The key words, as they relate to Phillis, are "contrary instincts." For when 20 we read the poetry of Phillis Wheatley—as when we read the novels of Nella Larsen or the oddly false-sounding autobiography of that freest of all black women writers, Zora Hurston—evidence of "contrary instincts" is everywhere. Her loyalties were completely divided, as was, without question, her mind.

But how could this be otherwise? Captured at seven, a slave of wealthy, dot- 21 ing whites who instilled in her the "savagery" of the Africa they "rescued" her from . . . one wonders if she was even able to remember her homeland as she had known it, or as it really was.

Yet, because she did try to use her gift for poetry in a world that made her 22 a slave, she was "so thwarted and hindered by . . . contrary instincts, that she . . . lost her health. . . ." In the last years of her brief life, burdened not only with the need to express her gift but also with a penniless, friendless "freedom" and several small children for whom she was forced to do strenuous work to feed, she lost her health, certainly. Suffering from malnutrition and neglect and who knows what mental agonies, Phillis Wheatley died.

So torn by "contrary instincts" was black, kidnapped, enslaved Phillis that 23 her description of "the Goddess"—as she poetically called the Liberty she did not have—is ironically, cruelly humorous. And, in fact, has held Phillis up to ridicule for more than a century. It is usually read prior to hanging Phillis's memory as that of a fool. She wrote:

> The Goddess comes, she moves divinely fair,
> Olive and laurel binds her *golden* hair.
> Wherever shines this native of the skies,
> Unnumber'd charms and recent graces rise. [My italics]

It is obvious that Phillis, the slave, combed the "Goddess's" hair every morn- 24
ing; prior, perhaps, to bringing in the milk, or fixing her mistress's lunch. She
took her imagery from the one thing she saw elevated above all others.

With the benefit of hindsight we ask, "How could she?"   25

But at last, Phillis, we understand. No more snickering when your stiff, 26
struggling, ambivalent lines are forced on us. We know now that you were not
an idiot or a traitor; only a sickly little black girl, snatched from your home and
country and made a slave; a woman who still struggled to sing the song that was
your gift, although in a land of barbarians who praised you for your bewildered
tongue. It is not so much what you sang, as that you kept alive, in so many of
our ancestors, *the notion of song.*

Black women are called, in the folklore that so aptly identifies one's status in 27
society, "the *mule* of the world," because we have been handed the burdens
that everyone else—*everyone* else—refused to carry. We have also been called
"Matriarchs," "Superwomen," and "Mean and Evil Bitches." Not to mention
"Castraters" and "Sapphire's Mama." When we have pleaded for understanding, our character has been distorted; when we have asked for simple caring,
we have been handed empty inspirational appellations, then stuck in the farthest corner. When we have asked for love, we have been given children. In
short, even our plainer gifts, our labors of fidelity and love, have been knocked
down our throats. To be an artist and a black woman, even today, lowers our
status in many respects, rather than raises it: and yet, artists we will be.

Therefore we must fearlessly pull out of ourselves and look at and identify 28
with our lives the living creativity some of our great-grandmothers were not
allowed to know. I stress *some* of them because it is well known that the majority of our great-grandmothers knew, even without "knowing" it, the reality of
their spirituality, even if they didn't recognize it beyond what happened in the
singing at church—and they never had any intention of giving it up.

How they did it—those millions of black women who were not Phillis Wheatley, 29
or Lucy Terry or Frances Harper or Zora Hurston or Nella Larsen or Bessie
Smith; or Elizabeth Catlett, or Katherine Dunham, either—brings me to the title
of this essay, "In Search of Our Mothers' Gardens," which is a personal account
that is yet shared, in its theme and its meaning, by all of us. I found, while thinking about the far-reaching world of the creative black woman, that often the
truest answer to a question that really matters can be found very close.

In the late 1920s my mother ran away from home to marry my father. Marriage, 30
if not running away, was expected of seventeen-year-old girls. By the time she
was twenty, she had two children and was pregnant with a third. Five children
later, I was born. And this is how I came to know my mother: she seemed a
large, soft, loving-eyed woman who was rarely impatient in our home. Her
quick, violent temper was on view only a few times a year, when she battled with
the white landlord who had the misfortune to suggest to her that her children
did not need to go to school.

She made all the clothes we wore, even my brothers' overalls. She made all 31
the towels and sheets we used. She spent the summers canning vegetables and
fruits. She spent the winter evenings making quilts enough to cover all our beds.

During the "working" day, she labored beside—not behind—my father in 32
the fields. Her day began before sunup, and did not end until late at night. There

was never a moment for her to sit down, undisturbed, to unravel her own private thoughts; never a time free from interruption—by work or the noisy inquiries of her many children. And yet, it is to my mother—and all our mother who were not famous—that I went in search of the secret of what has fed the muzzled and often mutilated, but vibrant, creative spirit that the black woman has inherited, and that pops out in wild and unlikely places to this day.

But when, you will ask, did my overworked mother have time to know or care about feeding the creative spirit? 33

The answer is so simple that many of us have spent years discovering it. We have constantly looked high, when we should have looked high—and low. 34

For example: in the Smithsonian Institution in Washington, D.C., there hangs a quilt unlike any other in the world. In fanciful, inspired, and yet simple and identifiable figures, it portrays the story of the Crucifixion. It is considered rare, beyond price. Though it follows no known pattern of quilt-making, and though it is made of bits and pieces of worthless rags, it is obviously the work of a person of powerful imagination and deep spiritual feeling. Below this quilt I saw a note that says it was made by "an anonymous Black woman in Alabama, a hundred years ago." 35

If we could locate this "anonymous" black woman from Alabama, she would turn out to be one of our grandmothers—an artist who left her mark in the only materials she could afford, and in the only medium her position in society allowed her to use. 36

As Virginia Woolf wrote further, in *A Room of One's Own:* 37

Yet genius of a sort must have existed among women as it must have existed among the working class. [Change this to "slaves" and "the wives and daughters of sharecroppers."] Now and again an Emily Bronte or a Robert Burns [change this to "a Zora Hurston or a Richard Wright"] blazes out and proves its presence. But certainly it never got itself on to paper. When, however, one reads of a witch being ducked, of a woman possessed by devils [or "Sainthood"], of a wise woman selling herbs [our root workers], or even a very remarkable man who had a mother, then I think we are on the track of a lost novelist, a suppressed poet, of some mute and inglorious Jane Austen. . . . Indeed, I would venture to guess that Anon, who wrote so many poems without signing them, was often a woman. . . .

And so our mothers and grandmothers have, more often than not anonymously, handed on the creative spark, the seed of the flower they themselves never hoped to see: or like a sealed letter they could not plainly read. 38

And so it is, certainly, with my own mother. Unlike "Ma" Rainey's songs, which retained their creator's name even while blasting forth from Bessie Smith's mouth, no song or poem will bear my mother's name. Yet so many of the stories that I write, that we all write, are my mother's stories. Only recently did I fully realize this: that through years of listening to my mother's stories of her life, I have absorbed not only the stories themselves, but something of the manner in which she spoke, something of the urgency that involves the knowledge that her stories—like her life—must be recorded. It is probably for this reason that so much of what I have written is about characters whose counterparts in real life are so much older than I am. 39

But the telling of these stories, which came from my mother's lips as naturally as breathing, was not the only way my mother showed herself as an artist. 40

For stories, too, were subject to being distracted, to dying without conclusion. Dinners must be started, and cotton must be gathered before the big rains. The artist that was and is my mother showed itself to me only after many years. This is what I finally noticed:

Like Mem, a character in *The Third Life of Grange Copeland,* my moth- 41 er adorned with flowers whatever shabby house we were forced to live in. And not just your typical straggly country stand of zinnias, either. She planted ambitious gardens—and still does—with over fifty different varieties of plants that bloom profusely from early March until late November. Before she left home for the fields, she watered her flowers, chopped up the grass, and laid out new beds. When she returned from the fields she might divide clumps of bulbs, dig a cold pit, uproot and replant roses, or prune branches from her taller bushes or trees—until night came and it was too dark to see.

Whatever she planted grew as if by magic, and her fame as a grower of 42 flowers spread over three counties. Because of her creativity with her flowers, even my memories of poverty are seen through a screen of blooms—sunflowers, petunias, roses, dahlias, forsythia, spirea, delphiniums, verbena . . . and on and on.

And I remember people coming to my mother's yard to be given cuttings 43 from her flowers; I hear again the praise showered on her because whatever rocky soil she landed on, she turned into a garden. A garden so brilliant with colors, so original in its design, so magnificent with life and creativity, that to this day people drive by our house in Georgia—perfect strangers and imperfect strangers—and ask to stand or walk among my mother's art.

I notice that it is only when my mother is working in her flowers that she 44 is radiant, almost to the point of being invisible—except as Creator: hand and eye. She is involved in work her soul must have. Ordering the universe in the image of her personal conception of Beauty.

Her face, as she prepares the Art that is her gift, is a legacy of respect she 45 leaves to me, for all that illuminates and cherishes life. She has handed down respect for the possibilities—and the will to grasp them.

For her, so hindered and intruded upon in so many ways, being an artist 46 has still been a daily part of her life. This ability to hold on, even in very simple ways, is work black women have done for a very long time.

This poem is not enough, but it is something, for the woman who literally 47 covered the holes in our walls with sunflowers:

> They were women then
> My mama's generation
> Husky of voice—Stout of
> Step
> With fists as well as
> Hands
> How they battered down
> Doors
> And ironed
> Starched white
> Shirts
> How they led
> Armies
> Headragged Generals

> Across mined
> Fields
> Booby-trapped
> Kitchens
> To discover books
> Desks
> A place for us
> How they knew what we
> *Must* know
> Without knowing a page
> Of it
> Themselves.

Guided by my heritage of a love of beauty and a respect for strength—in   48
search of my mother's garden, I found my own.

And perhaps in Africa over two hundred years ago, there was just such a   49
mother; perhaps she painted vivid and daring decorations in oranges and yel-
lows and greens on the walls of her hut; perhaps she sang—in a voice like
Roberta Flack's—*sweetly* over the compounds of her village; perhaps she wove
the most stunning mats or told the most ingenious stories of all the village sto-
rytellers. Perhaps she was herself a poet—though only her daughter's name is
signed to the poems that we know.

Perhaps Phillis Wheatley's mother was also an artist.   50

Perhaps in more than Phillis Wheatley's biological life is her mother's sig-   51
nature made clear.

For Discussion
and Writing

Reading and Thinking Critically

1. *Personal response:* Why does Walker discuss her mother's garden? What is
   the larger meaning of this garden, and how is it related to the creative, but
   often stifled spirit of generations of black women artists?
2. *Be alert to differences:* Walker alternates among types of writing in this essay.
   There is her own essayist's style; examples of poetry; and excerpts from
   Virginia Woolf's *A Room of One's Own.* What effects do these differences create for you?
3. *Broaden the context:* Walker takes on a large theme in this essay, concerning
   the suppression of black women and their creative inspirations. How does
   Walker's theme resonate in her essay's final line? In what way does Walker
   reach from the essay into your life and prove her assertion that her story is
   "yet shared, in its theme and its meaning, by all of us"?

Examining "In Search of Our Mothers' Gardens" as an Essay

1. In ¶29 Walker turns from the first part of the essay to the second, conclud-
   ing part. How does this paragraph function as a transition? Characterize
   Walker's focus in each of the essay's parts.
2. Walker uses the life of Phillis Wheatley as an extended example, and enlists
   Virginia Woolf to help readers understand the meaning of this example.
   Why?

3. Reread ¶s 30–41. How does Walker make a smooth transition into her discussion of her "mother's garden"?

Building Fly Rods and Living a Life
Michael Behrens

Michael Behrens, recent graduate of the University California, Berkeley, majored in Literature and now finds himself building fly rods for a living. Like many soon-to-be graduates and recent graduates, Behrens saw the world looming large before him. After finishing school, he worked for several months as a reporter for a small newspaper; he waited tables; and then, on reading an advertisement for fly rod makers, took a chance and applied—an impulsive move for which he is now grateful. As his title suggests, Behrens is up to more than explaining the construction of fly rods in this essay. Note that he does not (as Anna Quindlen does not) directly state a thesis. As you read, you might consider his reasons for this choice. In the sidebar to this piece, Behrens explains his motivation for writing.

1   Recently I spoke to a young man about my work, which is building fly rods. A good-natured, healthy Northern Californian was he: vegetarian, anti-caffeine, three triathlons finished last summer—and out of work for months. "Isn't it a sign of the affluence of our society that people can be employed full time making things like fly rods?" he asked me.

2   Ironically we were talking because his father had harbored hopes that his boy might cotton to fly rods. "It's just the sort of thing that could blossom into a career for him." Unfortunately for dad's plans, the son, who possessed the dreamy and sometimes petulant manner of a varsity athlete whose fields of glory are now only oft-recalled memories, chose to continue his wanderings through the maze of careerdom. "I can think of a lot of things I don't want to do," he confessed to me. "I just can't come up with anything I *do* want to do."

3   It is a great dilemma of our generation. Our conversation did prompt me to think of my own choices, but only long enough to recognize that my vegetarian friend, in his attitudes, embodied the malaise hanging about our collective twentysomething heads. This bewilderment, this overabundance of options, this jadedness—I was laboring under it all. That was before fly rods.

4   To appreciate their appeal it helps to understand their duties. Like jet fighters or any other human endeavor that flies in the face of Newton's first law, the ideal fly rod is strong, flexible, and as light as possible. It's the rapier of fishing poles.

5   The rods of African lemonwood and British Guinean greenheart and lancewood used by the English until the late nineteen hundreds recalled the simplicity and strength of their famed longbows, but, at lengths of up to eighteen feet, proved too unwieldy. Thus, from the 1860s on, rodmak-

ing belongs to Americans and their slimmer split cane rods—chief among them the Maine cabinetmaker and engineer named Hiram Leonard, whose work in the years following the Civil War anointed him as the grandfather of split-cane rods.

The "cane" of split cane was Tonkin bamboo. (Actually harvested 6 from the hillsides of the Kwangtung province of China, over the centuries a thousand monsoons have whipped it into the most pliant wood in the world.) After importation and up to twenty years of aging, the cane was split, glued into a hexagonal wand of six cane strips, and then painstakingly planed down to a tip (still containing all six strips of cane) often slimmer than a matchstick. Consuming hunreds of hours, the process contained about one hundred and fifty separate operations.

Cane rodmakers left lega- 7 cies of a life's work of split-cane rods scattered about the country. Like antique furniture or violins, these fly rods are distinguished by artisan. A fly fishing historian remembers his first glimpse, as an eight-year-old, of a fly rod made by the rodmaker Edward Payne, and now owned by the family doctor: "I found it strange that the doctor loved his gleaming four-ounce Payne so much that he utterly refused to fish with it. The old man laid it reverently on his red felt desktop in the lamplight and looked at the exquisite rod for hours. It obviously had the overtones of some religious relic" (Schwiebert 1).

Michael Behrens: My Commitment to This Essay

Having graduated from college and distanced himself from the world of assignments, Michael Behrens was under no obligation to write this essay. Yet he did—in an effort to understand something about himself and to relate this understanding to others. Behrens's personal statement gives you an insight into his motivations for writing, but it is *not* itself an essay. Why not? What are the differences between this statement and the essay? What are the similarities?

The "art" that I mention at the conclusion of this essay to me does not literally mean literature or painting. I actually meant "art" to connote something more like "meaning." Meaning, I suppose, is the art of human endeavor—we all hope that our lives mean something. In times past, only the elite intellectual caste of one kind or another wrestled with such doubts—only they had the leisure and the access to ideas. But in the second half of this century, America's sweeping middle class, educated in her huge universities, has democratized learning.

We had jobs for the engineers. But what of those who inherited a humanities education originally designed for either classics scholars or rich English dilettantes? We are brimming with ideas about meaningful things, we humanities majors; we are expected to become professionals; but few jobs are out there, and we find ourselves adrift, negotiating our way financially and spiritually. Is it any wonder that we vacillate, that we wander, that we're dubbed "slackers"? This essay is about fly rods and about finding meaning. It's set against an ongoing, generation-wide search for the good life.

Most crucial was a rod's 8 "action"—its ability to throw a pinpoint cast with a twitch of the caster's wrist. Therein lay the engineering complexities of the rodmaking craft. In 1865 a man wrote of a meeting with a talented but now obscure rodmaker named Charles Murphy: "I listened with wonder to the talk of angles, tapers, gluing, and other details, until I thought that the building up of a split-cane bamboo rod required more careful attention than the grinding of a lens for a great telescope" (Schwiebert 20).

Now, instead of bamboo from the Kmangtung province we have car- 9
bon graphite, which, in engineering qualities, has it all over cane. (Cane
rods are still made. Fabulously expensive, they possess the appeal of a
1969 Mercedes sports coupe—a high-performance anachronism.) The
American aerospace industry concocted graphite for use in thin-skinned
high-performance jet fighters, but post–Berlin wall it forms mountain bike
frames, golf club shafts, ski poles, and fly rods. Just as the English harvested the tropical woods of their Empire for their fishing rods, Americans
technological expeditions in the name of the Cold war have enriched the
leisure sports industry.

The company I work for began twenty years ago in the garage of an 10
engineer and tinkerer much like Charles Murphy. Now we are twenty
people working in a large warehouse. We sell fly rods in shops across the
country, and we export to Spain, England, France, Italy, and Norway.

But the craft remains the same. It's the craft that attracts me. Not just 11
craft in the sense of the actual trade, but the fact that my work claims a
history.

I work with a twenty-year-old machinist full of squirrelly energy and 12
as uncompromising in his craft as a curmudgeonly New England cabinetmaker. Does the fact that he labors daily upon an instrument designed to
catch trout, while others chase the cure for cancer, give him pause? In
1893, did Hiram Leonard similarly pause? If so, it was probably at the
proper time to ponder such matters—late at night after a few beers, and
secure in the knowledge that in the morning, one will rise and go back to
work.

I'm not anti-thought, you see, just dubious of the wisdom of always 13
analyzing, analyzing. My vegetarian friend, for example, possessed too
many opinions, and not enough passions. He reminded me of my studies
upon a university campus where, we were given to understand, everything was relative. In my field—literature—there was no right and wrong,
only opinions, and differences of opinion. Grades came down upon our
presentations of opinion like judgments from the Old Testament God—
that is to say, in unpredictable manner. Talent and hard work were usually rewarded. But was our work right? Not *right* in the moral sense—I
mean, had it at all approached *truth?*

A craftsman labors within realms of undisputable right and wrong. 14
There is, for instance, only one way to properly file a fly rod's ferrule, and
it takes months to learn. "This ferrule," I was told once early in my
apprenticeship, "has been *improperly* filed." This rejection of my work
braced me like a spray of icy water. Now I am imparting the same painful
lesson in ferrule-filing to another apprentice. We work at it late every
afternoon, painstakingly fine-tuning his skills. And then, our work done,
we'll take one of our rods outside and cast it for a few minutes. We'll
watch the line flick forward and unfurl in a tight, graceful loop. Its
rhythms will remind us that only at the farthest reaches of craftsmanship
will we find art.

Reading and Thinking Critically

1. *Personal response:* Assume you had spent thousands of dollars earning a degree and then took an apparently unrelated job upon graduation. What questions would you expect to encounter? How might you respond?
2. *Personal response:* Behrens majored in literature. What evidence do you see that his training has, indeed, prepared him for his work?
3. *Be alert to differences:* Behrens maintains that in a craft one can find absolute standards of right and wrong, and this appeals to him. By contrast, no one seemed willing to make firm judgments like this in his undergraduate major—literature. Why not? What accounts for these differences?

Examining "Building Fly Rods and Living a Life" as an Essay

1. Behrens does not state his thesis directly. Why not? How would you state his thesis?
2. Behrens devotes the middle of his essay to the craft of rodmaking. What attitudes about craftsmanship does he weave through his account?
3. How does Behrens's instruction to his apprentice in the last paragraph of the essay link Behrens to the tradition he has been writing about?
4. An essay need not resolve all confusions and answer all questions. In ¶12, Behrens raises a question about the relative value of various jobs: finding a cure for cancer versus building fly rods. Is one a more noble or a more worthy pursuit than the other? Why does Behrens *not* offer an answer?

Structures and Strategies

Prepare to Write: Explore Your Idea

Discovering Ideas

Whether you are assigned a topic to write on or are left to your own devices, you inevitably face the question: What is my idea? Like every essay, a familiar essay has at its heart an idea you want to convey. For Michael Behrens, the idea was that a craftsman's passionate devotion to a job turns work into art and can give life meaning. From beginning to end, Behrens advances this one idea: first, through the anecdote about the aimless vegetarian triathlete; next, through the history of fly rod building; and finally, through the reflection on his apprenticeship and his current relationship with an apprentice. Like Behrens, you face the challenge of presenting a *single* idea. Two techniques for generating ideas are reflecting on your experience and reading to spark ideas.

Reflect on Your Experience, and Write a Discovery Draft

The familiar essay is a form that draws on personal experience. So begin your thinking about a familiar essay with a personal experience or with an idea that fascinates you (or otherwise compels your attention). Then write a discovery draft—two or three pages of quickly made notes meant for your eyes alone, in which you go exploring. Without giving a thought to readers, write about whatever comes to mind concerning your topic. Often, a good place to begin is with a question: What *don't* I understand about this experience or idea? Your need to discover will give you a motivation to write.

Allow yourself some time away from your notes and then reread them. Next, underline the statements that, considered together, suggest an idea. Distill these statements into the clearest possible expression of that idea—into one or two sentences if you can. At this point your idea may not be fully defined, but you can use your uncertainty, once again, to motivate you in the next stage: writing a first, full draft meant for readers. Use your discovery draft to provide a place to *begin* your first draft. At the end of a discovery draft, you should address these questions:

> What do I think is my idea?
> Why do I want to write about this idea?
> Why should my readers care?

Read to Discover Ideas

Reading can help to spark ideas for a familiar essay. The strategy is to read and respond, using someone else's writing as a prompt for you to investigate your own ideas. This approach leads to the same discovery draft discussed above, the difference being that another person's writing, not your own experience, launches the draft. There is evidence in Alice Walker's essay that source materials by Phillis Wheatley, Virginia Woolf, and Jean Toomer helped to spark ideas. See especially ¶s 1–2, Walker's use of Toomer's observation of "black women whose spirituality was so intense, so deep, so *unconscious,* that they were themselves unaware of the richness they held"; and see ¶s 37–39, Walker's use of an excerpt from *A Room of One's Own.*

As in any essay, source materials can be brought to a familiar essay to advance your ideas (more on this in chapter 4, "Advance Your Idea Using Sources"). But sources can also help you to *have* ideas. It matters little whether you begin a discovery draft with your own experience or with the experiences of others, as expressed in their writing. Your goal is to generate ideas. If you can do this, you can move to the next stage, preparing a formal first draft, later versions of which will be given to readers.

Committing Yourself to an Idea

The very best writing is produced by those who have a personal stake in what they write. At times, this personal stake is discovered through writing; at other times, it precedes writing. In either event, you should be conscious of *not* letting readers see your work until you have adopted these attitudes:

- I write for myself and for my audience.
- I will find an approach to writing that lets me discover something personally significant.

You can find significance for both yourself and your readers in virtually any topic, provided you take your own experience seriously and are willing to explore the topic. The fly rod example demonstrates the point. Michael Behrens explores a topic unfamiliar to most of us, one that many would classify as "mere sport," and finds in it deep and resonant meaning. He is committed absolutely to his thesis: *A craftsman's passionate devotion to a job turns work into art and can give life meaning.* In the language of chapter 3, this is an ambitious, three-story thesis that creates a sense of tension. As readers, we want to know: How *does* work become art and create meaning? Fly rods aside, we want to understand this transformation since, like most people, we want to lead meaningful lives. Behrens's commitment to the idea of his essay creates a corresponding commitment in us to read and to take his ideas seriously. When you, like Behrens, show commitment to the idea of your essay, you stand a good chance of having readers make a commitment to *your* work.

Write: Clarify Your Idea and Make It Public

Creating Common Ground with Readers

Readers have no direct access to the events that prompted your essay. You need, therefore, to recreate these events so readers can understand the context in which your essay's idea emerged. Assume you are writing on the relationship between children and parents, perhaps on the idea of absentee parents: mothers or fathers who work long hours and who are seldom home. The idea of your essay will be remote if you continually write sentences at this level of abstraction: "Parents who work intensively out of the home are not available to help their sons and daughters through childhood's momentary crises." By contrast, you could help readers understand the full ramifications of your idea by relating a story of how, as a ten-year-old, you had a huge disagreement with your best friend and found no one home to console you and discuss the matter. By exploring an idea through particular experiences—by creating a common ground through which you *and* readers can examine an idea—you have the best possible chance of creating "a personal account that is yet shared."

Try to create common ground with readers in every paragraph using a variety of techniques: brief stories, descriptions, historical accounts, and references to books, articles, or current events. Whatever combination of techniques you use, your goal is to let the reader see and know *particular* people, places, things, and actions and then to explore your idea *through* these particulars. Several techniques that are especially useful for developing the parts of a familiar essay include narratives; descriptions; examples; historical accounts; references to published books, movies, or artwork; and references to current events. In any one essay, a writer will usually employ more than one technique.

Narratives (Anecdotes)

Recently I spoke to a young man about my work, which is building fly rods. A good-natured, healthy Northern Californian was he: vegetarian, anti-caffeine, three triathlons finished last summer—and out of work for months. . . .

—Michael Behrens

Descriptions

There are more-visible people in need. There are the legions of homeless, lying on the benches in Grand Central Terminal, huddled in doorways against the cold, carrying their lives on their backs, trading subsistence for life. In soup kitchens they lean over their meals as though in prayer and use the broth to warm as well as feed them, and use their dinnertime to stoke their beaten souls as well as their empty stomachs.

—Anna Quindlen

Examples

For example: in the Smithsonian Institution in Washington, D.C., there hangs a quilt unlike any other in the world. In fanciful, inspired, and yet simple and identifiable figures, it portrays the story of the Crucifixion. It is considered rare, beyond price. Though it follows no known pattern of quilt-making, and though it is made of bits and pieces of worthless rags, it is obviously the work of a person of powerful imagination and deep spiritual feeling. Below this quilt I saw a note that says it was made by "an anonymous Black woman in Alabama, a hundred years ago."

If we could locate this "anonymous" black woman from Alabama, she would turn out to be one of our grandmothers—an artist who left her mark in the only materials she could afford, and in the only medium her position in society allowed her to use.

—Alice Walker

Historical Accounts

The rods of African lemonwood and British Guinean greenheart and lancewood used by the English until the late nineteen hundreds recalled the simplicity and strength of their famed longbows, but, at lengths up to eighteen feet, proved too unwieldy. Thus, from the 1860's on, rod-making belongs to Americans and their slimmer split cane rods—chief among them the Maine cabinetmaker and engineer named Hiram Leonard, whose work in the years following the Civil War anointed him as the "grandfather of split-cane rods."

—Michael Behrens

References to Published Books, Movies, or Artwork

Not all gulls mate for life, but among those that do there can be a biological mandate for divorce. William Jordan reports in *Divorce Among the Gulls* that more than 25 percent of newly paired gulls separate after their first attempt to raise young. They break up for some of the same reasons humans do, primarily good old-fashioned incompatibility. . . .

—Jerry Dennis

References to Current Events

The latest news from the marriage wars is dire: 50 percent or more of the weddings performed in the United States in the next year are likely to end in divorce. Some sociologists predict the number will be closer to 60 percent, because the generation now reaching marrying age was raised in the divorce-racked sixties and seventies, and countless studies have demonstrated that children of divorced parents tend to become divorced themselves.

—Jerry Dennis

Tone and the Writing Occasion

As you saw in the more detailed discussions on writing occasion and common ground in chapter 3, *tone* describes the general attitude a writer takes toward readers. You have seen a variety of tones in the examples of familiar essays at the beginning of this chapter. In Alice Walker's "In Search of Our Mothers' Gardens," we find a writer who is making both an important personal discovery and a broader cultural discovery. The writer speaks of generations of black women whose creative voices have been suppressed. This grave topic demands a deeply serious tone. By contrast, the tone of Jerry Dennis's "Mates for Life" is nearly playful. He is no less committed to the idea of his essay than Walker is to hers, but Dennis's topic, the sociology of mating, gives him a wider range of tones from which to choose. Certainly the decline in stable marriages is a matter that can and has been treated as a serious problem, but Dennis approaches this topic from an unexpected angle (pair bonding in the wild and what it can teach us about human bonding). In this essay, at least, he is not interested in the social consequences of America's soaring divorce rate. As Dennis has approached it, his topic can sustain humor. And, like Walker, he is able to prompt in us a personal reflection, which is to say that writers can succeed in familiar essays with any tone, as long as the tone is matched carefully with an essay's topic.

To an extent, your choice of topics limits possibilities for your essay's tone. Some topics, like Walker's, must be treated with great seriousness. Others lend themselves to lighter treatments. In chapter 3, the writing occasion is described in the diagram shown on the facing page, the language of which can help you think about the tone most appropriate for your familiar essays.

If you think your topic lends itself to more than one tone, begin to narrow your options by reflecting on your purpose: Do you wish to explain, explore, persuade, suggest, or entertain? Think of your audience's familiarity with the topic and the range of their likely reactions. Think also of your own engagement with the topic. With what tone will you be most successful in exploring the idea? What is your mood when thinking of this topic: playful, serious, worried, outraged, confused, indignant, charmed,

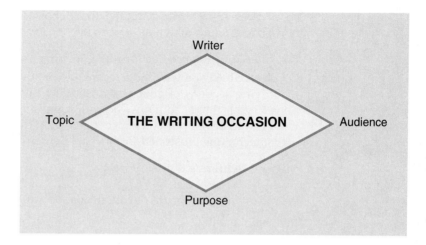

or intrigued? Only you can negotiate the many possibilities. Having thought the matter over, consciously choose a tone you think does justice to you, your topic, your purpose, *and* your audience; then use that tone consistently throughout your essay.

Planning a Structure

For virtually any essay, you do well to include a thesis—a single, clear statement of your essay's idea. The familiar essay is something of an exception in that writers often work indirectly. For strategic reasons, they will sometimes *not* state an essay's idea openly, in order to let readers come to that idea themselves. Recall the ideas of the essays that began this chapter:

Anna Quindlen:

Give of yourselves, reader, if only in some small way, and help this city's needy. (Quindlen does not state this idea directly.)

Michael Behrens:

A craftsman's passionate devotion to a job turns work into art and can give life meaning. (Behrens does not state this idea directly.)

Jerry Dennis:

"We ought to know a thing or two about the courtship rituals of humans, but we don't." (Dennis states his idea directly.)

Alice Walker:

"Guided by my heritage of a love of beauty and a respect for strength—in search of my mother's garden, I found my own." (Walker states her idea directly.)

Two of these essayists state their essay's idea directly; two do not. Note, however, that all four organize and develop their work with care, according to a thesis. Whether or not you directly state it, you should nonetheless have a thesis that governs every choice you make as a writer: choices about your essay's structure and tone; choices about examples, quotations, background materials, and so on.

Discover Your Essay's Sections by Quizzing Your Thesis

On pages 61–63 you will find a technique for "quizzing" a thesis and thus identifying sections of your essay. Conduct this quiz by directing questions to your thesis. Your answers will suggest the parts of the essay you will need to develop if you expect to develop the essay's idea fully. Here is that technique illustrated for Michael Behrens's thesis:

Michael Behrens's thesis: *why this?   what job?*

A craftsman's (passionate devotion) to (a job) turns work into art and can give life meaning.   *how does this happen?*   *how does this happen?*

What are the likely sections of an essay built on this statement? Behrens identified sections by answering his own questions:

What is the job being discussed?

> *Fly rod building.*

Why would a craftsman be passionately devoted to a job?

> *Give history of practices and materials. Stories about ownership.*

How does work become art?

> *The worker understands the history of the work and shares earlier values.*

How can work give life meaning?

> *Work can give one a sense of absolute values, or clear right and wrong, and of a place in history. Explore the consequences of not having a job to feel passionate about; explore the problem of "too many opinions and not enough passions."*

Your thesis is a contract in which you signal to readers your intention to present certain ideas and information. A fully developed essay is one in which every point of exploration and discussion suggested by the thesis is, in fact, explored and discussed. Michael Behrens understood that he should write an essay with these sections:

> Uncertainty, aimlessness of those who do not have a passion
> History of fly rods—devoted builders and users
> Modern fly rod building—connection to old ways, old values
> Meaning—and art—through work

Understanding Your Logic

As you begin the first draft of your essay, you must first understand your purpose for writing. Familiar essays lend themselves to a wide range of uses, from direct argument to quiet reflection: Anna Quindlen argues while Michael Behrens largely reflects. Though these presentations differ logically (because their purposes differ), both essays succeed; by examining the particulars of their own lives, the essayists have prompted us to think about ours. Ultimately, you want to prompt in readers such a reflection, but the logical strategies by which you do this will vary depending on your purpose. Two chapters in this book will help you to plan your essay's logic.

- When your purpose is to reflect or explain, see chapter 7 on writing explanations. That discussion is devoted to writing for academic occasions, but you can use the advice given there—on writing with clarity, for instance, or writing for various audiences—as you write a familiar essay.
- If you plan to argue, see chapter 11 (pages 403–484) for a detailed discussion on strategies for persuading readers.

Develop Sections by Exploiting a Tension

Having identified the likely sections of your essay, try presenting a paradox—a play of opposites—in each. Paradoxes create tension, and tension creates in readers a need for resolution. Here, for example, are the sections of Michael Behrens's essay and the tensions that he presents in developing them:

A. Open with the story of the vegetarian acquaintance.

   The vegetarian is sound in body but he's sick in his soul.

B. Present the story of fly rod building, first historical and then present-day: emphasize continuity of passion and values.

   The well-built fly rod will contradict Newton's first laws.

   Love (of fly rods) manifests itself in painstaking effort.

C. Return to vegetarian and what he lacks.

   Having opinions but lacking convictions is destructive.

D. Show the art in the craft and the meaning that comes from it.

   Rejection is valuable.

Michael Behrens develops the sections of his essay by exploring tensions. His strategy simultaneously keeps us engaged and allows him to develop his idea. The other writers whose essays began this chapter similarly develop one or more sections of their essays through tensions. Anna Quindlen, for instance, opens "A City's Needy" this way: "The most singular thing about need in New York City is . . . that need here is often so private, and so proud." We do not typically think of the needy in terms of pride. Quindlen sparks our interest, and we read on. A well-defined tension can organize the logic of sections of an essay, creating interest for readers and a plan by which you can advance your idea.

Advancing Your Idea with Sources

Your experience is the primary source in a familiar essay. Still, you may need to go to written source materials for facts, historical information, useful anecdotes and examples, or authoritative opinions. Whatever your needs, be sure that you put sources to *your* purposes in the essay and that the essay's focus remains on your idea. Every reference to a source should be an occasion through which you advance your idea.

Use an Anecdote or Quotation to Advance an Idea

Following are two passages from Ernest Schwiebert's *Trout Tackle*, which Michael Behrens uses in his essay. In the first example, Behrens quotes Schwiebert's story about the doctor and his Payne fly rod to further this point: that the split-cane rods are works of art—and, like antique furniture or violins, "are distinguished by artisan." Observe how Behrens first creates a context for Schwiebert and then makes a reference. As readers, we keep our focus on Behrens even as we are reading Schwiebert's words.

Behrens	*Schwiebert*
Cane rodmakers left legacies of a life's work of split-cane rods scattered about the country. Like antique furniture or violins, these fly rods are distinguished by artisan. A fly fishing historian remembers his first glimpse, as an eight-year-old, of a fly rod made by the rodmaker Edward Payne, and now owned by the family doctor: "I found it strange that the doctor loved his gleaming four-ounce Payne so much that he utterly refused to fish with it. The old man laid it reverently on his red felt desktop in the lamplight and looked at the exquisite rod for hours. It obviously had the overtones of some religious relic" (Schwiebert 1).	The first really fine fly rod that I ever saw was an eight-foot Payne owned by a physician in Chicago. It had been built by Edward Payne, one of the original apprentice disciples of Hiram Leonard in Bangor, and had been refinished by James Payne many years later. Their names meant nothing to an eight-year-old who was still more interested in catching fish than in the subtle rituals and liturgies of fishing. However, the craftsmanship and beauty of the rod were obvious, although I found it strange that the doctor loved his gleaming four-ounce Payne so much that he utterly refused to fish with it. The old man laid it reverently on his red felt desktop in the lamplight and looked at the exquisite rod for hours. It obviously had the overtones of some religious relic.
	It would be many years later before I fully understood that a skilled fisherman did have almost religious feelings about his tackle. It had great beauty and fished with elegance, and had the votive powers to reawaken memories of rivers past. It was my first exposure to the iconography of the split-cane rod.

Behrens	*Schwiebert*
Most crucial was the rod's "action"—its ability to throw a pinpoint cast with a twitch of the caster's wrist. Therein lay the engineering complexities of the rodmaking craft. In 1865 a man wrote of a meeting with a talented but now obscure rodmaker named Charles Murphy: "I listened with wonder to the talk of angles, tapers, gluing, and other details, until I thought that the building up of a split-cane bamboo rod required more careful attention than the grinding of a lens for a great telescope" (qtd. in Schwiebert 20).	Fred Mather was the distinguished fisherman and ichthyologist who later imported the brown trout to the United States, and his book *My Angling Friends* describes meeting the talkative Murphy at the Manhattan tackle shop of J.C. Conroy in 1865: I listened with wonder to the talk of angles, tapers, gluing, and other details, until I thought that the building up of a split-cane bamboo rod required more careful attention than the grinding of a lens for a great telescope.

In the second example, Behrens again mines a source for a memorable anecdote that develops his idea. Recall that Behrens's essay concerns the relationship between devotion to a craft and finding meaning in one's life. The quoted passage from Schwiebert's book on fishing tackle nicely suggests that larger meanings can emerge from an inanimate object, like a fly rod. When you integrate source materials into your essays, use the words of others to your own purpose. Make a point in your own words and *then*, to the extent you use them, draw on sources for support. For advice on smoothly integrating source materials into your essays, see chapter 4, pages 58–78.

Evaluate and Revise

General Evaluation

You will usually need at least two drafts to produce an essay that presents your idea clearly. The biggest changes in your essay will typically come between your first and second drafts. Any essay you write, including a familiar essay, will not be complete until you revise and refine your single compelling idea. In this book you will find two demonstrations of essays in the process of evolving from meandering first thoughts into finished products. First, see in chapters 12–14 general advice on the process of writing and revising, which includes first- and second-draft versions of a student paper. You will find another such demonstration in the "Student Writer at Work" sections at the end of chapters 1–5.

You revise and refine by evaluating your first draft, bringing to it many of the same questions you pose when evaluating any piece of writing. In chapter 5 you will find general guidelines for evaluating what you read, including:

- Are the facts accurate?
- Are the opinions supported by evidence?

- Are the opinions of others authoritative?
- Are assumptions clearly stated?
- Are key terms clearly defined?
- Is the presentation logical?
- Are all parts of the presentation well developed?
- Are dissenting points of view presented?

Address these same questions to the first draft of your familiar essays, and you will give yourself solid information by which to guide a revision.

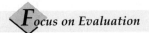

Focus on Evaluation

Have you been asked to write an evaluation of another writer's familiar easay? If so, you will base your evaluation on two sets of standards: first, you will apply specific standards for this type of writing, and second, you will need to apply the general standards for evaluation that are listed here and discussed at length in chapter 5, pages 87–102. See especially the "key points" for evaluation in chapter 5, pages 95–96.

Critical Points in a Familiar Essay

Significance

Readers are always entitled to ask: So what? How can I use this? In familiar essays, readers look for an opportunity to reflect on an idea that is significant to them as well as to the writer. Your goal, then, is to establish this significance quickly. There is no formula for success, and the four writers whose essays opened this chapter use four different strategies. The general strategy is to funnel the reader into an essay by introducing the topic, its significance, and your likely approach to it, all within two or three paragraphs. Readers who are not being paid to read (that is, anyone other than your composition teachers) will seldom give you more space than this to prove why they should be interested in your ideas. Having an efficient, clear strategy for opening is therefore very important.

Abstraction

The strength and appeal of a familiar essay resides in the writer's ability to give readers access to ideas through particular experiences. The moment ideas in the essay are expressed abstractly, as ideas only, the familiar essay disappears and we have something else—very often, philosophy. On this point, see the sentence on page 105, set against a paragraph by Jerry Dennis describing the grief of a sandhill crane. The single sentence is only an idea; the paragraph, excerpted from an essay, makes that idea understandable through specific details. Take special care to develop for each idea in your essay details through which the idea can be observed and understood.

Self-Interest

Because the familiar essay draws heavily on personal experience, writers can be tempted to focus exclusively on themselves and thus forget about their readers. In this case, readers will find nothing in the essay but a writer who screams: "Me! Me!"—and readers will turn away. While the familiar essay *is* very much about your experience, recall that it is also about something more: the reader's experience as it relates to yours. Therefore, keep readers in mind. Avoid letting your reflections on personal experience become the sole reason for writing. Work to create a common ground in every paragraph.

Occasions for Discussion and Writing

A Familiar Essay of Your Own

You are ready to begin work on your own familiar essay. One approach to choosing a topic is to review examples of the type of essay you will be writing. Consider rereading the essays that opened this chapter. You will find that the four authors—Quindlen, Dennis, Walker, and Behrens—write about topics they know well, either through direct experience or through careful reading. You will also find that these authors have a deep, personal involvement with their essay's topic: for Quindlen, this is poverty; for Walker, slavery; for Dennis, mating; and for Behrens, work. In choosing a topic for your essay, you too should be prepared for a deep involvement. In the best of cases, your motivation to write will be personal but your expression of ideas *in your essay* will be public and controlled. The examples amply demonstrate this double quality: in each essay you find someone writing for personal reasons, yet maintaining strict control over important elements of public expression—including the essay's reasoning, structure, sentence rhythm, and word choice.

To prepare for your familiar essay, select one of the examples that began this chapter, one that you find especially effective. Think critically about how this essay succeeds. You might respond to the questions following the piece; you might try writing a paragraph explaining what appeals to you most about the piece; you might reflect on the ways in which this essay could affect your own work. Once you have studied the piece and have a clear sense of how it succeeds, choose a topic for your own essay—a topic that you know well.

The Occasions sections of this chapter present two topics for writing: date rape and gender identity. If you prefer another topic, you might find suitable materials in the other Occasions sections in chapters 7–11:

Of course, you are not limited to these choices and should choose a topic according to your interests and experience. For detailed guidance on how you might organize your approach to writing a familiar essay, turn to the second "Occasion for Discussion and Writing" in this chapter, pages 158–164. That "Guide to the Assignment" provides a structured approach to the writing task may help you work through your first draft and revision, whatever your topic.

A note on using sources: Three of the four writers whose essays began the chapter draw on source materials to advance their ideas. You can—and are encouraged to—do the same, with the caution that writers who use sources should never let source materials overtake their essays. The psychological focus of your essay should remain yours alone. In writing a first draft, be sure that your voice predominates and that sources, even if essential to your essay's success, play a subordinate role.

I. Date Rape and Campus Policy

At some point during orientation week or in formal campus bulletins, most college administrations alert incoming students about the issue of date rape. Depending on the statistics you trust, one in four or one in seven women will be victimized by rape or attempted rape; and very often, the perpetrator will be someone the woman knows. Seeking to prevent sexual violence on campus, colleges have directly addressed the problem of date rape through educational programs before the fact and through disciplinary hearings after. The candid language with which administrators discuss sexual matters has offended many students and parents. But colleges have made the decision that it is better that some people be offended than even one student be harmed because a perpetrator did not clearly understand what constitutes rape or sexual assault.

In 1990, the students of Antioch University in Ohio initiated an effort that resulted two years later in a formal campus "Sexual Offense Policy." *Consent* is the defining feature of this policy: if students would engage in sex, their activity must be consensual, that is, agreed to verbally, by both partners, at every step along the way. Antioch's policy has generated a debate on the extent to which campuses should "get into the sex business." Newspaper columnists, television talk-show hosts, and magazine feature writers have given the matter national attention.

Now it is your turn to respond. Read and comment on the Antioch policy, and also on the essay paired with it by Camille Paglia: "Rape and Modern Sex War." You will find Paglia disputing a key assumption underlying the policy—that sexual relations exist in a social world and can be made subject to social regulation. Paglia views sex as more dangerously hormonal than words can negotiate, and so she finds policies like Antioch's flawed. The readings have been paired to generate a strong personal response on the basis of which you can launch into group discussions and, if you choose, write an essay. First read the selections with care. Working by yourself, do the following:

- Summarize the main idea of each selection.
- List the points of conflict between the Antioch policy and Paglia.
- Respond in writing to each of the selections.

Having done this, work in small groups and discuss the issues raised by these selections. The goal of group discussion will be to distinguish and clarify the views of group members.

The Antioch College Sexual Offense Policy
Introduction to the Policy

The statistics on the frequency of sexual violence on college campuses today 1 are alarming. While we try to make Antioch a safe environment for everyone, we still have problems here. There is date and acquaintance rape, and stranger rape, and, while the majority of perpetrators are men and majority of victims are women, there are also female perpetrators and male victims. There are also many students who have already experienced sexual violence before arriving at Antioch; healing from that experience may be an integral part of their personal, social and academic lives while they are here. . . .

Antioch has two policies, a sexual harassment policy and a sexual offense 2 policy, which have been designed to help deal with these problems when they occur on campus and/or when they involve an Antioch community member. Read these policies; you are responsible for knowing them. Under the sexual offense policy:

- All sexual contact and conduct between any two people must be consensual;
- Consent must be obtained verbally before there is any sexual contact or conduct;
- If the level of sexual intimacy increases during an interaction (i.e., if two people move from kissing while fully clothed—which is one level—to undressing for direct physical contact, which is another level), the people involved need to express their clear verbal consent before moving to that new level;
- If one person wants to *initiate* moving to a higher level of sexual intimacy in an interaction, *that person is responsible for getting the verbal consent of the other person(s) involved before moving to that level;*
- If you have had a particular level of sexual intimacy before with someone, you must still ask each and *every* time;
- If you have a sexually transmitted disease, you must disclose it to a potential sexual partner.

Don't ever make any assumptions about consent: they can hurt someone 3 and get you in trouble. Also, do not take silence as consent; it isn't. Consent must be clear and verbal (i.e., saying: yes, I want to kiss you also).

Special precautions are necessary if you, or the person with whom you 4 would like to be sexual, are under the influence of alcohol, drugs, or prescribed medication. Extreme caution should always be used. Consent, even verbal consent, may not be meaningful. Taking advantage of someone who is "under the influence" is never acceptable behavior. If, for instance, you supply someone with alcohol and get her/him drunk so that person will consent to have sex with you (figuring you wouldn't get "as far" if that person were sober), then their consent may be meaningless and you may be charged under the sexual offense policy. If you are so drunk that you act with someone totally inappropriately (in a way maybe you wouldn't if you were sober), or if you are so drunk you don't hear "no," you may still be charged under the sexual offense policy.

If you have a hard time knowing or setting your own personal boundaries, 5 or respecting other people's boundaries, you may have a harder time if alcohol or drugs are involved. For truly consensual sex, you and your partner(s) should be sober to be sexual.

Rape and Modern Sex War
Camille Paglia

Rape is an outrage that cannot be tolerated in civilized society. Yet feminism, 1 which has waged a crusade for rape to be taken more seriously, has put young women in danger by hiding the truth about sex from them.

In dramatizing the pervasiveness of rape, feminists have told young women 2 that before they have sex with a man, they must give consent as explicit as a legal contract's. In this way, young women have been convinced that they have been the victims of rape. On elite campuses in the Northeast and on the West Coast, they have held consciousness-raising sessions, petitioned administrations, demanded inquests. At Brown University, outraged, panicky "victims" have scrawled the names of alleged attackers on the walls of women's restrooms. What marital rape was to the '70s, "date rape" is to the '90s.

The incidence and seriousness of rape do not require this kind of exagger- 3 ation. Real acquaintance rape is nothing new. It has been a horrible problem for women for all of recorded history. Once fathers and brothers protected women from rape. Once the penalty for rape was death. I come from a fierce Italian tradition where, not so long ago in the motherland, a rapist would end up knifed, castrated, and hung out to dry.

But the old clans and small rural communities have broken down. In our 4 cities, on our campuses far from home, young women are vulnerable and defenseless. Feminism has not prepared them for this. Feminism keeps saying the sexes are the same. It keeps telling women they can do anything, go anywhere, say anything, wear anything. No, they can't. Women will always be in sexual danger.

One of my male students recently slept overnight with a friend in a pas- 5 sageway of the Great Pyramid in Egypt. He described the moon and sand, the ancient silence and eerie echoes. I will never experience that. I am a woman. I am not stupid enough to believe I could ever be safe there. There is a world of solitary adventure I will never have. Women have always known these somber truths. But feminism, with its pie-in-the-sky fantasies about the perfect world, keeps young women from seeing life as it is.

We must remedy social injustice whenever we can. But there are some 6 things we cannot change. There are sexual differences that are based in biology. Academic feminism is lost in a fog of social constructionism. It believes we are totally the product of our environment. This idea was invented by Rousseau. He was wrong. Emboldened by dumb French language theory, academic feminists repeat the same hollow slogans over and over to each other. Their view of sex is naive and prudish. Leaving sex to the feminists is like letting your dog vacation at the taxidermist's.

The sexes are at war. Men must struggle for identity against the over- 7 whelming power of their mothers. Women have menstruation to tell them they are women. Men must do or risk something to be men. Men become masculine only when other men say they are. Having sex with a woman is one way a boy becomes a man.

College men are at their hormonal peak. They have just left their mothers 8 and are questing for their male identity. In groups, they are dangerous. A woman going to a fraternity party is walking into Testosterone Flats, full of prickly cacti and blazing guns. If she goes, she should be armed with resolute alertness. She should arrive with girlfriends and leave with them. A girl who lets herself get dead drunk at a fraternity party is a fool. A girl who goes upstairs alone with a brother at a fraternity party is an idiot. Feminists call this "blaming the victim." I call it common sense.

For a decade, feminists have drilled their disciples to say, "Rape is a crime 9 of violence but not of sex." This sugar-coated Shirley Temple nonsense has exposed young women to disaster. Misled by feminism, they do not expect rape from the nice boys from good homes who sit next to them in class.

Aggression and eroticism are deeply intertwined. Hunt, pursuit, and capture are biologically programmed into male sexuality. Generation after generation, men must be educated, refined, and ethically persuaded away from their tendency toward anarchy and brutishness. Society is not the enemy, as feminism ignorantly claims. Society is woman's protection against rape. Feminism, with its solemn Carry Nation repressiveness, does not see what is for men the eroticism or fun element in rape, especially the wild, infectious delirium of gang rape. Women who do not understand rape cannot defend themselves against it.

The date-rape controversy shows feminism hitting the wall of its own broken promises. The women of my '60s generation were the first respectable girls in history to swear like sailors, get drunk, stay out all night—in short, to act like men. We sought total sexual freedom and equality. But as time passed, we woke up to cold reality. The old double standard protected women. When anything goes, it's women who lose.

Today's young women don't know what they want. They see that feminism 12 has not brought sexual happiness. The theatrics of public rage over date rape are their way of restoring the old sexual rules that were shattered by my generation. Because nothing about the sexes has really changed. The comic film *Where the Boys Are* (1960), the ultimate expression of '50s man-chasing, still speaks directly to our time. It shows smart, lively women skillfully anticipating and fending off the dozens of strategies with which horny men try to get them into bed. The agonizing date-rape subplot and climax are brilliantly done. The victim, Yvette Mimieux, makes mistake after mistake, obvious to the other girls. She allows herself to be lured away from her girl friends and into isolation with boys whose character and intentions she misreads. *Where the Boys Are* tells the truth. It shows courtship as a dangerous game in which the signals are not verbal but subliminal.

Neither militant feminism, which is obsessed with politically correct language, nor academic feminism, which believes that knowledge and experience are "constituted by" language, can understand pre-verbal or non-verbal communication. Feminism, focusing on sexual politics, cannot see that sex exists in and through the body. Sexual desire and arousal cannot be fully translated into verbal terms. This is why men and women misunderstand each other.

Trying to remake the future, feminism cut itself off from sexual history. It 14 discarded and suppressed the sexual myths of literature, art, and religion. Those myths show us the turbulence, the mysteries and passions of sex. In mythology we see men's sexual anxiety, their fear of women's dominance. Much sexual violence is rooted in men's sense of psychological weakness toward women. It takes many men to deal with one woman. Woman's voracity is a persistent motif. Clara Bow, it was rumored, took on the USC football team on weekends. Marilyn Monroe, singing "Diamonds Are a Girl's Best Friend," rules a conga line of men in tuxes. Half-clad Cher, in the video for "If I Could Turn Back Time," deranges a battleship of screaming sailors and straddles a pink-lit cannon. Feminism, coveting social power, is blind to woman's cosmic sexual power.

To understand rape, you must study the past. There never was and never 15 will be sexual harmony. Every woman must take personal responsibility for her sexuality, which is nature's red flame. She must be prudent and cautious about where she goes and with whom. When she makes a mistake, she must accept the consequences and, through self-criticism, resolve never to make that mistake again. Running to Mommy and Daddy on the campus grievance committee is unworthy of strong women. Posting lists of guilty men in the toilet is cowardly, infantile stuff.

The Italian philosophy of life espouses high-energy confrontation. A male 16 student makes a vulgar remark about your breasts? Don't slink off to whimper and simper with the campus shrinking violets. Deal with it. On the spot. Say, "Shut up, you jerk! And crawl back to the barnyard where you belong!" In general, women who project this take-charge attitude toward life get harassed less often. I see too many dopey, immature, self-pitying women walking around like melting sticks of butter. It's the Yvette Mimieux syndrome: Make me happy. And listen to me weep when I'm not.

The date-rape debate is already smothering in propaganda churned out by 17 the expensive Northeastern colleges and universities, with their overconcentration of boring, uptight academic feminists and spoiled, affluent students. Beware of the deep manipulativeness of rich students who were neglected by their parents. They love to turn the campus into hysterical psychodramas of sexual transgression, followed by assertions of parental authority and concern. And don't look for sexual enlightenment from academe, which spews out mountains of books but never looks at life directly.

As a fan of football and rock music, I see in the simple, swaggering mas- 18 culinity of the jock and in the noisy posturing of the heavy metal guitarist certain fundamental, unchanging truths about sex. Masculinity is aggressive, unstable, combustible. It is also the most creative cultural force in history. Women must reorient themselves toward the elemental powers of sex, which can strengthen or destroy.

The only solution to date rape is female self-awareness and self-control. A 19 woman's number one line of defense is herself. When a real rape occurs, she should report it to the police. Complaining to college committees because the courts "take too long" is ridiculous. College administrations are not a branch of the judiciary. They are not equipped or trained for legal inquiry. Colleges must alert incoming students to the problems and dangers of adulthood. Then colleges must stand back and get out of the sex game.

Individual Response: Date Rape and Campus Policy

Read the two selections, "The Antioch College Sexual Offense Policy" and "Rape and Modern Sex War."

1. Write a one-paragraph summary of each selection (see pages 85–87 for a discussion on writing summaries).

2. List the points of conflict between the Antioch policy and Paglia. To help you reflect on the conflicts, consider the following questions. (You might want to keep two lists—the likely Antioch response to these questions and the Paglia response.)

   - To what extent is sex, and the way we view it, a *social* relationship, as opposed to a purely physical one?

   - What is the relationship between what we say we feel and the hormonal urgings of the body?

   - Who takes what responsibility in sexual encounters?

   - In what ways does verbal consent alter traditional (pursuer/pursued) sexual interactions between men and women?

   - "Use common sense!" What beliefs about individual responsibility underlie this conventional advice? How do these beliefs compare with those implied by the Antioch policy?

3. For each selection, write a page of response notes. Your goal is to read these pieces and have a clear, strong reaction. For instance, if the administration at your school handed you the Antioch policy and said: "Abide by this," how would you respond? How do you respond when you read in Paglia: "There never was and never will be sexual harmony. Every woman must take personal responsibility for her sexuality, which is nature's red flame." You might begin your responses with references to specific lines in each selection.

Group Response: Date Rape and Campus Policy

1. As a group, compare your individual summaries of both the Antioch policy and Paglia's essay. Your first goal as a group is to agree on the content of these selections.

2. As a group, compare your reactions to the second Individual Response activity, listing the points of conflict between the Antioch policy and Paglia. You may want to organize the discussion by the questions posed in the activity. Again, the group should be able to agree on where the selections differ.

3. Beginning with one of the selections, take turns reading your response notes to the group. After each group member reads his or her response to a selection, have a discussion. One person should be assigned to take brief notes: the goal is to identify the range of responses to these selections. Having completed a round of discussion for the first of the readings, turn to the second reading and repeat the activity.

4. The Antioch policy has generated a great deal of national discussion. Use each of the following excerpts from various commentators to launch a group discussion. The goal is not to agree, necessarily, but to distinguish as clearly as possible the different positions among group members.

The outcry largely results from the fact that the [Antioch] rules undermine [the] traditional erotic [heterosexual encounter—with the man as the initiator, and the woman as the gatekeeper].

Eric Fassin, The New York Times, 26 Dec. 1993

The policy . . . is not puritanical; it is not anti-romantic; it does not reimpose the perspectives of the 1950s. The Antioch College Policy was developed by students' initiatives and direct involvement to deal with the realities they face in the 1990s.

Alan E. Guskin, President, Antioch University,
Antioch Record Media Supplement, 19 Nov. 1993

The main thread running through critiques of the policy is that freedom consists of individuals acting according to their private conscience.

We think this notion of people as isolated, unattached actors is a myth. In reality, people live and act always with other people, connected by a thick web of beliefs, traditions and rituals. . . . Freedom needs to be defined not as the absence of outside influences, but as the presence of opportunities to live a vital, engaged life.

Elizabeth Sullivan and Gabriel Metcalf,
Antioch Record Media Supplement, 19 Nov. 1993

Projecting an Essay: Date Rape and Campus Policy

1. You have read the Antioch policy and Paglia's essay. Your group has discussed individual versus community responsibility regarding sex. Now consider *your* campus's policy regarding date rape. Get a copy of the college's policy and distribute it to the group. (If no policy exists, see number 2.)

2. Using the Antioch policy, Paglia's essay, and your group discussions as background, respond to your college's policy—at first, individually and then, having shared your responses, as a group. If no college policy exists, decide if you want the college to adopt one. Offer clear reasons for your position.

3. Write a discovery draft concerning your college's policy (or lack of policy) regarding date rape. Your goal is to generate an idea that could guide the writing of a familiar essay. See pages 486–499 for advice on writing a discovery draft and devising a working thesis.

4. Distribute your working thesis to the group. As a group, quiz each statement (see Structures and Strategies, page 128 and pages 61–63) and devise a structure for a likely essay.

5. For each section of your projected essay, devise a common ground: a particular experience that you know well, through which you could explore the idea of that section.

6. Option: Write a familiar essay, based on your plan.

II. Exploring Gender Identity

Boys wear blue and wrestle; girls wear pink and play with dolls. Girls excel in languages and the arts; boys prefer math and science. How do these and other gender stereotypes evolve, and why are they so persistent? The selections in this Occasions section present you with an opportunity to reflect on how we acquire our sense of what is appropriately masculine and feminine. As it turns out, starting at a very young age, girls and boys are given clear, gender-specific messages. In the first selection, "Masculine/Feminine," Prudence Mackintosh wonders whether there might not be some biological (as opposed to social) reason that daughters of her friends play with dolls while the "primal physicalness" of her sons "causes the walls of [her] house to pulsate on rainy days." In "The Androgynous Man," Noel Perrin comments on a "manliness" test he once took—and apparently failed. The section concludes with a chapter from a much-publicized report on gender bias, published by the American Association of University Women.

Your Writing Assignment

Write a familiar essay guided by an insight you have concerning gender-role stereotyping in American culture. Explore and develop your insight in the context of a particular event from which you learned something about gender stereotyping. You should know this event well: you should have watched it, participated in it, or somehow have been affected by it. Assume that readers know neither you nor the event you are describing. While your personal experience will be your primary source for this essay, you may also refer to the readings in this section.

Masculine/Feminine

Prudence Mackintosh

The following essay presents a double opportunity: first, to think about the gender-identity issues you will be writing on later, and second, to use the terms introduced in the "Structures and Strategies" section to examine an essayist's strategies in creating an effective product. As you read "Masculine/Feminine" for the first time, bear three questions in mind.

- What is Mackintosh's idea in this essay? Does she state it directly? If you believe she has been indirect and has not included a thesis in the essay, write a version of this thesis yourself.
- What is Mackintosh's purpose? To what extent is she writing to reflect and explore? To what extent is she writing to persuade her readers?
- How does Mackintosh use personal experience as a base from which to make herself understood?

I had every intention to raise liberated, nonviolent sons whose aggressive tendencies would be mollified by a sensitivity and compassion that psychologists claim were denied their father's generation.   1

I did not buy guns or war toys (although Grandmother did). My boys even 2 had a secondhand baby doll until the garage sale last summer. I did buy Marlo Thomas' *Free to Be You and Me* record, a collection of nonsexist songs, stories, and poems, and I told them time and time again that it was okay to cry and be scared sometimes. I overruled their father and insisted that first grade was much too early for organized competitive soccer leagues. They know that moms *and dads* do dishes and diapers. And although they use it primarily for the convenient bathroom between the alley and the sandpile, my boys know that the storeroom is now mother's office. In such an environment, surely they would grow up free of sex-role stereotypes. At the very least wouldn't they pick up their own socks?

My friends with daughters were even more zealous. They named their 3 daughters strong, cool unisex names like Blakeney, Brett, Brook, Lindsay, and Blair, names that lent themselves to corporate letterheads, not Tupperware party invitations. These moms looked on Barbie with disdain and bought trucks and science kits. They shunned frilly dresses for overalls. They subscribed to Feminist Press and read stories called "My Mother the Mail Carrier" instead of "Sleeping Beauty." At the swimming pool one afternoon, I watched a particularly fervent young mother, ironically clad in a string bikini, encourage her daughter. "You're so strong, Blake! Kick hard, so you'll be the strongest kid in this pool." When my boys splashed water in Blakeney's eyes and she ran whimpering to her mother, this mom exhorted, "You go back in that pool and shake your fist like this and say, 'You do that again and I'll bust your lights out.' " A new generation of little girls, assertive and ambitious, taking a backseat to no one?

It's a little early to assess the results of our efforts, but when my seven-year- 4 old son, Jack, comes home singing—to the tune of—"Frère Jacques"—"Farrah Fawcett, Farrah Fawcett, I love you" and five minutes later asks Drew, his five-year-old brother, if he'd like his nose to be a blood fountain, either we're back-sliding or there's more to this sex-role learning than the home environment can handle.

I'm hearing similar laments from mothers of daughters. "She used to tell 5 everyone that she was going to grow up to be a lawyer just like Daddy," said one, "but she's hedging on that ambition ever since she learned that no one wears a blue fairy tutu in the courtroom." Another mother with two sons, a daughter, and a very successful career notes that, with no special encouragement, only her daughter keeps her room neat and loves to set the table and ceremoniously seat her parents. At a Little League game during the summer, fearful that this same young daughter might be absorbing the stereotype "boys play while girls watch," her parents readily assured her that she too could participate when she was eight years old. "Oh," she exclaimed with obvious delight, "I didn't know they had cheerleaders."

How does it happen? I have my own theories, but decided to do a little read- 6 ing to see if any of the "experts" agreed with me. I was also curious to find out what remedies they recommended. The books I read propose that sex roles are culturally induced. In simplistic terms, rid the schools, their friends, and the television of sexism, and your daughters will dump their dolls and head straight for the boardroom while your sons contemplate nursing careers. *Undoing Sex Stereotypes* by Marcia Guttentag and Helen Bray is an interesting study of efforts to overcome sexism in the classroom. After reading it, I visited my son's very traditional school and found it guilty of unabashedly perpetuating the myths that feminists abhor. Remember separate water fountains? And how, even if the line was shorter, no boy would be caught dead drinking from the girls' fountain and vice versa? That still happens. "You wouldn't want me to get cooties, would you, Mom?" my son says, defending the practice. What did I expect in a school where the principal still addresses his faculty, who range in age from 23 to 75, as "girls"?

Nevertheless, having been a schoolteacher myself, I am skeptical of neatly 7 programmed nonsexist curriculum packets like Guttentag and Bray's. But if you can wade through the jargon ("people of the opposite sex, hereafter referred to as POTOS"), some of the observations and exercises are certainly thought-provoking and revealing. In one exercise fifth-grade students were asked to list adjectives appropriate to describe women. The struggle some of the children had in shifting their attitudes about traditional male roles is illustrated in this paragraph written by a fifth-grade girl who was asked to write a story about a man using the adjectives she had listed to describe women:

> Once there was a boy who all his life was very *gentle.* He never hit anyone or started a fight and when some of his friends were not feeling well, he was *loving* and *kind* to them. When he got older he never changed. People started not liking him because he was *weak, petite,* and he wasn't like any of the other men—not strong or tough. Most of his life he sat alone thinking about why no one liked him. Then one day he went out and tried to act like the other men. He joined a baseball team, but he was no good, he always got out. Then he decided to join the hockey team. He couldn't play good. He kept on breaking all the rules. So he quit the team and joined the soccer team. These men were *understanding* to him. He was really good at soccer, and was the best on the team. That year they won the championship and the rest of his life he was happy.

After reading this paragraph it occurred to me that this little girl's self- 8 esteem and subsequent role in life would be enhanced by a teacher who spent less time on "nonsexist intervention projects" and more time on writing skills. But that, of course, is not what the study was meant to reveal.

The junior high curriculum suggested by *Undoing Sex Stereotypes* has 9 some laudable consciousness-raising goals. For example, in teaching units called "Women's Roles in American History" and "The Socialization of Women and the Image of Women in the Media" teenagers are encouraged to critically examine television commercials, soap operas, and comic books. But am I a traitor to the cause if I object when the authors in another unit use *Romeo and Juliet* as a study of the status of women? Something is rotten in Verona when we have to consider Juliet's career possibilities and her problems with self-actualization. The conclusions of this project were lost on me; I quit reading when the author began to talk about ninth-graders who were "cognitively at a formal operational level." I don't even know what my "external sociopsychological situation" is. However, I think I did understand some of the conclusions reached by the kids:

> "Girls are smart."
> "If a woman ran a forklift where my father works, there would be a walkout."
> "Men cannot be pom-pom girls."

Eminently more readable, considering that both authors are educators of 10 educators, is *How to Raise Independent and Professionally Successful Daughters,* by Drs. Rita and Kenneth Dunn. The underlying and, I think, questionable assumption in this book is that little boys have been reared correctly all along. Without direct parental intervention, according to the Dunns, daughters tend to absorb and reflect society's values. The Dunns paint a dark picture indeed for the parents who fail to channel their daughters toward professional success. The woman who remains at home with children while her husband is involved in the "real world" with an "absorbing and demanding day-to-day commitment that brings him into contact with new ideas, jobs, and people (attractive self-actualized females)" is sure to experience lowered IQ, according to the Dunns. They go on to predict the husband's inevitable affair and the subsequent divorce, which leaves the wife emotionally depressed and probably financially dependent on her parents.

Now I'm all for women developing competency and self-reliance, but the 11 Dunns' glorification of the professional is excessive. Anyone who has worked longer than a year knows that eventually any job loses most of its glamour. And the world is no less "real" at home. For that matter, mothers at home may be more "real" than bankers or lawyers. How is a corporate tax problem more real than my counseling with the maid whose boyfriend shot her in the leg? How can reading a balance sheet compare with comforting a five-year-old who holds his limp cat and wants to know why we have to lose the things we love? And on the contrary, it is my husband, the professional, who complains of lowered IQ. Though we wooed to Faulkner, my former ace English major turned trial lawyer now has time for only an occasional *Falconer* or Peter Benchley thriller. Certainly there is value in raising daughters to be financially self-supporting, but there is not much wisdom in teaching a daughter that she must achieve professional success or her marriage probably won't last.

In a chapter called "What to Do from Birth to Two," the authors instruct 12 parents to introduce dolls only if they represent adult figures or groups of figures. "Try not to give her her own 'baby.' A baby doll is acceptable only for dramatizing the familiar episodes she has actually experienced, like a visit to the doctor." If some unthinking person should give your daughter a baby doll, and she likes it, the Dunns recommend that you permit her to keep it without exhibiting any negative feelings, "but do not lapse into cuddling it or encouraging her to do so. Treat it as any other object and direct attention to other more beneficial toys." I wonder if the Dunns read an article by Anne Roiphe called "Can You Have Everything and Still Want Babies?" which appeared in *Vogue* a couple of years ago. Ms. Roiphe was deploring the extremes to which our liberation has brought us. "It is nice to have beautiful feet, it may be desirable to have small feet, but it is painful and abusive to bind feet. It is also a good thing for women to have independence, freedom and choice, movement, and opportunity; but I'm not so sure that the current push against mothering will not be another kind of binding of the soul. . . . As women we have thought so little of ourselves that when the troops came to liberate us we rushed into the streets leaving our most valuable attributes behind as if they belonged to the enemy."

The Dunns' book is thorough, taking parents step-by-step through the ele- 13 mentary years and on to high school. Had I been raising daughters, however, I think I would have flunked out in the chapter "What to Do from Age Two to Five." In discussing development of vocabulary, the Doctors Dunn prohibit the use of nonsensical words for bodily functions. I'm sorry, Doctors, but I've experimented with this precise terminology and discovered that the child who yells "I have to defecate, Mom" across four grocery aisles is likely to be left in the store. A family without a few poo-poo jokes is no family at all.

These educators don't help me much in my efforts to liberate my sons. And   14
although I think little girls are getting a better deal with better athletic training
and broader options, I believe we're kidding ourselves if we think we can raise
our sons and daughters alike. Certain inborn traits seem to be immune to parental and cultural tampering. How can I explain why a little girl baby sits on a
quilt in the park thoughtfully examining a blade of grass, while my baby William
uproots grass by handfuls and eats it? Why does a mother of very bright and
active daughters confide that until she went camping with another family of
boys, she feared that my sons had a hyperactivity problem? I'm sure there are
plenty of rowdy, noisy little girls, but I'm not just talking about rowdiness and
noise. I'm talking about some sort of primal physicalness that causes the walls
of my house to pulsate on rainy days. I'm talking about something inexplicable
that makes my sons fall into a mad, scrambling, pull-your-ears-off-kick-your-
teeth-in heap just before bedtime, when they're not even mad at each other. I
mean something that causes them to climb the doorjamb with honey and peanut
butter on their hands while giving me a synopsis of *Star Wars* that contains only
five intelligible words: "And then this guy, he 'pssshhhhhh.' And then this thing
went 'vronggggg.' But this little guy said, 'Nong-neee-nonh-nee.' " When Jack
and Drew are not kicking a soccer ball or each other, they are kicking the chair
legs, the cat, the baby's silver rattle, and, inadvertently, Baby William himself,
whom they have affectionately dubbed "Tough Eddy." Staying put in a chair for
the duration of a one-course meal is torturous for these boys. They compensate
by never quite putting both feet under the table. They sit with one leg doubled
under them while the other leg extends to one side. The upper half of the body
appears committed to the task at hand—eating—but the lower extremities are
poised to lunge should a more compelling distraction present itself. From this
position, I have observed, one brother can trip a haughty dessert-eating sibling
who is flaunting the fact he ate all his "sweaty little peas." Although we have
civilized them to the point that they dutifully mumble, "May I be excused,
please?" their abrupt departure from the table invariably overturns at least one
chair or whatever milk remains. This sort of constant motion just doesn't lend
itself to lessons in thoughtfulness and gentleness.

Despite my encouragement, my sons refuse to invite little girls to play any-   15
more. Occasionally friends leave their small daughters with us while they run
errands. I am always curious to see what these females will find of interest in my
sons' roomful of Tonka trucks and soccer balls. One morning the boys suggested that the girls join them in playing Emergency with the big red fire trucks and
ambulance. The girls were delighted and immediately designated the ambulance
as theirs. The point of Emergency, as I have seen it played countless times with
a gang of little boys, is to make as much noise with the siren as possible and to
crash the trucks into each other or into the leg of a living-room chair before you
reach your destination.

The girls had other ideas. I realized why they had selected the ambulance.   16
It contained three dolls: a driver, a nurse, and sick man on the stretcher. My boys
have used that ambulance many times, but the dolls were always secondary to
the death-defying race with the fire trucks; they were usually just thrown in the
back of the van as an afterthought. The girls took the dolls out, stripped and re-
dressed them tenderly, and made sure that they were seated in their appropriate places for the first rescue. Once the fire truck had been lifted off the man's
leg, the girls required a box of BandAids and spent the next half hour making
a bed for the patient and reassuring him that he was going to be all right. These

little girls and my sons had seen the same NBC "Emergency" series, but the girls had apparently picked up on the show's nurturing aspects, while Jack and Drew were interested only in the equipment, the fast driving, and the sirens. . . .

Of course, I want my sons to grow up knowing that what's inside a woman's head is more important than her appearance, but I'm sure they're getting mixed signals when I delay our departure for the swimming pool to put on lipstick. I also wonder what they make of their father, whose favorite aphorism is "beautiful women rule the world." I suppose what we want for these sons and the women they may marry someday is a sensitivity that enables them to be both flexible and at ease with their respective roles, so that marriage contracts are unnecessary. When my sons bring me the heads of two purple irises from the neighbor's yard and ask, "Are you really the most beautiful mama in the whole world like Daddy says, and did everyone want to marry you?" do you blame me if I keep on waffling? 17

The Androgynous Man
Noel Perrin

Noel Perrin opens his essay by recounting a crisis concerning his gender identity when he was a young man. Having taken a sex-role identity test, he was mortified to discover that he was "barely masculine at all." His discussion of masculine and feminine identities follows, and he introduces the term androgyny.

The summer I was 16, I took a train from New York to Steamboat Springs, Colo., where I was going to be assistant horse wrangler at a camp. The trip took three days, and since I was much too shy to talk to strangers, I had quite a lot of time for reading. I read all of *Gone With the Wind*. I read all of the interesting articles in a couple of magazines I had, and then I went back and read all the dull stuff. I also took all the quizzes, a thing of which magazines were even fuller then than now. 1

The one that held my undivided attention was called "How Masculine/Feminine Are You?" It consisted of a large number of inkblots. The reader was supposed to decide which of four objects each blot most resembled. The choices might be a cloud, a steam-engine, a caterpillar, and a sofa. 2

When I finished the test, I was shocked to find that I was barely masculine at all. On a scale of 1 to 10, I was about 1.2. Me, the horse wrangler? (And not just wrangler, either. That summer, I had to skin a couple of horses that died—the camp owner wanted the hides.) 3

The results of that test were so terrifying to me that for the first time in my life I did a piece of original analysis. Having unlimited time on the train, I looked at the "masculine" answers over and over, trying to find what it was that distinguished real men from people like me—and eventually I discovered two very simple patterns. It was "masculine" to think the blots looked like man-made objects, and "feminine" to think they looked like natural objects. It was masculine to think they looked like things capable of causing harm and feminine to think of innocent things. 4

Even at 16, I had the sense to see that the compilers of the test were using rather limited criteria—maleness and femaleness are both more complicated than that—and I breathed a huge sigh of relief. I wasn't necessarily a wimp, after all. 5

That the test did reveal something other than the superficiality of its mak- 6
ers I realized only many years later. What it revealed was that there is a large
class of men and women both, to which I belong, who are essentially androgynous. That doesn't mean we're gay, or low in the appropriate hormones, or
uncomfortable performing the jobs traditionally assigned our sexes. (A few years
after that summer, I was leading troops in combat and, unfashionable as it now
is to admit this, having a very good time. War is exciting. What a pity the 20th
century went and spoiled it with high-tech weapons.)

What it does mean to be spiritually androgynous is a kind of freedom. Men 7
who are all-male, or he-man, or 100% red-blooded Americans, have a little biological set that causes them to be attracted to physical power, and probably also
to dominance. Maybe even to watching football. I don't say this to criticize them.
Completely masculine men are quite often wonderful people: good husbands,
good (though sometimes overwhelming) fathers, good members of society.
Furthermore, they are often so unself-consciously at ease in the world that other
men seek to imitate them. They just aren't as free as androgynes. They pretty
nearly have to be what they are; we have a range of choices open.

The sad part is that many of us never discover that. Men who are not 100% 8
red-blooded Americans—say those who are only 75% red-blooded—often fail
to notice their freedom. They are too busy trying to copy the he-men ever to
realize that men, like women, come in a wide variety of acceptable types. Why
this frantic imitation? My answer is mere speculation, but not casual. I have
speculated on this for a long time.

Partly they're just envious of the he-man's unconscious ease. Mostly they're 9
terrified of finding that there may be something wrong with them deep down,
some weakness at the heart. To avoid discovering that, they spend their lives
acting out the role that the he-man naturally lives. Sad.

One thing that men owe to the women's movement is that this kind of fail- 10
ure is less common than it used to be. In releasing themselves from the single
ideal of the dependent woman, women have more or less incidentally released
a lot of men from the single ideal of the dominant male. The one mistake the
feminists have made, I think, is in supposing that all men need this release, or
that the world would be a better place if all men achieved it. It wouldn't. It would
just be duller.

So far I have been pretty vague about just what the freedom of the androg- 11
ynous man is. Obviously it varies with the case. In the case I know best, my own,
I can be quite specific. It has freed me most as a parent. I am, among other
things, a fairly good natural mother. I like the nurturing role. It makes me feel
good to see a child eat—and it turns me to mush to see a 4-year-old holding a
glass with both small hands, in order to drink. I even enjoyed sewing patches on
the knees of my daughter Amy's Dr. Dentons when she was at the crawling
stage. All that pleasure I would have lost if I had made myself stick to the notion
of the paternal role that I started with.

Or take a smaller and rather ridiculous example. I feel free to kiss cats. Until 12
recently it never occurred to me that I would want to, though my daughters have
been doing it all their lives. But my elder daughter is now 22, and in London.
Of course, I get to look after her cat while she is gone. He's a big, handsome
farm cat named Petrushka, very unsentimental, though used from kittenhood to
being kissed on the top of the head by Elizabeth. I've gotten very fond of him
(he's the adventurous kind of cat who likes to climb hills with you), and one night

I simply felt like kissing him on the top of the head, and did. Why did no one tell me sooner how silky cat fur is?

Then there's my relation to cars. I am completely unembarrassed by my inability to diagnose even minor problems in whatever object I happen to be driving, and don't have to make some insider's remark to mechanics to try to establish that I, too, am a "Man With His Machine." 13

The same ease extends to household maintenance. I do it, of course. Service people are expensive. But for the last decade my house has functioned better than it used to because I have had the aid of a volume called "Home Repairs Any Woman Can Do," which is pitched just right for people at my technical level. As a youth, I'd as soon have touched such a book as I would have become a transvestite. Even though common sense says there is really nothing sexual whatsoever about fixing sinks. 14

Or take public emotion. All my life I have easily been moved by certain kinds of voices. The actress Siobhan McKenna's, to take a notable case. Give her an emotional scene in a play, and within ten words my eyes are full of tears. In boyhood, my great dread was that someone might notice. I struggled manfully, you might say, to suppress this weakness. Now, of course, I don't see it as a weakness at all, but a kind of fulfillment. I even suspect that the true he-men feel the same way, or one kind of them does, at least, and it's only the poor imitators who have to struggle to repress themselves. 15

Let me come back to the inkblots, with their assumption that masculine equates with machinery and science, and feminine with art and nature. I have no idea whether the right pronoun for God is He, She, or It. But this I'm pretty sure of. If God could somehow be induced to take that test, God would not come out macho and not feminismo either, but right in the middle. Fellow androgynes, it's a nice thought. 16

The Classroom as Curriculum

American Association of University Women

In 1992, the American Association of University Women (AAUW) published a study entitled How Schools Shortchange Girls: A Study of Major Findings on Girls and Education. *The authors say their report is "a synthesis of all the available research on the subject of girls in school. . . . [and] presents compelling evidence that girls are not receiving the same quality, or even quantity, of education as their brothers." The AAUW report gained instant, nationwide attention and prompted several U.S. Senators to introduce legislation protecting girls from unequal treatment in publicly funded schools. Chapter 2 of the report, "The Classroom as Curriculum," examines what students from preschool to college learn about gender from the ways in which teachers interact differently with girls and boys.*

Students can learn as much from what they experience in school as they can from the formal content of classroom assignments. Classroom interactions, both with the teacher and other students, are critical components of education. These interactions shape a school. They determine in large measure whether or not a school becomes a community: a place where girls and boys can learn to value 1 themselves and others, where both the rights and the responsibilities of citizens are fostered.

Teacher-Student Interactions

Whether one looks at preschool classrooms or university lecture halls, at female [2] teachers or male teachers, research spanning the past twenty years consistently reveals that males receive more teacher attention than do females.[1] In preschool classrooms boys receive more instructional time, more hugs, and more teacher attention.[2] The pattern persists through elementary school and high school. One reason is that boys demand more attention. Researchers David and Myra Sadker have studied these patterns for many years. They report that boys in one study of elementary and middle school students called out answers eight times more often than girls did. When boys called out, the typical teacher reaction was to listen to the comment. When girls called out, they were usually corrected with comments such as, "Please raise your hand if you want to speak."[3]

It is not only the attention demanded by male students that explains their [3] greater involvement in teacher-student exchanges. Studies have found that even when boys do not volunteer, the teacher is more likely to solicit their responses.[4]

The issue is broader than the inequitable distribution of teacher *contacts* [4] with male and female students; it also includes the inequitable *content* of teacher comments. Teacher remarks can be vague and superficial or precise and penetrating. Helpful teacher comments provide students with insights into the strengths and weaknesses of their answers. Careful and comprehensive teacher reactions not only affect student learning, they can also influence student self-esteem.[5]

The Sadkers conducted a three-year study of more than 100 fourth-, sixth- [5] and eighth-grade classrooms. They identified four types of teacher comments: praise, acceptance, remediation, and criticism.

They found that while males received more of all four types of teacher com- [6] ments, the difference favoring boys was greatest in the more useful teacher reactions of praise, criticism, and remediation. When teachers took the time and made the effort to specifically evaluate a student's performance, the student receiving the comment was more likely to be male.[6] These findings are echoed in other investigations, indicating that boys receive more precise teacher comments than females in terms of both scholarship and conduct.[7]

The differences in teacher evaluations of male and female students have [7] been cited by some researchers as a cause of "learned helplessness," or lack of academic perseverance, in females. Initially investigated in animal experiments, "learned helplessness" refers to a lack of perseverance, a debilitating loss of self-confidence.[8] This concept has been used to explain why girls sometimes abandon while boys persistently pursue academic challenges for which both groups are equally qualified.[9]

One school of thought links learned helplessness with attribution theory. [8] While girls are more likely to attribute their success to luck, boys are more likely to attribute their success to ability. As a result of these different causal attributions, boys are more likely to feel mastery and control over academic challenges, while girls are more likely to feel powerless in academic situations.[10]

Studies also reveal that competent females have higher expectations of fail- [9] ure and lower self-confidence when encountering new academic situations than do males with similar abilities.[11] The result is that female students are more likely to abandon academic tasks.[12]

However, research also indicates that the concepts of learned helplessness [10] and other motivation constructs are complex. Psychologist Jacquelynne Eccles and her colleagues have found that there is a high degree of variation within each individual in terms of motivational constructs as one goes across subject areas. New evidence indicates that it is too soon to state a definitive connection between a specific teacher behavior and a particular student outcome.[13] Further research on the effects of teacher behavior and student performance and motivation is needed.

The majority of studies on teacher-student interaction do not differentiate [11] among subject areas. However, there is some indication that the teaching of certain subjects may encourage gender-biased teacher behavior while others may foster more equitable interactions. Sex differences in attributing success to luck versus effort are more likely in subject areas where teacher responses are less frequent and where single precise student responses are less common.[14]

Two recent studies find teacher-student interactions in science classes par- [12] ticularly biased in favor of boys.[15] Some mathematics classes have less biased patterns of interaction overall when compared to science classes, but there is evidence that despite the more equitable overall pattern, a few male students in each mathematics class receive particular attention to the exclusion of all other students, male and female.[16]

Research on teacher-student interaction patterns has rarely looked at the [13] interaction of gender with race, ethnicity, and/or social class. The limited data available indicate that while males receive more teacher attention than females, white boys receive more attention than boys from various racial and ethnic minority groups.[17]

Evidence also suggests that the attention minority students receive from [14] teachers may be different in nature from that given to white children. In elementary school, black boys tend to have fewer interactions overall with teachers than other students and yet they are the recipients of four to ten times the amount of qualified praise ("That's good, but . . .") as other students.[18] Black boys tend to be perceived less favorably by their teachers and seen as less able than other students.[19] The data are more complex for girls. Black girls have less interaction with teachers than white girls, but they attempt to initiate interaction much more often than white girls or than boys of either race. Research indicates that teachers may unconsciously rebuff these black girls, who eventually turn to peers for interaction, often becoming the class enforcer or go-between for other students.[20] Black females also receive less reinforcement from teachers than do other students, although their academic performance is often better than boys.[21]

In fact, when black girls do as well as white boys in school, teachers attribute [15] their success to hard work but assume that the white boys are not working up to their full potential.[22] This, coupled with the evidence that blacks are more often reinforced for their social behavior while whites are likely to be reinforced for their academic accomplishments, may contribute to low academic self-esteem in black girls.[23] Researchers have found that black females value their academic achievements less than black males in spite of their better performance.[24] Another study found that black boys have a higher science self-concept than black girls although there were no differences in achievement.[25]

The Design of Classroom Activities

Research studies reveal a tendency beginning at the preschool level for schools [16] to choose classroom activities that will appeal to boys' interests and to select presentation formats in which boys excel or are encouraged more than are girls.[26] For example, when researchers looked at lecture versus laboratory classes, they found that in lecture classes teachers asked males academically related questions about 80 percent more often than they questioned females; the patterns were mixed in laboratory classes.[27] However, in science courses, lecture classes remain more common than laboratory classes.

Research indicates that if pupils begin working on an activity with little introduction from the teacher, everyone has access to the same experience. Discussion that follows after all students have completed an activity encourages more participation by girls.[28] In an extensive multistate study, researchers found that in geometry classes where the structure was changed so that students read the book and did problems *first* and *then* had classroom discussion of the topic, girls outperformed boys in two of five tests and scored equally in the other three. Girls in the experimental class reversed the general trend of boys' dominance on applications, coordinates, and proof taking, while they remained on par with boys on visualizations in three dimensions and transformations. In traditional classes where topics were introduced by lecture first and then students read the book and did the problems, small gender differences favoring boys remained.[29]   17

Successful Teaching Strategies

There are a number of teaching strategies that can promote more gender-equitable learning environments. Research indicates that science teachers who are successful in encouraging girls share several strategies.[30] These included using more than one textbook, eliminating sexist language, and showing fairness in their treatment and expectations of both girls and boys.   18

Other research indicates that classrooms where there are no gender differences in math are "girl friendly," with less social comparison and competition and an atmosphere students find warmer and fairer.[31]   19

In their 1986 study, *Women's Ways of Knowing,* Belenky, Clinchy, Goldberger, and Tarule point out that for many girls and women, successful learning takes place in an atmosphere that enables students to empathetically enter into the subject they are studying, an approach the authors term "connected knowing." The authors suggest that an acceptance of each individual's personal experiences and perspectives facilitates students' learning. They argue for classrooms that emphasize collaboration and provide space for exploring diversity of opinion.[32]   20

Few classrooms foster "connected learning," nor are the majority of classrooms designed to encourage cooperative behaviors and collaborative efforts. The need to evaluate, rank, and judge students can undermine collaborative approaches. One recent study that sampled third-, fifth-, and seventh-grade students found that successful students reported fewer cooperative attitudes than did unsuccessful students. In this study the effects of gender varied as a function of grade level. Third-grade girls were more cooperative than their male peers, but by fifth grade the gender difference had disappeared.[33] Other studies do not report this grade level-gender interaction, but rather indicate that girls tend to be more cooperative than boys but that cooperative attitudes decline for all students as they mature.[34]   21

Some educators view the arrival of new classroom organizational structures as a harbinger of more effective and more equitable learning environments. "Cooperative learning" has been viewed as one of these potentially more suc-   22 cessful educational strategies. Cooperative learning is designed to eliminate the negative effects of classroom competition while promoting a cooperative spirit and increasing heterogeneous and cross-race relationships. Smaller cooperative work groups are designed to promote group cohesion and interdependence, and mobilize these positive feelings to achieve academic objectives.[35] Progress and academic performance are evaluated on a group as well as an individual basis; the group must work together efficiently or all its members will pay a price.[36] A number of positive results have been attributed to cooperative learning groups, including increasing cross-race friendships, boosting academic achievement, mainstreaming students with disabilities, and developing mutual student concerns.[37]

However, positive cross-sex relationships may be more difficult to achieve [23] than cross-race friendships or positive relationships among students with and without disabilities. First, as reported earlier in this report, there is a high degree of sex-segregation and same-sex friendships in elementary and middle school years.[38] Researchers have found that the majority of elementary students preferred single-sex work groups.[39] Second, different communication patterns of males and females can be an obstacle to effective cross-gender relationships. Females are more indirect in speech, relying often on questioning, while more direct males are more likely to make declarative statements or even to interrupt.[40] Research indicates that boys in small groups are more likely to receive requested help from girls; girls' requests, on the other hand, are more likely to be ignored by the boys.[41] In fact, the male sex may be seen as a status position within the group. As a result, male students may choose to show their social dominance by not readily talking with females.[42]

Not only are the challenges to cross-gender cooperation significant, but [24] cooperative learning as currently implemented may not be powerful enough to overcome these obstacles. Some research indicates that the infrequent use of small, unstructured work groups is not effective in reducing gender stereotypes, and, in fact, increases stereotyping. Groups often provide boys with leadership opportunities that increase their self-esteem. Females are often seen as followers and are less likely to want to work in mixed-sex groups in the future.[43] Another study indicates a decrease in female achievement when females are placed in mixed-sex groups.[44] Other research on cooperative education programs has reported more positive results.[45] However, it is clear that merely providing an occasional group learning experience is not the answer to sex and gender differences in classrooms.

Problems in Student Interactions

The ways students treat each other during school hours is an aspect of the infor- [25] mal learning process, with significant negative implications for girls. There is mounting evidence that boys do not treat girls well. Reports of student sexual harassment—the unwelcome verbal or physical conduct of a sexual nature imposed by one individual on another—among junior high school and high school peers are increasing. In the majority of cases a boy is harassing a girl.[46]

Incidents of sexual harassment reveal as much about power and authority [26] as they do about sexuality; the person being harassed usually is less powerful than the person doing the harassing. Sexual harassment is prohibited under Title IX, yet sex-biased peer interactions appear to be permitted in schools, if not always approved. Rather than viewing sexual harassment as serious misconduct, school authorities too often treat it as a joke.

When boys line up to "rate" girls as they enter a room, when boys treat 27 girls so badly that they are reluctant to enroll in courses where they may be the only female, when boys feel it is good fun to embarrass girls to the point of tears, it is no joke. Yet these types of behaviors are often viewed by school personnel as harmless instances of "boys being boys."

The clear message to both girls and boys is that girls are not worthy of 28 respect and that appropriate behavior for boys includes exerting power over girls—or over other, weaker boys. Being accused of being in any way like a woman is one of the worst insults a boy can receive. As one researcher recently observed:

> *"It is just before dismissal time and a group of very active fourth-graders are having trouble standing calmly in line as they wait to go to their bus. Suddenly one of the boys grabs another's hat, runs to the end of the line, and involves a number of his buddies in a game of keep-away. The boy whose hat was taken leaps from his place in line, trying to intercept it from the others, who, as they toss it back and forth out of his reach, taunt him by yelling, 'You woman! You're a woman!' When the teacher on bus duty notices, she tells the boys that they all have warnings for not waiting in line properly. The boys resume an orderly stance but continue to mutter names—'Woman!' 'Am not.' 'Yes, you are.'—under their breath."*

Margaret Stubbs, October 1990

Harassment related to sexual orientation or sexual preference has received 29 even less attention as an equity issue than heterosexual sexual harassment.[47] Yet, examples of name calling that imply homophobia, such as "sissy," "queer," "gay," "lesbo," are common among students at all levels of schooling. The fourth-grade boys who teased a peer by calling him a "woman" were not only giving voice to the sex-role stereotype that women are weaker than and therefore inferior to men; they were also challenging their peer's "masculinity" by ascribing feminine characteristics to him in a derogatory manner. Such attacks often prevent girls, and sometimes boys, from participating in activities and courses that are traditionally viewed as appropriate for the opposite sex.

When schools ignore sexist, racist, homophobic, and violent interactions 30 between students, they are giving tacit approval to such behaviors. Environments where students do not feel accepted are not environments where effective learning can take place.

Implications

Teachers are not always aware of the ways in which they interact with students. 31 Videotaping actual classrooms so that teachers can see themselves in action can help them to develop their own strategies for fostering gender-equitable education. The use of equitable teaching strategies should be one of the criteria by which teaching performance is evaluated.

Research studies indicate that girls often learn and perform better in same- 32 sex work groups than they do in mixed-sex groupings. Additional research is needed, however, to better understand the specific dynamics of these interactions, particularly the circumstances under which single-sex groupings are most beneficial. Single-sex classes are illegal under Title IX, but usually single-sex work groups within coed classes are not. Teachers should be encouraged to "try out" many different classroom groupings, not only in mathematics and science classes but across a wide range of subject matter. It is critical that they carefully observe the impact of various groupings and write up and report their findings.

Notes

[1]See for example, J. Brophy and T. Good, *Teacher-Student Relationships: Causes and Consequences* (New York: Holt, Rinehart, and Winston, 1974); M. Jones, "Gender Bias in Classroom Interactions," *Contemporary Education* 60 (Summer 1989):216–22; M. Lockheed, *Final Report: A Study of Sex Equity in Classroom Interaction* (Washington, DC: National Institute of Education, 1984); M. Lockheed and A. Harris, *Classroom Interaction and Opportunities for Cross-Sex Peer Learning in Science,* paper presented at the Annual Meeting of the American Educational Research Association, New York, April 1989; M. Sadker and D. Sadker, "Sexism in the Classroom: From Grade School to Graduate School," *Phi Delta Kappan* 68 (1986):512; R. Spaulding, *Achievement, Creativity and Self-Concept Correlates of Teacher-Pupil Transactions in Elementary School* (Cooperative Research Project No. 1352), (Washington, DC: U.S. Department of Health Education and Welfare, 1963).

[2]L. Serbin et al., "A Comparison of Teacher Responses to the Pre-Academic and Problem Behavior of Boys and Girls," *Child Development* 44 (1973):796–804; M. Ebbeck, "Equity for Boys and Girls: Some Important Issues," *Early Child Development and Care* 18 (1984): 119–31.

[3]D. Sadker, M. Sadker, and D. Thomas, "Sex Equity and Special Education," *The Pointer* 26 (1981):33–38.

[4]D. Sadker and M. Sadker, "Is the OK Classroom OK?," *Phi Delta Kappan* 55 (1985): 358–67.

[5]J. Brophy, "Teacher Praise: A Functional Analysis," *Review of Educational Research* 51 (1981):5–32; A. Gardner, C. Mason, and M. Matyas, "Equity, Excellence and 'Just Plain Good Teaching!' " *The American Biology Teacher* 51 (1989):72–77.

[6]M. Sadker and D. Sadker, *Year 3: Final Report, Promoting Effectiveness in Classroom Instruction* (Washington, DC: National Institute of Education, 1984).

[7]D. Baker, "Sex Differences in Classroom Interactions in Secondary Science," *Journal of Classroom Interaction* 22 (1986): 212–18; J. Becker, "Differential Treatment of Females and Males in Mathematics Classes," *Journal for Research in Mathematics Education* 12 (1981):40–53; L. Berk and N. Lewis, "Sex Role and Social Behavior in Four School Environments," *Elementary School Journal* 3 (1977):205–21; L. Morse and H. Handley, "Listening to Adolescents: Gender Differences in Science Classroom Interaction," in *Gender Influences in Classroom Interaction,* L. Wilkerson and C. Marrett, eds., (Orlando, FL: Academic Press, 1985), pp. 37–56.

[8]M. Seligman and S. Maier, "Failure to Escape Traumatic Shock," *Journal of Experimental Psychology* 74 (1967):1–9.

[9]C. Dweck and N. Repucci, "Learned Helplessness and Reinforcement Responsibility in Children," *Journal of Personality and Social Psychology* 25 (1973):109–16; C. Dweck and T. Goetz, "Attributions and Learned Helplessness," in *New Directions in Attribution Research,* J. Harvey, W. Ickes, and R. Kidd, eds., (Hillsdale, NJ: Erlbaum, 1978).

[10]See for example, K. Deaux, "Sex: A Perspective on the Attribution Process," in *New Directions in Attribution Research;* C. Dweck and E. Bush, "Sex Differences in Learned Helplessness: I. Differential Debilitation with Peer and Adult Evaluators," *Developmental Psychology* 12 (1976):147–56; C. Dweck, T. Goetz, and N. Strauss, "Sex Differences in learned Helplessness: IV. An Experimental and Naturalistic Study of Failure Generalization and Its Mediators," *Journal of Personality and Social Psychology* 38 (1980):441–52; L. Reyes, *Mathematics Classroom Processes,* paper presented at the Fifth International Congress on Mathematical Education, Adelaide, Australia, August 1984; P. Wolleat et al., "Sex Differences in High School Students' Causal Attributions of Performance in Mathematics," *Journal for Research in Mathematics Education* 11 (1980):356–66; D. Phillips, "The Illusion of Incompetence among Academically Competent Children," *Child Development* 55 (1984):200–16; E. Fennema et al., "Teachers' Attributions and Belief about Girls, Boys, and Mathematics," *Educational Studies in Mathematics* 21 (1990): 55–69.

[11]E. Maccoby and C. Jacklin, *The Psychology of Sex Differences* (Stanford, CA: Stanford University Press, 1974); E. Lenney, "Women's Self-Confidence in Achievement Settings," *Psychological Bulletin* 84 (1977):1–13; J. Parsons and D. Ruble, "The Development of Achievement-Related Expectancies," *Child Development* 48 (1977):1075–79; Dweck, Goetz, and Strauss, "Sex Differences in Learned Helplessness: IV"; J. Goetz, "Children's Sex Role Knowledge and Behavior: An Ethnographic Study of First Graders in the Rural South," *Theory and Research in Social Education* 8 (1981):31–54.

[12]W. Shepard and D. Hess, "Attitudes in Four Age Groups Toward Sex Role Division in Adult Occupations and Activities," *Journal of Vocational Behavior* 6 (1975):27–39; C. Dweck and E. Elliot, "Achievement Motivation," in *Handbook of Child Psychology,* vol. 4, P. Mussen and E. Hetherington, eds., (New York: Wiley, 1983); R. Felson, "The Effect of Self-Appraisals of Ability on Academic Performance," *Journal of Personality and Social Psychology* 47 (1984):944–52; M. Stewart and C. Corbin, "Feedback Dependence among Low Confidence Preadolescent Boys and Girls," *Research Quarterly for Exercise and Sport* 59 (1988): 160–64.

[13]J. Eccles-Parsons et al., "Sex Differences in Attributions and Learned Helplessness," *Sex Roles* 8 (1982):421–32; J. Eccles-Parsons, C. Kaczala, and J. Meece, "Socialization of Achievement Attitudes and Beliefs: Classroom influences," *Child Development* 53 (1982):322–39; J. Eccles, "Expectancies, Values and Academic Behaviors," in *Achievement and Achievement Motives,* J. Spence, ed., (San Francisco, CA: W.H. Freeman and Co., 1983); J. Eccles, *Understanding Motivation: Achievement Beliefs, Gender-Roles and Changing Educational Environments,* address before American Psychological Association, New York, 1987.

[14]B. Licht, S. Stader, and C. Swenson, "Children's Achievement Related Beliefs: Effects of Academic Area, Sex, and Achievement Level," *Journal of Educational Research* 82 (1989):253–60.

[15]J. Kahle, "Why Girls Don't Know," in *What Research Says to the Science Teacher—the Process of Knowing,* M. Rowe, ed., (Washington, DC: National Science Testing Association, 1990), pp. 55–67; V. Lee, "Sexism in Single-Sex and Coeducational Secondary School Classrooms," paper presented at the annual meeting of the American Sociological Association, Cincinnati, OH, August 8, 1991.

[16]J. Eccles, "Bringing Young Women to Math and Science," in *Gender and Thought: Psychological Perspectives,* M. Crawford and M. Gentry, eds., (New York: Springer-Verlag, 1989), pp. 36–58; Licht et al., "Children's Achievement Related Beliefs."

[17]Sadker and Sadker, *Year 3*; L. Grant, "Race-Gender Status, Classroom Interaction and Children's Socialization in Elementary School," in *Gender Influences in Classroom Interaction,* L. Wilkinson and C. Marrett, eds., (Orlando, FL: Academic Press, 1985), pp. 57–75.

[18]Grant, "Race-Gender Status," p. 66.

[19]C. Cornbleth and W. Korth, "Teacher Perceptions and Teacher-Student Interaction in Integrated Classrooms," *Journal of Experimental Education* 48 (Summer 1980):259–63; B. Hare, *Black Girls: A Comparative Analysis of Self-Perception and Achievement by Race, Sex and Socioecomonic Background,* Report No. 271, (Baltimore, MD: John Hopkins University, Center for Social Organization of Schools, [1979]).

[20]S. Damico and E. Scott, "Behavior Differences Between Black and White Females in Desegregated Schools," *Equity and Excellence* 23 (1987):63–66; Grant, "Race-Gender Status." See also J. Irvine, "Teacher-Student Interactions: Effects of Student Race, Sex, and Grade Level," *Journal of Educational Psychology* 78 (1986):14–21.

[21]Damico and Scott, "Behavior Differences;" Hare, "Black Girls: A Comparative Analysis."

[22]Damico and Scott, "Behavior Differences;" L. Grant, "Black Females 'Place' in Integrated Classrooms," *Sociology of Education* 57 (1984):98–111.

[23]Damico and Scott, "Behavior Differences."

[24]D. Scott-Jones and M. Clark, "The School Experience of Black Girls: The Interaction of Gender, Race and Socioeconomic Status," *Phi Delta Kappan* 67 (March 1986):20–526.

[25]V. Washington and J. Newman, "Setting Our Own Agenda: Exploring the Meaning of Gender Disparities Among Blacks in Higher Education," *Journal of Negro Education* 60 (1991):19–35.

[26]E. Fennema and P. Peterson, "Effective Teaching for Girls and Boys: The Same or Different?" in *Talks to Teachers,* D. Berliner and B. Rosenshine, eds., (New York: Random House, 1987), pp. 111–25; J. Stallings, "School Classroom and Home Influences on Women's Decisions to Enroll in Advanced Mathematics Courses," in *Women and Mathematics: Balancing the Equation,* S. Chipman, L. Brush, and D. Wilson, eds., (Hillsdale, NJ: Erlbaum, 1985), pp. 199–224; S. Greenberg, "Educational Equity in Early Education Environments," in *Handbook for Achieving Sex Equity Through Education,* S. Klein, ed., (Baltimore, MD: John Hopkins University Press, 1985), pp. 457–69.

[27]D. Baker, "Sex Differences in Classroom Interactions in Secondary Science," *Journal of Classroom Interaction* 22 (1986):212–18.

[28]D. Jorde and A. Lea, "The Primary Science Project in Norway," in *Proceedings of Growth GSAT Conference,* J. Kahle, J. Daniels, and J. Harding, eds., (West Lafayette, IN: Purdue University, 1987), pp. 66–72.

[29]P. Flores, "How Dick and Jane Perform Differently in Geometry: Test Results on Reasoning, Visualization and Affective Factors," paper presented at American Educational Research Association Meeting, Boston, MA, April 1990.

[30]J. Kahle, *Factors Affecting the Retention of Girls in Science Courses, and Careers: Case Studies of Selected Secondary Schools* (Reston, VA: The National Association of Biology Teachers, October 1983).

[31]Eccles, "Bringing Young Women to Math and Science."

[32]M. Belenky et al., *Women's Ways of Knowing—The Development of Self, Body, and Mind* (New York: Basic Books, Inc., 1986).

[33]G. Engelhard and J. Monsaas, "Academic Performance, Gender and the Cooperative Attitudes of Third, Fifth and Seventh Graders," *Journal of Research and Development in Education* 22 (1989):13–17.

[34]A. Ahlgren and D. Johnson, "Sex Differences in Cooperative and Competitive Attitudes from 2nd Through the 12th Grades," *Developmental Psychology* 15 (1979):45–49; B. Herndon and M. Carpenter, "Sex Differences in Cooperative and Competitive Attitudes in a Northeastern School," *Psychological Reports* 50 (1982):768–70; L. Owens and R. Straton, "The Development of Co-operative Competitive and Individualized Learning Preference Scale for Students," *Journal of Educational Psychology* 50 (1980):147–61.

[35]S. Sharon et al., eds., *Cooperation in Education* (Provo, UT: Brigham Young University Press, 1980); S. Bossert, *Task Structure and Social Relationships* (Cambridge, MA: Harvard University Press, 1979); W. Shrum, N. Cheek, and S. Hunter, "Friendship in the School: Gender and Racial Homophily," *Sociology of Education* 61 (1988):227–39.

[36]E. Aronson, *The Jigsaw Classroom* (Beverly Hills, CA: Sage, 1978); D. DeVries and K. Edwards, "Student Teams and Learning Games: Their Effects on Cross-Race and Cross-Sex Interaction," *Journal of Educational Psychology* 66 (1974):741–49; P Okebukola, "Co-operative Learning and Students' Attitude to Laboratory Work," *Social Science and Mathematics* 86 (1986):582–90; R. Slavin, "How Student Learning Teams Can Integrate the Desegregated Classroom," *Integrated Education* 15 (1977):56–58.

[37]N. Blaney et al., "Interdependence in the Classroom: A Field Study," *Journal of Educational Psychology* 69 (1977):121–28; D. DeVries and K. Edwards, "Student Teams and Learning Games: Their Effects on Cross-Race and Cross-Sex Interaction," *Journal of Educational Psychology* 66 (1974):741–49; Sharon et al., *Cooperation in Education;* R. Slavin, "Cooperative Learning," *Review of Educational Research* 50 (1980):315–42; R. Slavin, "Cooperative Learning and Desegregation," in W. Hawley ed., *Effective School Desegregation* (Berkeley, CA: Sage, 1981); R. Weigle, P. Wiser, and S. Cook, "The Impact of Cooperative Learning Experiences on Cross-Ethnic Relations and Attitude," *Journal of Social Issues* 3 (1975):219–44.

[38]M. Hallman, *The Evolution of Children's Friendship Cliques* (ERIC Document Reproduction Service no. ED 161556, 1977); R. Best, *We've All Got Scars: What Boys and Girls Learn in Elementary School* (Bloomington, IN: University Press, 1983); J. Eccles-Parsons, "Sex Differences in Mathematics Participation," in M. Steinkamp and M. Machr, eds., *Women in Science* (Greenwich, CT: JAI Press, 1984); M. Hallman and N. Tumma, "Classroom Effects on Change in Children," *Sociology of Education* 51 (1978): 170–282.

[39]M. Lockheed, K. Finklestein, and A. Harris, *Curriculum and Research for Equity: Model Data Package* (Princeton, NJ: Educational Testing Service, 1979).

[40]B. Eakins and R. Eakins, "Sex Roles, Interruptions, and Silences in Conversation," in B. Thorne and N. Henley, eds., *Sex Differences in Human Communication* (Boston, MA: Houghton Mifflin, 1978); N. Henley and B. Thorne, "Women Speak and Men Speak: Sex Differences and Sexism in Communications, Verbal and Nonverbal," in A. Sargent, ed., *Beyond Sex Roles* (St. Paul, MN: West Publishing Company, 1977); R. Lakoff, *Languages and Women's Place* (New York; Harper Colophone Books, 1976); D. Tannen, *You Just Don't Understand: Women and Men in Conversation* (New York: William Morrow, 1990).

[41]L. Wilkinson, J. Lindow, and C. Chiang, "Sex Differences and Sex Segregation in Students' Small-Group Communication," in L. Wilkinson and C. Marret, eds., *Gender Influences in Classroom Interaction* (Orlando, FL: Academic Press, 1985), pp. 185–207.

[42]J. Berger, T. Conner, and M. Fisek, eds., *Expectation States Theory: A Theoretical Research Program* (Cambridge, MA: Winthrop, 1974); M. Lockheed and A. Harris, "Cross-Sex Collaborative Learning in Elementary Classrooms," *American Educational Research Journal,* 21 (1984):275–94.

[43]Lockheed and Harris, "Cross-Sex Collaborative Learning."

[44]C. Weisfeld et at., "The Spelling Bee; A Naturalistic Study of Female Inhibitions in Mixed-Sex Competitions," *Adolescence* 18 (1983):695–708.

[45]For example, M. Lockheed and A. Harris, "Classroom Interaction and Opportunity for Cross-Sex Peer Learning in Science," *Journal of Early Adolescence* (1982):135–43.

[46]S. Strauss, "Sexual Harassment in the School: Legal Implications for Principals," *National Association of Secondary School Principals Bulletin* (1988):93–97; N. Stein, ed. *Who's Hurt and Who's Liable: Sexual Harassment in Massachusetts Schools,* 4th ed. (Quincy, MA: Massachusetts Department of Education, 1986).

[47]D. Grayson, "Emerging Equity Issues Related to Homosexuality," *Peabody Journal of Education* 64 (1989):132–45.

A Guide to the Assignment

This guide is designed to help you through the process of writing a familiar essay on the ways in which you learned about gender stereotyping. Key elements in this guide parallel the organization of the Structures and Strategies section on pages 122–132, and you should look to appropriate sections in the chapter for further guidance. You will prepare to write, write, advance your idea with sources, and then evaluate and revise. Here, once again, is your assignment:

Write a familiar essay guided by an insight you have concerning gender-role stereotyping in American culture. Explore and develop your insight in the context of a particular event from which you learned something about gender stereotyping. You should know this event well: you should have watched it, participated in it, or somehow have been affected by it. Assume that readers know neither you nor the event you are describing. While your personal experience will be your primary source for this essay, you may also refer to the readings in this section.

Prepare to Write: Explore Your Idea

Discovering Ideas

A familiar essay gives you a chance to write "a personal account that is yet shared." Having read the selections in this section and thought about gender identity in American culture, you are ready to reflect on related issues in your life. Your goal is to explore an idea through the particulars of your own experience in a way that prompts readers to reflect on their experience.

Reflect on Your Experience—and Write a Discovery Draft

From what event in your life have you learned a great deal about gender stereotyping? Choose this event with care, and then make it the subject of a discovery draft. As you begin to write, think about a confusing moment concerning this event—perhaps about conflicting expectations of how boys and girls "ought" to behave. What about the event still perplexes you? No one but you will read this discovery draft. Aim to write three or four pages.

After a few hours, return to your work and mark any phrase or sentence that stands out for you. You are hunting for an idea that is substantial enough to guide the first full draft of your essay. What counts as a substantial idea is a subjective matter, but look for ideas that you think bear further development. Faced with several possibilities, give preference to the idea that you do not understand fully. Uncertainty can motivate you to explore more in your writing.

The idea that emerges from your discovery draft will become the working thesis of your first draft. Do not be alarmed if your idea seems vague at this point. You will have opportunity to develop and refine as you continue to write. You should, however, be able to respond to these questions:

- Why do I *need* to write about this idea?
- Why should my readers care about this idea?

If you feel unsure of your answers, return to your discovery draft in search of an idea to which you can feel more committed. If need be, restart the process with a new discovery draft and choose a *different* event about which to write.

Read to Discover Ideas

The Occasions readings can help to spark ideas for an essay. Begin a discovery draft based on a single statement from Mackintosh, Perrin, or the AAUW report. Ideally, this statement should have prompted some strong response, which you can develop in your discovery draft. Reread and highlight statements in your discovery draft. Again, your goal is to generate a working thesis for the first full draft of your essay.

Committing Yourself to an Idea

Recall the attitudes of writers whose commitment sparks interest in their readers:

- I write for myself and for my audience.
- I will find some approach to my writing that lets me discover something personally significant.

Before beginning your first draft, take a few minutes to consider these questions: What are your *personal* reasons for writing the essay? What do you want to learn about yourself and about gender stereotypes? The strength and the appeal of your familiar essay will be rooted in your commitment to its central idea. Evaluate the level of this commitment as it is expressed in your thesis. In the language of chapter 3 (pages 39–57), are you making a one-, two-, or three-story commitment to this essay?

When you take your experience seriously and find significance in the ideas embedded in that experience, your readers will do the same. Your commitment can prompt readers to reflect on their own experience.

Write: Clarify Your Idea and Make It Public

Creating Common Ground with Readers

Work to establish a common ground with readers: tell stories, give examples, recount a history. Create in virtually every paragraph specific contexts through which readers can understand ideas. If you open a paragraph with a general statement like "a working mother who enjoys work sets a good example for children," then you should provide as support the details from *your* mother's working life and the direct way in which this became an example for you. By exploring an idea through particular experiences, you create a common ground through which you *and* readers have access to that idea.

Planning a Structure

Before sitting down to write your first draft, revise and refine your working thesis. State your essay's idea as clearly as possible. Then quiz your thesis, following the example on page 123 in Structures and Strategies, and the more extensive advice given on pages 61–63. Based on answers to your own questions, devise a structure for your essay.

Understanding Your Logic

Ultimately, as the writer of a familiar essay, you would like your observations to become an occasion for readers to reflect on their own lives. There are many ways to achieve this goal, depending on your purpose. If you want to change your reader's thinking about gender identity, you will be arguing. If you want readers to watch closely as you reflect on your or another's gender identity, you will be writing primarily to explain or explore. These purposes differ, and the logic you will use to advance the ideas in these essays will also differ. For advice on planning the logic of your essay, see chapter 7 on explanation and chapter 11 on argument.

◆ **S**uggestions for Writing with a Computer

In the early stages of writing familiar essays, it can be helpful to give yourself permission to wander off on tangents. Because writing at a keyboard is faster than a typewriter and it frees you from having to hit the return key at the end of each line and changing every sheet of paper, computers can enhance tangential asides and stream-of-consciousness interludes. Such unexpected turns can sometimes develop into crucial ingredients for a familiar essay.

As you write your draft and focus on developing your main idea, grant yourself the time to pursue various notions that come to mind, even if you're not sure how they relate to your ongoing essay. When you feel the urge to pursue an interesting idea, skip a line and type a bracket or two in boldface before pursuing this tangent. When you feel you've exhausted this digression, close the passage with more brackets. Then pick up where you left off.

When you have finished the draft, reread the essay and decide what you should do with these tangential asides. Some of these passages will truly be diversions and will have to be deleted; others might contain some germ of an idea that can be put to use in the essay, even if the prose itself does not belong in the essay. You might even find that some of these tangents do in fact belong in the body of your text. Whatever the case, realize that whether you use them or discard them, pursuing tangents is a legitimate part of writing many essays, especially familiar ones.

After thinking about your essay, use the cut and paste tools to restructure your essay, accommodating any of the more relevant tangents.

To the extent possible, present a tension—a play of opposites—in each section of your essay. The tension will not only give you a plan for writing, as you set one idea against another and resolve differences; it will also give your readers a motivation for reading, as they wonder how differences are resolved. See the Structures and Strategies section on this point, pages 122–135.

Writing Your First Draft

Write your first draft by completing one section of the essay at a sitting. Each section will likely consist of several paragraphs. A section may take you from a half-hour to several hours (or more) to write. By drafting one section of your essay at a sitting, you will see clearly two important relationships: first, of one paragraph to others *within* a section and, second, of whole blocks of paragraphs—of entire sections—to other sections as well as to your essay's overall idea. Unless your essay is very ambitious and grows very long, you should be able to finish your draft in four or five sittings. For further discussion of what constitutes a section of an essay, see pages 493–494. And, generally, see the material on writing a first draft on pages 486–498.

Advance Your Idea with Sources

Personal experience will be your main source in writing a familiar essay. Still, you may need to go to written source materials for facts, historical information, useful anecdotes and examples, or authoritative opinions; the readings present you with appropriate materials for doing this.

You are the one who determines how sources should be used. Have in mind a clear idea that you want to develop in each of your essay's sections, and then go to the readings to see what your sources offer. A social scientific article, the chapter from the AAUW report, provides a wealth of documented, reliable information that you can draw on to advance a particular idea in your essay. (You may want to go to the library and track down one or more of the sources referred to in the article.) Noel Perrin and Prudence Mackintosh give you first-person accounts that may prove equally useful, depending on your needs.

When you refer to sources, bear in mind strategies for incorporating them smoothly into your writing. (See chapter 4, pages 58–77 for details.) Introduce an idea into your essay, creating a context in which a source will be meaningful; introduce the author and the source; quote, summarize, or paraphrase the source; and then comment on how the source relates to the point you are making.

Evaluate and Revise

General Evaluation

Your primary challenge in revising a first draft is to make certain that the idea you thought you were writing about is the one you have developed in the draft. The act of writing will almost always refine your initial idea; on occasion, your writing will substantially alter your essay's idea, in which case you will have more work to do in revision. For extensive discussion on strategies for revision, see chapters 13 and 14.

Critical Points in a Familiar Essay

Pinpoint the essay's idea and reexamine its structure: Reread your first draft to determine, *exactly,* your essay's idea. Expect that your idea will have changed, at least partially. Again, distill this idea into a single statement, a thesis. And again, quiz that thesis to determine parts of the essay that follow from it (pages 61–63). Add, delete, and otherwise refine your essay's sections to ensure a close fit between the final expression of your idea and the essay's overall structure.

Revisit the essay's common ground: Determine how successfully you have created a common ground for readers: Have you consistently developed ideas *through* the particulars of a story, example, and so on? Wherever you have lapsed into making abstract presentations, revise and provide details to make your point clear. Remember: readers need details about particular people, places, things, and events.

Suggestions for Collaborative Writing

To create that all-important ground for your reader you must not only have clear and vivid examples, but also make sure these examples are persuasive and relevant. When writing a familiar essay, it is easy for writers to remain too much inside their own subjective understanding, assuming their insights and the examples used to support them are objective when in fact they might be tainted by unrecognized biases, stereotypes, or exaggeration.

For example, a student might write, "My little brother was like every other sister's little brother: smelly, sweaty, sloppy, and completely self-absorbed within his private world of bugs, dinosaurs, and monster movies." While the writer has sought to avoid abstraction by means of colorful example, readers who know that many male siblings do not fit this characterization might stop at this point in the reading, unwilling to share the reader's perspective. Some minor revising could make a lot of difference: "My little brother was like hundreds of other little brothers. . . ."

Exchange first drafts with another student. Read the essay with an eye toward how to make the common ground not only more vivid, but free of unjustified opinions and assumptions as well. Are there any examples that seem to you unwarranted? unclear? misplaced? If so, give the writer suggestions on how to revise any passages so that the reactions of other readers might be better anticipated.

Heighten tensions: As you reread, check to see if the tensions you thought you were developing in various sections of the essay are in fact present. Often you will need to heighten these tensions by clarifying contradictions or by more clearly expressing problems and puzzles. Use the beginning of each section to lay out a tension and create in your readers a desire to continue reading.

Pass the "so what" test: Readers can be brutal and quick in their assessment of an essay. One of the first questions they will ask of a piece is: "Why does this writing matter to me?" Your most challenging job in revision is to ensure that readers respond favorably, and you can do this by demonstrating that your essay's idea is significant to *you*. Believe in what you are writing. Demonstrate through the energy of your essay, through the care you give to it at all levels (and this includes your willingness to revise until you correct *all* errors of grammar, punctuation, usage, and spelling), that you take your own ideas seriously. Readers cannot help but be impressed by such commitment. When *you* are engaged by your own essay, readers will be engaged as well.

7

Explanation

Definitions and Examples

The first and simplest type of iron furnace was called a bloomery, in which wrought iron was produced directly from the ore. The ore was heated with charcoal in a small open furnace, usually made of stone and blown upon with bellows. Most of the impurities would burn out, leaving a spongy mass of iron mixed with siliceous slag (iron silicate). This spongy mass was then refined by hammering, reheating, and hammering some more, until it reached the desired fibrous consistency. During the hammering, the glasslike slag would be evenly distributed throughout the iron mass. This hammered slab of wrought iron, or "bloom," was then ready to forge into some usable object. There were many furnaces of this type in Colonial America, but they were later almost entirely replaced by cold-blast furnaces. The main drawback of this direct method of making wrought iron was its limited production. On the other hand, a bloomery required a much smaller investment of money and labor to set up and operate than did a blast furnace.

The first blast furnaces used a cold blast of air to feed the fire. They produced not wrought iron, but pig iron, which was cast into sand molds, called pigs, directly from the furnace. The pig was then reheated and cast into usable items, or treated in a finery and made into wrought iron or, less often, refined into steel. Blast furnaces of the nineteenth century were usually about twenty-five or thirty feet high. They consisted of an outer shell of rock with an inner lining of refractory brick and were capable of producing about two tons of pig iron daily. Four main ingredients are necessary to produce pig iron: iron ore, charcoal, limestone, and a continuous blast of air. The charcoal, an almost pure carbon fuel, aided by the air blast, burns, creating enough heat to reduce the ore to a molten state. Some of the impurities in the ore escape in the form of gasses, and most of the remainder combine with the limestone, which is the flux, to produce molten slag. The result is a relatively pure molten iron upon which the molten slag floats. The slag is tapped off into the waste area, and the iron is tapped into sand molds in the casting area.

Foxfire 5

The preceding paragraphs are an explanation. The topic is specific; we learn *what, how,* and *why* at a level appropriate to our interest and needs; we see (mostly) the thing being explained, not the writer. When we read an explanation, if it is a good explanation, we learn things outside our experience—something about the process of making pig iron, for instance. In the selections that begin on page 168, you will read and learn about the stomach's digestion of food; about how one applies for and maintains credit; about the uses of science, particularly bloodstain analysis, in solving crimes; and about the advantages and disadvantages of using genetically engineered organisms in agriculture. These are all explanations, and the variety of subject matter suggests that in any course you take and in whatever business or profession you find yourself, you will be asked to explain. To explain well, you will employ a variety of techniques—defining, showing a process, reviewing a history, classifying, illustrating, and describing—all in order to help readers understand your topic.

Sometimes you will write papers and reports devoted entirely to explanation; just as often, you will write arguments in which you devote *part* of a discussion to explaining. Either way, you set for yourself the task of making something clear to readers.

Clarity and Development

Clear explanation requires an unquestioned understanding of the topic being explained and a willingness to revise until the explanation is right. You will need to understand the topic well enough to be able to divide it into parts and examine each component. As you explain the individual parts, you will need to define, show a process, provide illustrations or a history, and so on through direct and audience-appropriate language. David Macaulay has met these criteria in his account of death and tomb building in ancient Egypt:

Death in ancient Egypt was considered the beginning of a new life in another world. This life, assuming certain precautions were taken, would last forever. Because life on earth was relatively short, Egyptians built their houses of mud. They built their tombs of stone since life after death was eternal.

The Egyptians believed that besides a physical body everyone had a soul called a ba and a spiritual duplicate of themselves called a ka. When the body died an individual's ba continued to live here on earth, resting within the body at night. His or her ka, on the other hand, traveled back and forth between the earth and the other world. Eternal life depended on both the ba and the ka being able to identify the body. For this reason corpses were preserved by the process of mummification.

The tomb into which the body was placed had two main functions. It was designed to protect the body from elements and from thieves who might try to steal the gold and precious objects placed in and around the coffin and it also had to serve as a house for the ka. The more important the person, the greater his tomb. . . . The burial chamber of the king was protected by a manmade mountain of stone called a pyramid. Its four triangular sides spreading below a single peak represented the rays of the sun shining down over the pharaoh, linking him directly and for all time to . . . the [sun] god.

—David Macaulay

Given its intended, general audience, Macaulay's explanation is clear and effective in matters both large and small. In large matters, Macaulay has broken the very broad topic of death among ancient Egyptians into four parts: the spiritual dimension, mummies, tombs, and pyramids. He anticipates questions we might have about each part: What did the ancient Egyptians believe about the afterlife? Why did they mummify their dead? Why were tombs for the dead made of stone? and Why were the tombs of the pharaohs built into the shape of a pyramid? In offering answers to these questions, Macaulay develops the parts of his topic, and he does so in language that we understand.

Macaulay also lets us know how each part of his larger topic is related to other parts. If we should wonder, for instance, about the relation of mummification to the Egyptians' spiritual beliefs, we are satisfied to learn that the Egyptians preserved their dead because they believed that in the afterlife, the ba and the ka must recognize the body of the deceased. For an audience of general readers, this explanation works well.

Audience

To judge the effectiveness of your explanations, look to the needs of your audience. Had Macaulay been writing for Egyptologists, he would not have written on what, for experts, would have been common knowledge. Certainly, he would have explained some element of original research in language that was considerably more detailed than the overview above. To take a second example: the writers of the iron-making piece state in the preface to their book that their discussion of iron-making was "not intended to be a how-to article" but rather an overview of an industry integral to development in rural Georgia. This statement of intention is important. While the paragraphs on iron making clearly distinguish between wrought iron and pig iron and the types of furnaces that produced them, they do not provide, and were not intended to provide, enough information for readers to make iron. Given a specific purpose and audience—to provide for nonexperts a general background to an industry—the explanation is well developed.

As a reader, you know when writers have miscalculated your familiarity with a topic and have pitched their work at too high or too low a level. The dangers of miscalculation are clear: readers will turn away and consider useless any explanation that is either too difficult or too simple. As a writer of explanations, be sure that you have carefully considered the needs of your readers. Use the audience needs analysis in the Structures and Strategies section (page 180) to help you in this regard.

Examples of Explanations

Four examples of explanations follow, the first three of which were written by professionals. These concern the workings of the stomach, the intricacies of obtaining credit, and the role of science in solving crimes. The fourth example was written by a student interested in agricultural yields and the ways in which genetic engineering might boost crop production in her native country. Different as they are in subject matter, these examples share qualities essential to all effective explanations: each writer divides a topic into parts; each part is developed and related to other parts and to the larger topic; and the language is appropriate for a specific audience, in this case, general readers. Questions follow that will prompt your thinking about each selection as an example of explanation.

The Stomach: Holding and Churning
Helena Curtis

Many of the explanations you read will appear in textbooks. The following account of how the human stomach works is taken from Helena Curtis's Biology, *second edition. Curtis directs her explanation to the first-year biology student. You will find the language technical, yet you will not find this a barrier to understanding the main points of the explanation. Most terms can be understood in context. Notice how Curtis divides her topic into parts and is careful to relate the parts to one another.*

The stomach is essentially a collapsible, elastic bag, which, unless it is fully distended, lies in folds. Distended, it holds two to four quarts of food. The mucosal layer is very thick and contains numerous gastric pits. . . . Mucus-secreting epithelial cells cover the surface of the stomach and also line the gastric pits. Within the pits lie the parietal cells, which produce hydrochloric acid, and the chief cells, which produce pepsinogen.

As a consequence of the HCl secretion, the pH of gastric juice is normally between 1.5 and 2.5, far more acid than any other body fluid. The burning sensation you feel if you vomit or regurgitate food is caused by the acidity of gastric juice acting on unprotected membranes. Normally, the mucus forms a barrier between the stomach epithelium and the gastric juices and so prevents the stomach from digesting itself. The HCl kills most bacteria and other living cells in the ingested food and also loosens the tough, fibrous components of tissues and erodes the cementing substances between cells. It initiates the conversion of pepsinogen to its active form, pepsin, by splitting off a small portion of the molecule. Once pepsin is formed, it acts on other molecules of pepsinogen to form more pepsin. Pepsin, which breaks proteins down into peptides, is active only at the low pH of the normal stomach.

With the exception of small molecules such as glucose and alcohol, little food is absorbed through the stomach. (Because alcohol is absorbed through the stomach, its effects are much more rapid when the stomach is empty.)

The stomach is under both neural and hormonal control. Anticipation of 4 food and the presence of food in the mouth stimulate churning movements of the stomach and the production of gastric juices. Fear and anger decrease motility. When food reaches the stomach, its presence causes the release of a hormone, gastrin, from gastric cells into the bloodstream. This hormone acts on the cells of the stomach to increase their secretion of gastric juices.

In the stomach, as a result of the action of the mucus, the pepsin, the 5 hydrochloric acid, and the churning motions, food is converted from a solid into a semiliquid mass. The stomach empties gradually through the pyloric sphincter, which separates the stomach and small intestine; the food mass is forced out, little by little, by peristalsis. The stomach is usually empty by the end of 4 hours after ingestion of a meal.

For Discussion and Writing

Reading and Thinking Critically

1. *Personal response:* One reaction to an effective explanation is often: "Oh, I didn't know that." What have *you* learned from Curtis's explanation?
2. *Broaden the context:* You can expect explanations to differ according to disciplinary focus. Curtis is a biologist, and a particular perspective guides her explanation. From what other perspectives might this topic be explained? Try writing a brief description of the stomach from one of these perspectives.
3. *Challenge the reading:* What assumptions has Helena Curtis made about you as a reader? Were these assumptions accurate, in your view?

Examining "The Stomach" as an Explanation

1. Into what parts has Curtis divided her discussion?
2. In which phrases in this explanation does Curtis link parts, showing one part related to others?
3. Where is Curtis in this explanation? Do you hear her voice?

Credit and Loans

The following explanation of "Credit and Loans" appears in The New York Public Library Desk Reference. *This explanation differs considerably from the one you just read, and the difference resides largely in the intended audience. As you read, ask: What assumptions does the writer of this explanation make about my background? my level of interest? my familiarity with the credit industry?*

One key to enhancing personal finances is through credit. With loans, credit 1 cards, revolving charge plans at department stores, and other methods of delaying payment, people obtain goods and services for which they otherwise would have to wait. Of course, use of credit results in debts and interest charges that must be paid to maintain a good credit rating and ensure the availability of more credit.

Getting credit is a fairly straightforward procedure. You can apply to a bank 2 for a loan or a bank credit card, such as Visa or MasterCard, or to a department store or gasoline company for a revolving charge account, by filling out an application form. These companies will ask about your income, employment history, length and type of residence, credit history, and major assets (car, home, etc.) in order to determine your creditworthiness.

A positive credit history—meaning that you have received credit and made   3
payments on time—is one of the strongest recommendations for further credit. If you have never had credit before, a good first step is to obtain a department store or gasoline company credit card, which is often easier to get, or to take out a small loan at a bank where you keep a savings and/or a checking account. Having a reasonably large amount of money in the bank also can help persuade issuers to provide you with credit.

When looking to obtain credit, especially once creditworthiness has been   4
established, comparison shopping is very important. Different states have different limits on the amount of interest that can be charged on consumer loans and bank cards. Interest rates on loans can range from less than 2 percent per month to 36 percent per year or more; credit card rates range from under 15 percent to 30 percent or more per year. You do not need to be a resident of a state to get credit from lending institutions headquartered there, and you can apply by mail.

The amount of indebtedness you should assume is not easy to calculate.   5
The credit-granting institution bases its decision on your gross income and expenses. Your own decision about how much credit you should use is harder to come by. Calculating the amount of money you have available from your income after deducting monthly expenses will give you some idea of what you can afford, although other factors—such as ever-decreasing balances in your checking and savings accounts, use of overdrafts or credit to cover regular expenses, and difficulty making payments on credit lines you already have—may suggest that additional credit is not a good idea.

Problems that can arise from credit, such as billing errors or unfair denial   6
of credit, can be remedied under federal regulations. The Fair Credit Billing Act requires that, if you notify a creditor in writing about an error on a bill, your complaint must be acknowledged within 30 days and resolved within 90 days. The Equal Credit Opportunity Act requires creditors to give a reason if you are denied credit and prohibits discrimination based on race, sex, age, marital status, color, religion, national origin, or receipt of public assistance.

If you are denied credit on the basis of a negative report from a credit bureau, you can obtain the information that agency supplied to the creditor free of   7
charge if you request it within 30 days of being turned down or for a small fee at any time. You can challenge the accuracy of any item in your credit file; this will force the credit bureau to investigate the item and remove it if it cannot be substantiated. Any item in your file also can be amended at your request to include a 100-word explanation that will be added to your file.

For Discussion and Writing

Reading and Thinking Critically

1. *Personal response:* What personal experiences have you had in obtaining credit and using a credit card? Have you found any parts of this explanation useful both in reflecting on your own experiences and in planning strategies for obtaining and using credit in the future?

2. *Broaden the context:* Attitudes toward debt-financing often vary among generations. Interview parents and grandparents and ask (assuming they are not offended by the intrusion) about how they paid for things when they began their working lives. Compare attitudes. What do you find?
3. *Challenge the reading:* The writer of any explanation makes decisions about what information to include and to exclude. Given your experiences with obtaining and using credit, would you have added any information to this explanation? Would you have omitted any? Why?

Examining "Credit and Loans" as an Explanation

1. Examine the first sentence of this explanation. What motivation does the writer provide for our reading about credit and loans?
2. The first sentence rests on an argument that is not being supplied by the writer. What is this argument? Even if you disagree with it, is the explanation that follows the argument useful? Explain.
3. Into what parts does the writer divide this discussion?

Science and the Hunt for the Criminal

Stuart S. Kind

In the article that follows, Stuart S. Kind reviews the uses of scientific techniques in solving crimes. A former forensic scientist who lives in Great Britain, Kind suggests that "crime investigation is a high-grade intellectual problem" demanding all the insights that science can offer. Throughout his explanatory essay, we sense his fascination with this intellectual problem. He writes: "it is hoped that sufficient has been said to interest the general reader and to stimulate the professionally interested to enquire further." This use of the passive voice ("it is hoped"), which masks the active "I hope," does little to hide this author's enthusiasm. From the history he provides of bloodstain analysis in murder investigations to his observation that forensic investigators rely on the scientific method, Kind lingers with his subject and takes pleasure in sharing material with readers.

As you read, notice that Kind uses several strategies to develop his topic: he provides a history, reviews a process, and offers examples.

It would be difficult, if not impossible, to decide when and where science was 1
first applied in the catching and convicting of criminals. One difficulty is that the use of the word "science" in its present sense dates only from the early nineteenth century. But man has been using his ingenuity in crime investigation for far longer than that.

The accumulation of special knowledge and inventiveness has been a hall- 2
mark of our approach to all types of problem-solving, not least in those fields where science and medicine are applied to legal problems. Common questions addressed to the expert may include:

"Did the deceased die a natural death or was he the victim of a criminal assault?"

"Under what circumstances did the deceased meet his death?"

"When did he die and who was responsible?"

"What is the significance of these marks or deposits left at the scene-of-crime?"

"Is there anything to show that a particular suspect is associated with the crime?"

"Is there anything which would allow a particular suspect to be excluded from suspicion?"

These are sample questions and are chosen in relation to the crime of mur- 3 der simply because it is that particular unlawful act which human societies tend to regard as the most serious. However, science is applied to a myriad of crimes of which only a comparatively small proportion are murders. Theft, burglary, sexual assault, fraud, arson, forgery, illicit drug dealing and terrorist offences also figure largely in the forensic scientist's daily work and this list is by no means complete.

Stuart S. Kind: My Commitment to This Essay

As you can probably tell from his essay, Stuart S. Kind immensely enjoys his work; he is also committed to having the public understand what forensic scientists do. Still, this statement describing his commitment is *not* itself an essay. Why not? What are the differences between this statement and the essay? What are the similarities?

Many forensic scientists are required to communicate their results to nonscientists such as police officers, trial lawyers, and juries, but others (for example, in research) have little opportunity to do so. In the absence of this front-line communication practice there is a constant tendency for forensic scientists, in common with all scientists, to restrict communication to peer groups. In this way new words are invented, and old ones invested with new meanings, until a new "priesthood" appears, speaking a new dialect. This leads to lack of comprehension or, even worse, faulty comprehension by nonspecialists.

A helpful factor in avoiding this drift into dialect is for the scientist regularly to write expository *articles in addition to experimental papers. I do this and encourage others to do so. I chose* Impact of Science on Society *for this article because of its wide international circulation in educational circles.*

The forensic scientist's inge- 4 nuity has been applied to many of the questions outlined above but the present article will deal only with two illustrative and major topics of daily interest in the affairs of the crime investigator. Other subjects of forensic interest will be left to possible future articles.

Blood Stains

A commonly occurring factor in 5 crime investigation is bloodstaining; however, it was not until the beginning of the nineteenth century that the importance of this, as criminal evidence, began to be explicitly recognised.

In one English multiple murder 6 investigation in 1811 it was recorded that expert advice was sought to establish whether certain stains were of paint or of blood. However, it is doubtful if this represents the first forensic examination of bloodstains.

A discussion which took place 7 in 1828 at the French *Académie Royale de Médecine* shows that French experts, at least, had concerned themselves for some time with the problem of the detection of bloodstains. It is recorded that a vigorous, and sometimes acrimonious, exchange on the subject took place between the famous scholars François Raspail and Mathieu Orfila.

Raspail didn't believe it was possible, by chemical or microscopical means, 8 to distinguish between blood and many other substances. Orfila believed that it was. History has proved Orfila right, but the only immediate result of the debate, at the time, was that Raspail was fined fifteen francs for illegally practicing medicine. It has always been a hazardous venture to defy the establishment.

Neither Orfila nor Raspail could have imagined the progress which was to 9 be made in the characterisation of bloodstains. Throughout the rest of the nineteenth century steady progress was made in the subject. An English textbook of 1868 (Guy's *Principles of Forensic Medicine*) devotes ten pages to the subject of bloodstains and mentions spectroscopic and microscopic crystal tests which would be accepted even today as reliable proof that a stain was a bloodstain.

The identification of the species origin of blood was a different matter. 10 Although evidence touching on this problem was sometimes given in court, mainly on the basis of microscopical examination, it was viewed with great caution by many lawyers and scientists. It was not until the end of the nineteenth century when work, predominantly by German scientists, established a safe way of establishing the species origin of blood. This was done by the use of serum from animals injected with different bloods.

It was found that an animal (usually a rabbit) reacted by producing a spe- 11 cific factor in its blood against the species of blood injected. This specific material was then used as a reagent in what became known as the "precipitin test for blood." The method is still in daily use in various forms in forensic science and medico-legal laboratories throughout the world.

The discrimination of blood from different individuals became a developing 12 possibility with the discovery of the human blood groups by the Austrian pathologist, Landsteiner, in 1901. Although Landsteiner's studies were made from the standpoint of clinical problems, they initiated a series of researches which has culminated in a method whereby the genetic blueprint of the human individual can be partly recovered from a bloodstain left at a scene-of-crime. This "DNA profiling" means that, in some cases, the forensic biologist can enter the witness box and state, with what amounts to certainty, that "this individual gave rise to that bloodstain."

Mark Evidence

Much of the best physical evidence in crime investigation comes from the exam- 13 ination of distinctive marks left at the scene of the crime. The comparison of these marks with something known to be associated with a suspect can often yield unique evidence. The instinctive knowledge that such marks can be unique seems to be an integral part of human nature.

Sisyphus, a figure in Ancient Greek mythology, knew it well when he 14 marked the hooves of his cattle with notches. Because of this, when the master thief Autolycus denied stealing the cattle, Sisyphus was able to prove that he was lying.

In more recent times accounts of such "shape" evidence become more fre- 15 quent. One such account relates to the murder of Edward Culshaw in Lancashire, England in 1784. Culshaw was shot in the head by a muzzle-loading gun. The surgeon who carried out the postmortem examination recovered a piece of paper, used as a wad, from the wound.

This wad had been used to retain the powder and shot in the barrel of the 16 gun and to provide a gas-tight seal in front of the expanding hot gases that pushed the shot out of the barrel. The wad was found to have been torn from a larger sheet of paper. The remainder of this sheet of paper was found in the possession of a suspect, who was convicted and hanged on the evidence.

Nowadays, firearm evidence is much more complex than in the eighteenth 17 century, although a case is recorded in the USA where, almost two hundred years after the case described above, a similar set of circumstances arose. In this case a home-loaded shotgun cartridge was used in the commission of a murder and the piece of newspaper which was used as a wad was discharged into the fatal wound, just as it had been in the eighteenth century English murder. A similar piece of newspaper, with a matching torn edge, was found in possession of the suspect.

Modern firearm evidence, much of it developed in the USA, deals with the same principles in a more sophisticated way. Distinctive marks made on bullets as they pass through the barrel of a gun, or on cartridge cases when they are struck by firing pins and breech blocks, are the modern stock-in-trade of the firearms examiner. These marks can be characteristic of an individual gun and thus provide the evidence that a particular bullet, or cartridge case, has been fired in a specified gun.   18

In addition to these examinations the firearms examiner may be expected to assess the trajectories of bullets and compare them with their supposed firing points. He may also be asked to perform chemical analyses of traces found on hands and clothing to see if these yield proof that the individual in question has recently fired a gun.   19

. . .

Crime Investigation Systems

Crime investigation has much in common with all other forms of enquiry including scientific research, and, like scientific research, one has yet to produce a universal formula for success. None the less it is possible to identify certain patterns in crime investigation and to use these patterns both in the design of enquiries in individual cases and in the design of standing systems for crime investigation.   20

When a crime is committed and becomes the subject of investigation the first stage in the hunt for the criminal is the recording of information relative to the crime. This information is largely undifferentiated at the beginning and much of it may subsequently prove to be of no value in the investigation, but it must be noted, even if only mentally, in case it proves to be relevant.   21

The next stage is that in which the investigator, using his knowledge of the crime and his experience of similar past crimes, maps out in his mind the whole range of possibilities. This particular stage is a frankly speculative one and its effectiveness is proportional to the experience and competence of the investigator. It is the production of all useful conjectures, the drawing of a boundary around all the possibilities.   22

Next these conjectures are examined and those selected which appear to be the most plausible under the circumstances. Finally lines of enquiry are selected to test the conjectures, starting with the most likely ones first.   23

Much of this process is carried out instinctively by the experienced detective, who indeed may not be able explicitly to identify the stages by which he works. But the explicit identification of the stages provides a framework of useful mental pegs to the detective and, more important, allows the identification of those interlocking, overlapping and closely correlated parameters which are the basic stuff of crime investigation.   24

These include the identities of victims and suspects, the timing and sequence of events, the location of events, the cause of death, methods of information transfer, the listing of those known individuals likely on past records to be associated with a particular type of crime (the "form"), the listing of individuals and classes who could have committed the offence (the "frame") and many other parameters.   25

The handling of large amounts of information such as are generated in   26
modern crime investigation has led to a proliferation of computer systems
designed to help the police in the processing of this information. These systems
allow information to be input, and for the updated database to be interrogated,
from different terminals. They allow the search and comparison of different data
fields, and give aid in the problem of deciding priorities. . . .

The Future in Crime Investigation

This short article can only give an outline of a restricted part of scientific crime   27
investigation. Many aspects of the subject have not even been touched upon,
but it is hoped that sufficient has been said to interest the general reader and to
stimulate the professionally interested to enquire further.

Much progress in the future will rest upon the recognition that, in other than   28
its routine application, crime investigation is a high-grade intellectual problem.
Many university scientists are interested in the social and individual causes of
crime, but comparatively few are interested in the "who?" of crime rather than
the "why?" It is hoped that this article will help to stimulate that interest.

The writer will forward any queries he receives to relevant destinations. A mod-   29
ern booklist on the subject is available from the author's address.

References

Clément, J. L. *Sciences légales et police scientifique,* Paris, Masson S. A., 1987.

Kind, S. S. *The Scientific Investigation of Crime,* Harrogate Forensic Science Services Ltd,
HG2 OBG, UK, 1987.

For Discussion and Writing

Reading and Thinking Critically

1. *Personal response:* How successfully has Kind explained to you the workings of forensic science with respect to bloodstain analysis and mark evidence? Did he make accurate assumptions about you as a reader? What,
   specifically, have you learned from this explanatory essay?
2. *Be alert to differences:* Perhaps you have read novels or watched television
   shows or movies in which a forensic scientist steps forward to solve a
   crime. What differences can you observe between fictionalized portrayals
   of forensic scientists and Kind's portrayal?
3. *Broaden the context:* Kind broadens the context of forensics as a science —as
   a method of inquiry into a "high-grade intellectual problem." Locate the
   places where you are conscious of his broadening the context.

Examining "Science and the Hunt" as an Explanation

1. Examine ¶s 5–12 and describe the method by which Kind develops the
   point he is making.
2. How does Kind attempt to interest the reader in the subject of his explanation?
3. Reread the opening and closing paragraphs of this essay. How has Kind
   "framed" his explanation; that is, how has he set his explanation of forensic science in a specific context that helps focus our view?

Genetically Engineered Organisms and the Environment

Josefa Pinto

In this next example of an explanatory essay, student Josefa Pinto writes on the advantages and disadvantages of using genetically engineered organisms in agriculture. Like Stuart Kind, Pinto mixes techniques in developing her explanation: she provides historical background, she classifies benefits and dangers, and (through the use of quotation) she reviews the process of genetic manipulation.

Food shortage is a topic close to home (literally) for Pinto, as you will see in the sidebar to her essay. Pinto has a personal interest in exploring the ways in which genetic engineering could improve crop yield. Having investigated the new technology, Pinto devotes herself to an explanation. Except for a brief editorial remark at the end of her paper, she does not directly suggest her own cautious approach to the applications of genetic engineering to agriculture. We see evidence of her caution and fair-mindedness in her review of benefits and potential harms.

Forty years ago, 2.5 billion people lived on this planet. By 1980, that number grew to 4.5 billion. Today, 5.5 billion people are living on an Earth of ever dwindling resources. Many difficult questions arise from this century's dramatic rise in population, but none is as immediately urgent as the question of food. How will everybody be fed? With only so much arable land, we have limited options: We can control population growth, using severe measures like China. But to this point, most nations have been unwilling to restrict couples to bearing only one child. Another option is to increase the food supply with improved fertilizers, seed stocks, irrigation systems, and farming techniques. Progress in these areas has done much to improve crop yield around the world; but no development offers greater possibilities for boosting crop yields and alleviating hunger than genetic engineering. Here is a technology that promises both dramatic benefits and, if critics are to be believed, dramatic (even catastrophic) harm.

Genetic engineering is the name given to the techniques by which scientists alter or combine genes (hereditary material) in an organism. Genes, which are a part of all living cells, carry chemical information that determines an organism's characteristics. Genes have often been called the "blue prints" of life. By changing an organism's genes, scientists can manipulate the organism's traits and the traits of its descendants—something that farmers have been doing with seed selection and grafting techniques for centuries, but a process that can be dramatically speeded with the direct manipulation of genetic materials. The process of manipulation is fascinating. Scientists "invade" the plant they want to improve with specially loaded bacteria, which carry desired genetic traits such as frost or pest resistance. Ingrid Wickelgren, writing for *Science News*, describes one process by which this invasion is carried out:

> Using a sterilized paper punch, scientists remove disks from plant leaves, generating wounded tissue that [the carrier] bacteria can penetrate. Hav-

ing endowed the bacteria with the gene of interest [which will encourage frost resistance, etc.], the researchers mix them with the disks, where the bacteria insert the new DNA into the nucleus of one or more plant cells. The disks are then placed on a selective medium that allows them to form an outer ring of cells, each capable of growing into a whole plant. (122)

These genetically altered "whole plants" show resistance to frost and pests; they give greater yields; some can create their own fertilizer. Through the manipulation of genetic materials, scientists hope to produce flawless organisms that will meet today's and tomorrow's food requirements. The science of genetically engineering organisms began in the early 1900s based on the experiments and ideas of the Austrian monk, Gregory Mendel. During the 1800s, through his cross-breeding experiments, Mendel laid the foundation for future experiments in genetic engineering. By the 1970s, American geneticists began developing techniques for isolating and altering genes. They discovered that a soil bacterium known as *Agrobacterium* was nature's own genetic engineer and could exchange pieces of DNA (the raw material of genes) with startling frequency (Carey 18). On June 30, 1981, biologists Jack Kemp of the Department of Agriculture and Timothy Hall of the University of Wisconsin first harvested the bacterium's power. The first experiment consisted of using a microbe or microorganism to slip a bean plant gene into a sunflower plant. Later, in 1982, bacterially produced insulin became the first recombinant DNA drug approved by the Food and Drug Administration for use by people. By 1987 and 1988, genes were being transferred into higher organisms such as plants and animals (Cherfas 878). Presently, genetic engineers have produced most of the economically important varieties of plants and animals, such as flowers, vegetables, grains, cows, horses, and dogs.

3

Josefa Pinto: My Commitment to This Essay

Josefa Pinto was required by her instructor to write an explanatory essay; but she was also able to discover very personal reasons for writing and thus claimed this essay as her own. This personal statement gives you an insight into Pinto's motivations for writing but it is *not* itself an essay. Why not? What are the differences between this statement and the essay? What are the similarities?

In my country, we have a serious problem with malnutrition, both in the countryside and in the cities. In years when farmers cannot grow enough, the government must buy food from overseas, but we do not have the hard currency to do so, and we go deeper and deeper into debt. We must be able to feed our people. For this reason, I investigated in my paper a new technology that may help us to solve our food crisis.

Scientists have discovered the benefits and uses of genetically engineered organisms in agriculture. One important example is the ice-minus bacterium created by Steve Lindow and Nicholas Panopoulos. Realizing a bacterium commonly found in plants produces a protein that helps ice to form, these scientists removed the unfavorable gene and thereby prevented ice from forming on greenhouse plants (Carey 18). Others have manipulated genetic materials to create tobacco that kills attacking insects and to produce plants that resist herbicides. Geneticists hope in 20 to 40 years to produce plants such as corn and other grains that "fix" their own

4

nitrogen—that will be able to extract nitrogen from the atmosphere without relying on nitrifying bacteria. If such a plant could be created, U.S. farmers would save $3 to $4 billion annually in fertilizer costs and could save one third of all crops lost each year to pests. Ultimately, geneticists hope to use the same amounts of land, fertilizer, and pesticide while producing greater yields; this method of increasing productivity could be most beneficial to countries with limited usable land (Pimentel 25).

Early experiments seem promising, but there are certain dangers and [5] problems involved with the use and release of genetically engineered organisms into the environment. One such problem is the limited research into and knowledge about these organisms. As Francis Sharples, former member of the Recombinant DNA Advisory Committee stated, "Knowledge of the biotic and antibiotic interactions of most species in mixed populations in natural ecosystems is extremely limited. Currently the unknowns far outweigh the knowns where the ecological properties of microbes are concerned"(44). Many scientists are concerned with marketing fruits, vegetables, and grains after such a limited amount of research. There are documented health hazards that can result from consumer use of genetically engineered products. Studies have shown that "shuffling' genes has elevated plant toxins. This was the case in the 1960s when scientists bred a new kind of potato that caused human illness. The gene mixing had increased the plant's natural toxins to dangerous levels, thereby forcing the United States Department of Agriculture to recall the poisonous product from the market. Although some scientists argue that illness may be detected within two weeks of consumption, long-term effects are unknown.

Perhaps the most dangerous problem associated with genetic engi- [6] neering is the one that has not yet been encountered: our inability, in theory, to control organisms or to predict their behavior, once released into the open environment. Some scientists argue that laboratory testing may not be an accurate prediction of an organism's behavior once it is released. According to Francis Sharples, "so many factors interact in the environment to determine where there will be trouble, that predictions of just which species introductions will cause ecological disruptions is nearly beyond the ability of ecologists and population biologists"(41). There is also the concern for the possibility of having weeds or toxic plants (like poison ivy) capture a gene for herbicide resistance to environmentally safe herbicides, thereby forcing scientists to use much harsher and more dangerous chemicals to control weed growth. As Cornell ecologist David Pimentel argues, "You can stop using pesticides, but once you put one of these microbes out there the damn thing will reproduce and grow and we'll never get rid of it"(16). Past experiences have left ecologists skeptical of our ability to control specially released organisms: experiments such as the release of the gypsy moth and the introduction of the Kudzu vine have caused ecological havoc and billions of dollars in damage. What happens if something goes wrong with an organism once it has been released into the environment? Once it has been released and found an appropriate habitat, the organism may not only reproduce and spread but might also evolve in ways that will benefit its existence—not ours (Sharples 40).

Those in favor of genetic engineering argue that the exchange of genes 7 taking place during laboratory experiments is merely an imitation of what is done in nature all the time. In other words, genetic engineering is a natural process that is being reproduced by humans. Scientists are confident that strict regulation and principles of agreement between private companies and government agencies will ensure the safety and efficiency of any genetically engineered organism (Hanson 24). Furthermore, American molecular biologists fear that additional road blocks to their research will cause them to fall behind European competitors—and that the United States will lose its lead in yet another area of technology. The dilemmas over genetic engineering are, at their root, based on a struggle between the advancement of knowledge and competition on the one hand and the need for safety on the other. Ecologists who oppose the uses of genetically engineered organisms in the open environment argue that the genetic engineer, today, is a 20th-century sorcerer's-apprentice playing with a technology that is not fully understood (Pimentel 14). Others question the consequences of "playing God." They feel that humans do not know enough about life to manipulate its forms. This may be true, but when faced with challenges humankind must respond. Earth's population explosion is a challenge of the severest sort. If science can help us to feed the billions of new people who will soon share this planet with us, then we should pursue and act on scientific knowledge.

But we should also exercise caution. As Albert Einstein once advised, 8 "Concern for man himself and his fate must always form the chief interest of all technical endeavors, in order that the creation of our minds, and I would add, our laboratories, shall be a blessing and not a curse" (qtd. in Wickelgren 124). Our search for perfection must not blind us to the consequences and dangers that the search may bring.

Works Cited

Carey, John, and Dave Allen. "Brave New World of Super Plants: Genetic Tinkering Promises Enormous Benefits for Agriculture, But Is It Safe?" *International Wildlife* Nov. 1986: 16–18.

Cherfas, Jeremy. "Transgenic Crops Get a Test in the Wild." *Science* Feb. 1991: 878.

Hanson, David. "Field Test Approval of DNA Product Draws Criticism." *Chemical and Engineering News* 25 Nov. 1985: 24–25.

Pimentel, David. "Down on the Farm: Genetic Engineering Meets Ecology." *Technology Review* Jan. 1987: 24–31.

Sharples, Frances E. "Genetic Engineering Raises Environmental Concerns." *Genetic Engineering: Opposing Viewpoints.* Ed. William Dudley. San Diego: Greenhaven P, 1990. 39–45.

Wickelgren, Ingrid. "Please Pass the Genes: Experts Weigh Worries of Engineered Ills in New Food Crops." *Science News* 19 Aug. 1989: 120–24.

For Discussion and Writing

Reading and Thinking Critically

1. *Personal response:* Must one be a geneticist or an agricultural engineer to write clearly about matters related to these fields? Does Pinto's grasp of her material provide sufficient background for writing a clear and effective explanation for nonexperts?
2. *Be alert to differences:* Having read Pinto's personal commitment statement in the sidebar, what evidence do you see in the essay of Pinto's personal involvement? Were you satisfied with how visible or invisible you found her to be?
3. *Challenge the reading:* In your view, did Pinto give balanced treatment to her coverage of the possible benefits and harms of genetic engineering in agriculture?

Examining "Genetically Engineered Organisms" as an Explanation

1. What are the parts of the topic that Pinto develops?
2. How does Pinto link these parts within the paper?
3. What three different strategies for development can you find Pinto using in this explanatory essay?

Structures and Strategies

Explanation or Argument?

At the beginning of this chapter, explanation was defined as a type of writing that shows the *what, how,* and *why* of a topic at a level appropriate to a reader's interests and needs. You have seen four examples of explanatory writing, enough to now complicate the definition somewhat; we could call these explanations low-level arguments, attempts by writers to keep readers focused on a topic *as objectively as possible.* These last four words are meant to acknowledge that explanatory statements and essays can be challenged, in which case they must be termed *arguments.*

Explanations are often the result of arguments. The cause of the tides, the motion of the planets, the effects of acid rain, the process by which HIV infection is transmitted—at some point all of these topics were subject to debate. Now, by virtue of scientific argument they are no longer subject to debate: we say that we know the *what, why,* and *how* of them. We write explanations about HIV in books or in essays, and we call this writing objective—that is, until it is challenged by someone who says: "This is wrong!" At this point, a debate begins and what was once thought to be an objective, purely explanatory account becomes highly charged.

In principle, any explanatory statement can be seen as argumentative, including the first paragraph of this chapter on the production of iron (see page 165). An expert in iron production could conceivably challenge the Foxfire account or offer to explain the process in other terms. But as long as writers direct our attention to the thing, event, or process being examined (as the Foxfire writers do) and not to strongly held views about this thing, event, or process, we can call the writing explanatory, or we can term it a low-level argument. In high-level arguments you find the strongly held views of the writer taking center stage. The presentation of these views ("That was a *miserable* movie!") requires specialized strategies and structures, which you will find discussed in chapter 11.

Prepare to Write: Explore Your Idea

Discovering Ideas

Whether you are assigned a topic or are left to your own devices, you inevitably face the question: What is my idea? Like every essay, an explanatory essay has at its heart an idea that you want to convey. Stuart Kind's idea was that forensic science presents the researcher with high-grade intellectual problems that must be approached systematically, with a method resembling that of other scientists. From beginning to end, Kind advances this one idea in his essay. Like Kind, you face the challenge of explaining a *single* idea. What will this idea be? Following are several strategies to help you define one.

Reflect on Your Experience

Use your experience as a resource in discovering an idea. Reflect on what you know well and on what interests you, and then ask: What skill have I mastered, what knowledge do I have, that will allow me to help others understand? In "Science and the Hunt for the Criminal," Stuart Kind writes on forensic science. Bloodstain analysis and mark evidence are topics of daily attention to the forensic scientist, and Kind is able to use his mastery to generate impressive and fascinating details for his essay. If the topic of an essay is left to you, work from your strengths and interests.

Frequently, you will be assigned essay topics in areas that fall outside your experience. When this happens, you should conduct enough research to gain experience on a topic, if only enough to become a limited expert. If you have any choice about your topic, gravitate to one about which you are eager to learn. Research will stimulate you; through reading, you will gain experience and, fairly quickly, you will have a new expertise that you can explain to others.

Read to Discover Ideas

Reading can help substantially in sparking ideas for explanatory essays. Consider this strategy: take advantage of the thinking that others have done on a topic by listing their categories for discussion and determining if these categories can help you to generate parts of your own essay. Josefa Pinto did exactly this. She began with one general textbook article that discussed various applications of genetic engineering: waste management, cloning, mining, medicine, and agriculture. Realizing that she could not discuss with any level of detail *all* of these subtopics, and guided by her own interests, Pinto chose one subtopic: agriculture. She then sought an article written by an expert in the genetic manipulation of plant materials and found a suitable piece written by an entomologist at Cornell, David Pimentel, for *Technology Review.*

She relied on this more narrowly focused article, "Down on the Farm: Genetic Engineering Meets Ecology," to subdivide her topic further, so that she could begin identifying a particular focus for her explanatory essay. Following is an excerpt from Pimentel's article. On reading this piece, Pinto had one guiding question: *What are the parts of my topic?*

> The agricultural benefits from gene splicing and other genetic-engineering techniques could be enormous. Scientists will develop products that will increase food production, reduce fertilizer use, and decrease the need for costly, environmentally dangerous pesticides. But genetically engineered agricultural products could also cause sobering ecological, social, and economic problems. . . .
>
> Genetically engineered farm products will almost surely have a broad range of uses in coming decades Consider the benefits that will result when organisms such as bacteria, viruses, fungi, nematodes, and insects are engineered to control insect pests, weeds, and plant diseases. The savings could be enormous since more than one-third of all U.S. crops—worth about $50 billion—are annually lost to pests. Pesticide costs could also drop by as much as $500 million. In addition, some pest outbreaks would decrease if fewer chemicals were used. This is because pesticides now destroy many natural enemies of insect pests, allowing their populations to rebound to alarming sizes.
>
> By increasing crop yields, genetic engineering could also reduce the amount of land needed for agriculture. Geneticists expect to be able to use biotechnology to increase the proportion of the crops that can be harvested—usually the fruit—while reducing the proportion of stems, roots, and male sex parts, which are usually not used as food. Thus, the same amounts of land, fertilizer, and pesticide would yield more food. These results would be especially advantageous in areas of the world where arable land is limited.

—David Pimentel

Based on her reading of Pimentel, Pinto was able to understand the likely parts of her topic: the benefits of genetic engineering as applied to agriculture, the dangers, the process (how is it done?), the history, and the necessary safeguards. Pinto realized that she might not pursue each of these subtopics in her paper, but she wanted to begin by identifying as many parts of the topic as she could. She identified two additional general articles in her initial research, and these solidified for her the various subtopics she would consider discussing. Once she made this division into subtopics, she searched for articles devoted to each and in this way generated the material needed for a first draft.

Investigate the Needs of Your Readers

Closely defining your readers' needs and then writing to meet those needs is something you should do for all types of writing. In order to discover ideas for an explanatory essay, you may give readers even greater consideration and let their needs help narrow your idea. In fact, many books are commissioned in just this way: editors review the needs of the marketplace, generate project ideas, and then seek out writers. For your essays, determine your readers' interests and needs and then find the point of intersection with your own interests and abilities.

You might well adopt this approach in sparking ideas for the writing assignment that concludes this chapter. There you will be asked to write an essay explaining the process by which you chose a college to an audience of juniors at your old high school—students who are about to begin this same process. Before thinking about the essay in terms of your own experience, you might ask: What aspect of the decision-making process will interest these high-school students? What do they need from me? Responding to these questions might well give you an idea to launch your essay.

Committing Yourself to an Idea

The very best writing is produced by those who are committed to their ideas, who have a personal stake in what they write. In chapter 2, you found that such writers generally adopt two attitudes:

- I write for myself and for my audience.
- I will find an approach to writing that lets me discover something personally significant.

Consider once again Stuart Kind's essay, "Science and the Hunt for the Criminal." Recall that Kind organizes his essay inductively; that is, he presents the two parts of his essay's idea toward the end, in separate paragraphs. In ¶28 he writes that "Crime investigation is a high-grade intellectual problem" that (he says in ¶20) "has much in common with all other forms of enquiry." Observe the relationship between the idea of his essay and Kind's statement of his reasons for writing:

> Many forensic scientists are required to communicate their results to nonscientists such as police officers, trial lawyers and juries but others (for example in research) have little opportunity to do so. In the absence of this front-line communication practice there is a constant tendency for forensic scientists, in common with all scientists, to restrict communication to peer groups. In this way new words are invented, and old ones invested with new meanings, until a new "priesthood" appears, speaking a new dialect. This leads to lack of comprehension or, even worse, faulty comprehension by nonspecialists.
>
> A helpful factor in avoiding this drift into dialect is for the scientist regularly to write *expository* articles in addition to experimental papers. I do this and encourage others to do so. I chose *Impact of Science on Society* for this article because of its wide international circulation in educational circles.

Kind's interest in presenting his specialty to nonscientists explains his commitment to this essay. He explicitly wants to stimulate our interest in the "who" of crime (see his last paragraph), and to do so he decides to explain what he does, his assumption being that an explanation by one who is fascinated with the topic might well fascinate readers. He is right. You see in this essay a personal motive and enthusiasm that is evident throughout. Kind's interest in his own topic interests readers. You, too, can engage readers by making a commitment to the idea in your explanatory essays.

Write: Clarify Your Idea and Make It Public

In planning and writing the first draft of any essay, you can expect to clarify your ideas. Writing is not only an act that communicates information you already possess but is also an act of discovery, and you should expect to deepen your insights as you write. You will do so in the context of making what insights you already have public. Your first consideration will be your readers. Who are they? What do they know? How will you make what *you* know available to them?

Creating Common Ground with Readers

Readers are more likely to understand and recall particular cases that illustrate an idea than they are to understand and recall that same idea expressed abstractly. We can more easily understand the parallel methods used to solve a pair of murders separated by two hundred years (see Kind, ¶s 15–17) than we can abstract phrasings like "the continuity of forensic methods." Readers want and need particulars, and your job as a writer is to provide them. Chapter 3 contains a discussion on creating "common ground" with readers; it presents strategies for presenting an idea through particulars. The discussion here will alert you to strategies especially useful for creating common ground in explanatory essays. Your choice of details in an essay will be guided by your assessment of your readers' needs and interests.

Tone and the Writing Occasion

How much an audience knows about a topic will directly affect what information you present and how you explain it. Observe how one writer, psychologist B. F. Skinner, alters the level of an explanation depending on his audience. In this first example, he writes on the topic of conditioned behavior for a general audience.

> It takes rather subtle laboratory conditions to test an animal's full learning capacity, but the reader may be surprised at how much he can accomplish even under informal circumstances at home. Since nearly everyone at some time or other has tried, or wished he knew how, to train a dog, a cat, or some other animal, perhaps the most useful way to explain the learning process is to describe some simple experiments which the reader can perform himself.
>
> "Catch your rabbit" is the first item in a well-known recipe for rabbit stew. Your first move, of course, is to choose an experimental subject. Any available animal—a cat, a dog, a pigeon, a mouse, a parrot, a chick-

en, a pig—will do. (Children or other members of your family may also be available, but it is suggested that you save them until you have had practice with less valuable material.) Suppose you choose a dog.

The second thing you will need is something your subject wants, say food. This serves as a reward or—to use a term which is less likely to be misunderstood—a "reinforcement" for the desired behavior.

Writing for a general audience, Skinner is careful *not* to use technical, complex language. Observe him discussing the same topic with fellow psychologists. Both his vocabulary and format change when he writes for colleagues in the *Journal of General Psychology:*

A conditioned reflex is said to be conditioned in the sense of being dependent for its existence or state upon the occurrence of a certain kind of event, having to do with the presentation of a reinforcing stimulus. A definition which includes much more than this simple notion will probably not be applicable to all cases. At almost any significant level of analysis a distinction must be made between at least two major types of conditioned reflex. These may be represented, with examples, in the following way (where S = stimulus, R = response, $(S–R)$ = reflex, $\rightarrow$ = "is followed by," and [ ] = "the strength of" the enclosed reflex):

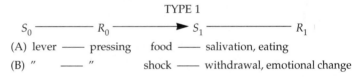

TYPE 1

S_0 ————— R_0 —————→ S_1 ————— R_1

(A) lever —— pressing   food —— salivation, eating

(B) "   —— "   shock —— withdrawal, emotional change

Clearly, then, your expectations about your audience determine a great deal about what your topic is and how you write about it. Use the questions below to conduct an audience needs analysis, which will help to clarify who, *exactly*, will be reading your explanation. Based on the needs of this carefully defined audience, decide on the complexity with which you will treat your topic, on the level of language you will use, and on the nature and number of your examples.

Audience Needs Analysis

Pose these general questions, regardless of your purpose:

- Who is the reader? What is the reader's age, sex, religious background, educational background, and ethnic heritage?
- What is my relationship with the reader?
- What impact on my presentation—on choice of words, level of complexity, and choice of examples—will the reader have?
- Why will the reader be interested in my paper? How can I best spark the reader's interest?

If you are writing to explain, pose these questions as well:

- What does the reader know about the topic's history?
- How well does the reader understand the topic's technical detail?
- What does the reader need to know? want to know?

- What level of language and content will I use in discussing the topic, given the reader's understanding?

Topic and the Writing Occasion

Carefully choose the topic you want to explain, making sure that it satisfies both the objectives of the assignment and the needs of your intended audience. The following principle may help you to determine how general, or how narrowly defined, your topic should be:

> The more specific the information needs of your audience, the narrower your topic.

If you intended to write an explanatory essay on biotechnology, the general topic of Josefa Pinto's paper, and a professor asked that you limit your explanation to five pages, you would face an impossible task. The topic is immense, and you would need to narrow the topic by identifying and choosing among subtopics. Josefa Pinto did just this, choosing the subtopic of the uses of genetic engineering in agriculture. For her audience of nonexperts, she wrote with an appropriate level of detail, in a language that was accessible. She correctly understood that none of her readers would be experts in the field who would demand technical language and detailed instructions on splicing genes from one plant into another.

Would Pinto's explanation, adequate for a general audience, have been adequate for an audience of biologists specializing in the field? No. To find an explanation useful, an audience wants information suited to its needs; experts might want to see information on the use of particular chemicals, the development of new procedures, or the careful identification of a problem. Nonexperts, unable to use such information, would prefer the overview and the language that Pinto provides. What counts as useful in an explanation depends heavily on your audience and will shift from one audience to the next.

Planning a Structure

Whatever your topic, you will likely explain by dividing it into parts and developing an explanation for each part. "Topical development" is by far the most common method for developing explanatory essays. You can identify parts by asking questions of, or quizzing, your thesis. (See pages 61–63 for details on this technique.) Pose as many questions as possible regarding your thesis; your answers will suggest the likely parts of an essay. Here is how Josefa Pinto quizzed her thesis:

Define. How does this work?

Future? What's the history?

The genetic manipulation of plants is a technology that promises both dramatic benefits and, if critics are to be believed, dramatic (even catastrophic) harm.

What's the debate?

What are these?

Having read this thesis, a reader expects to see developed and explained all points either implied or suggested directly. Here are those points, as determined by Pinto:

- a definition (what is the genetic manipulation of plants?)
- process (how is this manipulation done?)
- brief history
- classification
    benefits of genetically altering plants
    dangers of genetically altering plants
- a report on the debate

Contrast this explanatory thesis and the following argumentative thesis:

> Biologists who manipulate the genetic makeup of plants in a lab cannot be trusted to do accurately, and with wisdom, what has taken Nature millions of years in the wild.

An argumentative thesis promises an essay in which the writer's debatable idea receives the main emphasis in the essay. The explanatory thesis, by contrast, involves no such debate. The focus remains on objects, events, conditions, processes, or ideas—on presenting the parts in order to give readers information that they can put to use.

Developing Parts

You can develop the parts of an essay in a variety of ways: by providing a historical overview, by describing, by giving examples, by explaining a process, by developing a definition, by classifying, and by comparing and contrasting. Most often, you will rely on a variety of these techniques in any one essay, as is the case with the examples that begin this chapter. (Josefa Pinto uses five separate techniques for development; Stuart Kind uses three.)

Illustrations of each of these techniques for development follow. For the most part, the illustrations are limited to single paragraphs; however, the principles that organize these paragraphs can just as easily be extended to multiple paragraphs.

Historical Overview

One common way to develop a point you are making is to recount its history for readers. In his essay at the beginning of this chapter, Stuart Kind does exactly this. Historical accounts usually take several paragraphs to develop.

> A commonly occurring factor in crime investigation is bloodstaining; however, it was not until the beginning of the nineteenth century that the importance of this, as criminal evidence, began to be explicitly recognised.
>
> In one English multiple murder investigation in 1811 it was recorded that expert advice was sought to establish whether certain stains were

of paint or of blood. However, it is doubtful if this represents the first forensic examination of bloodstains.

A discussion which took place in 1828 at the French *Académie Royale de Médecine* shows that French experts, at least, had concerned themselves for some time with the problem of the detection of bloodstains. It is recorded that a vigorous, and sometimes acrimonious, exchange on the subject took place between the famous scholars François Raspail and Mathieu Orfila.

Raspail didn't believe it was possible, by chemical or microscopical means, to distinguish between blood and many other substances. Orfila believed that it was. History has proved Orfila right, but the only immediate result of the debate, at the time, was that Raspail was fined fifteen francs for illegally practising medicine. It has always been a hazardous venture to defy the establishment.

Neither Orfila nor Raspail could have imagined the progress which was to be made in the characterisation of bloodstains. Throughout the rest of the nineteenth century steady progress was made in the subject. An English textbook of 1868 (Guy's *Principles of Forensic Medicine*) devotes ten pages to the subject of bloodstains and mentions spectroscopic and microscopic crystal tests which would be accepted even today as reliable proof that a stain was a bloodstain.

The identification of the species origin of blood was a different matter. Although evidence touching on this problem was sometimes given in court, mainly on the basis of microscopical examination, it was viewed with great caution by many lawyers and scientists. It was not until the end of the nineteenth century when work, predominantly by German scientists, established a safe way of establishing the species origin of blood. This was done by the use of serum from animals injected with different bloods.

It was found that an animal (usually a rabbit) reacted by producing a specific factor in its blood against the species of blood injected. This specific material was then used as a reagent in what became known as the "precipitin test for blood." The method is still in daily use in various forms in forensic science and medico-legal laboratories throughout the world.

Description

All writers must make observations and describe what they see. What counts as an accurate and worthwhile description will vary according to circumstance, but generally it can be said that a writer who can evoke in us a clear sense of sight, feeling, smell, hearing, or taste earns our admiration. Consider this sentence from Bruce Chatwin's *In Patagonia*: "The wind blew the smell of rain down the valley ahead of the rain itself, the smell of wet earth and aromatic plants." This is a fine sentence. It evokes in us not only a feeling for the scene that Chatwin saw but also a recollection of our own experience. Everyone has smelled rain coming in advance of a storm. Everyone has smelled wet earth and an aromatic plant, perhaps an orchid or gardenia on prom night. Now mingle these smells as Chatwin does and have the scent carried on a moist wind, in a valley that is likely lush with vegetation. If one sentence can evoke such a clear sense of place, think what a well-written paragraph can do! Following is a description of the promenade—the walkway—on the Brooklyn Bridge. The author does a fine job of letting us see the bridge, even if we have never been there.

> On most traffic bridges the only foot passage is a pavement alongside rushing vehicles. Here the walk is a promenade raised above the traffic; one can lean over the railing and watch cars speeding below. The promenade is wide enough for benches—for walkers and for cyclists. Old-fashioned lamp posts remind the walker that it is, after all, a thoroughfare. But the walk is narrow enough for the promenader to reach over and touch the large, round cables, wrapped in wire casing, or the rough wire rope of the vertical suspenders. Crossing the verticals is a rigging of diagonal wire ropes—stays, attached somewhere below to the floor of the roadway.
>
> —Alan Trachtenberg, *Brooklyn Bridge: Fact and Symbol*

Example

An example is a particular case of a more general point. Development by example is one of the most common methods of developing parts of an explanatory essay. Examples *show* readers what you mean; if an example is vivid, readers will have a better chance of remembering your point. It is very common for writers to include an example along with other strategies for development. Several transitions are commonly used to introduce examples: *for example, for instance, a case in point, to illustrate.* In the following paragraph, Rachel Carson describes how methods of insect control can affect fish.

> Wherever there are great forests, modern methods of insect control threaten the fishes inhabiting the streams in the shelter of the trees. One of the best-known examples of fish destruction in the United States took place in 1955, as a result of spraying in and near Yellowstone National Park. By the fall of that year, so many dead fish had been found in the Yellowstone River that sportsmen and Montana fish-and-game administrators became alarmed. About 90 miles of the river were affected. In one 300-yard length of shoreline, 600 dead fish were counted, including brown trout, whitefish, and suckers. Stream insects, the natural food of trout, had disappeared.
>
> —Rachel Carson, *Silent Spring*

Sequential Order/Process

If you have ever cooked a meal by following a recipe, you have read a sequence of steps, a process. Such explanations do not explain the causes of a particular outcome: they will not, for instance, explain the chemical reactions that cake batter undergoes when placed in an oven. A process will show carefully sequenced events. The range of possibilities is endless: What is the process by which people fall in love? by which children learn? by which steel is made? by which a poem is written? by which a computer chip is manufactured? Each of these cases, different as they are, requires a clear delineation of steps. In presenting a process, you will typically use transitions that show sequence in time: *first, second, after, before, once, next, then,* and *finally.*

> Making a chip is a complex process. Most manufacturers now use what Heilmeier calls the "dip and wash" technique. A diagram of electronic circuitry is designed by a scientist on a computer terminal. Photographic machines produce hundreds of reproductions of the display and reduce them in size until their individual components are in the micron range. A photographic negative, or mask, is made of the patterns. Ultraviolet light is then projected through the mask onto a thin, 4-inch wafer of silicon that has been treated with photo resist, a light-sensitive material. Just like a film, the photo resist is developed, and the tiny patterns of the chips' circuitry emerge on the silicon's surface. The wafer is dipped in acid, which eats away the silicon where there is no photo resist. A layer of metal can be deposited for the interconnections between circuits, then another layer of photo resist. Some wafers take ten or more etched layers. Once all the layers are formed on the wafer, the chips are sawed out, fine wire leads are connected and they are ready for use in electronic devices.
>
> —Merrill Sheils, "And Man Created the Chip"

Definition

Definitions are always important. In explanatory writing, readers can learn the meaning of terms needed for understanding difficult concepts. Once a term is defined, it can be clarified with examples or descriptions. The paragraph that follows is explanatory in character—more or less announcing its definition.

> When we are hungry, we think of McDonald's or Godfather's Pizza. When we actually go to these fast food places, we never worry about whether they will have enough Big Macs or pizzas for us. Shouldn't we worry about it? How do they know that we are coming? Of course, they do not know that *we* are coming, but they know that someone will. In a market economy, stores tend to carry products that customers want and customers usually find products that they want at their favorite stores. A market economy is one in which competition works through the interaction of supply and demand. Individual sellers pursue private interests by selling the quantity and charging the price that will maximize their profits. Individual buyers, on the other hand, pursue private interests by selecting the bundle of goods and services that will maximize their satisfaction. There is no order imposed from above, but there is a sense of orderliness in the market.
>
> —Semoon Chang, *Modern Economics*

Division and Classification

Division (also called *analysis*) and classification are closely related operations. A writer who divides a topic into parts to see what it is made of performs an analysis. A *classification* is a grouping of like items. The writer begins with what may appear at first to be bits of unrelated information.

Gradually, patterns of similarity emerge and the writer is able to establish categories by which to group like items. In the example that follows, Brian Fagan considers the various locations at which archaeological digs are made and then classifies or groups the digs according to common features. Because establishing categories is a matter of judgment, another writer might well classify archaeological sites differently. Fagan's paragraph begins with his topic sentence. Notice that once he defines various classes, he devotes a sentence or two to developing each.

> Archaeological sites are most commonly classified according to the activities that occurred there. Thus, cemeteries and other sepulchers like Tutankhamun's tomb are referred to as **burial sites.** A 20,000-year-old Stone Age site in the Dnieper Valley of the Ukraine, with mammoth-bone houses, hearths, and other signs of domestic activity, is a **habitation site.** So too are many other sites, such as caves and rockshelters, early Mesoamerican farming villages, and Mesopotamian cities—in all, people lived and carried out greatly diverse activities. **Kill sites** consist of bones of slaughtered game animals and the weapons that killed them. They are found in East Africa and on the North American Great Plains. **Quarry sites** are another type of specialist site, where people mined stone or metals to make specific tools. Prized raw materials, such as obsidian, a volcanic glass used for fine knives, were widely traded in prehistoric times and profoundly interest the archaeologist. Then there are such spectacular **religious sites** as the stone circles of Stonehenge in southern England, the Temple of Amun at Karnak, Egypt, and the great ceremonial precincts of lowland Maya centers in Central America at *Tikal,* Copán, and Palenque. **Art sites** are common in southwestern France, southern Africa, and parts of North America, where prehistoric people painted or engraved magnificent displays of art.
>
> —Brian Fagan, *Archaeology*

Comparison/Contrast

To *compare* is to discuss the similarities between people, places, objects, events, or ideas. To *contrast* is to discuss differences. The writer developing such a paragraph conducts an analysis of two or more subjects, studying the parts of each and then discussing the subjects in relation to each other. Specific points of comparison and contrast make the discussion possible. Suppose you are comparing and contrasting a computer and the human brain. Two points you might use to make the discussion meaningful are the density with which information is packed and the speed with which information is processed. You could analyze a computer and a human brain in light of these two points, and presumably your analysis would yield similarities *and* differences.

Paragraphs of comparison and contrast should be put to some definite use in a paper. It is not enough to point out similarities and differences; you must *do* something with this information: three possibilities would be to classify, evaluate, or interpret. When writing your paragraph, consider two common methods of arrangement: by subject or point by point.

Arrangement by Subject:	Following a topic sentence in which you signal that a comparison is coming, you discuss each subject separately within the paragraph. First you discuss computers—their density of information, and then the speed with which they process information. Next, you discuss the human brain—its density of information, and then the speed with which it processes information. Either in the separate discussions within the paragraph or at the end you would review similarities and differences.
Arrangement, Point by Point:	This method allows you to mingle observations about computers and brains. After your topic sentence, raise your first *point* of comparison and contrast—density of information. Then follow with a discussion of *both* computers and brains. Next, raise your second point of comparison and contrast—speed at which information is processed. Again, follow with a discussion of *both* computers and brains.

When the comparisons you want to make are relatively brief, arrangement by subject works well. Readers are able to hold in mind the first part of the discussion as they read the second. When comparisons are longer and more complex, a point-by-point discussion helps the reader to focus on specific elements of your comparative analysis. Paragraphs developed by comparison and contrast use transition words such as: *similarly, also, as well, just so, by contrast, conversely, but, however, on the one hand/on the other,* and *yet.*

The following outlines demonstrate the ways a writer can organize a comparative analysis by subject or point by point.

Arrangement by Subject

Topic sentence (may be shifted to other positions in the paragraph)
Introduce Subject A
   Discuss Subject A in terms of the first point to be discussed
   Discuss Subject A in terms of the second point to be discussed
Introduce Subject B
   Discuss Subject B in terms of the first point to be discussed
   Discuss Subject B in terms of the first point to be discussed
Conclude with a summary of similarities and differences.

Arrangement, Point by Point

Topic sentence (may be shifted to other positions in the paragraph)
Introduce the first point to be compared and contrasted
   Discuss Subject A in terms of this point
   Discuss Subject B in terms of this point
Introduce the second point to be compared and contrasted
   Discuss Subject A in terms of this point
   Discuss Subject B in terms of this point

In the following paragraph, John Morreall organizes his comparative discussion by subject. First, he discusses his Subject A: the person with a sense of humor and the traits associated with this view of the world. Then Morreall discusses his Subject B: the person who lacks a sense of humor and the traits associated with this view of the world. Morreall concludes the paragraph with a topic sentence that makes a general point about humor and places the comparison and contrast in a larger perspective.

> When the person with a sense of humor laughs in the face of his own failure, he is showing that his perspective transcends the particular situation he's in, and that he does not have an egocentric, overly precious view of his own endeavors. This is not to say that he lacks self-esteem—quite the contrary. It is because he feels good about himself at a fundamental level that this or that setback is not threatening to him. The person without real self-esteem, on the other hand, who is unsure of his own worth, tends to invest his whole sense of himself in each of his projects. Whether he fails or succeeds, he is not likely to see things in an objective way; because his ego rides on each of the goals he sets for himself, any failure will constitute personal defeat and any success personal triumph. He simply cannot afford to laugh at himself, whatever happens. So having a sense of humor about oneself is psychologically healthy. As A. Penjon so nicely said, it "frees us from vanity, on the one hand, and from pessimism on the other by keeping us larger than what we do, and greater than what can happen to us."
>
> —John Morreal, *Taking Laughter Seriously*

In the following paragraph, Carl Sagan uses a point-by-point arrangement to compare and contrast the human brain with a computer. First, he examines the two subjects with respect to the density with which their information is packed; next, he examines the two subjects with respect to the speed with which they process information.

> How densely packed is the information stored in the brain? A typical information density during the operation of a modern computer is about a million bits per cubic centimeter. This is the total information content of the computer, divided by its volume. The human brain contains, as we have said, about 10^{13} bits in a little more than 10^3 cubic centimeters, for an information content of $10^{13} / 10^3 = 10^{10}$, about ten billion bits per cubic centimeter; the brain is therefore ten thousand times more densely packed with information than is a computer, although the computer is much larger. Put another way, a modern computer able to process the information in the human brain would have to be about ten thousand times larger in volume than the human brain. On the other hand, modern electronic computers are capable of processing information at a rate of 10^{16} to 10^{17} bits per second, compared to a peak rate ten billion times slower in the brain. The brain must be extraordinarily cleverly packaged and "wired," with such a small total information content and so low a processing rate, to be able to do so many significant tasks so much better than the best computer.
>
> —Carl Sagan, *The Dragons of Eden*

Understanding Your Logic

You can be just as strategically minded in planning an essay of explanation as you are planning any other type of essay. You have seen in "Science and the Hunt for the Criminal" that Stuart Kind arranges his explanation inductively; that is, he provides a series of cases that illustrate the methods of forensic science and then, near the very end, he presents his essay's idea. Kind's logic is as follows: since very few people understand what forensic scientists do, opening an essay with sweeping generalizations about that science would not have been especially helpful to readers. Generalizations are effective when they bring a pattern of coherence to numerous individual cases. Without the benefit of such cases, readers have little use for generalizations. Kind therefore opens with particulars that give readers the base of experience needed to make generalizations about forensic science.

Josefa Pinto, by contrast, introduces her explanatory essay with her idea: "[N]o development offers greater possibilities for boosting crop yields and alleviating hunger than genetic engineering. Here is a technology that promises both dramatic benefits and, if critics are to be believed, dramatic (even catastrophic) harm." Pinto opens with the problem of increasing population and the threat of global hunger. Most readers, she assumes, are aware of the issue; most have read about it or at least have seen the haunting photographs of starving children. Working with the confidence that she and her readers share a common base of experience, Pinto immediately presents her idea and then follows with particulars that develop this idea.

Choose an overall logic for your essay based on your estimate of the readers' familiarity with your topic. The greater the readers' familiarity, the more reason you have to open with your idea; the less the readers' familiarity, the more reason you have to delay your idea until you have created in the essay a base of details that can make later general statements meaningful. Also consider this: If you divide your idea into parts and present one part at a time, as most writers of explanations do, be sure to remind readers of your larger idea at all points in the essay. Parts should be clearly related to each other *and* to the whole. In Stuart Kind's essay, the explanations of bloodstain analysis and mark evidence are themselves related and, at every point, illustrate the essay's larger idea: that forensic science presents high-grade intellectual problems. In sum, before you can be assured that readers understand the logic of your explanation, you must understand this logic yourself.

Advance Your Idea with Sources

If you are not an expert on a topic, but find yourself writing an essay on it, how will you prepare an explanation? In fact, this was Josefa Pinto's problem in writing the paper on genetic engineering and agriculture. What can you do?

- Read enough to gain a general understanding.
- Read so that, relative to your audience, you know a considerable amount about your topic.

The discussion that follows suggests several ways in which you can use source materials to advance the idea of your explanatory essay.

Use General Sources to Identify Parts of the Topic

If you are new to a topic and need a quick overview about its constituent parts, read an encyclopedia entry (from a specialized encyclopedia if possible). Referring to such sources in an essay is generally frowned on (because the researcher hasn't consulted primary sources); nonetheless, reading encyclopedia entries can be a useful strategy when beginning an investigation. Aimed at a general audience, these books usually divide broad topics into constituent parts, one of which might become the focus of your essay. Encyclopedia entries can be especially helpful in historical research, where common knowledge is not undergoing rapid, and constant, revision.

Use Sources to Clarify Procedures and to Check the Reliability of Experts

Clarifying Basic Procedures

If you are not an expert on a topic, you will not be able to draw on personal experience when explaining basic procedures. Especially if the topic is at all technical, you will need to rely on sources to clarify first for you, and then for your reader, how things get done. The "thing" in question for Josefa Pinto was the process of manipulating the genetic materials of plants. Pinto's first task was to read about this process and to understand the process herself. She needed an overview for nonexperts and found this photo caption in a sidebar to an article by Ingrid Wickelgren in *Science News:*

> Gene insertion: Using a sterilized paper punch, scientists remove disks from plant leaves (left), generating wounded tissue that *Agrobacterium tumefaciens* bacteria can penetrate. Having endowed the bacteria with the gene of interest, the researchers mix them with the disks, where the bacteria insert the new DNA into the nucleus of one or more plant cells. The disks are then placed on a selective medium that allows them to form an outer ring of cells (above), each capable of growing into a whole plant.

Having found this explanation, Pinto asked herself: "Can I trust it?" As a nonexpert, she had no experience by which to verify the accuracy of the procedure she had just read. The fact that the procedure appeared in a reputable journal was reassuring, but Pinto wanted a reliability check. For this, she turned to another source, which she found in John Carey's "Brave

New World of Super Plants." Carey's credit line identified him as a senior editor of *International Wildlife*, the journal in which his selection appeared. When Pinto read the following, she was confident that the account by Ingrid Wickelgren, read earlier, was accurate:

> In a recent experiment at Washington University in St. Louis, for example, biologist Roger Beachy and co-workers created the first genetically-engineered virus-resistant plants. The researchers began by copying a gene from tobacco mosaic virus (TMV), a scourge of both tobacco and tomatoes. They then spliced the gene into *Agrobacterium*, added the bacterium to small bits of tomato and tobacco leaves, and regenerated whole plants from genetically altered pieces. The resulting plants were thus "vaccinated" against TMV; by making one part of the virus, as instructed by their new gene, they prevented the virus from causing the disease.
>
> —John Carey

Pinto now knew that the first explanation of how genetic material is manipulated in plants was accurate. She then faced a second decision: *How* should she use the explanation in her paper? Should she quote? paraphrase? summarize? In chapter 4 you will find a discussion of strategies for referring to source materials. Here, we can observe that Pinto felt she needed the authority of an acknowledged expert when providing readers with the *how-to*s of genetic manipulation.

Checking the Reliability of Experts

When you refer to experts in your papers, you want to be sure that their views are trustworthy. Again, if you are not an expert yourself, you face some difficulty in verifying the accuracy of sources. If you find yourself in this bind, consider three strategies:

- Look for the author's credit line to assure yourself that an opinion has been developed in a reputable academic or research-oriented context.
- Place some value on professional journals, the articles of which must pass peer reviews.
- Look for an author's work referred to in other sources to confirm that author's reputation.

An author's work is not necessarily reliable because it was developed in an academic environment or because it appeared in a reputable journal and was cited by other authors. Nonetheless, these reliability checks will serve you well when you write explanatory papers on unfamiliar topics. First, consider an author's credit line, which is useful to the extent that you can be assured that materials were developed in an academic context where research is challenged and subject to rigorous public debate.

Next, consider the sources in which you find your authors. The authors of Pinto's sources had published in "refereed" journals that accept pieces for publication only on the advice of well-respected, university-level specialists who read and judge the worthiness of article submissions. Finally, look for often-cited names. If you read enough on your topic, you will invariably find certain names reappearing. Seek out the work of these authors and learn why their views are getting attention. Even without being an expert yourself, you will be able to tell if an author is getting positive, negative, or mixed attention. To the extent it is positive, you should judge the author's work reliable and consider referring to that work in your paper. Josefa Pinto found a piece by Cornell researcher David Pimentel very helpful. Before relying too heavily on his work, however, she wanted to make sure that Pimentel was a respected voice on the genetic manipulation of plant materials. She was reassured on finding the following piece in *Science News:*

> Agriculture's extensive experience with the introduction of biological agents for pest control can offer insight for the safe and effective release of genetically engineered organisms, says David Pimentel, an entomologist at Cornell University in Ithaca N.Y. Around the world more than 100 programs employing natural, although perhaps foreign, enemies of targeted pests are considered fully effective. On the average, it has taken the introduction of about 20 parasites or predators to find one that is successful for pest control.
>
> Pimentel has surveyed data from 447 attempts at biological control to identify factors that increase the likelihood of success. He finds that although most potential biocontrol agents come from the native habitat of the pest, new associations—for instance, parasites of a related species from a distant location—tend to be more successful. Examples include the control of prickly pear cactus in Australia by a South American moth that naturally feeds on the tiger pear, and the control of the European rabbit in Australia by a virus introduced from the South American tropical forest rabbit.
>
> The advantage of new associations is that no genetic balance between resistance and virulence factors has evolved between host and parasite. "Changing the genetic makeup of a parasite by genetic engineering should, by a similar principle, make the new parasite genotype a highly effective biocontrol agent," Pimentel says. "At the same time, when the genetic makeup of an organism is changed, extreme caution must be exercised before it is released to be sure that it will not be a hazard to the ecological system."
>
> —Julie Ann Miller

Use Sources to Identify a Debate

In an explanatory essay you will not enter into a debate on your topic, but you can present this debate to readers and identify salient points. The fact that a topic is controversial is useful and important information, and you advance your essay considerably when you can report on a debate. Having read several sources on the genetic manipulation of plants, Josefa Pinto soon realized that virtually every author was taking sides in the argument by supporting a relatively quick release of genetically altered plants into the environment or by supporting a ban against such releases. Pinto read fifteen or so articles, enough to feel confident that she could accurately represent this debate to readers. In her explanatory essay, she does *not* take sides beyond making a cautionary statement in her conclusion that "our search for perfection must not blind us to the consequences and the dangers that the search may bring." To identify and report on a debate, read source materials with questions such as these in mind:

- What is the argument about?
- What side is the author taking?
- Why is the argument significant?
- What are the separate but related issues being argued?
- How can this argument be resolved?
- What are the consequences of this argument?

Without being an expert on a particular topic, you can use sources to become something of a *local* expert relative to your audience—your classmates and, perhaps, your instructor. Read sources to learn enough about your topic to write with authority. Specifically, read to identify parts, to clarify and confirm the basic procedures, to confirm the reliability of experts, and to identify a debate.

Evaluate and Revise

General Evaluation

You will usually need at least two drafts to produce an essay that presents your idea clearly. The biggest changes in your essay will typically come between your first and second drafts. In this book you will find two demonstrations of essays in the process of turning from meandering first thoughts into finished products. First, see the general advice on the process of writing and revising in chapters 13 and 14, which includes first- and second-draft versions of a student essay. You will find another such demonstration in chapter 1. No essay you write, including an explanatory essay, will be complete until you revise and refine its single compelling idea.

You revise and refine by evaluating your first draft, bringing to it many of the same questions you pose when evaluating any piece of writing. In chapter 5 you will find general guidelines for evaluating what you read, including:

- Are the facts accurate?
- Are opinions supported by evidence?
- Are the opinions of others authoritative?
- Are my assumptions clearly stated?
- Are key terms clearly defined?
- Is the presentation logical?
- Are all parts of the presentation well developed?

Address these same questions to the first draft of your essay, and the answers will give you solid information by which to guide a revision.

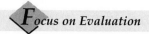

Have you been asked to write an evaluation of another writer's essay of explanation? If so, you will base your evaluation on two sets of standards. First, you will apply specific standards for this type of writing as listed here in "Critical Points." At the same time, you will need to apply the general standards for evaluation that are listed here and discussed at length in chapter 5, pages 92–96. See especially the "key points" for evaluation in chapter 5, pages 95–96.

Critical Points in an Explanatory Essay

An essay of explanation, above all, must be useful to readers. *Usefulness* is the single most important criterion, so to the extent possible reread your drafts from your readers' point of view. Pose these questions:

- Is the idea of this explanation clear?
- What are the parts of this explanation?
- How are these parts related to each other and, simultaneously, to the larger idea?
- How closely are the language and the examples of this explanation matched to the readers' abilities and interests?
- What will readers understand or be able to do, having read this explanation?

Read and revise the drafts of your explanatory essays until you can answer these questions to what you think will be your readers' satisfaction. These same questions can be put to use when evaluating any essay of explanation.

Occasions for Discussion and Writing

An Explanatory Essay of Your Own

You are ready to begin work on your own explanatory essay. One approach to choosing a topic is to review examples of the type of essay you will be writing. Consider rereading the essays that opened this chapter. You will find that the four authors—Curtis, the (anonymous) author of "Credit and Loans," Kind, and Pinto—write about topics they know well either through direct experience or through careful reading. You will also find that two of these authors have a deep, personal involvement with their essay's topic: Stuart Kind writes on his profession, forensic science; Josefa Pinto writes on increasing agricultural yields for her native country. In choosing a topic for your essay, you too can take a deep interest. In the best of cases, your motivation to write will be personal but your expression of ideas *in your essay* will be public and controlled. The Kind and Pinto examples amply demonstrate this double quality: in each essay you find someone writing for personal reasons, yet maintaining strict control over important elements of public expression—including the essay's reasoning, structure, sentence rhythm, and word choice.

To prepare for your explanatory essay, select one of the examples that began this chapter, one that you find especially effective. Think critically about how this essay succeeds. You might respond to the questions following the piece; you might try writing a paragraph explaining what appeals to you most about the piece; you might reflect on the ways in which this essay could affect your own work. Once you have studied the piece and have a clear sense of how it succeeds, choose a topic for your own essay—a topic that you know well.

The Occasions sections present two topics for writing: the rising costs of college and the college admissions process. If you prefer another topic, you might find suitable materials in the other Occasions sections in chapters 6 and 8–11:

Chapter 6: Date Rape and Campus Policy, 135–141
            Exploring Gender Identity, 142–164
Chapter 8: Analyzing the Content of Advertising, 257–264
            Analyzing the Content of Television Shows, 264–280
Chapter 9: High-School Dress Codes, 318–322
            Community Tensions (The Riots at Crown Heights), 322–341
Chapter 10: Poems by Langston Hughes, 374–380
            Short Stories by Kate Chopin, James Joyce, 380–402
Chapter 11: Television and Literacy, 445–455
            Cultural Consequences of Technology, 455–484

Of course, you are not limited to these choices and should choose a topic according to your interests and experience. For detailed guidance on how you might organize your approach to writing an explanatory essay, turn to the second Occasion for discussion and writing in this chapter, pages 224–230. That "Guide to the Assignment" provides a structured approach to the writing task that may help you work through your first draft and revision, whatever your topic.

A note on using sources: Three of the four writers whose essays began the chapter draw on source materials to advance their ideas. You can—and are encouraged to—do the same, with the caution that writers who use sources should never let source materials overtake their essays. The psychological focus of your essay should remain yours alone. In writing a first draft, be sure that your voice predominates and that sources, even if essential to your essay's success, play a subordinate role.

I. The Rising Costs of College

You need no introduction to the sticker shock that greets students seeking a college diploma. Four-year, public colleges cost on average $8000 per year for students who live on campus; the price is $17,000 for students at private four-year schools. If present trends continue, the cost for a diploma in the year 2000 will range from $75,000 to $300,000. Neither institutions nor individual students can soon expect relief from the intense financial pressures besetting higher education, according to Daniel Cheever, Jr., former president of Wheelock College, who addresses these matters in his essay "Higher and Higher Ed."

Cheever argues that the time has come "to ask basic questions, to conceptualize fundamentally different ways—less costly ways—of providing education." The argument follows a classic problem/solution format (see chapter 9): We have a problem, he insists, and we can resolve that problem only by taking certain actions. In the first part of such an essay, a writer must explain or argue that a problem exists. It is so apparent that the cost of college education is problematic that Cheever does not need to argue in this case. His readers readily concede the point and follow him through his explanation to learn just how serious the problem is.

Cheever's essay is followed by a second piece on the same topic, titled "Tuition at Public Colleges Is Up." Jean Evangelauf, writing for *The Chronicle of Higher Education*, reports on the latest cost figures from The College Board, which tracks tuition figures at more than 3,000 colleges and universities. In addition to her essay, Evangelauf provides summary information in tabular form that you should find useful. You have the following tasks in responding to these materials. First, read the selections with care. Working by yourself, do the following:

- Summarize the main idea of each selection. Evangelauf has written an explanatory article; Cheever has written an argumentative one.
- Identify where in his article Cheever is explaining and identify *how* he is explaining. Mark the point at which he turns to argument.

Having done this, work in small groups and use the information from Evangelauf's article to check the accuracy of assumptions and information in Cheever's article. Evaluate the effectiveness of Cheever's explanations and then work on sketching an explanatory essay on a topic related to the cost of college education.

Higher and Higher Ed

Daniel S. Cheever, Jr.

Daniel S. Cheever Jr. is president of Massachusetts Higher Education Assistance Corporation, a guarantor for federal student loans. He was president of Wheelock College from 1983 to 1991.

Many, perhaps most, of today's kindergarten students will not be able to go to college. When they are ready 12 years from now, a college education will cost more than almost any American family can afford. 1

How much will college cost when today's kindergartener is ready to attend? Four years at a first-rate private institution like Harvard could cost $267,000 unadjusted for inflation—$75,000 for the senior year alone—if tuition, fees, books and housing expenses increase only 7 percent annually. If annual increases are 8 percent, which has been the average rate of increase over the last 20 years, then four years at Harvard, Boston University, Lehigh and many other private universities will cost more than $300,000. Tuition for the senior year will be $85,000. 2

Costs at more typical liberal arts or comprehensive private colleges will be less, but not much less. Using the College Board's average annual total expenses, a degree at these colleges will cost $175,000 to $200,000, with senior-year tuition of $50,000 or more. And there are far more colleges with total costs closer to those of Harvard than one might think. 3

It will be cheaper to attend a public university, but still very expensive. The total cost of educating a student at a public institution is not much less than at a private college. Tuition is lower because the taxpayer picks up about 80 percent of the tab. Even with the taxpayer's subsidy, if today's kindergartener chooses to attend the University of Massachusetts, it would cost that student $75,000 for four years and the taxpayer four times that amount. 4

These numbers don't even cover the total cost of educating a student at either a public or private college. Much of the total cost is not passed on to the student because it is covered by funds from other sources: endowment income, annual giving, research grants, income from other operations and, at public colleges, state appropriations. At some universities, tuition and fees are less than one-half of the actual cost of education. Thus to educate today's kindergartener at Harvard may cost more than $600,000, of which the student will be charged $267,000 to $300,000 depending on how fast tuition rises in the next 12 years. 5

The bad news gets worse. These projections may err on the low side. Tuition increases may be higher than 7 percent annually, and could very likely consume a greater portion of family income in any event. Real wages, adjusted for inflation, have fallen 19 percent since 1972 for nonsupervising workers. For middle-class families, median family income adjusted for inflation has risen only 6

$2,000 since 1970, and that small gain is largely because of the entry of women into the labor market. From 1980 to 1987, after adjusting for inflation, family incomes rose only 6 percent, while tuition increased 30 percent, five times as much. And most colleges today point to unmet financial needs that could drive tuition even higher than 7 percent per year: deferred maintenance, faculty salaries, employee benefits, greater amounts of financial aid from institutional revenues and the recruitment of underrepresented populations.

For a college to cost less than these projected amounts would require sev- 7 eral improbable events to occur. Annual increases would have to average less than 7 percent, which seems unlikely given past history and current financial pressures. Exceptions exist: Boston University has announced a tuition increase of only 4 percent and no increase in room and board charges for next year. But tight price control of this nature can last for only two or three years, and, given past history and unmet future needs, 4 percent is very unlikely to be the average increase over the next 12 years even with low inflation.

Higher education is labor-intensive. Therefore, it faces strong upward pres- 8 sure for its "people costs": salary increases, new positions, office space and support staff, technical support staff for scientific and administrative computer functions, increased medical premiums and expenses for other benefit programs ranging from day care to workman's compensation. Much of its labor force is senior in years of service, and therefore expensive, as well as tenured. Many futurists predict these expense pressures for "people costs" will intensify during the next decade, not diminish. Thus it is unlikely that cost pressures on college campuses will diminish.

Limiting annual increases in tuition and fees to less than 7 percent also 9 would require making tough choices. Higher education is highly decentralized with faculties retaining much control over curriculum and course requirements, which therefore set requirements for staffing. In a collegial environment, both faculty and administrative decision makers find it hard to choose among competing priorities, with the danger that all priorities may be deemed important, the cost added up, and the bill sent to students.

Public institutions have a special problem in addition to the inherent pres- 10 sures to increase costs faced by all colleges. Public institutions are dependent on public appropriations from state legislatures. Presently 30 states have serious budget deficits, and many already have slashed state tax funds appropriated for higher-education operating expenses. Higher-education funding nationally has dropped from 8.3 percent of state spending in 1982 to 6.9 percent in 1991. The downward spiral is accelerating. In New England, for example, state tax appropriations fell 4.5 percent in 1991 and have fallen almost 7 percent since 1990. In Massachusetts, some public campuses have endured budget cuts of over 30 percent, and the overall state budget for higher education has been slashed from $780 million to $484 million in only three years. Now, higher education must compete for funds as never before. Gary Cox, executive director of the Kentucky Council on Higher Education, warns, "Do you put people out of nursing homes to pay for higher education? It's a terrible choice."

What will happen when a public institution like the University of Massa- 11 chusetts, the University of Vermont or the University of California charges the student $75,000 to $100,000 and a private institution like Harvard or Lehigh charges anywhere from $270,000 to $300,000? Some students will still attend college, a few of them because they will come from families of substantial wealth and more because they and their families will have borrowed to the absolute limit. But no proposals currently in Congress to reauthorize student aid programs include increases in student grant and loan eligibility sufficient to provide the money for tomorrow's college bills.

Some will argue that these tuition and fee projections are simplistic or too 12 gloomy, that family incomes will rise sufficiently to keep college affordable, or that colleges will be able to reduce prices. Perhaps. But in the period from the mid-1970s to the late 1980s, the average tuition (not counting room and board) at private institutions rose from 16 percent to 22 percent of family income, a jump of almost 50 percent. Public institutions fared better; average tuitions rose from only 4.1 percent to 4.8 percent of family income, but this was still an increase of 17 percent. And when the taxpayer's burden is included, then public education costs also become a large and increasing percentage of the taxpayer's family income.

The National-Economy Factor

Michael S. McPherson and Morton O. Shapiro, two Williams College econo- 13 mists, assert that the affordability of college will depend most on strong performance by the American economy, which would boost family income and increase federal and state support for higher education. But few economists predict a robust US economy for the next 12 years. And despite many periods of real economic growth since 1940, McPherson and Shapiro point to "a persistent tendency for college costs to grow more rapidly than inflation." That trend cannot continue forever without college becoming unaffordable for most Americans.

As larger and larger numbers of students are denied the chance to go to 14 college, some colleges will close. Their campuses will resemble today's abandoned manufacturing plants. Other colleges will have to merge. Ironically, colleges have struggled through a long-term decline of 25 percent in the traditional college-age population, a decline that finally bottoms out in two years and then rises slightly. Enrollments actually have risen, thanks in part to admission of more non-traditional and part-time students. But that market may be saturated, and just as colleges think they have survived this drop in their applicant pool, the second whammy will hit them, as students decide not to apply because they cannot afford higher education or because they have chosen the community college close to home.

What can colleges do to avoid being hurt when their speculative bubble 15 bursts, as it inevitably will when families realize they cannot afford the public or private tuitions of tomorrow? Some educators have advanced imaginative proposals such as reorganizing the undergraduate curriculum so that a bachelors degree can be achieved in three years instead of four. Such proposals are unlikely to be adopted. Students and their families will resent being deprived of 25 percent of what previously had been deemed necessary for undergraduate education. Already some critics believe that higher education has curtailed students' time on campus far too much.

Other proposals such as income-contingent loans or college-savings IRAs 16 may be taken more seriously. But they face political and financial hurdles that may take years to resolve, and tuitions will march upward in the meantime. The public continues to oppose new taxes, which is how income-contingent proposals will be perceived. (Income-contingent loans are based on the recipient's income; the repayment schedule begins at small amounts and as the student's earnings increase over time, the repayments also increase.) Thus it seems improbable that higher education can quickly win public support for a new $2,700 tax on a $40,000 income, which is what one income-contingent plan would require. The federal deficit poses an obstacle to quick passage of deferred-financing proposals like college IRAs, and even they would not permit enough capital to accumulate to pay a $300,000 tuition bill.

Cost-Cutting Now Underway

Most colleges will cut costs to avoid catastrophe. Many have already begun to do so. Yale has laid off 100 staff, and a faculty committee recommends further cuts of 10 percent of its academic programs (and Yale still faces $1 billion in deferred maintenance). Boston University will trim $20 million from a $600 million operating budget. Northeastern is seeking $40 million in cuts, and department chairs at Columbia have told the administration they will not participate in further budget cuts to reduce the still-remaining $30 million deficit. But cutting costs works only for a year or two before it bumps up against fundamental questions about how colleges are organized to accomplish their purpose. [17]

Cut-and-slash budget reduction creates other problems, too. Students are hurt. As courses are eliminated or postponed, for example, students suddenly discover they cannot get the courses necessary to complete a program or graduate. Reportedly, on some campuses students who have completed (and paid for) four years of full-time study do not have diplomas. On others, students cannot gain admission to financially-strapped colleges. "If we get no more money, we'll take no more students," declared the chancellor of the California State University system. [18]

Cost-cutting alone will not work because, in the absence of a new vision, it is not a long-term solution. After a year or two of serious cost-cutting, many colleges will face again the relentless upward pressure to increase expenses, albeit from a lower base. Tuitions will resume their steady rise, and, eventually, families or taxpayers will not be able to afford higher education once again. [19]

That is why real long-term savings can only come from restructuring how colleges are organized to accomplish their purposes. Some of our great research universities and a few PhD-granting institutions may be able to survive in their present form, but most other colleges will need to face basic questions about faculty-student ratios, teaching loads, the length of the academic year, the real value of research or scholarship activity and the administrative services that they can afford to offer students and employees. "You've got to either change, or you'll lose," is how Boston College's dean of enrollment describes it. [20]

The colleges that survive will he those that change in fundamental ways, those that figure out how to reorganize and restructure the delivery of their curriculum and administrative services at far less cost without sacrificing quality. To do so, they will need vision and courage. [21]

Restructuring: How and Where?

How to restructure? No one really knows. All we know is that we must try if we are to avoid tomorrow's financial crisis in higher education and preserve equal opportunity for all who qualify for admission. There may be success stories already, just waiting to be told. More likely, each campus will have to create its own program to reduce costs without undue harm to quality. That's why one place where money could be spent usefully is in support of innovative pilot programs to restructure or develop new models of higher education. Consortia of universities could be encouraged to collaborate instead of compete, and colleges [22] could benefit from grants to act as "shock absorbers" as they make the transition to different, less costly institutions.

Where to restructure? Everywhere. Research conducted by the Pew Charitable Trust, the US Department of Education and others report that the fastest-growing segment of higher-education budgets has been administrative costs. The upward pressure on tuition rates flows from the proliferation of administrative functions and departments. Some of this proliferation results from colleges' attempts to respond to new needs; increasingly, for example, colleges are asked to attend to the emotional health of their students, which has led to expansion of counseling and other programs in student development. Other administrative programs have emerged to fill gaps caused by faculty abdication of traditional faculty roles. On many campuses, faculty used to advise their students, but increasingly the faculty has reduced its academic advising. By default, advising has become an administrative function coordinated by an expensive administrative office. Still other administrative functions are responses to increased regulation of higher education by federal and state government. All these, and more, need to be restructured to reduce costs on a long-term permanent basis. That will require a willingness of all partners—government, students, families, faculty and staff—to accept less from the institution or to do more for it. 23

The public will need to be vigilant about one tempting money-saving measure. It is a lot cheaper to have courses taught by teaching assistants or part-time faculty than by professors or full-time faculty, but the negative consequences for students and for the academy can be high if the primary reason is cost-saving rather than the opportunity to bring unusually talented people to the faculty. 24

The future also may see specialization and differentiation among colleges. Liberal arts colleges will stop emulating comprehensive institutions or even each other, in contrast to the expansionist dreams of the 1970s and 1980s, which turned some undistinguished public or private colleges into "universities" in name only. In the '90s, campuses will develop and emphasize their separateness rather than their similarity. A major new center on one campus will not be matched by its neighbor; rather, comparable effort and money might go into innovative programs in another area or simply not be spent. Some successful colleges of the future will have focused on their core business and appealed to far narrower market segments to avoid a duplication of program and expense, which propels tuitions upward. 25

The Role of Technology

Technology, also, will command a central role in the successful restructuring of visionary institutions. Many colleges have made enormous investments in technology, particularly computers, for everything from library resources to laboratory experiments. There have been great educational benefits. But this investment has not yet transformed the fundamental way—and cost—of how courses are taught. Professors lecture, students listen, teaching assistants or junior faculty lead discussion groups of sections, students read—the basic economic model is not so different from the 1960s or the 1950s despite this investment in technology. 26

The future also will see concentrated efforts to increase government funding for higher education. At the federal level, increased grant limits and eligibility as well as expansion of the student-loan program seem inevitable. At state 27 levels, higher education will focus on gaining a larger share of the state revenue pie despite intense competition from other interests. Ironically, providing more money both helps and also makes the situation worse. By providing greater capital, we may remove whatever restraint exists to limit tuition increases.

While some may dispute some of the specific projections cited above, it 28 seems likely that every reader would agree that higher education has a serious institution-threatening problem. The cost of a college education already is very high and seems likely to continue increasing faster than annual increases in inflation and family income. This trend, which has existed for many years and caused today's problem, cannot continue forever. Both public and private institutions will cost too much for many families to afford. Furthermore, it seems unlikely that adequate relief will come from either federal or state governments. One or the other may provide some financial assistance, but it seems unrealistic to expect that these sources alone will solve our problem. Higher education has to solve its own problems.

Already most colleges are looking carefully at ways to cut costs. But this 29 cost-cutting is not examining basic questions about how a college is organized to provide for the advancement of knowledge and student learning. It is time to ask basic questions, to conceptualize fundamentally different ways—less costly ways—of providing education. Higher education will have to make hard choices. It will not be able to satisfy every need or respond to every constituent. The colleges that ask, and answer, basic questions about how to educate students in less expensive ways will be the colleges that survive.

Tuition at Public Colleges Is Up

Jean Evangelauf

Jean Evangelauf, a journalist, wrote this article for The Chronicle of Higher Education *(21 Oct. 92).*

Tuition at public colleges and universities climbed at double-digit rates for the 1 second year in a row, increasing three times as fast as the rate of inflation.

Figures released last week by the College Board show that undergraduate 2 tuition and required fees at public four-year institutions average $2,315 this year, 10 percent more than last year. At public two-year colleges, tuition also rose 10 percent, to an average of $1,292. Those increases represent a slowdown from last year's increases of 12 percent and 13 percent, respectively.

For the 12 months ending in September, the Consumer Price Index in- 3 creased 3 percent. The Higher Education Price Index also went up 3 percent during the last year. That index, which tracks the cost of goods and services purchased by colleges, is compiled by Research Associates of Washington, a company that specializes in research on education finance.

"Given the state of the economy and its impact on state budgets, many peo- 4 ple expected much larger increases this year, particularly in the public sector," said Donald M. Stewart, the board's president, in a statement accompanying its annual tuition report.

Many financially strapped public colleges in such states as California and 5 New York raised tuition substantially this year to make up for shortfalls in state support. Over all, state appropriations for higher education are 1 percent below the level of two years ago.

Seventeen states, including some with the largest public-college enrollment, are supplying less money to colleges this year than they did in 1990–91. 6

Private colleges kept their percentage increases in tuition to last year's lev- 7 els. At private four-year institutions, tuition again went up 7 percent to an average of $10,498. At private two-year colleges, tuition rose to 6 percent, to an average of $5,621.

"Facing Extraordinary Pressure"

Despite the sharp increases, public-college tuition remains a "bargain," accord- 8 ing to Kent Halstead, director of Research Associates. He said his analysis showed that public-college students had paid about 28 percent of full instructional costs in 1991–92, up from about 21 percent in the late 1970's.

"Where else can you buy anything that provides such immediate direct ben- 9 efits to you as an individual and pay less than one-third of the cost?" he asked.

However, both he and others expressed fear that spiraling tuition increases 10 could shut low-income people out of college.

"We're all concerned about the heavy increases in tuition," said C. Peter 11 McGrath, president of the National Association of State Universities and Land-Grant Colleges. "We need the public to understand that if tuition increases get too burdensome, there is a real danger that access and opportunity will be cut back."

He noted that states were having difficulty juggling competing demands in 12 their limited budgets. "Colleges have to cut back and be as flinty-eyed as possi-

Average College Costs This Year

	Public colleges		Private colleges	
	Resident	Commuter	Resident	Commuter
4-year colleges				
Tuition and fees	$2,315	$2,315	$10,498	$10,498
Books and supplies	528	528	531	531
Room and board*	3,526	1,549	4,575	1,762
Transportation	497	843	487	794
Other	1,205	1,238	936	1,036
Total	$8,071	$6,473	$17,027	$14,621
2-year colleges				
Tuition and fees	$1,292	$1,292	$ 5,621	$ 5,621
Books and supplies	502	502	512	512
Room and board*	—	1,592	3,750	1,558
Transportation	—	926	517	812
Other	—	970	866	941
Total	—	$5,282	$11,266	$ 9,444

Note: The figures are weighted by enrollment to reflect the charges incurred by the average undergraduate enrolled at each type of institution.
*   Room not included for commuter students
—   Insufficient data
Source: The College Board

Year-by-Year Changes in Tuition and Fees at 4-Year Institutions

	Public	Private
1982–83	+20%	+13%
1983–84	+12	+11
1984–85	+ 8	+ 9
1985–86	+ 9	+ 8
1986–87	+ 6	+ 8
1987–88	+ 6	+ 8
1988–89	+ 5	+ 9
1989–90	+ 7	+ 9
1990–91	+ 7	+ 8
1991–92	+12	+ 7
1992–93	+10	+ 7

Note: Beginning in 1987–88, data are weighted by enrollment.

Source: The College Board

ble, to make sure they aren't spending scarce resources in ways that aren't helpful," Mr. McGrath said.

Private colleges are facing "absolutely extraordinary pressure" this year 13 because they are trying to hold down their tuition increases and provide aid to needy students, said Richard F. Rosser, president of the National Association of Independent Colleges and Universities.

Private colleges need help in making higher education available to low- 14 income students, he said. "The federal and state governments should be doing this, but they are falling down in their responsibility," he said. He criticized the federal government for failing to increase spending on Pell Grants, the major source of aid for needy undergraduates.

"We've simply got to do a better job of getting people to understand the 15 investment in education has a greater payoff than almost anything else we could do in our country," Mr. Rosser said.

One bright spot in this year's cost report is the slower growth in room and 16 board charges at four-year institutions. Such charges went up 5 percent this year, compared with 6 percent last year. The cost of on-campus housing and meals averages $4,575 at private colleges, and $3,526 at public ones.

Over all, the total budget for students who live in campus housing, includ- 17 ing the cost of tuition and fees, room and board, books and supplies, transportation, and other expenses, averages $8,071 at public four-year institutions, $17,027 at private four-year colleges, and $11,266 at private two-year colleges. Figures for resident students at public community colleges are not available because of insufficient data.

The average total budget for commuter students ranges from $5,282 at 18 public two-year colleges to $14,621 at private four-year colleges.

Figures Weighted by Enrollment

The College Board averages are based on the reports of 2,181 colleges and uni- 19 versities that provided cost information for both 1991–92 and 1992–93. The colleges were asked to give information on the tuition and fees charged to first-

Range of 1992–93 Tuition at 4-Year Colleges

	Number of colleges	Average tuition and fee	Percentage of total enrollment
Private Institutions			
$15,000 or more	100	$16,661	15.6%
14,000–14,999	29	14,533	3.1
13,000–13,999	34	13,444	3.3
12,000–12,999	61	12,447	6.0
11,000–11,999	82	11,492	8.0
10,000–10,999	104	10,442	10.6
9,000– 9,999	110	9,529	10.5
8,000– 8,999	138	8,483	10.0
7,000– 7,999	118	7,466	7.7
6,000– 6,999	97	6,480	6.7
5,000– 5,999	84	5,498	4.7
4,000– 4,999	84	4,477	5.2
3,000– 3,999	66	3,576	2.0
2,000– 2,999	45	2,556	5.5
1,000– 1,999	7	1,621	0.1
Less than $1,000	10	457	1.0
Total	1,169	—	100.0%
Public Institutions			
$3,000 or more	96	$ 3,689	17.8%
2,500–2,999	107	2,745	20.9
2,000–2,499	84	2,236	15.6
1,500–1,999	150	1,718	25.5
1,000–1,499	100	1,344	18.8
Less than $1,000	17	873	1.4
Total	554	—	100.0%

Note: Includes only those institutions that provided final or estimated 1992–93 tuition and fees by September 10, 1992.
Source: The College Board

year, full-time undergraduates based on a nine-month academic year of 30 semester hours or 45 quarter hours. The figures are weighted by enrollment to reflect the costs incurred by the average undergraduate.

In addition to the tuition charged to resident students, out-of-state students attending public institutions are charged an average tuition supplement of $3,668 at four-year colleges and $2,440 at two-year colleges. Those figures are not weighted by enrollment.

One hundred institutions are charging tuition and required fees of $15,000 or higher this year, exclusive of room and board, according to the College Board. Landmark College, which provides education to students with learning disabilities, is the nation's most costly institution, with tuition and required fees of $21,200. Other expensive institutions include Bennington College ($19,780), Hampshire College ($19,030), Tufts University ($18,344), and Reed College ($18,190).

In its report the College Board also calculated the 1992–93 tuition without 22 taking enrollment into account, to show the costs charged by the average institution. Both approaches give similar tuition averages for all institutions except private four-year institutions. The unweighted tuition average for such colleges is $8,879, reflecting the fact that enrollments are larger at the more-expensive private colleges.

Individual Response: The Rising Costs of College

Read the two selections, "Higher and Higher Ed" and "Tuition at Public Colleges Is Up."

1. Write a one-paragraph summary of each selection (see pages 81–87 for a discussion on writing summaries).

2. Cheever devotes a considerable part of his essay to explanation. Identify where he explains and the various techniques by which he explains. See the Structures and Strategies section (pages 180–193), where you will find a discussion of the following techniques for explanation: historical review, description, example, sequential order/process, definition, division and classification, and comparison/contrast.

3. Read Evangelauf closely and highlight information that you think could help you to confirm the accuracy of Cheever's essay. Consider Evangelauf's article as a resource that can add to or detract from your confidence in Cheever.

Group Response: The Rising Costs of College

1. As a group, agree on where Cheever develops the idea of his essay through explanation. Because this is a lengthy selection, you may want to divide the work as follows: Cheever's introduction and first section, "The National-Economy Factor," "Cost-Cutting Now Underway," "Restructuring: How and Where?" and "The Role of Technology" (through to the end).

2. As a group, identify Cheever's techniques for explaining the problem of escalating costs. Agree on *how* Cheever explains.

3. As a group, identify points where Evangelauf and Cheever overlap. At what points do these writers discuss the same categories of information? Does information in one source confirm information in the other? For instance, Cheever assumes an annual increase in college costs of 8 percent. Does Evangelauf's article confirm this assumption?

4. As a group, review notes you have made on the explanatory parts of Cheever's essay and reach some consensus about the quality of Cheever's explanation. How effective a job has he done in explaining the rising costs of college? For guidance on evaluating explanations, see the discussion on in the Structures and Strategies section of this chapter, pages 198–199.

Projecting an Essay: The Rising Costs of College

1. Generate a list of topics related to the rising cost of college that you would like to have explained. Choose a general topic. Have each group member locate two sources on this topic.

2. Working with materials the group has generated, define a *specific* topic that could be explained in a brief essay. Divide this topic into parts (see page 187).

3. Each group member should outline an explanation for one part of this topic. (For possible strategies, see the Structures and Strategies discussion on development, pages 187–193.) The outline should suggest the types of information that would ideally be included in an explanation of this part. If the sources the group has assembled provide this information, so much the better: refer to a source and to a page number. If the group's sources do not provide the information, simply suggest in the outline what material would be needed. Do not conduct further research at this point.

4. Meet to consider how the parts that have been developed in outline form might be worked together to become an explanatory essay. First decide on a thesis. Quiz this thesis and determine the parts of an essay that would follow from it (see pages 61–63). Assume an audience of students who have not read either Cheever or Evangelauf.

5. Prepare an outline of your group's explanatory essay.

6. Option: Conduct the research needed to complete the essay, and then write a draft.

II. Choosing a College

When did you first begin to think about college, not as some distant possibility but as a *real* place that your would have to choose? Were you fifteen, sixteen? At the time, did you feel experienced enough to make momentous decisions about your future? Now that you are situated at a college, do you in retrospect think you were experienced enough? What were your needs in looking for a school? What were your questions? Did you know enough about college life, both intellectual and social, to have good questions? And who were your counselors, both official and unofficial? Were the teachers and guidance professionals at your high school knowledgeable? Did you welcome your parents into the decision-making process? Did you ever feel vaguely embarrassed by their presence on campus visits? How significantly did the rising cost of college and its financing figure into your planning?[1]

These and related questions, which you have so recently puzzled through, form the substance of this Occasions section. The following selections concern the process of college admissions: advice given by both professional counselors and students. Your larger purpose in reading is to

---

[1]On this point, see the articles in the preceding section.

reflect on the process that led to your choosing a specific school. Two of the readings were written by active deans of admission at four-year colleges; one was written by a professional counselor who runs his own advisory agency for students choosing schools; one selection was written by students at the *Yale Daily News*; and another was compiled by guidance counselors at a public high school in Massachusetts. These readings share an assumption that the process of choosing a college can be confusing and stressful, as well as rewarding when a good match is found between a school and a student's interests and abilities. Now that you are attending college, you are in a unique position to reread representative passages from college guides in light of your own decision-making process.

Your Writing Assignment

Prompted by your reading of the selections in this Occasions section, reflect on the decision-making process that led to your choosing a college. Reconstruct this process for students who are now juniors at your old high school. Having explained what led you to your decision, can you recommend your process to others who will soon be applying to colleges themselves? What worked for you in your selection process, and what didn't work? Your purpose in this essay is primarily to explore and explain; but having done this, you will have earned the right to judge your strategies. Seriously consider submitting this essay to your former high-school's newspaper. Others can benefit from both your experience and your self-criticism.

Getting Started on Choosing Colleges
William M. Shain

William M. Shain is Dean of Admission at Macalester College in St. Paul, Minnesota. In this brief essay, Shain has assembled for parents and their sons and daughters "a list of mistakes [he's] seen students make in applying to colleges, along with ways to avoid" them. As you read, reflect on your own experiences in applying to college. Did you make any of the errors that Shain discusses? More generally, to what extent do you think it is possible to avoid errors before making them?

Twenty-five years ago, when I graduated from secondary school, choosing a 1
college was a relatively simple proposition. I visited half a dozen schools, all within two hundred miles of home, and paid little attention to the six pieces of unsolicited mail I received from other institutions of higher education. My idea of a thoughtful application strategy was to apply to three schools, all of them in the Ivy League.

    The world has changed a lot in more than two decades, and the field of col- 2
lege admission certainly shows it. Students now begin thinking about college as early as junior high school, and I have even talked with parents of students as young as first grade! A student of any ability level can expect to receive enough

promotional material from colleges to fill a few shopping bags. And the most selective institutions in the country are now twice as hard to get into as they were when I applied.

This situation puts a heavy burden on students choosing a college, as well   3
as on their families and on the colleges. Much of the resulting anxiety and intensity, however, can be eased if a student simply uses common sense. To help, I have assembled a list of mistakes I've seen students make in applying to colleges, along with ways to avoid these common errors. Share this list with your teen.

Don't attempt to change yourself to fit the college. First of all, the search   4
for the perfect college must begin with the old adage "Know thyself." Too often, I see students trying to present themselves—or change themselves—to match a particular college or university. This posture strikes me as risky and even irrational. The point of choosing a college is to find an institution that meets your needs, rather than to sacrifice your sense of self on some institutional altar. The risk, of course, is that you end up at a college far less suited to your personality and learning needs than the school you might have found by a more thoughtful search process.

The best way to find this proverbial "fit" between student and institution is   5
to present yourself as accurately as possible throughout the college admission process. This not only will enable an institution to get a better sense of whether or not you are likely to flourish on its campus but may even enhance your chances for admission. Back when I was a high school teacher, one overzealous parent completely rewrote her son's college application, including the essays. The result was a marvelously articulate and sophisticated presentation, with superb polish and tone. However, all of us who wrote recommendations for the student honestly described a candidate whose verbal abilities were ordinary but who had some special strengths: warmth, curiosity, creativity, and humor. These qualities were abundantly evident in the essay the student had written, but Mom had found the information frightening and had vetoed it. The resulting hybridized file ended up faring less well than I would have predicted had the student done his own work.

Don't abandon common sense in investigating colleges. It is important   6
that you use simple good sense in evaluating colleges and universities Once you have set your personal criteria, your investigation should be active and should include a campus visit where possible. It is also important to remember that just as an applicant does not want to be evaluated solely on the basis of his or her SAT scores, so a college does not want to be evaluated solely on the basis of its students' average SAT scores. Actually, you should be careful about making distinctions between institutions with generally similar statistics, since no two institutions compute admission or other data in exactly the same way.

Don't let yourself be excessively influenced by college guidebooks. Good   7
sense also dictates using some discretion with college guidebooks, which in general seem to range in value from the somewhat worthwhile to the downright misleading. Remember that few publications annually update all data for all institutions covered. Be skeptical of figures that seem unusual compared to those of other institutions, and inquire how the institution involved has computed, for example, a claim that 90 percent of each senior class goes on to graduate school. And, of course, although the guidebooks that evaluate colleges are often fun to read, they are also judgmental. Their conclusions may well be based on values other than your own. just as you maintain a healthy skepticism about

restaurant and movie reviews, remember that you should use your own judgment concerning reviews of educational institutions as well.

Don't spend too much time and effort in trying to gain a "competitive 8 *edge" in the college admission process.* The onset of the college admission process shouldn't lead you to change your general approach to life. I find it distressing that so many students seem to mortgage their junior and senior years to getting into college. They attend counseling sessions and visit colleges, both good uses of their time. But they also take practice SATs repeatedly, spend huge amounts of their spare time on review courses of various sorts, and sometimes even work with independent college counselors when their own school already offers excellent college guidance. A heavy dose of these activities erodes the exuberance of the last two years of secondary school. Ironically, these activities may also indirectly reduce a student' chances of admission. Most selective institutions base their decision on ratings that include both academic and extracurricular factors. Six to ten hours a week of college admission cramming takes time away from both course work and activities and can easily reduce a student's level of achievement in the very areas that colleges evaluate when making their admission decisions. And why live in a crisis mode for two years? If the same time and energy were devoted to traditional school activities, an application file might, in fact, become stronger.

Don't let the results of the college admission process affect your self- 9 *esteem.* Retain your normal perspective about yourself and your world throughout the college admission process. In our admission office at Macalester, we try to use terms like *denial of admission* rather than *rejection,* since the latter term has emotional overtones that are not really appropriate to the decision we made. An admission decision is made on a *file,* not on a person. No admission process can accurately rank several thousand adolescents. Almost without exception, admission offices are populated by earnest, hardworking educators doing the best they can, but every office on occasion will underrate a student who ends up a Rhodes scholar somewhere else or will offer admission to a student whose years on campus turn out to be substandard in every respect. It seems both sane and healthy for students and their families to retain a mature perspective on what actually happens in the admission process, and not to take the results—positive or negative—too much to heart.

Don't compromise your integrity in your interactions with colleges. 10 Most important of all, students and their families should hold fast at all times to their normally high standards of ethical behavior. This means that applications should be accurate in word *and* spirit. You should not apply to more than one early decision plan if each requires you to enroll if admitted. And since an enrollment deposit (or other type of matriculation commitment) is a binding promise to attend a college, it is unethical to promise to attend more than one college or university.

Finally, the best antidote to the anxieties of a college search is for families 11 to function normally. The college admission process can be a largely enjoyable mutual endeavor. Campus visits, especially during the summer, can be interesting trips for the entire family, and you can profitably compare your perceptions of a campus with those of other family members. Several individuals working together can generate more and better questions to ask an admission officer— at a campus visit or in a letter—than can one person operating independently.

In general, I recommend that students and parents see college admission as   12
an extension of normal living. Families should work together as they normally
do, students should continue the school patterns that have always served them
well, and most of all, families should evaluate institutions carefully through the
filter of their own values. When a normal routine is combined with a thoughtful
and persistent search for good information, the chances are pretty close to 100
percent that the entire college admission process will end well and be enjoyable
along the way.

The Insider's Guide to the Colleges: Getting In
The Staff of the Yale Daily News

*Working on the assumption that the people prospective college students need
to hear from most are* actual *college students, the staff of the* Yale Daily News
compiled their Insider's Guide to the Colleges, *in which the following excerpt
appears. "Getting In" differs significantly in tone and approach from the other
selections in this section in that the writers regard the application process as
something of a game to be played. Nonetheless, these student writers do not for
an instant underestimate the seriousness or the importance of this game, and
they encourage student readers of their guide to adopt a strategy that will lead
to a reasoned choice. As you read the frank appraisals in this selection (for example, beware of guidance counselors "who want to keep their track records unblemished"), review your own experiences. In retrospect, how helpful to you
would the advice have been from "insiders" at the colleges that appealed to you?*

The task of applying to college can seem as intimidating as the weight of this   1
book. In the spring of your sophomore year in high school your aunt Millie,
whom you haven't seen in three years, pinches your cheek and asks you where
you're going to college. *How should I know,* you think to yourself. That fall, your
mother tells you that the boy down the street with the 4.0 grade point average
is taking the SAT prep course for the fifth time to see if he can get a perfect score
and win millions in scholarship money. You reply that you're late for school. You
keep ducking the subject, but the hints keep coming. With increasing regularity,
dinner table conversations turn toward college. Pretty soon a few of your friends
are visiting the guidance office periodically to talk to counselors or leaf through
college catalogs. Finally, you decide to make an appointment yourself.

When you first talk to your counselor, preferably as soon as possible in your   2
junior year, you may have only just begun to feel comfortable in high school.
College still seems far away, but picking and getting into a good one takes a lot
of work. The earlier you begin the search, the better. A visit to your counselor
is a good way to start. Most are very helpful, but a few should make you wary—
such as those who don't want to disappoint anybody, and those who want to
keep their track records unblemished. The first group will assure you that you
don't have a thing to worry about getting into the college of your choice. Although these counselors may be paying you a hard-earned compliment, it still
pays to read everything you can about the schools that interest you and to follow application procedure carefully. The second group will tell you not to apply
to any school whose admissions they consider "too competitive," and will try to
limit your alternatives. Listen to reason, but trust your instincts. Getting a sense

of how helpful your counselor will be is important. The good ones can be enormously valuable as advisors and confidants throughout the admissions process.

The next step is to read, ask questions, and read some more! Leaf through 3 this book and read about any college that catches your eye. Try to get a general idea of what you're looking for. What do you want in a college? A strong science department? A friendly atmosphere? Or maybe just a great social life? While your academic needs should be your primary concern at the outset, be wary of concentrating on only one or two academic departments and making them the sole basis of your judgments. In college, most people change their mind two or three times before finally settling on a major. If you do change your major midway through your sophomore year, you don't want it to affect the overall quality of your course work or force you to transfer because your college doesn't offer a good program in your new area of interest.

We realize that you can't possibly think of all the angles. No one can say 4 for sure what your interests will be three or four years from now, or what things will ultimately prove most important to you at the college you attend. But by taking a hard look at yourself now, and proceeding carefully as you begin looking at the colleges, you can be reasonably sure that you're investigating the right colleges for the right reasons.

In the early winter of your junior year, you'll receive your PSAT scores . . . 5 Unless you requested otherwise, you'll also be deluged with mail from colleges throughout the nation. The College Search Service of the College Board provides these colleges with the names and addresses of students who scored in various percentiles, and the schools crank out thousands of form letters to those whose scores show promise.

Making sense of your flood of mail may at first seem impossible. Glossy 6 brochures tend to portray a diverse group of beaming students frolicking happily and thinking deep thoughts on every page. "They're all the same," recalled one college freshman, happy to be finished with the process. Each brochure speaks of "rich diversity" and "academic rigor" and dozens of other high-minded ideals that are often in reality nothing more than hollow catch-phrases. Likewise, any campus can look beautiful through the lens of an admissions office photographer. Just remember, the building that looks so picturesque in the fading twilight could be part of the law school, miles from where the undergraduates study and live.

Also note that the schools who select you for their mailing might not be the 7 ones you would choose, but instead the ones that would choose *you!* Schools could choose to recruit you for any number of reasons: You could be from a part of the country the school feels is under-represented in its student body, or your test scores could be higher than their average, and they would like you to bring them up! Chances are you will have to take the initiative to get the mailing information on some of the schools that truly interest you.

Brochures and viewbooks can be useful if they are read critically. What 8 themes does the college stress most? What isn't mentioned? What does the SAT or ACT profile look like? Look for hard facts to back up the flowery prose. If nothing else, viewbooks reveal something about how the college perceives itself, as well as what it aspires to be. It isn't much to go on, but then again you don't have time to do a thorough analysis of all 2,000 four-year colleges in the nation.

There's one source of information that's often overlooked just because it's 9 close at hand (though sometimes for other reasons): your parents. They, and other adults who know you well, probably have some good ideas about which schools you ought to consider. Take their advice seriously and investigate the alternatives they suggest. Adults frequently have a better perspective on you as an individual than would most people in your age group. Do not, however, let anyone dictate which colleges you "must" consider. It's important to come to an understanding with your parents early on that the college choice is ultimately yours alone. You are the one who has to live with that choice for four years, not them. If money is a potential problem, reach an agreement on that as well. How much can your family afford to pay? Some colleges might offer substantial financial aid. How much will you be expected to contribute? It's much better to deal with these questions in the opening months of the process than to wait until later when emotions are running high.

There are two important things to bear in mind as you consult the opinions   10
of others. First, every piece of advice you'll get will be a reflection of a particular person's own life experiences and is likely to be highly subjective. Second, opinions are frequently based on stereotypes that are often false, outdated, or misleading. Still, these are the short-cuts most applicants use to begin narrowing their choices, an unfortunate but necessary phase. The more people you talk to, the more perspective you can gain on the colleges you are considering. The primary purpose of this book is to give you an *inside* look at the colleges. If you like what you've heard about a particular school, follow up with some careful research; find out if it really lives up to its name.

As the field narrows, you should begin to dig deeper. See what the guides   11
have to say about schools that interest you. Do you know anyone in college? Do you know anyone who knows anyone in college? Talk to them. You don't have to interview everyone you know, but you may find that real students are your best resource. Don't be afraid to ask "real" questions (For example, is State U really the party school it's made out to be?). Get the "facts" from your college guides, and opinions and insights from the people who really know the school—the students. College nights and visits from admissions officers can also be useful because you get to see and talk to a representative of the college in the flesh. As with the viewbooks, read between the lines. College reps are there to sell the school and will be reluctant to confess any serious problems with it. It's up to you to be critical in evaluating what they say.

All the things we've been mentioning are just bits and pieces, but if you start   12
adding them up, you'll begin to get an idea of what it's like on each campus. We realize that at this early stage college may still seem miles away. Being editor of the school paper or winning the league championship often seems thousand times more important than reading through stacks of college literature that all looks much the same a way. You'll be tempted to put off thinking about college until later (much later). Resist the temptation. Getting off on the right foot is important, and it takes some effort.

The College Visit

The Guidance Staff, Brookline Public High School

The guidance staff at the public high school in Brookline, Massachusetts, created for its students a handbook, "Choice, Not Chance: Career and College Planning." In addition to providing timetables for college decision making and general recommendations about the application process, the handbook offers a set of questions for students going on campus visits. Virtually all the handbooks

*available, those published commercially and those created by high-school guid-
ance departments, encourage students to visit schools that interest them, the
assumption being that in the visit the special character of a school reveals itself.
As you read the questions that visiting a college should answer, consider the
questions that you, having already selected a school, would add to or delete from
this list. Did you visit the campus you are now attending? Was the visit helpful?
Did it, in fact, reveal the character of the school to you?*

In the preliminary search for "*the*" college, a student may find that several col-   1
leges meet most of his/her requirements. One or two of these schools may be
a better choice than the others, however. The only valid way to determine which
is right is to visit the college campus.

THE VISIT SHOULD ENABLE THE STUDENT TO:

1. Meet with admissions people in order to obtain an idea of what they expect.
2. Get a feeling for the academic and social atmosphere.
3. See the facilities to be used for study, living, recreation, etc.
4. Talk with students now in attendance.
5. Appraise the community in which the college is located.

The visit should be carefully planned. The following is a list of suggestions to help   2
in preparation for a college visit.

1. Make arrangements with the Admissions Office by writing or phoning well
   in advance (preferably a month).
2. If possible, the student visitor should inform the college of his/her special
   areas of interest when writing for the appointment. This will help the admissions people to plan a more meaningful visit.
3. Refer to the college catalog to review basic concerns before leaving for the
   visit.
4. Be prepared to give the admissions officers accurate and up-to-date information concerning courses now being taken, SAT's or ACT's, approximate
   rank, number of students in your high school graduating class, extra-curric-
   ular activities that you have participated in, special awards, significant interests and experiences both in and out of school. (It is a good idea to prepare
   an outline to take with you listing all of the pertinent data.)
5. The visit and interview will determine the personal impression made on
   the admissions officer; obviously, some care should be given to dress and
   grooming.
6. Plan to spend at least half a day (full day preferred) at each college. In addition to making a tour of the campus, the student should try to:
   (a) Sit in on a class.
   (b) Have a meal on campus.
   (c) Browse in the library.
   (d) Engage students (other than tour guides) in conversation (upperclassmen,
       if possible).
   (e) Spend some time in the student center or union.
   (f) Spend some time in the community (city, town).
   (g) Read copies of the school and local newspapers.
7. Keep notes on your visit(s). Do not rely on memory, particularly if other college visits are to follow.

8. Be sure to write thank you notes to all those officials who gave their time to you.
9. After returning home, discuss your impressions with your college counselor and your parents.

Many things can be learned in an attempt to personalize the college selection 3 process. Here are some sample questions that your visit should answer:

1. Are there adequate educational facilities for the department or major area of your interest?
2. Are laboratory facilities up-to-date? Are they adequate?
3. Do freshmen have the opportunity to take courses with "top" professors?
4. What is the typical class size? for freshmen? for upperclassmen?
5. Are the library facilities sufficient? open stacks? Would you want to spend a great deal of time there? What are the hours for student use?
6. Does the campus have appeal, in general?
7. How near is the college to the local community? Are there community stores and other facilities readily accessible to students?
8. Is the campus clean and orderly? Do the students exhibit a pride in the school's appearance?
9. What is the condition of the buildings?
10. What are the dormitories like? Must freshmen live in dorms? Will you be allowed to decorate your room? How many to a room or suite? What are the basic dorm regulations? Hours? Are there study facilities in the dorm? Quiet hours?
11. Where are the dining facilities located?
12. What activities go on at the student union?
13. Are there fraternity and/or sorority houses? What are the differences in cost (as compared to dorm living)? What percentage of the students are in fraternities and sororities? What effect do these organizations have on student life as a whole?
14. Is religious affiliation significant? Are there required courses in religion? Must students attend Chapel?
15. Are there good athletic facilities? Intercollegiate? Intramural? Men's athletics? Women's athletics?
16. What is the relationship between students/faculty/administration?
17. Do the students seem serious about the educational experience or it there a "country club" atmosphere?
18. What are the financial aid opportunities? Work opportunities? Scholarships (academic or merit)? Athletic grants?
19. What are the unique programs? Foreign study opportunity?
20. What percentages of students go on to graduate school? And to which graduate schools?
21. What cultural activities are available on or near the campus? Are speakers, plays, musicians and other artists brought to campus?
22. Do the majority of students remain on the campus for weekends or do they tend to leave for home or elsewhere?

The Interview

Anthony F. Capraro, III

Anthony Capraro, president of a college counseling service in New York, was asked by the editors of Barron's Profiles of American Colleges *to advise students who are going on interviews. Advice on the interview, like advice on visiting campuses and writing application essays, is a staple of college guides. If you interviewed at any schools, recall your experiences as you read this selection. Again, consider this question: To what extent does advice help the prospective student before the fact of interviewing, visiting campuses, or essay writing? Project yourself into the assignment later in this section: When you are writing your own essay, to what extent will you feel comfortable advising others—as opposed to counseling them to advise themselves as they gain experience in their own application process?*

The interview is a contrived situation that few people enjoy, of which many 1 people misunderstand the value, and about which everyone is apprehensive. However, no information from a college catalog, no friend's friend, no high school guidance counselor's comments, and no parental remembrances from bygone days can surpass the value of your college campus visit and interview. This firsthand opportunity to assess your future alma mater will confirm or contradict other impressions and help you make a sound college acceptance.

Many colleges will recommend or request a personal interview. It is best to 2 travel to the campus to meet with a member of the admissions staff if you can; however. if you can't, many colleges will arrange to have one of their representatives, usually an alumnus, interview you in your hometown.

Even though the thought of an interview might give you enough butterflies 3 to lift you to the top of your high school's flagpole, here are some tips that might make it a little easier.

1. **Go prepared.** Read the college's catalog ahead of time so you won't ask "How many books are in your library?" or "How many students do you have?" Ask intelligent questions that introduce a topic of conversation that you want the interviewer to know about you. The key is to distinguish yourself in a positive way from thousands of other applicants. Forge the final steps in the marketing process you have built up since your first choices in the college admission process were taken back in junior high school. The interview is your chance to enhance those decisions.

2. **Nervousness** . . . is absolutely and entirely normal. The best way to handle it is to admit it, out loud, to the interviewer. Miles Uhrig, director of admission at Tufts University, sometimes relates this true story to his apprehensive applicants: One extremely agitated young applicant sat opposite him for her interview with her legs crossed, wearing loafers on her feet. She swung her top leg back and forth to some inaudible rhythm. The loafer on her top foot flew off her foot, hit him in the head, ricocheted to the desk lamp and broke it. She looked at him in terror, but when their glances met, they both dissolved in laughter. The moral of the story—the person on the other side of the desk is also a human being and wants to put you at ease. So admit to your anxiety and don't swing your foot if you're wearing loafers! (By the way, she was admitted.)

3. **Be yourself.** Nobody's perfect, and everyone knows nobody's perfect, so admit to a flaw or two before the interviewer goes hunting for them. The truly impressive candidate will convey a thorough knowledge of self.

4. **Interview the interviewer.** Don't passively sit there and allow the interviewer to ask all the questions and direct the conversation. Participate in this responsibility by assuming an active role. A thoughtful questioner will accomplish three important tasks in a successful interview:

a. **demonstrate interest,** initiative, and maturity for taking partial responsibility for the content of the conversation;

b. **guide the conversation** to areas where he/she feels most secure and accomplished; and

c. **obtain answers.**

Use your genuine feelings to react to the answers you hear. If you are delighted to learn of a certain program or activity, show it. If you are curious, ask more questions. If you are disappointed by something you learn, try to find a path to a positive answer or . . . consider yourself lucky that you discovered this particular inadequacy in time.

5. **Parents do belong** in your college decision process as your advisers! Often it is they who spend the megabucks for your next four years, and they can provide psychological support and a stabilizing influence for sensible, rational decisions. In essence, the sage senior will find constructive ways to include parents in the decision-making process as catalysts, without letting them take over (as many are apt to do). You may want your parents to meet and speak briefly to your interviewer. That's fine to do before or after, but not during your interview time.

6. **Practice makes perfect.** Begin your interviews at colleges that are low on your list of preferred choices, and leave your first-choice colleges until last. If you are shy, you will have a chance to practice vocalizing what your usually silent inner voice tells you. Others will have the opportunity to commit their inevitable first blunders where it won't count as much.

7. **Departing impressions.** There is a remarkable tendency for the student to base final college preferences on the quality of the interview only, or on the personal reaction to the interviewer as the personification of the entire institution. Do not do yourself the disservice of letting it influence an otherwise rational selection, one based on institutional programs, students, services, and environment. After the last good-bye and thank you has been smiled, and you exhale deeply on your way out the door, go ahead and congratulate yourself. If you used the interview properly you will know whether or not you wish to attend that college and why.

8. **Send a thank-you note** to your interviewer. A short and simple handwritten or typed note will do; and if you forgot to mention something important about yourself at the interview, here's your chance.

The College Essay
Theodore O'Neill

Theodore O'Neill is the Director of College Admission at the University of Chicago. "The only useful tip," he says, "for students who want to write proper college application essays is this: Let yourselves be heard in your writing." Like "knowing yourself," the advice to let yourself be heard is easy to give and difficult to achieve, as O'Neill acknowledges. He and other admission directors insist that the application essay provides crucial, balancing information that shows the person in an application as someone who is more than a profile in numbers. As you read, reflect on the essays you wrote and on their success in revealing you both to yourself and to various admission committees.

Most people involved with the college admission process agree that too many 1 hours are spent, too much energy is expended, and too many tears are shed over the whole business. Everyone wishes the process could be as humane as possible. When looking for a solution, students, parents, and admission officers alike point to the college application essay as the piece that is most struggled over.

Why not, then, get rid of the essay? Doing so would certainly have a few 2 obvious and immediate benefits. It would eliminate the all-night bouts of writing before the deadline, the crumpled balls of paper, the Federal Express expenses. It would allow admission officers to spend more time with their families and friends in February and March, when they are usually reading mountains of application essays. Most important (and anyone who has tried to compose a "personal statement" at any point in his or her life knows how great a benefit this would be), it would relieve applicants of the pain of struggling to reveal themselves on paper and would protect them from the risk of subjecting their self-revelations to the judgment of perfect strangers.

The question is, would eliminating the essay make the admission process 3 more humane? And if it would, wouldn't basing everything on numbers, as some state universities find that they must, make it even more humane? Then, at least, no person would have to say no to any other person; the admission decision would be strictly impartial. (Dear Applicant: We regret that we cannot accept you for admission. Don't take this personally. Your numbers simply don't match up with our numbers.) For that matter, why not go one step further? Why not relegate admission decisions to a national computer matching service, as some people are seriously proposing? Then in the spring a student would get one thick acceptance letter and *no* thin rejection letters. Wouldn't this be the ultimate in humane responses?

The answer, of course, is no. It's ridiculous to suggest that the computer- 4 ized or institutionalized response is the most humane. Philosophers have told us since the beginning of time that what is most humane is the conscious and distinctive use of language. The way to make a college application a real human affair is to model it on correspondence or, when possible, a conversation, not on a measurement. What a college needs to be able to do is to judge the whole person, and in order to do that, it needs to hear a voice that resonates with the human qualities of the academically qualified applicant. The only useful tip, then, for students who want to write proper college application essays is this: Let yourselves be heard in your writing. Don't try to ape someone else or to sound the way you think colleges want you to sound. Speak in your own voice.

Speaking in one's own voice should be easy, but we all know that it isn't. 5 Young children, up to a certain point, always speak in their own way, and polished writers find a style that says something honest about them. The rest of us, however, have other things to wrestle with in order to get our own true selves on paper. We *can* do it—anyone can. There is a voice down there, and we know it when we hear it, but we often have to make many frustrating false starts before it emerges.

When an essay is submitted that is truly representative of the student, the 6 college admission process begins to make sense. Since the model for application reading should be interpretation rather than measurement (because success in college relates to character and motivation much more than to things more easily gauged), the essay and interview provide the context in which to interpret everything else, such as transcripts and test scores. If a student can write with some thoughtfulness and self-knowledge, he or she is already doing much of what is asked for in college. Essay writing is taken as primary evidence of something crucial to collegiate study.

Perhaps the essay makes the whole business of applying to college more 7 daunting, but at least in acknowledging its importance we in admission are making a pact with applicants that says, "If you sweat over the essay, we will, too. We will do *our* best to reveal ourselves to you by trying to describe our college with a voice that is distinctive and true to the institution. We will not make vague, intrusive demands ('Say something about yourself'); we will pose questions that interest us and allow you to write intimately without having to write directly about yourself." The pact makes saying no harder but makes saying yes so much more satisfactory, so much more humane.

A Guide to the Assignment

This guide is designed to help you through the process of writing an explanatory essay on your decision-making process in choosing a college. Key elements in this guide parallel the organization of the Structures and Strategies section in this chapter, and you should look to appropriate sections in the chapter for further guidance. You will prepare to write, write, and then evaluate and revise. Here, once again, is your assignment:

Prompted by your reading of the selections in this section, reflect on the decision-making process that led to your choosing a college. Reconstruct this process for students who are now juniors at your old high school. Having explained what led you to your decision, can you recommend your process to others who will soon be applying to colleges themselves? What worked for you in your selection process, and what didn't work? Your purpose in this essay is primarily to explore and explain; but having done this, you will have earned the right to judge your strategies. Seriously consider submitting this essay to your former high-school's newspaper. Others can benefit from both your experience and your self-criticism.

Prepare to Write: Explore Your Idea

Discovering Ideas

The purpose of an explanatory essay is to show readers the *what, how,* and *why* of a topic in ways that are appropriate to the readers' needs and that keep the readers' focus largely on the thing being explained, not on the writer who is explaining. Given this purpose, you do well to choose topics for explanation according to two principles: explain what you know well or can learn about in a reasonably brief amount of time and explain something that interests you.

Reflect on Your Experience

Explanatory writing puts you in the role of teacher, and you never want to teach something that you don't know. The first principle, then, in sparking ideas for explanatory writing is to work from your experience: What object, process, or skill have you mastered, and how can you use this mastery to give others what they need to know? In an essay about how you chose a college, you obviously have a unique vantage point. Use your knowledge. At the top of a page, write "What I understand about applying to colleges." At the top of another page, write "What confuses me still about the process." Explore your experience. Fill each page with notes, and you will very likely spark ideas for an essay.

Divide Your Topic into Parts

Very often, you will have many more ideas about a topic when you think about its parts as opposed to when you think about it as a whole. Take the example of applying to college. Rather than wrestling with the whole, divide the topic in any way that occurs to you. Here are a few possibilities: the beginning, middle, and end of the process; a successful process versus an unsuccessful one; specific tasks in the process—initial choices, campus visits, applications, interviews, and so on. No method of dividing a topic is inherently better than another. The goal is to begin thinking of *parts*. Write "Applications process—parts" at the top of a page. Divide the topic in any of the ways just suggested or in ways that seem sensible to you. Once you generate an initial list—say, three or four items—work the same exercise: ask, "What are the parts of each item?" Complete two or three cycles of this activity, and you will have generated a good amount of information on which to write. On pages 11–13, you will see this technique presented visually as a tree diagram and as a mapping strategy.

Read to Discover Ideas

Source materials can help you to spark ideas for an essay. This Occasions section consists of selections representative of an entire industry, both inside academia and outside, devoted to helping teenagers make intelligent choices about college. You can use these materials to spark ideas for your essay. There are three strategies you can pursue. First, take advantage of the thinking that others have done by listing the categories they have used in writing about your same topic. For instance, you have seen authors discuss the following topics: gaining self-knowledge before applying; needing to impress others; visiting campuses; interviewing; and writing essays of application. Use these categories to reflect on your own experience. You might want to place each category at the top of a page and then fill that page with notes.

Second, read the Occasions selections and highlight any statements that prompted an immediate response from you. Copy these statements onto blank sheets and explain your reactions. You are sure to generate ideas for your essay. Third, observe how the writers have organized their explanations, and adopt some of their strategies. Here are three organizational plans you have seen: italicized statements that prompted paragraphs of explanation; lists of questions; and numbered items that prompted paragraphs. Any of these forms, or some combination of them, might appeal to you in thinking about presenting your own explanation.

*S*uggestions for Collaborative Writing

Just as source materials can help spark ideas, so too can discussions with other people. Professional writers are constantly trying their ideas out on others, thereby receiving abundant feedback that will eventually assist them in their revisions.

Begin by coming up with several good general questions that will prompt detailed, specific response. For example, if you were speaking to adults who had already gone to college, you might ask: "If you knew as an incoming freshman what you know now, what would you have done differently in deciding what college to attend?" Make a list of all the insights you hear from their answers, and refer back to this information when writing your draft. Or, if speaking to college students, ask: "What were the most important requirements that determined where you went to college? Are there any other requirements that you can think of now that you wish you'd thought of as a high school student?"

Such questions can foster conversations that will elicit questions and ideas that can have major implications for your essay. Get into the habit of constantly talking with students, roommates, teachers, family members, and anyone who will listen to you discuss your assignment for a few minutes. Keep track of all the information you pick up so you can refer to it as you begin writing.

Committing Yourself to an Idea

Recall the attitudes of writers whose commitment sparks interest in their readers:

- I write for myself and for my audience.
- I will find some approach to my writing that lets me discover something personally significant.

Before beginning your first draft, take a few minutes to consider this question: What will be your *personal* connection to explaining your process of applying to college? The fact that your essay is about your experience does not guarantee that you will be committed to your topic. Your goal is to find something of value in your experience, something worth explaining to yourself. Do this and you will help to engage your readers.

Write: Clarify Your Idea and Make It Public

All statements and essays are to some extent argumentative. When you say, "That sweater is brown," others have the right to disagree and respond, "No—it's a chocolate-gray." But if these statements can be characterized as arguments at all, they must be called low-level arguments in that the intention is to describe and account for an object. When writers focus on an object, not on their strongly held views about it, the purpose of writing can be called explanatory. Strongly expressed views indicate a high-level argument, as in "That sweater is *ugly!*" For more on the distinction between low- and high-level arguments, see Structures and Strategies, pages 180–181.

Creating Common Ground with Readers

As you prepare a draft of your explanatory essay, keep your readers clearly in mind. Your goal is to explain a topic that should be of interest, and you can reasonably hope that readers will learn something. Because you and your actions are the focus of this essay, you may be tempted to intrude with strongly held views. For the bulk of this essay, avoid the temptation. Work to keep your focus on the process of making a decision: on what you did, why, and how. Your recreation of events and processes will provide your common ground with readers.

You are writing for juniors at your former high school, in the hope that they will read the essay in the school paper. Recreate for yourself the needs and interests of sixteen-year-old students. How will you address them? Consider these questions, in addition to others that you may want to pose:

- Do your readers know enough to know which questions to ask?
- To what extent are your readers feeling frightened, overwhelmed, or excited? How do high-school juniors show these emotions?
- Will the timing of your essay (fall, winter, spring) affect the topics that will interest readers?
- What special, local circumstances become factors in the decision-making process for students from this school?
- What do juniors at your former high school need from *you?*
- To what extent will your having graduated from the same high school be important to your readers? How can you take advantage of your special relationship with these readers?

These questions, in addition to your own, should help you to visualize your readers. Once you do this, devise strategies for creating common ground with them: What are the *particular* stories, facts, and quotations through which you can make your idea known to these students?

Planning a Structure

Would you describe your decision-making process as organized, disorganized, purposeful, haphazard, hopeful, depressed, excited, fear-inducing, or challenging? Indicate as much in your thesis. Once you have successfully related your process in this essay, you will have earned the right to some editorializing and, perhaps, some self-criticism. In your conclusion you might respond to these questions: Did your process lead to an informed and effective decision? Would you recommend your process to others? Your thesis might hint at your responses to these or related questions, but the clear emphasis in your thesis and in your essay should be on explanation.

Understanding Your Logic

Following the discussion in Structures and Strategies (pages 186–187) and in chapter 4 (pages 61–63), quiz your thesis to identify parts of your essay. Devise a plan for developing each part. You have seen in this chapter explanations and examples of various strategies for development: presenting a historical overview, providing examples, recounting a process, offering definitions, dividing and classifying, and comparing and contrasting. All of these methods of development are open to you. Find some combination that lets you show the what, how, and why of your decision-making process. Before writing, understand whether you are presenting material inductively—working from specific statements of evidence to your thesis—or deductively—presenting specific evidence after, and in support of, your thesis. See pages 425–426 for a discussion on this decision.

Writing Your First Draft

Write one section of the essay at a sitting. Perhaps you have four sections: gathering materials on colleges; reading brochures and narrowing the possibilities; visiting schools; and completing applications. Each section of the essay will likely consist of several paragraphs. A section may take you from half an hour to several hours to write. By drafting at least one section of your essay at a sitting, you will see clearly two important relationships: first, of one paragraph to others *within* a section and, second, of whole blocks of paragraphs—of entire sections—to other sections as well as to your essay's overall idea. Unless your thesis is very ambitious and the essay grows very long, you should be able to finish your draft in four or five sittings. For further discussion of what constitutes a section of your essay, see pages 493–494. And, generally, see the material on writing a first draft on pages 486–498.

Suggestions for Writing with a Computer

In the course of writing your essay, from its earliest origins right up until the final stages, you should be collecting information. Information comes, not just in the form of research, but from insights, observations, memories, anecdotes, snippets of conversation, and chance discoveries. As you think about your essay throughout the day, you will probably begin to notice things that might end up influencing your essay: a poster advertising a lecture, a newspaper article, or a memory of something that happened to you years ago.

As you collect this information, be sure to record it right away. At the end of the day write all of this information down in a file on your computer titled "Misc." or "Notes." As you record ideas and observations, write them out in complete sentences, even paragraphs. You'll discover that a lot of this information can be pasted directly into your essay at a later time.

The more time you spend writing your essay, the larger you Misc. file should grow. Refer to this evolving file continually: when you incorporate something into your essay, delete it from the file (so you won't forget and use it again). You can return to this file whenever you feel writer's block coming on or your revision process is at a standstill; chances are there will be something in there you can use to get going again.

Advance Your Idea with Sources

You can use the sources in this Occasions section in a variety of ways to advance the idea of your explanatory essay. One indirect way has been suggested in the "discovering ideas" section: let the Occasions readings create for you categories by which to generate ideas and organize your discussion. Review each selection and list topics of interest to each writer. Use these same categories—for instance, interviews, campus visits, application essays, and common mistakes—to stimulate and organize thinking about your own decision-making process. (If you choose the cost of college as a category, see the two reading selections on pages 202–211.) You can also use sources more directly, following suggestions in this chapter:

- Use sources to clarify procedures.
- Use sources to check the reliability of experts.
- Use sources to identify a debate—which for the purposes of this essay you will report on, not participate in.
- Use sources to lend credibility to your explanations.

To write an explanation with authority, you should know more about your topic than your audience does. Given your experiences and the reading you have done in this section, you know far more than high-school juniors about the process of deciding on a college. Relatively speaking, you *are* an authority. Draw source materials into your essay to complement your own insights. The Occasions section will provide you with pertinent facts, opinions, and examples.

See chapter 4 for demonstrations of using sources to provide facts, examples, and authoritative opinions and also for specific strategies for introducing sources into an essay. In particular, see the section on "Sources and Cycles of Development," pages 61–68. Here you will get advice on keeping your essay focused on *your idea,* not on your source; you will learn how to link sources to create a synthesis; and you will find strategies for summarizing, paraphrasing, and quoting.

Evaluate and Revise

General Evaluation

Your primary challenge in revising the first draft of an explanatory essay is to ensure that you have a single, clear idea that you want to communicate about the thing, event, or process being explained. The biggest changes in your essay will likely come between your first and second drafts. Your explanatory essay will not be complete until you revise and refine its single compelling idea.

Critical Points in an Explanatory Essay

Be sure that your explanatory essay—or one that you are reading and evaluating—is a low-level argument that keeps the reader's focus on the topic, event, or process being explained, *not* on your (or the writer's) strongly held opinions. (See pages 180–181 for more on the distinction between low- and high-level arguments.) Specifically, evaluate these elements:

- How effectively does the essay divide the topic being explained into parts?
- How thoroughly developed are these parts?
- To what extent has the writer presented material in a language and at a level of detail that is appropriate for the intended audience?
- Does the essay show the reader what, why, and how?

Analysis

Definitions and Examples

An analysis is an argument in which you study the parts of something to understand how it works, what it means, or why it might be significant. The writer of an analysis uses an analytical tool: a *principle* or *definition* on the basis of which an object, an event, or a behavior can be divided into parts and examined. Here are excerpts from two analyses of L. Frank Baum's *The Wizard of Oz*:

> At the dawn of adolescence, the very time she should start to distance herself from Aunt Em and Uncle Henry, the surrogate parents who raised her on their Kansas farm, Dorothy Gale experiences a hurtful reawakening of her fear that these loved ones will be rudely ripped from her, especially her Aunt (Em—M for Mother!). [Harvey Greenberg, *The Movies on Your Mind* (New York: Dutton, 1975)]

> [*The Wizard of Oz*] was originally written as a political allegory about grass-roots protest. It may seem harder to believe than Emerald City, but the Tin Woodsman is the industrial worker, the Scarecrow [is] the struggling farmer, and the Wizard is the president, who is powerful only as long as he succeeds in deceiving the people. [Peter Dreier, "Oz was Almost Reality," *Cleveland Plain Dealer* 3 Sept. 1989.]

As these paragraphs suggest, what you discover through an analysis depends entirely on the principle or definition you use to make your insights. Is *The Wizard of Oz* the story of a girl's psychological development, or is it a story about politics? The answer is *both*. In the first example, psychiatrist Harvey Greenberg applies the principles of his profession and, not surprisingly, sees *The Wizard of Oz* in psychological terms. In the second example, a newspaper reporter applies the political theories of Karl Marx and, again not surprisingly, discovers a story about politics.

Different as they are, these analyses share an important quality: each is the result of a specific principle or definition being used as a tool to divide an object into parts to see what it means and how it works. The writer's choice of analytical tool simultaneously creates and limits the possibilities for analysis. Thus, working with the principles of Freud, Harvey Greenberg was going to see *The Wizard of Oz* in psychological, not political, terms; working with the theories of Karl Marx, Peter Dreier could only have understood the movie in terms of the economic relationships among characters. It's as if the writer of an analysis who adopts one analytical tool puts on a pair of glasses and sees an object in a specific way. A second writer, using a different tool (and a different pair of glasses), sees the object differently.

You might protest: Are there as many analyses of *The Wizard of Oz* as there are people to read it? Yes, or at least as many analyses as there are analytical tools. This does not mean that all analyses are equally valid or useful. The writer must convince the reader. In creating an essay of analysis, the writer must organize a series of related insights, using the analytical tool to examine first one part and then another of the object being studied. To read Harvey Greenberg's essay on *The Wizard of Oz* is to find paragraph after paragraph of related insights—first about Aunt Em, then the Wicked Witch, then Toto, and then the Wizard. All these insights point to Greenberg's single conclusion: that "Dorothy's 'trip' is a marvelous metaphor for the psychological journey every adolescent must make."[1] Without Greenberg's analysis, we probably would not have thought about the movie as a psychological journey, which is precisely the power of an analysis: its ability to reveal objects or events in ways we would not otherwise have considered.

The writer's challenge is to convince readers that (1) the analytical tool being applied is legitimate and well matched to the object being studied; and (2) the analytical tool is being used systematically to divide the object into parts and to make a coherent, meaningful statement about these parts and the object as a whole.

Examples of Analyses

Four examples of analyses of increasing length and complexity follow. The first three examples are written by professional writers. The fourth is written by a student, in response to assignment in his sociology class. Each analysis illustrates the two defining features of analysis just discussed: a statement of an analytical principle or definition, and the use of that principle or definition in closely examining an object, behavior, or event. As you read, try to identify these features. Questions for discussion follow each example.

---

[1]See Harvey Greenberg, *Movies on Your Mind* (New York: Dutton, 1975).

The Comfort of Diners

John B. Levine

These paragraphs were excerpted from an article by John B. Levine in the Boston Sunday Globe, *July 18, 1993 (54). Levine teaches psychiatry at Harvard Medical School and prepared his observations on diners for a paper he delivered at a conference of the Society for Commercial Archeology. As you read ¶1, observe how he draws on the work of another writer to establish a principle by which he will analyze his "ideal" diner in ¶2.*

There is something comforting and familiar about eating in old restaurants. Liz   1
Logan, a New York Times food writer, has characterized this feeling as an "anti-dote to the nervous breakdown." In describing Mocca, a Hungarian restaurant on 2d Avenue near E. 82d Street in New York, she enumerates as essential features: comfort food; waiters and waitresses who have served the same customers for a long time; and cross-generational clientele. Repeated ordering of the same standard dish also contributes to "a modest payoff of completely reliable satisfaction." The result is "a sense of soul, resonance and continuity." The outer landscape calms the inner landscape.

We would look for much of the same in an ideal diner: comforts of home   2
without the disadvantages; echoes of the pleasures of the extended family. The ritual of eating and talking is reduced to its essentials. One sits down to a plate of hash browns, two eggs over easy, fried ham and toast for the pleasure of the familiar. Diners may have first-rate food, made with fresh local ingredients and the owner's personal flair, but culinary adventure is not the point. One is seeking comfort.

For Discussion and Writing

Reading and Thinking Critically

1. *Personal response:* Recall a diner at which you've had a meal, if possible, one that you know well. What do you expect in terms of food and people when you go to the diner?
2. *Challenge the reading:* To what extent does Levine's analysis of diners as places of *comfort* make sense to you, given your familiarity with the diner(s) described above?
3. *Broaden the context:* Identify other places in our culture where people seek *comfort.* List these, and then forge connections among these places. What makes them comfortable? In a larger sense, what is it we are looking for when we seek comfort?

"The Comfort of Diners" as an Example of Analysis

1. What analytical tool (principle or definition) does Levine use in this brief analysis?
2. How does Levine establish the validity of this tool?
3. How does Levine apply this tool in defining his "ideal" diner?

The Plug-In Drug

Marie Winn

The following analysis of television viewing as an addictive behavior appeared originally in Marie Winn's 1977 book, The Plug-In Drug. *A writer and media critic, Winn has been interested in the effect of television on both individuals and the larger culture. In this passage, she carefully defines the term* addiction *and then applies it systematically to the behavior under study.*

The word "addiction" is often used loosely and wryly in conversation. People 1 will refer to themselves as "mystery book addicts" or "cookie addicts." E. B. White wrote of his annual surge of interest in gardening: "We are hooked and are making an attempt to kick the habit." Yet nobody really believes that reading mysteries or ordering seeds by catalogue is serious enough to be compared with addictions to heroin or alcohol. The word "addiction" is here used jokingly to denote a tendency to overindulge in some pleasurable activity.

People often refer to being "hooked on TV." Does this, too, fall into the 2 lighthearted category of cookie eating and other pleasures that people peruse with unusual intensity, or is there a kind of television viewing that falls into the more serious category of destructive addiction?

When we think about addiction to drugs or alcohol we frequently focus on 3 negative aspects, ignoring the pleasures that accompany drinking or drug-taking. And yet the essence of any serious addiction is a pursuit of pleasure, a search for a "high" that normal life does not supply. It is only the inability to function without the addictive substance that is dismaying, the dependence of the organism upon a certain experience and an increasing inability to function normally without it. Thus people will take two or three drinks at the end of the day not merely for the pleasure drinking provides, but also because they "don't feel normal" without them.

Real addicts do not merely pursue a pleasurable experience one time in 4 order to function normally. They need to *repeat* it again and again. Something about that particular experience makes life without it less complete. Other potentially pleasurable experiences are no longer possible, for under the spell of the addictive experience, their lives are peculiarly distorted. The addict craves an experience and yet is never really satisfied. The organism may be temporarily sated, but soon it begins to crave again.

Finally, a serious addiction is distinguished from a harmless pursuit of plea- 5 sure by its distinctly destructive elements. Heroin addicts, for instance, lead a damaged life: their increasing need for heroin in increasing doses prevents them from working, maintaining relationships, from developing in human ways. Similarly alcoholics' lives are narrowed and dehumanized by their dependence on alcohol.

Let us consider television viewing in the light of the conditions that define 6 serious addiction.

Not unlike drugs or alcohol, the television experience allows the participant 7 to blot out the real world and enter into a pleasurable and passive mental state. The worries and anxieties of reality are as effectively deferred by becoming absorbed in a television program as by going on a "trip" induced by drugs or alcohol. And just as alcoholics are only vaguely aware of their addiction, feeling that they control their drinking more than they really do ("I can cut it out any time I want—I just like to have three or four drinks before dinner"), people similarly overestimate their control over television watching. Even as they put off other activities to spend hour after hour watching television, they feel they could easily resume living in a different, less passive style. But somehow or other while the television set is present in their homes, the click doesn't sound. With television pleasures available, those other experiences seem less attractive, more difficult somehow.

A very heavy viewer (a college English instructor) observes: 8

"I find television almost irresistible. When the set is on, I cannot ignore it. I can't turn it off. I feel sapped, will-less, enervated. As I reach out to turn off the set, the strength goes out of my arms. So I sit there for hours and hours."

Self-confessed television addicts often feel they "ought" to do other things— 9 but the fact that they don't read and don't plant their garden or sew or crochet or play games or have conversations means that those activities are no longer as desirable as television viewing. In a way the lives of heavy viewers are as imbalanced by their television "habit" as a drug addict's or an alcoholic's. They are living in a holding pattern, as it were, passing up the activities that lead to growth or development or a sense of accomplishment. This is one reason people talk about their television viewing so ruefully, so apologetically. They are aware that it is an unproductive experience, that almost any other endeavor is more worthwhile by any human measure.

Finally it is the adverse effect of television viewing on the lives of so many 10 people that defines it as a serious addiction. The television habit distorts the sense of time. It renders other experiences vague and curiously unreal while taking on a greater reality for itself. It weakens relationships by reducing and sometimes eliminating normal opportunities for talking, for communicating.

And yet television does not satisfy, else why would the viewer continue to 11 watch hour after hour, day after day? "The measure of health," writes Lawrence Kubie, "is flexibility . . . and especially the freedom to cease when sated." But heavy television viewers can never be sated with their television experiences— these do not provide the true nourishment that satiation requires—and thus they find that they cannot stop watching.

For Discussion and Writing

Reading and Thinking Critically

1. *Personal response:* To what extent does Winn describe you in her discussion of the addicted television viewer? Does her analysis alarm you? give you resolve to change? amuse you?
2. *Broaden the context:* What do you know about addiction, generally? Does television viewing qualify as addictive behavior? Is Winn's definition of addiction acceptable to you? (And if it is not, how is her analysis damaged?)
3. *Challenge the reading:* Winn writes: "And yet television does not satisfy, else why would the viewer continue to watch hour after hour, day after day?" Can you answer this in ways that might contradict Winn?

"The Plug-In Drug" as an Example of Analysis

1. In the first part of her essay, Winn offers a four-part definition of the *addicted* individual. What are the four elements of her definition?
2. In the second part of the essay, locate the places where Winn uses each of the parts of her definition to analyze television viewing as addictive.

3. In what ways does Winn's choice of analytical tools focus her attention on *particular* features of television viewing? List other behaviors associated with television viewing that Winn does not consider, given her focus on addiction.

In Search of the Arab

Jack Shaheen

Jack Shaheen is an Arab American much concerned with the negative portrayals of Arabs on television. As you will see in the sidebar to this piece, Shaheen undertook his analysis to illustrate in precise ways how Arabs are stereotyped in the media. Like Levine and Winn, he is careful to state the principle of analysis he will use in studying Arab stereotypes. Like Levine but unlike Winn, he announces that principle without defending it, assuming the reader will agree that the principle is a valid one.

When I think of the word "Arab," I see the 150 million people in the great expanse of the Arab world, most of whom share a common cultural heritage, religion and history. 1

They are city dwellers, suburbanites, farmers and villagers who live in twenty-one different countries. Many wear Western-styled dresses, trousers, shirts, ties and coats. Some Arab men cover their heads with a small embroidered or crocheted cap, over which they place the traditional *kufiyah,* a white or checkered cloth which is folded diagonally and kept in place by two rings of thick black wool called the *agal.* Some Arab women go veiled in the streets or wear just head scarves of smoke-thin chiffon or opaque black crepe. Other women wear the latest fashions from Paris and London and New York. Still others wear the traditional *abaya* (chiffon gowns). The variety of white, brown and black-skinned Arab men, women and children defies stereotyping. 2

• • •

Still, the Arab stereotype has been part of our culture ever since cameras started cranking. Motion pictures of the early 1900s presented Arabia as an exotic land, with harems and seductive belly dancers. Many of today's perceptions can be traced to *the* motion picture of the 1920s, *The Sheik,* starring Rudolph Valentino. The film spurred the practice of lumping Arabs—Egyptians, Iraqis, Lebanese, Bahrainis and others—as a collective group. The film also spawned the illusion of the romantic sheik who abducts young ladies and confines them in his desert tent. Valentino's character turns out to be, despite his burnoose and desert tan, none other than a Scottish earl, who had been abandoned in the Sahara as a baby. A Scotsman, not an Arab, turns out to be the great lover and seducer of English ladies. 3

Television has replaced the movie's seductive sheik of the 1920s with the hedonistic oil sheik of the 1980s. In today's films and television shows, Arabs do not only pursue women, but a host of things, like American real estate, businesses and government officials. 4

"The great enemy of truth is very often not the lie—deliberate, continued and dishonest—but the myth, persistent, persuasive and unrealistic," said Presi- 5 dent John F. Kennedy. TV writers employ many myths about Arabs. Here are [two] of them.

• • •

ALL ARABS ARE MOSLEMS. A host of simple-minded cliches about Moslems 6 and Islam exists. When the hostage crisis in Iran occurred, most Westerners began to view all Moslems, the followers of Islam, as Arab or Iranian militants seeking to return the world to the 14th century. There is, however, great diversity in Islam, a religion that covers one-seventh of the earth's inhabitable area and includes a sixth of its population. To judge all Moslems as the same is as futile as judging all Christians and Jews in the same way. Most of the world's 800 million Moslems are not fatalistic radicals. Like most Christians and Jews, they, too, devoutly believe in and respect God and seek to live a good life in peace with others.

Many educated people con- 7 fuse the Arab world with the Moslem world. Geographically, Arab countries stretch along Northern Africa and into the Middle East. But the Moslem world overlaps the Arab world and stretches far beyond to most of Africa continuing eastward through India, Indonesia and the Philippines. Not all of the Arab world's 150 million people are Moslem, though many, of course, are both.

Former news correspondent, 8 radio announcer and author, Edward J. Byng, writes in his book *The World of the Arabs,* "Our Western picture of Islam and of the Arabs is a pitiful caricature of the reality. It is the result of thirteen hundred years of religious propaganda." In Arabic, "Islam" means submission to God. A religion that celebrated its 1400th anniversary in 1981, Islam provides an all-inclu-

Jack Shaheen: My Commitment to This Essay

In the preface to his book, from which this excerpt is taken, Jack Shaheen explains his personal motivation for writing. This statement is *not* itself an essay. Why not? What are the differences between this statement and his analysis of the portrayal of Arabs on television? What are the similarities?

*M*uch *of my philosophy about stereotyping stems from what I learned as a child from my mother, Nazara, and my grandparents, Naffa and Jacob. Their origins were in Lebanon, an Arab country with a rich heritage of ethnic and religious diversity. Our home in the steel city of Clairton, Pennsylvania, was a center for ethnic sharing—food, conversation, traditions and sometimes tears for those friends and relatives left behind in the "old country." The neighborhood consisted of people named Patellis, Mesco, Henderson, Geletko and Drnach, and was more like a family. We exchanged food—Arabic meat pies for sausage and lasagna. We exchanged thoughts—"Truman acts like a Republican"—and respect—"Your priest is a good man." It was a happy, innocent time.*

• • •

As a working, middle-class family living on the outskirts of Pittsburgh, we never experienced the sting of today's ethnic slurs. Nor were our neighbors insulted by stereotypes. One's heritage did not matter. People accepted you for what you were. Contact, not media imagery, shaped personal relationships.

My memories of the past, when people were looked upon as individuals—and current stereotypes, that paint ethnic groups with a broad brush—led me to write about the portrayal of Arabs on TV. Ethnic stereotypes and caricatures corrupt the imagination, narrow our vision and blur reality. My hope in writing this book is to eventually see a more balanced view of Arabs on television: to find in Arab television characters the equivalent of my mother, Nazara, and my grandparents, Jacob and Naffa, people who had compassion for all *other peoples. This work is also for my children and others, so as they grow up, they will experience the joy of accepting people as they are.*

sive system for social and religious conduct based upon the Koran (divine revelations) and the teachings of the prophet Mohammed. It is monotheistic and shares values and traditions with Christianity and Judaism. For example, Abraham (Ibrahim, in Arabic) is considered by Moslems as the father of all monotheistic people and is thus revered in Islam. Mohammed is the *last* prophet, following the footsteps of Abraham, Moses and Jesus. Islam's most basic acts of faith are usually called "The Five Pillars of Islam"—Profession of Faith, Prayer, Almsgiving, Fasting and Pilgrimage.

But on TV entertainment programs, when performers refer to "Allah" or 9 Islam, viewers do not see devout worshipers. TV often shows Islam as a religion that permits a man to have many wives and concubines and condones beheadings and stoning people to death. Although "Allah" means God, when performers say "Allah" on TV it is usually with the intent of evoking laughter, cynicism, or the image of some vaguely pagan deity.

• • •

ALL PALESTINIANS ARE TERRORISTS. The TV image fails to reflect the true 10 diversity of 4.4 million Palestinians who mostly live as exiles, scattered throughout the Middle East and beyond. During three decades of dispersal, Palestinians have developed an intense sense of community. They yearn to once again have a home they can call their own.

The stereotype obscures the peaceable Palestinian multitude—those men 11 and women who work as diplomats, doctors, professors, artists, farmers, engineers, shopkeepers and homemakers.

Former President Jimmy Carter has said that any permanent solution to the 12 Arab-Israeli conflict would require Israel "to honor Palestinian rights." Carter explained, "I see hundreds of thousands of Palestinians deprived of a home, deprived of a right to own property, deprived of a right to assemble, deprived of right of free speech, deprived of a right to vote and . . . approaching a generation under military rule. . . . This is not only contrary to established world custom, but it's also directly in violation of the heritage of the Jews and it is anomalous in an Israeli nation."

Viewers mainly see Palestinians as an evil mass of masked faces. This slant 13 ed view persists in spite of some balanced documentaries, newscasts, magazine and newspaper reports about the Palestinian people which show that most of them want peace.

• • •

The Arab world will number 300 million people by the year 2000. Its nat 14 ural settings of rolling deserts, forested mountains, white beaches and lush green river banks are ripe for the cinematographer's lens. There are untold stories to be heard within Arab communities. The emerging conflicts of individuals building nations while attempting to maintain valued religious and social traditions are many. Will their nations become so "modern" that social unity and faith decline? Will Arab folklore and language continue to survive alongside innovative ideas? Or will the technological future mute the Arab traditions of humor, poetry and song? Will the educated young, those who have studied at Arab universities or in Europe and the United States, continue to care for their parents at home? Or will they feel this is the responsibility of the state, of institutions? Will Western dress, already an accepted style in most Arab countries, reflect an actual change in social roles and attitudes?

The drama of the Arab world awaits the television artist. But in order to 15 capture such drama, the artist must first have a sincere motivation to care and to perceive. The artist might better follow those guidelines established by the Anti-Defamation League of the B'nai B'rith and "put an end forever to unjust and unfair discrimination against and ridicule of any sect or body of citizens."

Most perceptions of Arabs today come not from real knowledge but from 16
faulty and simplistic assumptions. The writer and producer, in cooperation with
broadcast standards officials, will convey a truer image when they begin to *see*
Arabs—indeed all people—as the multifaceted beings they are.

*For Discussion
and Writing*

Reading and Thinking Critically

1. *Personal response:* To what extent have you accepted the stereotyped portrayal of Arabs in the media? Put another way: To what extent have you previously recognized the complexity and variety of Arab life, as discussed by Shaheen in ¶s1–2 and 14?
2. *Broaden the context:* Reread President Kennedy's statement about myths. What other myths can you think of that are the "great enemy of truth"?
3. *Be alert to differences:* To what extent in your own viewing of television and movies are you aware of the stereotyped portrayals of Arabs that Shaheen discusses? Can you think of a particular movie or show in which Arabs are presented sympathetically—a show in which the director has captured "the drama of the Arab world"?

"In Search of the Arab" as an Example of Analysis

1. What principle of analysis does Shaheen use in examining Arab portrayals in the media? (See ¶5.)
2. In what ways do ¶s1–2 prepare the reader for the principle Shaheen will use in analyzing Arab portrayals in the media? What is the function of ¶s3–4?
3. In ¶5, Shaheen announces that he will examine two myths, which he does in two blocks of paragraphs: ¶s6–9 and ¶s10–13. Examine these sets of paragraphs. How does Shaheen organize them? How does he use his analytic principle?
4. What is the purpose of ¶s14–16? How are these paragraphs consistent with ¶s1–2, and how do they stand in contrast to the myths that Shaheen discusses in ¶s6–13?

STUDENT PAPER

The Coming Apart of a Dorm Society
Edward Peselman

*Edward Peselman wrote this paper as a first-semester sophomore, in response
to the following assignment from his sociology professor:*

Read chapter 3, "The Paradoxes of Power," in Randall Collins' *Sociological Insights: An Introduction to Non-Obvious Sociology* (2nd ed., 1992). Use any of Collins' observations to examine the sociology of power in a group with which you are familiar. Write for readers much like yourself: freshmen or sophomores who have taken one course in sociology. Your object in this paper is to use Collins as a way of learning something "nonobvious" about a group to which you belong or have belonged.

As you will see in the sidebar to this analysis, Peselman had compelling reasons to write about a somewhat troubling and confusing event in his past.

During my first year of college, I lived in a dormitory, like most fresh- 1
men on campus. We inhabitants of the dorm came from different cultural
and economic backgrounds. Not surprisingly, we brought with us many
of the traits found in people outside of college. Like many on the outside,
we in the dorm sought personal power at the expense of others. The gaining and maintaining of power can be an ugly business, and I saw people
hurt and in turn hurt others all for the sake of securing a place in the
dorm's prized social order. Not until one of us challenged that order did
I realize how fragile it was.

Randall Collins, a sociologist at the University of California, Riv- 2
erside, defines the exercise of power as the attempt "to make something
happen in society" (1992, p. 61). A society can be understood as something as large and complex as "American society"; something more sharply defined—such as a corporate or organizational society; or something smaller still—a dorm society like my own, consisting of six 18-year-old men who lived at one end of dormitory floor in an all male dorm.

Edward Peselman: My Commitment to This Essay

Edward Peselman was assigned to write an analytical essay for his sociology course. Through a careful choice of topics, he was able to discover a strong motivation to write, which he shares in his personal commitment statement. The statement is *not* itself an essay. Why not? What are the differences between this statement and the essay? What are the similarities?

When I got this assignment on power from my sociology professor, I knew immediately what I'd be writing about. Sometimes I see the people I lived with last year, and I think about how our relationship ended. It was a strange group of people. We didn't have much in common, but we still hung out. Insults were a big part of how we got along. Strange—and embarrassing!

I never examined my dorm experience in any particularly thoughtful way. I certainly never saw it "sociologically." The assignment about power and the reading in Randall Collins sparked an immediate connection to the dorm. Collins helped me to figure out, in a bit more detail, what was going on.

In my freshman year, my 3
society was a tiny but distinctive social group in which people exercised power. I lived with two roommates, Dozer and Reggie. Dozer was an emotionally unstable, excitable individual who vented his energy through anger. His insecurity and moodiness contributed to his difficulty in making friends. Reggie was a friendly, happy-go-lucky sort who seldom displayed emotions other than contentedness. He was shy when encountering new people, but when placed in a socially comfortable situation he would talk for hours.

Eric and Marc lived across the hall from us and therefore spent a con- 4
siderable amount of time in our room. Eric could be cynical and was often blunt: he seldom hesitated when sharing his frank and sometimes unflat-tering opinions. He commanded a grudging respect in the dorm. Marc could be very moody and, sometimes, was violent. His temper and stub-born streak made him particularly susceptible to conflict. The final mem-

ber of our miniature society was Benjamin, cheerful yet insecure. Benjamin had certain characteristics which many considered effeminate, and he was often teased about his sexuality—which in turn made him insecure. He was naturally friendly but, because of the abuse he took, he largely kept to himself. He would join us occasionally for a pizza or late-night television.

Together, we formed an independent social structure. Going out to 5 parties together, playing cards, watching television, playing ball: these were the activities through which we got to know each other and through which we established the basic pecking order of our community. Much like a colony of baboons, we established a hierarchy based on power relationships. According to Collins, what a powerful person wishes to happen must be achieved by controlling others. Collins's observation can help to define who had how much power in our social group. In the dorm, Marc and Eric clearly had the most power. Everyone feared them and agreed to do pretty much what they wanted. Through violent words or threats of violence, they got their way. I was next in line: I wouldn't dare to manipulate Marc or Eric, but the others I could manage through occasional quips. Reggie, then Dozer, and finally Benjamin.

Up and down the pecking order, we exercised control through macho 6 taunts and challenges. Collins writes that "individuals who manage to be powerful and get their own way must do so by going along with the laws of social organization, not by contradicting them" (p. 61). Until mid year, our dorm motto could have read: "You win through rudeness and intimidation." Eric gained power with his frequent and brutal assessments of everyone's behavior. Marc gained power with his temper—which, when lost, made everyone run for cover. Those who were not rude and intimidating drifted to the bottom of our social world. Reggie was quiet and unemotional, which allowed us to take advantage of him because we knew he would back down if pressed in an argument. Yet Reggie understood that on a "power scale" he stood above Dozer and often shared in the group's tactics to get Dozer's food (his parents were forever sending him care packages). Dozer, in turn, seldom missed opportunities to take swipes at Benjamin, with references to his sexuality. From the very first week of school, Benjamin could never—and never wanted to—compete against Eric's bluntness or Marc's temper. Still, Benjamin hung out with us. He lived in our corner of the dorm, and he wanted to be friendly. But everyone, including Benjamin, understood that he occupied the lowest spot in the order.

That is, until he left mid-semester. According to Collins, "any social 7 arrangement works because people avoid questioning it most of the time" (p. 74). The inverse of this principle is as follows: when a social arrangement is questioned, that arrangement can fall apart. The more fragile the arrangement (the flimsier the values on which it is based), the more quickly it will crumble. For the entire first semester, no one questioned our rude, macho rules and because of them we pigeon-holed Benjamin as a wimp. In our dorm society, gentle men had no power. To say the least, ours was not a compassionate community. From a distance of one year, I am shocked to have been a member of it. Nonetheless, we had created a mini-society that somehow served our needs.

At the beginning of the second semester, we found Benjamin packing up his room. Marc, who was walking down the hall, stopped by and said something like: "Hey buddy, the kitchen get too hot for you?" I was there, and I saw Benjamin turn around and say: "Do you practice at being such a _____ , or does it come naturally? I've never met anybody who felt so good about making other people feel lousy. You'd better get yourself a job in the army or in the prison system, because no one else is going to put up with your _____ ." Marc said something in a raised voice. I stepped between them, and Benjamin said: "Get out." I was cheering.   8

Benjamin moved into an off-campus apartment with his girlfriend. This astonished us, first because of his effeminate manner (we didn't know he had a girlfriend) and second because none of the rest of us had been seeing girls much (though we talked about it constantly). Here was Benjamin, the gentlest among us, and he blew a hole in our macho society. Our social order never really recovered, which suggests its flimsy values. People in the dorm mostly went their own ways during the second semester. I'm not surprised, and I was more than a little grateful. Like most people in the dorm, save for Eric and Marc, I both got my lumps and I gave them, and I never felt good about either. Like Benjamin, I wanted to fit in with my new social surroundings. Unlike him, I didn't have the courage to challenge the unfairness of what I saw.   9

By chance, six of us were thrown together into a dorm and were expected, on the basis of proximity alone, to develop a friendship. What we did was sink to the lowest possible denominator. Lacking any real basis for friendship, we allowed the forceful, macho personalities of Marc and Eric to set the rules, which for one semester we all subscribed to— even those who suffered.   10

The macho rudeness couldn't last, and I'm glad it was Benjamin who brought us down. By leaving, he showed a different and a superior kind of power. I doubt he was reading Randall Collins at the time, but he somehow had come to Collins' same insight: as long as he played by the rules of our group, he suffered because those rules placed him far down in the dorm's pecking order. Even by participating in pleasant activities, like going out for pizza, Benjamin supported a social system that ridiculed him. Some systems are so oppressive and small minded that they can't be changed from the inside. They've got to be torn down. Benjamin had to move, and in moving he made me (at least) question the basis of my dorm friendships.   11

Reference

Collins, R. 1992. *Sociological Insight: An Introduction to Non-Obvious Sociology.* 2nd ed. New York: Oxford University Press.

Reading and Thinking Critically

1. *Personal response:* By using analytical tools borrowed from Randall Collins, has Peselman gained insight into his freshman-year dorm experiences?
2. *Be alert to differences:* How does what Peselman observes about power relationships in a college dormitory correspond with what you know of such relations? If you can identify a dorm society of which you are a part, do you see power relations at work? How different are the rules that establish the pecking order in your dorm from the macho rules that Peselman describes?
3. *Challenge the reading:* Are you satisfied with the extent to which Peselman, as the writer and observer, includes himself in his own analysis? To what extent does he stand outside the behavior he is analyzing? Would you make any suggestions to him in this regard?
4. *Challenge the reading:* In ¶2, Peselman wants to extend Collins' use of "society" as a broad term to something much smaller, the "mini" society of a dorm. Does this extension seem fair to you?

"The Coming Apart of a Dorm Society" as an Example of Analysis

1. What is the function of ¶1? Though Peselman does not use the word "sociology," what signals does he give that this will be a paper that examines the social interactions of a group?
2. Peselman introduces Collins in ¶2. Why?
3. What does Peselman accomplish in ¶s3–4? How does his use of Collins in ¶5 logically follow the presentation in ¶s3–4?
4. The actual analysis in this paper takes place in ¶s5–11. Point to where Peselman draws on the work of Randall Collins, and explain how he uses Collins to gain insight into dorm life.

Structures and Strategies

Prepare to Write: Explore Your Idea

Discovering Ideas

Whether you are assigned a topic to write on or are left to your own devices, you inevitably face this question: What is my idea? Like every essay, an analysis has at its heart an idea you want to convey. For Edward Peselman, it was the idea that a social order based on flimsy values is not strong enough to sustain a direct challenge to its power, and thus will fall apart eventually. From beginning to end, Peselman advances this one idea: first, by introducing readers to the dorm society he will analyze; next, by introducing principles of analysis (from Randall Collins); and finally, by examining his dorm relationships in light of these principles. The entire set of analytical insights coheres as an essay because the insights are *related* and point to Peselman's single idea. Following are three techniques for generating ideas for analysis.

Reflect on Your Experience

Peselman's essay offers a good example of the personal uses to which analysis can be put. Peselman reflected on his own experience and, as he says in his personal commitment statement, "knew immediately what [he'd] be writing about." Notice that he gravitated toward events in his life that confused him and about which he wanted some clarity. Such topics can be especially fruitful for analysis because you know the particulars well and can provide readers with details; there is a puzzle to the topic that interests you; and there is a prospect, through the application of your analytical tool, for understanding. When you select from your experience topics to analyze, you provide yourself with a motivation to write and learn. When you are motivated in this way, you spark the interest of readers, who will want to follow you in your effort to make meaning of your experience.

Choose to Analyze an Event, Object, or Behavior That Readers Know Well But Will Not Have Considered from Your Particular Angle

Harvey Greenberg's analysis of *The Wizard of Oz* (discussed at the beginning of this chapter, pages 231–232) shows the advantages of analyzing a topic familiar to readers. Greenberg could assume that most people had seen *The Wizard of Oz* and probably remembered it as a pleasant childhood film. Very likely, Greenberg also understood that his readers had not thought systematically about the film in the ways a psychiatrist would. When you analyze an event, object, or behavior that readers know well but have not examined systematically as part of an analysis, you instantly create the potential to write an essay that will show something new. Recall John Levine's topic—diners. We've all been to diners, but have we considered them in just the way that he has, as places of comfort? *No*, and because we have not, we read on. Marie Winn writes of television viewing. We all watch television, but how many of us have thought systematically about our viewing habits in terms of addiction? Winn motivates us to read. Analyzing familiar objects can thus challenge you to show readers something new; and such analyses can motivate readers to look with interest on a novel way of seeing something they thought they understood or, perhaps, had never perceived a need to consider seriously.

Read to Discover Ideas

In a later section of this chapter ("Advance Your Idea with Sources"), you will learn to locate in books and articles the analytical tools needed to examine specific events, objects, and behaviors. Often in assigning an analytical essay, your professor will choose this tool for you. Edward Peselman, for example, was asked to use "any of [Randall] Collins' observations [on power] to examine the sociology of power in a group with which you are familiar." Peselman used Collins as directed, but at one point he extended one of Collins's principles:

According to Collins, "any social arrangement works because people avoid questioning it most of the time" (p. 74). The inverse of this principle is as follows: when a social arrangement is questioned, that arrangement can fall apart. The more fragile the arrangement (the flimsier the values on which it is based), the more quickly it will crumble.

Notice how Peselman is able to think independently with the analytical principle Collins offers. Peselman *reasons* with this principle. He generates a new and related principle, which he puts directly to use in analyzing his dorm society (see ¶s7–9). Allow your reading to stimulate your own thinking about analytical principles and definitions. Showing independence in this regard is a sign that you have your own ideas about the principles being applied and that you are using them thoughtfully.

Committing Yourself to an Idea

The very best writing is produced by those who have a personal stake in what they write. At times, this personal stake is discovered through writing; at other times, it precedes writing. In either event, you should be conscious of *not* letting readers see your work until you have adopted these attitudes:

- I write for myself and for my audience.
- I will find an approach to writing that lets me discover something personally significant.

You can find significance for both yourself and your readers in virtually any event, behavior, or object you wish to analyze. The key is to be thorough and systematic in the application of an analytical principle. Using Randall Collins as a guide, Edward Peselman returns again and again to the events of his freshman year in the dormitory. We sense that Peselman himself wants to know what happened in that dorm. He writes: "I saw people hurt and in turn hurt others all for the sake of securing a place in the dorm's prized social order." There's a silent judgment being made here. Peselman does not approve of what happened, and the analysis he launches is meant to help him understand. Such personal commitment to the events and behaviors being analyzed creates for readers an equal and parallel commitment: we want stay with this essay to learn what happened. When you commit yourself to the idea of your essay, readers will follow into your analysis.

Write: Clarify Your Idea and Make It Public

Creating Common Ground with Readers

Readers may or may not be familiar with the object, event, or behavior you wish to analyze. Harvey Greenberg could assume that readers had seen *The Wizard of Oz*. He did not, therefore, need to summarize the movie before launching into his analysis. Edward Peselman, by contrast, could be sure that readers would not know anything about the events and behaviors in his dormitory. He therefore took special care to present the cast of characters (see ¶s 3–4) that readers would need in order to follow an analysis. One of your early tasks is to determine how much of the event, behavior, or object being analyzed you will need to recreate for readers.

You have a related concern, as well: to determine the extent to which readers are familiar with or agree with the analytical tool you are using. When presenting to audiences who understand or are likely to accept this tool, you don't need to do much more than state it before putting it to use. This is Jack Shaheen's strategy (pages 236–239). He offers no reasons why we should accept the principle (in ¶5) that myths are the enemy of truth, beyond his attributing the statement to a figure he believes we are likely to trust, John F. Kennedy. If that statement were spoken by someone completely unknown to readers, then readers would have *no* reason to accept it as a legitimate principle for analysis. In that case, Shaheen would have likely felt an obligation to discuss the principle and demonstrate its usefulness.

Tone and the Writing Occasion

Recall that an analysis is an argument, an effort to demonstrate to readers that an event, object, or behavior has a particular meaning and significance. This demonstration of significance is a serious business, and the tone of an analysis is accordingly earnest and direct. There is little room for playfulness, even when you are analyzing an object or behavior that readers might consider light-hearted. For instance, in analyzing diners John Levine takes a topic that we don't typically consider weighty enough to discuss in serious tones, but he does just that, suggesting diners are places of comfort. The tone of an analysis usually matches the form's serious purpose. We see this tone demonstrated in each of the examples that begin this chapter.

Planning a Structure

An analysis is a two-part argument. The first part states and establishes the writer's agreement with a certain principle or definition.

Part One of the Argument

This first argument essentially takes this form:

Claim #1: Principle "X" (or definition "X") is valuable.

Principle "X" can be a theory as encompassing and abstract as the statement that *myths are the enemy of truth.* Principle "X" can be as modest as the definition of a term—for instance, "addiction" or "comfort." As you move from one subject area to another, the principles and definitions you use for analysis will change, as these assignments illustrate:

Sociology: Write an essay in which you place yourself in American society by locating both your absolute position and relative rank on each single criterion of social stratification used by Lenski & Lenski. For each criterion, state whether you have attained your social position by yourself or if you have "inherited" that status from your parents.

Literature: Apply principles of Jungian psychology to Hawthorne's "Young Goodman Brown." In your reading of the story, apply Jung's principles of the *shadow, persona,* and *anima*.[2]

Physics: Use Newton's second law ($F = ma$) to analyze the acceleration of a fixed pulley, from which two weights hang: m_1 (.45 kg) and m_2 (.90 kg). Explain in a paragraph the principle of Newton's law and your method of applying it to solve the problem. Assume your reader is not comfortable with mathematical explanations: do not use equations in your paragraph.

Finance: Using Guidford C. Babcock's "Concept of Sustainable Growth" [*Financial Analysis* 26 (May–June 1970): 108–114], analyze the stock price appreciation of the XYZ Corporation, figures for which are attached.

The analytical tools to be applied in these assignments change from discipline to discipline. Writing in response to the sociology assignment, you would use sociological principles developed by Lenski and Lenski. In your literature class, you would use principles of Jungian psychology; in physics, Newton's second law; and in finance, a particular writer's concept of "sustainable growth." But whatever discipline you are working in, the first part of your analysis will clearly state which (and whose) principles and definitions you are applying. For audiences unfamiliar with these principles, you will need to explain them; if you anticipate objections, you will need to argue that they are legitimate principles capable of helping you as you conduct an analysis.

Part Two of the Argument

In the second part of an analysis, you *apply* specific parts of your principle or definition to the topic at hand. Regardless of how it is worded, this second argument in an analysis can be rephrased to take this form:

Claim #2: By applying Principle (or definition) "X," we can understand ___(topic)___ as ___(conclusion based on analysis)___.

This is your thesis, the main idea of your analytical essay. Fill in the first blank with the specific object, event, or behavior you are examining. Fill in the second blank with your conclusion about the meaning or significance of this object, based on the insights made during your analysis. In

---

[2]Analysis of literature presents a special case. See chapter 10 for details.

the case of John Levine, the object in question is a diner, and his claim can be expressed as follows:

> By applying observations offered by Liz Logan, we can understand *diners* as *places of comfort.*

Marie Winn completes the second claim of her analysis this way:

> By applying the four-part definition I've just presented, *television viewing* can be understood as *an addiction.*

And Jack Shaheen completes the second claim of his analysis as follows:

> By applying President Kennedy's observation that myths are the enemy of truth, we can see *the depictions of Arabs on television* as a *distortion of the truth about Arabs.*

Unless you are asked to follow a specialized format, especially in the sciences or the social sciences, you can present your analysis as an essay by following the guidelines below. As you move from one class to another, from discipline to discipline, the principles and definitions you use as the basis for your analyses will change, but the following basic components of analysis will remain the same:

- Create a context for your essay of analysis. Introduce and summarize for readers the object, event, or behavior to be analyzed. Present a strong case about why an analysis is needed: give yourself a motivation to write, and give readers a motivation to read. Consider setting out a problem, puzzle, or question to be investigated.

- Introduce and summarize the key definition or principle that will form the basis of your analysis. Plan to devote the first part of your analysis to arguing for the validity of this principle or definition *if* your audience is not likely to understand it or if they are likely to think that the principle or definition is *not* valuable.

- Analyze your topic. Systematically apply elements of this definition or principle to parts of the activity or object under study. You can do this by directing specific questions, based on your analytic principle or definition, to the object. Discuss what you find part by part (organized, perhaps, by question), in clearly defined sections of the essay.

- Conclude by stating clearly what is significant about your analysis. When considering your essay as a whole, what new or interesting insights have you made concerning the object under study? To what extent has your application of the definition or principle helped you to explain how the object works, what it might mean, or why it is significant?

Understanding Your Logic

Turning Key Elements of a Principle or Definition into Questions

Prepare for an analysis by developing questions based on the definition or principle you are going to apply, and then by directing these questions to the activity or object to be studied. The method is straightforward: state as clearly as possible the principle or definition to be applied. Divide the principle or definition into its parts and, using each part, develop a question. For example, Jack Shaheen used as his analytic principle this insight from President Kennedy: *Myths are the enemy of truth.*

Shaheen divided his principle for analysis into three parts, and he created three questions:

1. Specifically, what myths about Arabs have been presented on television?
2. What is the truth about Arabs, with regard to these myths?
3. How have the myths damaged the truth?

Directing Your Questions to the Object under Analysis

In his analysis of Arab portrayals on television (pages 236–239), Shaheen poses these questions to the two myths he identifies: "All Arabs are Moslems" and "All Palestinians are Terrorists." For each myth, he answers his three questions. Here is his analysis of the first myth:

Specifically, what myths about Arabs have been presented on television?

Many educated people confuse the Arab world with the Moslem world.

What is the truth about Arabs, with regard to these myths?

Geographically, Arab countries stretch along Northern Africa and into the Middle East. But the Moslem world overlaps the Arab world and stretches far beyond to most of Africa continuing eastward through India, Indonesia and the Philippines. Not all of the Arab world's 150 million people are Moslem, though many, of course, are.

How have the myths damaged the truth?

TV often shows Islam as a religion that permits a man to have many wives and concubines and condones beheadings and stoning people to death. Although "Allah" means God, when performers say "Allah" on TV it is usually with the intent of invoking laughter, cynicism, or the image of some vaguely pagan deity.

The other writers whose analyses open this chapter follow the same logic in their essays: each takes a principle or definition for analysis, converts it to questions, and then uses the questions to identify parts of and to make insights into the object being examined. For instance, Marie Winn develops a four-part definition of addiction, each part of which is readily turned into a question which she then directs at a specific behavior: television viewing. Her analysis of television viewing is then developed in four parts that can be understood as *responses* to each of her analytical questions.

Developing the Paragraph-by-Paragraph Logic of Your Essay

The following paragraph from Edward Peselman's essay illustrates the typical logic of a paragraph in an analytical essay:

Up and down the pecking order, we exercised control through macho taunts and challenges. Collins writes that "individuals who manage to be powerful and get their own way must do so by going along with the laws of social organization, not by contradicting them" (p. 61). Until mid year, our dorm motto could have read: "You win through rudeness and intimidation." Eric gained power with his frequent and brutal assessments of everyone's behavior. Marc gained power with his temper—which, when lost, made everyone run for cover. Those who were not rude and intimidating drifted to the bottom of our social world. Reggie was quiet and unemotional, which allowed us to take advantage of him because we knew he would back down if pressed in an argument. Yet Reggie understood that on a "power scale" he stood above Dozer and often shared in the group's tactics to get Dozer's food (his parents were forever sending him care packages). Dozer, in turn, seldom missed opportunities to take swipes at Benjamin, with references to his sexuality. From the very first week of school, Benjamin could never—and never wanted to—compete against Eric's bluntness or Marc's temper. Still, Benjamin hung out with us. He lived in our corner of the dorm, and he wanted to be friendly. But everyone, including Benjamin, understood that he occupied the lowest spot in the order.

We see in this example paragraph the typical logic of analysis.

The writer introduces a specific analytical tool.   Peselman quotes a line from Randall Collins:

> "[I]ndividuals who manage to be powerful and get their own way must do so by going along with the laws of social organization, not by contradicting them."

The writer applies this analytical tool to the object being examined.
Peselman states *his* dorm's law of social organization.

> Until mid year, our dorm motto could have read: "You win through rudeness and intimidation."

The writer uses the tool to identify and then examine the meaning of parts of the object.   Peselman shows how each member (the "parts") of his dorm society conforms to the laws of "social organization":

> Eric gained power with his frequent and brutal assessments of everyone's behavior. Marc gained power with his temper—which, when lost, made everyone run for cover. Those who were not rude and intimidating drifted to the bottom of our social world. . . .

An essay of analysis takes shape when a writer creates a series of such paragraphs and then links them with an overall logic. Here is the logical organization of Edward Peselman's essay:

The Coming Apart of a Dorm Society

¶1: Introduction states a problem—provides a motivation to write and to read.

¶2: Randall Collins is introduced—the author whose work will provide principles for analysis.

¶s3–4: Background information is provided—the cast of characters in the dorm.

¶s5–9: The analysis takes place—specific parts of dorm life are identified and found significant, using principles from Collins.

¶s10–11: Summary and conclusion are provided—the freshman dorm society disintegrated for reasons set out in the analysis. A larger point is made: Some oppressive systems must be torn down.

Advance Your Idea with Sources

When you are given an assignment that asks for analysis, be prepared to bring two specific strategies for reading to source materials that might provide you with principles and definitions.

- **Look for a sentence that makes a general statement about the way something works.** The statement may strike you as a rule or a law. The line that Jack Shaheen quotes from John F. Kennedy has this quality: "The great enemy of truth is very often not the lie—deliberate, continued and dishonest—but the myth, persistent, persuasive and unrealistic." Such statements are generalizations, conclusions to sometimes complicated and extensive arguments. You can use these conclusions to guide your own analyses as long as you are aware that for some audiences, you will need to recreate and defend the arguments that resulted in these conclusions.

- **Look for statements that take this form: "X" can be defined as (or "X" consists of) the following: A, B, and C.** The specific elements of the definition—A, B, and C—are what you use to identify and analyze parts of the object being studied. You've seen an example of this approach in Marie Winn's four-part definition of addiction, which she uses to analyze television viewing. As a reader looking for definitions suitable for conducting an analysis, you might come across Winn's definition of addiction and then use it for your own purposes, perhaps to analyze the playing of video games as an addiction.

Following is a page from *Sociological Insight* by Randall Collins; Edward Peselman used a key sentence from this extract as an analytical tool in his essay on power relations in his dorm (see page 241). Notice that Peselman underlines the sentence he will use in his essay:

Try this experiment some time. When you are talking to someone, make them explain everything they say that isn't completely clear. The result, you will discover, is a series of uninterrupted interruptions:

A: Hi, how are you doing?
B: What do you mean when you say "how"?
A: You know. What's happening with you?
B: What do you mean, "happening"?
A: Happening, you know, what's going on.
B: I'm sorry. Could you explain what you mean by "what"?
A: What do you mean, what do I mean? Do you want to talk to me or not?

It is obvious that this sort of questioning could go on endlessly, at any rate if the listener doesn't get very angry and punch you in the mouth. But it illustrates two important points. First, virtually everything can be called into question. We are able to get along with other people not because everything is clearly spelled out, but because we are willing to take most things people say without explanation. Harold Garfinkel, who actually performed this sort of experiment, points out that there is an infinite regress of assumptions that go into any act of social communication. Moreover, some expressions are simply not explainable in words at all. A word like "you," or "here," or "now" is what Garfinkel calls "indexical." You have to know what it means already; it can't be explained.

"What do you mean by 'you'?"

"I mean *you, you!*" About all that can be done here is point your finger.

The second point is that people get mad when they are pressed to explain things that they ordinarily take for granted. This is because they very quickly see that explanations could go on forever and the questions will never be answered. If you really demanded a full explanation of everything you hear, you could stop the conversation from ever getting past its first sentence. The real significance of this for a sociological understanding of the way the world is put together is not the anger, however. It is the fact that people try to avoid these sorts of situations. They tacitly recognize that we have to avoid these endless lines of questioning. Sometimes small children will start asking an endless series of "whys," but adults discourage this.

<u>In sum, any social arrangement works because people avoid questioning it most of the time</u>. That does not mean that people do not get into arguments or dispute about just what ought to be done from time to time. But to have a dispute already implies there is a considerable area of agreement. An office manager may dispute with a clerk over just how to take care of some business letter, but they at any rate know more or less what they are disputing about. They do not get off into a . . . series of questions over just what is meant by everything that is said. You could very quickly dissolve the organization into nothingness if you followed that route: there would be no communication at all, even about what the disagreement is over.

Social organization is possible because people maintain a certain level of focus. If they focus on one thing, even if only to disagree about it, they are taking many other things for granted, thereby reinforcing their social reality.

The statement that Peselman has underlined—"any social arrangement works because people avoid questioning it most of the time"—is the end result of an argument that takes Collins several paragraphs to develop. Peselman agrees with the conclusion and uses it in ¶7 of his essay. Observe that for his own purposes Peselman does *not* reconstruct Collins's argument. He selects *only* Collins's conclusion and then imports that into his essay. Once he identifies in Collins a principle he can use in his analysis, he converts the principle into questions that he then directs to his topic: life in his freshman dorm. Two questions follow directly from Collins's insight:

1. What was the social arrangement in the dorm?
2. How was this social arrangement questioned?

Peselman clearly defines his dormitory's social arrangement in ¶s3–6 (with the help of another principle borrowed from Collins). Beginning with ¶7, he explores how one member of his dorm questioned that arrangement:

> That is, until he left mid-semester. According to Collins, "any social arrangement works because people avoid questioning it most of the time" (p. 74). The inverse of this principle is as follows: when a social arrangement is questioned, that arrangement can fall apart. The more fragile the arrangement (the flimsier the values on which it is based), the more quickly it will crumble. For the entire first semester, no one questioned our rude, macho rules and because of them we pigeon-holed Benjamin as a wimp. In our dorm society, gentle men had no power. To say the least, ours was not a compassionate community. From a distance of one year, I am shocked to have been a member of it. Nonetheless, we had created a mini-society that somehow served our needs.

Evaluate and Revise

General Evaluation

You will usually need at least two drafts to produce an essay that presents your idea clearly. The biggest changes in your essay will typically come between your first and second drafts. In this book you will find two demonstrations of essays in the process of turning from meandering first thoughts into finished products. First, see the general advice on the process of writing and revising in chapters 13 and 14, which include first- and second-draft versions of a student paper. You will find another such demonstration in the "Student Writer at Work" sections at the end of chapters 1–5. In fact, that student writer makes use of analysis in his work. See the final draft of his essay, pages 3–5.

No essay that you write, including an analysis, will be complete until you revise and refine your single compelling idea: your analytical conclusion about what the object, event, or behavior being examined means or how it is significant. You revise and refine by evaluating your first draft, bringing to it many of the same questions you pose when evaluating any piece of writing. In chapter 5 you will find general guidelines for evaluating what you read, including these:

- Are the facts accurate?
- Are opinions supported by evidence?
- Are the opinions of others authoritative?
- Are my assumptions clearly stated?
- Are key terms clearly defined?
- Is the presentation logical?

- Are all parts of the presentation well developed?
- Are dissenting points of view presented?

Address these same questions to the first draft of your analysis, and you will have solid information to guide your revision.

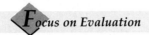

Focus on Evaluation

Have your been asked to write an evaluation of another writer's essay of analysis? If so, you will base your evaluation on two sets of standards. First you will apply specific standards for this type of writing as listed here in "Critical Points." At the same time, you will need to apply the general standards for evaluation that are listed here and discussed at length in chapter 5, pages 92–96. See especially the "key points" for evaluation in chapter 5, pages 95–96.

Critical Points in an Analytical Essay

Write an Analysis, Not a Summary

The most common error made in writing analyses, which is *fatal* to the form, is to present readers with a summary only. For analyses to succeed, you must *apply* a principle or definition and reach a conclusion about the object, event, or behavior you are examining. By definition, a summary includes none of your own conclusions. Summary is naturally a part of analysis; you will need to summarize the object or activity being examined and, depending on the audience's needs, summarize the principle or definition being applied. But in an analysis, you must take the next step and share insights that suggest the meaning or significance of some object, event, or behavior.

Make Your Analysis Systematic

Analyses should give the reader the sense of a systematic, purposeful examination. Marie Winn's analysis illustrates the point: she lays out four elements of a definition she will use to analyze television viewing, she takes up each element in turn, and she applies this element to her topic. Winn is admirably systematic in her method, and we are never in doubt about her purpose.

Imagine another analysis in which a writer lays out four elements of a definition but then applies only two, without explaining the logic for omitting the others. Or imagine an analysis in which the writer offers a principle for analysis but directs it to only a half or a third of the object being discussed, without providing a rationale for doing so. In both cases, the writer would be failing to deliver on a promise basic to analyses: once a principle or definition is presented, it should be thoroughly and systematically applied.

Evaluate Your Analytical Tool

Essential to any analysis is the validity of the principle or definition being applied, the analytical tool. Make yourself aware, both as writer and reader, of a tool's strengths and limitations. Pose these questions of the analytical principles and definitions you use: Are they accurate? Are they well accepted? Do *you* accept them? What are the arguments against them? What are their limitations? Since every principle or definition used in an analysis is the end product of an argument, you are entitled—even obligated—to challenge it. If the analytical tool is flawed, then the analysis that follows from it will be flawed also.

Answer the "So What" Question

An analysis should make readers *want* to read. It should give readers a sense of getting to the heart of the matter, that what is important in the object or activity under analysis is being laid bare and discussed in revealing ways. If when rereading the first draft of your essay, you cannot imagine readers saying, "I never thought of _____ this way," then something may be seriously wrong. Reread closely to determine why the essay might leave readers flat and exhausted, as opposed to feeling that they have gained new and important insights. Closely reexamine your own motivations for writing. Have *you* learned anything significant through the analysis? If not, neither will readers, and they will turn away. If you have gained important insights through your analysis, communicate them clearly. At some point, pull together your related insights and say, in effect: "Here's how it all adds up."

Occasions for Discussion and Writing

**An Analytical Essay of
Your Own**

You are ready to begin work on your own analytical essay. One approach to choosing a topic is to review examples of the type of essay you will be writing. Consider rereading the essays that opened this chapter. You will find that the four authors—Levine, Winn, Shaheen, and Peselman—write about topics they know well either through direct experience or through careful reading. You will also find that at least two of these authors have a deep, personal involvement with their essay's topic: Jack Shaheen, of Arab descent, writes on media stereotypes of Arabs; and Edward Peselman writes of power relations in his college dormitory. In choosing a topic for your essay, you too can take a deep interest. In the best of cases, your motivation to write will be personal, but your expression of ideas *in your essay* will be public and controlled. The Shaheen and Peselman examples amply demonstrate this double quality: in each essay you find someone writing for personal reasons, yet maintaining strict control over important elements of public expression—including the essay's reasoning, structure, sentence rhythm, and word choice.

To prepare for your analytical essay, select one of the examples that began this chapter, one that you find especially effective. Think critically about how this essay succeeds. You might respond to the questions following the piece; you might try writing a paragraph explaining what appeals to you most about the piece; you might reflect on the ways in which this essay could affect your own work. Once you have studied the piece and have a clear sense of how it succeeds, choose a topic for your own essay—a topic that you know well.

The next two Occasions sections present two topics for writing: analyzing the content of advertising and analyzing the content of television shows. If you prefer another topic, you might find suitable materials in the other Occasions sections in chapters 6–7 and 9–11:

Chapter 6: Date Rape and Campus Policy, 135–141
Exploring Gender Identity, 142–164

Chapter 7: The Rising Costs of College, 201–212
The College Admissions Process, 212–230

Chapter 9: High-School Dress Codes, 318–322
Community Tensions (The Riots at Crown Heights), 322–341

Chapter 10: Poems by Langston Hughes, 374–380
Short Stories by Kate Chopin, James Joyce, 380–402

Chapter 11: Television and Literacy, 445–455
Cultural Consequences of Technology, 455–484

Of course, you are not limited to these choices and should choose a topic according to your interests and experience. For detailed guidance on how you might organize your approach to writing an analytical essay, turn to the second Occasion for discussion and writing in this chapter, pages 274–278. That "Guide to the Assignment" provides a structured approach to the writing task that may help you work through your first draft and revision, whatever your topic.

A note on using sources.   All of the writers whose essays begin the chapter draw on source materials to advance their ideas. You can—and are encouraged to—do the same, with the caution that writers who use sources should never let source materials overtake their essays. The psychological focus of your essay should remain yours alone. In writing a first draft, be sure that your voice predominates and that sources, even if essential to your essay's success, play a subordinate role.

I. Analyzing an Advertisement

Each of us sees and hears hundreds of advertisements daily. Busy as we are, we seldom have time to reflect on the ways in which advertisers construct ads to influence our buying habits. But influence us they do, with a content that is both visually and verbally complex. Ads consist of an explicit, or obvious, content and an implicit, or suggested, one. The implicit content of advertisements is the subject of our discussion. In this Occasions section, you will find an advertisement and two reading selections. As with the brief *Wizard of Oz* example analyses that opened this chapter (see pages 231–232), the two analyses you bring to the single advertisement will yield different insights. Study the award-winning advertisement for Lee jeans (see page 258) and then read the two selections. Working by yourself, do the following:

- Summarize the reading selections. In a paragraph, describe the advertisement for Lee jeans.
- Respond to the selections and to the advertisement.
- Identify principles or definitions you use could use for analysis.
- Conduct an analysis: systematically apply at least one principle or definition from each selection to the advertisement.
- Compare the results of your analyses.

Having done this, work in small groups and discuss your analytical insights.

Sources for Identifying Analytical Tools

Two reading selections follow, from which you will be able to draw principles and definitions to analyze the Lee ad. This first selection appears in a textbook on advertising by Dorothy Cohen of Hofstra University.

We've had to fit into their workplace, their government and their clubs. Do we really have to fit into their jeans?

Women have had to fight for the vote. Women have had to fight for equal pay. At times, women have even had to fight to be called women.

And if you were to ask almost anyone, the fight has been well worth it.

However, does that mean women should have to fight their way into jeans that were made for men?

At Lee, we have a somewhat untraditional point of view. You see, unlike other manufacturers, we believe a woman's place is in women's jeans.

We build jeans the way a woman is built, because we think it should be just as easy for a woman to find a pair of jeans that fit as it is for a man. You might say that we're an equal opportunity jeansmaker.

(Is it really any wonder so many women out there have at least a couple pairs of Lee Jeans in their closets?)

What's more, because not all women are alike, not all Lee Jeans are alike. In addition to our popular Relaxed Fit Jeans, for example, Lee also accommodates you with classic Regular Fit and our new Loose Fit Jeans.

So you don't have to wear jeans made for anybody but you. After all, just because women want to wear the pants these days, that doesn't mean they have to be somebody else's.

Lee
The brand that fits.

Elements of an Effective Layout

Dorothy Cohen

Fundamentally a good layout should attract attention and interest and should provide some control over the manner in which the advertisement is read. The message to be communicated may be sincere, relevant, and important to the consumer, but because of the competitive "noise" in the communication channel, the opportunity to be heard may depend on the effectiveness of the layout. In addition to attracting attraction, the most important requisites for an effective layout are balance, proportion, movement, utility, clarity, and emphasis. 1

Balance

Balance is a fundamental law in nature and its application to layout design formulates one of the basic principles of this process. *Balance* is a matter of weight distribution; in layout it is keyed to the *optical center* of an advertisement, the point which the reader's eye designates as the center of an area. In an advertisement a vertical line which divides the area into right and left halves contains the center; however the optical center is between one-tenth and one-third the distance above the mathematical horizontal center line. . . . 2

In order to provide good artistic composition, the elements in the layout must be in equilibrium. Equilibrium can be achieved through balance, and this 3 process may be likened to the balancing of a seesaw. The optical center of the advertisement serves as the fulcrum or balancing point, and the elements may be balanced on both sides of this fulcrum through considerations of their size and tonal quality.

The simplest way to ensure formal balance between the elements to the right and left of the vertical line is to have all masses in the left duplicated on the right in size, weight, and distance from the center. . . . Formal balance imparts feelings of dignity, solidity, refinement, and reserve. It has been used for institutional advertising and suggests conservatism on the part of the advertiser. Its major deficiency is that it may present a static and somewhat unexciting appearance; however, formal balance presents material in an easy-to-follow order and works well for many ads. 4

To understand informal balance, think of children of unequal weight balanced on a seesaw; to ensure equilibrium it is necessary to place the smaller child far from the center and the larger child closer to the fulcrum. In informal balance the elements are balanced, but not evenly, because of different sizes and color contrast. This type of a symmetric balance requires care so that the various elements do not create a lopsided or topheavy appearance. A knowledge of a sense of the composition can help create the feeling of symmetry in what is essentially asymmetric balance. 5

Informal balance presents a fresh, untraditional approach. It creates excitement, a sense of originality, forcefulness, and, to some extent, the element of surprise. Whereas formal balance may depend on the high interest value of the illustration to attract the reader, informal balance may attract attention through the design of the layout. . . . 6

Proportion

Proportion helps develop order and creates a pleasing impression. It is related to balance but is concerned primarily with the division of the space and the emphasis to be accorded each element. Proportion, to the advertising designer, is the relationship between the size of one element in the ad to another, the amount of space between elements, as well as the width of the total ad to its depth. Proportion also involves the tone of the ad: the amount of light area in relation to dark area and the amount of color and noncolor.[1] 7

As a general rule unequal dimensions and distances make the most lively design in advertising. The designer also places the elements on the page so that each element is given space and position in proportion to its importance in the total advertisement and does not look like it stands alone. . . . 8

Movement

If an advertisement is to appear dynamic rather than static, it must contain some movement. *Movement* (also called *sequence*) provides the directional flow for the advertisement, gives it its follow-through, and provides coherence. It guides the reader's eye from one element to another and makes sure he or she does not miss anything. 9

Motion in layout is generally from left to right and from top to bottom—the direction established through the reading habits of speakers of Western lan- 10

---

[1]Roy Paul Nelson, *The Design of Advertising,* 4th ed., (Dubuque, IA: Wm. C. Brown Co., 1981), p. 118.

guage. The directional impetus should not disturb the natural visual flow but should favor the elements to be stressed, while care should be taken not to direct the reader's eye out of the advertisement. This can be done by the following:

—*Gaze motion* directs the reader's attention by directing the looks of the people or animals in an ad. If a subject is gazing at a unit in the layout, the natural tendency is for the reader to follow the direction of that gaze; if someone is looking directly out of the advertisement, the reader may stop to see who's staring.

—*Structural motion* incorporates the lines of direction and patterns of movement by mechanical means. An obvious way is to use an arrow or a pointed finger. . . . Sequence can also be achieved by building the layout in accordance with certain letters of the alphabet, (*S, J, C, V, Z,* and *O*).

Unity

Another important design principle is the unification of the layout. Although an   11
advertisement is made up of many elements, all of these should be welded into a compact composition. Unity is achieved when the elements tie into one another by using the same basic shapes, sizes, textures, colors, and mood. In addition, the type should have the same character as the art.

A *border* surrounding an ad provides a method of achieving unity. Sets of   12
borders may occur within an ad, and, when they are similar in thickness and tone, they provide a sense of unity.

Effective use of white space can help to establish unity. . . . *White space* is   13
defined as that part of the advertising space which is not occupied by any other elements; in this definition, white space is not always white in color. White space may be used to feature an important element by setting it off, or to imply luxury and prestige by preventing a crowded appearance. It may be used to direct and control the reader's attention by tying elements together. If white space is used incorrectly, it may cause separation of the elements and create difficulty in viewing the advertisement as a whole.

Clarity and Simplicity

The good art director does not permit a layout to become too complicated or   14
tricky. An advertisement should retain its clarity and be easy to read and easy to understand. The reader tends to see the total image of an advertisement; thus it should not appear fussy, contrived, or confusing. Color contrasts, including tones of gray, should be strong enough to be easily deciphered, and the various units should be clear and easy to understand. Type size and design should be selected for ease of reading, and lines of type should be a comfortable reading length. Too many units in an advertisement are distracting; therefore, any elements that can be eliminated without destroying the message should be. One way in which clarity can be achieved is by combining the logo, trademark, tag line, and company name into one compact group.

Emphasis

Although varying degrees of emphasis may be given to different elements, one   15
unit should dominate. It is the designer's responsibility to determine how much emphasis is necessary, as well as how it is to be achieved. The important element may be placed in the optical center or removed from the clutter of other elements. Emphasis may also be achieved by contrasts in size, shape, and color, or the use of white space.

The second reading selection is excerpted from the essay "Women: Invisible Cages" by Brigid Brophy. Brophy wrote this selection in 1963, but the sentiments she expressed then are far from being dated. In 1991, in her bestselling *Backlash,* Susan Faludi wrote: "The word may be that women have been 'liberated,' but women themselves seem to feel otherwise. Repeatedly in national surveys, majorities of women say they are still far from equality." Brophy makes the same point when she writes about *apparent* liberation and invisible cages. Read Brophy to identify principles and definitions you can use to analyze the advertisement for Lee jeans.[3]

from Women: Invisible Cages

Brigid Brophy

All right, nobody's disputing it. Women are free. At least, they *look* free. They even feel free. But in reality women in the western industrialized world today are like the animals in a modern zoo. There are no bars. It appears that cages have been abolished. Yet in practice women are still kept in their place just as firmly as the animals are kept in their enclosures. The barriers which kept them in now are invisible. 1

It is about forty years since the pioneer feminists, several of whom were men, raised such a rumpus by rattling the cage bars—or created such a conspicuous nuisance by chaining themselves to them—that society was at last obliged to pay attention. The result was that the bars were uprooted, the cage thrown open: whereupon the majority of the women who had been held captive decided they would rather stay inside anyway. 2

To be more precise, they *thought* they decided; and society, which can with perfect truth point out "Look, no bars," *thought* it was giving them the choice. There are no laws and very little discrimination to prevent western, industrialized women from voting, being voted for or entering the professions. If there are still comparatively few women lawyers and engineers, let alone women presidents of the United States, what are women to conclude except that this is the result either of their own free choice or of something inherent in female nature? 3

Many of them do draw just this conclusion. They have come back to the old argument of the anti-feminists, many of whom were women, that women are unfit by nature for life outside the cage. And in letting this old wheel come full cycle women have fallen victim to one of the most insidious and ingenious confidence tricks ever perpetrated. 4

In point of fact, neither female nature nor women's individual free choice has been put to the test. As American Negroes have discovered, to be officially free is by no means the same as being actually and psychologically free. A society as adept as ours has become at propaganda—whether political or commercial—should know that "persuasion," which means the art of launching myths and artificially inducing inhibitions, is every bit as effective as force of law. No doubt the reason society eventually agreed to abolish its anti-woman laws was that it had become confident of commanding a battery of hidden dissuaders 5

---

[3]You can also use this selection as a source for your written analysis of a television show. See the assignment on page 264.

which would do the job just as well. Cage bars are clumsy methods of control, which excite the more rebellious personalities inside to rattle them. Modern society, like the modern zoo, has contrived to get rid of the bars without altering the fact of imprisonment. All the zoo architect needs to do is run a zone of hot or cold air, whichever the animal concerned cannot tolerate, round the cage where the bars used to be. Human animals are not less sensitive to social climate.

The ingenious point about the new-model zoo is that it deceives both sides 6 of the invisible barrier. Not only can the animal not see how it is imprisoned; the visitor's conscience is relieved of the unkindness of keeping animals shut up. He can say "Look, no bars round the animals," just as society can say "Look, no laws restricting women" even while it keeps women rigidly in place by zones of fierce social pressure.

There is, however, one great difference. A woman, being a thinking ani- 7 mal, may actually be more distressed because the bars of her cage cannot be seen.

Individual Response: Analyzing an Advertisement

Carefully study the advertisement for Lee jeans and read the two selections: "Elements of an Effective Layout" and the excerpt from "Women: Invisible Cages."

1. Summarize the reading selections. In a paragraph, describe the advertisement for Lee jeans.

2. Identify in each selection at least one principle or definition that you could apply in analyzing the advertisement. For detailed advice on reading to identify analytical tools, see "Advance Your Idea with Sources," pages 251–253.

3. Convert the principles or definitions you have found into questions. For advice on this point, see pages 248–249.

4. Conduct an analysis: systematically apply at least one principle or definition from each selection to the Lee advertisement.

5. Compare your analytical insights. What conclusions can you draw about the application of multiple analytical tools to a single object for analysis?

6. In what ways have the analytical tools you've used given you access to the advertisement that you wouldn't otherwise have had? In what ways, simultaneously, have these tools *limited* your vision? How can the same tool that limits be responsible for giving you analytical access?

Group Response: Analyzing an Advertisement

1. As a group, take turns identifying the analytical principles and definitions you found in the reading selections. Someone should keep a record of the group's discussion.

2. Compare the insights group members made on the basis of "Elements of an Effective Layout." To what extent are group members' insights similar?

3. What makes the Lee jeans advertisement successful or unsuccessful in terms of layout? In your response, try to devise a comprehensive, thesis-like statement that accounts for as many of your analytical insights as possible.

4. Compare the insights group members made on the basis of "Women: Invisible Cages." To what extent are your group members' insights similar?

5. In terms of the psychology of gender relations and gender identity that Brophy discusses, what do you think is the appeal of this Lee jeans advertisement? In your response, try to devise a comprehensive, thesis-like statement that accounts for as many of your analytical insights as possible.

6. Discuss the different insights your group has made into the Lee jeans advertisement. Are the two sets of insights based on principles and definitions found in the two reading selections at all comparable? To what extent do your analytical insights point to similar elements of the advertisement?

7. Do you find that either of the reading selections yields a better analysis of the ad? How do you define *better?*

8. Brainstorm on other analytical approaches to this advertisement that might prove revealing.

9. As a group, take up a question you considered individually: In what ways have the analytical tools you've used given you access to the advertisement that you wouldn't otherwise have had? In what ways, simultaneously, have these tools *limited* your vision? How can the same tool that limits be responsible for giving you analytical access?

Projecting an Essay: Analyzing an Advertisement

1. As a group, plan to write a detailed sketch of an analysis of the Lee jeans advertisement. Your first decision is to determine which of the two reading selections the group wants to use.

2. Each member of the group should reread the agreed-on selection and systematically identify every possible principle or definition that might be suitable for analyzing the advertisement.

3. Create a master list of these principles and definitions. As a group, convert each principle and definition into a question, and then direct this question to the advertisement. Record your responses and photocopy your group's notes so that each member has a full set.

4. Individually, review your group's notes for analysis. Realizing that you could not use all the insights your group has made in a single essay, choose five or six related insights that you think suggest some overall coherence about the ad: what the ad means, how it works, or why it is significant. Write out this statement of coherence. This will become your proposed working thesis for the group's projected essay. The five or six related insights will become paragraph- (or multi-paragraph-) length analyses of the ad, which you will present as support for your thesis.

5. As a group, review each member's selection of notes and his or her working thesis statement. Agree on which statement is most compelling. Explicitly discuss what makes for a compelling thesis in an analytical essay.

6. Having agreed on which working thesis the group will pursue in its projected essay, review *all* the notes for analysis that would support this thesis. Choose five or six to include in the projected essay.

7. Based on your group's selection of a working thesis and a corresponding set of analytical insights, create a detailed outline of your projected essay.

8. Option: Write an essay based on the group's outline.

II. Analyzing the Content of Television Shows

This Occasions section consists of three selections, any one of which you can use to analyze the content of a television show. Each selection provides you with many analytical tools: principles and definitions you can apply to the show of your choice. These tools differ from one another significantly, so your analysis of a show will depend wholly on which tool you select. In the first article, Michael Parenti argues that television shows, in addition to their entertainment value, have a political content. Gary Selnow follows with a report on a "values analysis" of prime-time television. More than you might think, reports this author, the "medium . . . [demonstrates] a wide-ranging set of positive personal values." In the third and final selection, Marsha E. Williams and John C. Condry explore the portrayals of minorities on television and find that over the years, "the programming and advertisements on television have hardly changed at all, at least from the perspective of peoples of color." These writers share a key assumption: that television has a powerful educational effect. What that effect is perceived to be depends on the questions they—and you—pose.

Your Writing Assignment

Using one of the three selections in this Occasions section, analyze the content of a television show: a 30- or 60-minute situation comedy, cartoon, or drama. The goal of your analysis is to make a statement about what the show means, how it works, or why it is significant. The show should be one that you watch regularly so that you have a clear sense of its characters, audience, and recurring or developing themes. If possible, arrange to videotape the segment so that you can watch it several times. Write for an audience of college students your same age. Do *not* assume that your audience has seen the show to be analyzed or has read the materials on which you will base your analysis.

Following the readings, you will find a guide to the assignment that will help you through the process of writing and revising your analysis.[4]

---

[4]In the preceding section, you will find a selection by Brigid Brophy, "Women: Invisible Cages." You can use this selection, in addition to those in this Occasions section, as a source for principles and definitions by which to analyze a television show.

Political Entertainment
Michael Parenti

A frequent commentator on radio and television, Michael Parenti is the author of five books, all with radical themes: Democracy for the Few; Power and Powerlessness; Inventing Reality: The Politics of the Mass Media; The Sword and the Dollar: Imperialism, Revolution, and the Arms Race; *and* Make-Believe Media: The Politics of Entertainment, *in which the following selection appears. Parenti claims that television shows have a political content, and he suggests what that content might be.*

Make-believe. The term connotes the playful fantasies of our childhood, a pleasant way of pretending. But in the world created by movies and television, make-believe takes on a more serious meaning. In some way or other, many people come to believe the fictional things they see on the big and little screens. The entertainment media are the make-believe media; they make us believe.

Today, very little of our make-believe is drawn from children's games, storytelling, folktales, and fables, very little from dramas and dreams of our own making. Instead we have the multibillion-dollar industries of Hollywood and television to fill our minds with prefabricated images and themes. Nor are these just idle distractions. I will argue that such images often have real ideological content. Worse still, they discourage any critical perception of the great and sometimes awful realities of our lives and sociopolitical system, implanting safe and superficial pictures in our heads. Even if supposedly apolitical in its intent, the entertainment industry is political in its impact.

How can we speak of Hollywood films and television shows as being "purely" entertainment when they regularly propagate certain political themes and carefully avoid others? To borrow Robert Cirino's phrase: "We're being more than entertained."[1] Hollywood and television are permeated with class, racial, gender, and other political biases. George Gerbner argues that all media carry a "hidden curriculum" of values and explanations about how things happen.[2] The sociologist Hal Himmelstein believes that through its settings, music, words, and stories, television has become "one of our society's principal repositories of ideology."[3] A leading communications critic, Herbert Schiller, writes that "one central myth dominates the world of fabricated fantasy; the idea that [media] entertainment and recreation are value-free, have no point of view, and exist outside . . . the social process."[4] Another critic, Erik Barnouw, concludes: "Popular entertainment is basically propaganda for the status quo."[5]

In accord with those observations, I will try to demonstrate in the chapters ahead that over the years, films and television programs have propagated images and ideologies that are supportive of imperialism, phobic anticommunism, capitalism, racism, sexism, militarism, authoritarian violence, vigilantism, and anti–working-class attitudes. More specifically, media dramas teach us that:

- Individual effort is preferable to collective action.
- Free enterprise is the best economic system in the world.
- Private monetary gain is a central and worthy objective of life.
- Affluent professionals are more interesting than blue-collar or ordinary service workers.
- All Americans are equal, but some (the underprivileged) must prove themselves worthy of equality.

- Women and ethnic minorities are not really as capable, effective, or interesting as White males.

- The police and everyone else should be given a freer hand in combating the large criminal element in the United States, using generous applications of force and violence without too much attention to constitutional rights.

- The ills of society are caused by individual malefactors and not by anything in the socioeconomic system.

- There are some unworthy persons in our established institutions, but they usually are dealt with and eventually are deprived of their positions of responsibility.

- U.S. military force is directed only toward laudable goals, although individuals in the military may sometimes abuse their power.

- Western industrial and military might, especially that of the United States, has been a civilizing force for the benefit of "backward" peoples throughout the Third World.

- The United States and the entire West have long been threatened from abroad by foreign aggressors, such as Russians, Communist terrorists, and swarthy hordes of savages, and at home by unAmerican subversives and conspirators. These threats can be eradicated by a vigilant counterintelligence and by sufficient doses of force and violence.

The Hollywood director Cecil B. deMille once said that if you want to send 5 a message use Western Union. Hollywood is strictly an entertainment business and not a purveyor of social messages or political causes, he maintained. In fact, Hollywood, like television, is very much in the business of sending political messages. Certainly not the kind of reformist or dissident messages that deMille objected to, but ones—like those listed above—with which he felt comfortable, so comfortable that he did not think they had political content.

What the media actually give us is something that is neither purely enter- 6 tainment nor purely political. It is a hybrid that might be called "political entertainment." The entertainment format makes political propagation all the more insidious. Beliefs are less likely to be preached than assumed. Woven into the story line and into the characterizations, they are perceived as entertainment rather than as political judgments about the world. When racial subjugation is transmuted into an amusing Sambo and imperialist violence into an adventuresome Rambo, racism and imperialism are more likely to be accepted by viewers, who think they are merely being entertained. "Beliefs, attitudes, and values are more palatable and credible to an audience when they are molded and reinforced by characters and program plots than when they are preached by a newscaster or speaker for a particular cause."[6] To quote Schiller:

> For manipulation to be most effective, evidence of its presence should be nonexistent. When the manipulated believe things are the way they are naturally and inevitably, manipulation is successful. In short, manipulation requires a false reality that is a continuous denial of its existence.
>
> It is essential, therefore, that people who are manipulated believe in the neutrality of their key social institutions. They must believe that government, the media, education, and science are beyond the clash of conflicting social interests.[7]

Notes

1. Robert Cirino, *We're Being More Than Entertained* (Honolulu: Lighthouse Press, 1977).

2. George Gerbner, Larry Gross, and William Meldoy, eds., *Communication Technology and Social Policy* (New York: Wiley, 1973).

3. Hal Himmelstein, *Television Myth and the American Mind* (New York: Praeger, 1984), p. 3.

4. Herbert Schiller, *The Mind Managers* (Boston: Beacon Press, 1973), pp. 79–80.

5. Erik Barnouw, "Television as a Medium," *Performance,* July/August 1972, cited in Schiller, *The Mind Managers,* p. 80.

6. Ralph Arthur Johnson, "World without Workers: Prime Time's Presentation of Labor," *Labor Studies Journal,* 5, Winter 1981, p. 200.

7. Schiller, *The Mind Managers,* p. 11.

Values in Prime-Time Television
Gary W. Selnow

Gary W. Selnow is Associate Professor in the Department of Communication Studies at Virginia Polytechnic Institute and State University. The following selection appeared in the Journal of Communication *in 1990. Selnow uses an eighteen-item inventory, devised by the Baltimore City Public Schools, to analyze the values content of television shows.*

In the past several years, low dealings of people in high places, including government and religious figures and Wall Street notables, have inspired a heightened interest in personal values in the United States. With this attention comes a desire to discover causes for the perceived impoverishment of values. Prominent among scores of candidates, including drug abuse, the breakdown of the family, and a general population-wide abandonment of religious beliefs, is the unhealthy influence of television. It has been argued that television's sexual and violent content is eroding a sense of values among the viewing public (see 33). Consequently, some seek to reduce this type of content and encourage more temperate programing (see 8).

There is also a growing sense that responsibility for teaching values should be shifted from family and church, where it once resided, to third-party institutions, most notably community organizations and schools. Some have suggested that television, too, should move from being part of the problem to part of the remedy.

Only a handful of studies have dealt with television and values. Sutherland and Siniawsky (32) found that, contrary to popular belief, soap operas do not condone immoral behaviors; other authors argue that soap operas do help legitimize taboo behaviors (19, 25). Chesebro (7) described the communication strategies used to convey values on television; and in earlier work (31) I examined the moral codes that undergird the resolution of problems on television.

This article describes how values are portrayed on prime-time network television programs. After cataloguing the occurrence of "values incidents" according to a well-accepted inventory of values, it describes the characters involved, characterizes the instructional potential for viewing audiences, and considers the disposition of values as favorable or unfavorable. It then looks at the prominence of values incidents in a story line and at how fully the values are explained. Finally, it examines how values incidents are structured and linked.

Although values have been defined in many ways (e.g., 1, 4, 20, 23), most 5 definitions converge on Rokeach's statement that a value is "a type of belief, centrally located within one's total belief system, about how one ought or ought not to behave. . . . Values are thus abstract ideals, positive or negative, not tied to any specific attitudes, object or situation" (29, p. 124). Developing a coding scheme based on such a description is a difficult undertaking. Values involve considerable subjectivity, emotional weightlifting, and individual interpretation bound up in ideology and group perspective. Selecting a typology of values, therefore, was critical.

This study used an 18-item inventory developed by the Baltimore 6 **City Public Schools.** The BCPS taxonomy, selected following an exhaustive review of existing value classification schemes (e.g., 2, 14, 26, 28), provides bold, clear statements and so avoids problems inherent to vague value concepts (see 21). Moreover, since the program serves as the basis for classroom instruction, it defines each item clearly and includes a complete set of lesson plans illustrating the precise meaning of each category. Such elaborate documentation helped us apply the instrument uniformly and consistently.

The BCPS values program was chosen, however, primarily for its invento- 7 ry and substance. Baltimore designers selected items that were universal and contributed to a well-rounded education. These items offer "a set of key tenets or a common core of beliefs built around positive character and good citizenship objectives which exist within a pluralistic society" (27, p. 2). Items derive from other school and church programs, traditional citizenship courses, and psychology literature. The package reflects basic Judeo-Christian tenets but clearly is not religious in nature. It concerns personal, social, and national values, and so represents more than a single perspective. In short, this values taxonomy, developed by a mainstream school system and since adopted widely by other school systems as a standard for values instruction (16), provides a well-accepted cross-section of values and presents them in a form easily adaptable to television content analysis.

The BCPS Values Inventory consists of ten "personal values" and eight "cit- 8 izenship values."[1] The personal values generally involve a set of individual philosophies related to self-perceptions and an outlook toward others. Embedded in this inventory are notions of right and wrong and a sense of global standards for human rights and human obligations:

1. Personal integrity and honesty rooted in respect for the truth, intellectual curiosity, and love of learning.
2. A sense of duty to self, family, school, and community.
3. Self-esteem rooted in the recognition of one's potential.
4. Respect for the rights of all persons regardless of their race, religion, sex, age, physical condition, or mental state.

---

[1]In the original BCPS scheme these categories were called "character objectives" and "citizen objectives." The categories appear here in slightly edited form.

5. A recognition of the rights of others to hold and express differing views, combined with the capacity to make discriminating judgments among competing opinions.
6. A sense of justice, rectitude, and fair play, or a commitment to them.
7. A disposition of understanding, sympathy, concern, and compassion for others.
8. A sense of discipline and pride in one's work; respect for the achievement of others.
9. A respect for one's property and the property of others, including public property.
10. Courage to express one's conviction.

The citizenship values deal with an individual's responsibilities to the state; [9] they avoid social norms and customs governing human relationships. These culture-specific values outline an individual's commitment to a democratic philosophy:

1. Patriotism; love, respect, and loyalty to the United States; a willingness to correct its imperfections by legal means.
2. An understanding of the rights and obligations of a citizen in a democratic society.
3. An understanding that other societies in the world do not enjoy the rights and privileges of a democratic government.
4. Respect for the U.S. Constitution, the rule of law, and the right of *every* citizen to enjoy equality under the law. An understanding of the Bill of Rights and a recognition that all rights are limited by other rights and obligations.
5. Respect for legitimate authority at the local, state, and federal level.
6. Allegiance to the concept of democratic government and opposition to totalitarian rule. A recognition that such government is limited by the separation of powers and by the countervailing role of other institutions in a pluralistic society—principally the family, religion, the school, and the private sector of the economy.
7. Recognition of the need for an independent court system to protect the rights of all citizens.
8. An acceptance of all citizenship responsibilities at the local, state, and national levels, and a commitment to preserve and to defend the United States and its democratic institutions.

We defined a values incident as an event, behavior, or verbal reference [10] revealing any one, or any substantive portion, of the 18 values articulated in the BCPS taxonomy. Incidents ranged from passing references, in one or two lines of dialogue, to central subplot themes.

• • •

The personal values that are endemic to American culture are deeply [11] **embedded in the programming material of its most favored entertainment medium.** These values are played out in endless scenarios and in countless dialogues, and range in magnitude from subplot foundations to passing observations. They appear in many forms and are expressed by many types of characters at various levels of involvement. If the strength of a lesson grows with the frequency of its exhibition and with the variance of conditions under which it is displayed, then television's lessons are remarkably coherent and congruent with the beliefs of churches, schools, and commercial institutions. If the cumulative effects of television's themes and patterns move audiences toward perceptions of mainstream values (e.g., 11, 12), the value themes identified here also may play an important role in perpetuating established cultural norms.

Most important, values observed in this program sample are shown to be "good" not only by their positioning but by their close association with characters representing state authority. Because law enforcement characters are over-represented among characters involved with positive values (as they are among *all* prime-time characters), displays of positive values are linked strongly and disproportionately with authority and power figures. Such displays help perpetuate the cultural norm that associates goodness and positive values with the state, power, and recognized authority. Television, therefore, not only projects a values system but reinforces the association of such values with mainstream authority institutions.   12

Amid television's admittedly dramatic accounts of sex and violence, the medium is also demonstrating a wide-ranging set of positive personal values. Viewers see entire programs, not just controversial portions. With evidence that television portrays a range of positive personal values, this article argues that its effects may lie not only in the demonstration of power but also in the teaching of the standards of individual morality.   13

References

1. Allport, G. W., P. E. Vernon, and G. Lindzey. *A Study of Values.* Boston: Houghton Mifflin, 1960.

2. Bales, R. and A. Couch. "The Value Profile: A Factor Analytic Study of Value Statements." *Sociological Inquiry* 39, 1969, pp. 3–17.

3. Bandura, A. *Social Learning Theory.* Morristown, N.J.: General Learning Press, 1971.

4. Bem, D. J., *Beliefs, Attitudes, and Human Affairs.* Belmont, Cal.: Brooks/Cole, 1970.

5. Blau, P. and O. Duncan. *The American Occupational Structure.* New York: John Wiley, 1967.

6. Busby, L. J. "Sex-role Research on the Mass Media." *Journal of Communication* 25(4), Autumn 1975, pp. 107–131.

7. Chesebro, J. W. "Communication, Values, and Popular Television Series—A Four-Year Assessment." In H. Newcomb (Ed.), *Television: The Critical View* (4th ed.). New York: Oxford University Press, 1987, pp. 16–54.

8. Christian Leaders for Responsible Television. "Statement of Concern." Tupelo, Mississippi, February 3, 1986.

9. Dominick, J. "Crime and Law Enforcement on Prime-Time Television." *Public Opinion Quarterly* 37(2), Summer 1973, pp. 241–250.

10. Donnagher, P. C., R. W. Poulos, R. M. Liebert, and E. S. Davidson. "Race, Sex and Social Example: An Analysis of Character Portrayals on Interracial Television Entertainment." *Psychological Reports* 38, 1976, pp. 241–250.

11. Gerbner, G. "Television's Populist Brew: The Three B's." *Etc.: A Review of General Semantics* 44(1), 1987, pp. 3–8.

12. Gerbner, G., L. Gross, M. Morgan, and N. Signorielli. "Political Correlates of Television Viewing." *Public Opinion Quarterly* 48(1B), Spring 1984, pp. 283–300.

13. Gerbner, G., L. Gross, M. Morgan, and N. Signorielli. "Aging with Television: Images on Television Drama and Conceptions of Social Reality." *Journal of Communication* 30(1), Winter 1980, pp. 37–47.

14. Gordon, L. V. *The Survey of Personal Values.* Chicago: Science Research Associates, 1960.

15. Greenberg, B. S. "Television and Role Socialization: An Overview." In D. Pearl, J. B.

Lazar, and L. Bouthilet (Eds.), *Television and Behavior: Ten Years of Scientific Progress and Implications for the Eighties.* Volume 2. Washington, D.C.: U.S. Department of Health and Human Services, 1982, pp. 179–190.

16. Green, Sharon, Education Specialist and Program Coordinator, Baltimore City Public Schools. Telephone conversation, August 25, 1988.

17. Hodge, R. and D. Tripp. *Children and Television.* Stanford, Cal.: Stanford University Press, 1986.

18. Holsti, O. R. *Content Analysis for the Social Sciences and Humanities.* Reading, Mass.: Addison-Wesley, 1969.

19. Katzman, N. "Television Soap Operas: What's Been Going on Anyway?" *Public Opinion Quarterly* 36(2) Summer 1972, pp. 200–212.

20. Kluckholn, C. "Values and Value Orientations in the Theory of Action: An Exploration in Definition and Classification." In T. Parsons and E. A. Shils (Eds.), *Toward a General Theory of Action.* Cambridge, Mass.: Harvard University Press, 1951, pp. 388–433.

21. Kraft, V. *Foundations for a Scientific Analysis of Value.* London: D. Reidel, 1981.

22. McNeil, J. C. "Feminism, Femininity, and the Television Series: A Content Analysis." *Journal of Broadcasting* 19(3), Summer 1975, pp. 259–271.

23. Maslow, A. H. (Ed.). *New Knowledge in Human Values.* Chicago: Henry Regnery, 1970.

24. Meyrowitz, J. "Television and the Obliteration of Childhood: The Restructuring of Adult/Child Information Systems." In S. Thomas (Ed.), *Studies in Mass Communication and Technology.* Norwood, N.J.: Ablex, 1984, pp. 151–167.

25. Modeleski, T. "The Search for Tomorrow in Today's Soap Operas." *Film Quarterly* 33, 1979, pp. 12–21.

26. Moos, R. H. *Evaluating Educational Environments.* San Francisco: Jossey-Bass, 1979.

27. Pinderhughes, A. G., J. Sarnecki, and G. Green. "Status Report on the Character and Citizenship Education Program in the Baltimore City Schools." City of Baltimore, Department of Education, Baltimore, Md., 1987.

28. Rokeach, M. *The Nature of Human Values.* San Francisco, Jossey-Bass, 1973.

29. Rokeach, M. *Beliefs, Attitudes, and Values.* San Francisco, Jossey-Bass, 1980.

30. Seggar, J. F. "Imagery of Women in Television Drama: 1974." *Journal of Broadcasting* 19(3), Summer 1975, pp. 273–282.

31. Selnow, G. W. "Solving Problems on Prime Time Television." *Journal of Communication* 36(2), Spring 1986, pp. 63–72.

32. Sutherland, J. C. and S. J. Siniawsky. "The Treatment and Resolution of Moral Violations on Soap Operas." In E. J. Whetmore (Ed.), *Mediamerica.* Belmont, Cal.: Wadsworth, 1985, pp. 317–325.

33. Yen, M. "A Morality Who's Who." *Publishers Weekly,* July 11, 1986, p. 42.

Living Color: Minority Portrayals and Cross-Racial Interactions on Television

Marsha E. Williams and John C. Condry

Marsha E. Williams and John C. Condry teach in the Department of Human Development and Family Studies at Cornell University. The following appeared in a paper they presented at the 1989 Conference of The Society for Research in Child Development. The authors conclude that hardly any progress has been made in portraying peoples of color on television.

Controversy surrounding the portrayal of racial and ethnic minorities on tele- [1] vision is almost as old as the medium itself. Peoples of color have historically been both underrepresented and misrepresented on television. During the early years, nonwhites comprised fewer than 3% of all character portrayals (Smythe, 1953). By the early 1970s, however, this figure had increased to approximately 11% (U.S. Commission on Civil Rights, 1977), and there it remained throughout most of this decade (Greenberg, 1982). Although Blacks have always been television's most visible minority group, parity with the U.S. census data has yet to be achieved. Furthermore, minority characters, be they Blacks, Asians, Native Americans, or Latinos, have traditionally been less diverse, less dignified, and less positive than either white characters or real life minorities.

Stereotypic black roles of the 1950s and early 1960s gave way to more   2 subtle indicators of racism in the 1970s (see MacDonald, 1983, for a historical review). For example, Black characters tended to be younger and poorer, and less likely to be cast in professional occupations, dramatic or romantic roles (Greenberg, 1982; Berry, 1980; Graves, 1980). Moreover, Blacks on television were more likely to appear in segregated environments, with a great percentage of minority's appearance time concentrated in a very small percentage of the programs (Weigel & Howes, 1982; Weigel, Loomis, & Soja, 1980).

The misrepresentation of other minority groups persisted through the   3 1970s as well. Native American organizations protested the depiction of Indians as savage, ignorant, and cowardly warriors. However, the popularity of television westerns rendered the protests futile. Asian portrayals on television paralleled those in motion pictures. Women were either docile and submissive, or seductive and sexy. Asian men tended to be cunning and sly villains, or superwise, Charlie Chan-type detectives. They, too, were featured in limited occupational roles such as laundry men, waiters, or karate experts. Finally, television's Hispanics were typically poor and unemployed barrio-dwellers, or aggressive and hostile gang members (Greenberg, 1982).

This article focuses on the programming frequently watched by children in   4 America. Specifically, the present study reports a content analysis designed to investigate the nature of minority portrayals and cross-racial relationships on television programs and commercials broadcast during 1987. Although no formal hypotheses were tested, the analysis was guided by several questions of interest: Are minorities still underrepresented and misrepresented on television, as earlier research indicated? If so, to what degree? How are interactions between white and minority characters portrayed? Do they exist? If so, how frequently? Are they voluntary or involuntary interactions? Do they occur more frequently among children or adults?

· · ·

Discussion

The findings reported in this study are strikingly similar to those reported in pre-   5 vious content analyses. Studies analyzing television content during the 1970s found that minority appearances on dramatic programs averaged approximately 11% during that decade (Greenberg, et al., 1980; Seggar, Hafen, & Hannon-Gladden, 1981). That the present study reports a figure smaller than 10% does not reflect a decrease in minority representation, but rather an increase in the type of broadcasting included in the sample. This study included all of the programs and advertisements (with few exceptions, as described in the Method section) aired heavy children's viewing hours, and thus provided a more valid representation of the "environment" of television. Advertisements, although they represent less than 13 minutes of broadcasting per hour (Condry, 1987; Condry, Bence, & Scheibe, 1988), bombard the television viewer with character portrayals. In this study, an average hour of television consisted of 71 commercial characters (65 white, 6 nonwhite) compared to only 22 program characters (19 white, 3 nonwhite). Thus, the inclusion of advertisements provides an important addition to our fund of knowledge about the structure of television.

For comparative purposes, however, the present sample was divided, and [6] analysis was conducted on fictional programs only (movies, situation comedies, and dramas). The results indicate that nonwhites comprised 14.5% of the total characters, a gain of 3.5% over the Greenberg, et al., and Seggar, et al., studies. While this increase is encouraging, it is not necessarily indicative of a general trend in television broadcasting. Fictional characters represent only 15% of the total number of appearances in the present sample.

The nature of minority portrayals has remained virtually unchanged as well. [7] Character analysis revealed several ways in which television minorities are less prestigious than whites. They appear as children with much greater frequency, and as such are more limited in both authority and responsibility. Although minority characters are just as likely to be employed as whites, they generally hold lower status jobs. Furthermore, nonwhites are rarely cast as friends and neighbors, but they frequently appear as both perpetrators and victims of criminal and delinquent acts more so than white characters.

Nearly 40% of television's minorities have no contact with whites. When [8] cross-racial interactions do occur, however, an interesting trend emerges. Children and teens typically engage in positive, social interactions with white characters. In other words, cross-racial friendships among youth were commonplace outside of the classroom. By adulthood, however, positive social interaction with whites had sharply diminished. Adults' cross-racial relations, though predominantly positive, tended to be limited to less voluntary job-related situations. These findings suggest the degree to which the broadcasting industry has accepted integration in American society. Socially, friendships among minority and white children and adolescents are acceptable, but by adulthood, both white and nonwhite individuals are expected to have outgrown the tendency to interact socially.

• • •

The study presented here shows that, like the viewing audience, the pro- [9] gramming and advertisements on television have hardly changed at all, at least from the perspective of peoples of color. This finding should not be taken lightly, even though exceptions (e.g., "The Cosby Show") are singled out with justifiable pride by network officials. Television may have come some distance since "Beulah" and "Amos 'N Andy," but this research suggests that it still has a long way to go.

References

Berry, G. L. (1980). Children, television, and social class roles: The medium as an unplanned educational curriculum. In E. L. Palmer & A. Dorr (Eds.), *Children and the faces of television* (pp. 71–81). New York: Academic Press.

Berry, G. L., & Mitchell-Kernan, C. (1982). *Television and the socialization of the minority child.* New York: Academic Press.

Collins, W. A. (1983). Interpretation and inference in children's television viewing. In J. Bryant & D. R. Anderson (Eds.), *Children's understanding of television* (pp. 125–150). New York: Academic Press.

Collins, W. A. (1979). Children's comprehension of television content. In E. Martella (Ed.), *Children communicating: Media and development of thought, speech, and understanding.* Beverly Hills, CA.: Sage.

Condry, J. C. (1987) TV as educator. *Action in Teacher Education, Journal of the Association of Teacher Educators, 9*(2), 15–26.

Condry, J. C., Bence, P., & Scheibe, C. (1988). Non-program content of children's television. *Journal of Broadcasting and Electronic Media, 32*(3), 255–270.

Graves, S. B. (1982). The impact of television on the cognitive and affective development of minority children. In G. L. Berry & C. Mitchell-Kernan (Eds.), *Television and the socialization of the minority child* (pp. 37–67). New York: Academic Press.

Greenberg, B. S. (1988). Some uncommon television images and the drench hypothesis. In S. Oskamp (Ed.), *Television as a social issue* (pp. 88–102). Newbury Park, CA.: Sage.

Greenberg, B. S. (1982). Television and role socialization: An overview. In D. Pearl, L. Bouthilet, & J. Lazar (Eds.), *Television and behavior: Ten years of scientific progress and implication for the eighties. Vol. 2. Technical reviews* (pp. 179–190). Rockville, MD: NIMH.

Greenberg, B. S., Simmons, K. W., Hogan, L., & Atkin, C. K. (1980). The demography of fictional characters. In B. S. Greenberg (Ed.), *Life on television.* Norwood, NJ: Ablex.

Greenberg, B. S., & Burek-Neuendorf, K. (1980). Black family interactions on television. In B. S. Greenberg (Ed.), *Life on television.* (pp. 35–46). Norwood, NJ: Ablex.

Greenberg, B. S. (1972). Children's reactions to TV blacks. *Journalism Quarterly, 69*(1), 5–14.

MacDonald, J. F. (1983). *Blacks on white TV: Afro-Americans in television since 1948.* Chicago: Nelson-Hall.

Nielsen Report on Television (1988). Northbrook, IL: A.C. Nielsen Co.

Seggar, J. F., Haren, J. K., & Hannonen-Gladden, H. (1981). Television's portrayals of minorities and women in drama and comedy drama, 1971–1980. *Journal of Broadcasting, 25,* 277–288.

Smythe, D. W. (1954). Reality as presented by television. *Public Opinion Quarterly, 18,* 143–156.

United States Commission on Civil Rights (1977). *Window dressing on the set: Women and minorities in television.* Washington, DC: Government Printing Office.

Weigel, R. H., & Howes, P. W. (1982). Race relations on children's television. *Journal of Psychology, 3*(1), 109–112.

Weigel, R. H., Loomis, J. W., & Soja, M. J. (1980). Race relations on prime-time television. *Journal of Personality and Social Psychology, 39,* 884–893.

A Guide to the Assignment

This guide is designed to help you through the process of writing your essay of analysis. Key elements of this guide parallel the organization of the Structures and Strategies section in this chapter, and you should look to appropriate sections in the chapter for further guidance. You will prepare to write, write, advance your idea with sources, and then evaluate and revise. Begin with rereading your writing assignment:

Using one of the three selections in this section, analyze the content of a television show: a 30- or 60-minute situation comedy, cartoon, or drama. The goal of your analysis is to make a statement about what the show means, how it works, or why it is significant. The show should be one that you watch regularly so that you have a clear sense of its characters, audience, and recurring or developing themes. If possible, arrange to videotape the segment so that you can watch it several times. Write for an audience of college students your same age. Do *not* assume that your audience has seen the show to be analyzed or has read the materials on which you will base your analysis.[5]

Prepare to Write: Explore Your Idea

Discovering Ideas

Activities that follow are designed to promote your thinking about an idea that you want to pursue in your analysis.

Reflect on Your Experience

You can begin this project with your object of analysis: a television show. Reflect on the shows that you watch, and select one that you know well. Before sitting down to watch the next segment of this show, spend some time writing what you know and think about it. Reflect on the characters, plot, setting, and recurring themes—on as many elements as occur to you. Having done this, return to your writing and highlight any topic that especially interests you and about which you'd like to know more. List these topics.

Read to Spark Ideas

You could also begin this project with a principle for analysis that you find especially compelling. The selections in the Occasions section provide you with numerous possibilities for identifying analytical principles or definitions. Any one of the three readings presents you with many choices. At this point, it is enough to identify a principle or definition that you think would make a useful tool for analyzing a television show. Write the reasons you think this tool would be useful.

Match an Analytical Tool to a Topic for Analysis

An important challenge will be to make a good match between an analytical principle and the television show you choose. The tool you choose for conducting your analysis will determine and limit the possibilities of what you see. If you use Parenti, expect to make observations about politics; if you use Selnow, expect to make observations about core values; if you use Williams and Condry, expect to make observations about race. Think carefully, then, about what interests you in the television show and about which one of the Occasions readings will come closest to helping you think about this show in terms that you find interesting.

---

[5]You will find in the preceding section a selection by Brigid Brophy, "Women: Invisible Cages." You can use this selection, in addition to those in this Occasions section, as a source for principles and definitions by which to analyze a television show.

◆ *Suggestions for Collaborative Writing*

Make plans with another student to watch the same episode of the same television show, but make sure that you are both viewing the show from different perspectives: If you are using Parenti and focusing on political themes, the other student should make observations about core values or race while using Selnow or Williams and Condry.

After you've both watched the same show and recorded your observations, discuss your findings. What insights has the other person come up with that you didn't notice? How might these observations enhance and complicate your analysis? How have each of you brought to the text—that is, the television show—new questions and perspectives that must now be considered in each of your analyses?

Committing Yourself to an Idea

Recall the attitudes of writers whose commitment sparks interest in their readers:

- I write for myself and for my audience.
- I will find some approach to my writing that lets me discover something personally significant.

Well before beginning your first draft, take some time to understand your *personal* connection to analysis. Know why you're conducting it (aside from the obvious—that your professor has asked you to write). If possible, identify some puzzle or problem in the television show that interests you, and then choose one of the readings to help you find a resolution. Motivate yourself to make a discovery about the show, and you will simultaneously motivate your audience to read.

Write: Clarify Your Idea and Make It Public

Creating Common Ground with Readers

Creating common ground with readers involves presenting particular details though which you will develop ideas. In the context of this assignment, you will create common ground in two ways:

1. You will need to explain and argue for the validity of the principle or definition you use. Since you cannot be sure that your audience will accept these as valid, merely announcing them is not enough. You will need to justify, for instance, your use of Parenti's political approach to entertainment.

2. You will also need to summarize the television show that you choose. Be especially alert to introducing characters, giving an overview of the plot, and identifying themes.

Planning a Structure

Plan your analysis by sections. Given the writing assignment, you can identify the two sections noted immediately above: a summary of the show and an introduction to the principles you will be applying (in addition to an argument supporting the legitimacy of these principles). Beyond these sections, you should devote separate paragraphs to using the analytical tools you have identified. Apply each tool to identify parts of the television show to be analyzed and to discuss, in light of your principle or definition (borrowed from Parenti, Selnow, or Williams and Condry), the meaning or significance of these parts. For an illustration of this, see Edward Peselman's essay, ¶s5–9. At some point in your essay, you will need to pull together these separate paragraphs of analytical insight and make an overall statement about what the object under analysis (the television show) means, how it works, or why it is significant.

Suggestions for Writing with a Computer

After writing a draft of your analysis, it's a good idea to analyze the form your analysis takes. One way to do this using the computer is to divide the screen into two parallel columns. Insert your analysis in the column on the left. Use the empty column on the right to write a succinct analysis of what the paragraph on the left is doing. Comment on the goal of each paragraph and the reason for its appearance at this point in the draft. If any questions or new ideas come to mind while you are writing these analyses, put them down as well. When you are finished, read your analytical commentary. Do you notice anything different about the structure of your essay? What new ideas do you now have for improving this structure?

Understanding Your Logic

Decide on where to locate your thesis—at the beginning of the essay or at the end. This strategic decision will be based, in part, on your sense of the audience's likely response to your essay. If you expect opposition, build the essay toward your thesis, which you will locate at the end (your thesis and conclusion will occur together). This inductive arrangement is illustrated in the essay by Marie Winn (pages 234–235). If you expect agreement or at least a neutral response, consider stating your thesis outright, at the beginning, as Edward Peselman does (page 240).

Deductive Arrangement

Introduction—topic and thesis.

Introduction of analytical principle and reasons why readers should accept it.

Summary of the television show to be analyzed.

Analysis, in paragraphs. Each paragraph will respond to a specific question for analysis (see "Advance Your Idea with Sources," below).

Conclusion.

Inductive Arrangement

Introduction—topic (but *no* thesis).

Introduction of analytical principle and reasons why readers should accept it.

Summary of the television show to be analyzed.

Analysis, in paragraphs. Each paragraph will respond to a specific question for analysis (see "Advance Your Idea with Sources," below).

Conclusion and thesis.

Writing Your First Draft

Begin your first draft by writing one section of your essay at a sitting. This advice assumes that you have a working thesis; that you know approximately where in the essay you will summarize the television show you are examining, and that you have a plan for introducing and applying principles and definitions for analysis. The first draft of a section may take you from a half-hour to several hours to write. By drafting at least one section of your essay at a sitting, you will see clearly two important relationships: first, of one paragraph to others *within* a section and, second, of whole blocks of paragraphs—of entire sections—to other sections as well as to your essay's overall idea. You should be able to finish your draft in four or five sittings. For further discussion of what constitutes a section of your essay, see pages 493–494. And, generally, see the material on writing a first draft on pages 486–498.

Advance Your Idea with Sources

The following notes will help you to identify principles and definitions for analysis in the Occasions readings and to convert these into questions for analysis.

Parenti

Parenti offers a list of images and themes that, he says, "are supportive of imperialism, phobic anticommunism, capitalism, racism, sexism, militarism, authoritarian violence, vigilantism, and anti–working-class attitudes." The underlying principle on which Parenti is basing his insights appears in his second paragraph:

> [The prefabricated images and themes of Hollywood] have real ideological content . . . [and] discourage any critical perception of the great and sometimes awful realities of our lives and sociopolitical system, implanting safe and superficial pictures in our heads.

Work with this underlying principle and its parts: prefabricated images, ideological content, and discouragement of critical perception. Develop specific questions based on these parts, as follows: What are prefabricated images, and to what extent do you find them in this television show? As for "ideological content," which may seem the most difficult element of Parenti's statement, Parenti himself suggests what he means. See his bulleted list of themes, another term for which is "ideological content." Use as many of these as you want to convert to questions and make preliminary notes for your essay of analysis, but choose only two or three to write about in your first draft.

Selnow

Selnow writes that after an "exhaustive review" he has selected the Baltimore City Public Schools' eighteen-item inventory for analyzing the values content of television shows. You can use any of these eighteen items as analytical tools. Note that Selnow writes: "Embedded in this inventory are notions of right and wrong and a sense of global standards for human rights and human obligations." What are these notions and standards? Answer this question and you will have identified the underlying principles on which the inventory is based. Converting any item of the inventory into a question for analysis should be straightforward. Here's an example, based on item #2: "To what extent does the television show I'm examining communicate a sense of self, family, school, and community?"

You will need to decide how many items of the inventory you will use in your analysis of the television show. In preparing notes on which to base an analysis, you might use all the items, as Selnow has in his study. In actually writing your paper, you should be more selective and choose from your notes a few items that seem to illuminate the show you are examining.

Williams and Condry

If you have an interest in racial portrayals, you will work with the questions for analysis developed by Williams and Condry. The authors believe that television images are powerful and that images of minorities have historically been inaccurate (see ¶1). This selection helps you take a step toward conducting an analysis by offering specific questions based on racial concerns (see ¶4). Use any or all of the authors' questions in making notes for your own analysis. In writing the first draft of your essay, use at least one question, but not more than three, to guide your inquiry.

Directing Questions to the Object under Analysis

Once you have identified the principles or definitions with which you want to work, convert them into questions and you will be ready to begin making analytical insights. (For more on this point, see Structures and

Strategies, pages 248–249.) Your questions for analysis will help you to identify the parts of the television show you are examining.

You may make many notes while preparing for your essay as you apply various questions for analysis, identify parts, and gain insights into the television show. When the time comes to write a first draft, however, choose from your notes *related* insights, along with their corresponding principles for analysis, so that you can make a clear, overall statement about the television show's meaning or significance.

Evaluate and Revise

General Evaluation

Your primary challenge in revising a first draft is to ensure that the idea you thought you were writing about turns out, in fact, to be the one you have developed in the draft. The act of writing will virtually always refine your initial idea; on occasion, your writing will substantially alter your essay's idea, in which case you will have more work to do in revision. For extensive discussion on strategies for revision, see chapters 13 and 14.

Critical Points in an Analysis

In an essay of analysis, your main concerns in revision can be expressed as three questions:

1. Have you made your analytical principle clear and shown that it is useful?
2. Have you clearly summarized the object you are examining (the television show) so readers have a context in which to understand your analytical insights?
3. Have you systematically applied your analytical tools to the object you are studying?

Beyond these questions, consider these points:

- Have you gone well beyond a summary in writing this essay?
- Have you provided yourself with a strong motivation to write and learn? Have you simultaneously provided readers with a motivation to read?
- Have you evaluated your analytical tools, satisfying yourself that they are fair and generally acceptable?
- Have you been systematic in applying these tools?

Problem/Solution Essays

Definitions and Examples

The cost of books has tripled in the last 15 years, and readers are getting ripped off.

Advertisers manipulate children into buying harmful and unnecessary products.

The high failure rate of condoms makes them a risky defense against sexually transmitted diseases.

Big-time college sports programs undermine the purpose of college education.

Rising book prices, advertisements aimed at the defenseless, condom failure, big-money sports: all of these are problems, and as such they excite our interest. Problems create tension, and tension creates a need for resolution. The goal of a problem/solution essay is to raise a problem and then resolve it, or at least point to a resolution. If advertisers manipulate children, what protection *can* we offer? If condoms fail, what *should* we do to battle the spread of sexually transmitted diseases? The essay's first part—establishing that a problem exists—is implied by these "if" clauses. With the problem defined, the writer then moves to an argument about action: what we *should* do and how we *can* help.

The writer will offer either a solution or a proposal for solving the problem. A solution is appropriate when the tension created by the essay's problem can be resolved, more or less, by means of argument in the essay itself. A proposal is appropriate when the resolution of a problem involves action beyond the essay (as you will see illustrated in the following example). You will always find two parts to a problem/solution essay. The length and complexity of these parts will vary, depending on the problem being addressed and the solution being offered. When the writer is confident that readers will agree that a problem exists, the writer can explain the problem. For readers who need convincing, however, the writer must argue that the problem exists and is somehow relevant to the readers. By whatever means, the writer must make a problem the *readers'* problem. Only then will readers consider taking action, and action is the essay's reason for being. Once readers acknowledge a problem, they naturally ask: What should we do? How can we help? Ready with an answer, the writer presents a plan. Let's examine a brief problem/solution essay.

Reader Rip-Off

Tony Rothman

Why has the cost of books nearly tripled in the past 15 years when the cost of electronics is going down? And why, when most authors have written their books on computer, do large publishers refuse to accept their disks, which would bypass the expensive typesetting process? 1

The replies I get to these questions are fairly uniform, and none of them makes any sense. The price of paper has skyrocketed, I'm told. Not all disks are compatible with the company's computer system. It's difficult to keep track of corrections on disk. It's cheaper to send a manuscript to Hong Kong for typesetting than to do it electronically onshore. 2

Take the point about increasing paper costs. Of the production costs of a book—which include typesetting, printing, and binding—about 15 percent is for paper. Even if the cost of paper has increased over the last decade by a factor of five, if all other things are held constant, the production costs should have increased by only 13 percent. Yet cover prices have tripled. 3

Disk compatibility is no longer a serious dilemma: Most word processors can produce ASCII files, which can be read by almost all systems. Indeed, many smaller publishers work from authors' disks. 4

What is the alternative? Join, for a moment, in a thought experiment and see if it's possible to reduce the cover price of books by a factor of three while providing a product that's as convenient as a book, as easy to read—and as legal. And all using existing technology. Start by breaking down the cost of a book. A typical discount schedule is roughly as follows: If the cover price of a book is $20, then at least 40 percent, or $8, will go to the retailer. Of the remaining $12, perhaps $3 will go to the distributors who ship the books from the printers to the bookstores. Of the remaining $9, it might cost $3 actually to produce the book. The author receives $2 and the publisher keeps $4. All these numbers vary considerably, but as a rule of thumb a book's cover price is six to eight times the production cost. 5

Like pantyhose and toy cars, books are priced by the manufacturer. That is, the publisher fixes the cover price and gives retailers a discount. Switching to markup pricing would undoubtedly stimulate competition and lower the cost of books. In the above example, if the distributor took a 30 percent markup on the book as it came from the publisher ($9) and the retailer took 50 percent on that, the cover price would be $18. 6

The next tactic is to eliminate retailers and distributors. This is the princi- 7
ple behind mail order. A $20 book can often be sold in this way for $12, a substantial savings but still not the stated goal.

What if we placed a small printing plant right in the bookstore and elec- 8
tronically shipped a book direct from the publisher? In other words, a customer
browses in a store where one copy of each book is on display, along the lines
of most video stores, then, having made a choice, has the book printed on the
spot. Such a system would be of little comfort to Rizzoli, but it could handle un-
illustrated books, which are the majority.

A print-on-demand system has numerous advantages. It effectively elimi- 9
nates distribution costs and also eliminates book returns. Roughly 40 percent of
all books printed are never sold. By abolishing both returns and distribution
costs, the $20 book could be sold for about $10.50. At the same time, the
retailer's rent goes down since shelf space is saved, and the concept of "out of
print" disappears; any book on a publisher's master disk is always in print.
Books can also be printed from libraries. All this scheme requires is a letter-qual-
ity printer that can print and bind a book in about a minute—so as not to wear
out the customer's patience—at 1.5 cents a page. Such machines are almost
available.

I find print on demand an aesthetically pleasing idea, but the next step is 10
even more delightful. Eliminate publishers altogether. Books could be printed on
demand directly from authors' home computers. A central on-line clearinghouse
might provide catalogs and advertisements for a small fee. Then the cover price
is roughly the author's royalty plus printing plus the retailer's markup, which
could amount to $7.50.

Tony Rothman presents a problem/proposal essay. In ¶s1–4, assuming
that readers will not necessarily agree with him, he argues that books cost
too much. Rothman makes his argument primarily by countering (in
¶s3–4) the reasons publishers use to explain the rising cost of books. That
done, he moves to a proposal in ¶5, where he writes: "What's the alternative?" In response, he asks readers to imagine a new method for producing and distributing books. First, he presents a goal, "to reduce the cover
price of books by a factor of three," and then he presents a plan. Rothman
begins his proposal with a quick review of the current system of pricing a
book. Without this orienting information, we could not fully appreciate
the logic or the force of his proposal. The plan itself consists of three parts:
first (¶6), change the method by which books are marked up; next (¶s7–9),
eliminate retailers and distributors; and finally (¶10), eliminate publishers.

The tone of a problem/solution or problem/proposal essay is tied
closely to the seriousness and the immediacy of the problem being discussed. Rothman's problem is one we may grumble about on leaving a
bookstore but will probably not move us to swift and righteous action, as
would, for example, news that drug traffickers have been loitering on the
grounds of a local elementary school. The issue of a book's cover price *is*
a problem, though not a pressing or dangerous one, and Rothman chooses his tone accordingly: he sounds no alarms but, rather, invites the reader to join in his playful "thought experiment." More serious problems call

for a more serious and urgent tone, as you will see illustrated in the examples that follow.

Examples of Problem/Solution Essays

Four examples of problem/solution essays follow, the first two of which are the work of professional writers. The first concerns the problem of sexually transmitted diseases and how we can most reliably prevent their spread; the second addresses the problem of advertisements directed at children and how we can prevent children from being manipulated. Two student essays follow: one written in direct response to the immediately preceding piece on the problem of advertisements and the other on the problem of big-money sports on college campuses. Different as they are in subject matter, these problem/solution essays share essential qualities: The writer argues for or explains a problem, attempting to make that problem the reader's; the writer then attempts to resolve the tension thus created by offering a proposal or a solution. Questions follow that will prompt your thinking about these selections as examples of problem/ solution essays.

Condoms: Safer, But Not "Safe," Sex
Steven J. Sainsbury, M.D.

A problem as insidious as sexually transmitted diseases gives rise to heated debates on how that problem is best resolved. In their opening section, problem/solution essays often point to a cause and its direct effect. The solution that follows is an argument: change the events creating the problem and the problem will disappear. With medical problems, standard interventions might be a pill, a vaccine, or a surgical procedure. But in the case of AIDS, no such intervention has succeeded, for the problem's cause—the HIV virus—is too little understood. Still, the virus's pathways of transmission are understood, and the debate over AIDS has turned to behavioral interventions. In this essay (also found in chapter 3), an emergency-room physician argues that a widely accepted solution—condom use—is an imperfect, and indeed dangerous response to a grave problem. The author offers an alternative: abstinence.

My 15-year-old patient with pelvic pain lay quietly on the gurney, as I asked   1
her the standard questions.
    "Are you sexually active?"   2
    "Yes."   3
    "Are you using any form of birth control?"   4
    "No."   5
    "What about condoms?"   6
    "No."   7
    Her answers didn't surprise me. Nor was it surprising that her pain was due   8
to a rip-roaring gonorrheal infection, although it just as easily could have been

due to some other venereal disease, a tubal pregnancy or even AIDS. As a specialist in emergency medicine, I treat teenagers like this one every day. Most are sexually active. Condoms are used rarely and sporadically.

Yet in the midst of the AIDS epidemic, I continue to hear condoms touted 9 as the solution to HIV transmission. As part of a "safe sex" campaign, condoms are passed out in high schools, sold in college restroom dispensers and routinely discussed.

The message? Condoms equal safe sex. 10

Steven Sainsbury: My Commitment to This Essay

Steven Sainsbury is a physician whose work requires that he write—though not essays for the *Los Angeles Times,* where this piece first appeared. As this personal statement attests, Sainsbury had strong motivations for writing; yet the statement itself is *not* an essay. Why not? What are the differences between this statement and the essay? What are the similarities?

A career in emergency medicine requires an immersion in the problems of others. Illness, trauma, and death are not just everyday occurrences—they are the very essence of my caregiving. The inevitable tragedies are accepted and forgotten. But with the needless and preventable afflictions, it is different—they cause a level of frustration that cries out for action and change.

Teenage pregnancy, in which the mother and offspring are statistically doomed to poverty and unhappiness, is on the rise. So is the spread of venereal diseases such as gonorrhea, chlamydia, and herpes. Now comes AIDS. The acquisition of this disease means not only pain and suffering, but actual death. I watched a parade of patient after patient, usually extremely young, uneducated, and unmotivated, present with each of these maladies.

What was the solution? The press and public had decided that condoms would solve this growing menace. My experiences told me different. The population that was being sold "safe sex" didn't care. And, even if they did, the product they were expected to embrace was defective and full of holes—literally and figuratively.

I decided to speak out—to expose this tenet of political correctness for what it was: myth and folklore. So I did, never imagining that it would get such national attention and support.

As a physician, I wish that this 11 were true. Yet, to imply that the use of condoms will safeguard both sex partners from venereal disease, including AIDS, is not only a lie, it is a dangerous lie.

Consider the following two vital facts. 12

Fact No. 1: Condoms are not 13 being used. Many studies confirm this, including one survey among college women—a group we might presume to be as well-informed as any on the risks of herpes, genital warts, cervical cancer and AIDS. In 1989, only 41 percent insisted on condom use during sexual intercourse! If educated women cannot remember to use condoms, how can we expect teenagers or the uninformed to do so?

Fact No. 2: Condoms fail, and 14 fail frequently. Because of improper storage, handling and usage by consumers, the condom breakage rate during vaginal intercourse is 14 percent. Other high-risk behaviors, particularly anal intercourse, increase this rate significantly. For the person who averages sex three times a week, a 14 percent breakage rate equates to a condom failure every two weeks.

AIDS is a killer disease and 15 any measures taken to prevent its transmission must be 100 percent effective. For condoms to be the answer to AIDS, they must be used every time and can never break or leak. Neither criterion is ever likely to be met. Condoms may mean "safer" sex, but is "safer" acceptable for this deadly epidemic?

Suppose that, for unknown reasons, automobiles suddenly began to ex- 16 plode every time someone turned the ignition. Motorists were getting blown up all over the country. Finally, the government comes out with a solution. Just put this additive in the fuel, they say, and the risk of explosion will go down

90 percent. Would you consider the problem solved? Would you still keep driving your car? I doubt it. Then why do we accept condoms as the solution for AIDS?

There is one recommendation, and only one, that is guaranteed to prevent 17 the transmission of the AIDS virus and most other sexually transmitted diseases. A recommendation that lies buried in government reports but has always resided in common sense: that the only safe sex is no sex until one is ready to commit to a monogamous relationship with an uninfected person. The key words are *abstinence* and *monogamy.*

I can hear the moans already. Condom fans begin to reflexively murmur 18 words like *unrealistic, naive,* and *old-fashioned.* Well, perhaps a return to a few old-fashioned concepts is what's needed to stem the surging tide of AIDS, unwanted pregnancies and venereal disease. Just as we try to teach our children to be honest, kind and gentle, perhaps we can also teach them to be chaste.

American families are bombarded by continual images of unprincipled sex- 19 ual activity in movies, television and print media. Planned Parenthood found that there are roughly 20,000 sexual scenes *every year* on American television. Isn't it time to lend balance to the distorted and dangerous lifestyles portrayed as the norm for our society?

The French noblewoman Madame de Sevigne, writing in 1671, described 20 the condom as a "spider web against danger." Three centuries later, little has changed.

For Discussion and Writing

Reading and Thinking Critically

1. *Personal response:* What are the differences between agreeing with a logical point and agreeing with the author's conclusions? Can you, for instance, agree that condoms fail? And if you agree, can you agree that such failure poses a risk? This being so, examine your own activity or the activity of friends. Do you consider abstinence a realistic response to the problem of sexually transmitted disease?
2. *Broaden the context:* Compare Steven Sainsbury's argument for sexual abstinence to arguments for abstinence that you have heard from your priest, minister, or rabbi. Are the arguments the same? Explain.
3. *Challenge the reading:* In ¶15, Sainsbury argues by parallel case, suggesting that people would never accept a 90 percent assurance that the cars they drove were safe. People would insist on a 100 percent assurance. Does this parallel case persuade you? What are its strengths? its weaknesses?

Examining "Safer, But Not 'Safe,' Sex" as a Problem/Solution Essay

1. Why does Sainsbury open his essay with the anecdote about his 15-year-old patient? What is the problem he points to in this essay, and where does he raise it?
2. Does Sainsbury explain this problem? Does he argue that it exists? Explain.
3. Where does Sainsbury present his solution?

Should We Ban TV Advertising to Children?
YES

Peggy Charren

Founder and former president of Action for Children's Television (ACT), Peggy Charren has devoted her career to being an advocate for children's causes. In 1979, the Federal Trade Commission considered adopting the following regulation: "Ban all television advertising for any product which is directed to, or seen by, audiences composed of a significant portion of children who are too young to understand the selling purpose of or otherwise comprehend or evaluate the advertising." Charren argued in favor of the ban (which was not adopted). This brief form of her remarks appeared first in The National Forum *in the fall of 1979.* Note that in her essay, student writer Alison Tschopp argues directly against Charren's proposed ban (see page 293).*

It is beyond dispute that television is a major element in the lives of all Americans, especially children. Recent statistics bear this out. As of September, 1977, 98 percent of American households, 72.9 million homes, had at least one television set; 46 percent of those had more than one set; and 78 percent of television households have color sets. Approximately 33.3 million children between the ages of two and eleven live in households with television sets. The average household viewing time is six hours and ten minutes per day. Children age six to eleven view, on the average, 24 hours and 25 minutes of television per week.[1] Two-to-five-year-olds view an average of 27 hours and 25 minutes of television per week. Daily television viewing of six-to-eleven-year-old children peaks at eight p.m., when 44 percent of the six-to-eleven-year olds in television-owning households are watching television. The viewing of two-to-five-year-olds peaks at ten a.m. Saturday morning, when 36 percent are watching television.[2]

It has been estimated that two-to-five-year-olds view, on average, 20,746 television commercials per year, and that six-to-eleven-year-olds see 19,236 commercials a year.[3] The average two-to-eleven-year-old child is exposed to approximately five hours of advertising per week.

Television broadcast revenues were $5,889,000,000 in 1977.[4] It has been estimated that $660,765,000 of that amount was generated by television advertising of products which have strong appeal to children: candy, soft drinks, cereals, and toys.[5] It is clear that these expenditures would not continue to be made if they did not result in increased sales of the advertised products.

Figures of this magnitude raise significant questions. First, are children who request parents to purchase specific products capable of evaluating product claims made in advertisements? Second, are they basing their requests on factual information derived from advertisements or are their requests based on emotional appeals in the advertisements which are calculated to generate unreasoning responses? Finally, is it feasible to place upon parents the full responsi-

---

*In demonstration of the fact that a writer's views change, Charren says she would no longer argue for a ban on advertising to children—political realities being what they are. "Still," she says, "the interests of children must continue to be lobbied for," and Charren is involved in that effort.

bility for evaluating the products advertised to children and then mediating between children and television advertising?

The Child as Consumer

Advertisers who sell to children are asking the most impressionable and least 5 experienced members of the audience to make complex and reasoned consumer judgments. In order to make a meaningful purchase decision, the child, whose skills of analysis and judgment are still in a developmental stage, must answer an intricate series of questions: Is the product as it appears in the TV commercials? Is the product more desirable than other products in its category? Does the desire or need for the product justify its price? Does the product have limitations or potential harmful effects which should be considered? Is the price a reasonable and/or affordable one?

At every step of the consumer reasoning process, the child is at a disad- 6 vantage. Analysis of child-oriented commercials suggests that children are given little true consumer information, few facts about the price, durability, or nutritional value of a given product.[6] However, even if advertisers were to radically alter the commercial presentation of products, research on child development and consumer socialization indicates that most children would not be able to understand or evaluate commercials in a reasonable manner.

Central to the child's inability to evaluate commercial messages is the lack 7 of comprehension of the promotional or selling intent inherent in advertising. The report of the National Science Foundation, *Research on the Effects of Television Advertising on Children: A Review of the Literature and Recommendations for Future Research,* summarizes the findings:

> Younger children, particularly those below ages 8 or 9, either express confusion or base their discrimination of commercials on effect or on superficial perceptual cues, such as a commercial's shorter length. . . . A substantial proportion of children, particularly those below 8 years, express little or no comprehension of the persuasive intent of commercials.[7]

Since most young children do not comprehend an advertiser's motives, they 8 lack the reasonable skepticism which adults exhibit when evaluating commercials. Research findings have revealed that as many as half of all preschool children believe that all commercials arc true in a literal sense.[8] Findings such as these reflect the child's incomplete conception of the world. The egocentric nature of the young child as described in cognitive development theory suggests that he cannot see into the minds of others and that he cannot imagine that others see the world differently than he does.

Even though older children—ages 9 through 12—display some under- 9 standing of advertising messages as qualitatively distinct from other broadcast announcements, a strikingly small percentage of this age group understands commercials in adult terms. In research conducted at the Graduate School of Business at the University of Texas with children in the fourth and sixth grades, generally ages 8 through 11, less than 15 percent of the children questioned were able to differentiate between programs and commercials on the basis that "television commercials sell; make money."[9]

The cynicism manifested by some 9-to-12-year olds concerning TV adver- 10 tising may reflect no more than a lingering inability to comprehend the true nature of commercials. T. G. Bever, professor of psychology and linguistics at

Columbia University and a former associate of Piaget's Institute Scientifique D'Education in Geneva, describes his research with 10-year-olds:

> Rather than attempt to use skills that they recognize are too limited to differentiate effectively between the subtleties of truth and falsehood, right and wrong, the 10-year-olds resolve the conflict by adopting a rigid moral stance and an overgeneralized view of the world. They simplify the problem by assuming that advertising . . . always "lies!"[10]

Fantasy in Child-Directed Advertising

The inability of children, particularly that of preschoolers, to detect or comprehend the persuasive intent of commercials makes them especially vulnerable to the aspects of fantasy contained in many child-directed advertisements. Barbara Fowles, director of Children's Television Workshop, describes a preschool child's perception of television fantasy: [11]

> The child sees no boundaries between his own fantasies and objective reality. . . . A television reality, like a young child's thoughts, can flow freely between reality and fantasy.[11]

The common inclusion of imaginary beings and magical transformation of reality in many merchandising campaigns manipulate the preschool child's undeveloped sense of reality to promote desires for particular products. Fowles further defines the concept: [12]

> No four-year-old gives a second thought to the appearance of Tony the Tiger at the breakfast table of an ordinary child. This is not so much because he is jaded by television, as it is because, to his way of thinking, this is perfectly reasonable. If it can happen in his imagination, it can happen in fact.[12]

Research by Charles K. Atkin for Public Advocates, Inc. illustrates the impact that advertising appeals from imaginary television characters can have on young viewers. Interviews with one hundred children, ages 4–5 and 7–8, indicated that children recognized and liked the characters of Fred Flintstone and Barney Rubble utilized by General Foods to market its Cocoa Pebbles cereal. Moreover, half of the preschool children and three-quarters of the children from a low-income Mexican-American group believed that Fred and Barney were authorities who knew "about which cereals children should eat." Almost all of the children interviewed believed that Fred and Barney would like them more if they ate Cocoa Pebbles.[13]   [13]

Although children cannot evaluate commercials in a meaningful manner, there is little question that advertising does teach children to desire and request advertised products, but Donald Hendon, professor of business administration at Texas A & I University, notes, "Commercials are teaching something which may have little or no value, except to the companies involved."[14]   [14]

The disproportionate number of child-directed ads for highly sugared and/ or nutritionally questionable foods has generated mounting concern among doctors, dentists, parents, and other child-care providers. Adults may be able to inform themselves about the potential nutritional value of food products advertised to them, and consequently make more reasonable food choices. Children, however, do not have this advantage.   [15]

With the advent of child-directed TV advertising, family nutrition education [16] has been challenged by commercial suppliers who may or may not recognize their role as health educators. Dr. Joan Gussow, assistant professor of nutrition and education at Teachers' College, Columbia University, points out:

> The diet sold to children by television . . . is so impoverished that it makes it impossible for a child not to go wrong. Thus, whatever one may think of individual products or of individual commercials, it is clear that the diet children's television commercials are promoting is an imbalanced one.[15]

Although some members of the food industry have acknowledged that chil- [17] dren do need additional education in order to make reasoned food choices, efforts to supply these lessons on television has been, to this date, half-hearted. The disclosure by cereal advertisers that their product is "part of a balanced breakfast, rather than a complete meal in itself," constitutes no more than five seconds in most 30-second ads.

Research by Charles Atkin on the effectiveness of the "balanced breakfast" [18] tag line found that most children could not remember the components of a balanced breakfast, and that "only one child in seven could provide an adequate definition of the concept."[16] Moreover, two-thirds of the preschoolers tested believed that a bowl of cereal alone constituted a balanced meal, a misconception shared by two-thirds of the children under eight years old from a predominantly low-income Mexican-American sample population.

The Emotional Appeal of TV Advertising

Children are at an emotional, as well as a rational disadvantage, in facing the [19] TV advertising onslaught. Since any true assessment of advertising requires that children understand not only the reality of the advertised product, but also the role it can reasonably play in their lives, and since children lack the experience and developed world view to make such judgments, they may be manipulated by the advertiser's insistence. As Richard Feinbloom, Medical Director of the Family Health Care Program of Harvard Medical School, comments:

> To children, normally impulsive, advertisements for appealing things demand immediate gratification. An advertisement has the quality of an order, not a suggestion. The child lacks the ability to set priorities, to determine relative importance, and to reject some directives as inappropriate.[17]

Advertisers use children to carry messages about products to adult con- [20] sumers, a practice which often creates conflict for children who receive opposing messages from adults on television and adults in the home. Decisions about appropriate food and toy purchases have always required negotiation between parents and children, but the advent of child-directed TV advertising has markedly increased the incidence of these conflict situations.

Several studies have documented the experience of children who are the tar- [21] get of commercials for desirable products, but who are unable to persuade their parents to purchase the advertised items. Research by Charles K. Atkin of Michigan State University and John Rossiter and Thomas Robertson of the University of Pennsylvania suggests that these children experience considerable disappointment and unhappiness.[18] A recent study by Marvin E. Goldberg and Gerald J. Gorn confirms the role commercials play in producing frustration among children.[19] In this study, exposure to a toy commercial was shown significantly to change children's preferences from playing with friends in a sandbox to playing with the toy, even when it was postulated to the children that their mothers wished them to play with a tennis ball rather than the advertised toy.

Problems related to TV advertising are frequently cited by parents and other 22 child-care providers as a source of familial conflict. A national survey of over 1200 families by Yankelovich, Skelly, and White for "The General Mills American Family Report, 1976–77," concluded:

> Advertising is regarded as an industry which is not living up to its responsibilities to parents and children. One out of four parents mentions the "gimmies"—children always asking for things that they see advertised—as a major problem in raising children.[20]

The extent of parental displeasure over child-directed TV advertising is also 23 evaluated in the *NSF Report* which cites research compiled by Ward, Wackman, and Wartella in 1975. Almost 75 percent of the over 600 parents indicated "negative" or "strongly negative" responses to children's commercials.[21]

The continual recurrence of family conflict generated by TV commercials 24 may be particularly stressful among low-income families. Selling to children wrongly presupposes that children understand the value of money and are cognizant of their family's economic level. Moreover, since products currently advertised to children could be marketed directly to adults—consumers who have the necessary cognitive skills to make reasoned purchasing judgments—using children for their "pester power" is unconscionable and unnecessary.

Freedom to communicate messages, commercial or otherwise, is founded 25 on the existence of a freethinking, independent and non-captive audience. While modern television, with its intrusiveness and omnipresence, was obviously not envisioned by the founding fathers when they framed the first amendment, the content of programs broadcast over the airwaves clearly deserves free speech protection. But commercial speech, on television or elsewhere, has less constitutional protection, and none, the Supreme Court tells us, if the commercial message is unfair or deceptive.

It is advertising directed to children that Action for Children's Television is 26 most concerned with. It is believed that advertising directed to very young children is inherently deceptive and unfair and should be stopped. ACT believes that such a government-ordered restriction would not in any way violate the first amendment. It is unquestioned that the FTC has, by virtue of its charge from Congress, the power to prohibit advertisers from promoting their products by means of unfair or deceptive practices. A ban on television advertising directed to very young children, at least under age eight, would comply with the Commission's standard of unfairness and deception now recognized as valid, and thus would be a valid restriction on commercial speech.

For these reasons—and others not detailed in this abbreviated article— 27 Action for Children's Television supports a ban on television ads directed to children too young to understand the selling or persuasive intent of commercials, proposed by the Federal Trade Commission.

Robert Choate, president of the Council on Children, Media, and Mer- 28 chandising, has succinctly expressed the point of view we have tried to defend as follows:

> Advertising to children much resembles a tug of war between 200-pound men and 60-pound youngsters. Whether called an unfair practice or though subject to fairness doctrine interpretation, the fact remains that

any communication that has a $1,000-per-commercial scriptwriter, actors, lighting technicians, sound effects specialists, electronic editors, psychological analysts, focus groups, and motivational researchers with a $50,000 budget on one end and the 8-year-old mind (curious, spongelike, eager, gullible) with 50 cents on the other *inherently represents an unfair contest.*

Notes

1. A. C. Nielsen Co., *Nielsen Television 78* (1978), pp. 5, 6, 8, 10, 11.

2. *The Media Book* 1978 (New York: Min-Mid Publishing, 1978), pp. 301, 302.

3. National Science Foundation, *Research on the Effects of Television Advertising* on Children (1977), pp. 14, 15. Hereinafter called *NSF Report.*

4. Television/Radio Age (September 25, 1978), p. 40.

5. *Broadcasting* (February 27, 1978), p. 27.

6. See Charles Atkin and Gary Herald, "The Content of Children's Toy and Food Commercials," *Journal of Communication,* Vol. 27, No. 1 (Winter, 1977), pp. 107–114.

7. *NSF Report,* pp. 30, 31.

8. Scott Ward, et. al., *Children Learning to Buy: The Development of Consumer Information Processing Skills* (Cambridge: Marketing Science Institute, 1976).

9. Clara Ferguson, *Preadolescent Children's Attitudes Toward Television Commercials* (Austin, Texas: The University of Texas, 1975), p. 30.

10. T. F. Bever, et al., "Young Viewers' Troubling Response to TV Ads," *Harvard Business Review* (November/December, 1975), p. 116.

11. Barbara Fowles, "A Child and His Television Set: What is the Nature of the Relationship?" *Education and Urban Society,* Vol. 10, No. 1 (November, 1977), p. 93.

12. *Ibid.*

13. Charles K. Atkin and Wendy Gibson, *Children's Responses to Cereal Commercials,* report to Public Advocates, Inc. (San Francisco, 1978), p. 5.

14. Donald W. Hendon, Anthony F. McGann, and Brenda Hendon, "Children's Age, Intelligence and Sex as Variables Mediating Reactions to TV Commercials," *Journal of Advertising,* Vol. 7, No. 3 (Summer, 1978), p. 10.

15. Joan Gussow, "Counternutritional Messages of TV Ads Aimed at Children," *Journal of Nutritional Education* (Spring 1972), p. 50.

16. Atkin and Gibson, *Children's Responses to Cereal Commercials,* p. 2.

17. Richard I. Feinbloom, Statement submitted to the Federal Trade Commission, November, 1971, quoted by Charren in Hearings on Broadcast Advertising and Children Before House Committee on Interstate and Foreign Commerce, 94th Congress, 1st Session (July, 1975), p. 29.

18. Charles K. Atkin, "Parent-Child Communication in Supermarket Breakfast Cereal Selection," *Effects of Television Advertising on Children* (East Lansing, Michigan: Michigan State University, 1975); Thomas Robertson and John Rossiter, "Children's Consumer Satisfaction," Center for Research in Media and Children, University of Pennsylvania.

19. Marvin E. Goldberg and Gerald J. Gorn, "Some Unintended Consequences of TV Advertising to Children" *Journal of Research* 5 (June, 1978).

20. Yankelovich, Skelly and White, Inc. *Raising Children in a Changing Society: The General Mills American Family Report, 1976–1977* (Minneapolis, MN: General Mills, Inc., 1977), p. 36.

21. *NSF Report,* p. 134.

For Discussion and Writing

Reading and Thinking Critically

1. *Personal response:* Can you recall times when you were prompted by a commercial to go to your parents and ask them to buy you something? Did any conflicts ensue? Describe the exchange, or describe a time in which a commercial convinced you to buy something yourself. To what extent did the product match the appeal of the advertisement?
2. *Broaden the context:* Charren herself broadens the context of this argument to include a larger argument about infringements to free speech. Read Alison Tschopp's essay below, a direct response and challenge to Charren. Do you agree with Charren that a ban on advertising to children does not violate the advertiser's right to free speech?
3. *Be alert to differences:* What has changed in the sixteen years since this article was published? Is Charren's argument any more or less valid than it was in 1979?

Examining "Should We Ban TV Advertising" as a Problem/Solution Essay

1. In a sentence, express the problem that Charren presents. In a brief paragraph following this sentence, explain the particular ways, according to Charren, that advertisements are unfair when directed to children.
2. ¶25 represents a transition point in this essay. How does this take place?
3. Charren gives little space to developing her solution, relative to the attention she gives to defining the problem. Why might this be so?

STUDENT PAPER

Advertising to Children Should Not Be Banned

Alison Tschopp

Student writer Alison Tschopp, who is planning to be an attorney, read Peggy Charren's argument on banning advertising aimed at children and wrote her own problem/solution essay in response. Tschopp argues for the existence of a problem different than the one identified by Charren. Instead of claiming that advertisements directed at children are inherently deceptive (because the intended audience is not equipped emotionally or cognitively to view the ads), Tschopp focuses on family situations that permit children undue influence on important decision making. Observe how this redefinition of the problem—this alternate understanding of the problem's causes—has direct consequences for which solutions get proposed.

Are television commercials rotting the minds and bodies of our children? Some people think so, especially when it comes to advertisements for expensive toys and foods of questionable nutritional value. Impressionable children are easy prey for marketers, say the critics (Charren 14). And advertisements can perpetuate attitudes and myths that are harmful to children's development, such as the myth that girls are not as aggressive as boys or that boys are not sensitive enough to care for a baby-doll (Kilbourne 45).

We know that advertisers are persuasive, and we know that the power [2] of advertisements over children is directly related to the amount of television that children watch. According to a survey cited in a recent article by American Federation of Teachers President Albert Shanker, one-quarter of nine year olds in this country watch 42 hours of television each week (7)—approximately eight hours of which is devoted to advertisements. The most obvious way to eliminate the exposure to so much advertising is to limit television viewing. Still, we are not about to eliminate television from the American household. In a best-case scenario, we might reduce viewing time by half. If we could return our children to viewing a modest 25 hours of weekly television (the 1977 level), they would still be seeing nearly 260 hours of advertisements each year. Is this acceptable?

Alison Tschopp: My Commitment to This Essay

Alison Tschopp was required by a professor to write a problem/solution essay; in the process, she was able to discover very personal reasons for writing, and thus claimed the essay as her own. This personal statement gives you an insight into Tschopp's motivations for writing, but it is *not* itself an essay. Why not? What are the differences between this statement and the essay? What are the similarities?

I see a threat to the welfare of Americans, including children, by limiting our Constitutional right to free speech. I want my children to grow up in a society where they'll be free to say what's on their minds—even if this is dangerous, unpopular, or plain stupid—as many ads are. There's no way to stop assaults on free speech if we start chipping away at the First Amendment. Children are manipulated by ads—so let's ban the speech of advertisers. Communists pollute the minds of Americans—so let's ban Communists from speaking in public forums. Americans deserve the right to speak and *to listen. The marketplace of ideas will determine whether ideas have merit.*

Peggy Charren, president of [3] Action for Children's Television (ACT), a national consumer's group, says no and recommends banning television ads directed at children. Charren argues that our constitution's First Amendment, which protects freedom of speech, should be suspended to allow such a ban. She maintains that television ads directed at children do not deserve First Amendment protection on the grounds that, since children cannot fully appreciate the persuasive nature of advertisements, TV commercials are inherently unfair and deceptive (15).

Charren begins her argument by discussing the child consumer. She [4] criticizes companies that advertise to children for asking children to "make complex and reasoned consumer judgments" (13). She explains that, since children do not comprehend advertisers' motives, they are not armed with the reasonable skepticism with which adults evaluate advertisements—and that, therefore, the advertisers' right to free speech, at least with respect to children, should be limited. The right of free speech in our society is so important that anyone who proposes that we limit it bears a heavy burden of presenting a compelling argument. But Charren does not. First, she assumes that the skepticism portrayed by adult viewers of advertisements protects them (and could likewise protect children) from advertisers' power of persuasion. But realistically, few people are immune to the advertiser's art. In his article "The Language of Advertising Claims," Jeffrey Schrank asserts that skepticism does not protect consumers because advertising works "below the level of conscious awareness and it works even on those who claim immunity to its message" (156).

Most adult viewers in this country watch advertisements and believe 5 that "no attack is taking place" (Schrank 156), which is precisely the condition under which Charren claims that children watch televised advertising. Yet we hear no one arguing that because adults are being manipulated we should therefore ban television advertising. What we do hear—from the Supreme Court—is that when ads are blatantly deceptive or unfair, they are not protected by the First Amendment. Basically, the Court has said that it is never legal for an advertiser to lie—either to children or to adults.

But such protection is not enough for Charren, who believes that chil- 6 dren make, and should be protected in making, important consumer decisions. She argues that advertisements aimed at affecting these decisions are unfair, and that children are being persuaded improperly. To illustrate, she claims that ads, specifically for sugared cereals, are deceptive and teach children to make unreasonable food choices. She feels that advertisers' reminders that cereal is "part of a balanced breakfast" do not give children information sufficient for judging the issues. In support of her argument, she cites a study where two-thirds of the preschoolers tested believed that a bowl of cereal alone constituted a balanced meal (15).

Most parents know that preschoolers and children in grades 1 7 through 4 (through age 11) cannot be depended upon to choose for themselves, for instance, a well-balanced diet or to understand the principles of comparison shopping for price and quality. We do not expect that children make these decisions alone; parents are responsible for guiding their children's decisions. Young children do not have the resources to do the shopping. Parents do. Preschoolers do not make their own meals. Parents do. If children are not getting all their nutritional needs fulfilled, this is not caused by advertisers but by families that lack resources for making balanced choices. If children are duped into choosing poorly made or overpriced but cleverly advertised products, this is not the fault of advertisers but of a family situation that permits children to influence important consumer decisions without a counterbalancing influence from parents.

Parents play a key role in a child's development, nutritional and oth- 8 erwise. A parent's close involvement with children, not limiting the First Amendment, is the appropriate countermeasure to the power of advertisers. Let parents interact with their children and begin their own persuasive campaign! Perhaps children are being confused when messages seen on television advertisements conflict with messages heard at home. But conflict in itself is not "bad." Parents must guide their children towards appropriate conclusions in making most decisions: what clothes to wear; what cereal to eat; what toys are worthwhile. As children mature they must learn to evaluate and resolve such questions for themselves. Keeping the world, with its sometimes harmful and often confusing messages, from children does not offer protection. If that were the case, how high would we need to build walls to block out the everyday assaults on the lives of our children? Do we ban the evening news because of its frequently upsetting content? Do we stop talking about the threat of drugs? No. What we do is acknowledge to our children that dangers exist, and then we exercise parental judgment: we teach children and hope they learn well enough to one day manage on their own.

Children receive conflicting messages from a variety of sources which cannot be silenced: teachers, books, friends, and television programs. We have, from time to time, experimented in this country with limiting access to potentially damaging or offensive materials, such as books and movies. But these experiments have not withstood legal challenges. The courts have decided that Americans have the right to choose what they see or hear and that writers and others have the right to create what they wish. Certain extreme instances, like child pornography, are so offensive and damaging to the children being filmed that as a society we *have* said that such products are repugnant and should not be supported by viewers who argue it is their right to see such material. And, in part, this is the argument that Charren is making about advertisements directed at children. But as a society we have agreed to limit speech only in the most extreme cases. There is nothing in the making of advertisements that is as purposefully vulgar or hurtful as there is in child pornography. If anything, advertising more closely resembles the language of our everyday speech: we live, after all, in a consumer society and advertising is the language of consumerism. In this sense, Charren's real argument is with America's values, and on this point she may be right. But values cannot be legislated. They must be taught.

The task of shaping children's values, like their diets, is better addressed through ongoing discussions between parents and children than through limiting the right of free speech. There is no need to silence advertisers in order to teach values or protect the innocent and unskeptical. The right to free speech is protected by the Constitution because as a nation we believe that no one person is capable of determining which ideas are true and rational. Like media critic Jean Kilbourne, we may disagree with some of the messages being conveyed through advertising—say, the message that women are attractive only when they are young and thin (44). Like Peggy Charren, we can agree that advertisements can create stresses in a family's life (15). Nevertheless, we must allow all ideas a place in the market place. As Charles O'Neil, an advertiser and a defender of the medium, suggests, "[a]dvertising is only a reflection of society; slaying the messenger will not alter the fact" that potentially damaging or offensive ideas exist (196). If we disagree with the message sent in an ad, it is our responsibility to send children a different message.

Works Cited

Charren, Peggy. "Should We Ban TV Advertising to Children? YES." *National Forum: The Phi Kappa Phi Journal* 59.4 (1979): 13–16.

Kilbourne, Jean. "The Child as Sex Object: Images of Children in the Media." *The Educator's Guide to Preventing Child Abuse.* Ed. Mary Nelson and Kay Clark. Santa Cruz: Network Publications, 1986. 40–46.

O'Neil, Charles A. "The Language of Advertising." *Exploring Language.* 6th ed. Ed. Gary Goshgarian. New York: HarperCollins, 1992. 186–97.

Schrank, Jeffrey. "The Language of Advertising Claims." *Teaching About Doublespeak.* Urbana, IL: National Council of Teachers of English, 1976. 156–62.

Shanker, Albert. "Where We Stand: TV Chastity Belt." *New York Times* 7 Mar. 1993, sec. 4: 7.

For Discussion and Writing

Reading and Thinking Critically

1. *Personal response:* Were you aware of recent statistics on the amount of television that children watch each week? (See ¶2.) What is your response to these figures?

2. *Be alert to differences:* In ¶4, Tschopp tries to nullify a difference that Charren worked hard to establish. Charren suggests that children are not emotionally or cognitively equipped to react in a mature, skeptical way to ads. But neither, says Tschopp, are adults. Why is this elimination of a difference between children and adults important for Tschopp's argument?

3. *Challenge the reading:* Do you feel Tschopp has given fair weight to the significance of cultural pressures in a child's life? See ¶s7–8 particularly. Tschopp's response to Charren's argument about the influence of ads is to say, in effect: "Parents, do your jobs! Educate your kids—don't let advertisers do it." Is this response sufficient and realistic, in your view?

Examining "Advertising Should Not Be Banned" as a Problem/Solution Essay

1. Peggy Charren (pages 287–292) argued that advertisements directed at children are inherently deceptive. Tschopp concedes that ads can be persuasive, but she defines the problem differently by pointing to an altogether different cause. What, according to Tschopp, is the problem? How does she argue for this problem?

2. Where does Tschopp address an objection to her solution? How does she attempt to advance her own solution by responding to this objection?

3. Tschopp offers no proposal or specific plan of action here. Why not?

Athletes and Education
Jenafer Trahar

Student writer Jenafer Trahar is concerned with the impact of big-time college sports on education. In this problem/solution essay, Trahar assumes that readers will accept her claim that an overemphasis on sports is a problem. Accordingly, she explains the problem that interests her: she does not argue for it as, for instance, Peggy Charren does. Once Trahar dismisses attempted solutions, she offers her own proposal that, she believes, will "allow student-athletes to gain access to college but would also increase the chances of their actually receiving an education." As you read, consider the extent to which athletics poses a problem at your school. If a problem exists, how are administrators, students, and student-athletes dealing with it?

There have always been athletics on college campuses, but the presence of athletes posed no problems until the late nineteenth century. It was around this time that many colleges and universities began to rely on financial support from the alumni. What the alumni wanted was for their alma mater to be a winner. Sports became part of an important fund-raising activity for many campuses, particularly at midwestern and southern universities. Northeastern schools could always rely on their academic reputations for maintaining the flow of alumni money. Midwestern and southern schools, however, did not have a ready-made source of contributions and needed some attraction other than academics to get alumni interested in making donations (Naison 493–94). For many years, schools turned to building their sports programs at the expense of their academic ones. 1

Today, schools that field major football or basketball teams stand to make tens of thousands of dollars every time a game is played, not only from ticket sales but also from television revenue. Every time a game is televised, the schools involved make money. The payoff for the very best teams is enormous. For example, each team that advances to the Final Four of the NCAA basketball tournament earns its institution one million dollars. 2

One major problem with the commercialization of college sports is the exploitation of student-athletes, many of whom come to school on athletic scholarships. Frequently, student-athletes don't deserve to be admitted to a school. Many colleges routinely lower admission requirements for their ball players, and some schools will even waive requirements for that exceptional athlete who, without his sports abilities, might not have had a place on a college campus. Most kids not interested in academics would normally shun a college education. But for gifted athletes, college appears to be a road that leads to the pros. Or so they think. According to Richard Lapchick of the Center for the Study of Sport in Society, of every twelve thousand high school athletes who participate in sports in any one year, only one will subsequently play for a professional team. But the news gets even more grim: 3

[O]nly 1 in 50 will get a scholarship to play in college. And of the top players who receive scholarships in big-money sports like football and basketball, fewer than 30 per cent will graduate from college after four years. (xv)

Academically qualified or not, what these young men and women 4 may not realize in coming to college is that athletics is the only service their school is offering them. These kids spend so much time practicing and then studying play books that they barely have enough time to attend their required classes, let alone do the work for them. One football player described his schedule this way: "[T]wo to six, practice. Seven to eight, watch films. Eight to 10:30, go to study hall—where you just get plays from coaches" (Lichtenstein 47). The result of this preoccupation with sports is too often a player who has played through his athletic eligibility and who loses his scholarship because he has done poorly in his course work. The scholarship is revoked, and the student-athlete leaves the university without a degree. He was too busy to get one.

Though many reformers have sought to correct the exploitation of 5 student-athletes, no one has come up with a workable solution. Some have suggested that big-time sports be cut entirely out of colleges. The logic of this argument is that since sports seem inevitably to lead to commercialization, and since commercialization of sports leads inevitably to students being exploited, the only way to end exploitation is to take the money entirely out of college sports. This approach amounts to wishing for the purity—the amateur status—of an earlier time. Simply put, there is too much money involved now to ever go back. The days of amateurism are gone; sports have become too integral a part of college life, especially now that many schools depend heavily on the revenue their teams bring in.

The NCAA's Proposition 48 requires athletes to have a certain grade 6 point average, SAT score, and achievement scores in order to be accepted as students at a school. As John Thompson, basketball coach at Georgetown University, pointed out when Proposition 48 was initially discussed, the idea is not particularly fair to student-athletes who come from poor school districts where education suffers due to a lack of funding. Student-athletes should not be held responsible for their lack of achievement if that lack is due, in part, to overcrowded and underfunded classes (Asher B4).

The system of college athletics has been in place for so long now that 7 it's almost too late for change. Almost, but not quite. After nearly a century of student-athlete exploitation, the time has come not for a de-emphasis on sports but for a re-emphasis on education. What follows is a four-step outline of a reasonable, workable solution to addressing the exploitation of student-athletes. The first step we must take, before we can expect a change in the admission process, is to teach our educators that they must demand more from student-athletes. Study time must come to equal, if not exceed, playing time. There should be a required GPA for student-athletes. It should be a reasonable one, however: perhaps 2.0, taking into account the fact that student-athletes do have heavy athletic schedules. Athletics should be taken into account, not used as an excuse to defend unacceptable student performance in the classroom.

The second step in resolving the problem is to eliminate the sympathetic professor who is a "friend" to the student-athlete. Professors and administrators need to learn that the education of athletes is more important than the score of Saturday's game. All those people who think they're helping by letting student-athletes slide are really doing more harm than good. If it takes punishment to teach professors and administrators this, then punishment is what's needed. First, the grading process used for "helping" student-athletes should be reviewed. Any professor caught scaling for a student should be punished. (The punishment should be left up to the school to decide.) Second, efforts must be made to supervise student-athletes. Tutors can be assigned to each athlete, and an administrator from outside the athletic department can be assigned to organize (and enforce) study schedules for entire teams. Athletes who do not study will lose their eligibility. Professors who scale will be punished. With these strategies in place, the problem of poor academic performance among student-athletes should diminish over time.

The third step in addressing the exploitation of student-athletes is to reduce practice time. Schools must not trust coaches to see to it that students are studying enough. There needs to be a rigidly fixed amount of time on the field; once that time is over, so is practice. Period. No excuses for longer practice or sports-related study halls should be tolerated.

The final step in addressing the problem, perhaps the most important, is the creation of a special education center for the student-athlete. Such a center would be a place where an athlete could get honest help, from honest students who want to see athletes get an education—not a touchdown or home run. Of course the student tutors in these facilities would need supervision, but this could be easily arranged if the college administration were committed to helping the student-athlete.

Some might find fault in these recommendations, claiming that there isn't enough money available to make all these changes. But, of course, the money would come from the ticket sales and proceeds from televised games. Television contracts with the NCAA should be written to guarantee that a certain percentage of sports revenue be spent directly on supervising the education of student-athletes. Colleges with nationally competitive teams should each form a special committee from the Board of Trustees to oversee and to implement the recommendations I have offered.

We don't need to eliminate college sports. We probably couldn't anyway, what with all the money being made. Eliminating sports would do more harm than good, taking away both a source of pride in college life and an important source of revenue. Changing the admissions process to deny marginally prepared student-athletes would not be fair, since for many of these kids sports is their only avenue of exposure to college life and the possibility of a higher education. To eliminate the chance to attend college for marginal student-athletes would be heartless, because it places on them a burden they didn't make, a burden that should and can be lifted with the proper approach. That's why a plan that modifies the present system, not destroys it, makes the most sense. Let's take advantage of all the money that college sports generates and use that money to *really* educate the student-athlete. The proposals I have made would not only allow student-athletes to gain access to college but would also increase the chances of their actually receiving an education.

Works Cited

Asher, Mark. "The Rule Doesn't Kill the Problem." *Washington Post* 18 June 1985: B4.

Lapchick, Richard E., with Robert Malekoff. *On the Mark: Putting the Student Back in Student-Athlete.* Lexington, MA: Lexington Books, 1987.

Lichtenstein, Grace. "Playing for Money." *Rolling Stone* 30 Sept. 1982: 44–48.

Naison, Mark. "Scenario for Scandal." *Commonweal* 24 Sept. 1982: 493–497.

For Discussion and Writing

Reading and Thinking Critically

1. *Personal response:* To what extent does the pursuit of athletics pose a problem at your school? Do you see evidence of the problem that Trahar discusses in ¶s2–4?
2. *Challenge the reading:* Trahar presents a four-part proposal in ¶s7–10. Examine each part carefully, with an eye to its feasibility if it were applied to the athletics program at your school. To what extent do you find her proposal reasonable?
3. *Be alert to differences:* Think of two colleges, one where athletics is given a great deal of attention, and another where it is not. In your view, how do the philosophies of these schools differ with respect to athletics? Compare the educational experiences of student-athletes at these schools.

Examining "Athletes and Education" as a Problem/Solution Essay

1. What problem does big-time college sports pose?
2. Show how Trahar explains this problem, having assumed that the reader agrees with her.
3. Trahar makes a four-part proposal in the second part of her essay. Why does this topic merit a step-by-step plan, as opposed to the organization of other essays in which you find a solution?

Structures and Strategies

Imagine two people observing the same event, say, a college football game. One sees the game and the enthusiasm of the crowd on a crisp autumn day, and concludes that football contributes significantly to the culture of American colleges. The second observer is not enthusiastic. She sees a multimillion dollar stadium, national television coverage, and sponsors advertising heavily, and concludes that athleticism on campus is a hugely expensive and lucrative enterprise that undermines the values of a college education. One observer sees a problem; the other does not. Does a problem exist? What *is* the problem? How is the problem resolved? Responding clearly to these questions is the challenge you face when writing a problem/solution essay, a challenge you can meet through a process of preparing, writing, and revising.

Prepare to Write: Explore Your Idea

In chapters 13 and 14, you can read in some detail about approaching essay writing as a process. In those chapters you will see thorough demonstrations of how essays are written in stages. Writers gather materials and think of multiple approaches to an idea as they prepare to write; they write a first draft in which they express, explore, and refine the idea; and then they revise—they rewrite—until that idea is expressed clearly and all sections of the essay advance the idea. Typically, writers work through several versions of an essay before it reaches final form. Several specific strategies are presented here to help you think about preparing to write, writing, and revising a problem/solution essay.

Discovering Ideas

The burden of proof is always on the person who claims that a problem exists. In the absence of believing there is a problem, readers take no action. If you want readers to act, they must know exactly what is wrong, and you must develop good ideas for showing them. In addition to the general prewriting activities in chapter 1 that are offered to help you think creatively about ideas in your essay, you can consider the strategies for defining a problem discussed next.

Read to Discover Ideas

One way to spark ideas is to read widely, both to help you identify problems and to consider solutions. In an example essay beginning this chapter, student writer Jenafer Trahar (pages 298–301) used a source (Mark Asher, "The Rule Doesn't Kill the Problem," *Washington Post* 18 June 1985: B4) to spark ideas for an essay about the exploitation of student-athletes. The source did not provide Trahar with a solution, but rather prompted a line of thinking that led to a solution. Read the original source, along with two paragraphs from Trahar's essay:

A Source That Sparked Ideas

Proposition 48 [requires] a 700 minimum score (out of 1600) on the Scholastic Aptitude Test or a 15 (out of 36) on the American College Test and a 2.0 grade-point average (out of 4.0) in a core curriculum of 11 academic courses to be eligible for first-year eligibility in Division 1.

• • •

[Georgetown University basketball coach John] Thompson says athletes are not totally responsible for their academic problems. In fact, he said, "It may be a greater exploitation in stopping them from coming to some of these universities and not educating them than it is because a few kids took bribes and a few kids took drugs."

He disagrees strongly with educators who say Proposition 48 will serve as an incentive to black athletes to score 700 on the SATs and have a C average in a core curriculum.

"You can have all the rules in the world," he said. "The rule doesn't kill the problem. The problem starts in grade school; the problem starts in junior high school; the problem starts in high school."

The Source Used

The NCAA's Proposition 48 requires athletes to have a certain grade point average, SAT score, and achievement scores in order to be accepted as students at a school. As John Thompson, basketball coach at Georgetown University, pointed out when Proposition 48 was initially discussed, the idea is not particularly fair to student-athletes who come from poor school districts where education suffers due to a lack of funding. Student-athletes should not be held responsible for their lack of achievement if that lack is due, in part, to overcrowded and underfunded classes (Asher B4).

The system of college athletics has been in place for so long now that it's almost too late for change. Almost, but not quite. After nearly a century of student-athlete exploitation, the time has come not for a de-emphasis on sports but for a re-emphasis on education. . . .

Call Attention to a Difference between What Is Expected, or Desired, and What Is Actually the Case

People will accept as a problem any noticeable difference, or gap, between what they want to see and what they actually see. Tony Rothman's essay (pages 282–283) on the high cost of books is a good example. Recall the opening questions with which he launches the essay:

> Why has the cost of books nearly tripled in the past 15 years when the cost of electronics is going down? And why, when most authors have written their books on computer, do large publishers refuse to accept their disks, which would bypass the expensive typesetting process?

Rothman sets out the problem of his essay as a direct response to these questions, which rest on a difference between what he expects to see in the world of publishing and what he actually sees.

Call Attention to Damage, Disadvantage, or Danger

A classic method for establishing a problem is to point readers directly, and sometimes brutally, to negative effects. The more graphic the effects, the greater the impact on readers and the greater the likelihood that they will accept the problem as real. Peggy Charren (pages 287–292) devotes most of her essay to establishing the psychological, emotional, and dietary harm that comes from exposure to television advertisements. Here is a representative sentence from her essay:

> The disproportionate number of child-directed ads for highly sugared and/or nutritionally questionable foods has generated mounting concern among doctors, dentists, parents, and other child-care providers.

Charren's readers get a steady flow of evidence directed to a single claim: that TV advertising harms children. Charren establishes the problem for the reader with facts, examples, and opinions from experts. Steven Sainsbury (pages 284–286) defines the problem in his essay by pointing the reader to the physical harm that follows from the decision not to use condoms or from condom failure:

> [The girl's admission that she used no form of contraception] didn't surprise me. Nor was it surprising that her pain was due to a rip-roaring gonorrheal infection, although it just as easily could have been due to some other venereal disease, a tubal pregnancy, or even AIDS. As a specialist in emergency medicine, I treat teen-agers like this one every day.

Sainsbury's technique is very nearly brutal. He asks the reader to watch the pain of a teenager and then claims that the behavior responsible for her condition is the rule, not the exception.

Call Attention to a *Potential* Problem

A less dramatic but equally effective technique is to direct the reader's attention to a problem likely to occur if certain precautions are *not* taken. Perhaps as a projection based on present conditions, a writer glimpses a problem and imagines its full, negative impact. (This happens in the world of business when a negative trend constituting an actual or potential problem is spotted. Working groups then are assembled to reverse the trend.) When presenting a problem that is not yet at a crisis point, you should make every effort to show that the problem is real and potentially threatening; make the additional point that action now will be less costly and less disruptive than action taken later. An example:

> Preventable illnesses among children, such as measles, exact an extraordinarily high toll in lives and in money each year. It is estimated that, worldwide, for every $20 dollars spent in prevention through vaccine programs, the lives of one hundred children can be saved; for every $20 spent, $300 is saved in later hospital costs. We can prevent disease. We can save lives and money, but we must begin a vaccine drive—now.

Committing Yourself to an Idea

Readers will take a problem seriously to the extent that you do. One challenge you face in writing a problem/solution essay is to believe that a problem really exists and is worth not only your attention but the reader's. A real problem will create in your audience the motivation to read and consider solutions. In chapter 2, you read specific strategies for committing yourself to the idea of an essay. These strategies follow from two general attitudes that a writer adopts:

- I write for myself and for my audience.
- I will find some approach to my writing that lets me discover something personally significant.

Commitment through Reading

One strategy for both discovering and committing yourself to an idea is to read. Reading invites response, sometimes *passionate* response, as was the case when student writer Alison Tschopp found in Peggy Charren's essay (pages 287–292) an argument for protecting children from the manipulations of advertisers by limiting free speech. Tschopp was stirred to action. Considering a career in law at the time she wrote the essay, Tschopp had taken government and history courses and was familiar with the Constitution, which she thought was threatened. Here is the thesis from Tschopp's essay:

> A parent's close involvement with children, not limiting the First Amendment, is the appropriate counter-measure to the power of advertisers.

As a thesis, this statement shows a writer who is making a significant commitment to her work—a "three-story" thesis in the language of chapter 2 (where there is a discussion on ways to communicate commitment in your thesis statements). In her thesis, Tschopp promises to make connections among her source materials, and she introduces tension. Notice how she sets "parental involvement" against limits to the First Amendment as the appropriate countermeasure to "the power of advertisers." The essay that builds on a thesis with tension creates contrasts that interest readers. Tschopp obviously cares about protecting children *and* protecting the Constitution.

As a future attorney, Tschopp feels strongly about protecting the First Amendment, and so she's committed to the argument in her essay; she defines the problem as a lack of parental involvement, *not* as the advertisers' abuse of a constitutional right. Her solution follows from this same commitment. The way to lessen the impact of advertising on children is to improve parental presence. In this essay, Tschopp clearly wrote for her audience *and* for herself. She found an approach to a problem that let her discover and express an idea that was personally significant. Read the sidebar to Steven Sainsbury's essay on condom use and you will see that same commitment. You, too, should insist on making a personal commitment to the problems you address in a problem/solution essay. When you care, readers will care.

Write: Clarify Your Idea and Make It Public

Creating Common Ground with Readers

Readers are more likely to understand and recall particular cases that illustrate an idea than they are to understand and recall that same idea expressed as an abstract statement. We can easily imagine the weariness of a man condemned his whole life to roll an immense boulder to the top of a hill, only to see it roll down to the bottom every time he nears his goal. We can recall and understand this image more easily than we can abstract definitions of existential futility. Readers want and need particulars, and your job as a writer is to provide them. In chapter 3 you will find a discussion on creating "common ground" with readers; it offers strategies for presenting an idea through particulars. The discussion here will alert you to strategies that are especially useful for creating common ground in problem/solution essays. Your choice of details in an essay will be guided by your assessment of your readers' needs and interests.

Tone and the Writing Occasion

As shown in the more detailed discussions on writing occasion and common ground in chapter 3, *tone* describes the general attitude a writer takes toward readers. You have seen a variety of tones in the examples of problem/solution essays in this chapter: the flippant, breezy tone of Tony Rothman, proposing a solution to the rising prices of books; the angry and insistent tone of Peggy Charren, arguing to curtail the speech of advertisers; the here's-the-brutal-facts tone of Steven Sainsbury, insisting that sex with condoms is not acceptably safe; and the starkly critical tone of Alison Tschopp, arguing against Peggy Charren's solution to the manipulation of children by advertisers. Each writer chose his or her tone with care, matching tone to a specific writing occasion. In chapter 3, writing occasion is described in the diagram shown on page 307, the language of which will help you decide on the tone of your problem/solution essays.

The tone you adopt for a problem/solution essay can be determined based on the elements in this diagram. Your purpose is clear in a problem/solution essay. What about your audience and topic? How do you, as writer, negotiate these elements and arrive at a tone that will be appropriate for your writing occasion? Turn first to the topic of your essay: the "problem." How weighty is this problem? If it is not particularly pressing, if it has no tragic or lasting consequences, you might gain advantage by adopting a light-hearted tone, as Rothman does in his essay on book pricing. But when the topic is urgent—the spread of AIDS, for instance—the tone should be correspondingly serious, as indeed Steven Sainsbury's is in his essay.

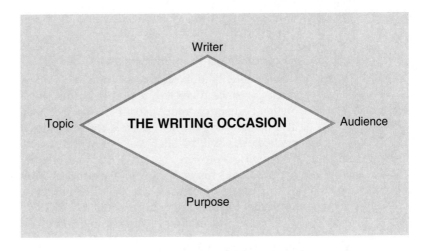

Think now of your readers and of the tone most likely to gain their attention and action. Why did Sainsbury adopt a tough, even brutal approach in his essay on condoms and sex? The decision he made was based on a careful review of his audience's likely reactions to the essay's topic. You will base your decisions concerning tone on these same factors. Sainsbury believed that his readers held a complacent attitude about sex with condoms, thinking erroneously that condoms ensured safe sex. In his statement on his reasons for writing the essay (see page 285), Sainsbury wrote that condoms are "defective and full of holes—literally and figuratively." His tough tone is calculated to shock readers out of complacency by exposing condom use as a myth of "political correctness." His tone is apparent from his opening example of the young girl with a "rip-roaring" gonorrheal infection.

Give careful thought to the tone of your problem/solution essays. The choices you make can work for you or against you in getting readers to take problems seriously and inspiring them to act. You will base decisions about tone on your assessments of the topic, the audience's relationship with this topic, and the relationship of these elements with the larger purpose of the essay: to present a problem and resolve it.

Explaining a Problem

When you can count on your readers' accepting your claim that a problem exists, then you can feel comfortable explaining that problem. You assume the readers' agreement—as Jenafer Trahar does in her essay at the beginning of this chapter—and devote your attention to providing as much pertinent explanatory information as possible. Chapter 7 is devoted to essays of explanation, and the first part of a problem/solution essay in which you explain a problem is, in fact, an explanatory essay. Numerous strategies are available to you in making an explanation: you can define the problem, recount its history, describe it, offer examples of it, and more (see pages 187–193). Your goal is to provide details that allow readers to see the problem clearly and to understand its significance and its causes.

Arguing That a Problem Exists

Often you will not be able to assume that readers agree with you, and you must convince them that a problem does, in fact, exist. Tony Rothman, Steven Sainsbury, and Alison Tschopp face this challenge in their essays at the beginning of this chapter. You should plan to argue when you expect readers will be skeptical—or will at least withhold judgment until your point is proven. As part of your argument, you may need to present the problem's history or provide examples; however, the overall purpose of this part of the essay will be to convince readers. (Chapter 11 offers strategies for presenting arguments that answer questions of fact.)

There are several ways you can present an argument:

- Make a **generalization** based on a specific case.

  A 15 year-old teen-ager's admission that, though sexually active, she does not use condoms is true of most sexually active teen-agers. (Steven Sainsbury)

- Show **cause and effect.**

  Book prices are high because of certain specific practices in the production, distribution, and mark-up scheduling of books. (Tony Rothman)

- Present a **parallel case.**

  If American drivers were told that their automobiles had a 10 percent likelihood of exploding, no one would drive. Users of condoms, which have a 14 percent failure rate, should be similarly wary. (Steven Sainsbury)

- Present an **analogy.**

  Advertising to children resembles a tug of war with 200 pound men on one side and 60 pound children on the other. (Peggy Charren)

- Vigorously **counter the arguments of others** who say that a problem either does not exist or has one cause when you maintain that it has another.

  Publishers are wrong in their contention that rising paper costs and disk incompatibilities raise the price of books. (Tony Rothman)

- **Make appeals to a respected authority.**

  The director of family health care at the Harvard Medical School states that to children, "advertisements for appealing things demand immediate gratification." (Peggy Charren)

Arguing for the existence of a problem means assembling evidence—facts, examples, and expert opinions—in support of your claim that the problem exists. Most arguments mix the preceding techniques, and you will probably want to do the same. See chapter 11 for a more detailed discussion of constructing arguments.

Planning a Structure

The problem/solution essay has a basic, two-part form. Writers adapt the form to their own needs, sometimes giving greater weight to the presentation of a problem, sometimes giving greater weight to the solution of that problem, and sometimes giving equal weight to both. The needs and expectations of readers largely determine the specific strategy adopted. For instance, Peggy Charren devotes most of her presentation to defining the problem of advertisements directed at children (see pages 287–292). Her audience, the Federal Trade Commission, was considering a proposal to ban such advertisements and Charren saw it as her role to define clearly and convincingly that a problem existed. Charren did not need to argue the advantages of one proposal versus another since only one proposal was being considered. She therefore gave virtually all her attention to presenting the problem. Jenafer Trahar, by contrast, weighted her problem/solution essay differently, giving more emphasis to her proposed solution since she assumed that readers would share her concern about the exploitation of student-athletes. Whatever weight a writer decides to give the different parts of the problem/solution essay, the essay invariably has two parts that can be presented in outline form:[1]

I. There is a serious problem.
   A. The problem exists and is growing. (Provide support for this statement.)
   B. The problem is serious. (Provide support.)
   C. Current methods cannot cope with the problem. (Provide support.)
II. There is a solution to the problem. (Your argumentative thesis, or claim, goes here.)
   A. The solution is practical. (Provide support.)
   B. The solution is desirable. (Provide support.)
   C. We can implement the solution. (Provide support.)

Understanding Your Logic

The solution to a problem, the second part of your essay, follows directly from the problem's cause. Stating a problem is *not* the same as stating a cause. Peggy Charren and Alison Tschopp agree that children who watch television commercials can be duped into buying poorly made or overpriced goods and can exert pressure on parents, which creates conflict. What action would alleviate this problem? The answer depends *entirely* on what is seen to cause the problem. Charren claims that advertisements are themselves the cause, since ads manipulate children emotionally and

---

[1]Source: Adapted from Richard D. Rieke and Malcolm O. Sillars, *Argumentation and the Decision Making Process* (Glenview: Scott, Foresman, 1984) 163.

cognitively: Eliminate the ads and the problem should be solved. By contrast, Tschopp acknowledges that ads are persuasive, but she will not blame advertisers for manipulating children: "We live in a consumer society," she says, and "advertising is the language of consumerism." Tschopp points to a different cause:

> If children are duped into choosing poorly made or overpriced but cleverly advertised products, this is not the fault of advertisers but of a family situation that permits children to influence important consumer decisions without a counterbalancing influence from parents.

Tschopp then presents her own solution: "A parent's close involvement with children . . . is the appropriate countermeasure to the power of advertisers." The differing solutions follow directly from differing causes. Both solutions represent an intervention in the sequence of cause and effect. When actions lead to a negative effect, change the actions. Charren and Tschopp agree on this much. *Which* actions should be altered is the issue.

The course of action you suggest in the second part of your problem/solution essay involves an argument about policy, about what *ought* to be done. See strategies for arguing in support of proposed policies in chapter 11. Cause and effect will probably be one line of reasoning in support of your solution. To a greater or lesser extent, each of the essays that begin this chapter uses a cause-and-effect argument for its proposed solution. Other strategies will help you make an argument about policy: parallel case, analogy, emotional appeals, and appeals to authority. See pages 427–433 for details and illustrations.

Presenting a Solution or a Proposal?

In some cases, a problem you have identified may be resolved with reference to the available facts and without the need for extensive action on the reader's part. For instance, Alison Tschopp argues that the problem of poorly planned purchases (influenced by advertisements) is resolved by parental guidance. Tschopp is not about to offer *specific* guidelines for parent–child interactions, for no one set of guidelines would help all families. Her interest is in establishing a *general* principle of involvement as the appropriate response to the problem at hand. Steven Sainsbury also presents a solution in his essay.

In other cases, resolving a problem requires action by the reader, or by some governing body (a board of trustees, the state legislature, and so on). If there is a problem that compels you to action and motivates you to call on others to act, then prepare a proposal: a clear and detailed plan that can correct the problem if people follow it. See the essays by Tony Rothman and Jenafer Trahar for examples of specific proposals.

In order to trust your approach to a problem, readers will want to know that you have carefully considered alternate solutions and proposals. These solutions and proposals may have merit, and they may not. You should at the very least be aware of them, raise them before readers do, and respond to them.

Advance Your Idea with Sources

Because the problem/solution essay requires that you make arguments and/or explanations, you can draw on source materials the same way you would when writing either type of essay. In chapters 7 (explanation) and 11 (argument), see the "Advance Your Idea with Sources" section for specific advice on using sources. Following are several general headings from those discussions, with references to specific passages in the two student papers at the beginning of this chapter.

Read to Clarify the Background of Your Problem

Readers of a problem/solution essay often need a larger context, such as background information or a history, in order to understand a problem. Source materials can help in this regard. For instance, in introducing her essay, Jenafer Trahar needed to read a source to learn about the history of collegiate sports. She found information for her essay's first paragraph (see page 298) from an article by Mark Naison in *Commonweal*. Here is a passage from that source, and the corresponding paragraph from Trahar's essay:

A Source That Clarifies a Problem

When I first began reviewing the history of college sports, what immediately attracted my attention was how quickly American universities became involved in providing sports entertainment for their students and the general public. According to Frederick Rudolph, discussing the rise of college football in the late nineteenth century, "few movements so captured the colleges and universities. . . . At last, the American college and university had discovered something that all sorts of people cared about passionately." So quickly did the general public seize upon college football as a subject of enthusiasm and identification (aided by the proliferation of mass circulation newspapers) that university presidents, operating in a climate not always conducive to intellectual concerns, be-

The Source Used

There have always been athletics on college campuses, but the presence of athletes posed no problems until the late nineteenth century. It was around this time that many colleges and universities began to rely on financial support from the alumni. What the alumni wanted was for their alma mater to be a winner. Sports became part of an important fundraising activity for many campuses, particularly at midwestern and southern universities. Northeastern schools could always rely on their academic reputations for maintaining the flow of alumni money. Midwestern and southern schools, however, did not have ready-made sources of contributions and needed some attraction other than academics to get alumni interested in making donations (Naison 493–94). For many years,

gan consciously to use the sport as a vehicle for attracting financial and political support, whether from alumni, state legislators, or prospective students and contributors.

At some institutions, especially private colleges in the East, the tendency to exploit public interest in football to the fullest was partially checked by efforts to attract academically and financially elite student bodies, and to develop internationally respected research faculties and graduate schools. But at land-grant colleges in the midwestern and southern states, founded to provide practical training to farmers or specialized technical education conducive to the expansion of local industries, university administrators "often discovered that athletic victories were more important than anything else in convincing reluctant legislators to open the public purse." Indeed, the very features of the state institutions which made them most democratic—their responsiveness to public opinion, their commitment to making higher education available to broad sections of the populace, their insistence on a practical justification for the universities' existence—led them to assume major responsibility for the provision of sports entertainment for their states and regions.[2]

schools turned to building their sports programs at the expense of their academic ones.

Read to Support Your Claim Directly with Facts, Examples, and Opinions

Source materials can provide details that increase the likelihood of readers agreeing that a problem exists. For instance, Alison Tschopp found herself presenting an extended counterargument to Charren's argument written in 1979. Charren opened with statistics on the amount of television children watch. Tschopp needed to update the information, and she

---

[2]Mark Naison, "Scenario for Scandal," *Commonweal* 16 (1982): 494.

was able to do so with facts gleaned from an article by Albert Shanker (see pages 293–297). Here is an excerpt from Shanker's article and the corresponding passage from Tschopp's essay:

A Source That Provides Facts

Why do our kids do so badly in school? Lots of people will tell you it's because they spend too much time in front of a TV set. And it's true that the numbers are staggering. In 1990, one in four 9-year-olds spent six or more hours, seven days a week, watching TV. That's more than most adults spend at work and certainly more than these kids spend in school. It's also true that kids who watch lots of TV have poor test scores. What should we do?

The Source Used

We know that advertisers are persuasive, and we know that the power of advertisements over children is directly related to the amount of television that children watch. According to a survey cited in a recent article by American Federation of Teachers President Albert Shanker, one-quarter of nine year olds in this country watch 42 hours of television each week (7)—approximately eight hours of which is devoted to advertisements. The most obvious way to eliminate exposure to so much advertising is to limit television viewing.

Source materials can also provide authoritative opinions that can bolster your argument. For example, in order to establish the validity of her own argument, Alison Tschopp needed to shake a foundation of Charren's argument: the claim that because children are not emotionally or intellectually equipped to be critical of advertisements, advertisements aimed specifically at children are deceitful and should be banned. Using the work of a writer who has analyzed the rhetoric of advertising claims, Tschopp was able to make a counterargument that ads work subconsciously on adults as well as on children and yet "we hear no one arguing that because adults are being manipulated we should therefore ban television advertising." Here is the passage in Jeffery Schrank's "The Language of Advertising Claims" that provided Tschopp with the logic of her counterargument:

A Source That Provides Opinions

Although few people admit to being greatly influenced by ads, surveys and sales figures show that a well-designed advertising campaign has dramatic effects. A logical conclusion is that advertising works below the level of conscious awareness and it works even on those who claim immunity to its message. Ads are designed to have an effect while being

The Source Used

. . . The right of free speech in our society is so important that anyone who proposes that we limit it bears a heavy burden of presenting a compelling argument. But Charren does not. First, she assumes that the skepticism portrayed by adult viewers of advertisements protects them (and could likewise protect children) from advertisers' power of per-

laughed at, belittled, and all but ignored.

A person unaware of advertising's claim on him or her is precisely the one most defenseless against the adwriter's attack. Advertisers delight in an audience which believes ads to be harmless nonsense, for such an audience is rendered defenseless by its belief that there is no attack taking place.

suasion. But realistically, few people are immune to the advertiser's art. In his article "The Language of Advertising Claims," Jeffery Schrank asserts that skepticism does not protect consumers because advertising works "below the level of conscious awareness and it works even on those who claim immunity to its message" (156).

Read to Locate Arguments against Your Claim, So That You Can Respond

Before accepting your ideas as reasonable, readers usually want to be assured that you have considered arguments contrary to your own. (See chapter 11 on rebuttals, page 435.) For instance, before presenting her solution to the problem of exploitation of student-athletes, Jenafer Trahar reviewed previous proposals for reform—the most radical was by Robert Hutchins. Though she does not mention Hutchins by name, she responds to these passages:

A Source That Provides a Counterargument

Money is the cause of athleticism in the American colleges. Athleticism is not athletics. Athletics is physical education, a proper function of the college if carried on for the welfare of the students. Athleticism is not physical education but sports promotion, and it is carried on for the monetary profit of the colleges through the entertainment of the public.

• • •

1. Reduce admission to ten cents. . . . [to] cover the handling costs.
2. Give the director of athletics and the major coaches some kind of academic tenure, so that their jobs depend on their ability as instructors and their character . . . and not on the gates they draw.[3]

The Source Used

Though many reformers have sought to correct the exploitation of student-athletes, no one has come up with a workable solution. Some have suggested that big-time sports be cut entirely out of colleges. The logic of this argument is that since sports seem inevitably to lead to commercialization, and since commercialization of sports leads inevitably to students being exploited, the only way to end exploitation is to take the money entirely out of college sports. This approach amounts to wishing for the purity—the amateur status—of an earlier time. Simply put, there is too much money involved now to ever go back.

---

[3]Robert M. Hutchins. "Gate Receipts and Glory," *The Saturday Evening Post,* 3 Dec. 1983.

Evaluate and Revise

General Evaluation

You will usually need at least two drafts to produce an essay that presents your idea clearly. The biggest changes in your essay will typically come between your first and second drafts. In this book you will find two demonstrations of essays in the process of turning from meandering first thoughts into finished products. First, in chapters 13 and 14 you will find general advice on the process of writing and revising, which includes first- and second-draft versions of a student paper. You will find another such demonstration in the "Student Writer at Work" sections at the end of chapters 1–5.

No essay that you write, including a problem/solution essay, will be complete until you revise and refine the single compelling idea of your essay. You revise and refine by evaluating your first draft, bringing to it many of the same questions you pose when evaluating any piece of writing. In chapter 5 you will find general guidelines for evaluating what you read, including these:

- Are the facts accurate?
- Are opinions supported by evidence?
- Are the opinions of others authoritative?
- Are my assumptions clearly stated?
- Are key terms clearly defined?
- Is the presentation logical?
- Are all parts of the presentation well developed?
- Are dissenting points of view presented?

Address these same questions to the first draft of your problem/solution essays, and you will have solid information to guide a revision.

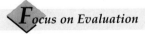

ocus on Evaluation

Have you been asked to write an evaluation of another writer's problem/solution essay? If so, you will base your evaluation on two sets of standards. First, you will apply specific standards for this type of writing as listed here in "Critical Points." At the same time you will need to apply the general standards for evaluation that are listed here and discussed at length in chapter 5, pages 92–96. See especially the "key points" for evaluation in chapter 5, pages 95–96.

Critical Points in a Problem/Solution Essay

In the problem/solution essay, you want to be sure that you have clearly addressed several issues and refined your thinking concerning them.

These issues can be framed as questions that follow from the key structures and strategies presented on the preceding pages:

- Is the problem you are writing about precisely defined?
- Will readers agree with your definition of the problem and its causes?
- Will readers, when presented with the problem, feel a need for action?
- Will readers find your proposal or solution reasonable?
- Have you responded to competing proposals or solutions?
- Have you demonstrated a clear cause-and-effect relationship between the problem and your proposal or solution?

These questions will get at the heart of a problem/solution essay whether that essay is yours in first-draft form, or someone else's that you are reading and evaluating. Pose these questions and study your writing (or someone else's) with care. A clear and careful response will direct you to a revised essay or, if needed, to a formal evaluation. For an example of how you might evaluate someone else's problem/solution essay, see Alison Tschopp's evaluation of Peggy Charren's presentation to the Federal Trade Commission, pages 293–297. You will find that Tschopp faults Charren for incorrectly defining the cause of a problem; Tschopp presents a competing cause and offers a competing solution. For more details on preparing formal evaluations, see the guidelines on pages 95–96.

Occasions for Discussion and Writing

A Problem/Solution Essay of Your Own

You are ready to begin work on your own problem/solution essay. One approach to choosing a topic is to review examples of the type of essay you will be writing. Consider rereading the essays that opened this chapter. You will find that the four authors—Sainsbury, Charren, Tschopp, and Trahar—write about topics they know well either through direct experience or through careful reading. You will also find that these authors have a deep, personal involvement with their essay's topic: Steven Sainsbury, a physician, wants to prevent disease; children's advocate Peggy Charren wants to ban manipulative advertisements; Alison Tschopp, a future attorney, wants to protect the First Amendment; and student Jenafer Trahar wants to see student-athletes assured an education. In choosing a topic for your essay, you too can take a deep interest. In the best of cases, your motivation to write will be personal, but your expression of ideas *in your essay* will be public and controlled. All of the opening examples amply demonstrate this double quality: in each essay you find someone writing for personal reasons, yet maintaining strict control over important elements of public expression—including the essay's reasoning, structure, sentence rhythm, and word choice.

To prepare for your problem/solution essay, select one of the examples that began this chapter, one that you find especially effective. Think critically about how this essay succeeds. You might respond to the questions following the piece; you might try writing a paragraph explaining what appeals to you most about the piece; you might reflect on the ways in which this essay could affect your own work. Once you have studied the piece and have a clear sense of how it succeeds, choose a topic for your own essay—a topic that you know well.

The next two Occasions sections present two topics for writing: high-school dress codes and community tensions (specifically, the riots at Crown Heights). If you prefer another topic, you might find suitable materials in the other Occasions sections in chapters 6–8 and 10–11:

Of course, you are not limited to these choices and should choose a topic according to your interests and experience. For detailed guidance on how you might organize your approach to writing a problem/solution essay, turn to the second Occasion for discussion and writing in this chapter, pages 336–341. That Guide to the assignment provides a structured approach to the writing task that may help you work through your first draft and revision, whatever your topic.

A note on using sources: All of writers whose essays begin the chapter draw on source materials to advance their ideas. You can—and are encouraged to—do the same, with the caution that writers who use sources should never let source materials overtake their essays. The psychological focus of your essay should remain yours alone. In writing a first draft, be sure that your voice predominates and that sources, even if essential to your essay's success, play a subordinate role.

I. Dress Codes in Public Schools

As a high-school student, how much thought did you, your friends, and your classmates give to clothes? Increasingly in schools around the country, discussion has been stirred over the merits of dress codes and uniform standards. Long the object of derision among those who value free expression, the idea of common dress among students has made something of a comeback. Points offered in favor of wearing uniforms and adopting a dress code include the following:

- In some schools, violence has erupted when one student demands another's clothing.
- Gang members sometimes identify themselves by wearing a certain hat, scarf, or T-shirt.
- Some students feel compelled, for social reasons, to spend more money on clothes than they can afford.
- Some clothing can be disruptive or aggressive, such as certain "message" T-shirts.
- Administrators claim that uniforms can generate a feeling of common purpose and school pride.
- Administrators also claim that uniforms equalize students, putting the relatively privileged and relatively poor on an equal footing.
- Students who are not spending hundreds of dollars for clothing can save money for college or work fewer hours in order to study more.

You have two tasks in responding to the materials for discussion that follow. First, read the following selections: "There Already Is a Dress Code," by Boston University senior Mariah Houton, and "Dress Codes and Uniforms," by freelance education writer Muriel Cohen. Working by yourself, do the following:

- Summarize the main idea of each selection.

- Comment on the strengths and weaknesses of each selection.
- Take a stand on the issue of school dress codes and uniforms.

Having done this, work in small groups and adopt a *group* position on the topic, debating your separate views until you reach a consensus. Then, as a group, propose a dress code (however minimally defined) or some standard for uniforms to be worn by high-school students.

There Already Is a Dress Code

Mariah Houton

I've been reading about Boston mayoral candidate Jim Brett's proposal to impose a dress code on Boston public school students. I'm a senior at Boston University, doing honors work, but three years ago I was a public school student in Boston. As I look back, I see how different my high school experience might have been if we had been forced to wear uniforms. Some say that uniforms mean coercion. But I remember that the pressure from my peers was far more coercive than any dress code.

This is how I had to dress in order to be a part of what I considered the in crowd at Boston Latin Academy. In order to leave for school by 7:15 a.m., I would get up at 5:30, shower and wash my hair, choose a coordinated outfit, iron it, dry my hair, style it, spray it and apply full makeup, including foundation, blush, eyeliner, mascara and lipstick. In order to achieve the big-hair look, I had to have a perm ($50 every four months) and used at least a bottle of hairspray per week. The spray coated the furniture, the floor and the walls in my bedroom with a sticky residue. In the evenings, I would watch television, exercise and do my nails, which were long and polished.

All told, I spent more time on my appearance than on my academic courses. Being rather shy, this was the only way I felt I could be accepted. Not every girl was as involved with her appearance as I was, but I was not unique. This was how we gained respect. I never even considered any other way of dressing.

Choice of the outfit was key; the ideal was never to wear the same coordinated outfit more than once every two weeks. Although many of us came from working-class families, the correct outfits weren't cheap. Skirts were almost never worn. I needed at least five pairs of designer jeans (Guess or Girbaud) costing about $56 each. I also needed at least five expensive sweatshirts such as Champion or Polo (from $30 to $100), plus sweaters, blouses, matching earrings, shoes coordinated with each outfit and a school bag from Esprit or the Gap.

It was also vital to own a leather jacket, designer windbreakers and denim jackets, as well as a wool coat. Even if I didn't outgrow it, fashion dictated a new winter coat every fall. Expensive jewelry completed the look: gold chains ($200), initial rings, diamond stud earrings ($300 and up).

Between classes, my friends and I gathered in the second-floor ladies room to primp, gossip and smoke. As soon as we were of legal working age (14), we all got jobs in order to afford our dress code when our parents refused to buy these things. None of us saved any of our earnings for college.

When I entered Boston University, I started fresh, like all my classmates. Lacking a peer group to compete with, I began studying instead. There were still cliques, but none was as intense as the cliques were in high school. Now, although it's still important for me to look good, my looks are no longer the center of my life. Ironically, once I stopped perming and spraying my hair, it looked prettier. Everyone tells me that I look much better now. In the mirror, I see a human being, not an image.

Latin Academy was a college preparatory school. Of the seven girls in my group, only three went on to college. I wonder if the time and effort we wasted on our appearance could have made the difference. If we had had uniforms, perhaps our intense competition would never have started. 8

Dress Codes and Uniforms

Muriel Cohen

Dress codes and school uniforms are two separate issues. Dress codes dictate 1
the rules that might bar wearing hats indoors or message T-shirts in the classroom. A rule for uniforms requires each student to wear an outfit specified by the school.

Here is where the element of choice comes into play. When parents send 2
their children to nonpublic schools, they accept the dress code or the school uniform spelled out in the school regulations. While parents and students in public schools are bound by rules on attendance and discipline, should they be subject to orders on what to wear? Can they transfer to another school?

While advocates argue that school uniforms and dress codes result in more 3
disciplined students, that may be specious. Parents who accept dress codes and school uniforms have already demonstrated to their children their interest and support for the school. That is a subtle and more important issue than whether all the girls wear plaid skirts or the boys wear neckties.

It would be better if [the candidates for mayor] promised the schools more 4
of what they need—books and computers and pencils and paper and teachers for art and music and science and math—than offering the rhetoric of . . . dress codes or uniforms, which offer more superficial than substantive change.

Individual Response: Dress Codes in Public Schools

Read the two selections, "There Already Is a Dress Code" and "Dress Codes and Uniforms."

1. Write a one-paragraph summary of each selection (see pages 81–87 for a discussion on writing summaries).

2. Having read these two selections, consider the issues involved in setting dress standards for high-school students. Based on your reading and on your personal insights, state as clearly as you can "the problem" regarding the dress of high-school students. Recall (from pages 302–304) that you have several strategies available to you for defining a problem:

Read to spark ideas regarding a problem.
Call attention to a difference between what is expected, or desired, and what is the case.
Call attention to damage, disadvantages, or danger.

Call attention to a *potential* problem.
You might also conclude that there is no problem.

3. Assume that you will need to convince others that the problem you have stated actually exists. See pages 308–309 and decide on how you would present such an argument. Sketch the argument in outline form. The sketch should be no longer than one page.

Group Response: Dress Codes in Public Schools

1. In a group of four, exchange and compare summaries you have written for "There Already Is a Dress Code" and "Dress Codes and Uniforms."

2. As a group, agree on the essential information of each selection. Where group members disagree, reread particular sentences or paragraphs and clarify what the author has stated.

3. Write a group summary of each section. Borrow language from individual summaries as you need to, and revise for consistency of style and smoothness of flow.

4. Having agreed on what the authors have stated, present to one another your own statements on the problem concerning the dress of high-school students. If you believe that no problem exists, say as much. Argue for your position, using the sketch you have prepared.

5. Immediately after each speaker presents, group members should discuss the presentation. The group response should be guided by these questions: Does a problem exist? If so, what exactly *is* the problem? How urgent is it? Why should anyone care about it? How does the problem as stated by this group member compare with the problem as stated by others?

6. After all group members have presented, discuss the issues and make an effort to agree that a particular problem exists. Those who feel there is no problem should state as much and should explain their reasons. The goal of this discussion is to arrive at one statement, however narrowly defined, with which all group members can agree. If this proves impossible, try for a pair of statements. (For subsequent activities, the group would then split into two smaller groups.)

Projecting an Essay: Dress Codes in Public Schools

1. As a group, state the problem regarding dress codes and uniforms for high-school students. As clearly as you can, list the causes of the problem.

2. Discuss the cause-and-effect thinking that will lead from the statement of your problem to a proposal for change. See pages 309–310 on cause-and-effect logic. These are your guiding questions: What action does the problem call for? What new action will break an undesirable cycle of cause and effect and lead to more desirable outcomes?

3. Devise a proposal, however modest, for addressing the problem you have defined. The proposal should be detailed and should lead to *specific* actions. As a group, clearly understand the goals of your proposal. If your proposal had its precise, intended effect, what would change—and why?

4. What problems or what objections do you foresee? Identify these, perhaps relying on the brief selections and the note that begin this section. Respond to objections or to any counterproposals you can name.

5. Devise an argument in support of your proposal (see pages 424–434). Remember: in an argument about policies (which is what your argument for a proposal is), you can appeal to your audience's emotions as well as to their sense of reason and respect for authority.

6. Orally present the problem to other groups or to your class. Present your proposal for alleviating that problem, and have a recorder in your own group take notes on any discussion that follows—especially on criticisms of your proposal.

7. In a final meeting as a group, prepare an outline of a problem/solution essay based on your group meetings and on your presentations to other groups. See page 309 for a suggested format. Be sure to raise and respond to any useful criticisms raised by others.

8. Option: Prepare a problem/solution essay, based on your group's discussions.

II. Community Tensions: The Example of Crown Heights

For three days and nights in August 1991, a race riot shook New York City in the Crown Heights section of Brooklyn. Scores of people were hurt and many businesses were looted as decades-old distrust between blacks and religious Jews gave way to violence. The incidents leading to the riot—a car accident, a dead six-year-old black child, and a retaliatory murder of a young Jewish scholar—will be detailed in the following selections. You will see evidence of a long-simmering and complicated problem that was waiting to boil over. You will also see difficult and slow, but encouraging, efforts being made to ease tensions in the neighborhood.

The purpose of your reading about Crown Heights is not to write about Crown Heights, per se, but to prompt your thinking about complex problems and solutions in your *own* community. In this Occasions section, the events and commentaries regarding Crown Heights provide an opportunity to recognize the complexity of problems and the creativity, commitment, and patience needed to effect equally complex solutions. You have two goals: First, read the selections that follow and think seriously on the factors that can complicate problems and make solutions difficult to achieve; and second, bring this same awareness to bear on a community-based problem that you know well.

Your Writing Assignment

Prompted by your reading about the Crown Heights riot, reflect on a community-based problem you both care about and know something about that exists close to your own home. Perhaps, like the problem between African Americans and Jewish Americans in Crown Heights, the problem you choose might involve miscommunication and mutual mistrust; the problem might concern the environment, town governance, fiscal or educational issues—whatever concerns you. The problem may not be dramatic in the sense that, if unchecked, it will lead to violence; still, it should be a *specific and real* problem for which real solutions are needed.

Write a problem/solution essay for readers *in your community,* alerting them to a problem in their midst, and to a likely solution. Write for publication on the OP-ED page of your town's newspaper. Specifically, your task is to argue that a problem exists and to present a proposal that is specific and detailed.

Rage and Atonement

Josh Getlin

Written two years after the Crown Height riots, this article reviews the specific incidents sparking the events of August 1991 as well as the community's long-standing tensions. A staff writer for the Los Angeles Times, *Josh Getlin also reports on the slow progress now being made toward resolving tensions.*

Crown Heights, N.Y.—Never again.   1

As he stands by his young son's grave on a sweltering afternoon, Carmel   2
Cato rises above private grief to issue a public warning. A message to the Hasidic Jews whose motorcade accidentally killed his boy, Gavin, two years ago, triggering New York's worst race riots in two decades.

"Nobody ever paid the price for this, nobody went to jail," says Cato, a soft-   3
spoken black man with tears in his eyes. "And it's because some lives are considered more important than others in Crown Heights. This must never happen again."

At almost the same moment 10,000 miles, away, Norman Rosenbaum   4
leaves his home in Australia and boards a plane for New York to resume his bitter quest for justice. Three hours after Gavin Cato died, an angry mob of blacks surrounded Rosenbaum's 29-year-old brother, Yankel, an Orthodox Jewish student, and stabbed him to death in the same Brooklyn neighborhood. "Kill the Jew," they shouted as he fell.

"The fury over my brother's death continues because a jury acquitted the   5
only man who was charged with the crime," says Rosenbaum. "His killers still walk the streets, free to do as they like, while the city does nothing. And so we Jews say it once more: Never again."

In Crown Heights, justice is a bad joke and wounds have yet to heal. The   6
deaths of Cato and Rosenbaum sparked three days of rioting in August, 1991, filling the front pages and shocking millions of New Yorkers. Now, two years after the storm broke over the neighborhood on a hot summer night, the personal, political and moral fallout continues.

At first glance, the community of brownstone apartments and brick homes   7
less than 15 minutes from Wall Street seems calm. Caribbean blacks go about their daily business with Hasidic Jews, a reclusive, Messianic group whose men wear black hats, long black coats and beards. But underneath that lid of civility is a caldron of animosity.

Last month, a two-volume state report blasted New York City Mayor David 8
Dinkins for failing to halt the violence as soon as it broke out. The key finding,
which the city's first black mayor does not dispute, was that he waited three
days to snuff out a riot that resulted in 190 injuries, mostly to police, and 124
arrests.

Dinkins explained that he and top aides didn't realize the riot was out of 9
control until the third night, despite widespread television coverage of the car-
nage. The report was a devastating indictment, a portrait of passivity under fire
that could become a key issue in the city's Nov. 2 mayoral election.

As might be expected, attorneys for both the Cato and Rosenbaum fami- 10
lies charged that their clients' rights had been violated. Last week, lawyers
representing Rosenbaum deposed Dinkins in a vitriolic public session, arguing
that he deliberately left Jews unprotected. Meanwhile, Attorney General Janet
Reno is deciding whether to re-try the Rosenbaum case on federal civil-rights
grounds.

The greatest pain, however, has been felt by blacks and Jews. Like the 11
1992 Los Angeles riots, Crown Heights raised troubling questions about race
relations. But the Brooklyn clash marked an unprecedented attack by blacks on
Jews, adding a disturbing new chapter to an already tense relationship. And
that, in turn, has spawned soul-searching in the Jewish community. Many non-
Orthodox Jews have long felt uneasy, about the Hasidim, spurning their religious fundamentalism and extreme political views. During the riots, some
national Jewish organizations remained silent about the violence against their
brethren, causing the rift to grow.

The Crown Heights controversy shows no signs of fading away—not for 12
Jews, blacks or anyone else—and has cast a pall over New York City.

"There's a sense of heaviness and pain in our community that all New 13
Yorkers still feel," Gov. Mario M. Cuomo said earlier this month at a ceremony
commemorating the two-year anniversary of the riots. "We can't forget what
happened. Yet we have to move on."

For some, that's the only choice. Amid the gloom, there are a few signs of 14
genuine progress in Crown Heights. A handful of activists has worked, to bring
Jews and blacks together, trying everything from face-to-face meetings and basketball games to multiracial rap concerts. They're hopeful, telling anyone who
will listen that grassroots communication can make a huge difference, especially among the neighborhood's youth. But they're also realistic.

"We're nowhere near where we want to be," says Richard Green, a black 15
community organizer who runs the Crown Heights Youth Collective. "There's
still a lot of negative stuff that's playing out here. People hear all the bad news
these days and tune out the rest."

Like so many other neighborhood problems, it began with a misunder- 16
standing.

On the night of Aug. 19, 1991, a police car was guiding two other vehi- 17
cles through Crown Heights. The caravan included Menachem Schneerson, the
Grand Rebbe and spiritual leader of the Lubavitchers—the formal name for the
branch of Hasidic Jews who live there.

As was his custom, the Rebbe was returning from the cemetery where he 18
visited the graves of his wife and predecessor. At 8:20 p.m., the last car in the
motorcade sped through a red light to keep up with the other vehicles and was
hit by another automobile.

The driver of the third car, Yosef Lifsh, careened onto a sidewalk, killing 7- 19
year-old Gavin Cato and injuring his 6-year-old cousin, Angela Cato.

Within seconds, a Hasidic-run ambulance company arrived at the scene, 20
where enraged onlookers had begun to beat up Lifsh.

When police arrived, they quickly urged the Lubavitchers to climb into their 21
own private ambulance and flee the scene for their own safety. At the same
moment, a city ambulance arrived and began taking care of the bleeding children.

In the confusion, a rumor spread like wildfire: The Jews took care of their 22
own, leaving two innocent black kids to die. And the cops let it happen.

Soon, bands of angry black people began roaming the neighborhood, trash- 23
ing Jewish businesses and attacking Hasidim. Minutes after Yankel Rosenbaum
was stabbed, police arrested a suspect and brought him before the dying man,
who lay crumpled on the hood of a car. He spat blood at the 16-year-old black
suspect and cried: "Why did you do this? I never did anything to you."

For the next 96 hours, Crown Heights went through hell. Large crowds of 24
blacks threw rocks at police and assaulted Jews, shouting "Heil Hitler!" Rioters
defaced buildings and looted stores, while black and Jewish protesters staged
counter-demonstrations.

All the while, hundreds of police followed orders and stood their ground, 25
failing to pursue rioters who were roaming at will through the 50-square-block
neighborhood. On the fourth day, the disturbance was finally snuffed when
Dinkins flooded the area with 2,000 officers.

It was war—fueled by the racism and ignorance that had festered in Crown 26
Heights for years. Angry and distrustful, the neighborhood's mostly Caribbean
blacks had clashed repeatedly with Hasidim over housing, crime and other
issues. There had been only sporadic attempts at dialogue, and ugly incidents
kept dividing the two hostile communities.

"We're paying now for that distance," says Rabbi Shea Hecht, one of the 27
leading Hasidic peacemakers and co-chair of a blue-ribbon community panel
formed after the riots to reduce tensions. "We have a long road to travel. I can't
kid you about that."

A key problem is that Crown Heights differs markedly from other urban 28
trouble spots. It may be the only place in the United States where a white community surrounded by black neighbors has refused to move, An estimated
170,000 blacks and 17,000 Lubavitchers reside in the area, and on some
blocks they live side by side, sharing the same streets and an uneasy peace.

"We don't understand the Jewish people very well," says T.J. Moses, a 16- 29
year-old black resident of Crown Heights. "But we have to try better. We've got
to forget what happened."

That may be a pipe dream, given the crush of media coverage. Crown 30
Heights, as every New Yorker knows, has become a near-obsession with reporters, rabblerousers and politicians.

Since the state report, Dinkins has accepted responsibility, repeatedly say- 31
ing "never again." But that hasn't silenced Jewish critics, nor has it quieted
Rudolph Giuliani, the Republican challenger and former U.S. Attorney who
leads Dinkins in the polls. Four years ago, the city's liberal Jewish voters supported Dinkins. Now, many say they are are undecided.

"Crown Heights left a real mark on the Jewish gut," says Jim Sleeper, a 32
journalist and author who has written about New York City ethnic relations.

"We've all heard stories from parents of Jewish kids getting beaten up by Irish kids years ago, but this mass attack and the ugliness of it was truly unprecedented. To a lot of Jews, it's been a watershed."

For many black residents, however, the events leading up to the riot merely 33 confirm what they'd come to believe about the Lubavitchers. They've long regarded the insular group with suspicion, never understanding why the men recited strange prayers in public. Some felt insulted that Hasidic women refused to shake hands with neighbors. Mostly, they chafed at the group's perceived clout at city hall—and their own corresponding political weakness.

Indeed, the police-led motorcade that killed Gavin Cato came to symbolize 34 this image.

In 1981, after threats on the Rebbe's life, Mayor Edward I. Koch assigned 35 an unmarked police car to escort Schneerson's biweekly caravans to the cemetery. Police had also been assigned to channel traffic from overflow crowds on the Jewish Sabbath. The result has been a persistent belief by many black residents that Hasidim receive more city services than blacks do.

Given these pressures, it's not surprising that the confusion and anger over 36 Cato's tragic death finally lit the torch in Crown Heights. Jews were outraged that blacks would equate Cato's accidental death with Rosenbaum's deliberate murder, but others saw it differently.

"Gavin, we won't let them bury you on the back pages," said the Rev. Al 37 Sharpton, a controversial black activist, at a ceremony marking the second anniversary of the boy's death.

"You're bigger than a 7-year-old now. You're the symbol of a whole system 38 of racism, and we're going to make sure the whole world knows what really happened in Crown Heights."

For years, the quiet Brooklyn neighborhood was nothing special. Like many 39 other New York melting pots, it was home to Irish, Italian, Jewish, German and black families, all of whom lived together fairly peaceably. Everything changed after World War II.

Suddenly, white families moved out of Crown Heights in droves, lured by 40 affordable homes in newly built suburbs. At the same time, a large number of Caribbean blacks and others streamed into the tree-lined community, attracted by its relatively cheap housing. In less than three decades, the once overwhelmingly white neighborhood became 70% black.

But the Lubavitchers stayed. They had invested a fortune in real estate and 41 had spent years developing local businesses. Their evangelical culture required a network of services all within walking distance—including synagogues, yeshivas (schools), markets and mikvahs (ritual baths for women). How could they duplicate this world in a Long Island subdivision?

In 1969, the Grand Rebbe labeled it a sin for Hasidim to sell housing to 42 non-Jews if it would harm the long-term interests of the Jewish community. Crown Heights was their home, he declared, and would remain so. The Lubavitchers consider the Rebbe their Messiah, his decisions their law.

Turning their backs on the modern world, Hasidim carefully observe 43 the strict Jewish commandments that have governed the sect since its origins in czarist Russia. Under a code of modesty, women are forbidden to touch men other than their husbands. Children attend special religious schools and summer camps. Their parents are leery of outsiders, including non-Orthodox Jews.

In a New York neighborhood wracked with change, they've kept to them- 44
selves and taken care of their own. Years ago, the Lubavitchers formed a community patrol and started their own ambulance service. Did black neighbors
complain? It really didn't matter.

"If I want to live in a ghetto, within my religious beliefs, that's my right in 45
this country," explains Rabbi Hecht. "It's not that we're antisocial. These are
ancient laws. We believe in 'live and let live.' We've never wanted to make trouble with anybody."

But violence flared between Hasidim and blacks. Over the years, the Luba- 46
vitchers blamed blacks for increased crime, while blacks protested that they were
being roughed up by vigilante groups. By the mid-'70s, racial tensions had
reached the breaking point.

"The Jews think the blacks are all muggers and rapists," said the Rev. 47
Clarence Norman Sr., the minister of First Baptist Church of Crown Heights,
in a 1975 interview. "And the blacks see the Jews as white people, as symbols
of oppression. Tension could be removed by dialogue."

Such dialogue would not begin until rioting tore the neighborhood apart 16 48
years later. And even then, politicians discovered that racial healing is a tricky
art.

Initial press accounts made Dinkins look like a hero in Crown Heights. The 49
New York media credited him with cracking down on violence and he was widely praised for cooling community tensions by sending a network of mayoral
advisers to neighborhood trouble spots.

Then stories surfaced about the confused police response, how scores of 50
officers had been hurt. Critics said cops weren't given the green light to crack
down until the third day—when Dinkins himself was pelted by rocks after visiting a Crown Heights school.

Meanwhile, the criminal justice system made everyone angry. A grand jury 51
failed to indict Lifsh, ruling Gavin Cato's death accidental. Rosenbaum's accused
killer was acquitted, amid charges the Brooklyn district attorney had badly bun-
gled the case.

Hasidic critics charged that Dinkins had gone easy on black rioters because 52
he didn't want to antagonize his political base, a charge the mayor heatedly
denied. Blacks, in turn, insisted that Cato's death had been swept under the rug.

Dinkins was taunted by Jewish demonstrators on a trip to Israel, and the 53
Amsterdam News, the city's leading black newspaper, editorialized that "a car-
ful of Jews" had murdered Cato.

Adding fuel to the fire, mayoral challenger Giuliani called the riot a po- 54
grom—a politically loaded word for the state-sponsored violence that plagued
Jews under the Russian czars. Then, during a New York speech in which Dinkins
urged public healing, hecklers called him a "Jew hater."

The normally low-key mayor erupted. Blasting back at his critics, he asked: 55
"In burying a 7-year-old boy and a quiet biblical scholar, did we bury decency,
too?"

By now, even Jews were slamming each other. Commentary, the conserv- 56
ative Jewish magazine, noted that Lubavitchers are law-abiding folk. But writer
Philip Gourevitch added acidly:

"The Hasidim of Crown Heights are no Gandhis. They tend to be openly 57
critical of blacks, and their criticisms often smack of bigotry. Moreover, their
uncompromising rejection of modern liberal society . . . makes them alien not

only to their black neighbors but to just about everyone else, including the majority of their fellow Jews."

In a stinging response to such thinking, New York Times columnist A.M. 58 Rosenthal addressed Jews who feel economically and morally superior to Lubavitchers, and who were quiet during the riots:

"Are the Hasidim a little too Jewish for them? Maybe they think only a certain *kind* of Jew gets beaten up. Sweethearts, by you, you are Park Avenue, by your wife, you are Park Avenue, but by an anti-Semite, you are a Hasid." 59

For Lubavitchers, it's an old war. Conceding that his group has to mend 60 fences, Rabbi Hecht says: "Sure, we were being attacked by blacks. But they weren't the real bad guys. Our enemies are the Jews on Long Island who aren't close to us. And they think *we're* the bad guys."

The political corpses are strewn all over Crown Heights. And Dinkins may 61 be the biggest loser of all.

But is it really that simple? Supporters point out that the mayor faced tough 62 tactical choices. Green, the veteran activist, says Dinkins' strategy of reaching out to residents instead of instantly cracking heads averted more bloodshed.

"We let people blow off steam in community meetings," he says. "And 63 what's the alternative? Were we supposed to kill 75 people and have 1,500 buildings go up in smoke? If we had, South-Central [Los Angeles] would have been a Halloween party by comparison."

Green shakes his head, idling his van on a quiet Crown Heights street: "We 64 don't have to love each other, but we have to respect each other. At some point, all this yelling has to stop and the healing has to begin. Like right now."

If there's any healing in the neighborhood, it mostly happens out of public 65 view.

The Crown Heights Coalition, a group of community leaders from both 66 sides, meets regularly to find common ground. They sponsor forums, publish newsletters and plant trees for peace in a local park. The goodwill is growing, but with adults it has limits.

As she chats with neighbors at the local mikvah, for example, resident 67 Bracha Levertov blames outside agitators for much of Crown Heights' troubles. Still, she says, many Hasidic Jews remain distrustful of their black neighbors, despite the need to build bridges.

"I know we need to communicate," Levertov says. "But when you see 68 toughs walking on your side of the street, you cross to the other side. I'm sorry. Feelings are feelings."

Several blocks away, Elisha Gill leans on a rake and concedes that both 69 sides have had their troubles. Yet Gill, a black homeowner, says it's nothing that can't be solved if people listen to each other.

As if by some magical clockwork, Green pulls up in his van and quietly 70 agrees: "This man [Gill] has the answer, he's got it right. We can't get angry. We gotta get busy. And that's what me and my buddy, Dave, are all about."

Almost on cue, David Lazerson strolls around the corner with two 71 teenagers, one black and one Hasidic. T.J. Moses and Yudi Simon give Green high-fives and then Lazerson gives him a bear hug. Slowly, the stereotypes fade.

"Me and T.J. got to be friends, and it's because we've been talking to each 72 other," says Simon, a cheerful kid wearing a yarmulke and T-shirt that reads "Increase the Peace."

T.J. grabs Simon in a playful hammerlock and nods in agreement: "It 73 wouldn't be possible for us, you know, without the good community stuff that Richard and David put together."

The two men couldn't be more different: Lazerson, a Lubavitcher with a 74 Ph.D. in special education, wears a New York Yankees skullcap, along with sneakers, baggy jeans and a black T-shirt reading "Laz" on the back.

Green, whose long dreadlocks end in a pony tail, has run the Crown 75 Heights Youth Collective for 16 years. Both men are in their mid-40s.

Soon after the riots ended, their respective communities tapped them to 76 bring black and Jewish youths together. At first, they held tense face-to-face meetings, trying to deal with myths and misunderstandings. There was a lot of pain. A lot to learn.

"I found out that they [Jews] are not all millionaires, you know, and that a 77 lot of them come from poor homes, too," says T.J. "I found out why they wear the kind of clothes they wear, what it means to them. Stuff like that. And that they're not all stuck up."

For his part, Yudi says he's learned that blacks are law-abiding people. He 78 was amazed to discover that they worry about safety, families, good grades and jobs like anybody else.

"They're very decent people, you know," he says, circling T.J. in a boxer's 79 crouch. "I like 'em. I've spent time with 'em. We can talk now. That didn't happen before."

Gradually, says Lazerson, the teen-age dialogue spilled onto the basketball 80 court, where kids learned to respect each other more. There have been some unforgettable moments—especially when the black teenagers came to play in the old gymnasium of a Jewish school.

"A black kid came up to me and said he couldn't play here," Lazerson 81 recalls. "When I asked why, he pointed out that there were large metal bolts sticking out of the backboard.

" 'Oh,' I said. 'You mean the rubber ball could get cut by the bolts?' And he 82 said, 'No, man, my hands. My hands could get cut on the backboard.'

"Not one to miss a good line, I answered: 'Uh, yeah, the yeshiva kids com- 83 plain about that all the time.' "

Music provides the best communication of all. Lazerson is also a rock musi- 84 cian and has performed several rap songs stressing racial harmony. One, in particular, seems to have caught on in the neighborhood and, without much urging, T.J. and Yudi perform an impromptu break-dance on the sidewalk while Lazerson recites the pulsing lyrics.

He claps his hands and the scene becomes surreal: Hasidim on nearby 85 stoops sway to the rhythm, while blacks put down groceries and boogie to the beat. The words are simple, yet they might be the last, best hope for Crown Heights. Something the old folks have forgotten:

Ain't talkin' in riddles, just callin' attention
To something so obvious, you shouldn't have to mention
Don't care where you came from, don't care where you've been
Don't care how you dress, or if your hair's a mess
Don't care if you're fat or where your bankroll's at
Cause all these things mean nothing, my friend
They don't really matter when you get to the end
In the final analysis . . . they all cause paralysis.

What the Hasidim Know

A. M. Rosenthal

Writing two years after the violence in Crown Heights, New York Times *columnist A. M. Rosenthal broadens the significance of the event by seeing past particular animosities to a graver problem: a challenge to our belief that America is the place where law is on the side of those who* prevent *persecution. Protection for the "oppressed or [the] endangered" was missing in Crown Heights, says Rosenthal, and he faults Mayor Dinkins for not having used the force of law to protect Jews in the same way that the force of law had been called on to protect the rights of blacks in the early years of the civil rights movement.*

Let's all put Crown Heights behind us—certainly, but not now, not yet.   1

To walk away from Crown Heights now, with its real meaning and the real 2 offense of New York City's government still unstated and unexamined, would make it more likely that some other riot, some other pogrom, against some other group would be committed somewhere in America. There can be hope after Crown Heights—but, as always, only when reality is faced.

We are told Crown Heights is a matter of Mayor David Dinkins's incom- 3 petence. Or—it is a matter of malarkey, that cockamamie story that he did not know how bad it was, nobody told him. Or—the police brass were paralyzed by their own inefficiency and timorousness.

All true, but they do not add up to the whole. What is left out is what the 4 Hasidim know, why the feeling of betrayal is so deep in them. To understand the crime, understand the victim.

The Mayor allowed one group of citizens to be persecuted, openly and vio- 5 lently, by another group of citizens, without providing the victims with the protection of the law. What Hasidim know is this: That passiveness strikes at the essential difference between America and the countries they or their parents fled in fear and disgust.

I doubt that any of the Hasidim are foolish enough to believe that in 6 America they would find a land where religious or racial hatred had been eliminated.

But they knew that in the old countries, the government and the police were 7 on the side of the pogromists. And they believed that in America it was the other way around—officials or police did not have to love you, but they would protect you against the rioters. For them, that was the difference—the law as shield, not knife.

In four days in 1991, they learned that was not true for them. In their own 8 neighborhood, they were set upon, beaten, reviled, one of them murdered— while the police, knowing and seeing, failed to protect them.

That, is what Hasidim know Crown Heights was about—the destruction of 9 the law, the destruction of faith in the law.

The bitterness of black violence against Jews is that for both groups every- 10 thing they fought and hope for rests on protection by the law, particularly against physical attack, in Selma or Brooklyn. Common self-interest in protective law brought Jews and blacks together in the civil rights struggle.

I do not understand why some Jews do not understand what is in the hearts 11 of the Hasidim, or are silent. They would not tolerate, for a moment, police or mayoral failure against riots in their own neighborhoods. 911 would damn well work. There would be no sympathetic clucks for "root cause" rationalizations.

Are the Hasidim a little too Jewish for them? Maybe they think only a cer- 12
tain *kind* of Jew gets beaten up. Sweethearts, by you, you are Park Avenue, by
your wife you are Park Avenue, but by an anti-Semite you are a Hasid.

All right, we all know that Jews can be among the most suicidal of God's 13
ostriches. But does everybody else have to be that thick too?

Why does Gov. Mario Cuomo say we should be grateful to the Mayor for 14
all the riots that did not happen? Surely he jests; St. John's turns out great lawyers, but lesser comedians.

Why does even the Mayor's opponent, Rudolph Giuliani, not get to the gut 15
of it—not one man's competence but belief and trust in the law?[4]

Why do not African-Americans who have most to gain from the law's pro- 16
tection against bigoted violence, not understand they have most to lose from the
destruction of that shield?

I understand the cheapjack black politicians who heat up the streets one day 17
and talk unctuously about brotherhood the next. But New York has African-
American officials, business people, journalists, clergy and union people who
despise them, easily enough to take leadership away from the slicksters. They
do not. Why?

As for Mayor Dinkins, his future depends on his inner strength. Can he 18
accept Crown Heights for what it was—not a mere chain of command foulup,
but his own failure to use the law to protect the oppressed or endangered? He
did not stop the buck. He did break the faith.

When that is understood by Mayor, public and press, New Yorkers can safe- 19
ly put those four days behind them; not now.

The Two Nations of Crown Heights

Andrew W. Cooper

Andrew W. Cooper, publisher and editor of The City Sun, *a weekly newspaper
in Brooklyn, New York, wrote this piece for the* New York Times *OP-ED page sixteen months after the riots. His prognosis for improved relations between Jews
and blacks is not good. Cooper explains his position in light of the long history
of confrontation between the two groups.*

Ever since the accidental death of young Gavin Cato and the slaying of Yankel 1
Rosenbaum ignited Crown Heights in August 1991, questions have been asked
about the deep antagonism between the black and Hasidic communities that
occupy much of the same turf in that torn neighborhood.

What is the history of the hostility and when did it start? The answers 2
depend partly on perception and partly on reality. The reality is that Crown
Heights originally was a secular Jewish community that gradually attracted a
large number of African-Americans and, more recently, West Indian immigrants.

Hasidic political ascendancy began with the partitioning of Crown Heights 3
by the city fathers in 1976 and 1977. Mayor Abraham Beame and City Council-

---

[4]Rudolf Giuliani defeated David Dinkins in New York's mayoralty race and was sworn
into office in January 1994. Giuliani quickly called on Attorney General Janet Reno to bring
civil rights charges against Lemrick Nelson, who had been acquitted on charges that he
murdered Yankel Rosenbaum. In late 1993, a new murder suspect was named.

man Theodore Silverman successfully argued for a separation of the community governing bodies—community boards, school districts, police liaisons. At the time, Mr. Silverman stated, "If we the City of New York were to partition Crown Heights, we would be acting in accord with American foreign policy because American policy was created to assist emerging nations."

In 1977, the Board of Estimate decided to keep all of New York City's communities intact except Crown Heights. The line was drawn down the middle of Eastern Parkway, dividing the community board and creating two "nations," separate and unequal. One community board's members were all black; on the other side, the Hasidim gained disproportionate power. 4

It was separatist and unlawful to give the Hasidic community what black residents saw as an unequal distribution of police protection and city services. Many blacks also complained of an escape route to Israel for accused Hasidic lawbreakers that was open by virtue of their dual citizenship. (Consider, among others, Yosef Lifsh, the driver of the car that killed Gavin Cato who went to Israel to avoid a civil suit.) As one black resident, Anthony Morris, cynically remarked, "Eastern Parkway, no; the Gaza Strip, yes." Throughout this process, the secular Jewish community maintained a deafening silence. 5

This is the reality black Crown Heights has lived with since the 1970's. Its resentment is deep and abiding and will continue until this division is remedied or, as City Councilwoman Mary Pinkett said, "until the police and other agencies begin to do their jobs without fear or political favor." 6

The two communities have an added problem of continued West Indian immigration and the beginnings of extensive Russian-Jewish immigration. The American black middle class and West Indian communities have not joined together, although recognition of their mutual interests is on the way. 7

The tragedy is that both West Indians and American blacks see the Hasidim, backed by the secular Jewish community and its resources, as their front-line enemy. 8

Many blacks view Mayor David Dinkins as a scapegoat used by the Hasidim to extract even more political and economic concessions from blacks. The presence of the Jewish Defense League in Crown Heights together with certain crazies, black and white, makes for a dangerous predicament. Andrew Stein and Rudolph Giuliani cheering on from the sidelines makes for a great show but adds to a very explosive mixture. 9

The black professionals of Crown Heights resent what they see clearly as the unequal application of laws that the Police Department is sworn to apply equally. Consider the arbitrary closing of streets at the insistence of the Hasidim so their religious parades and marches could take place unencumbered. This has forced black residents to abide by special parking and traffic rules. Sunday, a day of worship for Christian churchgoers, has frequently been disrupted by changes in public transportation routes with no regard for black sensitivities. 10

Black residents say that the police have not responded to complaints about double parking by the Hasidim and do not ticket Hasidic parking offenders. The perception that the Hasidim rule the community board and dominate public policy with no regard for black concerns—with arrogance and disdain—is another burr under the saddle of the Crown Heights middle class. 11

What is the future of Crown Heights? The prospects are not bright. So long as blacks perceive that Hasidic rule is at the expense of blacks and so long as the secular Jewish community maintains its silence—except to protest what is 12 perceived as injustice by blacks against the Hasidim and never the reverse—the Crown Heights pot will continue to boil.

To call David Dinkins a "Jew hater" and to label the entire black commu- 13
nity anti-Semitic because it protests injustices practiced against it is propaganda of the highest form and to say the least, a rather interesting form of racism.

Strained But Amicable Relations

Lynne Duke

Complicating our understanding of the problem between blacks and Jews in Crown Heights is their broader sociological relationship: both groups have been persecuted, both have fought stereotyping. In some respects, reports Lynne Duke of The Washington Post, *the riot in August 1991 was atypical of the normally "strained but amicable" relations between the two groups.*

Tensions between some blacks and Jews here continue to flare and wane only 1
to flare anew.

It has gotten so bad that a public event in Queens this month a heckler 2
branded the city's black mayor David N. Dinkins (D), a "Jew hater." And groups of Orthodox Jews in the Crown Heights and Williamsburg sections of Brooklyn twice this month have beaten and subdued black men they said were committing crimes.

As city leaders try to ease tensions and prevent the kind of street violence 3
in which a Jewish student died 16 months ago in Crown Heights, black and Jewish leaders around the country are trying to keep the New York tensions from damaging a relationship that historically has been strained.

Last week, the effort brought together Jesse L. Jackson, founder of the 4
National Rainbow Coalition, and Robert K. Lifton, president of the American Jewish Congress. The two announced in Washington that their groups will work together on issues ranging from Haitian refugees to family medical leave. They also plan to visit communities and college campuses across the country to promote ethnic harmony.

"There are problems," Jackson said of the black-Jewish tension in Crown 5
Heights, "but you cannot allow one or two bad loans to close a whole bank."

Meanwhile, black and Jewish activists rallied here earlier this month to 6
salute Dinkins with a standing ovation at Harlem's Apollo Theatre and show "The Liberators," a documentary about black U.S. soldiers who were the first to arrive to free the Jews from Nazi death camps.

Dinkins and several others, including Manhattan District Attorney Robert 7
M. Morgenthau, Jackson and, via videotape, Nobel Peace Prize winner Elie Wiesel, called for peace among the city's ethnic groups.

"Enough already," Rep. Charles B. Rangel (D-N.Y.) shouted to the crowd 8
of hundreds.

Experts in black-Jewish relations said they believe recent tensions in New 9
York have exaggerated what generally has been an amicable relationship between the two groups. Dinkins, in fact, enjoyed wide Jewish support in his bid to become the city's first black mayor.

"To jump to conclusions that what's happening in black-Jewish relations is 10
false," said Michael S. Miller, executive of New York's Jewish Community

Relations Council. "But to assert that what's happening in Crown Heights does not impact black-Jewish relations also is false."

The latest troubles erupted after the acquittal on Oct. 29 of Lemrick Nelson, 11 a black youth who had been charged in the killing of rabbinical student Yankel Rosenbaum. Rosenbaum was killed in August 1991 during the street violence in Crown Heights that broke out when a car in the motorcade of the leader of the Lubavitcher Hasidim sect of Orthodox Jews accidentally struck and killed a black child and seriously injured another.

Fueled by rumors that a private Jewish ambulance service had ignored the 12 injured children and cared for the Lubavitchers instead, angry mobs of blacks yelled epithets aimed at Jews. Rosenbaum, caught in a crowd, was stabbed to death.

Jews angered by the Nelson acquittal vented their anger at Dinkins, who 13 was blamed by some in Crown Heights for inadequate police response to the 1991 melee. And earlier this month, when Dinkins quickly condemned what police called a Crown Heights bias attack by 20 to 30 Jewish men on Ralph Nimmons, a homeless black man, some Jews accused Dinkins of being unsympathetic to their side of the story.

Since then, a group of Jews attacked another black man whom they said 14 they suspected of committing a crime, this time in the nearby Williamsburg section. Both cases remain under investigation as bias attacks, as do several other recent cases involving attacks on Jews by a Hispanic and by whites.

Several authorities on black-Jewish relations said that Crown Heights is in 15 many ways not representative of broader themes in the relationship. For instance, most blacks and Jews do not live as close to one another as do the ultra-orthodox Lubavitchers and their black neighbors, many of whom are of Caribbean origin.

Crown Heights also is atypical because of the nature of the Lubavitcher 16 sect. Members of the highly insular group separate themselves not only from blacks, but from more mainstream Jews, who they believe have less rigorous religious standards.

But authorities say the Crown Heights tensions underscore historic strains 17 between blacks and Jews, some dating back to the breakup of the old civil rights alliance in the late 1960s as black power adherents began to take greater control of a movement that included Jews in leadership roles.

In the 1970s and 1980s, the civil rights alliance split further as black and 18 Jewish advocacy groups clashed over quotas in the workplace. Tensions also have existed among the two groups over U.S. policy toward Israel and the Palestinians. Nation of Islam leader Louis Farrakhan and his followers have made critiques of Jews a centerpiece of their public speeches, often using language that Jews have condemned as antisemitic.

These controversies have been given wide media attention—some say far 19 wider than is deserved.

"The Jewish-black relationship ought not to be separated from the larger 20 white-black relationship in this kind of negative way . . . that suggests that there's a larger Jewish-black problem than there is a white-black problem," said Henry Siegman, executive director of the American Jewish Congress.

"In fact, I would say that despite the problems in Crown Heights, in New 21 York or wherever else they may exist, the relationship between the black community and the Jewish community stands out in that it is much more supportive, much more positive than is the overall black-white relationship in America," he said.

Gary Rubin, national affairs director for the American Jewish Committee, 22 pointed out that black and Jewish members of Congress, for instance, have formed a strong coalition. Blacks and Jews also voted in overwhelming numbers for President-elect Clinton.

Several authorities on black-Jewish relations said that both groups are over- 23 ly burdened with an expectation that they ought to be natural allies because they are both American minority groups who have suffered from prejudice and discrimination.

"There's a tendency of people who are close to one another to have high- 24 er expectations of one another, so that when conflict erupts there is an exaggerated sense of disappointment," said Siegman.

"I think that the problem with the black and Jewish communities is 25 that we expect so much of each other," said Rabbi Lynne Lansberg of the Marjorie Kovler Institute of Black-Jewish Relations. "There's an historical link and a sociological link. The historical link is obviously the fight for civil rights. And it's popular for people to say Jews were only involved in civil rights because there was something in it for them. But the fact is Jews could pass [as whites]. So I think it's very important to stress that Jews were involved in the civil rights movement then and now because it was and is the right thing to do."

But Julius Lester, a University of Massachusetts at Amherst professor of 26 Judaic and Near Eastern Studies who is black and also Jewish, said it is difficult for blacks to identify with Jews as fellow victims of oppression.

The two groups may each have a history of enslavement and oppression, 27 but in the American context blacks and Jews have fared quite differently: blacks have struggled well into the 20th century for basic rights in a majority white society, while Jews benefited because they can "partake of and share in the majority identity as whites," Lester wrote earlier this year in the journal Jewish Currents.

Before the advent of Korean merchants, many of the small business in black 28 urban neighborhoods were owned by Jewish merchants whose presence often was resented by blacks.

"Jews talk about they're oppressed and black people look at them and say 29 'You must be kidding me,' " Lester said in an interview. "And so you're talking about two different kinds of oppression."

What blacks may not easily understand, said Landsberg, is that for all their 30 affluence, many Jews remain insecure because of their history of oppression, including the death camps run by Nazi Germany.

"Underneath this masquerade of success in the Jewish community are peo- 31 ple who are scared and looking over their shoulders," she said. "We have the material goods, but we do not have the sense of security that generations of wealthy white Christian Americans have."

One answer, black and Jewish suggest, is to put aside historic tensions and 32 work together on common interests.

As Jackson and Lifton spoke to members about their groups' new joint 33 efforts, Jackson was asked if he thought they contributed to black-Jewish problems by calling New York "Hymietown" in the late 1980s.

Lifton, clearly annoyed with the question, answered it himself: 34

"Every single time we have a meeting or a conference or a discussion where we are trying to bring people together and to represent a healing opportunity, somebody comes up with past history. . . . we should stop always reopening old wounds and always harkening back to these kinds of questions. As far as I'm concerned it's time to put an end to 'Hymietown.' "

A Guide to the Assignment

This guide is designed to help you through the process of writing a problem/solution essay on a problem in a community you know well. Key elements in this guide parallel the organization of the Structures and Strategies section in this chapter, and you should look to appropriate sections in the chapter for further guidance on completing your assignment. You will prepare to write, write, and then evaluate and revise. Here, once again, is your assignment:

> Prompted by your reading about the Crown Heights riot, reflect on a community-based problem you both care about and know something about that exists close to your own home. Perhaps, like the problem between African Americans and Jewish Americans in Crown Heights, the problem you choose might involve miscommunication and mutual mistrust; the problem might concern the environment, town governance, fiscal or educational issues—whatever concerns you. The problem may not be dramatic in the sense that, if unchecked, it will lead to violence; still, it should be a *specific and real* problem for which real solutions are needed.
>
> Write a problem/solution essay for readers *in your community*, alerting them to a problem in their midst, and to a likely solution. Write for publication on the OP-ED page of your town's newspaper. Specifically, your task is to argue that a problem exists and to present a proposal that is specific and detailed.

Prepare to Write: Explore Your Idea

Discovering Ideas

Read the selections on the Crown Heights riot in order to identify the underlying problem. None of the articles in this Occasions sections completely identifies the entire problem or its causes, and you should expect a similar challenge in defining a problem in your own community. In the Crown Heights case, you will need to synthesize sources to get a sense of the whole: you will need to identify some causes that immediately precipitated the riot and some that were long-standing. The issues that gave rise to the riots are exceedingly complex. Your task is to recognize this complexity by reading the Occasions selections with care. You might bring these questions to the readings:

- What do Jewish Americans say happened at Crown Heights?
- What do African Americans say happened at Crown Heights?

- Why does each group feel that it was wronged?
- In what ways did public officials act to heal misunderstandings?
- In what ways did public officials act to inflame misunderstandings?
- In what ways has the larger history of interaction between groups contributed to the tensions at Crown Heights? How might such a broader context contribute to a solution?
- How do you define the problem between the Jewish- and African-American communities in Crown Heights?
- What solutions have been offered? Have they been effective?

The goal of these questions is to help you to define the problem at Crown Heights and to appreciate that problem's complexity. In responding to these and any other questions you have that might help you reach this goal, take notes as you read. Be prepared to speak about the problems and their causes. Recall these strategies for defining a problem:

Call attention to a difference between what is expected, or desired, and what is the case.
Call attention to damage, disadvantages, or danger.
Call attention to *potential* problems.

Now turn to your own essay and choose a problem to pursue—one complex enough to deserve your extended attention. Apply the same sorts of questions that you brought to the Crown Heights readings to the community-based problem you have identified. The result of your questioning should be two or three pages of notes.

Use your thinking about Crown Heights to inform your thinking about possible solutions in your own essay. Devise a proposal with concrete steps that you feel offers a realistic chance of relieving some of the damage, danger, or disadvantages that you have identified. Consider other proposals. Be as specific as you can in listing actions that people can take. Of each proposal, ask: Are the specific actions you have set out realistic? What impediments to progress can be foreseen? At what rate do you expect progress to be made? What would be clear evidence of progress? What counterproposals can you offer? What are their advantages and disadvantages? As you think on these and related questions, take notes. You will study these notes as you seek a direction in the essay's first draft.

Committing Yourself to an Idea

Recall the attitudes of writers whose commitment sparks interest in readers:

- I write for myself and for my audience.
- I will find some approach to my writing that lets me discover something personally significant.

Before beginning your first draft, take a few minutes to respond to these questions. What will be your *personal* connection to the problem in your community?

Write: Clarify Your Idea and
Make It Public

Creating Common Ground with Readers

What details will you provide to engage readers with the problem you have defined? To help in this matter, return to the Crown Heights selections and study each writer's techniques for engaging you. For instance, how do first-person accounts and stories of particular incidents capture your attention? How does well-chosen background material serve the same purpose? Use the readings as a guide to choosing details through which you will make clear your problem and proposed solution.

Remember that you are writing for readers of your local newspaper. Get recent copies of the newspaper and turn to the editorial pages. Read the editorials and the essays on the opposing (OP-ED) page. Answer these questions:

> What assumptions are being made about the readers' familiarity with issues?
> What assumptions are being made about the readers' interest in the issues?
> What assumptions are being made about the readers' level of education?
> What assumptions are being made about the readers' political affiliations?

To learn still more about your readers, you may want to pose the audience-related questions on page 42, which will prompt you with a series of questions. Understanding the needs and motivations of your readers is essential to the success of your problem/solution essay. You are writing to get readers to *act*. They must feel that the problem you present is theirs as well as yours.

Part 1 of the Essay

Recall that a problem/solution essay has two parts (see the recommended format on page 309). In the first part, for the purposes of this assignment, you will *argue* that a problem exists. Consult the Structures and Strategies section as well as chapter 11 (pages 426–434) for the lines of reasoning you can offer in support of your claim that a problem exists. The following strategies have been demonstrated in this chapter:

> Making generalizations
> Showing cause and effect
> Presenting a parallel case—perhaps the Crown Heights case
> Presenting analogies
> Countering another person's argument
> Presenting expert opinions

You will likely want to use a combination of strategies. Recall from the Crown Heights readings that problems seldom have single causes and correspondingly single, simple solutions. As you argue for the existence of your problem, be aware of its complexity. Force yourself to define the problem from the points of view of *all* concerned. To the extent possible, draw on source materials to advance the idea of your essay. You may need to take a few trips to your local library. Read and use sources, if you can, for the following reasons:

- To clarify the background of your problem.
- To support your claim directly with facts, examples, and opinions.
- To locate arguments against your claim, so that you can respond.

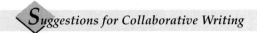

Suggestions for Collaborative Writing

Popular debates tend to be presented in an overly simplistic fashion. Hot topics are typically shown as existing within an either/or, pro versus con polarity, which seldom takes into consideration the range of complexities and nuances that inform the problem at hand. After writing your first draft, exchange papers with someone in your class. Make an outline of the problem as expressed within his or her draft, and then come up with a list of all the problems, questions, and unaddressed concerns you can think of that complicate the problem as it is presented in that essay. Work with each other to show how the problems you're seeking to solve are inherently more complex than they might seem. Afterward, revise your essay, taking into consideration any additional perspectives offered by your reader.

Part 2 of the Essay

Propose a plan of action to correct the problem you have defined. Your plan should be detailed enough to prompt debate on the merits of specific recommendations. The most compelling proposals are built on a direct link between a problem and its causes. Ask yourself: How do certain clearly definable actions lead to the problem I have identified? How can this cause-and-effect chain be broken by concrete actions that I will propose?

Argue for Your Plan

Your proposal will be an argument about what *ought* to occur; it is an argument about policy. See the Structures and Strategies discussion on pages 308–309 and chapter 11 for specific advice on arguing in favor of a policy. In addition to arguing cause and effect, you can present analogies and parallel cases, call on authorities to bolster your position, and appeal directly to readers' emotions.

Readers will expect you to acknowledge that proving direct cause and effect is difficult. At times, you may not be able to base your proposal on direct causal links. The best you may be able to do is present strongly suspected, but unproven, links. You might consider offering a partial or first-step solution. Acknowledge the difficulty of the problem and the need for a number of coordinated actions to be taken. The particular plan that you offer is admittedly partial, but it is designed to make an impact and is a reasonable first step.

Another way to show your awareness of the complexity of the problem is to review counterproposals. Show that others have acknowledged the problem, and discuss the merits of their proposed solutions. If you are feeling ambitious and want to propose a comprehensive solution, then your essay should reflect your understanding of each of the complex causes of the problem.

Advance Your Idea with Sources

Depending on the problem you discuss in your essay, you may not refer to the Crown Heights readings. But you will nonetheless need to refer to source materials in order to make your essay a fully public document to which readers can respond. Where will you locate sources and how will you use them to advance the idea of your problem/solution essay? As for *where*, you will likely need to consult local documents—your town's newspapers, for instance. Recall that you can use sources in a variety of ways to advance your essay. (See the cross-referenced discussions in this chapter's Structures and Strategies for details.)

- Read to help identify and commit yourself to an idea.
- Read to clarify the background of your problem.
- Read to support your claim directly with facts, examples, and opinions.
- Read to locate arguments against your claim, so that you can respond.

Suggestions for Writing with a Computer

Like many other essays, problem/solution essays often require that you consult a range of source materials in order for your claims and solutions to be credible. When working with a range of sources, you may find it increasingly difficult to organize supporting information as you revise your essay. You might try to put this information in small files on your disk, which you can quickly and easily refer to during the composing process. For example: put notes and quotations drawn from newspapers, journals, magazines, books, conversations, observations, and opinions into separate files. As you revise your essay, continually recheck this collection of source materials (which will most likely grow in size as you continue to think about your essay), pulling bits and pieces of evidence into your essay where appropriate. (Remember to delete information from your source file as you use it.)

See chapter 4 for demonstrations of using sources to provide facts, examples, and authoritative opinions and also for specific strategies for introducing sources into an essay. Particularly, see the section on "Sources and Cycles of Development," pages 61–68. Here you will get advice on keeping your essay focused on *your* idea, not on sources; you will learn how to link sources to create a synthesis; and you will find strategies for summarizing, paraphrasing, and quoting.

Evaluate and Revise

Your primary challenge in revising a first draft is to ensure that readers believe a problem exists and that it concerns them. Moreover, you must be confident that the solution you have proposed follows directly from this problem and attacks its causes. The act of writing a draft will virtually always refine your initial ideas. On occasion, your writing of the draft will substantially alter your ideas, in which case you will have more work to do in revision. For an extensive discussion on strategies for revision, see chapters 12–14. For the problem/solution essay in particular, remember the following critical points.

Critical Points in a Problem/Solution Essay

- Is the problem you are writing about precisely defined?
- Will readers feel a need for action when presented with this problem?
- Will readers find your proposal or solution reasonable?
- Have you responded to competing proposals or solutions?
- Have you demonstrated a clear cause-and-effect relationship between the problem and your proposal or solution?

You succeed with a problem/solution essay when you convince readers to act on a problem or to accept action by others. Having completed your first draft, try to see the essay through your readers' eyes. Is the problem, as presented, compelling? Does it touch readers' lives? Does it create in readers a tension that needs to be resolved? And is the essay's proposal likely to strike readers as sensible and manageable? In revising your essay, adjust the points you make and the way you make them in order to convince your readers.

Interpreting Literature

Definitions and Examples

You and three friends read a poem. Can you expect to agree on the poem's meaning or on whether this is a *good* poem? If the four of you could not agree, what would this suggest about the purposes and usefulness of poetry and of your reading poetry? Below you will find four statements, written by literary critics. Each has read Robert Frost's "Out, Out—," a narrative poem that tells of an accident at a saw mill, where a boy's hand is severed. (You can read the poem on page 374.)

> [Frost's] theme is the uncertainty and unpredictability of life, which may be accidentally ended at any moment, and the tragic waste of human potentiality which takes place when such premature death occurs.
>
> —Laurence Perrine

> Frost's story . . . symbolizes a tragic aspect of the human situation: the fact that man's economic means, for the very reason that they are mechanical in nature, can destroy him.
>
> —John Lynen

> [T]he boy dies. The point of his death, however, is not [as Perrine insists] the inscrutability of fate and the tenuousness of human existence. Rather it is the waste of life brought on by the well-meaning but insensitive parents' rushing the boy out of childhood into adulthood.
>
> —Weldon Thornton

> Frost's "Out, Out" is a poem of conflict between youth and the responsibility of adulthood and is strangely violent. . . . [T]he poem is alive with the conflict: before his death, the youth is struggling with the

responsibilities of age. Ironically, the boy is successful in his attempt to escape from the struggle. His escape is death.

—William Kelly

Four readers, four responses, little agreement: the *opposite* of what you might have expected or desired, but an accurate snapshot of how people respond to works of literature. Literature challenges us to make meaning, and meaning is something we come to individually. This is half the story. While we respond individually, we also exist in a larger culture that reads and responds. When people across the street, across the nation, and across the world read the same poems, novels, and dramas, the natural desire is to start a conversation. When this conversation takes place formally in academic settings, in journals, and in book reviews, it is called *literary criticism*.

No one expects that a single interpretation of a literary work will end all discussion about that text. We speak of interpretations—plural. The goal of reading and interpreting literature is to have readers of *your* interpretation make this acknowledgment: "I understand what you say, and I find it reasonable." Others may agree or disagree with your reading—your interpretation—of a poem or story, but in no event will people taking part in this exchange expect a single, correct reading because consensus is not the goal of arguments about literature.[1] A reading of a novel is not right or wrong in the sense that the statement "The world is round" is right or wrong. This observation does *not* mean that all opinions about works of literature are valid. Interpretations are stronger or weaker to the extent that the writer presents a convincing argument. Later in this chapter you will find specific strategies for arguing for your interpretation of a text. The assumption there, as here, is that one interpretation, presented with strong evidence, can clearly be more convincing than another.

Works of literature may be brief, as with this poem:

Airing Linen
Wash and dry,
sort and fold:
you and I
are growing old.

—Henry Taylor

Or consider the following very short story, which the poet X. J. Kennedy attributed to Thomas Bailey Aldrich:[2]

---

[1]This discussion is based directly on the work of Stephen Toulmin, Richard Rieke, and Allan Janik in *Introduction to Reasoning* (New York: Macmillan, 1979). See chapter 12, their "Introduction" to fields of argument, 195–202; and chapter 15, "Arguing about the Arts," 265–282. For a related discussion, see Richard D. Rieke and Malcolm O. Sillars, *Argumentation and the Decision Making Process*, 2nd ed. (Glenview: Scott, 1984).

[2]Cited in X. J. Kennedy, *Literature: An Introduction to Fiction, Poetry, and Drama*, 2nd edition, Boston: Little, Brown, 1979, p. 1.

A woman is sitting in her old, shuttered house.
She knows that she is alone in the whole world;
every other thing is dead.
    The doorbell rings.

And, of course, literary works can be quite long. But whatever its length, a poem, play, story, or novel presents readers with an opportunity to forge a relationship among (1) the world as the artist has observed it; (2) a *text* such as Frost's poem that somehow reflects the facts about or the author's impressions of the world; and (3) ourselves, the audience. This forged relationship is called *interpretation;* you will have an opportunity to observe and to make interpretations in this chapter.

A special mention must be made about the controversy associated with the word *literature.* Traditionally we have had what is termed a *literary canon,* a body of works that for generations scholars (and an obedient public) have regarded as important to Western culture: Shakespeare, Keats, Brontë, Shelley, Melville, and many more. However, given that authors are always creating new poems, plays, and novels, why are some of these texts added to the canon, the "important" list worthy of study, while others are excluded? Some critics have directed this same question backward in time and have caused something of a revolution in literary studies: What makes Shakespeare, Shelley, and the others worthy of being in the canon? Why do we call their work *literature* and teach them? Why aren't more women writers, more minorities, or more members of less industrial nations represented in what we call *literature?* Critics who challenge the traditional canon of literature fault the assumptions about race, class, and gender by which books have been designated as literature, and they are working to redefine which texts get studied in the nation's schools. Challenging the definition of literature may well become a guiding concern in one of your literature courses.

Examples of Interpretations of Literature

Three examples of interpretations of literature follow. One is written by a professional literary critic and two are composed by student writers. First, critic Martin Simpson offers an interpretation of Kate Chopin's "A Shameful Affair": the story, says Simpson, is about the awakening of a sexually repressed young woman. In her reading of James Joyce's "Counterparts," student Sarika Chandra sees an effort by essentially powerless characters to claim some authority in their lives. Student Ryan Kelly concludes with his response to a poem by Ted Hughes, "The Thought-Fox." The literary works referred to in these selections can be found in two locations in the chapter. Look for the short stories by James Joyce and Kate Chopin in the Occasions for Discussion and Writing, beginning on pages 380 and 387, respectively. Ted Hughes's poem, "The Thought-Fox," immediately precedes Ryan Kelly's essay.

Chopin's "A Shameful Affair"

Martin Simpson

A teacher of literature and a literary critic, Martin Simpson taught at Illinois State University when this piece was written. Note Simpson's use of the present tense, a convention in writing about literature. And note Simpson's continual references to Chopin's story as evidence for his interpretive claims. Chopin's "A Shameful Affair" appears later in this chapter, beginning on page 387.

Mildred Orme, in Kate Chopin's "A Shameful Affair," is a socially convention- 1
al and sexually repressed young woman who has come to the Kraummer farm to escape the sexual demands that were made on her in civilized, urban society. Chopin uses fertile nature imagery to show Mildred being drawn out of the realm of sheltered social convention and into a natural world that is rich with sensuous physical surroundings. Here Mildred is forced to recognize and struggle with her sexuality.

Mildred is obviously a young woman who has continually repressed the sex- 2
ual side of her nature. She is attracted to Fred Evelyn from the first time she sees him and goes out of her way to get his attention. After he has refused her request to drive her to church, she walks down to the river where she knows he will be fishing. She knows he will be alone, because earlier "all the other farmhands had gone forth in Sunday attire" (150). Even though it is obvious to the reader that Mildred is pursuing Fred, she conceals this knowledge from herself. She labels Fred as a "clumsy farmhand" and notes quite inaccurately that "farmhands are not so very nice to look at" (148). After she has had her sexual nature awakened by the kiss, she tells herself that the desire she feels for him is a "shameful whim that chanced to visit her soul, like an ugly dream" (152). Mildred has been able to avoid facing her sexual repression in the past only because she has been away in a civilized, urban environment where social conventions have allowed her to keep men at arm's length. She has "refused [her] half dozen offers" (149) and ironically has come to the farm to seek "the repose that would enable her to follow exalted lines of thought" (150).

The imagery that Chopin uses to describe the farm and Mildred's relation 3
to it reveals that Mildred has entered a sensuous environment that she is trying to resist by clinging to symbols of civilization. The farmhouse itself, as a man-made structure, can be considered an island of civilization amidst the "swelling acres [of] undulating wheat" that "gleam in the sun like a golden sea" (148) and connote pulsating fertility. At first Mildred remains "seated in the snuggest corner of the big front porch of the Kraummer farmhouse," behind her "Browning or her Ibsen" (148), which conveys the image of someone who is trying to isolate herself intellectually in a farmhouse that is itself isolated in an ocean of natural fertility.

Mildred has to abandon her island of civilized social convention when she 4
becomes interested in Fred Evelyn, and nature begins to take its effect on her when she does. She must go down a "long, narrow footpath through the bending wheat" (150) to encounter Fred at the river. This footpath is like a tunnel through the "yellow wheat" that reaches "high above her waist" (150) on either side, which suggests the nearly overwhelming aspect of the fecundity that is almost enveloping her. Mildred's close contact with her sensuous surroundings causes her own repressed sexuality to come to the surface. Her brown eyes

become "filled with a reflected golden light" (150) from the wheat as she passes through it, and her lips and cheeks become "ripe with color that the sun had coaxed there" (150). Nature has now begun to erode the self-control that Mildred has exercised over her passions.

Mildred's losing battle against the effects of the fertility around her is conveyed through Chopin's inspired use of imagery during the scene at the river. While she is watching Fred fish, Mildred is standing very still and "holding tight to the book she had brought with her" (150). The book is a sort of life-preserver (a repression-preserver, rather), a symbol of civilization and social restraint. When she "carefully" lays the book down and takes into her hands the phallic fishing pole that Fred gives her, she has given in to her sexual instincts. The voluntary act of setting aside the book and picking up the pole symbolically foreshadows her willing participation in the passionate kiss that follows.

After she has unwittingly and temporarily surrendered to her sexual desires at the river, Mildred once again retreats into her customary repressive behavior. When she feels the first moment of shame after Fred had kissed her, she determines to return to her room in the farmhouse. She will be isolated from nature there and she can "give calm thought to the situation, and determine then how to act" (151). Only when she is back on the "very narrow path" through "the wheat that [is] heavy and fragrant with dew" (153) is she able to admit to herself what Chopin has already shown to the reader in the scene at the river: she is partly responsible for Fred's impulsive kiss. Being greatly disturbed at this knowledge, she tells Fred that she hopes to someday be able to forgive herself (153).

Chopin's theme in "A Shameful Affair," the enlightened idea that sexual repression is harmful, is brought out by her contrasting images of civilized society and liberating natural fecundity. Mildred's consistent retreat from sexuality, associated with symbols of societal repression, causes her to become a troubled and confused young woman. She will never be a complete and healthy human being, Chopin is saying, until she comes to terms with the "golden, undulating sea" of her passions.

Reference

Chopin, Kate. "A Shameful Affair." *The Awakening and Selected Stories of Kate Chopin.* ed. Barbara H. Solomon. (New York: Signet, 1976) 148–53.

For Discussion and Writing

Reading and Thinking Critically

1. *Personal response:* Read "A Shameful Affair," on pages 387–391. What is *your* response to Kate Chopin's story? Do you feel a sexual tension at the heart of the story, as Simpson does?

2. *Be alert to differences:* Having read "A Shameful Affair," review every paragraph of Simpson's interpretation and note any differences between your responses and his. (For instance, in ¶2 Simpson writes that Mildred Orme is "obviously" repressed sexually. Is this obvious?) Each paragraph in the essay is an argument designed to convince you. Are you convinced?

3. *Challenge the reading:* If at any point Simpson does not convince you that his interpretation is valid, make a counterinterpretation. Just as he points to

passages in the story in support of his claim, you point to passages in support of your claim.

Examining "Chopin's 'A Shameful Affair' " as an Interpretive Essay

1. Aside from the opening and closing paragraphs, show how each paragraph in Simpson's essay illustrates a pattern of interpretive statement and support.
2. In terms of the overall argument of this essay, what is the function of ¶s2–6? What "tension" is developed in each paragraph?
3. How does ¶7 consolidate the claims in the previous paragraphs?

STUDENT PAPER

The Power of Alcohol and the Church in Joyce's "Counterparts"
Sarika Chandra

In the following interpretive essay, student Sarika Chandra examines the ways in which the main character of a short story by James Joyce uses alcohol in virtually the same way that his wife uses the Church—to gain power. Throughout this paper, you will find Chandra following the pattern of claim, reference to text, and comment that is a feature of all literary interpretation. Chandra pursues an option that your professors might require in interpretive essays: going beyond the story being interpreted, that is, beyond the primary source, to secondary sources. Watch as Chandra refers to Joyce scholars and experts on Irish social life in order to support her claim. Joyce's "Counterparts" appears in this chapter's Occasions for Discussion and Writing, pages 380–387.

"Counterparts" tells the story of a man named Farrington, who will 1 not do his job right and takes abuse from his boss for that. Farrington spends a long time drinking after work and when he gets home beats his son. However, Joyce tells much more in eleven pages than just another story about an abusive alcoholic. "Counterparts" is a story about how otherwise powerless people seek to gain control over their lives.

The story opens with a scene in which Farrington is being summoned 2 to the office of Mr. Alleyne, his boss. Farrington copies documents for a living, and this element of the story appears to have some basis in Joyce's childhood. Richard Ellman notes that "calligraphy enabled [Joyce's father, John] to work occasionally for a solicitor . . . named Aylward" (39). Calligraphy is similar in nature to Farrington's job of copying documents. Further, Ellman points out that "Aylward's office is probably that described in 'Counterparts,' where his name is changed to Alleyne" (39). However, nothing in Joyce's biography explains the complexity of "Counterparts."

Farrington sits in Alleyne's office, powerless, listening to this man 3 berate him for some job poorly done. Apparently, mistakes and the resulting humiliation are regular occurrences in this office. Aside from the abuse that he must take from Alleyne, Farrington is made powerless by the very nature of his profession. As a copyist, not even his work is his own: he must labor all day at copying someone else's words. Farrington is trapped, immediately by his boss and more generally by his job.

After work, Farrington looks forward to drinking, which he does every time he is humiliated. After the scene in Alleyne's office, he wants to go to the pub but he realizes that he has no money. Suddenly, he thinks of his watch and pawns it for six shillings. Now nothing else matters, for he is in the position to buy himself some power. At the pub, Farrington relates the incident in Alleyne's office to his companions. He claims that he looked coolly at Mr. Alleyne and said, "I don't think that that's a fair question to put to me" (93). Nosey Flynn and Davy Byrne say that this was the smartest thing they have heard. Farrington is pleased and he "[stands] a drink in his turn" (93). He repeats the same story to O'Halloran and Paddy Leonard and they too agree that the story was smart. Farrington stands another round of drinks. Higgens comes to the bar and praises Farrington for being cool in front of Mr. Alleyne.

Here Farrington is trying to get himself some power by buying people drinks and repeating his story in order to believe that he had some control at the office (which he didn't) and that he has control at the pub. But buying drinks leads to no real power or respect, since people take interest in Farrington for only so long as he pays for the whiskey. Nevertheless, interest for whatever reason pleases Farrington very much. Later, when the conversation strays away from his story, he buys another round. At the end of the evening, when all his money is gone, he is defeated at arm wrestling by Weathers. Again, Farrington is humiliated: "He had lost his reputation as a strong man, having been defeated twice by a mere boy" (97).

Frustrated, he goes home, where yet another attempt to gain power fails. He walks into a dark room in his house and "a little boy [comes] running down the stairs" (97). It is one of his five children, Tom, who says that his mother is at the chapel. Farrington responds, "That's right. . . . Did she

---

Sarika Chandra: My Commitment to This Essay

Sarika Chandra was required by her instructor to write an interpretive essay; but she was also able to discover very personal reasons for writing and claimed this essay as her own. This personal statement gives you an insight into Chandra's motivations for writing, but it is *not* itself an essay. Why not? What are the differences between this statement and the essay? What are the similarities?

On my first reading of "Counterparts" I was upset and found myself hating Farrington. I needed to understand this reaction, so I read the story a second and third time and discovered my feelings toward Farrington were complicated. He is a lost, desperate man who is powerless to change his life, so powerless that he grabs power by beating his young son. The act is sick and cowardly, but Joyce complicates the story and makes it more than a tale about parental abuse. Farrington himself is abused. His life as a copyist is depressing and repetitive. He's trapped and doesn't have a clue why, so all he can do is drink and lash out. His son is also trapped, living with this man. And though I don't see her, I am certain Farrington's wife is trapped. Husband and wife bully each other; father bullies son; supervisor bullies copyist. Here is a world without joy, where people grab for whatever gives them power and the barest threads of self-worth: Farrington grabs onto the bottle, while his wife and son grab onto the Church. Rereading this story and writing the essay helped explain my revulsion to Farrington.

think of leaving any dinner for me?" (97). Again, Farrington feels out of control, and this makes him nervous. He wants his wife home to serve him since a "servant" gives service to someone who by definition is powerful. But his wife is not home. Worse, he has to be informed of her absence by his young son. Farrington becomes a mimic and grows enraged: "At the chapel. At the chapel, if you please!" (97–98) and then tries to assert control by beating Tom, who cries "O pa! . . . Don't beat me, pa! And . . . I'll say a *Hail Mary* for you. . . ." (98).

Tom's attempt to save himself by offering a false prayer shows the influence of the church and of Farrington's wife on the home. Whereas Farrington escapes to a pub to gain power, his wife has only the chapel as a means of escape and a path to power. The Catholic church is extremely influential in Irish life. As Joyce put it, "Ireland has been . . . the most faithful daughter of the Catholic church. . . . Its faith was never once shaken seriously" (*Critical Writings* 169). In Joyce's day, women were welcome in church but certainly not in a pub. Married men were expected to socialize. According to one sociologist, pub life "was a means of enforcing the religiously inspired segregation of men and women that even marriage did not break down" (Stivers 86). Ability to drink was not only a display of manliness but also of a solidarity among men that excluded women:

> The men drink heavily. . . . The public houses are drab and uncomfortable. There is no provision but for hard drinking, and a respectable woman would not set foot inside one of these places. (Stivers 87)

Farrington's wife, unable to go to a pub, turns to the church both as a source of strength and as a source of control over her husband. Evidence for this control can be found in the story even though Farrington's wife is not directly present. Tom offers to say a prayer for his father, the implication being that his father needs help. A helper is someone in control, someone who has power and is willing to use it. In this case, power flows from the church, not from a bottle. Farrington's wife has done well in teaching her children how to combat a brutish father. As a child, Tom has only one weapon to fend off this man who has hit him "viciously" with a stick. Tom has the church, which he uses in an effort to save himself. This offer to make a prayer is false in the sense that it is motivated by self-defense. But we see also that Farrington is a man whose soul in fact needs help, so perhaps a prayer—any prayer—is legitimate.

In attempting to get power, Farrington uses alcohol and his wife and children use the chapel. It is hard to say which is more powerful from Joyce's point of view. In "Counterparts," alcohol is generally ineffective, but still it is strong enough an influence to evoke Tom's cry. Yet the story also shows that the chapel is effective in that it frustrates Farrington's desire for authority in his own home. But *effective* is not quite the right word, for Joyce has created a man who is powerless in his job and a home in which the wife "bullied her husband when he was sober and was bullied by him when he was drunk" (97). The characters in "Counterparts" are locked in a struggle for power, a struggle that everyone seems to be losing.

Works Cited

Ellman, Richard. *James Joyce.* Oxford: Oxford UP, 1982.

Joyce, James. "Counterparts." *Dubliners.* Ed. Robert Scholes and A. Walton Litz. New York: Cornell UP, 1989.

—. *The Critical Writings.* Ed. Ellsworth Mason and Richard Ellman. New York: Cornell UP, 1989.

Stivers, Richard. *A Hair of the Dog: Irish Drinking and American Stereotype.* University Park, PA: Pennsylvania State UP, 1976.

For Discussion and Writing

Reading and Thinking Critically

1. *Personal response:* Read James Joyce's "Counterparts," on pages 380–387, and respond. To what extent do you think this is a story about powerlessness?
2. *Challenge the reading:* Chandra compares and contrasts different efforts to claim power: Farrington's efforts through alcohol and his wife's efforts through the Church. Has Chandra clearly distinguished the similarities and the differences of these efforts?
3. *Be alert to differences:* Compare this interpretive essay by Chandra, a student, with Martin Simpson's essay. What similarities and differences do you observe? To what extent does Chandra write like a professional critic?

Examining "The Power of Alcohol and the Church" as an Interpretive Essay

1. Do you feel that Chandra has supported her claim about how powerless people gain power? Work with a specific paragraph and demonstrate the extent to which she develops a cycle of claim and support.
2. Note the difference between Chandra's references to Joyce's story, her primary source, and her references to secondary sources—to Ellmann in ¶2 and Stivers in ¶8. What do the secondary sources add to the essay?
3. How is the essay structured? Does the structure suit Chandra's purpose?

STUDENT PAPER

"The Thought-Fox"—A Response
Ryan Kelly

The paper that follows was written by student Ryan Kelly for an introductory literature course. Because his class was studying the formal elements of poetry, Kelly was expected to examine Ted Hughes's "The Thought-Fox" in light of such elements as "assonance" and "caesura." Kelly does not merely catalogue Hughes's techniques but, rather, shows how the poet uses technique to create certain effects. Like the other writers whose essays begin this chapter, Kelly works with a clear interpretive claim: "The Thought-Fox" is a poem "about how a poem—itself—gets written." Observe how Kelly refers repeatedly to specific lines in "The Thought-Fox" in support of his interpretive statements.

The Thought-Fox

I imagine this midnight moment's forest:
Something else is alive
Beside the clock's loneliness
And this blank page where my fingers move.

Through the window I see no star;
Something more near
Though deeper within darkness
Is entering the loneliness:

Cold, delicately as the dark snow
A fox's nose touches twig, leaf;
Two eyes serve a movement, that now
And again now, and now, and now

Sets neat prints into the snow
Between trees, and warily a lame
Shadow lags by stump and in hollow
Of a body that is bold to come

Across clearings, an eye,
A widening deepening greenness,
Brilliantly, concentratedly,
Coming about its own business

Till, with a sudden sharp hot stink of fox,
It enters the dark hole of the head,
The window is starless still; the clock ticks
The page is printed.

—Ted Hughes

Ted Hughes's "The Thought-Fox" is a poem watching itself in a mirror. That is, it is about how a poem—itself—gets written. To some extent, therefore, it is about the writing process in general, or even creativity in general.

The poem is written in the first-person, beginning with the words "I imagine." The reader may assume that the voice belongs to Hughes himself, though it very well may be spoken through a persona who happens to be a poet. There is no regular pattern of meter or rhyme. "The Thought-Fox" remains unpredictable, like its subject.

It is interesting that Hughes would have tipped the reader off with his title, for the first two stanzas try to create an air of mystery, as if some unknown thing were approaching.

The poem begins, as it will end, with the poet working alone in his room. Hughes suggests the focus and intensity of a poet at work right away by using a strongly alliterated line: "I imagine this midnight moment's forest." There is a meditative brooding feeling with these m-sounds that captures the reader's attention.

Hughes goes on to emphasize the solitude. He uses personification, pointing to the "clock's loneliness." He then repeats the word "loneliness" at the end of the next stanza. It is clear to the reader that the process of composition must represent a genuine isolation for the poet.

But he also writes, as early as line 2, that "Something else is alive." The 6 reader is confused and waits to find out. Hughes' repetition of the word "something" in the next stanza heightens the tension. Now it is something "more near" than the stars, but "deeper within darkness." The reader might pause here. It is easy to see now that something could be nearer than the stars, but less easy to grasp how it might lie "deeper within darkness." The answer, we later decide, is that the fox, since it is imaginary, does not belong to the physical world at all.

Hughes has done an excellent job of creating expectation and of giv- 7 ing the sense of some creature approaching. What is amazing is that the poet is referring to a mental event. We don't usually think of thought drawing near as if it were coming from some other place. We don't, for that matter, think of thought as an independent thing, outside our control. We say that we *have* thoughts. In this poem, it is almost as if the thoughts live lives of their own, and as if they have us.

Hughes is not talking about 8 abstract thought but something more along the lines of poetic inspiration. What comes to him as if from some other place is an *image*, a very concrete image of a fox.

Stanza three represents a dra- 9 matic change. The abstract words like "darkness" and "loneliness" suddenly yield to concrete descriptions. We meet the fox. Hughes uses his language to give the reader the impression of a fox's nose coming forward. He alliterates the d-sound in the first line—"Cold, delicately as the dark snow"—making the reader pronounce the words with great care (you cannot say the line rapidly). And his use of the caesura in the next line—"nose touches twig, leaf;"—makes us hesitate just like the fox.

Then, in an image that combines sound, rhythm, and even the appear- 10 ance of words, Hughes writes

> Two eyes serve a movement, that now
> And again now, and now, and now
> Sets neat prints into the snow

The repetition of "now" four times forces us to see the word as a foot- 11 print. And the rhythm, which is very nearly iambic, has just the slightest

---

Ryan Kelly: My Commitment to This Essay

Ryan Kelly was required by his instructor to write an interpretive essay; but he was also able to discover very personal reasons for writing and claimed this essay as his own. This personal statement gives you an insight into Kelly's motivations for writing, but it is *not* itself an essay. Why not? What are the differences between this statement and the essay? What are the similarities?

I first read Hughes's poem when I was sitting alone in a quiet, mostly dark room. His "midnight moment's forest" made me stop and look around the room and then look around my own head. Inside of me and outside, the world was quiet when I read, and the poem crept up on me like the thought fox did on the poet. This impression was clear enough that I expected the last line to be, "The page is read"! But it wasn't, and when I read and reread I had the idea that this poem was more about writing a poem than about reading one. Hughes's techniques seemed to support this interpretation, which pleased me. I thought I had a good understanding of the poem, and I wanted to communicate this in my essay.

jerky hesitation. By putting into our minds the picture of footprints in the snow, Hughes gets us ready for the final line of the poem, which will compare the printed page with the prints in the snow.

The fourth stanza has the fox coming closer. The animal is still wary, 12 and Hughes suggests this with an enjambment at the end of the second line. He writes: "a lame/shadow lags" and we have to pause for a moment, just long enough to feel the lagging.

Hughes uses another effective enjambment between the end of the 13 fourth and the beginning of the fifth stanza. The fox is "bold to come" "Across clearings." Here the sensation is of something breaking loose from cover and hurrying through the open. This is especially apparent when the poem is read aloud.

But after this brief rush, the poem slows down again. The poet builds 14 tension through the fifth stanza. He does this in several ways. On the one hand, he uses a great many long vowel sounds, especially in the first three lines. There are assonances between "eye" and "widening" and between "deepening" and "greenness." Further, lines 2 and 3 seem to use a dactylic rhythm, which is supposed to bring speed into a poem. On the other hand, he does things to slow the reader down. He sets long, multisyllable words alongside one another, which slows down pronunciation, and he fills the stanza full of caesuras so that the reader keeps pausing. Reading the stanza out loud, we feel frustrated, bottled-up.

The last stanza comes as a surprise. There is an immediate sense of re- 15 lease. The first line is packed with assonances ("sharp," "hot," and "fox") and alliterated word-sounds ("sudden," "sharp," "stink," and "fox"). After the long words in the previous stanza, these short words are like punches: "Till, with a sudden sharp hot stink of fox." It is the climax of the poem. The fox, which we have imagined to be outside in a snowfield, now "enters the dark hole of the head." It is a strange image, for the head is usually considered a solid, not a hole. But Hughes is making a metaphor. The hole is the inside of the head—that is, the imagination.

As soon as the fox has entered, the poem ends. And the end comes as 16 a surprise. We are suddenly back in the room, with the window and the clock. "The page is printed." The last word is a pun, with the print referring both to the tracks in the snow and letters put down on paper by the writer.

On one level the poem is about itself—about a poet imagining a fox 17 and writing of that experience. On another, "The Thought-Fox" suggests things about the nature of thought and inspiration in general. Hughes wants us to feel the process, and the paradox, how the thoughts and images may be inside us, but how they seem to come from elsewhere. This inside/outside paradox may explain why it is that the fox, which Hughes tells us right away is part of what he imagines, can also be described as moving toward him from someplace else.

Interestingly, Hughes' descriptions in the last two lines of the poem 18 are cold and detached, much as they were before the fox appeared. He seems to be suggesting, without ever saying so in words, that it is the imagination that gives life to things. For when the act of imagining—writing—ends, we are left with a starless window and a ticking clock—two bleak images.

For Discussion and Writing

Reading and Thinking Critically

1. *Personal response:* "The Thought-Fox" is brief enough for you to read several times. Do so, and answer these questions: What is this poem about? How do you know this?
2. *Be alert to differences:* If you have never studied poetry formally, what differences can you observe between your explanation of how "The Thought-Fox" achieves its meaning and Ryan Kelly's explanation?
3. *Challenge the reading:* One criticism of careful, line-by-line analyses is that too much analysis can lessen one's pleasure of a literary text. What do you gain by reading Kelly's close analysis of "The Thought-Fox"? Do you lose anything? In either case, point to lines or paragraphs in the essay to support your response. If you want to argue that literary explanations diminish a reader's enjoyment, be prepared to explain how one enjoys a poem without such efforts as Kelly's and how explanations may detract. Conversely, you may want to argue (as your literature professors will argue) that close readings *enhance* enjoyment. Explain.

Examining " 'The Thought-Fox'—A Response" as an Interpretive Essay

1. Choose one paragraph and explain Kelly's pattern of making interpretive statements and then referring to the poem.
2. Examine Kelly's use of present-tense verbs.
3. Describe the structure of this essay, and comment on its effectiveness.

Structures and Strategies

Interpretive essays about a poem, a play, a short story, or a novel are arguments. To write an interpretive essay, begin with a personal response and reread until you are sure of that response. Then read again to find passages that you can refer to in your essay to support your interpretation. The goal is to convince readers that this interpretation is reasonable. In this section you will find specific strategies for reading and responding to a literary work; for *re*reading that work to confirm your interpretive hunches about it; and for writing an essay in which you argue for the reasonableness of your claim *on the basis of specific references to the literary work.*

Prepare to Write: Explore Your Idea

Discovering Ideas

Whether you are assigned a topic to write on or are left to your own devices, you inevitably face the question: What is my idea? Like every essay, an interpretative essay must have at its heart an idea that you want to convey—a point illustrated by the three example essays at the beginning of this chapter. Martin Simpson's idea is that Chopin's "A Shameful Affair" concerns a sexual awakening; Sarika Chandra's idea is that characters in Joyce's "Counterparts" use the bottle or the Church to gain power and self-esteem; Ryan Kelly's idea is that Ted Hughes's "The Thought-Fox" is a poem about writing a poem. Like each of these writers, you need to advance a single idea in every section of your interpretive essays. What will this idea be? Following are strategies to help you define an interpretive statement that you can use as the basis for writing an essay.

Respond Personally to the Literary Work

Writing about literature is premised on the belief that the text you are examining is worthy of your extended reflection. If you have not thought about what you've read, if you haven't responded to it personally, you can hardly expect to write about it with conviction. Several questions can help prompt a personal response on a first reading:

- What do I feel when reading this material? Why do I feel this way?
- Does this text make me *want* to read? Why or why not?
- What about this text is worth reading a second time?
- How am I challenged by or changed in response to this text?
- With what questions does this text leave me?
- What differences do I see between the author's observations of the world and my observations? How can I explain these differences?

Personal responses based on these and related questions can make you want to know more about what you've read. If on completing a story, drama, or poem you find yourself, for instance, *moved, offended, challenged, saddened, confused, needled,* or *intrigued,* you will have an immediate and even pressing reason to return for a second reading. Sometimes you may need to brainstorm (see pages 9–11) after a first reading in order to understand your particular response to a text. What follows is a demonstration of such a brainstorming session. Sarika Chandra, whose essay appears at the beginning of this chapter, spent five minutes writing out her response to "Counterparts," a short story by James Joyce (see pages 380–387). Read the concluding paragraphs of "Counterparts," along with Chandra's marginal notes. The story concerns a man named Farrington, who in this scene returns home from a night of heavy drinking—paid for by pawning his watch and prompted by a disagreement with his boss.

At this point, Farrington's lost his name.

A very sullen-faced man stood at the corner of O'Connell Bridge waiting for the little Sandymount tram to take him home. He was full of smouldering anger and revengefulness. He felt humiliated and discontented; he did not even feel drunk; and he had only twopence in his pocket. He cursed everything. He had done for himself in the office, pawned his watch, spent all his money; and he had not even got drunk. He began to feel thirsty again and he longed to be back again in the hot reeking public-house. He had lost his reputation as a strong man, having been defeated twice by a mere boy. His heart swelled with fury and, when he thought of the woman in the big hat who had brushed against him and *Pardon!* his fury nearly choked him.

His tram let him down at Shelbourne Road and he steered his great body along in the shadow of the wall of the barracks. He loathed returning to his home. When he went in by the side-door he found the kitchen empty and the kitchen fire nearly out. He bawled upstairs:

—Ada! Ada!

His wife was a little sharp-faced woman who bullied her husband when he was sober and was bullied by him when he was drunk. They had five children. A little boy came running down the stairs.

—Who is that? said the man peering through the darkness.

—Me, pa.

—Who are you? Charlie?

—No, pa. Tom.

—Where's your mother?

—She's out at the chapel.

—That's right . . . Did she think of leaving any dinner for me?

—Yes, pa. I—

—Light the lamp. What do you mean by having the place in darkness? Are the other children in bed?

The man sat down heavily on one of the chairs while the little boy lit the lamp. He began to mimic his son's flat accent, saying half to himself: *At the chapel. At the chapel, if you please!* When the lamp was lit he banged his fist on the table and shouted:

—What's for my dinner?

—I'm going . . . to cook it, pa, said the little boy.

The man jumped up furiously and pointed to the fire.

—On that fire! You let the fire out! By God, I'll teach you to do that again!

He took a step to the door and seized the walking-stick which was standing behind it.

—I'll teach you to let the fire out! he said, rolling up his sleeve in order to give his arm free play.

[margin notes: F's defeated, powerless in his job & in the bar | This miserable? Is there any joy in this man's life? | Again, no name | I'd be terrified too! The bully | Is this the only way he can feel good about himself—by beating a kid?]

The little boy cried *O, pa!* and ran whimpering round the table, but the man followed him and caught him by the coat. The little boy looked about him wildly but, seeing no way of escape, fell upon his knees.

—Now, you'll let the fire out the next time! said the man, striking at him viciously with the stick. Take that, you little whelp!

The boy uttered a squeal of pain as the stick cut his thigh. He clasped his hands together in the air and his voice shook with fright.

—O, pa! he cried. Don't beat me, pa! And I'll . . . I'll say a *Hail Mary* for you . . . I'll say a *Hail Mary* for you, pa, if you don't beat me . . . I'll say a *Hail Mary.* . . .

The man could use some salvation. What a grim life.

Chandra wrote for several minutes after she read these final paragraphs of Joyce's story. Here is her response:

> Farrington is a lost, desperate man. His powerlessness depresses me. He's so powerless that he grabs the only power left to him by beating his young son. It's a sick thing to do and it's cowardly and it gets me mad, a father taking out his troubles on a boy this way. I'd hate Farrington if his situation at work weren't so miserable. He's trapped and doesn't have a clue about what's trapping him. His son is trapped, living in a house with this man. Although I don't see her, I bet his wife is feeling trapped, too. Husband and wife bully each other. There's no happiness in this world. People grab for whatever gives them power and security: the father grabs the bottle, the mother and son grab onto the Church.

Read Secondary Sources to Spark Ideas

In addition to your personal responses to a literary work, which is the primary way you will generate ideas for interpretive essays, you can read and respond to secondary sources: the work of other interpreters of this same text or of biographers who have studied the life and times of the author. In your school library you should be able to locate criticism on many of the writers you read in your literature courses; you will certainly be able to find criticism on the writers whose work appears in this chapter: James Joyce, Kate Chopin, Langston Hughes, Robert Frost, and Ted Hughes. To further spark ideas for her essay, Sarika Chandra searched for secondary sources on "Counterparts" and found the work of Joyce scholar Richard Ellmann; here Ellmann discusses the occasional jobs held by John Joyce, the author's father:

> Besides the £11 a month from his pension, collected punctually each month at David Drimmie and Sons, John Joyce picked up a little money here and there. His calligraphy enabled him to work occasionally for a solicitor on the quays named Aylward;* he had a random occupation as advertisement canvasser for the *Freeman's Journal*; and at election times he could always depend upon the usual small jobs to make him momentarily affluent and, necessarily, drunk. (39)

Ellmann adds the footnote at the asterisk: "Aylward's office is probably that described in 'Counterparts,' where his name is changed to Alleyne for reasons explained on p. 16." Turning to that page in Ellmann's *James Joyce,* Chandra found that the writer's father had once worked with a man named Henry Alleyne who swindled Joyce and others out of some money. Ellmann writes that "James Joyce liked paying off his father's scores" and gave Mr. Alleyne "the name of the unpleasant employer in the story 'Counterparts.'"

Chandra found the biographical information useful in introducing her essay, and she refers directly to Ellmann's work in her second paragraph. She concludes that paragraph this way: "[N]othing in Joyce's biography explains the complexity of 'Counterparts.'" Chandra then turns directly to her idea about powerlessness and begins pointing the reader to lines from the story. In this particular case, a secondary source provided an idea for making an important transition in the essay. In other cases, secondary sources can spark ideas by prompting your agreement or disagreement. The possibilities are many, and it is usually worth your time to read what others have written about the author whose work you are reading.

Committing Yourself to an Idea

Once you have responded to the text you are reading and have a definite idea about it, commit yourself to the idea by *re*reading. Determine just how valuable this idea is in making the text have meaning for you and, potentially, for readers. Your goal is to find in separate passages patterns of meaning that make your initial idea seem reasonable.

Specifically, try to convert your personal response to the text into a pointed question, and ask: *Why? How? What are some examples?* Guided by this question, reread in order to gain insights into how the text works and how you think it achieves meaning in one particular way (with respect to your question). If you have trouble deciding on a question to guide your second reading, reflect again on your response to the text. Find some line, some gesture, some interaction among characters that prompts a response in you. Begin, again, from there.

You may find yourself writing papers for literature courses in which you approach your topic according to the viewpoints of various schools of literary criticism.[3] Without naming these schools here and introducing

---

[3]Scholars who write professionally about and teach poetry, plays, and fiction are called *literary critics;* and critics affiliate themselves with one of several approaches to literature— so-called "schools" of literary criticism, each of which regards texts differently and, based on its approach, poses distinctive questions. Some critics read *Moby Dick,* for instance, and ask: What is the psychological basis of the relationship between Ishmael and Queequeg? Some read and ask: What echoes can we find of Melville's years at sea? Some look at the public's initial rejection of the novel and ask: Why and when did this work come to be regarded as an American classic? The possible angles from which to study a literary work are many; each suggests its own set of questions, its own set of problems worth investigating, and its own rules about what counts as acceptable, supporting evidence. Readers find patterns of meaning in a text depending on the questions they ask. The questions that guide your reading, then, are of paramount importance. Questions reveal your assumptions about what you think is important.

you to complicated terminologies and methods, you might pose some of the following questions, in addition to the questions prompted by your personal response, to find patterns of meaning in a text. These questions assume that you have already completed a close first reading.

- What circumstances of the author's life does the text reflect?
- In what ways does the text exist in a relationship with other texts by the same author and with other texts from the same time period?
- How might the text shift its meaning from one reader to the next? from one audience to the next, over time?
- What is the reader's role in making this text meaningful?
- How does the text reflect certain cultural assumptions about gender, race, or culture in the author's and the reader's times?
- What psychological motives underlie the characters' actions?
- What are the economic or power relationships among characters?

When you want to maintain your focus on a poem, play, or work of fiction itself (as opposed to considering the reader's responses or various influences on the author), you can pose the following questions, arranged by category. These questions are often appropriate for introductory survey courses in literature.

Characterization Who are the main characters? What are their qualities? Is each character equally important? Equally well developed?

Language What devices such as rhyme (identical sounds), meter (carefully controlled rhythms), and pauses does the author use to create special emphasis? How does the author use metaphors and choose words to create visual images? In what ways are these images tied to the meaning of the text?

Narrator, Point of View Who is speaking? What is the narrator's personality and how does this affect the telling? Is the narrator omniscient in the sense that he or she can read into the thoughts of every character? If not, how is the narrator's vision limited?

Plot How does the writer sequence events so as to maintain the reader's attention? Which actions are central? How are other, subsidiary actions linked to the central ones? What patterning to the plot do you see? Are there ways in which the plot's structure and theme are related?

Structure In what ways can you (or does the author) divide the whole poem or story into component parts—according to theme? plot? setting? stanza? How are these parts related?

Setting Where does the story take place? How significant is the setting to the meaning of the text?

Symbolism Are any symbols operating, any objects that (like a flag) create emotional, political, religious, or other associations for readers? If so, how do these symbols function in the poem, story, or play?

Theme What large issues does this text raise? Through which characters, events, or specific lines are the questions raised? To what extent does the text answer these questions?

As you work with a key question to guide your second reading of a text, make notes in the margin wherever you feel the text provides details that you think add to a pattern of meaning. Sarika Chandra converted her personal response to "Counterparts" into this question: *In what way do characters show power or powerlessness in this short story?* The question builds directly on the response she made in her five-minute brainstorming session (see page 357), in which her main concern was with power and powerlessness. Chandra uses her question to tease out details in the text that will subsequently provide her with evidence needed to argue for her interpretation. Observe how Chandra's marginal notes call attention to potential evidence for her claim:

Defeated & powerless at the office

Defeated and powerless at the bar

He cursed everything. He had done for himself in the office, pawned his watch, spent all his money; and he had not even got drunk. He began to feel thirsty again and he longed to be back again in the hot reeking public-house. He had lost his reputation as a strong man, having been defeated twice by a mere boy.

• • •

Powerless at home, unless he's drunk

His wife was a little sharp-faced woman who bullied her husband when he was sober and was bullied by him when he was drunk. They had five children. A little boy came running down the stairs.

—Who is that? said the man, peering through the darkness.

—Me, pa.

—Who are you? Charlie?

—No, pa. Tom.

—Where's your mother?

—She's out at the chapel.

The chapel the one place F.'s wife can go to get beyond his abuse. God is more powerful than F.

—That's right. . . . Did she think of leaving any dinner for me?

—Yes, pa. I—

—Light the lamp. What do you mean by having the place in darkness? Are the other children in bed?

F. knows it (↑) too; she's beyond his reach.

The man sat down heavily on one of the chairs while the little boy lit the lamp. He began to mimic his son's flat accent, saying half to himself: *At the chapel. At the chapel, if you please!* When the lamp was lit he banged his fist on the table and shouted:

—What's for my dinner?

• • •

F.'s pathetic grab for power by beating his son

—I'll teach you to let the fire out! he said, rolling up his sleeve in order to give his arm free play.

The little boy cried *O, pa!* and ran whimpering round the table, but the man followed him and caught him by the coat. The little boy looked about him wildly but, seeing no way of escape, fell upon his knees.

—Now, you'll let the fire out the next time! said the man, striking at him viciously with the stick. Take that, you little whelp!

The boy uttered a squeal of pain as the stick cut his thigh. He clasped his hands together in the air and his voice shook with fright.

The boy, as w/his mother, some measure of power over F. through the church.

—O, pa! he cried. Don't beat me, pa! And I'll . . . I'll say a *Hail Mary* for you . . . I'll say a *Hail Mary* for you, pa, if you don't beat me . . . I'll say a *Hail Mary*. . . .

Based on your first and second readings of a text, you should be ready to make an interpretive statement that you are committed to arguing. This statement will be your essay's idea—its argumentative thesis. Here is Chandra's idea:

> "Counterparts" is a story about how otherwise powerless people seek to gain control over their lives.

A writer will be more or less committed to a thesis, and this level of commitment sets a tone for the entire essay (see the discussion in chapter 2). What marks Chandra's as an ambitious, "three-story" thesis (in the language of chapter 2) is that she is hinting at connections among parts of the story that are not obviously connected. Beyond this, Chandra introduces tension into this idea with the opposites "powerless" and "control." Presenting this tension was foremost on her mind when writing the essay, as these lines from her personal commitment statement suggest:

> [Farrington] is a lost, desperate man who is powerless to change his life. . . . Husband and wife bully each other; father bullies son; supervisor bullies copyist. Here is a world without joy, where people grab for whatever gives them power and the barest threads of self-worth: Farrington grabs onto the bottle, while his wife and son grab onto the Church. Rereading this story and writing the essay helped explained my revulsion to Farrington.

These lines from Chandra's personal commitment statement, along with her thesis, express the core idea of her essay and communicate to us the level of her commitment. Without her core idea, the essay could not be written. Without her commitment to this idea, she would have lacked a motivation to write and would have failed to provide us with a motivation to read. What Chandra must now do is begin to make public her personal insights and commitment: she needs to think of her audience and build a common ground with them; she needs to communicate the pattern of meaning she has found in Joyce's story; and she needs to consider strategies for arguing convincingly.

Write: Clarify Your Idea and Make It Public

In planning and writing the first draft of any essay, you can expect to clarify your ideas for yourself. Writing is not only an act that communicates information you already possess, it is an act of discovery, and you should expect to deepen your insights as you write. You will do so in the context of making public the insights you already have. Your first consideration will be your readers. Who are they? What do they know? How will you make what *you* know available to them?

Creating Common Ground with Readers

The common ground you share with readers in an interpretive essay is the poem, story, play, or novel that you are discussing. Readers will either have read the text(s) or not. For those who have not, you must provide enough background information about characters and actions to enable readers to follow your discussion. Even for those readers who have read a work, you will need to provide enough background to refresh their memories and direct their attention as you refer to particular lines. To create a common ground with readers, you will use summary and quotation, in effect recreating the text in your essay.

A **plot summary** is a brief description of characters and events that provides readers enough context to follow your discussion. Plot summaries are written in the historical present tense. Consider these sentences from Chandra's paper. Present-tense verbs are boldfaced:

> After work, Farrington **looks** forward to drinking, which he **does** every time he **is** humiliated. After the scene in Alleyne's office, he **wants** to go to the pub but he **realizes** he has no money. Suddenly, he **thinks** of his watch and **pawns** it for six shillings.

Variations from the present tense may be needed from time to time to clarify sequences of events. Past-tense verbs will be needed in the essay at those points where you discuss actual historical moments in an author's life. (You will see this in Onwuchekwa Jemie's essay on Langston Hughes. See pages 367–370, particularly ¶s2–6.) For the most part, use present-tense verbs because the events of the text are always present to readers: readers will find the same actions, in the same order, in the text no matter how many times they return to it.

As part of your plot summaries, you will often quote from the text in order to recreate a scene or an image for your reader. This example continues the paragraph above, from Sarika Chandra:

> . . . At the pub, Farrington relates the incident in Alleyne's office to his companions. He claims that he looked coolly at Mr. Alleyne and said, "I don't think that's a fair question to put to me" (93). Nosey Flynn and Davy Byrne say that this was the smartest thing they have heard. Farrington is pleased and he "[stands] a drink in his turn" (93).

Remember: the purpose of the plot summary is to create a context in your essay so that you can refer to a text in ways that support your interpretation. Your job is to orient readers so that they know *where* you are referring and what is happening at the point of reference. Once you have situated the reader in this way, then you make your point. To review, you will use plot summaries in two forms in your essay:

- You will write a summary of the entire story, poem, play, or novel early in your essay.

- Then, throughout the essay, you will summarize and recreate for readers a particular scene or image *every* time you want to make an interpretive claim. Your summary points readers to a new location in the text. Once you are at this location with the reader, make a claim and then refer to a specific line for evidence.

Often you will make your interpretive observation about the line you have referred to immediately following your plot summary, sometimes in the same sentence:

> Frustrated by his loss at arm wrestling, Farrington returns home, where yet another attempt to gain power fails.

"[W]here yet another attempt to gain power fails" is not part of Chandra's summary, but rather an observation about the story that followed from her guiding question (*In what ways do characters show power or powerlessness?*) and that she makes in her essay to support her claim. To ensure that readers can follow her discussion, Chandra summarizes portions of "Counterparts" throughout her essay so that her observations will have a specific reference and will make sense to her readers. You will need to provide more plot summary to create common ground for readers who are unfamiliar with the text(s) you are interpreting; less summary is necessary for readers who are familiar with the text. In either case, you will need to recreate this text in your essay as you point readers to passages that form patterns of meaning.

Tone and the Writing Occasion

The tone you adopt in an interpretive essay will vary less than your tone for other essays, since the interpretive essay is a specialized argument intended largely for your professor and for classmates in a literature class. The characteristic tone of the interpretive essay might be described as one of confident, satisfied discovery at having made sense of a literary work. You can detect this tone in excerpts from the two student essays at the beginning of this chapter:

> The poem begins, as it will end, with the poet working alone in his room. Hughes suggests the focus and intensity of a poet at work right away by using a strongly alliterated line: "I imagine this midnight moment's forest." There is a meditative, brooding feeling with these m-sounds that captures the reader's attention.
>
> —Ryan Kelly

> Farrington sits in Alleyne's office, powerless, listening to this man berate him for some job poorly done. Apparently, mistakes and the resulting humiliation are regular occurrences in this office. Aside from the abuse he must take from Alleyne, Farrington is made powerless by the very nature of his profession. As a copyist, not even his work is his own: he must labor all day at copying someone else's words. Farrington is trapped, immediately by his boss and more generally by his job.
>
> —Sarika Chandra

These confident, present-tense observations point readers to particular passages of a text and then explain why these passages are meaningful. The writers can be confident because they are convinced about the pattern they have found. Their job in the essay is to convince readers. And because interpretation is by definition a personal act, these example interpretive essays and the ones you write will reflect a sense of personal discovery. At times, you may be moved to communicate your discovery with an excited "Aha—I've found it!" tone.

Planning a Structure

Once you have read and reread a text and have a clear interpretive statement in mind, as well as a firm sense of which passages in the text support this interpretive statement, you can plan a structure for your first draft. See chapter 4 on "Advancing Your Idea with Sources," and especially the section on "Quizzing the Thesis" (pages 61–63) for advice on planning a sketch based on your initial thesis. Here is how Sarika Chandra quizzed her thesis:

What's the story?   How are they powerless?

"Counterparts" is a story about how otherwise powerless people seek to

gain control over their lives.

How do they gain control?   What are the details?

From this thesis and the questions she posed, Chandra was able to sketch an outline for her first draft.

> Plot summary of basic situation—Farrington's powerlessness
> Farrington and Joyce, connection—reference to secondary source
> Farrington buying drinks—buys power: references to text
> Farrington abusing son—grasps for power: references to text
> Farrington's wife and child going to Church—prays for power (or endurance?): references to text
> Women not welcome in Irish pubs, no power that way for F's wife: reference to secondary source

Chandra used this sketch as a guide to selecting passages in "Counterparts" and in secondary sources that helped her support the claim that Joyce had written a story about how "otherwise powerless people seek to gain control over their lives." You will find on reading the paper that Chandra's sketch is built directly from the notes she made in her second reading and that her second reading followed directly from the question that evolved from her first, personal response to the story.

"Counterparts" is a story rich with meaning and, like any work of literature, yields itself to many interpretations. The point to remember is that whatever pattern you find in a text, you are obligated to show readers why, given all the patterns that *could* be found, this one is reasonable and worth their consideration. You demonstrate the worthiness of an interpretive claim by repeatedly referring the reader to the text—a primary source—and when pertinent, to secondary sources.

Understanding Your Logic

The logic used to argue for your interpretation of a literary work reverses the logic by which you discovered patterns of meaning in the text. Typically, a reader makes discoveries inductively, forging tentative connections among separate lines or scenes and only slowly realizing that a pattern of meaning exists. In your essay, you *begin* by stating this pattern in the clearest terms possible, and then you provide evidence in support of it. Here, for example, are the opening paragraphs from Ryan Kelly's and Sarika Chandra's essays:

> Ted Hughes's "The Thought-Fox" is a poem watching itself in a mirror. That is, it is about how a poem—itself—gets written. To some extent, therefore, it is about the writing process in general, or even creativity in general.
>
> —Ryan Kelly

> "Counterparts" tells the story of a man named Farrington, who will not do his job right and takes abuse from his boss for that. Farrington spends a long time drinking after work and when he gets home beats his son. However, Joyce tells much more in eleven pages than just another story about an abusive alcoholic. "Counterparts" is a story about how otherwise powerless people seek to gain control over their lives.
>
> —Sarika Chandra

Clearly, Kelly and Chandra did not begin their first readings of the poem and the short story with these understandings. Through careful reading and rereading, they worked slowly toward these statements of interpretation. Then in writing their essays, they reversed the discovery process and began their essays with their interpretations. This is a *deductive* arrangement. Open the essay with your thesis, and follow with references to specific lines or scenes.

Cycles of Development

The specific lines and scenes to which you refer readers become the evidence in your argument. Writers of interpretive essays follow a clear pattern when referring readers to a text; this pattern can be called a *cycle of development:*

- First, locate the reader at a specific point in a play, poem, or story by explaining what is happening, who is speaking, and so on.
- Second, make an interpretive statement about the poem or story.
- Third, present evidence for this interpretation by referring to a specific line or scene, either by quoting or by summarizing.
- Finally, comment on the line or scene referred to and show how this reference supports your interpretation. Move on to a new, related claim and begin a new cycle of development.

Here's how this cycle of development looks in a paragraph written by a noted literary critic, Lionel Trilling, who is writing on "The Greatness of *Huckleberry Finn.*" Trilling's interpretive claim is that Huck Finn is a character who sympathizes with the misfortunes of others:

[Huckleberry Finn's] sympathy is quick and immediate. When the circus audience laughs at the supposedly drunken man who tries to ride the horse, Huck is only miserable: "It wasn't funny to me . . . ; I was all of a tremble to see his danger." When he imprisons the intending murderers on the wrecked steamboat, his first thought is of how to get someone to rescue them, for he considers "how dreadful it was, even for murderers, to be in such a fix. I says to myself, there ain't no telling but I might come to be a murderer myself yet, and then how would I like it?" But his sympathy is never sentimental. When at last he knows that the murderers are beyond help, he has no inclination to false pathos. "I felt a little bit heavy-hearted about the gang, but not much, for I reckoned that if they could stand it I could." His will is genuinely good and therefore he has no need to torture himself with guilty second thoughts.

The logic of this paragraph is as follows: Trilling makes two related claims in this paragraph: first, that Huck's "sympathy is quick and immediate"; and second, that this "sympathy is never sentimental." He refers the reader to specific passages that support his claim and, after a final quoted passage, makes this comment: "[Huck's] will is genuinely good and therefore he has no need to torture himself with guilty second thoughts." With this interpretive comment, Trilling cements the relationship between the claims he has made and the evidence he has offered. He has argued effectively. In one brief paragraph, then, Lionel Trilling demonstrates the cycle of claim, reference, and comment that is basic to writing about literature. You, too, will make use of this cycle.

An analysis of a literary text—that is, an entire essay devoted to interpretation—is built by linking many such cycles, according to an overall plan or thesis. Trilling's paragraph is one cycle in a larger essay. Virtually every paragraph in the larger essay shows this same cycle of claim, support, and comment. Each paragraph-level cycle advances the overall interpretation of the essay. Reread Sarika Chandra's or Ryan Kelly's essays and you will see how full cycles of development link together to form a persuasive whole. (For more on cycles of development, see chapter 4, pages 61–68.)

Advance Your Idea with Sources

One of the more difficult aspects of learning to write interpretive essays about literature is knowing how to weave source materials into your work. When should you quote? How much should you quote? To what extent should your voice predominate in the essay (as opposed to the voice of the author whose work you are analyzing)? How can you maneuver your discussion of one text—for instance, a poem—into a discussion of another text by the same author (or by a different author)? When should you go beyond primary sources to secondary sources?

Several principles can be observed in the work of professional writers and put to use in your own writing:

- Work consistently with the pattern of claim, reference to a text, and comment discussed and illustrated above.

- Refer to secondary sources to supplement your original ideas.
- Organize your discussion by ideas, not by sources (see chapter 4, pages 61–63).

In the following essay-length excerpt from *Langston Hughes: An Introduction to the Poetry,* Onwuchekwa Jemie demonstrates an effective use of primary and secondary sources. In this passagie, Jemie attempts to establish the importance of music, particularly jazz, in Hughes's poetry by drawing on primary sources—Hughes's poetry—as well as on his autobiography and secondary sources in order to support the claim that "Hughes's major poetry lives and breathes, to use his own phrase, in the 'shadow of the blues.' " Turn to this chapter's second "Occasion for Discussion and Writing," pages 391–397, to find most of the source materials to which Jemie refers. As you read, bear these questions in mind:

- Jemie is convincing, so much so that the essay reads more as a presentation of facts than as an interpretation. But Jemie *is* interpreting. Choose a passage in this essay and point to Jemie's cycle of claim and support.
- Why does Jemie devote ¶s2–4 to explaining the rise of jazz in the 1920s? How are sources used in these paragraphs?
- At what points in the essay does Jemie tend to use secondary sources? At what points does Jemie use primary sources?

The Jazz Poet

Onwuchekwa Jemie

[Langston] Hughes recognized music as the quintessential Afro-American art. 1 Into music more than any other art form, black people from earliest times have poured their daily concerns. Music accompanied the African, newly arrived in the Americas, at work in the slavemaster's house and in his fields, and at work or play in the slave quarters. From slavery to freedom, music has provided a salve for the cut and hurt soul and body. It has served as an ecstasy-inducer, an escape, a manifestation and affirmation of the transcendent beauty of life.

Hughes's experience with black music began in early youth: 2

> It was fifty years ago the first time I heard the Blues on Independence Avenue in Kansas City. Then State Street in Chicago. Then Harlem in the twenties with J. P. and J. C. Johnson and Fats and Willie the Lion and Nappy playing piano—with the Blues running all up and down the keyboard through the ragtime and the jazz. House rent party cards. I wrote *The Weary Blues.* . . .[1]

He came to maturity in the 1920s, a decade of overwhelming importance for the development and diffusion of black music, and the classic age of both jazz and blues. From their homes in the lower Mississippi River region (for jazz, New Orleans in particular), jazz and blues had traveled north with the Great Migration and established themselves in various regional centers, especially Kansas City, Chicago, and New York. And through the 1920s each of these regions developed its own styles and orientations (Kansas City jazz, for instance, was noted for its strong blues orientation), but not in isolation: all the while a process of cross-fertilization, of fusion and diffusion, was taking place. This cross-fertilization, and the spread of black music on the national and international scene, was greatly facilitated by the introduction of commercial phonograph recordings of black music in 1923. In fact the so-called jazz age may be said to have properly begun in 1923 when black music first became readily available on phonograph records.

It was during that same decade that Fletcher Henderson, based in New 3 York, developed precision in jazz instrumentation, introduced orchestral arrangements, and organized the jazz orchestra into what was to become the Big Band. Many of the best known names in jazz, including Coleman Hawkins, J. C. Higginbotham, Russell Procope, Benny Carter, Ben Webster, Don Redman, Cootie Williams, Dicky Wells, and Eddie Barefield played in Henderson's band at one time or another. Even Louis Armstrong, the first great jazz virtuoso, played briefly with Henderson before returning to Chicago to found his famous Hot Five and Hot Seven groups. And it was in the 20s that Armstrong established what came to be regarded as the standard jazz structure, including solo and improvisation, and introduced the trumpet as the prime solo instrument (a preeminence which the trumpet was to enjoy until the 1940s when Charlie Parker supplanted it with the saxophone). And while these developments were taking place, Duke Ellington, a young man, was learning his craft and was to emerge in the following decade as one of the great jazz leaders.

It was also in the 1920s that the classic blues structure was established: 4 three lines of lyric, the second line a repetition in whole or part of the first line, the third line rhyming with the first two. The era was dominated by women singers, worthy successors to Ma Rainey, with Bessie Smith as "Empress" and Ida Cox, Victoria Spivey, and the other Smiths—Mamie, Laura, Clara and Trixie—in attendance. These singers were frequently accompanied by jazz orchestras. Toward the end of the 20s, however, commercial interest in classic blues declined, and by 1929 the blues women had been forced out of the spotlight and out of the recording studios. The recording industry had discovered fresh sources: male blues singers who had recently migrated north to Chicago. And the depression ushered in the era of Blind Lemon Jefferson, Bill Broonzy, Tampa Red, and Georgia Tom (Thomas A. Dorsey, "Father of Gospel Music") and their Chicago city blues.[2]

In 1921 Hughes persuaded his father to send him to college in New York 5 rather than in Europe, out of "an overwhelming desire to see Harlem. . . . the greatest Negro city in the world."[3] And he more than saw Harlem: he attended shows, followed the progress of black musicians, singers, and actors, and sat up in the gallery night after night watching Noble Sissle and Eubie Blake's "Shuffle Along"—the black musical which became the prototype of the Broadway musical comedy.[4]

Hughes, in short, was from his early youth a sensitive and involved witness 6 to the growth and maturation of what in the mid-1920s emerged as classic black music; and even in that early era black music was universally acknowledged as the greatest indigenous American music (as against the musics inherited from Europe), and was enjoyed and imitated the world over. In tune as he was with the currents of life around him, it is not surprising that he came to regard this music as a paradigm of the black experience and a metaphor for human life in general. "The rhythm of life / Is a jazz rhythm," he declared in 1926.[5] Conversely, a poem in jazz rhythm has the rhythm of life; to capture the rhythm of jazz is to capture (an aspect of, a slice of) life. And the rhythm of life: long, incantive, endless like the jazz, with its riffs and breaks and repetitions, with love and joy and pain interchanging, alternating in "Overtones, / Undertones, / To the rumble of street cars, / To the swish of rain"[6]—the hard fierce beat of street cars and rain an appropriate urban metaphor for the movements and vibrations and cycles of which human life is composed.

Jazz is everyone's life, everyone's heartbeat: "Jazz is a heartbeat—its heart-   [7] beat is yours"[7]—whoever you may happen to be and even if you cannot comprehend or define it. Recalling Louis Armstrong's rebuke—"Lady, if you have to ask what it is, you'll never know"—Hughes says: "Well, I wouldn't be so positive. The lady just might know—without being able to let loose the cry—to follow through—to light up before the fuse blows out."[8] The lady may feel and know in her marrows "the meanings and rhythms of jazz" even if she is unable to articulate them.

Again, jazz is "a montage of a dream deferred. A great big dream—yet to   [8] come—and always *yet*—to become ultimately and finally true."[9] And that same or other lady, "dressed so fine," who has not bop but Bach on her mind, if she was to listen she would surely hear, "way up in the treble" of the Bach, that same music of a dream deferred, that same "tingle of a tear," of mixed sorrow and hope that is jazz.[10] Jazz is process-music, a dynamic force whose thrust is forwards towards the future. It is anti-static, developing, moving. Its impulse is recalcitrant, rebellious, revolutionary. With its free and easy, open-ended improvisational construction, its invitation to joy and the uninhibited movements of the body, jazz constitutes rebellion in a puritan society. It goes against the grain of the accepted and expected in music (Western music) and in life (Puritan Christian life). It challenges the established: Western industrial society and its weary materialism, its demand of "work, work, work," its destruction of human beings with inhuman machineries. Jazz carries within it the vision of an alternative mode of life; and just as continued black existence in circumstances of deprivation is a reproach to American democracy, so is jazz (and by extension, all black music and culture) a rival and subverter of the mainstream culture.

It should of course be pointed out that this view of jazz as a music of revolt   [9] is not entirely original with Hughes. It is adapted from J. A. Roger's essay of the year before.[11] Also, the bohemian rebellion in the America of the 1920s, of which the Harlem Renaissance was a manifestation, generally viewed black music and culture in this light. And this view is in keeping with the history of European thought of the last half millenium which, surveying the world through the elaborate manichean binoculars of Judeo-Christianity, saw in the non-Western world, its manners and morals, an exotic "other" antithetical to the West, a magnetic pole whose powerful attraction is fatal to "civilization" and "reason," whose embrace would mean drastic change or revolution. What Hughes did was to convert this idea into an operative principle of black art.

When Hughes speaks of jazz in these terms he is to be understood to mean   [10] black music in general. Jazz in this broad sense stands for the Afro-American Spirit out of which the total musical culture flows. Jazz, he says, is a big sea "that washes up all kinds of fish and shells and spume and waves with a steady old beat, or offbeat."[12] That Spirit, that sea, is the source of blues, gospel, and rock and roll, as it was of spirituals, work songs, field hollers, shouts, and ragtime. These varied emanations of the Spirit come and go: "A few more years and Rock and Roll will no doubt be washed back half forgotten into the sea of jazz."[13] And other forms will emerge and take its place.

Life, too, is such a sea: "Life is a big sea / full of many fish. / I let down   11
my nets / and pull."[14] And literature: "Literature is a big sea full of many fish.
I let down my nets and pulled. I'm still pulling."[15] Jazz and literature are the
same sea of life out of which all things of human significance and meaning
emerge, and to which they return. Jazz, literature, and life share the same heartbeat and constitute a unity. Each is a metaphor for the others; in their structures
and significances they parallel and illuminate and reinforce one another.

Hughes therefore proposes to pour life as he knows it into the molds so   12
magnificently provided by black music. He proposes to do in literature what others were doing in music, to create, in effect, a literary equivalent of black music.
He wants to create literature that is as *rooted* in the life of the folk and as *deep*
and *accessible* to them as black music is. Literature in which the masses of black
people would find their life experiences reflected and illuminated; in which the
community would find itself expressed.

Notes

1. Hughes, "Jazz as Communication," *The Langston Hughes Reader* (New York, George
Braziller, 1958), pp. 492–94.

2. See Alain Locke, *The Negro and His Music* [1936] (New York, Arno, 1969); Marshall
Stearns, *The Story of Jazz* (Oxford Univ. Press, 1956); Andre Hodeir, *Jazz: Its Evolution
and Essence* (New York, Grove, 1956); Gunther Schuller, *Early Jazz* (Oxford Univ. Press,
1967); Maude Cuney-Hare, *Negro Musicans and Their Music* (New York, Associated Publishers, 1936).

3. *Big Sea,* p. 62.

4. Ibid., p. 85.

5. "Lenox Avenue: Midnight," *Weary Blues,* p. 39.

6. Ibid.

7. "Jazz as Communication."

8. Ibid. This rebuke, sometimes attributed to Fats Waller, is part of jazz lore.

9. Ibid.

10. "Lady's Boogie," *Montage of a Dream Deferred* (New York, Henry Holt, 1951), p. 44.

11. J. A. Rogers, "Jazz at Home," in Locke, *The New Negro,* pp. 216–24.

12. "Jazz as Communication."

13. Ibid.

14. Epigraph, *Big Sea.*

15. Ibid., p. 335.

Evaluate and Revise

General Evaluation

You will usually need at least two drafts to produce an essay that presents
your idea clearly. The biggest changes in your essay will typically
come between your first and second drafts. In this book you will find
two demonstrations of essays in the process of turning from meandering
first thoughts into finished products. First, see the general advice on
the process of writing and revising in chapters 12–14, which includes
first- and second-draft versions of a student paper. You will find another

such demonstration in the "Student Writer at Work" sections at the end of chapters 1–5.

No essay that you write, including an interpretive essay, will be complete until you revise and refine your single compelling idea. You revise and refine by evaluating your first draft, bringing to it many of the same questions you pose when evaluating any piece of writing. In chapter 5 you will find general guidelines for evaluating what you read, including these:

- Are opinions supported by evidence?
- Are the opinions of others authoritative?
- Are my assumptions clearly stated?
- Are key terms clearly defined?
- Is the presentation logical?
- Are all parts of the presentation well developed?
- Are dissenting points of view presented?

Address these same questions to the first draft of your interpretive essays, and you will have solid information to guide your revision.

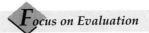

Focus on Evaluation

Have you been asked to write an evaluation of another writer's interpretation of literature? If so, you will base your evaluation on two sets of standards. First, you will apply specific standards for this type of writing as listed here in "Critical Points." At the same time, you will need to apply the general standards for evaluation that are listed here and discussed at length in chapter 5, pages 92–96. See especially the "key points" for evaluation in chapter 5, pages 95–96.

Critical Points in an Interpretive Essay

An essay of interpretation must make nonobvious connections among the parts of the poem, story, play, or novel that you are examining. Your interpretive statement (see pages 361–364) is what holds these observations together and makes your numerous references to the text coherent. The relationship of parts to the whole is therefore especially important: every time you refer readers to specific lines or scenes, show how these lines or scenes relate to the larger pattern of meaning you have discovered in the text.

Statements of interpretation will be as convincing as your presentation of evidence. Therefore, whenever you claim that a particular line or scene in a text is meaningful, you need to provide a full cycle of development:

- Make your interpretive claim.
- Refer to a specific line or scene.
- Comment on how this reference is meaningful *and* how it is related to your overall interpretation.

If you can provide full cycles of development for each interpretive claim that you make, and if you can link these claims together with an overall interpretation, then you stand a good chance of convincing readers that your approach to a text is reasonable and worth their consideration.

Occasions for Discussion and Writing

A Literary Interpretation of Your Own

You are ready to begin work on your own literary interpretation. One approach to choosing a topic is to review examples of the type of essay you will be writing. Consider rereading the essays that opened this chapter. You will find that the three authors—Simpson, Chandra, and Kelly—write about literary works they have come to know well through careful, repeated reading. You will also find in the personal commitment statements evidence that the two student authors had a personal stake in their essays: Joyce's "Counterparts" stirred Sarika Chandra to anger; Hughes's "The Thought-Fox" moved Ryan Kelly to quiet, thoughtful reflection. In choosing a literary work on which to write, you too can build on a personal response. In the best of cases, your motivation to write will be personal but your expression of ideas *in your essay* will be public and controlled. All of the opening examples amply demonstrate this double quality: in each essay you find someone writing for personal reasons, yet maintaining strict control over important elements of public expression—including the essay's reasoning, structure, sentence rhythm, and word choice.

To prepare for your essay of interpretation, select one of the examples that began this chapter, one that you find especially effective. Think critically about how this essay succeeds. You might respond to the questions following the piece; you might try writing a paragraph explaining what appeals to you most about the piece; you might reflect on the ways in which this essay could affect your own work. Once you have studied the piece and have a clear sense of how it succeeds, choose a poem or short story about which to write.

The Occasions sections of this chapter offer you several opportunities: Robert Frost's poem "Out, Out—," accompanied by interpretive responses; James Joyce's "Counterparts"; Kate Chopin's "A Shameful Affair"; and selected poems and essays by Langston Hughes. Of course, you may choose to write on some other work(s) of literature. Still, you can turn in this chapter to pages 398–402 for detailed guidance on how you might approach and organize an interpretive essay.

A note on using sources: All of writers whose essays began the chapter draw heavily on the literary works they are interpreting. You should do the same, with the caution that writers who use sources should never let source materials overtake their essays. The psychological focus of your essay should remain yours alone. In writing a first draft, be sure that your voice predominates and that sources, even if essential to your essay's success, play a subordinate role.

I. Debating the Meaning of a Poem

One of the assumptions underlying this chapter is that when we speak of interpreting a poem, story, play, or novel, we must speak in the plural—of interpretations. This assumption is based on the belief that interpretations are more or less convincing, not right or wrong. The selections that follow—multiple interpretations of a poem by Robert Frost—demonstrate this assumption at work. First, read the poem and form your own opinions about it.

"Out, Out—"

The buzz-saw snarled and rattled in the yard
And made dust and dropped stove-length sticks of wood,
Sweet-scented stuff when the breeze drew across it.
And from there those that lifted eyes could count
Five mountain ranges one behind the other   5
Under the sunset far into Vermont.
And the saw snarled and rattled, snarled and rattled,
As it ran light, or had to bear a load.
And nothing happened: day was all but done.
Call it a day, I wish they might have said   10
To please the boy by giving him the half hour
That a boy counts so much when saved from work.
His sister stood beside them in her apron
To tell them "Supper." At the word, the saw,
As if to prove saws knew what supper meant,   15
Leaped out at the boy's hand, or seemed to leap—
He must have given the hand. However it was,
Neither refused the meeting. But the hand!
The boy's first outcry was a rueful laugh,
As he swung toward them holding up the hand   20
Half in appeal, but half as if to keep
The life from spilling. Then the boy saw all—
Since he was old enough to know, big boy
Doing a man's work, though a child at heart—
He saw all spoiled "Don't let him cut my hand off—   25
The doctor, when he comes. Don't let him, sister!"
So. But the hand was gone already.
The doctor put him in the dark of ether.
He lay and puffed his lips out with his breath.
And then—the watcher at his pulse took fright.   30
No one believed. They listened at his heart.
Little—less—nothing!—and that ended it.
No more to build on there. And they, since they
Were not the one dead, turned to their affairs.

A debate concerning this poem began in 1956 when Laurence Perrine, in *Sound and Sense* (his introduction to poetry), argued that the poem's "theme is the uncertainty and unpredictability of life." Eleven years later, Weldon Thornton, a professor of literature at the University of North

Carolina, suggested that Perrine "implied a mistaken interpretation of the poem." A challenge was made and, over the years, a debate ensued.

This is no large debate, certainly, confined as it is to a single poem (and not one of Frost's better-known ones at that). Still, the selections you find here do represent how readers of literature make claims and counterclaims about literary texts. You are about to observe—and, if you choose, enter into—a debate. Arguing for interpretations is what your professors do as writers, and this is what they will ask of you in their courses: that you read a literary text with care, infer a pattern of meaning, make a claim about that pattern, and then argue in support of the claim by pointing repeatedly to specific lines in the text. You have already seen four essay-length examples of argument-making about literary texts in this chapter (the three essays that began the chapter, and the essay concerning Langston Hughes). In the chapter's "Structures and Strategies" section, you also saw specific techniques for constructing arguments in support of interpretive claims. What you have not yet seen is an extended debate on a *single* text. The points of view that follow invite you, as a critical reader of Frost's poem, to formulate your own understanding. You will be asked to do exactly this in the questions that follow these selections. You have two tasks in reading these materials. First read the selections with care. Working by yourself, do the following:

- Find a pattern of meaning in Frost's "Out, Out—" and make an interpretive claim.
- Support this claim with references to specific lines of the poem. Be prepared to explain to group members how these lines form a pattern of meaning.
- Read and respond to each of the professionally written interpretations of the poem. Which of these do you find most convincing? Be prepared to defend your choice to group members.

Then, work in small groups, comparing your evaluations of the professional pieces and exchanging your own interpretations of Frost's poem. Debate among yourselves which of the student interpretations is most convincing.

Laurence Perrine (1956)

Robert Frost in "Out, Out—" makes his meaning entirely clear even for the reader who does not recognize the allusion contained in his title. His theme is the uncertainty and unpredictability of life, which may be accidentally ended at any moment, and the tragic waste of human potentiality which takes place when such premature deaths occur. A boy who is already "doing a man's work" and gives every promise of having a useful life ahead of him is suddenly wiped out. There seems no rational explanation for either the accident or the death. The only comment to be made is, "No more to build on there." 1

Frost's title, however, is an allusion to one of the most famous passages in all English literature, and it offers a good illustration of how a poet may use allu- 2 sion not only to reinforce emotion but also to help define his theme. The passage is that in *Macbeth* in which Macbeth has just been informed of his wife's death. A good many readers will recall the key phrase. "Out, out, brief candle!" with its underscoring of the tragic brevity and uncertainty of life that can be snuffed out at any moment. For some readers, however, the allusion will summon up the whole passage in act V, scene 5, in which this phrase occurs. Macbeth's words are:

> She should have died hereafter;
> There would have been a time for such a word.
> To-morrow, and to-morrow, and to-morrow
> Creeps in this petty pace from day to day
> To the last syllable of recorded time;   5
> And all our yesterdays have lighted fools
> The way to dusty death. Out, out, brief candle!
> Life's but a walking shadow, a poor player,
> That struts and frets his hour upon the stage
> And then is heard no more. It is a tale   10
> Told by an idiot, full of sound and fury,
> Signifying nothing.

Macbeth's first words underscore the theme of premature death. The boy also "should have died hereafter." The rest of the passage, with its marvelous evocation of the vanity and meaninglessness of life, expresses neither Shakespeare's philosophy nor, ultimately, Frost's, but it is Macbeth's philosophy at the time of his bereavement, and it is likely to express the feelings of us all when such tragic accidents occur. Life does indeed seem cruel and meaningless, a tale told by an idiot, signifying nothing, when human life and potentiality are thus without explanation so suddenly ended.

John F. Lynen (1960)

Even when [Frost] seems most determined to do no more than describe a scene   1
or episode, his imagery has a significance which extends outward to range upon range of meaning. In " 'Out, Out—,' " for example, he tells the story of how a boy loses his hand by accident while cutting wood at a buzz saw and dies only a few hours after. The effect of pathos is so intense that one may at first suppose that this constitutes the poem's main value. But sad events do not in themselves create moving poetry. Though Frost may seem only to describe, actually he has so managed his description that the boy's story symbolizes realities present everywhere in the human situation. The key to the poem's meaning is to be found in the fact that the loss of the hand causes almost immediate death:

> But the hand!
> The boy's first outcry was a rueful laugh,
> As he swung toward them holding up the hand
> Half in appeal, but half as if to keep
> The life from spilling. Then the boy saw all—
> Since he was old enough to know, big boy
> Doing a man's work, though a child at heart—
> He saw all spoiled.

Ordinarily an accident of this sort would not be mortal, especially when, as in this case, modern medical attention is within reach. "The doctor put him in the dark of ether," and there is no *physical* reason why he should not have recovered. His death is caused, rather, by his recognition of what the loss of a hand signifies in terms of his life: "the boy saw all— . . . He saw all spoiled." At the end

> They listened at his heart.
> Little—less—nothing!—and that ended it.
> No more to build on there.

The "all" that the boy sees is the complete and irretrievable ruin of his life. Any merely medical explanation of his death is irrelevant. He does not die of shock or a too intense sorrow but of his realization of the truth. It cannot be a matter of enduring great pain for a time or of learning to get along as a cripple. There is no choice; he *must* die, and the reader will understand the poem to the extent that he sees why this is so.

All is spoiled because of the very nature of the world in which the boy lives. 2 The long opening description has the important function of defining this world. It is, of course, the rural world, the scene of the accident being the farmyard where the boy, along with others, is cutting firewood. Frost pictures the setting as a sort of rustic amphitheatre with the snarling saw at its center and, extending away in the distance,

> Five mountain ranges one behind the other
> Under the sunset far into Vermont.

One should also note that the boy is working, not just playing at work as children elsewhere might, and that the work is expected of him. This emphasizes the fact that in his world a man's livelihood, even at an early age, depends upon hard physical labor. For him, then, the loss of the hand means not only a painful abnormality, but perhaps even the loss of his ability to survive.

Weldon Thornton (1967)

Robert Frost's " 'Out, Out—' " has been included in several poetry textbooks 1 with comments or questions which imply what seems to me a mistaken interpretation of the poem. Most of the editorial comments suggest that the themes of the poem are the uncertainty and unpredictability of life and regret at the apparently meaningless death of the young boy. For example, Laurence Perrine includes the poem in his *Sound and Sense: An Introduction to Poetry,* and says that its "theme is the uncertainty and unpredictability of life, which may be accidentally ended at any moment, and the tragic waste of human potentiality which takes place when such premature deaths occur. A boy who is already 'doing a man's work' and gives every promise of having a useful life ahead of him is suddenly wiped out. There seems no rational explanation for either the accident or the death. The only comment to be made is, 'No more to build on there' " (2nd ed., New York, 1963, p. 115). Also, in their *Understanding Poetry,* Cleanth Brooks and Robert Penn Warren say that in this poem Frost "felt in the fatal accident to an obscure farm boy the pathos and horror of the unreasonable and unpredictable end that at any moment may come to life" (3rd ed., New York, 1960, p. 28).

But scrutiny of the poem reveals several details not explained by this inter- 2 pretation, and suggests a psychological complexity which it misses. As we look into the poem, we realize that the young boy is deftly characterized and that his accident is not entirely accidental. The poem reveals a psychological drama played out between the boy and his family. The climax of this drama is the boy's moving his hand into the saw, in an inarticulate and self-destructive protest against the insensitivity of the family which wishes to hurry him into the responsibilities of adulthood.

Frost suggests the boy's dissatisfaction as early as line 5 when he says, "And 3 from there those that lifted eyes could count / Five mountain ranges one behind the other. Under the sunset far into Vermont." The distinction implicit in "Those that lifted eyes" focuses the important difference between the boy and his parents. He, being young, and feeling restrained by the work, cannot keep his eyes and thoughts off the mountains; the father, an adult, finds nothing in the mountains to tempt him from his work. Frost makes this even clearer when he says, "Call it a day, I wish they might have said / To please the boy by giving him the half hour / That a boy counts so much when saved from work." But the father is not aware of this. A few lines later Frost again points toward the essential fact about the boy when he describes him as a "big boy / Doing a man's work, though a child at heart."

From such hints as these, we can reconstruct the boy's thoughts and feel- 4 ings leading up to his accident. All day the boy has been at work, and all day the feeling has been growing within him that he is held captive by the work and by the parents who keep him at it. He feels that he is being kept from things he wants to do, that life is being stolen from him. His sister's call to supper provides just the break in the continuity of the day's work which permits the boy's subconscious impulse to act on the dissatisfaction it has been harboring: he moves his hand toward the saw. That this is what the boy does should be clear from the way Frost describes it, when he says the saw

> As if to prove saws knew what supper meant,
> Leaped out at the boy's hand, or seemed to leap—
> He must have given the hand. However it was,
> Neither refused the meeting.

In this undeniably realistic poem, the personification of the saw most reasonably implies what the other lines say, that the boy gave the hand. Not that the boy intended to kill himself; what he rather wanted was not death but harm, some basis for saying "Look what you have done to me, have made me do to myself." And this view is supported by the boy's next action: "The boy's first outcry was a rueful laugh, / As he swung toward them holding up the hand / Half in appeal, but half as if to keep / The life from spilling." Only half of the boy's thought is on saving his life; with the other half he holds toward them "in appeal" the emblem of the life they have deprived him of.

When the boy cries to have the already severed hand saved, his cry is not 5 to his parents but to his sister, since he feels that she, also called into labor and responsibility too soon, will understand him better than they. But of course it is too late, and the boy dies. The point of his death, however, is not the inscrutability of fate and the tenuousness of human existence. Rather it is the waste of life brought on by the well-meaning but insensitive parents' rushing the boy out of childhood into adulthood.

Individual Response: Debating the Meaning of Frost's "Out, Out—"

1. Find a pattern of meaning in "Out, Out" and make an interpretive claim. Write that claim on a sheet of paper.

2. Identify the different parts of your claim. (See the example of Sarika Chandra's quizzing her claim—or thesis—and identifying parts of an essay.)

3. Support the parts of your claim with references to specific lines in the poem. Be prepared to explain to group members how these lines, considered together, form a pattern of meaning.

4. Write a brief response to the three interpretations of the poem, and decide which one you think is most convincing. Be prepared to defend your choice to group members.

5. In one or two paragraphs, respond to the question: What key issues in the poem are being debated by Perrine, Lynen, and Thornton?

6. How does your interpretation of "Out, Out—" stand in relation to those of the professionals? Do you feel your interpretation is as authoritative as theirs? Explain.

Group Response: Debating the Meaning of Frost's "Out, Out—"

1. Verbally exchange your interpretation of "Out, Out—" with group members. Present your pattern of meaning and have group members respond. Group members should explain why they do or do not find your interpretation convincing.

2. As a group, explain what you think are the key issues being debated by Perrine, Lynen, and Thornton. To what extent has your group raised these same issues in question 1, above?

3. As a group, review your individual reactions to the three professional critics. Can the group reach any consensus on which writer is the most convincing? In a class-wide discussion, the group should be able to defend its choice.

4. As a group, reflect on the way in which you have conducted your discussion of one another's interpretations of Frost's poem. Compare your discussions of "Out, Out—" with the way in which Perrine, Lynen, and Thornton have conducted their discussions. What similarities and differences do you observe?

Projecting an Essay: Debating the Meaning of Frost's "Out, Out—"

1. The group should select one student interpretation of "Out, Out—" and plan to sketch an interpretive essay, following the suggestions set out in the Structures and Strategies section of this chapter.

2. State the interpretive claim as a sentence. Each group member should take this sentence, quiz it to define its (and the essay's likely) component parts, and then reread the poem, searching for lines that might support the interpretation.

3. As a group, consider everyone's suggestions for supporting the interpretive claim, and select those lines of the poem that offer the most convincing support.

4. Sketch an essay. As a group, write a one-paragraph summary of the poem—for the most part, in the present tense. Compare your summary with those of other groups, and refine it. In each section of your proposed essay, plan to discuss specific lines of the poem.

5. As a group, write out one section of the essay, making sure to complete a full cycle of development of claim, reference to the text, and comment.

6. Option: Write a draft of the essay, based on your group's outline.

II. The Work of James Joyce, Kate Chopin, and Langston Hughes

This Occasions section presents you with opportunities to practice skills discussed earlier and demonstrated in the previous selections. James Joyce's "Counterparts," you may recall, is the subject of Sarika Chandra's essay (pages 347–350); Kate Chopin's "A Shameful Affair" is the subject of Martin Simpson's interpretive essay (pages 345–346); and selected poems by Langston Hughes, along with related autobiographical and secondary sources, are the sources used by Onwuchekwa Jemie (pages 367–370). These selections appear in this section both as a reference for your reading of these essays and as an occasion for you to write interpretive essays yourself.

Your Writing Assignment

Select a story, poem, or set of poems (and in the case of Hughes, related materials) as the subject of an interpretive essay. Your goal is to read, to discover a pattern of meaning, and then to present this pattern to readers by referring to specific lines of the text. You should be conscious throughout of using full cycles of claim, reference, and comment, as discussed in the Structures and Strategies section of this chapter.

"Counterparts"

James Joyce

James Joyce (1882–1941), a giant of Irish literature and arguably the most influential twentieth-century writer in English, was born in Dublin and educated in Jesuit schools. On graduation from University College in 1902, Joyce moved to Europe and visited his homeland intermittently. His works include a collection of stories, Dubliners *(1914), in which "Counterparts" appears; his first novel, A*

Portrait of the Artist as a Young Man *(1916); and the novels* Ulysses *(1922) and* Finnegan's Wake *(1939).*

The bell rang furiously and, when Miss Parker went to the tube, a furious voice 1
called out in a piercing North of Ireland accent:

—Send Farrington here! 2

Miss Parker returned to her machine, saying to a man who was writing at 3
a desk:

—Mr. Alleyne wants you upstairs. 4

The man muttered *Blast him!* under his breath and pushed back his chair 5
to stand up. When he stood up he was tall and of great bulk. He had a hanging face, dark wine-coloured, with fair eyebrows and moustache: his eyes bulged
forward slightly and the whites of them were dirty. He lifted up the counter and,
passing by the clients, went out of the office with a heavy step.

He went heavily upstairs until he came to the second landing, where a door 6
bore a brass plate with the inscription *Mr. Alleyne.* Here he halted, puffing with
labour and vexation, and knocked. The shrill voice cried:

—Come in! 7

The man entered Mr. Alleyne's room. Simultaneously Mr. Alleyne, a little 8
man wearing gold-rimmed glasses on a clean-shaven face, shot his head up over
a pile of documents. The head itself was so pink and hairless that it seemed like
a large egg reposing on the papers. Mr. Alleyne did not lose a moment:

—Farrington? What is the meaning of this? Why have I always to complain 9
of you? May I ask you why you haven't made a copy of that contract between
Bodley and Kirwan? I told you it must be ready by four o'clock.

—But Mr. Shelley said, sir— 10

—*Mr. Shelley said, sir.* . . . Kindly attend to what I say and not to what *Mr.* 11
Shelley says, sir. You have always some excuse or another for shirking work.
Let me tell you that if the contract is not copied before this evening I'll lay the
matter before Mr. Crosbie. . . . Do you hear me now?

—Yes, sir. 12

—Do you hear me now? . . . Ay and another little matter! I might as well 13
be talking to the wall as talking to you. Understand once for all that you get a
half an hour for your lunch and not an hour and a half. How many courses do
you want, I'd like to know. . . . Do you mind me now?

—Yes, sir. 14

Mr. Alleyne bent his head again upon his pile of papers. The man stared 15
fixedly at the polished skull which directed the affairs of Crosbie & Alleyne,
gauging its fragility. A spasm of rage gripped his throat for a few moments and
then passed, leaving after it a sharp sensation of thirst. The man recognised the
sensation and felt that he must have a good night's drinking. The middle of the
month was passed and, if he could get the copy done in time, Mr. Alleyne might
give him an order on the cashier. He stood still, gazing fixedly at the head upon
the pile of papers. Suddenly Mr. Alleyne began to upset all the papers, searching for something. Then, as if he had been unaware of the man's presence till
that moment, he shot up his head again, saying:

—Eh? Are you going to stand there all day? Upon my word, Farrington, 16
you take things easy!

—I was waiting to see . . . 17

—Very good, you needn't wait to see. Go downstairs and do your work. 18

The man walked heavily towards the door and, as he went out of the room, 19 he heard Mr. Alleyne cry after him that if the contract was not copied by evening Mr. Crosbie would hear of the matter.

He returned to his desk in the lower office and counted the sheets which 20 remained to be copied. He took up his pen and dipped it in the ink but he continued to stare stupidly at the last words he had written: *In no case shall the said Bernard Bodley be* . . . The evening was falling and in a few minutes they would be lighting the gas: then he could write. He felt that he must slake the thirst in his throat. He stood up from his desk and, lifting the counter as before, he passed out of the office. As he was passing out the chief clerk looked at him inquiringly.

—It's all right, Mr. Shelley, said the man, pointing with his finger to indi- 21 cate the objective of his journey.

The chief clerk glanced at the hat-rack but, seeing the row complete, 22 offered no remark. As soon as he was on the landing the man pulled a shepherd's plaid cap out of his pocket put it on his head and ran quickly down the rickety stairs. From the street door he walked on furtively on the inner side of the path towards the corner and all at once dived into a doorway. He was now safe in the dark snug of O'Neill's shop, and filling up the little window that looked into the bar with his inflamed face, the colour of dark wine or dark meat, he called out:

—Here, Pat, give us a g.p., like a good fellow. 23

The curate brought him a glass of plain porter. The man drank it at a gulp 24 and asked for a caraway seed. He put his penny on the counter and, leaving the curate to grope for it in the gloom, retreated out of the snug as furtively as he had entered it.

Darkness, accompanied by a thick fog, was gaining upon the dusk February 25 and the lamps in Eustace Street had been lit. The man went up by the houses until he reached the door of the office, wondering whether he could finish his copy in time. On the stairs a moist pungent odour of perfumes saluted his nose: evidently Miss Delacour had come while he was out in O'Neill's. He crammed his cap back again into his pocket and re-entered the office, assuming an air of absent-mindedness.

—Mr. Alleyne has been calling for you, said the chief clerk severely. Where 26 were you?

The man glanced at the two clients who were standing at the counter as if 27 to intimate that their presence prevented him from answering. As the clients were both male the chief clerk allowed himself a laugh.

—I know that game, he said. Five times in one day is a little bit. . . . Well, 28 you better look sharp and get a copy of our correspondence in the Delacour case for Mr. Alleyne.

This address in the presence of the public, his run upstairs and the porter 29 he had gulped down so hastily confused the man and, as he sat down at his desk to get what was required, he realised how hopeless was the task of finishing his copy of the contract before half past five. The dark damp night was coming and he longed to spend it in the bars, drinking with his friends amid the glare of gas and the clatter of glasses. He got out the Delacour correspondence and passed out of the office. He hoped Mr. Alleyne would not discover that the last two letters were missing.

The moist pungent perfume lay all the way up to Mr. Alleyne's room. Miss 30 Delacour was a middle-aged woman of Jewish appearance. Mr. Alleyne was said to be sweet on her or on her money. She came to the office often and stayed a long time when she came. She was sitting beside his desk now in an aroma of perfumes, smoothing the handle of her umbrella and nodding the great black feather in her hat. Mr. Alleyne had swivelled his chair round to face her and thrown his right foot jauntily upon his left knee. The man put the correspondence on the desk and bowed respectfully but neither Mr. Alleyne nor Miss Delacour took any notice of his bow. Mr. Alleyne tapped a finger on the correspondence and then flicked it towards him as if to say: *That's all right: you can go.*

The man returned to the lower office and sat down again at his desk. He   31 stared intently at the incomplete phrase: *In no case shall the said Bernard Bodley be . . .* and thought how strange it was that the last three words began with the same letter. The chief clerk began to hurry Miss Parker, saying she would never have the letters typed in time for post. The man listened to the clicking of the machine for a few minutes and then set to work to finish his copy. But his head was not clear and his mind wandered away to the glare and rattle of the public-house. It was a night for hot punches. He struggled on with his copy, but when the clock struck five he had still fourteen pages to write. Blast it! He couldn't finish it in time. He longed to execrate aloud, to bring his fist down on something violently. He was so enraged that he wrote *Bernard Bernard* instead of *Bernard Bodley* and had to begin again on a clean sheet.

He felt strong enough to clear out the whole office single-handed. His body   32 ached to do something, to rush out and revel in violence. All the indignities of his life enraged him. . . . Could he ask the cashier privately for an advance? No, the cashier was no good, no damn good: he wouldn't give an advance. . . . He knew where he would meet the boys: Leonard and O'Halloran and Nosey Flynn. The barometer of his emotional nature was set for a spell of riot.

His imagination had so abstracted him that his name was called twice before   33 he answered. Mr. Alleyne and Miss Delacour were standing outside the counter and all the clerks had turned round in anticipation of something. The man got up from his desk. Mr. Alleyne began a tirade of abuse, saying that two letters were missing. The man answered that he knew nothing about them, that he had made a faithful copy. The tirade continued: it was so bitter and violent that the man could hardly restrain his fist from descending upon the head of the manikin before him.

—I know nothing about any other two letters, he said stupidly.   34

—*You—know—nothing.* Of course you know nothing, said Mr. Alleyne.   35 Tell me, he added, glancing first for approval to the lady beside him, do you take me for a fool? Do you think me an utter fool?

The man glanced from the lady's face to the little egg-shaped head and back   36 again; and almost before he was aware of it, his tongue had found a felicitous moment:

—I don't think, sir, he said, that that's a fair question to put to me.   37

There was a pause in the very breathing of the clerks. Everyone was   38 astounded (the author of witticism no less than his neighbours) and Miss Delacour, who was a stout amiable person, began to smile broadly. Mr. Alleyne flushed to the hue of a wild rose and his mouth twitched with a dwarf's passion. He shook his fist in the man's face till it seemed to vibrate like the knob of some electric machine:

—You impertinent ruffian! You impertinent ruffian! I'll make short work of   39 you! Wait till you see! You'll apologise to me for your impertinence or you'll quit the office instanter! You'll quit this, I'm telling you, or you'll apologise to me!

He stood in a doorway opposite the office watching to see if the cashier 40
would come out alone. All the clerks passed out and finally the cashier came out
with the chief clerk. It was no use trying to say a word to him when he was with
the chief clerk. The man felt that his position was bad enough. He had been
obliged to offer an abject apology to Mr. Alleyne for his impertinence but he
knew what a hornet's nest the office would be for him. He could remember the
way in which Mr. Alleyne had hounded little Peake out of the office in order to
make room for his own nephew. He felt savage and thirsty and revengeful,
annoyed with himself and with everyone else. Mr. Alleyne would never give him
an hour's rest; his life would be a hell to him. He had made a proper fool of
himself this time. Could he not keep his tongue in his cheek? But they had never
pulled together from the first, he and Mr. Alleyne, ever since the day Mr. Alleyne
had overheard him mimicking his North of Ireland accent to amuse Higgins and
Miss Parker: that had been the beginning of it. He might have tried Higgins for
the money, but sure Higgins never had anything for himself. A man with two
establishments to keep up, of course he couldn't. . . .

He felt his great body again aching for the comfort of the public-house. The 41
fog had begun to chill him and he wondered could he touch Pat in O'Neill's. He
could not touch him for more than a bob—and a bob was no use. Yet he must
get money somewhere or other: he had spent his last penny for the g.p. and
soon it would be too late for getting money anywhere. Suddenly, as he was fin-
gering his watch-chain, he thought of Terry Kelly's pawn-office in Fleet Street.
That was the dart! Why didn't he think of it sooner?

He went through the narrow alley of Temple Bar quickly, muttering to him- 42
self that they could all go to hell because he was going to have a good night of
it. The clerk in Terry Kelly's said *A crown!* but the consignor held out for six
shillings; and in the end the six shillings was allowed him literally. He came out
of the pawn-office joyfully, making a little cylinder of the coins between his
thumb and fingers. In Westmoreland Street the footpaths were crowded with
young men and women returning from business and ragged urchins ran here
and there yelling out the names of the evening editions. The man passed
through the crowd, looking on the spectacle generally with proud satisfaction
and staring masterfully at the office-girls. His head was full of the noises of tram-
gongs and swishing trolleys and his nose already sniffed the curling fumes of
punch. As he walked on he preconsidered the terms in which he would narrate
the incident to the boys:

—So, I just looked at him—coolly, you know, and looked at her. Then I 43
looked back at him again—taking my time, you know. *I don't think that that's
a fair question to put to me,* says I.

Nosey Flynn was sitting up in his usual corner of Davy Byrne's and, when 44
he heard the story, he stood Farrington a half-one, saying it was as smart a thing
as ever he heard. Farrington stood a drink in his turn. After a while O'Halloran
and Paddy Leonard came in and the story was repeated to them. O'Halloran
stood tailors of malt, hot, all round and told the story of the retort he had made
to the chief clerk when he was in Callan's of Fownes's Street; but, as the retort
was after the manner of the liberal shepherds in the eclogues, he had to admit
that it was not so clever as Farrington's retort. At this Farrington told the boys
to polish off that and have another.

Just as they were naming their poisons who should come in but Higgins! 45
Of course he had to join in with the others. The men asked him to give his version of it, and he did so with great vivacity for the sight of five small hot whiskies

was very exhilarating. Everyone roared laughing when he showed the way in which Mr. Alleyne shook his fist in Farrington's face. Then he imitated Farrington, saying *And here was my nabs, as cool as you please,* while Farrington looked at the company out of his heavy dirty eyes, smiling and at times drawing forth stray drops of liquor from his moustache with the aid of his lower lip.

When that round was over there was a pause. O'Halloran had money but 46 neither of the other two seemed to have any; so the whole party left the shop somewhat regretfully. At the corner of Duke Street Higgins and Nosey Flynn bevelled off to the left while the other three turned back towards the city. Rain was drizzling down on the cold streets and, when they reached the Ballast Office, Farrington suggested the Scotch House. The bar was full of men and loud with the noise of tongues and glasses. The three men pushed past the whining match-sellers at the door and formed a little party at the corner of the counter. They began to exchange stories. Leonard introduced them to a young fellow named Weathers who was performing at the Tivoli as an acrobat and knock-about *artiste*. Farrington stood a drink all round. Weathers said he would take a small Irish and Apollinaris. Farrington, who had definite notions of what was what, asked the boys would they have an Apollinaris too; but the boys told Tim to make theirs hot. The talk became theatrical. O'Halloran stood a round and then Farrington stood another round, Weathers protesting that the hospitality was too Irish. He promised to get them in behind the scenes and introduce them to some nice girls. O'Halloran said that he and Leonard would go but that Farrington wouldn't go because he was a married man; and Farrington's heavy dirty eyes leered at the company in token that he understood he was being chaffed. Weathers made them all have just one little tincture at his expense and promised to meet them later on at Mulligan's in Poolbeg Street.

When the Scotch House closed they went round to Mulligan's. They went 47 into the parlour at the back and O'Halloran ordered small hot specials all round. They were all beginning to feel mellow. Farrington was just standing another round when Weathers came back. Much to Farrington's relief he drank a glass of bitter this time. Funds were running low but they had enough to keep them going. Presently two young women with big hats and a young man in a check suit came in and sat at a table close by. Weathers saluted them and told the company that they were out of the Tivoli. Farrington's eyes wandered at every moment in the direction of one of the young women. There was something striking in her appearance. An immense scarf of peacock-blue muslin was wound round her hat and knotted in a great bow under her chin; and she wore bright yellow gloves reaching to the elbow. Farrington gazed admiringly at the plump arm which she moved very often and with much grace; and when, after a little time, she answered his gaze he admired still more her large dark brown eyes. The oblique staring expressing in them fascinated him. She glanced at him once or twice and, when the party was leaving the room, she brushed against his chair and said *O, pardon!* in a London accent. He watched her leave the room in the hope that she would look back at him, but he was disappointed. He cursed his want of money and cursed all the rounds he had stood to Weathers. If there was one thing that he hated it was a sponge. He was so angry that he lost count of the conversation of his friends.

When Paddy Leonard called him he found that they were talking about feats 48 of strength. Weathers was showing his biceps muscle to the company and boasting so much that the other two had called on Farrington to uphold the national honour. Farrington pulled up his sleeve accordingly and showed his biceps muscle to the company. The two arms were examined and compared and finally it was agreed to have a trial of strength. The table was cleared and the two men rested their elbows on it, clasping hands. When Paddy Leonard said *Go!* each was to try to bring down the other's hand on to the table. Farrington looked very serious and determined.

The trial began. After about thirty seconds Weathers brought his oppo- 49 nent's hand slowly down on to the table. Farrington's dark wine-coloured face flushed darker still with anger and humiliation at having been defeated by such a stripling.

—You're not to put the weight of your body behind it. Play fair, he said.   50

—Who's not playing fair? said the other.   51

—Come on again. The two best out of three.   52

The trial began again. The veins stood out on Farrington's forehead, and 53 the pallor of Weathers' complexion changed to peony. Their hands and arms trembled under the stress. After a long struggle Weathers again brought his opponent's hand slowly on to the table. There was a murmur of applause from the spectators. The curate, who was standing beside the table, nodded his red head towards the victor and said with loutish familiarity:

—Ah! that's the knack!   54

—What the hell do you know about it? said Farrington firecely, turning on 55 the man. What do you put in your gab for?

—Sh, sh! said O'Halloran, observing the violent expression on Farrington's 56 face. Pony up, boys. We'll have just one little smahan more and then we'll be off.

A very sullen-faced man stood at the corner of O'Connell Bridge waiting 57 for the little Sandymount tram to take him home. He was full of smouldering anger and revengefulness. He felt humiliated and discontented; he did not even feel drunk; and he had only twopence in his pocket. He cursed everything. He had done for himself in the office, pawned his watch, spent all his money; and he had not even got drunk. He began to feel thirsty again and he longed to be back again in the hot reeking public-house. He had lost his reputation as a strong man, having been defeated twice by a mere boy. His heart swelled with fury and, when he thought of the woman in the big hat who had brushed against him and *Pardon!* his fury nearly choked him.

His tram let him down at Shelbourne Road and he steered his great body 58 along in the shadow of the wall of the barracks. He loathed returning to his home. When he went in by the side-door he found the kitchen empty and the kitchen fire nearly out. He bawled upstairs:

—Ada! Ada!   59

His wife was a little sharp-faced woman who bullied her husband when he 60 was sober and was bullied by him when he was drunk. They had five children. A little boy came running down the stairs.

—Who is that? said the man peering through the darkness.   61

—Me, pa.   62

—Who are you? Charlie?   63

—No, pa. Tom.   64

—Where's your mother?   65

—She's out at the chapel.   66

—That's right . . . Did she think of leaving any dinner for me?   67

—Yes, pa. I—   68

—Light the lamp. What do you mean by having the place in darkness? Are 69
the other children in bed?

The man sat down heavily on one of the chairs while the little boy lit the 70
lamp. He began to mimic his son's flat accent, saying half to himself: *At the
chapel. At the chapel, if you please!* When the lamp was lit he banged his fist
on the table and shouted:

—What's for my dinner? 71

—I'm going . . . to cook it, pa, said the little boy. 72

The man jumped up furiously and pointed to the fire. 73

—On that fire! You let the fire out! By God, I'll teach you to do that again! 74

He took a step to the door and seized the walking-stick which was stand- 75
ing behind it.

—I'll teach you to let the fire out! he said, rolling up his sleeve in order to 76
give his arm free play.

The little boy cried *O, pa!* and ran whimpering round the table, but the man 77
followed him and caught him by the coat. The little boy looked about him wildly but, seeing no way of escape, fell upon his knees.

—Now, you'll let the fire out the next time! said the man, striking at him 78
viciously with the stick. Take that, you little whelp!

The boy uttered a squeal of pain as the stick cut his thigh. He clasped his 79
hands together in the air and his voice shook with fright.

—O, pa! he cried. Don't beat me, pa! And I'll . . . I'll say a *Hail Mary* for 80
you . . . I'll say a *Hail Mary* for you, pa, if you don't beat me . . . I'll say a *Hail
Mary*. . . .

"A Shameful Affair"

Kate Chopin

*Kate Chopin (1851–1904) is a much-admired nineteenth-century American
writer known widely for her novel* The Awakening *(1899) and for two collections
of short stories,* Bayou Folk *(1894) and* A Night in Arcadie *(1987). Chopin began
her career as a published writer when she was thirty-eight years old, after her
husband died and she was left to care for six children.*

Mildred Orme, seated in the snuggest corner of the big front porch of the 1
Kraummer farmhouse, was as content as a girl need hope to be.

This was no such farm as one reads about in humorous fiction. Here were 2
swelling acres where the undulating wheat gleamed in the sun like a golden sea.
For silver there was the Meramec—or, better, it was pure crystal, for here and
there one might look clean through it down to where the pebbles lay like green
and yellow gems. Along the river's edge trees were growing to the very water,
and in it, sweeping it when they were willows.

The house itself was big and broad, as country houses should be. The mas- 3
ter was big and broad, too. The mistress was small and thin, and it was always
she who went out at noon to pull the great clanging bell that called the
farmhands in to dinner.

From her agreeable corner where she lounged with her Browning or her 4
Ibsen, Mildred watched the woman do this every day. Yet when the clumsy
farmhands all came tramping up the steps and crossed the porch in going to
their meal that was served within, she never looked at them. Why should she?

Farmhands are not so very nice to look at, and she was nothing of an anthro-polgist. But once when the half dozen men came along, a paper which she had laid carelessly upon the railing was blown across their path. One of them picked it up, and when he had mounted the steps restored it to her. He was young, and brown, of course, as the sun had made him. He had nice blue eyes. His fair hair was dishevelled. His shoulders were broad and square and his limbs strong and clean. A not unpicturesque figure in the rough attire that bared his throat to view and gave perfect freedom to his every motion.

Mildred did not make these several observations in the half second that [5] she looked at him in courteous acknowledgment. It took her as many days to note them all. For she singled him out each time that he passed her, meaning to give him a condescending little smile, as she knew how. But he never looked at her. To be sure, clever young women of twenty who are hand-some, besides, who have refused their half dozen offers and are settling down to the conviction that life is a tedious affair, are not going to care a straw whether farmhands look at them or not. And Mildred did not care, and the thing would not have occupied her a moment if Satan had not intervened, in offering the employment which natural conditions had failed to supply. It was summer time; she was idle; she was piqued, and that was the beginning of the shameful affair.

"Who are these men, Mrs. Kraummer, that work for you? Where do you [6] pick them up?"

"Oh, ve picks 'em up everywhere. Some is neighbors, some is tramps, and [7] so."

"And that broad-shouldered young fellow—is he a neighbor? The one who [8] handed me my paper the other day—you remember?"

"Gott, no! you might yust as well say he was a tramp. Abet he vorks like a [9] steam ingine."

"Well, he's an extremely disagreeable-looking man. I should think you'd be [10] afraid to have him about, not knowing him."

"Vat you vant to be 'fraid for?" laughed the little woman. "He don't talk no [11] more un ven he vas deef und dumb. I didn't t'ought you vas sooch a baby."

"But, Mrs. Kraummer, I don't want you to think I'm a baby, as you say, a [12] coward, as you mean. Ask the man if he will drive me to church tomorrow. You see, I'm not so very much afraid of him," she added with a smile.

The answer which this unmannerly farmhand returned to Mildred's request [13] was simply a refusal. He could not drive her to church because he was going fishing.

"Aber," offered good Mrs. Kraummer, "Hans Platzfeldt will drive you to [14] church, oder verever you vants. He vas a goot boy vat you can trust, dat Hans."

"Oh, thank him very much. But I find I have so many letters to write tomor- [15] row, and it promises to be hot, too. I shan't care to go to church after all."

She could have cried for vexation. Snubbed by a farmhand! a tramp, per- [16] haps. She, Mildred Orme, who ought really to have been with the rest of the family at Narragansett—who had come to seek in this retired spot the repose that would enable her to follow exalted lines of thought. She marveled at the problematic nature of farmhands.

After sending her the uncivil message already recorded, and as he passed [17] beneath the porch where she sat, he did look at her finally, in a way to make her positively gasp at the sudden effrontery of the man.

But the inexplicable look stayed with her. She could not banish it. [18]

It was not so very hot after all, the next day, when Mildred walked down 19 the long narrow footpath that led through the bending wheat to the river. High above her waist reached the yellow grain. Mildred's brown eyes filled with a reflected golden light as they caught the glint of it, as she heard the trill that it answered to the gentle breeze. Anyone who has walked through the wheat in midsummer-time knows that sound.

In the woods it was sweet and solemn and cool. And there beside the river 20 was the wretch who had annoyed her, first, with his indifference, then with the sudden boldness of his glance.

"Are you fishing?" she asked politely and with kindly dignity, which she 21 supposed would define her position toward him. The inquiry lacked not pertinence, seeing that he sat motionless, with a pole in his hand and his eyes fixed on a cork that bobbed aimlessly on the water.

"Yes, madam," was his brief reply. 22

"It won't disturb you if I stand here a moment, to see what success you will 23 have?"

"No, madam." 24

She stood very still, holding tight to the book she had brought with her. Her 25 straw hat had slipped disreputably to one side, over the wavy bronze-brown bang that half covered her forehead. Her cheeks were ripe with color that the sun had coaxed there; so were her lips.

All the other farmhands had gone forth in Sunday attire. Perhaps this one 26 had none better than these working clothes that he wore. A feminine commiseration swept her at the thought. He spoke never a word. She wondered how many hours he could sit there, so patiently waiting for fish to come to his hook. For her part, the situation began to pall, and she wanted to change it at last.

"Let me try a moment, please? I have an idea." 27

"Yes, madam." 28

"The man is surely an idiot, with his monosyllables," she commented in- 29 wardly. But she remembered that monosyllables belong to a boot's equipment.

She laid her book carefully down and took the pole gingerly that he came 30 to place in her hands. Then it was his turn to stand back and look respectfully and silently on at the absorbing performance.

"Oh!" cried the girl, suddenly, seized with excitement upon seeing the line 31 dragged deep in the water.

"Wait, wait! Not yet." 32

He sprang to her side. With his eyes eagerly fastened on the tense line, he 33 grasped the pole to prevent her drawing it, as her intention seemed to be. That is, he meant to grasp the pole, but instead, his brown hand came down upon Mildred's white one.

He started violently at finding himself so close to a bronze-brown tangle that 34 almost swept his chin—to a hot cheek only a few inches away from his shoulder, to a pair of young, dark eyes that gleamed for an instant unconscious things into his own.

Then, why ever it happened, or how ever it happened, his arms were hold- 35 ing Mildred and he kissed her lips. She did not know if it was ten times or only once.

She looked around—her face milk white—to see him disappear with rapid 36 strides through the path that had brought her there. Then she was alone.

Only the birds had seen, and she could count on their discretion. She was 37 not wildly indignant, as many would have been. Shame stunned her. But through it she gropingly wondered if she should tell the Kraummers that her chaste lips had been rifled of their innocence. Publish her own confusion? No! Once in her room she would give calm thought to the situation, and determine then how to act. The secret must remain her own: a hateful burden to bear alone until she could forget it.

And because she feared not to forget it, Mildred wept that night. All day 38 long a hideous truth had been thrusting itself upon her that made her ask herself if she could be mad. She feared it. Else why was that kiss the most delicious thing she had known in her twenty years of life? The sting of it had never left her lips since it was pressed into them. The sweet trouble of it banished sleep from her pillow.

But Mildred would not bend the outward conditions of her life to serve any 39 shameful whim that chanced to visit her soul, like an ugly dream. She would avoid nothing. She would go and come as always.

In the morning she found in her chair upon the porch the book she had left 40 by the river. A fresh indignity! But she came and went as she intended to, and sat as usual upon the porch amid her familiar surroundings. When the Offender passed her by she knew it, though her eyes were never lifted. Are there only sight and sound to tell such things? She discerned it by a wave that swept her with confusion and she knew not what besides.

She watched him furtively, one day, when he talked with Farmer Kraummer 41 out in the open. When he walked away she remained like one who has drunk much wine. Then unhesitatingly she turned and began her preparations to leave the Kraummer farmhouse.

When the afternoon was far spent they brought letters to her. One of them 42 read like this:

"My Mildred, deary! I am only now at Narragansett, and so broke up not 43 to find you. So you are down at the Kraummer farm, on the Iron Mountains. Well! What do you think of that delicious crank, Fred Evelyn? For a man must be a crank who does such things. Only fancy! Last year he chose to drive an engine back and forth across the plains. This year he tills the soil with laborers. Next year it will be something else as insane—because he likes to live more lives than one kind, and other. Quixotic reasons. We are great chums. He writes me he's grown as strong as an ox. But he hasn't mentioned that you are there. I know you don't get on with him, for he isn't a bit intellectual—detests Ibsen and abuses Tolstoi. He doesn't read 'in books'—says they are spectacles for the shortsighted to look at life through. Don't snub him, dear, or be too hard on him; he has a heart of gold, if he is the first crank in America."

Mildred tried to think—to feel the intelligence which this letter brought to 44 her would take somewhat of the sting from the shame that tortured her. But it did not. She knew that it could not.

In the gathering twilight she walked through the wheat that was heavy and 45 fragrant with dew. The path was very long and very narrow. When she was midway she saw the Offender coming toward her. What could she do? Turn and run, as a little child might? Spring into the wheat, as some frightened four footed creature would? There was nothing but to pass him with the dignity which the occasion clearly demanded.

But he did not let her pass. He stood squarely in the pathway before her, 46 hat in hand, a perturbed look upon his face.

"Miss Orme," he said, "I have wanted to say to you, every hour of the past 47 week, that I am the most consummate hound that walks the earth."

She made no protest. Her whole bearing seemed to indicate that her opin- 48
ion coincided with his own.

"If you have a father, or brother, or any one, in short, to whom you may 49
say such things—"

"I think you aggravate the offense, sir by speaking of it. I shall ask you never 50
to mention it again. I want to forget that it ever happened. Will you kindly let
me by."

"Oh," he ventured eagerly, "you want to forget it! Then, maybe, since you 51
are willing to forget, you will be generous enough to forgive the offender some
day?"

"Some day," she repeated, almost inaudibly, looking seemingly through 52
him, but not at him—"some day—perhaps; when I shall have forgiven myself."

He stood motionless, watching her slim, straight figure lessening by degrees 53
as she walked slowly away from him. He was wondering what she meant. Then
a sudden, quick wave came beating into his brown throat and staining it crim-
som, when he guessed what it might be.

Selected Poems and Essays
Langston Hughes

*Langston Hughes (1902–1967) was a widely read and respected African-
American poet, associated with the Harlem Renaissance and known for collections such as* The Weary Blues *(1926). Hughes was a prolific writer not only of
poetry but of essays, plays, and novels as well as an autobiography,* The Big Sea
(1940).

*The selections that follow are the sources referred to in Onwuchekwa Jemie's
essay "The Jazz Poet," which you will find on pages 367–370. Consider two strategies for reading this material by (and about) Hughes. You might read Jemie's
essay first and then later examine the source materials. Or you might first form
your own opinions about Hughes's poetry and then read Jemie's essay.*

From *Montage of a Dream Deferred*

Note: In terms of current Afro-American popular music and the sources
from which it has progressed—jazz, ragtime, swing, blues, boogie-woogie,
and be-bop—this poem on contemporary Harlem, like be-bop, is marked
by conflicting changes, sudden nuances, sharp and impudent interjections,
broken rhythms, and passages sometimes in the manner of the jam session, sometimes the popular song, punctuated by the riffs, runs, breaks,
and disc-tortions of the music of a community in transition.

L.H.

Dream Boogie

Good morning daddy!
Ain't you heard
The boogie-woogie rumble
Of a dream deferred?

Listen closely:
You'll hear their feet
Beating out and beating out a—

You think
It's a happy beat?

Listen to it closely:
Ain't you heard
something underneath
like a—
        What did I say?

Sure,
I'm happy!
Take it away!
Hey, pop!
Re-bop!
Mop
        Y-e-a-h!

Theme for English B

The instructor said,

    Go home and write
    a page tonight
    And let that page come out of you—
    Then, it will be true.

I wonder if it's that simple?

I am twenty-two, colored, born in Winston-Salem.
I went to school there, then Durham, then here
to this college on the hill above Harlem.
I am the only colored student in my class.
The steps from the hill lead down into Harlem,
through a park, then I cross St. Nicholas,
Eighth Avenue, Seventh, and I come to the Y,
the Harlem Branch Y, where I take the elevator
up to my room, sit down, and write this page:

It's not easy to know what is true for you or me
at twenty-two, my age. But I guess I'm what
I feel and see and hear. Harlem, I hear you:
hear you, hear me—we two—you, me talk on this page.
(I hear New York, too.) Me—who?

Well, I like to eat, sleep, drink, and be in love.
I like to work, read, learn, and understand life.
I like a pipe for a Christmas present,
or records—Bessie, bop, or Bach.

I guess being colored doesn't make me not like
the same things other folks like who are other races.
So will my page be colored that I write?
Being me, it will not be white.
But it will be a part of you, instructor.
You are white—
yet a part of me, as I am a part of you.
That's American.

Sometimes perhaps you don't want to be a part of me.
Nor do I often want to be a part of you.
But we are, that's true!
As I learn from you,
I guess you learn from me—
although you're older—and white—
and somewhat more free.

This is my page for English B.

Boogie: 1 A.M.

Good evening, daddy!
I know you've heard
The boogie-woogie rumble
Of a dream deferred
Trilling the treble
And twining the bass
Into midnight ruffles
Of cat-gut lace.

Lady's Boogie

See that lady
Dressed so fine?
She ain't got boogie-woogie
On her mind—

But if she was to listen
I bet she'd hear,
Way up in the treble
The tingle of a tear.
    Be-bach!

Dream Boogie: Variation

Tinkling treble,
Rolling bass,
High noon teeth
In a midnight face,
Great long fingers
On great big hands,
Screaming pedals
Where his twelve-shoe lands,
Looks like his eyes
Are teasing pain,
a Few minutes late
For the Freedom Train.

Harlem

What happens to a dream deferred?

    Does it dry up
    like a raisin in the sun?
    Or fester like a sore—
    And then run?

Does it stink like rotten meat?
Or crust and sugar over—
like a syrupy sweet?

Maybe it just sags
like a heavy load.

Or does it explode?

Same in Blues

I said to my baby,
Baby, take it slow.
I can't, she said, I can't!
I got to go!

There's a certain
amount of traveling
in a dream deferred.

Lulu said to Leonard,
I want a diamond ring.
Leonard said to Lulu,
You won't get a goddamn thing!

A certain
amount of nothing
in a dream deferred.

Daddy, daddy, daddy,
All I want is you.
You can have me, baby—
but my lovin' days is through.

A certain
amount of impotence
in a dream deferred.

Three parties
On my party line—
But that third party,
Lord, ain't mine!

There's liable
to be confusion
in a dream deferred.

From river to river
Uptown and down,
There's liable to be confusion
when a dream gets kicked around.

You talk like
they don't kick
dreams around
Downtown.

I expect they do—
But I'm talking about
Harlem to you!

from *Weary Blues*

Lenox Avenue: Midnight

The rhythm of life
Is a jazz rhythm,
Honey.
The gods are laughing at us.

The broken heart of love,
The weary, weary heart of pain,—
    Overtones,
    Undertones,
To the rumble of street cars,
To the swish of rain.

Lenox Avenue,
Honey.
Midnight,
And the gods are laughing at us.

Epigraph to *The Big Sea*

Life is a big sea
full of many fish.
I let down my nets
and pull.

Jazz as Communication

You can start anywhere—Jazz as communication—since it's a circle, and you 1
yourself are the dot in the middle. You, me. For example, I'll start with the blues.
I'm not a Southerner. I never worked on a levee. I hardly ever saw a cotton field
except from the highway. But women behave the same on Park Avenue as they
do on a levee: when you've got hold of one part of them the other part escapes
you. That's the Blues!

Life is as hard on Broadway as it is in Blues-originating-land. The Brill 2
Building Blues is just as hungry as the Mississippi Levee Blues. One communicates to the other, brother! Somebody is going to rise up and tell me that nothing that comes out of Tin Pan Alley is jazz. I disagree. Commercial, yes. But so
was Storyville, so was Basin Street. What do you think Tony Jackson and Jelly
Roll Morton and King Oliver and Louis Armstrong were playing for? Peanuts?
No, money, even in Dixieland. They were communicating for money. For fun,
too—because they had fun. But the money helped the fun along.

Now; To skip a half century, somebody is going to rise up and tell me Rock 3
and Roll isn't jazz. First, two or three years ago, there were all these songs about
too young to know—*but.* . . . The songs are right. You're never too young to
know how bad it is to love and not have love come back to you. That's as basic
as the Blues. And that's what Rock and Roll is—teenage *Heartbreak Hotel*—
the old songs reduced to the lowest common denominator. The music goes way
back to Blind Lemon and Leadbelly—Georgia Tom merging into the Gospel
Songs—Ma Rainey, and the most primitive of the Blues. It borrows their gut-
bucket heartache. It goes back to the jubilees and stepped-up Spirituals—Sister
Tharpe—and borrows their I'm-gonna-be-happy-anyhow-in-spite-of-this-world
kind of hope. It goes back further and borrows the steady beat of the drums of
Congo Square—that going-on beat—and the Marching Bands' loud and blatant

yes!! Rock and roll puts them all together and makes a music so basic it's like the meat cleaver the butcher uses—before the cook uses the knife—before you use the sterling silver at the table on the meat that by then has been rolled up into a commercial filet mignon.

A few more years and Rock and Roll will no doubt be washed back half for- 4 gotten into the sea of jazz. Jazz is a great big sea. It washes up all kinds of fish and shells and spume and waves with a steady old beat, or off-beat. And Louis must be getting old if he thinks J. J. and Kai—and even Elvis—didn't come out of the same sea he came out of, too. Some water has chlorine in it and some doesn't. There're all kinds of water. There's salt water and Saratoga water and Vichy water, Quinine water and Pluto water—and Newport rain. And it's all water. Throw it all in the sea, and the sea'll keep on rolling along toward shore and crashing and booming back into itself again. The sun pulls the moon. The moon pulls the sea. They also pull jazz and me. Beyond Kai to Count to Lonnie to Texas Red, beyond June to Sarah to Billy to Bessie to Ma Rainey. And the Most is the It—the all of it.

Jazz seeps into words—spelled out words. Nelson Algren is influenced by 5 jazz. Ralph Ellison is, too. Sartre, too. Jacques Prevert. Most of the best writers today are. Look at the end of the *Ballad of the Sad Cafe*. Me as the public, *my* dot in the middle—it was fifty years ago, the first time I heard the Blues on Independence Avenue in Kansas City. Then State Street in Chicago. Then Harlem in the twenties with J. P. and J. C. Johnson and Fats and Willie the Lion and Nappy playing piano—with the Blues running all up and down the keyboard through the ragtime and the jazz. House rent party cards. I wrote *The Weary Blues:*

Drowning a drowsy syncopated tune . . . . . . etc. . . . *Shuffle Along* was 6 running then—the Sissle and Blake tunes. A little later *Runnin' Wild* and the Charleston and Fletcher and Duke and Cab. Jimmie Lunceford, Chick Webb, and Ella. Tiny Parham in Chicago. And at the end of the Depression times, what I heard at Minton's. A young music—coming out of young people. Billy—the male and female of them—both the Eckstein and the Holiday—and Dizzy and Tad and the Monk. Some of it came out in poems of mine in *Montage of a Dream Deferred* later. Jazz again putting itself into words:

POEMS FROM "MONTAGE"

But I wasn't the only one putting jazz into words. Better poets of the heart of 7 jazz beat me to it. W. C. Handy a long time before. Benton Overstreet. Mule Bradford. Then Buddy DeSilva on the pop level. Ira Gershwin. By and by Dorothy Baker in the novel—to name only the most obvious—the ones with labels. I mean the ones you can spell out easy with a-b-c's—the word mongers— outside the music. But always the ones of the music were the best—Charlie Christian, for example, Bix, Louis, Joe Sullivan, Count.

Now, to wind it all up, with you in the middle—jazz is only what you 8 yourself get out of it. Louis's famous quote—or misquote probably—"Lady, if you have to ask what it is, you'll never know." Well, I wouldn't be so posi- tive. The lady just might know—without being able to let loose the cry—to follow through—to light up before the fuse blows out. To me jazz is a mon- tage of a dream deferred. A great big dream—yet to come—and always yet— to become ultimately and finally true. Maybe in the next seminar—for Saturday—Nat Hentoff and Billy Strayhorn and Tony Scott and the others on that panel will tell us about it—when they take up "The Future of Jazz." The

Bird was looking for that future like mad. The Newborns, Chico, Dave, Gulda, Milt, Charlie Mingan. That future is what you call pregnant. Potential papas and mamas of tomorrow's jazz are all known. But THE papa and THE mama—maybe both—are anonymous. But the child will communicate. Jazz is a heartbeat—its heartbeat is yours. You will tell me about its perspectives when you get ready.

From *The Big Sea*

We were riding in a bowl of pine trees, with the distant rim of the mountains   1
all around and the sky very blue. For once, my father did not seem to be in a hurry. He let his horse mosey along, biting at the wayside grass. As we rode, my father outlined a plan he had made up in his mind for me, a plan that I had never dreamed of before. He wanted me to go to Switzerland to college, perhaps to Basle, or one of the cantons where one could learn three languages at once, French, German, and Italian, directly from the people. Then he wanted me to go to a German engineering school. Then come back to live in Mexico.

The thought of trigonometry, physics, and chemistry in a foreign language   2
was more than I could bear. In English, they were difficult enough. But as a compromise to Switzerland and Germany, I suggested Columbia in New York—mainly because I wanted to see Harlem.

My father wouldn't hear of it. But the more I thought of it, the better I liked   3
the idea myself. I had an overwhelming desire to see Harlem. More than Paris, or the Shakespeare country, or Berlin, or the Alps, I wanted to see Harlem, the greatest Negro city in the world. *Shuffle Along* had just burst into being, and I wanted to hear Florence Mills sing. So I told my father I'd rather go to Columbia than to Switzerland.

My father shut up. I shut up. Our horses went on down the mountain into   4
the blue shadows. We didn't talk much for days. At home he gave me several involved problems in bookkeeping to do and told me to stop spending so much time with the Mexicans, promenading in the Portales in the evening. But his advice went in one ear and out the other. I liked the Portales, but I didn't like bookkeeping.

· · ·

Living in New York was higher than my father had anticipated, and he   5
asked every month for an accounting of my expenses, penny by penny. Since I had always spent it all, "All gone" seemed to me a sufficient accounting to give, simple and clear. But it did not please my father.

About that time, my mother and step-father had parted again. My mother   6
came to New York to live, so I had to use my allowance to help her until she found a job. My father kept wondering why I ran out of money so quickly. But I didn't have enough for college, my mother, and me, too.

What an upleasant winter! I didn't like Columbia, nor the students, nor any-   7
thing I was studying! So I didn't study. I went to shows, read books, attended lectures at the Rand School under Ludwig Lewisohn and Heywood Broun, missed an important exam in the spring to go to Bert Williams's funeral, sat up in the gallery night after night at *Shuffle Along,* adored Florence Mills, and went to Chinatown with Chun. I even acquired a small Mandarin vocabulary.

Of course, I finished the years without honors. I had no intention of going   8
further at Columbia, anyhow. I felt that I would never turn out to be what my father expected me to be in return for the amount he invested. So I wrote him

and told him I was going to quit college and go to work on my own, and that he needn't send me any more money.

He didn't. He didn't even write again.   9

A Guide to the Assignment

This guide is designed to help you through the process of writing an interpretive essay about a literary work. Key elements in this guide parallel the organization of this chapter, and you should look to appropriate sections in the chapter for further guidance. You will prepare to write, write, advance your idea with sources, and then evaluate and revise. Here, once again, is your assignment:

> Select a story, poem, or set of poems (and in the case of Hughes, related materials) as the subject of an interpretive essay. Your goal is to read, to discover a pattern of meaning, and then to present this pattern to readers by referring to specific lines of the text. You should be conscious throughout of using full cycles of claim, reference, and comment, as discussed in the Structures and Strategies section of this chapter.

Prepare to Write: Explore Your Idea

As you begin your reading for this essay, recall that interpreting a work of literature involves pointing to a pattern that you believe makes a text meaningful. The process goes something like this: while reading, you begin to notice certain details that you think are related. At first, the relationship may not be well defined, but as you read and reread, the relationship—the pattern of meaning that you see—becomes clear and you can express it as a formal statement. Your statement becomes the basis on which to return to the text and identify specific lines that confirm the existence of the pattern you have found. In your essay, these same lines become evidence in an effort to convince readers that your interpretation is reasonable and worthy of serious consideration.

Discovering Ideas

Select one of the writers in this Occasions section and read his or her work. Read and respond personally to the text. In the Structures and Strategies section, you found these questions to help prompt a personal response on a first reading:

- What do I feel when reading this material? Why do I feel this way?
- Does this text make me *want* to read? Why or why not?
- What about this text is worth reading a second time?
- How am I challenged by or changed in response to this text?
- With what questions does this text leave me?
- What differences do I see between the author's observations of the world and my observations? How can I explain these differences?

On finishing your first reading, write for ten or fifteen minutes and record your response, much the way Sarika Chandra did on page 357.

Committing Yourself to an Idea

Review what you have written as a personal response and write a single statement summarizing that response. Convert that statement to a question by asking *Why? How? What are some examples?* Guided by your question, reread in order to gain insights into how the text works and how you think it achieves meaning in one particular way (with respect to your question). If you have trouble deciding on a question to guide your second reading, reflect again on your response to the text. Find some line, some gesture, some interaction among characters that prompts a response in you. Begin again from there. Your goal in this second reading is to identify specific lines of a story or poem that confirm your personal response.

Based on your first and second readings of a text, make a single interpretive statement that you are committed to arguing. This statement will be your essay's idea—its argumentative thesis. As you read and reread this thesis, ask yourself: What is my personal commitment? In writing an essay based on this thesis, will I learn something personally valuable? Revise your thesis if need be until you feel that you are committed to it. (For a discussion of thesis and commitment, see chapter 2, pages 28–31.)

Suggestions for Collaborative Writing

Pair up with a classmate who is writing about the same poem or story. Individually, sketch an outline of the text, writing a line-by-line interpretation of the poem or a more general interpretation of the short story. Then, try to articulate in a single paragraph the emerging pattern of meaning within the text that you want to bring to the reader's attention.

When finished, share your findings with your classmate. Where have your interpretations overlapped? Where have they diverged dramatically? Do the other person's analyses raise any question you ought to consider as you write your own draft? Can you help your partner strengthen his or her ideas as a result of your own interpretation? What do your differing analyses and interpretations tell you about the nature of commenting on literary texts?

Write: Clarify Your Idea and Make It Public

Creating Common Ground with Readers

Write a present-tense summary of the poem or story you are examining. The summary need not be longer than a paragraph, but it should explain essential elements for readers who have not read the piece: narrator, actors, actions, mood, central idea, and any other aspects you decide are important. Your goal is to recreate the story or poem in your essay. Consider placing this paragraph early in the essay in order to provide readers with orienting information. Then, each time you make an interpretive claim and refer to a specific line of text, lead up to that line with a present-tense summary describing what is happening in the story or poem at that point. Here's an example from Ryan Kelly's essay:

> The poem begins . . . with the poet working alone in his room. Hughes suggests the focus and intensity of a poet at work right away by using a strongly alliterated line: "I imagine this midnight moment's forest." There is a meditative, brooding feeling with these M-sounds that captures the reader's attention.

The first statement of this paragraph opens with a present-tense verb that points readers to a specific place in the poem that Kelly is about discuss. Having located the reader in the poem, Kelly then makes his interpretive claim: "Hughes suggests the focus and intensity of a poet at work right away by using a strongly alliterated line." Kelly quotes a line and then comments: "There is a meditative, brooding feeling with these M-sounds that captures the reader's attention." In this brief paragraph, Kelly has demonstrated the cycle of claim, reference, and comment essential to writing about literature. Take special care to locate readers in a story or poem before you make a claim and point to a specific line.

Planning a Structure

Quiz your thesis: look at the example on page 364 in Structures and Strategies, and see the more extensive discussion on pages 61–63 in chapter 4. Your goal is to identify all parts of an essay that would follow from your thesis. Having done this, develop a sketch of a likely essay. (For an example, turn to the sketch of Sarika Chandra's essay, page 364.) Now return to the poem or story and choose specific lines or scenes that you will present as evidence that demonstrates the pattern you have found.

Understanding Your Logic

The logic of your essay will *reverse* the logic through which you discovered a pattern of meaning in the poem or story. Typically, a reader makes discoveries inductively, forging tentative connections among separate lines or scenes and only slowly realizing that a pattern of meaning exists. In your essay, *begin* by stating this pattern in the clearest terms possible; then, provide evidence for your interpretation.

As you refer readers to specific parts of the text in order to support your interpretation, remember to use full cycles of development:

- First, locate the reader at a specific point in a play, poem, or story by explaining what is happening, who is speaking, and so on.
- Second, make an interpretive statement about the poem or story.
- Third, present evidence for this interpretation by referring to a specific line or scene, either by quoting or by summarizing.

- Finally, comment on the line or scene referred to and show how this reference supports your interpretation. Move on to a new, related claim and begin a new cycle of development.

◆ Suggestions for Writing with a Computer

If you have been adhering to the cycle of development concept discussed in Structures and Strategies, you will find that your essay contains a number of these cycles. Locate each cycle as it appears in your essay. Within that cycle, identify where you've made a claim, where you've made a reference to the text, and where you've commented on that text.

Isolate these different cycles from one another by skipping several lines between each one. Experiment by rearranging the order of the cycle: What happens when you make the reference first, then the claim, and then the comment? What happens when you allow the comment to come first, then the reference, and then the claim? Are there some places where you can vary this cyclical order to avoid having your final essay become overly predictable in its structure? When should you not deviate from this order? Use your cut and paste tools to rearrange and modify certain sections of the essay.

Writing Your First Draft

You have prepared to write. Now assemble your interpretive claim (your thesis), a sketch of your essay, and the specific lines you will refer to in support of your claim. Write your first draft, one section of the essay at a sitting. You might try beginning with a direct statement of your thesis (save the introduction for later), followed by a paragraph that summarizes the text you are interpreting. Continue by writing one cycle of development at a time: locate your reader at a specific point in the text, make a claim, refer to a specific line, and comment. This done, move to a new, related cycle of development and repeat the process until you have completed your first draft.

Advance Your Idea with Sources

An essay of interpretation is based on the assumption that you will be referring to a literary text throughout, and strategies for doing this have been discussed extensively in this chapter. When referring to a poem or story in this Occasions section, bear these principles in mind:

- Work consistently with the pattern of claim, reference to a text, and comment discussed in the chapter.
- Organize your discussion by ideas, not by sources (see chapter 4, pages 61–63).

If you choose to write on the poetry of Langston Hughes, you will have sources beyond the literary work available to you: a statement on jazz, passages from Hughes's autobiography, and Jemie's essay. If you want to refer to sources beyond the poetry, do so only to supplement your original ideas.

Your professor may ask that you use secondary sources in your essay on Joyce, Chopin, or Hughes and you are certain to find such materials in your college's library. Even without your professor's prompting, consider going to the library once you have developed your own interpretation. Consult the library catalogue for holdings on Joyce, Chopin, or Hughes. Also consult the *MLA International Bibliography of Books and Articles on Modern Languages and Literatures.*

Evaluate and Revise

General Evaluation

You will revise your interpretive essay as you would any essay: for large-scale concerns like unity and coherence, for smaller-scale matters like paragraph development, and for still smaller-scale matters like sentence style and correctness. For general strategies on revising your first draft, see chapter 12–14.

Critical Points in an Interpretive Essay

A successful interpretive essay has several key features you will want to check when revising your essay. First and foremost, your interpretive claim—your essay's thesis—should communicate a pattern of meaning that you have found in the literary work. What is the evidence for this pattern? You will answer this question by pointing readers to specific lines in the text. Every such reference should be presented as a cycle of development. Direct these questions at your draft:

- Does each reference in support of your interpretation locate your reader at a *particular* point in the poem or story? Does each summarizing or locating statement provide all the information needed for your reader to understand the reference you are about to make?
- Do you make a clear interpretive claim before referring the reader to a specific line or scene? Your claim should state how the line you are about to refer to is meaningful.
- Do you follow the above with a *specific* reference?
- Do you then comment on how the poem or story demonstrates the claim you are making?

Your essay should consist of interlinked cycles of development. Each cycle should lead logically from one to the next; and all cycles should be related to your overall interpretive claim. Revise until you have achieved this goal.

CHAPTER 11

Argument

Definitions and Examples

Do not expect your undergraduate, college education to prepare you for a *specific* job. Seventy percent of college graduates take jobs unrelated to their majors, and what is true of them is likely to be true of you. What, then, is the value of college? No single answer could satisfy everyone, but most would accept this as a partial response: *a college education can help you to think critically.* The importance of thinking critically cannot be overstated, according to Robert Ornstein of the Institute for the Study of Human Knowledge. "Solutions to the significant problems facing modern society demand a widespread, qualitative improvement in thinking and understanding," he says. "We need a breakthrough in the *quality* of thinking employed both by decision-makers at all levels of society and by each of us in our daily affairs." Effective, strategic thinkers are needed urgently and are appreciated everywhere, and you will do well to make clear thinking an explicit goal of your studies. Specifically, learn to identify and solve problems; to plan strategically; to challenge others and yourself; and to generate new ideas and information. Do this, and no matter what your career, college will have served you well.

This is an argument, an attempt to change your mind through reasoned discussion. While this argument is brief, it consists of the same parts that characterize *any* argument: claim, support, and reasoning.[1] The relationship among these parts is what gives an argument its force. No argument is possible unless claim, support, and reasoning are brought together to make a convincing whole.

---

[1]The approach to argument taken here is based on the work of Stephen Toulmin, as developed in *The Uses of Argument* (Cambridge: The University Press, 1958).

Claims

Any paper that you write in college will have a claim, a single statement that crystallizes your purpose for writing and governs the logic and development of the paper. The claim, also called an *argumentative thesis*, will express your view on a subject. Your goal in the argument is to defend your claim as being true, probable, or desirable. Because the claim is a specialized case of thesis statements for all varieties of writing, the discussion here assumes that you have read chapter 2, pages 27–31.

Answering Questions with Your Claim

Arguments provide answers to one of three types of questions: questions of *fact, value,* or *policy*.

Claims That Answer Questions of Fact

A *question of fact* can take the following forms:

> *Does X exist?*
> *Does X lead to Y?*
> *How can we define X?*

The first question can be answered with a *yes* or *no*. The second question leads to an argument about cause and effect. If one thing leads to or causes another, the writer must show how this happens. The third question is an argument about definitions. At times, definitions can be presented without debate; at other times, writers will argue to define a term in a particular way and then will build an entire presentation based on that definition.

Once established as true, a statement of fact can be used as evidence in other arguments. For instance, in a problem/solution argument the writer must establish that a problem exists; once this fact is established, the writer can make a second argument in support of a particular solution.

Example Theses

Extrasensory perception does not exist.

Chronic fatigue syndrome *is* real, though its causes are not entirely understood.

Stories describing near-death experiences have not withstood scientific scrutiny.

Claims That Answer a Question of Value

A *question of value* takes the form: *What is X worth?* You make an argument about values when at the conclusion of a hearty meal you pat your belly and smile. In more academic circumstances, scholars argue about value when they review and comment on one another's work—for instance, calling a theory *powerful* or elegant. Determinations of value are based on standards called *criteria* that are explicitly stated and then used to judge the worth of the object under review.

Example Theses

So-called "cold fusion," if it proves practical, will have tremendous economic and humanitarian value.

Though it raises useful questions, Eric Smith's research linking intelligence and birth order is flawed.

Nabokov's *Lolita* is a great novel.

Claims That Answer a Question of Policy

A *question of policy* takes the form: *What action should we take?* Politics is a major arena for arguments of policy. In this arena, arguments help to determine which legislative actions are taken and how huge sums of money are spent. *Should the legislature raise taxes? Should the United States support totalitarian regimes?* These questions about what *ought* to be done prompt arguments based on claims of policy.

Example Theses

Funding decisions for NASA should be based on a coherent, long-term approach to space exploration.

Eventually, taxes will have to be raised if the government cannot reduce our massive national debt.

More businesses should provide on-site daycare facilities.

Defining Terms in the Claim

In order to provide the basis for a sound argument, all words of a claim must be carefully defined so that people are debating the same topic. Consider this claim, which answers a question of policy: *The United States should not support totalitarian regimes.* Unless the term *totalitarian regimes* is clearly defined (and distinguished, say, from authoritarian regimes), the argument could not succeed. The writer, the reader, and various experts referred to in the argument might define and use the word *totalitarian* differently. If this happened, a reader could not be sure about what is being argued and no meaningful exchange of ideas would take place. Take care to examine your claims and, if one term or another requires it, actually write a paragraph of definition into your argument. If you suspect that your audience will not accept your definition, then you will need to argue for it. Entire arguments are sometimes needed to define complex terms, such as *honor*. If a key term in your claim is not complicated, then a paragraph or even a sentence of definition will suffice. With terms well defined, argumentation can begin.

Supporting the Claim

You can offer facts, opinions, and examples as support for your claims. A **fact** is a statement that can be verified, proven true or false. As a writer you should be able to verify facts on demand, and most often you will do this by referring to an authoritative source. (This is one of the reasons for documenting your papers.) In most circumstances once facts are presented and accepted by experts in a given field, the rest of us can be content to accept them as well. Facts are constantly being updated and revised as a consequence of research. It is therefore essential that you refer to the most recent sources possible.

An **opinion** is a statement of interpretation and judgment. Opinions are themselves arguments and should be based on evidence in order to be convincing. Opinions are not true or false in the way that statements of fact are. Rather, opinions are more or less well supported. You do your own argument a service by referring to the opinions of experts who agree with you. An **example** is a particular instance of a statement you are trying to prove. The statement is a generalization, and by offering an example you are trying to demonstrate that the generalization is correct.

Presenting Reasons for Your Claim

Reasoning in an argument is the pattern of thinking used to connect statements of support to a claim. Formally, these types of reasoning are referred to as *lines of argument.* The three types of reasoning ask readers to accept support for a claim on the grounds of logic, emotion, or authority. In writing papers for your courses, you will most often appeal to your reader's logic. Two specific types of appeal to logic are generalization and cause and effect. You will make generalizations, arguing that what is true in one case is true in others, as in this statement:

Plastic litter kills animals.

You will also argue by cause and effect, trying to convince readers that one event or condition is directly responsible for another, as in this statement:

Insect problems arose with the practice of intensive, single-crop farming.

These and other strategies for reasoning with your reader will be discussed in detail in this chapter's Structures and Strategies section. For now, observe how all arguments can be examined in light of claims, support, and reasoning. Recall the example paragraph that begins this chapter. Three kinds of support are offered for the claim that *a college education can help you to think critically.* Each statement of support is connected to the claim by a specific type of reasoning.

Analysis: The example paragraph consists of three sets of statements that support the claim. Each is based on a corresponding type of reasoning. Claim, support, and reasoning function as one persuasive whole:

[1]**Support:**   Fact (most students take jobs unrelated to their major)
Reasoning: Appeal to logic (a generalization—what's true of most will be true of you)

Claim (about value):

> A college education can help you to think critically (and thinking critically is a good thing).

[2]**Support:**   Opinion (statement by Robert Ornstein: quality thinking is needed)
Reasoning: Appeal to authority (Ornstein is an expert on thinking and learning; his testimony is valuable)

[3]**Support:**   Opinion (statement by writer: make critical thinking a goal of college)
Reasoning: Appeal to emotion (self-interest will lead you to agree)

Key Term Defined: Critical thinking is the ability to identify and solve problems, to plan strategically, to challenge ideas, and to generate ideas.

While writing an argument, you should attempt to pull claim, support, and reasoning together so that you construct a persuasive whole. If you discover that the parts are not fitting together as expected, you may need to modify your claim.

Examples of Arguments

Following are four examples of arguments. The first three—on learning science, on reasons to carry a handgun, and on America's 200th birthday—were written by professionals: they are arguments you would read in a newspaper or a magazine. The final argument, on the advantages of an all-volunteer army, was written by a student. Different as these arguments are in terms of their topics and their intended audiences, each illustrates how a writer pulls together claim, support, and reasoning to create a convincing whole. Questions for discussion and writing follow each selection.

To Light the Fire of Science, Start with Some Fantasy and Wonder

Chet Raymo

Chet Raymo is a professor of physics at Stonehill College in Easton, Massachusetts. This essay, the argumentative claim for which appears both in the title and (twice) in the selection itself, was first published in Raymo's regular column, "Science Musings," in the Boston Globe *on December 21, 1992. The charm of this argument lies partially in Raymo's taking apparently unconnected pursuits—the reading of children's literature and the practice of good science—and supporting their connection in convincing ways. In the process, he makes his own love of science and of children's literature clear to all.*

Every year about this time I am asked by friends and colleagues to recommend 1
good science books for kids, to fill the remaining hollows in Santa's pack.

There are lots of terrific science books out there, and a good place to find 2
them is the children's book section of the Museum of Science shop. But my
advice to parents is: Don't be overly worried about providing science books for
your kids. Expose them to good children's literature, and the science will take
care of itself.

Over the years I have often referred to children's books in this column, 3
including the nonsense books of Dr. Seuss, Antoine de Saint-Exupery's "The
Little Prince," Lewis Carroll's "Alice in Wonderland" and "Through the
Looking-glass," L. Frank Baum's "Wizard of Oz," Kenneth Grahame's "The
Wind in the Willows" and Felix Salten's "Bambi."

All of these in essays about science.   4

What's the connection?   5

Children's books capture the curious, willing-to-be-surprised, "let's pretend" 6
quality of good science. Children's books are full of the playfulness that is part
of all first-rate science. And, like science, children's books insist upon the reality of the unseen.

Science books for children are packed full of interesting information. What 7
most of these books do not convey is the story of how the information was
obtained, why we understand it to be ture, and how it might embellish the landscape of the mind. For many children—and adults, too—science *is* information,
a mass of facts. But facts are not science any more than a table is carpentry.

Science is an attitude toward the world—curious, skeptical, undogmatic and 8
sensitive to beauty and mystery. The best science books for children are the ones
that convey these attitudes. They are not necessarily the books labeled "science."

From a "science" book we might learn that a flying bat might snap up 15 9
insects per minute, or that the frequency of its squeal can range as high as
50,000 cycles per second. Useful information, yes.

But consider the information in this poem from Randall Jarrell's "The Bat- 10
Poet":

> *A bat is born*
> *Naked and blind and pale.*
> *His mother makes a pocket of her tail*
> *And catches him. He clings to her long fur*
> *By his thumbs and toes and teeth.*
> *And then the mother dances through the night*
> *Doubling and looping, soaring, somersaulting—*
> *Her baby hangs on underneath.*

Oh what wondrous information! Even the rhythm of the poem ("naked and 11
blind and pale"; "thumbs and toes and teeth") mimics the flight of mother and
child, doubling and looping in the night.

More: 12

> *The mother eats the moths and gnats she catches*
> *In full flight; in full flight*
> *The mother drinks the water of the pond*
> *She skims across. Her baby hangs on tight.*

That wonderful line—"In full flight; in full flight"—conveys the single most important fact about bats: their extraordinary aviator skills. Jarrell's repeated phrase conveys useful facts about chiropteran dining; it also lets the child feel in her bones what it is to be a bat. 13

In Jarrell's book, the Bat-Poet recites his poem about bats to a chipmunk. Afterwards, he asks, "Did you like the poem?" 14

The chipmunk replies, "Oh, of course. Except I forgot it was a poem. I just kept thinking how queer it must be to be a bat." 15

The Bat-Poet says, "No, it's not queer. It's wonderful." 16

That's what good children's literature does—makes us feel the queerness and wonderfulness of nature. It's the best possible introduction to science. 17

Albert Einstein wrote: "When I examine myself and my methods of thought, I come to the conclusion that the gift of fantasy has meant more to me than any talent for abstract, positive thinking." The best time—perhaps the only time—to acquire the gift of fantasy is childhood. We live in an age of information. Too much information can swamp the boat of wonder, especially for a child. What children need is not more information, but fantasy. 18

Einstein also wrote: "The most beautiful experience we can have is the mysterious. It is the fundamental emotion which stands at the cradle of all true art and true science." At first, this might seem a strange thought. We are frequently asked to believe that science is the antithesis of mystery. Nothing could be further from the truth. Mystery invites the attention of the curious mind. Unless we perceive the world as mysterious—queer and wonderful—we will never be curious about what makes it tick. 19

For Discussion and Writing

Reading and Thinking Critically

1. *Personal response:* When you were a child, you read children's books and listened to them at bedtime. What is new to you in Raymo's discussion of children's literature? Can you think of one instance in which a story prompted you to engage in the "let's pretend" mode of thinking (see ¶6 on page 408) that Raymo finds so useful to scientific thinking?
2. *Be alert to differences:* Raymo includes two very different types of writing in this piece: his own essayist's style and his references to the "Bat-Poet" by Randall Jarrell (see ¶s 10–16 on pages 408–409). How do these differences in style and tone of writing reinforce Raymo's claim?
3. *Broaden the context:* Think of the science curriculum in your high school. To what extent were you invited to "think" like a scientist in the world? Did your teachers cultivate in you a sense of mystery and wonder? What might be the cornerstones of a science curriculum, following the principles laid out by Raymo?

Examining "To Light the Fire" as an Example of Argument

1. What is Raymo's claim?
2. What types of support does Raymo offer for his claim? Look for facts, examples, and opinions.
3. With what reason does Raymo link each type of support to his claim?

On Our Birthday—America as Idea

Barbara Tuchman

Barbara Tuchman, a recipient of two Pulitzer Prizes, was a highly respected historian whose writing won both critical acclaim and popular success. Her books include Guns of August *(1962),* Stilwell and the American Experience in China *(1971), and* A Distant Mirror *(1979). In the following essay, Tuchman argues that the founding "idea" of America, an idea battered and abused over the past two hundred years, is alive and still guiding the country. This essay was published originally in 1976, "On Our Birthday."*

The United States is a nation consciously conceived, not one that evolved 1
slowly out of an ancient past. It was a planned idea of democracy, of liberty of conscience and pursuit of happiness. It was the promise of equality of opportunity and individual freedom within a just social order, as opposed to the restrictions and repressions of the Old World. In contrast to the militarism of Europe, it would renounce standing armies and "sheathe the desolating sword of war." It was an experiment in Utopia to test the thesis that, given freedom, independence, and local self-government, people, in Kossuth's words, "will in due time ripen into all the excellence and all the dignity of humanity." It was a new life for the oppressed, it was enlightenment, it was optimism.

Regardless of hypocrisy and corruption, of greed, chicanery, brutality, and 2
all the other bad habits man carries with him whether in the New World or Old, the founding idea of the United States remained, on the whole, dominant through the first hundred years. With reservations, it was believed in by Americans, by visitors who came to aid our Revolution or later to observe our progress, by immigrants who came by the hundreds of thousands to escape an intolerable situation in their native lands.

The idea shaped our politics, our institutions, and to some extent our 3
national character, but it was never the only influence at work. Material circumstances exerted an opposing force. The open frontier, the hardships of homesteading from scratch, the wealth of natural resources, the whole vast challenge of a continent waiting to be exploited, combined to produce a prevailing materialism and an American drive bent as much, if not more, on money, property, and power than was true of the Old World from which we had fled. The human resources we drew upon were significant: Every wave of immigration brought here those people who had the extra energy, gumption, or restlessness to uproot themselves and cross an unknown ocean to seek a better life. Two other factors entered the shaping process—the shadow of slavery and the destruction of the native Indian.

At its Centennial the United States was a material success. Through its sec- 4
ond century the idea and the success have struggled in continuing conflict. The Statue of Liberty, erected in 1886, still symbolized the promise to those "yearning to breathe free." Hope, to them, as seen by a foreign visitor, was "domiciled in America as the Pope is in Rome." But slowly in the struggle the idea lost ground, and at a turning point around 1900, with American acceptance of a rather half-hearted imperialism, it lost dominance. Increasingly invaded since then by self-doubt and disillusion, it survives in the disenchantment of today, battered and crippled but not vanquished.

What has happened to the United States in the twentieth century is not 5
a peculiarly American phenomenon but a part of the experience of the West.

In the Middle Ages plague, wars, and social violence were seen as God's punishment upon man for his sins. If the concept of God can be taken as man's conscience, the same explanation may be applicable today. Our sins in the twentieth century—greed, violence, inhumanity—have been profound, with the result that the pride and self-confidence of the nineteenth century have turned to dismay and self-disgust.

In the United States we have a society pervaded from top to bottom by contempt for the law. Government—including the agencies of law enforcement—business, labor, students, the military, the poor no less than the rich, outdo each other in breaking the rules and violating the ethics that society has established for its protection. The average citizen, trying to hold a footing in standards of morality and conduct he once believed in, is daily knocked over by incoming waves of venality, vulgarity, irresponsibility, ignorance, ugliness, and trash in all senses of the word. Our government collaborates abroad with the worst enemies of humanity and liberty. It wastes our substance on useless proliferation of military hardware that can never buy security no matter how high the pile. It learns no lesson, employs no wisdom, and corrupts all who succumb to Potomac fever.

Yet the idea does not die. Americans are not passive under their faults. We expose them and combat them. Somewhere every day some group is fighting a public abuse—openly and, on the whole, not withstanding the FBI, with confidence in the First Amendment. The U.S. has slid a long way from the original idea. Nevertheless, somewhere between Gulag Archipelago and the featherbed of cradle-to-the-grave welfare, it still offers a greater opportunity for social happiness—that is to say, for well-being combined with individual freedom and initiation—than is likely elsewhere. The ideal society for which mankind has been striving through the ages will remain forever beyond our grasp. But if the great question, whether it is still possible to reconcile democracy with social order and individual liberty, is to find a positive answer, it will be here.

For Discussion and Writing

Reading and Thinking Critically

1. *Personal response:* How accustomed are you to thinking of America as an "idea"? Over the years, what has been your involvement with this idea? To what extent do you take it for granted?
2. *Challenge the reading:* Tuchman arranges her argument as a series of smaller claims tied to a larger one. Consider any one of these smaller claims, such as: "What has happened to the United States in the twentieth century is not a peculiarly American phenomenon but a part of the experience of the West." What would you need to know, as a reader, to feel comfortable accepting this claim? Do you accept the claim?
3. *Broaden the context:* If you are an immigrant to this country, compare the "idea" to which Tuchman refers in her essay to the "idea" guiding events in the country where you were born. Is there a difference? If you are a native born American and have traveled abroad, reflect on this same contrast.

Examining "On Our Birthday" as an Example of Argument

1. Where does Tuchman locate the claim of this argument? Why might she have chosen this location?

2. Sketch Tuchman's argument. What are the points she makes, and why has she made them in this particular order?

3. Examine Tuchman's support for her claims. What types of support does she offer? Where? Does Tuchman convince you with her evidence?

A Peaceful Woman Explains Why She Carries a Gun

Linda Hasselstrom

You have doubtless read pieces on gun control—on why an American's constitutional right to bear arms must be guaranteed or, by contrast, why we must ban or limit handguns and semi-automatic weapons in the interest of a civil society. And, no doubt, you have a view about gun control yourself. In the selection that follows, Linda Hasselstrom, a writer who lives and works in South Dakota, argues for the wisdom of her (not all women's—but of one woman's) carrying a pistol. Hasselstrom reports that reaching her decision was difficult, and possible only after years of soul searching.

Linda Hasselstrom: My Commitment to This Essay

Linda Hasselstrom worked for ten years sorting through her conflicting thoughts on handgun possession. Her motivation for writing is clear, but this statement is *not* itself an essay. Why not? What are the differences between this statement and the essay? What are the similarities?

Three ideas guided me through more than ten years of writing and revising this essay before it was published:

First, I believe that humans must accept some responsibility for their safety and well-being, rather than expecting government, society, law enforcement, or other entities to furnish protection on demand.

Second, media attention often focuses on dramatic incidents involving weapons, in an atmosphere where discussion becomes emotional. I thought a calm, reasoned discussion of the options, without drama or hyperbole, might be useful to individuals who had not yet made such decisions.

Third, my decision to protect myself with a gun had been made carefully, calmly, after considerable thought, to fit specific circumstances; I take full responsibility for the consequences of the decision. I hoped my method might help other people find their own solution to the problem of safety in an increasingly violent world.

1   I am a peace-loving woman. But several events in the past 10 years have convinced me I'm safer when I carry a pistol. This was a personal decision, but because handgun possession is a controversial subject, perhaps my reasoning will interest others.

2   I live in western South Dakota on a ranch 25 miles from the nearest large town; for several years I spent winters alone here. As a freelance writer, I travel alone a lot—more than 100,000 miles by car in the last four years. With women freer than ever before to travel alone, the odds of our encountering trouble seem to have risen. And help, in the West, can be hours away. Distances are great, roads are deserted, and the terrain is often too exposed to offer hiding places.

3   A woman who travels alone is advised, usually by men, to protect herself by avoiding bars and other "dangerous situations," by approaching her car like an Indian scout, by locking doors and windows. But these precautions aren't always enough. I spent years following them and still found myself in dangerous situations. I began to resent the idea that just because I am female, I have to be extra careful.

A few years ago, with another woman, I camped for several weeks in the 4 West. We discussed self-defense, but neither of us had taken a course in it. She was against firearms, and local police told us Mace was illegal. So we armed ourselves with spray cans of deodorant tucked into our sleeping bags. We never used our improvised Mace because we were lucky enough to camp beside people who came to our aid when men harassed us. But on one occasion we visited a national park where our assigned space was less than 15 feet from other campers. When we returned from a walk, we found our closest neighbors were two young men. As we gathered our cooking gear, they drank beer and loudly discussed what they would do to us after dark. Nearby campers, even families, ignored them; rangers strolled past, unconcerned. When we asked the rangers point-blank if they would protect us, one of them patted my shoulder and said, "Don't worry, girls. They're just kidding." At dusk we drove out of the park and hid our camp in the woods a few miles away. The illegal spot was lovely, but our enjoyment of that park was ruined. I returned from the trip determined to reconsider the options available for protecting myself.

At that time, I lived alone on the ranch and taught night classes in town. 5 Along a city street I often traveled, a woman had a flat tire, called for help on her CB radio, and got a rapist who left her beaten. She was afraid to call for help again and stayed in her car until morning. For that reason, as well as because CBs work best along line-of-sight, which wouldn't help much in the rolling hills where I live, I ruled out a CB.

As I drove home one night, a car followed me. It passed me on a narrow 6 bridge while a passenger flashed a blinding spotlight in my face. I braked sharply. The car stopped, angled across the bridge, and four men jumped out. I realized the locked doors were useless if they broke the windows of my pickup. I started forward, hoping to knock their car aside so I could pass. Just then another car appeared, and the men hastily got back in their car. They continued to follow me, passing and repassing. I dared not go home because no one else was there. I passed no lighted houses. Finally they pulled over to the roadside, and I decided to use their tactic: fear. Speeding, the pickup horn blaring, I swerved as close to them as I dared as I roared past. It worked: they turned off the highway. But I was frightened and angry. Even in my vehicle I was too vulnerable.

Other incidents occurred over the years. One day I glanced out a field below 7 my house and saw a man with a shotgun walking toward a pond full of ducks. I drove down and explained that the land was posted. I politely asked him to leave. He stared at me, and the muzzle of the shotgun began to rise. In a moment of utter clarity I realized that I was alone on the ranch, and that he could shoot me and simply drive away. The moment passed, the man left.

One night, I returned home from teaching a class to find deep tire ruts in 8 the wet ground of my yard, garbage in the driveway, and a large gas tank empty. A light shone in the house; I couldn't remember leaving it on. I was too embarrassed to drive to a neighboring ranch and wake someone up. An hour of cautious exploration convinced me the house was safe, but once inside, with the doors locked, I was still afraid. I kept thinking of how vulnerable I felt, prowling around my own house in the dark.

My first positive step was to take a kung fu class, which teaches evasive or 9 protective action when someone enters your space without permission. I learned to move confidently, scanning for possible attackers. I learned how to assess danger and techniques for avoiding it without combat.

I also learned that one must practice several hours *every* day to be good at 10 kung fu. By that time I had married George; when I practiced with him, I learned how *close* you must be to your attacker to use martial arts, and decided a 120-pound woman dare not let a six-foot, 220-pound attacker get that close unless she is very, very good at self-defense. I have since read articles by several women who were extremely well trained in the martial arts, but were raped and beaten anyway.

I thought back over the times in my life when I had been attacked or threat- 11 ened and tried to be realistic about my own behavior, searching for anything that had allowed me to become a victim. Overall, I was convinced that I had not been at fault. I don't believe myself to be either paranoid or a risk-taker, but I wanted more protection.

With some reluctance I decided to try carrying a pistol. George had always 12 carried one, despite his size and his training in martial arts. I practiced shooting until I was sure I could hit an attacker who moved close enough to endanger me. Then I bought a license from the county sheriff, making it legal for me to carry the gun concealed.

But I was not yet ready to defend myself. George taught me that the most 13 important preparation was mental: convincing myself I could actually *shoot a person*. Few of us wish to hurt or kill another human being. But there is no point in having a gun—in fact, gun possession might increase your danger—unless you know you can use it. I got in the habit of rehearsing, as I drove or walked, the precise conditions that would be required before I would shoot someone.

People who have not grown up with the idea that they are capable of pro- 14 tecting themselves—in other other words, most women—might have to work hard to convince themselves of their ability, and of the necessity. Handgun ownership need not turn us into gunslingers, but it can be part of believing in, and relying on, *ourselves* for protection.

To be useful, a pistol has to be available. In my car, it's within instant reach. 15 When I enter a deserted rest stop at night, it's in my purse, with my hand on the grip. When I walk from a dark parking lot into a motel, it's in my hand, under a coat. At home, it's on the headboard. In short, I take it with me almost everywhere I go alone.

Just carrying a pistol is not protection; avoidance is still the best approach 16 to trouble. Subconsciously watching for signs of danger. I believe I've become more alert. Handgun use, not unlike driving, becomes instinctive. Each time I've drawn my gun—I have never fired it at another human being—I've simply found it in my hand.

I was driving the half-mile to the highway mailbox one day when I saw a 17 vehicle parked about midway down the road. Several men were standing in the ditch, relieving themselves. I have no objection to emergency urination, but I noticed they'd dumped several dozen beer cans in the road. Besides being ugly, cans can slash a cow's feet or stomach.

The men noticed me before they finished and made quite a performance out 18 of zipping their trousers while walking toward me. All four of them gathered around my small foreign car, and one of them demanded what the hell I wanted.

"This is private land, I'd appreciate it if you'd pick up the beer cans." 19

"What beer cans?" said the belligerent one, putting both hands on the car 20 door and leaning in my window. His face was inches from mine, and the beer fumes were strong. The others laughed. One tried the passenger door, locked: another put his foot on the hood and rocked the car. They circled, lightly thumping the roof, discussing my good fortune in meeting them and the benefits they were likely to bestow upon me. I felt very small and very trapped and they knew it.

"The ones you just threw out," I said politely. 21

"I don't see no beer cans. Why don't you get out here and show them to 22 me, honey?" said the belligerent one, reaching for the handle inside my door.

"Right over there," I said, still being polite, "—there, and over there." I 23 pointed with the pistol, which I'd slipped under my thigh. Within one minute the cans and the men were back in the car and headed down the road.

I believe this incident illustrates several important principles. The men were 24 trespassing and knew it; their judgment may have been impaired by alcohol. Their response to the polite request of a woman alone was to use their size, numbers, and sex to inspire fear. The pistol was a response in the same language. Politeness didn't work; I couldn't match them in size or number. Out of the car, I'd have been more vulnerable. The pistol just changed the balance of power. It worked again recently when I was driving in a desolate part of Wyoming. A man played cat-and-mouse with me for 30 miles, ultimately trying to run me off the road. When his car passed mine with only two inches to spare, I showed him my pistol, and he disappeared.

When I got my pistol, I told my husband, revising the old Colt slogan, "God 25 made men *and women,* but Sam Colt made them equal." Recently I have seen a gunmaker's ad with a similar sentiment. Perhaps this is an idea whose time has come, though the pacifist inside me will be saddened if the only way women can achieve equality is by carrying weapons.

We must treat a firearm's power with caution. "Power tends to corrupt, and 26 absolute power corrupts absolutely," as a man (Lord Acton) once said. A pistol is not the only way to avoid being raped or murdered in today's world, but, intelligently wielded, it can shift the balance of power and provide a measure of safety.

For Discussion and Writing

Reading and Thinking Critically

1. *Personal response:* Does Hasselstrom convince you of *her* need to carry a pistol?
2. *Personal response:* Hasselstrom describes herself as constantly alert to danger. She "rehearses," mentally, with her pistol (see ¶s14–16). At what price do you think Hasselstrom buys her security? Would this be too high a price for you?
3. *Broaden the context:* In the United States, far fewer people live in the country than in urban centers. Transpose the logic of Hasselstrom's argument to a city. Does her argument still hold up?

Examining "A Peaceful Woman" as an Example of Argument

1. What indications do you find in this article that Hasselstrom is arguing for the validity of *her* decision, as opposed to arguing that all women, and men for that matter, should carry a pistol?
2. Examine the ways in which Hasselstrom appeals both to your emotions and to your sense of logic in this argument.

3. Block out each of the anecdotes that Hasselstrom relates. Then offer an observation on her strategy in preparing this argument.

The Volunteer Army: A Good Idea
Michele Pelletier

Student writer Michele Pelletier prepared the next argument in response to the following assignment from her history professor:

In our study this semester of American history, post–World War II, we have touched on many topics including the emergence of America as a world power, the Presidency and assassination of JFK, the Vietnam conflict, racial and civil unrest of the 60s, the feminist revolt, and more. Choose one aspect of these or other topics and define it narrowly, so that you can discuss this in detail, in 6 or 7 pages.

- Your paper should be an argument.
- Your paper should show a span of time.
- Your paper should show some sensitivity to the ways in which popular attitudes related to the topic you are discussing reflect historical events.

To become interested in writing this argument, Pelletier needed a topic to which she could develop a personal commitment. She found this when she reviewed her lecture notes on the Gulf War. Pelletier realized that if there had been a draft, her brothers might have been called to service, which got her thinking about the merits of an all-volunteer army versus a drafted one. The following excerpts restate key ideas from the essay presented in chapter 4 (pages 69–72).

Michele Pelletier: My Commitment to This Essay

Michele Pelletier was required by her instructor to write an interpretive essay, but she was also able to discover very personal reasons for writing and claimed this essay as her own. This personal statement gives you an insight into Pelletier's motivations for writing, but it is *not* itself an essay. Why not? What are the differences between this statement and the essay? What are the similarities?

At the time of the Gulf War, the topic of the draft was at the center of many conversations. My roommates and I debated whether women should be drafted if there was a draft. (I said yes.) Many of us debated whether being a student was a legitimate exemption from the draft. (I said no.) Quick as it was, the war was very real and the prospect of a draft being restored seemed equally real. If called, I would have served. But it worried me that I, who am hardly capable of squashing an ant, could be called on to kill a person. There are many people in this country who would volunteer to go to war—and they would make better soldiers than someone like me. I'd rather serve in a different capacity. Some prefer not to fight, and there is no good reason to make them.

Since the abolition of compulsory draft laws in 1973, the United States has had an all volunteer army. As recently as 1990, in anticipation of and then in the wake of the Persian Gulf War, powerful voices in Congress were calling for hearings to examine reinstituting the military draft. Senator Nunn of Georgia and others have argued that young men and women should give something back to the country that has nurtured and protected them, and one such means of giving would be national military service. If the draft is reinstituted, we young men and women of college age, along with our younger siblings, would be the ones who served. We who will be affected must take a hard look at this debate in order to decide which type of army is most effective and offers America the best possible value morally, militarily, and economically.

Armies of volunteers and conscripts are today's versions of the mili- 2 tias and mercenary forces that existed in the 15th and 16th centuries. . . .

There are no compelling reasons that we should return to a draft. An 11 all volunteer army gives us a far better value: a better value morally— individuals who serve willingly satisfy the State's need for protection and their own need to earn a living; a better value militarily—better prepared, better trained, longer-serving soldiers increase military effectiveness; and a better value economically—the volunteer army saves money.

For Discussion and Writing

Reading and Thinking Critically

1. *Personal response:* Does Pelletier convince you? Before answering, try to construct the most damaging possible counterargument to Pelletier's discussion. Has she considered and effectively dismissed counterarguments? Has she anticipated yours?
2. *Challenge the reading:* Talk with someone who is presently in the all-volunteer Army. Discuss with that person the merits of the draft versus volunteering for duty. Possibly review some points in Pelletier's argument. Does your interview confirm Pelletier's insights?
3. *Be alert to differences:* Compare Pelletier's method of arguing with Linda Hasselstrom's in "A Peaceful Woman Explains Why She Carries a Gun." What differences do you observe in the ways they support their claims?

Examining "Volunteer Army" as an Example of Argument

1. Reread Pelletier's "conversation" with Socrates in ¶s3–5 on pages 69–70. Why does she call on the famous philosopher here? How does she use the quoted passage from *Crito* to help structure the remainder of her argument?
2. In this argument, how does Pelletier appeal to both the reader's sense of reason and respect for authority?
3. Where, and how effectively, does Pelletier deal with would-be counterarguments to her own?
4. Pelletier locates her claim at the end of her argument. Why?

Structures and Strategies

Given a claim you want to make—for example, that your city should build a $500 million convention center—there are many ways to argue: there is no single, correct way. You will have choices to make based on the needs of your readers and on your familiarity with the topic. Where, for instance, will you locate the claim of your argument? Directly, at the beginning, or at the end, where you can benefit from careful consensus building? Will you play on readers' emotions (on their civic pride)? How will you reason? Will you refer to similar cases (convention building successes and failures in other cities)? Will you argue by cause and effect (that convention centers bring in direct and indirect revenues)? Will you refer to the experiences of experts (perhaps local business people)? Knowing what you want to argue is the beginning of your work. Knowing *how* to argue involves a consideration of strategies that you can develop through a process of preparing to write, writing, and revising.

Prepare to Write: Explore Your Idea

In chapters 12–14, you can read in some detail about approaching essay writing as a process. In those chapters you will see through demonstrations how essays are written in stages: writers gather materials and think of multiple approaches to an idea as they prepare to write; they write a first draft in which they express, explore, and refine their idea; and then they revise—they rewrite—until that idea is expressed clearly and all sections of the essay advance the idea. Typically, writers work through several versions of an essay before it reaches final form. In the discussion here, you will find several specific strategies to help you think about preparing to write, writing, and revising an argument.

Discovering Ideas

An argument must have at its core an idea—*your* idea—that you think is correct, reasonable, and worth a reader's serious consideration. You want readers to agree with you, but first you must know your own mind. Aside from the general prewriting activities on pages 7–21 that are offered to help you think creatively about ideas for your essay, you can consider the strategies presented in the following sections.

Reflect on Your Experience

Experience is a powerful shaper of opinion. The first place to look for ideas about which to argue is your own past. Comb through events of your life—physical, intellectual, and emotional—and search for some direct connection to topics on which you might write. Reflect on the significance of these events and you may well discover both an idea and a motivation. Such was the case with Michele Pelletier, whose history professor asked that she prepare a course-related argument. With the Gulf War recently over, the military draft was much in the news and on the minds of students, as Pelletier reports in her personal commitment statement:

> At the time of the Gulf War, the topic of the draft was at the center of many conversations. My roommates and I debated whether women should be drafted if there was a draft. (I said yes.) Many of us debated whether or not being a student was a legitimate exemption from the draft. (I said no.)

Pelletier reflected on her recent experience and found a topic to which she was personally connected and which satisfied her history professor's assignment. She began thinking about her argument in personal terms. You can do the same.

Read to Spark Ideas

One way to spark ideas is to read about your topic. If you must create the essay's topic yourself, review course notes and assigned readings. List as possible topics for argument any material that prompted in you a response, positive or negative. If a professor has assigned the topic, your focus has already been narrowed. Now locate essays, articles, or book chapters on this topic. Read and respond; it is very likely that at least one selection will prompt in you an idea for writing.

This was Michele Pelletier's experience. Her history professor had asked that she write about some topic discussed, if only briefly, during the semester. Her argumentative essay was supposed to "show a span of time" and "show some sensitivity to the ways in which popular attitudes related to the topic . . . reflect[ed] historical events." Pelletier chose the military draft. As she assembled sources that could help her generate ideas, she reassembled pertinent materials from her history course, she went to the library, and then she considered a source she had read for her philosophy course—Plato's *Crito*, in which Socrates argues that individuals owe a debt of obedience to the State in which they live. Pelletier saw a direct relationship between this ancient text and her present-day essay. Observe that her response in the margin—"How to pay the obligation?"— guides her use of the source in the essay itself, both in setting up the source and in responding to it:

A Source That Sparked Ideas

For, having brought you into the world, and nurtured and educated you, and given you and every other citizen a share in every good which we had to give, we further proclaim to any Athenian by the liberty which we allow him, that if he does not like us when he has become of age and has seen the ways of the city, and made our acquaintance, he may go where he pleases and take his goods with him. None of us laws will forbid him or interfere with him. Anyone who does not like us and the city, and who wants to emigrate to a colony or to any other city, may go where he likes, retaining his prop-

The Source **Used**

Some argue a position that has much merit: that the state, which nurtures and protects the individual, has the moral right to ask that individual for service. Balancing the needs of the state against the rights of the individual is an ancient concern, dating at least to the times of classical Greece. In one of Plato's dialogues, *Crito*, Socrates explains the State's position. (The "we" in this passage refers to the collective voice and authority of Athens.)

For, having brought you into the world, and nurtured and educated you, and given you and every other citizen a share in every good which

How best to pay the obligation?

erty. But he who has experience of the manner in which we order justice and administer the State, and still remains, has entered into an implied contract that he will do as we command him. And he who disobeys us is, as we maintain, thrice wrong; first, because in disobeying us he is disobeying his parents; secondly, we are the authors of his education; thirdly, because he has made an agreement with us that he will duly obey our commands; and he neither obeys them nor convinces us that our commands are unjust; and we do not rudely impose them, but give him the alternative of obeying or convincing us;—that is what we offer, and he does neither.

we had to give, we further proclaim to any Athenian by the liberty which we allow him, that if he does not like us when he has become of age and has seen the ways of the city, and made our acquaintance, he may go where he pleases and take his goods with him. None of us laws will forbid him or interfere with him. . . . But he who has experience of the manner in which we order justice and administer the State, and still remains, has entered into an implied contract that he will do as we command him. (102)

In this passage, Socrates argues that a citizen who enjoys the privileges and securities of living under State protection owes that State obedience. . . . It is true: we owe the society that nurtures us a debt. But how best that debt is paid and to what extent the citizens who "owe" are entitled to participate in deciding on payment—these are difficult questions that have been debated through the centuries.

Identify Tensions

One way to think of an argument is to see it as a play of tensions in which understandably opposing needs come into conflict and require that you take a position. You can identify ideas for argument by pointing to difficult decisions, yours or someone else's, and examining conflicting needs. For instance, young professionals who consider putting off having a family know that having children early on can interrupt a flowering career but, on the positive side, will result in their being relatively young when the children leave home; having children later allows careers to develop but can create a tremendous energy drain for older parents. You could certainly formulate an argument that explores the tensions of young professionals considering when, and whether, to begin a family. In your search for ideas about which to argue, identify difficult choices. There you will find *tension*—always a fruitful place to begin.

Linda Hasselstrom's argument on why she carries a gun illustrates this approach. As a reporter who often traveled alone, Hasselstrom felt vulnerable in the presence of men who used their size to intimidate her. She needed to protect herself, but she also realized that protection came with a price: eternal vigilance. In exchange for carrying a gun and balancing the power between herself and men, Hasselstrom became conscious of potential assaults at every moment. While in public spaces, she would mentally rehearse situations in which she would use her gun so that, when needed, she could act. The tension is clear: protection from harm on the one hand and vigilance, which might be described as a necessary paranoia, on the other. Hasselstrom's readers might well ask: Is safety worth this price? Hasselstrom built her essay around a tension. You can do the same in choosing topics for your own arguments.

Take Sides in a Debate

A *debate* can be defined as a tension that has erupted into a heated public discussion. Gun control, health care reform, the military draft, and abortion rights are LARGE issues of public policy about which people disagree, sometimes violently. One way to find ideas for an argument is to search out public debates and then take sides. When writing an argument about current affairs, you will seldom need to go further than a local newspaper or a weekly news magazine. When writing an argument about a topic specific to one of your courses, review your assigned readings and locate two or more authors who address the same topic and hold different opinions. Make this topic the focus of your argument, and state your claim.

For example, in a history of science course you might be assigned an argumentative essay that draws on sources read for class. Knowing that debates can provide you with topics for argument, you could review the semester's reading and settle on the famous debate between Galileo and the Church. In a letter dated August 4, 1597, Galileo wrote to the astronomer Johannes Kepler:

> I have been for many years an adherent of the Copernican system, and it explains to me the causes of many of the appearances of nature which are quite unintelligible on the commonly accepted hypothesis [that the sun revolves around the earth].

In 1633, the Holy Inquisition condemned Galileo for supporting the view that the earth revolved around the sun:

> The proposition that the earth is not the centre of the [universe] and does not move from its place is absurd and false philosophically and formally heretical, because it is expressly contrary to the Holy Scripture.

The debate between Galileo and the Church would be an excellent starting point for an argument. You might approach the debate in two ways: you could take sides yourself (in the Galileo case this would not be appropriate, given what you know of astronomy) or you could consider what the debate suggests about some larger issue (in the Galileo case, perhaps the relationship between individual scientists and institutional bodies such as the Church or governing scientific bodies). The key is to use the debate somehow to launch your own argument. Where people have disagreed, there is room for your own opinion. *Every* discipline of study has its debates, both present-day and historical. Search these out as fruitful places to begin an argument of your own. (You will find an extended example of a debate in literary scholarship on pages 374–380.)

Committing Yourself to an Idea

Readers take an argument seriously to the extent that a writer does. One obligation you have in presenting an argument is to believe in your position. Your interest and involvement will help to secure the reader's interest and involvement. In chapter 2, you will find specific strategies for committing yourself to the idea of an essay. These strategies follow from two general attitudes:

- I write for myself and for my audience.
- I will find some approach to my writing that lets me discover something personally significant.

Commitment through Reading

One strategy both for sparking and committing yourself to an idea is to read. Reading invites response, as was the case with student writer Michele Pelletier when reading the words attributed to Socrates in Plato's *Crito*. As Pelletier read, she saw great merit in the argument that individuals owe a debt of service to their country. Prior to reading Plato, Pelletier had planned to argue against the draft on military and economic grounds alone. But the Socrates' argument provided a moral center to her argument, and having quoted a passage from this source she was able to write this:

> It is true: we owe the society that nurtures us a debt. But how best that debt is paid and to what extent the citizens who "owe" are entitled to participate in deciding on payment—these are difficult questions that have been debated through the centuries. The position of Socrates, as applied to military service, leads directly to an army of draftees: The State has a need for protection. Citizens owe the State a debt. The State calls young men, and they come.
>
> If the State institutes a draft for the purposes of protection, then we are within our rights to ask: Does an army of draftees, necessarily, offer the best possible protection? If we can demonstrate that an all volunteer force *better* serves the security interests of the State, then it should follow that we do not need a draft. If the State wants to claim its moral debt from citizens, fine: let that debt be paid with some other, non-military service.

Pelletier argued her case against the mandatory draft all the more forcefully because she agreed with the principle set down by Socrates. Commitment to her idea—that there are no good reasons for reinstituting a mandatory draft—would have been weakened had she not acknowledged the moral arguments for the draft. Here is Pelletier's statement on her reasons for writing the essay:

> At the time of the Gulf War, the topic of the draft was at the center of many conversations. My roommates and I debated whether women

should be drafted if there was a draft. (I said yes.) Many of us debated whether or not being a student was a legitimate exemption from the draft. (I said no.) Quick as it was, the war was very real and the prospect of a draft being restored seemed equally as real. If called, I would have served. But it worried me that I, who am hardly capable of squashing an ant, could be called on to kill a person. There are many people in this country who would volunteer to go to war—and they would make better soldiers than someone like me. I'd rather serve in a different capacity. Some prefer not to fight, and there is no good reason to make them.

Observe the personal involvement. Pelletier was able to write an essay that satisfied her needs as well as those of her history teacher. She took the issue of the military draft seriously and personally. This statement is not yet an essay—there is much work to do, but it reveals the spark at the center of the essay, without which the essay would not have been worth writing or reading. You can, and should, personally commit yourself to the idea of your essay. Find in your topic personal reasons for writing.

Write: Clarify Your Idea and Make It Public

In planning and writing the first draft of any essay, you can expect to clarify your ideas for yourself. Writing is not only an act that communicates information you already possess, but is an act of discovery, and you should expect to deepen your insights as you write. You will do so in the context of making what insights you already have public. Your first consideration will be your readers. Who are they? What do they know? How will you make what *you* know available to them?

Creating Common Ground with Readers

Readers are more likely to understand and recall particular cases that illustrate an idea than they are to understand and recall that same idea expressed as an abstract statement. For instance, we can easily imagine the fear of a woman traveling alone, whose car is surrounded by obviously drunk men—one of the predicaments that Linda Hasselstrom relates in her essay on why she carries a gun. For readers, the tangible fear the writer creates is far more compelling and memorable than this: *Women who travel alone frequently are threatened and need protection.* In chapter 3 you will find a discussion on creating "common ground" with readers, on strategies for presenting the ideas of your essay through particular, memorable details. Here you will read about common ground in the context of arguments that you write. The principle to bear in mind is this: your choice of common-ground details in an essay will be guided by your sense of the readers' needs and interests.

Tone and the Writing Occasion

As you will see in the more detailed discussions on writing occasion and common ground in chapter 3, *tone* describes the general attitude a writer takes toward readers. You have seen a variety of tones in the examples of argumentative essays in this chapter, among them: Chet Raymo's musing, conversational argument on why good children's literature provides an excellent imaginative foundation for future scientists; Linda Hasselstrom's fear-evoking rationale for carrying a handgun; and Barbara Tuchman's scholarly, historical argument on the "idea" of America and its persistence, even in challenging times. Each writer chose his or her tone with care, matching it to a specific writing occasion. Raymo was writing for parents in the market for Christmas presents that would promote scientific thinking in their children; Hasselstrom was writing for people who had not yet made up their minds on the wisdom of carrying a handgun for protection; Tuchman was writing on the occasion of America's 200th birthday, to readers who may have been feeling that the America beginning its third century had lost its direction. Tone varies from essay to essay, depending on topic and audience. The tone you adopt for an argument can be determined based on the elements in the diagram below.

Let's apply the language of this diagram to your arguments. Your purpose in an argument is clear: change a reader's mind through reasoned discussion. What of audience and topic? How will you, as writer, negotiate these elements and arrive at a tone appropriate for a specific writing occasion? The decisions that you make can be explored through the work of one writer, Linda Hasselstrom. Hasselstrom understood, both for herself and her readers, that the determination to carry a handgun for protection was a momentous personal decision. The debate surrounding handgun use had been loud and emotional. In her statement of reasons for writing the essay, Hasselstrom wrote: "[M]edia attention often focuses on dramatic incidents involving weapons, in an atmosphere where discussion becomes emotional. I thought a calm, reasoned discussion of the options, without drama or hyperbole, might be useful to individuals who had not yet made such decisions."

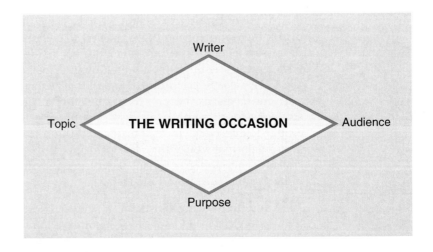

With this very specific audience in mind—*individuals who had not yet made such decisions*—she set about providing reasons why she chose to carry a handgun. What would persuade such individuals that for a woman who often traveled alone a handgun represented a sensible means of protection? If you have read Hasselstrom's essay (pages 412–415), the answer is clear: particular fear-evoking stories that are harrowing enough to make any person in similar circumstances consider making the same choice. Hasselstrom writes of a camping trip, of being harassed while driving on a highway, and of being threatened by drunken men; the particular details provide a rationale for her decision and make a strong appeal to readers who might similarly fear for their safety. The tone of this essay is serious, unemotional, but disturbing. The details through which Hasselstrom develops her idea make the essay memorable.

You create a tone for your essays through your choice of words and your choice of common-ground details. The decisions you make—just like the decisions made by the authors of the essays at the beginning of this chapter—depend on the topic and on a sense of the readers' needs and expectations. As you write, consciously decide on a tone—amused, concerned, outraged, understanding, and so on—and then choose your words and details accordingly. The tone you set in an argument can work for you or against you in advancing your idea.

Planning a Structure

Arguments do not have a set structure that you are obligated to follow. Structure follows from the needs of a particular essay, and as long as you are aware of your claim and your strategies for supporting it in designing your arguments, any structure can work. Over the centuries, however, classic structures for argumentation have emerged, one being the problem/solution essay discussed in chapter 9. Another time-honored structure is the five-part essay summarized next.

Writing an Argument

The following steps illustrate the classic five-part structure of writing an argument.

1. Introduce the topic to be argued. Establish its importance.
2. Provide background information so that readers will be able to follow your discussion.
3. State your claim (your argumentative thesis) and develop your argument by making a logical appeal based on the following factors: generalization, causation, sign, analogy, parallel case, or authority. Support your claims with facts, opinions, and examples. If appropriate, mix an emotional appeal or an appeal to authority with your logical appeals.
4. Acknowledge counterarguments and treat them with respect. Rebut these arguments. Reject their evidence or their logic or concede some validity and modify your claim accordingly. Be flexible: you might split the counterarguments and rebut them one at a time at different locations in the

paper; or you might begin the paper with a counterargument, rebut it, and then move on to your own claim.

5. A useful way to conclude is to summarize the main points of your argument. Then remind readers of what you want them to believe or do.

Note: This five-part structure for argument does not suggest, necessarily, a five-paragraph argument. Arguments can be considerably longer than five paragraphs.

Inductive and Deductive Arrangements

Inductive and deductive arrangements have to do with where you place your claim in an argument. Induction moves from support—particular facts, examples, and opinions—to a claim. A great deal of scientific and technological argument proceeds this way. The writer makes certain observations, finds patterns in those observations, and then makes a claim about those observations. Visually, the process could be represented as in the diagram on the left, below.

Deductive arrangement, shown in the diagram on the right, moves from a claim to support—to particular facts, opinions, and examples. A good deal of writing in the humanities, in politics, and in law proceeds this way. The writer begins with a general principle or claim, the truth, likelihood, or desirability of which is then proven.

What determines whether you will use an inductive or deductive arrangement for your argument? First, realize that in either approach you *begin* writing your argument with the identical information: in both cases, you know before the draft what your claim, support, and lines of reasoning will be. The decision to move inductively or deductively is a decision about strategy.

You can position the claim in your argument at the beginning, middle, or end of the presentation. Working with the five-part structure, you have

Induction	Deduction

flexibility in positioning your claim. One factor that can help determine placement is considering the members of your audience and the likelihood of their agreeing with you. When an audience is likely to be neutral or supportive, you can make your claim early on with the assurance that you will not alienate readers. When an audience is likely to disagree, plan to move your claim toward the end of the presentation, in that way giving yourself space to build consensus with your readers, step by step, until you reach a conclusion.

Readers tend to remember most clearly what they read last. Thus, you may want to present your reasons in support of your claim in the order of least to most emphatic. Conversely, you may want to offer your most emphatic reasons in support of a claim at the very beginning of the argument. In one strong move you might gain the reader's agreement and then cement that agreement with reasons of secondary importance. Any argument can be arranged in a variety of ways. Decisions you make about placing your claim and arranging your points of support will depend on your assessment of the members of your audience and their probable reactions to your views.

Understanding Your Logic

Reasoning in an argument is the pattern of thinking you use to connect statements of support to your claim. Formally, types of reasoning are referred to as **lines of argument.** There are three lines of argument available to you in presenting claims of fact, value, and policy. You can appeal to the reader's sense of logic, respect for authority, and emotion. The following chart summarizes the main lines of argument you can use when connecting supporting statements to a claim. To support a claim of fact, for instance, you would look to the chart and see that you could argue in any of six ways. There are five ways to argue for claims of value and five for claims of policy. In presenting a claim, you will typically offer several statements of support and, correspondingly, several lines of argument.

Matching lines of argument with types of claims

	Claims of Fact	Claims of Value	Claims of Policy
Appeals to Reason			
generalization	x	x	
causation	x		x
sign	x		
analogy	x	x	x
parallel case	x	x	x
Appeals to Authority	x	x	x
Appeals to Emotion		x	x

Adapted from Wayne Brockriede and Douglas Ehninger, "Toulmin on Argument: An Interpretation and Application," *Quarterly Journal of Speech* 46 (1960): 53.

Appealing to Logic

An appeal to reason is by far the most common basis for arguing in the academic world. This section demonstrates five of the most common appeals to logic. You can argue from generalization, from causation, from sign, from analogy, or from parallel case.

Argument from generalization   Given several representative examples of a group (of people, animals, paintings, trees, washing machines, whatever), you can infer a general principle or **generalization**—a statement that applies to other examples of that group. In order for a generalization to be fair, you must select an adequate number of examples that are typical of the entire group; you must also acknowledge the presence of examples that apparently disprove the generalization. Arguments from generalization allow you to support claims that answer questions of fact and value.

Sample Argument

As litter, plastic is unsightly and deadly. Birds and small animals die after getting stuck in plastic, six-pack beverage rings. Pelicans accidentally hang themselves with discarded plastic fishing line. Turtles choke on plastic bags or starve when their stomachs become clogged with hard-to-excrete, crumbled plastic. Sea lions poke their heads into plastic rings and have their jaws locked permanently shut. Authorities estimate that plastic refuse annually kills up to 2 million birds and at least 100,000 mammals.

—Gary Turbak, *"60 Billion Pounds of Trouble"*

Claim: Plastic litter kills animals.

Support: Birds, turtles, sea lions, and various mammals have died from plastic litter.

Reasoning: Generalization. Danger to the animals cited can be generalized to other animals that come into contact with plastic litter.

Argument from causation   In an argument from causation, you begin with a fact or facts about some person, object, or condition. (If readers are likely to contest these facts, then you must make an argument to establish them before pushing on with an argument from causation.) An argument from **causation** enables you to claim that an action created by that person, object, or condition leads to a specific result, or effect: Sunspots cause the aurora borealis. Dieting causes weight loss. Smoking causes lung cancer. Working in the opposite direction, you can begin with what you presume to be an effect of some prior cause: the swing of a pendulum, inattention among school children, tornadoes. Of this presumed effect, you ask: "What causes this?" If you are a scientist or social scientist, you might perform an experiment. Establishing a direct causal link is seldom easy, for usually multiple causes will lead to a single condition (think of the inattentive child at school). In arguing causation, therefore, you need to be sensitive to complexity. Arguments of causation allow you to support a claim that answers a question of fact or a claim that answers a question of policy. Cause-and-effect reasoning also allows you to use a problem/solution structure in your arguments. (See chapter 9.)

Sample Argument

Under primitive agricultural conditions the farmer had few insect problems. Those arose with the intensification of agriculture—the devotion of immense acreages to a single crop. Such a system set the stage for explosive increases in specific insect populations. Single-crop farming does not take advantage of the principles by which nature works; it is agriculture as an engineer might conceive it to be. Nature has introduced great variety into the landscape, but man has displayed a passion for simplifying it. Thus he undoes the built-in checks and balances by which nature holds the species within bounds. One important natural check is a limit on the amount of suitable habitat for each species. Obviously then, an insect that lives on wheat can build up its population to much higher levels on a farm devoted to wheat than on one in which wheat is intermingled with other crops to which the insect is not adapted.

—Rachel Carson, *Silent Spring*

Claim: Insect problems arose with the practice of intensive, single-crop farming.

Support: The variety of vegetation in natural habitats discourages infestation; natural habitats have "checks and balances."

Reasoning: Cause and effect. By creating one-crop farms and eliminating the checks and balances of natural habitats, farmers caused their own insect problems.

Argument from sign A sore throat and fever are signs of flu. Black smoke billowing from a window is a sign of fire. Risk taking is a sign of creativity. In an argument from **sign,** two things are correlated; that is, they tend to occur in the presence of one another. When you see one thing, you tend to see the other. A sign is *not* a cause, however. If your big toe aches at the approach of thunderstorms, your aching toe may be a sign of approaching storms, but it surely does not cause them. Economists routinely look to certain indexes (housing starts, for instance) as indicators, or signs, of the economy's health. Housing starts are *correlated with* economic health, often by means of a statistical comparison. If a sign has proven a particularly reliable indicator, then you can use it to support a claim that answers a question of fact.

Sample Argument

Anxiety over the body as a kind of wasteland is implicit in appeals in advertisements about retaining and restoring moisture. . . . Dry skin . . . [is] a sign of a woman who is all dried up and is not sexually responsive—and who may also be sterile. This is because water is connected, in our psyches, with birth. It is also tied to purity, as in baptismal rites when sin is cleansed from a person. All of this suggests that words and images that picture a body of a woman as being dehydrated and losing water have great resonance.

—Arthur Asa Berger, *"Sex as Symbol in Fashion Advertising"*

Claim: In advertisements, words and images of dehydration resonate for readers and viewers.

Support: Readers have profound psychological associations with dryness.

Reasoning: Sign. Dry skin is a sign of sterility and infertility, deeply resonant themes for men and women.

Argument from analogy   An argument from **analogy** sets up a comparison between the topic you are arguing and another topic that may at first appear unrelated. While suggestive and at times persuasive, an analogy actually proves nothing. There is always a point at which an analogy will break down, and it is usually a mistake to build an argument on analogy alone. Use analogies as you would seasonings in cooking. As one of several attempts to persuade your reader, an analogy spices your argument and makes it memorable. You can use analogies in support of claims that answer questions of fact, value, or policy.

Sample Argument

In closing, we might describe learning with an analogy to a well-orchestrated symphony, aimed to blend both familiar and new sounds. A symphony is the complex interplay of composer, conductor, the repertoire of instruments, and the various dimensions of music. Each instrument is used strategically to interact with other instruments toward a rich construction of themes progressing in phases, with some themes recurring and others driving the movement forward toward a conclusion or resolution. Finally, each symphony stands alone in its meaning, yet has a relationship to the symphonies that came before and those that will come later. Similarly, learning is a complex interaction of the learner, the instructional materials, the repertoire of available learning strategies, and the context, including the teacher. The skilled learner approaches each task strategically toward the goal of constructing meaning. Some strategies focus on understanding the incoming information, others strive to relate the meaning to earlier predictions, and still others work to integrate the new information with prior knowledge.

—Beau Fly Jones, et al., *"Learning and Thinking"*

Claim: Learning involves a complex blending of learner, materials, and context.

Support: In a symphony orchestra, meaning (sound) is created through interaction of musicians, conductor, composer, and history.

Reasoning: Analogy. The complex interactions needed to create symphonic music are analogous to the interaction needed to create meaning for a learner.

Argument from parallel case   While an analogy argues a relationship between two apparently unrelated people, objects, conditions, or events, an argument from parallel case argues a relationship between directly related people, objects, events, or conditions. The implicit logic is this: the way a situation turned out in a closely related case is the way it will (or should) turn out in this one. Lawyers argue from parallel case whenever they cite a prior criminal or civil case in which the legal question involved is similar to the question involved in a current case. Because the earlier case ended a certain way (with the conviction or acquittal of a defendant, or with a particular monetary award), so too should the present case have this outcome. An argument from parallel case requires that situations presented as parallel be alike in essential ways; if this requirement is not met, the argument loses force. The argument would also be weakened if someone could present a more nearly perfect parallel case than yours. You can use a parallel case in support of claims that answer questions of fact, value, or policy.

Sample Argument

Would registry of handguns stop the criminal from carrying the unregistered gun? No, and it might afflict the householder with some extra red tape. However, there is a valid argument for registry. Such a law might have no immediate effect, but we have to begin somewhere. We license automobiles and drivers. That does not stop automobile deaths, but surely the highways would be even more dangerous if populated with unlicensed drivers and uninspected cars.

—Adam Smith, *"Fifty Million Handguns"*

Claim: Registration can mark a modest beginning to resolving the problem of handguns.

Support: Cars and drivers are licensed.

Reasoning: Parallel case. The registration of guns will have a limited effect on deaths caused by guns, just as the registration of drivers and automobiles has a limited effect on the number of traffic deaths. Both efforts, however minimal, show a willingness to manage a problem.

Appealing to Authority

Two types of authority are important in arguments: the authority you bring as a writer and the authority of those who have expert knowledge on the topic that concerns you. Of the two types, *you* are the essential one, since you are present in every argument you make. From one argument to the next, you may or may not call on expert sources (according to your purpose and the needs of your audience).

Establishing yourself as an authority   Intangible elements such as trustworthiness, decency, thoroughness, and engagement are quite different from, but just as important as, the logical force you bring to an argument. An argument impinges on the will of your readers. It asks them to change their minds, and such a request will to some extent make anyone feel vulnerable. After all, you are asking the reader to admit: "I was wrong on that issue, or my thinking was unclear. I'll accept what *you* have to say." To make such a change requires something of an emotional submission ("I'll follow you on this point") as well as an intellectual one ("Your reasons are better than mine"). Before readers will agree, they need to trust the person who asks for their agreement; as a maker of arguments, you must therefore work to establish your trustworthiness—your authority to speak and make a claim. *Authority* in this sense is not the same as having expert knowledge; it has to do, rather, with establishing a presence that readers can yield to in a self-respecting way.

How do you establish this trust? Be honest, first of all. The point is so obvious it hardly seems worth making; but readers generally have a good nose for dishonesty. One whiff and they will turn away—for good. Beyond honesty, which is the main thing, strike a reasonable tone and choose a level of language appropriate for the occasion. Read thoroughly enough on your topic to establish that, although you are not an expert, you do know the important issues and are knowledgeable enough to have an opinion worth considering.

Referring readers to experts   As a writer, you greatly help your cause when you can quote experts on a subject who support your point of view. Realize, though, you are likely to find that experts disagree. For instance, in court cases both prosecution and defense present expert witnesses, sworn to tell the truth. One expert says a defendant is sane and competent to stand trial; a second expert says the opposite. No doubt, the experts *are* telling the truth. But expert *opinions* are just that: interpretations of facts. Facts usually lend themselves to multiple interpretations, and you should not be discouraged when authorities seem to contradict one another.

Whether you find contradictions or not, sources of authority must be authoritative. If they are not, any argument built on an appeal to authority will falter. One of your important challenges, then, both as a writer of arguments and as a critical reader, is to evaluate the worthiness of sources that you and others use. Is the expert testimony that you or others are drawing on truly expert? If you are not an expert in the field, how can you tell? A number of general guidelines should help you make this determination.

Once you have determined to the best of your ability that an expert whom you wish to quote is indeed expert, you must then identify those points in your discussion where appeals to authority will serve you well. You may want to mix appeals to authority with appeals to reason and, perhaps, to emotion. Appeals to authority can be used to support claims that answer questions of fact, value, and policy.

Sample Argument

Leo Marx claims that Melville's "Bartleby the Scrivener" is autobiographical.

Claim: Herman Melville's "Bartleby the Scrivener" is a story about Melville.

Support: Leo Marx says so.

Reasoning: Authority. Leo Marx is a respected literary critic who has taught at leading universities; his insights are valuable and are worth examining.

Using authoritative sources   The following list provides suggestions on how to use authoritative sources:[2]

1. Prefer acknowledged authorities to self-proclaimed ones.
2. Prefer an authority working within his or her field of expertise to one who is reporting conclusions about another subject.
3. Prefer first-hand accounts over those from sources who were separated by time or space from the events reported.
4. Prefer unbiased and disinterested sources over those who can reasonably be suspected of having a motive for influencing the way others see the subject under investigation.
5. Prefer public records to private documents in questionable cases.
6. Prefer accounts that are specific and complete to those that are vague and evasive.
7. Prefer evidence that is credible on its own terms to that which is internally inconsistent or demonstrably false to any known facts.
8. In general, prefer a recently published report to an older one.
9. In general, prefer works by standard publishers to those of unknown or "vanity" presses.
10. In general, prefer authors who themselves follow [standard] report writing conventions. . . .
11. When possible, prefer an authority known to your audience to one they have never heard of. . . .

Appealing to Emotion

Appeals to reason are based on the force of logic; appeals to authority are based on the reader's respect for the opinions of experts. By contrast, appeals to emotion are designed to tap the needs and values of an audience. Arguments based on appeals to reason and authority may well turn out to be valid; but validity does not guarantee that readers will *endorse* your position. For instance, you might establish with impeccable logic that the physical condition of your community's public schools has deteriorated badly, to the point of affecting the performance of students. While true, your claim may not carry force enough to persuade the Town Council to vote on a bond issue or to raise taxes—two actions that would generate the requisite money to renovate several buildings. To succeed in

---

[2]This material is quoted from Thomas E. Gaston and Bret H. Smith, *The Research Paper: A Common-Sense Approach* (Englewood Cliffs: Prentice-Hall, 1988) 31–33.

your effort or in any appeal to emotion, you must make your readers feel the same urgency to act that you do. The following includes an emotional appeal.

Sample Argument

Our children are sitting in schools where paint is flaking off the walls, where the heating plant works sixty percent of the time, where plumbing backs up repeatedly, where windows are cracked or broken and covered by cardboard to keep out the winter. No member of the Town Council would for a moment consider working in an office with such appalling conditions. You each would be indignant and would claim that the environment endangered your welfare. Yet these are precisely the conditions our children contend with now. To vote against a tax hike will be to condemn our children to circumstances that you personally would find intolerable.

—Linda Cohen, *"School Committee Hearing"*

Claim: You should vote for the tax increase.

Support: Our children attend a school that is in deplorable condition.

Reasoning: Emotion. The story of the conditions at the school is unsettling enough to convince town council members to vote for a tax increase, which will alleviate those conditions.

On the basis of an audience analysis, you can sketch a profile of your readers and consider strategies suited to winning their emotional support. Plan your emotional appeal by beginning with a claim that has already been supported by an appeal to reason. In your efforts to raise taxes for school renovation, you could show photographs, produce a list of items in need of repair, and quote expert witnesses who believe that children's learning suffers in deteriorating environments. Having argued by an appeal to reason, you can then plan an emotional appeal.

Making an emotional appeal   The following list provides suggestions on how to make an emotional appeal:

1. List the needs of your audience with respect to your subject: these needs might be physical, psychological, humanitarian, environmental, or financial.

2. Select the category of needs best suited to your audience and identify emotional appeals that you think will be persuasive.

3. In your appeal, place the issue you are arguing in your reader's lap. Get the reader to respond to the issue emotionally.

4. Call on the reader to agree with you on a course of action.

The limits of argument   In the real world, the best of arguments may sometimes fail to achieve its objective. Some subjects—for example, abortion or capital punishment—are so controversial or so tied to preexisting religious or moral beliefs that many people have long since made up their minds one way or the other and will never change them. Such subjects are so fraught with emotion that logical arguments are ineffective in persuading people to rethink their positions. Sometimes, also, your audience has a vested interest in not being persuaded by your arguments. (Perhaps your audience has a financial stake in holding to an opposing position.) When your audience feels significantly threatened by the prospect of your victory, you must realize that it is futile to continue insisting on the validity of your argument.

Making Rebuttals

By definition, arguments are subject to challenge, or to counterarguments. Because reasonable people will disagree, you must be prepared when arguing to acknowledge differences of opinion and to address them—for two reasons. First, by raising a challenge to your own position you force yourself to see an issue from someone else's perspective. This can be a valuable lesson in that challenges can prompt you to reevaluate and refine your views. In addition, challenges pique a reader's interest. Research shows that when tension (that is, disagreement) exists in an argument, readers maintain interest: they want to know what happens or how the argument is resolved.

Once you acknowledge opposing views, respond with a **rebuttal,** an argument of opposition. One type of response is to reject the counterargument by challenging its logic. If the logic is flawed, the counterargument will not weaken the validity of your argument. When you are confident in the position you are arguing, raise the most damaging argument against your position that you can, and then neutralize that challenge. If you do not raise objections, your readers inevitably will; better that you raise them on your terms so that you can control the debate.

Of course, one response to an opposing argument is *to let it change you.* After all, if you are arguing honestly, you are by definition participating in a reasoned exchange. This is to say, when arguing you should be available to accepting the views of others. Readers will appreciate, and take as a sign of your reasonableness, your ability to concede at least some of your opposition's points.

Advance Your Idea with Sources

You can read source materials with these purposes in mind as you prepare your arguments:

- to clarify the background of your topic
- to support your claim directly with facts, opinions, and examples
- to locate arguments against your claim
- to respond to arguments against your claim

In her essay at the beginning of this chapter (see pages 69–72 for the complete essay), student Michele Pelletier demonstrates all four types of reading in support of her argument. Notice she is careful to cite her sources. (See pages 613–628 for more on how to cite the work of others in your own papers.)

Read to Clarify the Background of Your Topic

To know your topic thoroughly, you will very often need to do background reading. Your purpose in this case is largely explanatory: to seek information to develop an understanding of facts and situations so that you can offer a suitable background for your audience and then begin your argument.

A Source That Clarifies Background

. . . During the Carter Administration, . . . the quality of the recruits declined sharply.

The Army was in particularly bad shape. In 1980, only 54% of its recruits had earned high school diplomas, down from 70% in 1964, the last year of the peacetime draft prior to the Vietnam buildup. In 1977–1980, 44% were in the lowest acceptable intelligence category (Category IV on the Armed Forces Qualifying Test), as opposed to 19% in 1964 and 17% in the first three years of the volunteer force.

In the 'Eighties, however, a round of pay increases, the restoration of some education benefits, and a renewed sense of the military as an honorable profession have reversed the trend. The services now regularly meet their recruitment goals. Last year 92% of recruits were high school graduates, including 91% in the Army. . . . Disciplinary problems have declined, fewer recruits are dropping out during the first term of enlistment, and more are reenlisting.

As a result, the U.S. now has a better educated and more experienced military than during the draft era.

—David Kelley, "Arms and the Man: In Terms of Quality, Morality, A Volunteer Military Beats the Draft." *Barron's* 30 Mar. 1987.

The Source Used

In what ways can an all volunteer army be shown to be superior to an army of draftees? First, in these days of sophisticated weaponry, we need a military made up of intelligent individuals who have the ability to learn the technical aspects of warfare. In order to use "smart bombs," night vision equipment, and advanced communications gear, soldiers must be well trained and experienced. During the draft era, the military was forced to take high school dropouts. College students were able to avoid the draft because of schooling. The result was an army "composed disproportionately of the poor, the less intellectually able, and the less idealistic"— which, as Michael Novak has pointed out—"is not healthy for our democracy" (847). Nor does such an army make for an effective fighting force.

Novak was writing in 1980, in response to an all volunteer army that was in disarray after the Vietnam war. Given the state of military affairs, Novak was arguing to reinstitute the draft. But in the 13 years since his essay appeared in *National Review*, his objections to the volunteer army have been met *without* resorting to a draft. In 1980, only 54% of recruits had high-school diplomas. Pay was bad and maintenance of weapons and aircraft was low. Today, 92% of recruits hold high-school diplomas (Kelley 11). Pay, maintenance, and morale has increased to the point that the forces are, according to former Secretary of Defense Cheney, "the highest-quality force in the nation's history" (qtd. in Barone and Gergen 45).

Read to Support Your Claim Directly with Facts, Opinions, and Examples

One frequently used technique for supporting a claim is to refer to the work of an acknowledged expert. In doing so, you borrow that expert's authority, thereby increasing your own authority. Michele Pelletier supports her argument with an appeal to authority when she quotes former Secretary of Defense, Dick Cheney, as saying that today's all-volunteer army is "the highest-quality force in the nation's history." You will also use facts and examples drawn from other sources to support your material. Pelletier draws statistical information into her argument from the same source, David Kelley, that she used to gain background information.

Read to Locate Arguments against Your Claim

In order for readers to take your argument seriously, you must demonstrate your awareness of counterarguments: the views of others who disagree with you. By acknowledging these views, you admit to readers that you recognize that not everyone thinks as you do. When you then rebut these arguments, readers gain confidence in your position. (See the discussion on page 435.) In the following sentence, from her essay on the all-volunteer army, Michele Pelletier quotes a source that neatly presents one reason *not* to maintain such an army; that is, she quotes a source that argues *against* her position:

> #### A Source That Argues against Your Claim
> With the moral and military arguments for the draft gone, some have objected to the volunteer army on political grounds, claiming that the "nation's volunteer Army concentrates the burden of military service and the risk of death on poor and working-class men" (Barone and Gergen 45).

Read to Respond to Arguments against Your Claim

You can draw on the work of others to help you rebut an argument counter to your own, whether you have raised that argument yourself or have quoted that argument, as Michele Pelletier has done. Pelletier turns to an economist, Gary Becker, to help her respond to the counterargument that the volunteer army "concentrates the burden of military service and the risk of death on poor and working-class men":

A Source That Counters a Criticism	*The Source Used*

... It is true that blacks constitute over 20% of the armed forces compared with only 12% of the civilian work force. But the Army is not staffed mainly by the lower classes, as demonstrated by the preponderance of high school graduates and by the fact that almost half of all recruits come from families with above-average incomes.

I believe the military deserves praise rather than criticism for offering black men and women better work opportunities than they can find in the private sector.

—Gary S. Becker. "Leave the Draft Where It Belongs: On History's Junk Heap." *Business Week* 25 Mar. 1991.

With the moral and military arguments for the draft gone, some have objected to the volunteer army on political grounds, claiming that the "nation's volunteer Army concentrates the burden of military service and the risk of death on poor and working-class men" (Barone and Gergen 45). Gary Becker, University Professor of Economics and Sociology at the University of Chicago, ably counters this view:

It is true that blacks constitute over 20% of the armed forces compared with only 12% of the civilian work force. But the Army is not staffed mainly by the lower classes, as demonstrated by the preponderance of high school graduates and by the fact that almost half of all recruits come from families with above-average incomes. (14)

Not only does Becker reject the criticism that an all volunteer military draws on the poor and working class, he praises the military for offering minorities a chance for advancement not found in the private sector.

Evaluate and Revise

General Evaluation

You will usually need at least two drafts to produce an essay that presents your idea clearly. The biggest changes in your essay will typically come between your first and second drafts. In this book you will find two demonstrations of essays in the process of turning from meandering first thoughts into finished products. First, see chapters 12–14 for general advice on the process of writing and revising, which includes first- and second-draft versions of a student paper. Another such demonstration is located in the "Student Writer at Work" sections at the end of chapters 1–5.

No essay, including an argument, will be complete until you revise and refine its single, compelling idea. You revise and refine by evaluating your first draft, bringing to it many of the same questions you pose when evaluating any piece of writing. Chapter 5 presents general guidelines for evaluating what you read, including these:

- Are the facts accurate?
- Are opinions supported by evidence?
- Are the opinions of others authoritative?
- Are my assumptions clearly stated?
- Are key terms clearly defined?
- Is the presentation logical?
- Are all parts of the presentation well developed?
- Are dissenting points of view presented?

Address these same questions to the first draft of your argumentative essays, and you will have solid information to guide your revision.

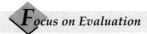

Focus on Evaluation

Have you been asked to write an evaluation of another writer's argumentative essay? If so, you will base your evaluation on two sets of standards. First, you will apply specific standards for this type of writing as listed here in "Critical Points." At the same time you will need to apply the general standards for evaluation that are listed here and discussed at length in chapter 5, pages 92–96. See especially the "key points" for evaluation in chapter 5, pages 95–96.

Critical Points in an Argumentative Essay

Whether you are evaluating your own arguments or someone else's, there are several common errors to watch for. Correct these errors in your own writing, and raise a challenge when you find them in the writing of others.

Defining Terms

Your evaluation of an argument should begin with its claim. Locate the claim and be sure that all terms are well defined. If they are not, determine whether the lack of definition creates ambiguities in the argument itself. For example, the term *generosity* might appear, without definition, in a claim. If that term and the claim itself were later illustrated with the example of a mall developer's "generously offering the main corridors of the mall for exhibitions, during the Christmas Season, of waste recycling demonstrations by Scouting troops," you might justifiably question the validity of the argument. If you define *generosity* as the giving of oneself freely and without any expectation of return, then you might wonder how generous the mall developer is really being. Certainly the increased traffic flow through the mall would boost business, and the supposed generosity might be an advertising ploy. As the reader of this argument, you would be entitled to raise a challenge; if you were the writer, you could by carefully defining terms avoid later challenges to your implied view of the word *generosity*. For instance, you could define the word as "any action, regardless of its motive, that results in the greatest good for the greatest number of people." This one sentence (specifically, the phrase *regardless of its motive*) lets you fend off the challenge, which you could rebut by saying: "Sure, the mall developer is increasing traffic to the mall, and probably profits as well; the developer is also educating an entire community about the importance of recycling. Here is a situation in which everyone wins. To be generous, you don't need to be a martyr."

Examining Inferences

As you have seen, the lines of inferences that a writer makes—generalization, causation, and so on—establish logical support for a claim. If you as the reader feel that the argument's inferences are not valid, then you are entitled to raise a challenge because if these inferences are flawed, the validity of the claim may be in doubt. Any of the following seven types of fallacies, or flaws, will undermine an argument's logic. The first four flaws specifically address the inferences you will use to make arguments from generalization, causation, sign, and analogy.

   1. *Faulty generalization.* Generalizations may be flawed if they are offered on the basis of insufficient data. It would not be valid, for instance, to make the generalization that left-handed people are clumsy because all three lefties of your acquaintance are clumsy. A more academic example: Assume you had administered a survey to students in your dorm. In studying the results you discovered that attitudes toward joining fraternities and sororities were evenly split. Slightly more than 50 percent wanted to join, a bit less than 50 percent did not. It would be a faulty generalization to claim on the basis of this one survey that students on your campus are evenly split on joining Greek organizations. In order for your generalization to be accurate, the survey would need to have been administered campus-wide, if not to every student, then at least to a representative cross-section.

   2. *Faulty cause and effect.* Two fallacies can lead a writer to infer incorrectly that one event causes another. The first concerns the ordering of events in time. The fact that one event occurs before another does *not* prove that the first event caused the second. (In Latin, this fallacy is known as *post hoc*, a brief form of *post hoc, ergo propter hoc*—after this, therefore because of this.) If the planets Venus and Jupiter were in rare alignment on the morning of the Mt. St. Helens eruption, it would not be logical to argue that an alignment of two planets caused the volcano to erupt. The second flaw in thinking that leads to a faulty claim of causation is the belief that events must have *single* causes. Proving causation is often complicated, for many factors usually contribute to the occurrence of an event. What caused the layoff of production-line workers at the General Motors plant in Framingham, Massachusetts? An answer to this question would involve several issues, including increased competition from foreign auto manufacturers, a downturn in the economy, the cost of modernizing the Framingham assembly line, a need to show stockholders that there were fewer employees on the payroll, and a decision to build more cars out of the country. To claim that *one* of these is the sole cause of the plant shutdown would be to ignore the complexity of the event.

3. *Confusing correlation with causation.* There is a well-known saying among researchers that *correlation does not imply causation.* In one study on creativity, researchers correlated *risk taking* and *a preference for the unconventional* with groups of people classified as creative. It would not be logical to infer from this correlation that creativity *causes* risk taking or a preference for the unconventional or that these traits *cause* creativity. The most that can be said is that the traits are associated or correlated with—they tend to appear in the presence of—creative people. Arguments made with statistical evidence are usually subject to this limitation.

4. *Faulty analogy.* The key components of an analogy must very nearly parallel the issues central to the argument you are making. The wrong analogy not only will *not* clarify, but also will positively confuse. For instance, an attempt to liken the process of writing to climbing a flight of stairs would create some confusion. The analogy suggests that the writing process occurs in clearly delineated steps, when progress in actual writing is seldom so neat. The stages of writing do not progress "step by step" until a final draft is achieved. It is more accurate to say that the process of writing loops back on itself and that the process of revision takes place not just at the end of writing (the last step) but throughout. So the stairs analogy might confuse writers who, reflecting on their own practices, do not see neat linear progress and therefore assume they must be doing something wrong. Analogies should enhance, not obscure, understanding.

5. *Either/or reasoning.* Assume that someone is trying to persuade you that the United States ought to intervene militarily in a certain conflict many thousands of miles from U.S. territory. At one point in the argument you hear this: "Either we demonstrate through force that the United States continues to be a world power or we take a back-seat, passive role in world affairs. The choice is clear." Actually, the choice is not at all clear. The person arguing has presented two options and has argued for one. But many possibilities for conducting U.S. foreign policy exist besides going to war or becoming passive. An argument will be flawed when its author preselects two possibilities from among many and then attempts to force a choice.

6. *Personal attacks.* Personal attacks, known in Latin as *ad hominem* arguments, challenge the person presenting a view rather than the view itself. You are entitled to object when you read or hear this type of attack: "The child psychologist on that talk show has no kids, so how can he recommend anything useful to me concerning my children?" Notice that the challenge is directed at the person who is presenting ideas, not at the ideas themselves. The psychologist's advice may well be excellent, but the *ad hominem* attack sidesteps the issues and focuses instead on personality. Here is a variant on the *ad hominem* argument: The speaker is giving what sounds like good advice on child rearing, but she is neither a psychologist nor an educator, so we really shouldn't base our actions on her views." In this case, the critic is dismissing a statement because the speaker is not an acknowledged expert. This kind of criticism can be legitimate if an argument is being directly based on the authority of that speaker's expertise, and you *should* give preference to sources that are authoritative. Nonetheless, it is sidestepping the other issues in an argument to dismiss an apparently useful observation by dismissing the person who holds it. At the very least, statements should be evaluated on their merits.

7. *The begged question.* Writers who assume the validity of a point that they should be proving by argument are guilty of begging the question. For instance, the statement "All patriotic Americans should support the President" begs a question of definition: What *is* a patriotic American? The person making this statement assumes a definition that he should in fact be arguing. By making this assumption, the writer sidesteps the issue of definition altogether. The point you want to make must be addressed directly through careful argument.

Examining Evidence

Arguments also can falter when they are not adequately or legitimately supported by facts, examples, statistics, or opinions. Refer to the following guidelines when using evidence.

Facts and Examples

1. *Facts and examples should fairly represent the available data.* An example cannot be forced. If you find yourself needing to sift through a great deal of evidence *against* a point you wish to make in order to find one confirming fact or example, take your difficulty as a sign and rethink your point.

2. *Facts and examples should be current.* Facts and examples need to be current, especially when you are arguing about recent events or are drawing information from a field in which information is changing rapidly. If, for example, you are arguing a claim about the likelihood of incumbent politicians being reelected, you should find sources that report on the most recent elections. If in your argument you are trying to show a trend, then your facts and examples should also be drawn from sources going back several years, if not decades.

3. *Facts and examples should be sufficient to establish validity.* A generalization must be based on an adequate number of examples and on representative examples. To establish the existence of a problem concerning college sports, for instance, it would not do to claim that because transcripts were forged for a handful of student-athletes at two schools a problem exists nationwide.

4. *Negative instances of facts and examples should be acknowledged.* If an argument is to be honest, you should identify facts and examples that constitute evidence *against* your position. Tactically, you are better off being the one to raise the inconvenient example than having someone else do this for you in the context of a challenge. For example, an argument might conclude that a particular advertising company has consistently misrepresented facts about its products. The arguer would be less than ethical to omit from the discussion several advertisements that were entirely legitimate in their treatment of facts. The wiser strategy would be for the arguer to address these negative examples (negative in the sense that they apparently disprove the claim), either turning them to advantage or at the very least neutralizing them.

Statistics

5. *Use statistics from reliable and current sources.* Statistics are a numerical compression of information. Assuming you do not have the expertise to evaluate procedures by which statistics are generated, you should take certain commonsense precautions when selecting statistical evidence. First, cite statistics from reliable sources. If you have no other way of checking reliability, you can assume that the same source cited in several places is reliable. The U.S. government publishes volumes of statistical information and is considered a reliable source. Just as with facts and examples, statistics should be current when you are arguing about a topic of current interest.

6. *Comparative statistics should compare items of the same logical class.* If you found statistical information on housing starts in New England in one source and in a second source found information on housing starts in the Southwest, you would naturally want to compare the numbers. The comparison would be valid only if the term "housing starts" was defined clearly in both sources. Lacking a definition, you might plunge ahead and cite the statistics in a paper, not realizing that one figure included apartment buildings in its definition of "housing" while the other included only single-family homes. Such a comparison would be faulty.

Expert Opinions

7. *"Experts" who give opinions should be qualified to do so.* Anyone can speak on a topic, but experts speak with authority by virtue of their experience. Cite the opinions of experts in order to support your claims. Of course you will want to be sure that your experts are, in fact, expert; and evaluating the quality of what they say can be troublesome when you do not know a great deal about a topic. You can trust a so-called expert as being an authority if you see that person cited as such in several sources. For experts who are not likely to be cited in academic articles or books, use your common sense. If you were arguing that birchbark canoes track better in the water than aluminum canoes, you would want to seek out a person who has considerable experience with both.

8. *Experts should be neutral.* You can disqualify an expert's testimony for possible use in your argument if you find that the expert will profit somehow from the opinions or interpretations offered. Returning to the example of the birchbark canoe: you would want to cite as an authority in your paper the person who has paddled hundreds of miles in both aluminum and birchbark canoes, not the one who earns a living making birchbark canoes.

Occasions for Discussion and Writing

An Argumentative Essay of Your Own

You are ready to begin work on your own argumentative essay. One approach to choosing a topic is to review examples of the type of essay you will be writing. Consider rereading the essays that opened this chapter. You will find that the four authors—Raymo, Tuchman, Hasselstrom, and Pelletier—write about topics they know well either through direct experience or through careful reading. You will also find that these authors have a deep, personal involvement with their essay's topic: Raymo, a physicist, explores the relationship between imaginative play and the practice of science; Tuchman's involvement is made clear through her reflection on the "idea" of America; Hasselstrom recounts the difficult decision to carry a handgun; and Pelletier takes a stand on the all-volunteer army. In choosing a topic for your argumentative essay, you too should be prepared for a deep involvement. In the best of cases, your motivation to write will be personal, but your expression of ideas *in your essay* will be public and controlled. The examples amply demonstrate this double quality: in each essay you find someone writing for personal reasons, yet maintaining strict control over important elements of public expression—including the essay's reasoning, structure, sentence rhythm, and word choice.

To prepare for your essay, select one of the examples that begin this chapter, one that you find especially effective. Think critically about how this essay succeeds. You might respond to the questions following the piece; you might try writing a paragraph explaining what appeals to you most about the piece; you might reflect on the ways in which this essay could affect your own work. Once you have studied the piece and have a clear sense of how it succeeds, choose a topic for your own essay—a topic that you know well.

The next two Occasions sections present two topics for writing: television and literacy, and the cultural consequences of technology. If you prefer another topic, you might find suitable materials in the other Occasions sections in chapters 6–10:

Chapter 10:   Poems by Langston Hughes, 374–380
                     Short Stories by Kate Chopin, James Joyce, 380–402

Of course, you are not limited to these choices and should choose a topic according to your interests and experience. For detailed guidance on how you might organize your approach to writing an argumentative essay, turn to the second Occasion for discussion and writing in this chapter, pages 476–483. This "Guide to the Assignment" provides a structured approach to the writing task that may help you work through your first draft and revision, whatever your topic.

A note on using sources: All four writers whose essays began the chapter draw on source materials to advance their ideas. You can—and are encouraged to—do the same, with the caution that writers who use sources should never let source materials overtake their essays. The psychological focus of your essay should remain yours alone. In writing a first draft, be sure that your voice predominates and that sources, even if essential to your essay's success, play a subordinate role.

I. Television and Literacy

When you were younger, did a parent say "Turn off that television! You watch too much." Whether this was true or not in your particular case, young people in this country watch plenty of television—on average, 20 hours each week. Many educators and many parents claim that watching television makes for passive, uncritical children who glue themselves to the tube instead spending (what the adults think of as) more productive time reading. The three selections that follow explore this criticism and the assumptions on which it is founded.

First, acknowledging what he calls the "staggering" amounts of television that American children watch, Albert Shanker, President of the American Federation of Teachers, discusses the virtues of the so-called "TV Chastity Belt." Television critic David Bianculli then makes a case for "teleliteracy" in an essay from his book of the same title. And sociologist Susan Neuman follows with an essay on "The Myth of the TV Effect," her conclusion to a study entitled *Literacy in the Television Age.* Each of these essays is an argument. After reading them, do the following:

- Summarize the claim—the argumentative thesis—of each selection.
- Identify all evidence that the authors use to support their claims.
- For each argument, identify the author's reasoning.

Having done this, work with classmates to adopt a group position on the following question: *Should parents limit or in any way supervise the amount of television that children watch?* As you read, try to answer this question for yourself. Your goal should be to bring to your first group discussions a well-developed point of view.

TV Chastity Belt

Albert Shanker

Why do our kids do so badly in school? Lots of people will tell you it's because 1
they spend too much time in front of a TV set. And it's true that the numbers
are staggering. In 1990, one in four 9-year-olds spent six or more hours, seven
days a week, watching TV. That's more than most adults spend at work and certainly more than these kids spent in school. It's also true that kids who watch
lots of TV have poor test scores. What should we do?

Some people talk about parents' cracking down, but a Miami entrepreneur 2
has invented a far more ingenious solution. It's a gadget that rations children's
television time and shuts off the set when a kid has used up his allotment.

Here's how it works. The parent enters Johnny's weekly ration of TV time 3
into a black box that controls the TV power supply. To turn on the TV, the kid
needs to punch in his four-digit ID number, and as he listens to MTV or plays a
game of Nintendo, a clock in the black box debits his account. When he's used
up his time, the set dies, and it's no more TV until next week. The gadget can
also black out whole time periods—for instance, between midnight and 6:00
a.m. so a kid can't sneak out of bed to watch an X-rated film.

This TV chastity belt has gotten enthusiastic notices in the *Washington* 4
Post, the *Boston Globe* and even *TV Guide.* Testimonials talk about how it has
restored tranquility to family life because parents don't have to say *no* all the
time and how it teaches kids to budget their time and make judgments about
what they really want. Above all, of course, it ensures that a youngster's weekly ration of television does not depend on his own discipline or self-control.

Gadgets like this are familiar in the adult world, too. Look at the self-lock- 5
ing refrigerator device for people who are desperate to lose weight or the cigarette case that can be programmed to release only a certain number of cigarettes
a day. You can also see it at the highest levels of the U.S. government in the
Gramm-Rudman bill and the proposed balanced budget amendment. Both are
based on the idea that people in Congress can't keep themselves from over-
spending, and what they need is a gadget that makes it impossible for them to
lose control.

But before we put this difficulty in saying *no* down to human nature—which 6
is the same thing as saying that youngsters can't do anything about it—there's
another angle. Kids in Japan, Germany, France, Sweden and Holland also have
TV sets, but as far as I know, there's been no wave of companies forming in
these countries to market TV chastity belts. Their kids watch far less television,
on average, than American youngsters. They also achieve at much higher levels. How come?

Most adults do what they must in order to get what they want, and kids are 7
no different. Youngsters in these other countries know that if they want to get
into university, it's not enough to squeak through high school. They must study
hard and pass a demanding examination. As for kids who are going right from
school to work, they know that the courses they have taken, the grades they
have gotten and their success on examinations will determine the kind of job
they get.

American kids see no good reason to turn off the TV and do their school- 8
work. A high school graduate who wants to go to college, and can swing it financially, will be able to find some school to accept him, no matter how little he

knows and how poor his grades. It's about the same for youngsters who are going right to work. Top companies don't hire new graduates—they prefer workers in their twenties who already have experience. And the companies that do hire new graduates seldom ask for a transcript or care what kind of record a kid has.

Too much television may lead to poor school performance, but we are not 9 going to take care of the problem by locking up the TV sets. Doing so might induce a handful of kids to start paying attention to their schoolwork, but the rest will find other ways of occupying their time. We must connect student achievement with what happens after graduation—with getting into college or getting a good job—and we must make the stakes visible to our students. Until we do that, we will not get the kind of improvement in student performance that we want and need—no matter how ingenious and successful we are at turning off the tube.

Teleliteracy[3]

David Bianculli

Woody Allen has his *Radio Days,* but he's older than I am. At thirty-eight, my 1 mass-media memories are vastly different. I have *Television Days,* and my earliest video recollections are a montage of brief, flickering, black-and-white images: test patterns and farm reports while waiting for the Saturday-morning cartoons to start. Heckle and Jeckle and Tom Terrific. Month-long countdowns for *Peter Pan* and *The Wizard of Oz.* Looney Tunes, the Road Runner, Gerald McBoing Boing, Captain Kangaroo's Grandfather Clock.

But TV was growing up as quickly as I was, and, for whatever reasons, my 2 parents allowed and even encouraged me to sample at will. Both of them were fervent supporters of John F. Kennedy, so I was allowed to stay up late to watch the Democratic convention and Nixon–Kennedy debates of 1960. Three years later, I watched, along with the rest of America, as the nation mourned JFK's assassination and, astoundingly, witnessed Jack Ruby's shooting of Lee Harvey Oswald on live TV. I was only ten, but that's not the kind of thing your forget. I matured a lot that weekend; so did television.

I had never seen real death on TV before, but, by then, the TV set was a 3 regular and reliable source of horror, thanks to *Alfred Hitchcock Presents, The Twilight Zone,* and a show called *Thriller,* hosted by Boris Karloff, that scared me to death. That, to me, was TV's dark side. On the light side, as I headed into the 1960s, my favorite programs were *Rocky and His Friends* and its closely related successor, *The Bullwinkle Show,* from which I developed my love of bad puns.

In the midsixties, my teen years, I nurtured tastes and ideas that, in retro- 4 spect, leave me less than proud. I loved *The Wild Wild West,* for example, and clearly recall telling a school friend that, based on the way Robert Conrad vanquished bad guys seven at a blow, I'd rather fight four or five guys at a time than

---

[3]Bianculli defines *teleliteracy* as "the demonstration of fluency in the language and content of TV."

just one. My friend fixed me with a glance that said, in essence, I watched too much TV. Looking back, I'm certain he was right.

Perhaps, though, my uncritical nature is what led me to become a TV crit- 5 ic by profession. I didn't just watch *Batman* and *Star Trek* and *Get Smart;* I also watched *Have Gun, Will Travel* and *The Defenders* and *Slattery's People.* I caught the Beatles on *The Ed Sullivan Show* and had my consciousness raised by *The Smothers Brother Comedy Hour.* I watched, with fascination, such unscripted TV events as the moon landing, the evening news reports from Vietnam, and the 1968 riots in Chicago. And surely, I'm not the only American male my age who, as a youth, was overcome by several significant and unfor- gettable emotions while watching Diana Rigg as Emma Peel on *The Avengers.*

It was television, almost as much as rock 'n' roll, that encouraged me to be 6 different, and think differently, in the late sixties. Tom and Dick Smothers paved the way for me, along with Patrick McGoohan's surrealistic, paranoid, and non- conformist *The Prisoner* series. When the new decade started, my tastes had evolved to encompass the unfettered, short-lived freedom of the PBS antholo- gy series *The Great American Dream Machine* (former home of Andy Rooney, Chevy Chase, Marshall Efron, and others) and the increasingly surrealistic TV addresses by President Richard M. Nixon.

In the first half of the seventies, reality far outstripped entertainment. Aside 7 from a few oddball shows, such as *Kolchak: The Night Stalker,* there wasn't much to compare with the freakishness of the Saturday Night Massacre or the Watergate hearings. Then, in the fall of 1975, came *Saturday Night Live,* which gave my generation a TV voice of its own for the first time. It also by coincidence, helped me find my voice as well: *Saturday Night Live* was the first TV series I reviewed as a professional TV critic, inaugurating my TV-review col- umn in Florida's *Gainesville Sun.*

I've changed employers many times since, but not my approach. I still watch 8 too much TV. I still find that *everything* I care about shows up on TV sooner or later, giving me a chance to think and write about music, politics, comedy, drama, science, even the business and technology of television. And, after all these years, I still get enthusiastic when I see good stuff—and upset when the networks mess it up or take it off. It's difficult to describe the joy I got when pre- viewing, and raving about, and steering readers toward, Dennis Potter's *The Singing Detective*—or my amazement when, while interviewing Kurt Vonnegut for this book, he turned out to be just as rabid a fan of that very same mini- series. I also enjoy the sense of continuity that comes when I introduce my own children to something as subversively entertaining as *The Simpsons,* which is to the nineties what *The Bullwinkle Show* was to the sixties.

Am I taking TV too seriously? Maybe—but I'd argue that many people don't 9 take TV seriously enough. The common and easy thing to do is to dismiss TV entirely, or to attack it for its obvious excesses and weaknesses. However, reject- ing the entire medium of television on the basis of *Charlie's Angels* is no more logical or defensible—or sporting—than rejecting the entire motion-picture industry on the basis of *Porky's.* Not too long ago, film was as maligned and mistrusted as TV is today, but the movies have since matured into an accepted and admired art form. Television, too, is a modern art, and it's on display— every night—in the largest gallery in the country. Yet perhaps because of that pervasiveness and familiarity, it's either taken for grated or targeted for abuse.

Anyone who still thinks of TV as a vast wasteland, though, hasn't checked out the scenery in quite a while.

And even television's past has a significant and continued impact on our present culture. That's where the concept of *teleliteracy* comes in: it's an acknowledgment and understanding of the elements of TV's past and present that are likely to survive well into the future. In essence, anyone who can discuss TV's coverage of the Gulf War or the William Kennedy Smith trial, or laugh knowingly at any of TV's parodies of Roseanne Arnold singing the national anthem, or who can mimic the theme song of *The Twilight Zone,* is demonstrating teleliteracy.

This differs a bit from *Cultural Literacy,* the concept put forth by Professor E. D. Hirsch, Jr., in his best-seller of the same name. The subtitle of that book, it should be remembered, is *What Every American Needs to Know.* By comparison, teleliteracy is, for that most part, What Every American Already Knows.

In the follow-up book *The Dictionary of Cultural Literacy,* written by Hirsch, Joseph F. Kett and James Trefil, the authors stated in their introduction that "cultural literacy, unlike expert knowledge, is meant to be shared by everyone." Sharing is one thing; remembering is another. Most of us "shared" *Beowulf* in junior high school, but that doesn't mean we could spout a cogent synopsis many years later.

I suggest that cultural literacy, while a fine idea, is applying its energies in the wrong direction. If you want to talk about knowledge that is shared by everyone, the area on which to focus is television. Television is our most common language, our most popular pastime, our basic point of reference; it's also where most of our children are first exposed to allusion, satire, and other "literary" concepts.

Look at *Sesame Street,* which is littered with characters and skits poking fun at literature (fairy tales), poetry (nursery rhymes), music, and even TV itself. Or *Square One TV,* a television show that teaches mathematics to preteens. Its most popular segment is "Mathnet," which borrows Jack Webb's monosyllabic *Dragnet* style to teach fractions and decimals. And is there really that much difference between a child's insistence on hearing the same bedtime story night after night and wanting to rewind and review an entertaining installment of *Shelley Duvall's Faerie Tale Theatre?*

As viewers age, and as television ages, the commonly shared experiences pile up. TV has now matured to the point where it's repeatedly self-referential, as when *The Wonder Years* lapses into a dream sequence based on *Star Trek,* or when *Newhart* ends its entire run with an episode suggesting the whole series was a dream—and putting Bob Newhart back into the character, bedroom and bed of his previous hit TV series, *The Bob Newhart Show.* Yes, these are inside jokes—but the point is that, with television, almost everyone's an insider.

Does this mean that literacy, at least in the cultural sense, is doomed to extinction? That the literati who in this century fondly cite the works of Franz Kafka will be usurped in the next century by *tele*literati who prefer to quote from the words of Ralph Kramden? No. But it's time to realize TV must be doing something right to reach and affect so many people, and that teleliteracy is something to be quantified and upgraded and utilized, not ignored.

The Myth of the TV Effect

Susan B. Neuman

[T]elevision as a medium is neither "intrinsically" good nor bad. In contrast to   1
popular conceptions, it is a resource which like any others, may be used or
abused. Unfortunately those who have condemned the television set as a
"mechanical rival," prescribing to do away with it altogether, have failed to
weigh its strengths and weaknesses. In doing so, they have ignored the possibilities of television as a means of extending children's interests and knowledge.
These critics have also created an unnecessarily adversarial distinction between
what has traditionally been defined as "entertainment" and what is classified as
"education"—a relationship which, in fact, may be more complementary than
conflicting.

It is true that by design, television is not an instrument of teaching. Yet the   2
medium may have much to offer in educational value. For example, television
is a remarkable disseminator of information. It has undoubtedly contributed to
the public's knowledge and understanding of current social and political events
(Comstock, 1978). Similarly, television is a primary medium in which many children today are introduced to a wide variety of stories and genres. These opportunities could be used more fruitfully to help children see the important
connections between their traditional school subjects and the different facets of
our culture.

Too often many adults, particularly those in the educational community,   3
have chosen to ignore television or even worse, have virulently attacked all uses
of the medium. Articulating this perception in a public address, Jankowski reported (1986):

> It is a source of constant amazement to me that the television set, an inert,
> immobile appliance that does not eat, drink or smoke, buy or sell anything,
> can't vote, doesn't have a job, can't think, can't turn itself on or off, and
> is used only at our option, can be seen as the cause of so much of society's
> ills by so many people in education.

Unfortunately, the assumption that media draw children's attention away   4
from learning has fostered a rather narrowly defined view of how literacy develops and how learning is thought to occur. Reading graded materials, such as
basal readers, has been viewed as the sine qua non in schools, sometimes at the
cost of equally important hands-on experiences or activities involving other
forms of symbolic representation. However, if children's ability to acquire literacy is said to be based on their prior knowledge, their conceptual understanding of language, and their uses of a variety of strategies, then there might be
many paths to that goal, some of which may actually lie outside the printed
page. For example, background knowledge derived from television, radio, and
other sources surely contributes to an individual's understanding and critical
thinking when reading about similar events in newspapers and texts. In this
respect, rather than compete, media may serve complementary functions.

Indeed, children's interests in stories are often enhanced by their presenta-   5
tion in more than one medium. Cooper (1984), for example, found that after
watching a televised version of a popular children's story, even the youngest
children wanted to discuss its meaning, to explore the fiction further, to mull it
over, and to go back to the book. We need to appreciate the special qualities

inherent in each medium, to expose children to multiple genres and media presentations, and to build important connections between them.

It is a fact that many children today are watching a great deal of televised fare that is inappropriate for their age and sophistication level. This concern raises two possible courses of action. If we take the position of technology determinist Neil Postman that "it is pointless to spend time or energy deploring television or even making proposals to improve it," then the only response is to lock the television set up, or do whatever is necessary to keep it away from the innocent eyes of children. But if we believe that television can offer the potential to complement and enliven children's literacy experiences, it is imperative that greater efforts be made both to improve the quality of programming, and children's viewing habits. These efforts need to involve not just parents, but all those concerned with children in our society. As Schramm, Lyle, and Parker found (1961):

> We have a resource in children and a resource in television. We are concerned that television should strengthen, not debilitate, the human resource. This end can be accomplished most easily not by unilateral activity on the part of the TV industry, or by parents or schools, but rather by mobilizing all the chief forces in society which bear on the television-child relationship. It must be a shared effort to meet a shared responsibility. (p. 188)

Television has the potential to extend learning and literacy well beyond the classroom walls. Whether it actually realizes its potential depends on the cooperative efforts and sense of public responsibility of broadcasters, the guidance and supervision of parents, and the skills and vision of educators building linkages between home and school learning.

References

Comstock, G. (1978). *Trends in the study of incidental learning from television viewing.* Syracuse, NY: Syracuse University. (ERIC Document Reproduction Service No. ED 168 605).

Cooper, M. (1984). Televised books and their effects on children's reading. *Uses of English, 35,* 41–49.

Jankowski, G. (1986). *Television and teachers: Educating each other.* (ERIC Document Reproduction Service, No. ED 268 600).

Schramm, W., Lyle, J., & Parker, E. (1961). *Television in the lives of our children.* Stanford, A: Stanford University Press.

Individual Response:
Television and Literacy

Read to understand and evaluate the preceding three arguments: "TV Chastity Belt," "Teleliteracy," and "The Myth of the TV Effect." For each selection, respond to the following. (As needed, see the cross-references to discussions earlier in the chapter.)

Understand the Readings
1. What is the author's claim? (See pages 403–406.)

Does the claim answer a question of fact? a question of value? a question
of policy?

What terms are essential to understanding the claim? What definitions do
you find?

2. What support does the author offer for his or her claim? (See pages 406–407.)

What facts are used?
Which examples?
Whose opinions?

3. For each instance of support, identify the author's reasoning. Consult the
chart on page 426 and, based on the claim you believe the author is making, note the various types of reasoning that are appropriate.

Has the author made any appeals to reason?
Has he or she argued from generalization (see page 428); causation (page
428); sign (page 429); analogy (page 430); or parallel case (page 431)?
Has the author made appeals to authorities?
Has the author appealed to emotions?

4. Has the author raised and responded to counterarguments?

Evaluate the Readings

1. Points you may want to consider when evaluating Shanker:

- Has Shanker convinced you that his claim is valid, or, at the very least,
  worth your serious consideration?

- Shanker is president of a national teacher's organization. He approaches
  the question of television viewing as an educator and as a concerned parent. Are you satisfied that the children's views on television watching are
  represented adequately in this argument? If not, why do you think Shanker has neglected them?

- Reread ¶s5–7. Do you believe that people cannot control their impulses,
  even self-destructive ones, and should have rules imposed on them from
  the outside?

- In ¶9, Shanker avoids making a direct cause-and-effect relationship
  between television watching and school performance. Still, he operates
  with an assumption about the educational value of television. What is
  this assumption?

2. Points you may want to consider when evaluating Bianculli:

- Bianculli obviously enjoys television and finds much to value in the
  medium. In ¶s1–7, he provides a personal account of his television viewing and why it was important. He then begins ¶9 with a question: "Am
  I taking TV too seriously?" Do you think he is?

- How do you respond to Bianculli's argument (¶9) "that many people
  don't take TV seriously enough"?

- What is your view of Bianculli's distinction (¶s10–13) between teleliteracy and cultural literacy? Is *teleliteracy* a term you find useful?

- Has Bianculli convinced you in this argument that "it's time to realize TV
  must be doing something right to reach and affect so many people, and

that teleliteracy is something to be quantified and upgraded and utilized, not ignored" (¶16)? How would you put the term to use? Would you make teleliteracy a goal for public schools?

3. Points you may want to consider when evaluating Neuman:

- Neuman claims in ¶s1–2 that critics have "created an unnecessarily adversarial distinction between what has traditionally been defined as 'entertainment' and what is classified as 'education'—a relationship which, in fact, may be more complementary than conflicting." What is your view of this distinction? To what extent does Neuman's characterization of television's critics apply to Albert Shanker?

- What is the "narrowly defined view of how literacy develops," according to Neuman (¶4)? Does your experience beyond the printed page confirm Neuman's impression that "there might be many paths to [literacy]"—that television, radio, and movies might enhance a student's ability to read?

- In her conclusion (¶7), Neuman writes that broadcasters, parents, and educators must cooperate if television is to achieve its potential "to extend learning and literacy well beyond the classroom walls." Reflect on your television viewing, past and present. Do you agree that television has such potential?

Group Response: Television and Literacy

Before deciding on a policy concerning the amount of television children should watch, discuss with group members some questions raised by Shanker, Bianculli, and Neuman.

1. To what extent will children control their impulses, even when these impulses work against their own best interests?

2. How is a child best motivated: by punishing negative behavior? by rewarding positive behavior? by appealing to the child's self-interest? by some combination of these?

3. To what extent are problems that we say exist among children (such as heavy television viewing) related to problems in the larger culture? If you believe there is a strong relation (as Shanker does), with what confidence—and with what expectations for success—can you address one set of problems without addressing the other?

4. What are the merits of television? Bianculli and Neuman have their views. Do you agree with them?

5. Identify in the selections you have read key assumptions about the worth of television programming and the relationship between television viewing and literacy. (For a discussion on assumptions, see chapter 5, pages 89–90.) As a group, identify your own assumptions.

7. Find where Bianculli and Neuman attack the critics of television. What do these critics say? How do Bianculli and Neuman respond? What are your group's positions?

8. The consensus you reach as a group regarding these questions will lead directly to a policy on limiting or otherwise supervising the television viewing of young people. Policies are plans of action designed to bring about desired ends. Policies always rest on assumptions about what is desirable, about how people behave and are motivated, and about how problems get resolved. Your group should be clear about its assumptions before setting out to design a policy.

◆Suggestions for Writing with a Computer

Exchange disks with another student, giving him or her a copy of a rough draft of an argument you have written.

Working at the computer, read your partner's rough draft, focusing in particular on the tone of the essay. How would you describe the tone of this rough draft? Is it reasonable and measured? Emotional? Sarcastic? Bitter? Humorous? Patronizing? Timid? Aggressive? Cynical? Wishy-washy? Dry?

Copy two passages from this draft, each no more than a paragraph in length. One passage should be an example of a place where you think the author's tone is appropriate and effective. Write a note to the author, telling the author exactly why the tone in this passage works for you. Point to specific examples.

Then copy a passage where the tone may be inappropriate or poorly developed. Point out to the author what you see as problems with the tone in this section. Then rewrite this passage, adopting a tone that might be more successful. Be sure to explain to the author why you have made your modifications. Afterward, discuss your findings and revisions.

Projecting an Essay: Television and Literacy

The goal of your group work is to sketch an argument in response to the following: *Should parents limit or in any way supervise the amount of television that children watch?* Your response will answer a question of policy, about what *ought* to be done. (See page 405 on claims that answer questions of policy, and page 427 for lines of reasoning you can present for such claims.) Your argument should appeal to a reader's sense of reason, emotion, and respect for authority. Choose one of two audiences: a room of twelve-year-old, avid television viewers, *or* a room of parents whose twelve-year-olds watch television. (Coordinate your choice of audience with other groups, so that both audiences are addressed.)

1. Bearing in mind your group discussions, agree on a policy for limiting or supervising the number of hours each week that young people watch television. Work with group members to define and defend a "reasonable" amount of time for television watching.

2. In the Structures and Strategies section of the chapter, consult the chart that summarizes which lines of argument are appropriate for claims of policy (page 427): you can appeal to reason (specifically, you can argue from cause, analogy, and parallel case); you can appeal to authority (for instance, to Shanker, Bianculli, or Neuman); and you can appeal to emotion.

3. Divide among the group responsibility for devising separate appeals in support of your claim. Each group member is responsible for producing various types of support—specific facts, opinions, and examples—consistent with the line of reasoning he or she is developing. Remember: appeals will be directed to a particular audience—either parents or children.

4. As a group, decide on the claim you will argue and on the general shape of the argument: which lines of support, facts, opinions, and examples will be used and where they will be located. One group member should serve as recorder and take notes, which will be typed and sent to other group members as soon as possible.

5. Exchange your outlined argument with another group. Evaluate the "critical points" of your partner-group's outline, based on the criteria on pages 439–443: What strengths do you find? What weaknesses? Report back to the partner group and expect a report from them. Based on their evaluation of your outline, identify counterarguments and plan responses (see page 435).

6. Prepare a final draft of your group's outline argument, attaching pertinent support materials (relevant facts, quotations from authorities, and examples).

7. Option: Prepare an argumentative essay, based on your group's discussions.

II. Technology and Change

Technology is a fundamental part of culture, and when technologies change, observes Margaret Mead and other anthropologists, so do other elements of culture, including "central values." Over the past two hundred years, the pace of technological innovation has been especially rapid, forcing on us both anticipated and unexpected changes. In inventing the steam engine, for instance, in 1769, James Watt may have foreseen the rise of industrial England, but he could not have foreseen the wretched living conditions among urban laborers of the next century; nor could he have well understood the social rupture in the move from cottage industries to the factory system. In our own day, the inventors of the first vacuum-tube, room-sized computers may have imagined how computers would revolutionize information management. But these pioneers probably did not foresee the revolution's underbelly: new possibilities for industrial sabotage, invasions of privacy, and government control and monitoring of its citizens.

Technologies have the power to alter our values, disrupting traditions and forcing us to revisit age-old questions and to pose new questions as well. The following readings offer you an occasion to explore several of these questions. An anthropologist, Margaret Mead, and a theologian,

Martin Marty, explore the ways in which new technologies challenge traditional beliefs. In demonstration of their point, you will read how the introduction of the wheel changed a Native American culture. These pieces provide a broader context for your reading of three additional selections on a modern-day technology, in vitro fertilization, that has brought joy to barren couples but has also sparked heated debate. Several controversial issues have arisen. For example, should women beyond their biological childbearing years (that is, should postmenopausal women) receive fertility treatments that enable them to give birth? The question is not academic. On July 18, 1994, a 62-year-old Italian gave birth to a healthy 7 lb., 4 oz. boy. When Riccardo enters college, his mother will be 80.

These selections form a mini-case library gathered to prompt your thinking about the often-difficult social and ethnical questions that new technologies force on us. The selections will provide you with ideas and source materials for an argumentative essay.

Your Writing Assignment

Accept for the moment this statement: Within 500 years, technology will have advanced to the point that our brains can accept plug-in, micro-chip modules, each of which can provide instant, expert abilities such as the ability to sight-read music or to think and speak in any language. In a six- or seven-page argument to be read by your classmates, explore these questions:

1. If you could choose a plug-in, micro-chip module right now, what instant, expert ability would you choose? Given this ability, what, if anything, would change fundamentally about you, about what makes you human?
2. What changes would you expect to see in a culture in which everyone, on demand, could become an instant expert?
3. To what extent would these changes, both personal and cultural, be for the good?

Read the following selections to prompt your thinking about technology and change. Following these selections, you will find a Guide to the Assignment that will help you through the process of writing and revising an argumentative essay.

Options

You have three options in writing this essay: the micro-chip module option described above, and these:

Option 2: Write on the changes and challenges associated with widespread use of "designer" in vitro fertilization (IVF). Assume that at some point in the future infertile *and* fertile couples as well as single women could select eggs and sperm from a bank, according to the specific traits they desire in a child. The child thus selected and born would *not* be genetically related to the parent(s).

Option 3: Write on the social and ethical questions surrounding any technology that interests you—in which case you can use the articles by Mead, Bliss, Spicer, and Marty in this chapter but will then need to do some additional library research.

Cultural Patterns and Technical Change
Margaret Mead

Margaret Mead, acclaimed anthropologist and author of numerous books and articles, was approached by the United Nations in the early 1950s with this question: How can we ease the disruptive effects of the technologies we introduce to Third World countries? Mead assembled a task force of anthropologists, physicians, public health officials, and mental health specialists to take on the question. In the brief passage that follows, excerpted from her introduction to the task force's final report, Mead lays bare a defining assumption of culture and cultural change. Written over forty years ago, Mead's views on cultural change are still widely shared.

Technical change is also as old as civilization and since time immemorial the ways of life of whole peoples have been transformed by the introduction of new tools and new technical procedures, as inventions like the plough, the domestication of animals, writing, the use of steam, the factory assembly line, and the internal combustion engine, have been diffused from one country to another. Relationships of relative dominance between two peoples, population balances, dynasties, and whole religious systems have been upset by some change in technology, just as the inventions which underlie technological change have themselves arisen from changing conceptions of nature and of man. 1

Nor is the attempt to control technological change new; monarchs have tried to introduce new practices among their people; merchants have attempted to keep within national borders some valuable technical process like the weaving of cloth, conquerors have educated the conquered so that they would fit in better with the scheme of conquest. 2

What is new is the assumption, on an international scale, of responsibility for introducing changes which are needed among peoples in areas of the world which can visibly benefit from the knowledge which the peoples of other areas have—of techniques which will increase production and conserve natural resources; of nutritional practices which will improve the well-being of a people; of public health practices which will lower the death rate, the incidence of epidemic and endemic disease, and rescue individuals now doomed to physical and mental illness. New also is the recognition and willingness to deal scientifically with the concomitant effects of such change. 3

Within this emerging world climate of opinion, in which international governmental and international voluntary, and national governmental and national voluntary agencies are all playing a role, this survey is designed to provide materials which will sensitize all those concerned with this world-wide task to the mental health implications of such introduced change in the living habits of whole populations. 4

The approach of this survey is based on the recognition that a culture is a systematic and integrated whole. "Culture" as used in this survey is an abstrac- 5 tion from the body of learned behaviour which a group of people, who share the same tradition, transmit entire to their children, and, in part, to adult immigrants who become members of the society. It covers not only the arts and sciences, religions and philosophies to which the word culture has historically applied, but also the system of technology, the political practices, the small intimate habits of daily life, such as the way of preparing or eating food, or of hushing a child to sleep, as well as the method of electing a prime minister or changing the constitution. This survey is based on the assumption, itself drawn from field work among many kinds of societies, that a change in any one part of the culture will be accompanied by changes in other parts, and that only by relating any planned detail of change to the central values of the culture is it possible to provide for the repercussions which will occur in other aspects of life.

The following case study on the introduction of the wheel into a Native American culture appears in a classic text of anthropology, Edward Spicer's Human Problems in Technological Change. *Written in the 1950s, like Mead's* Cultural Patterns and Technical Change, *Spicer's book offers several case studies that follow from a key anthropological assumption that he shares with Mead: cultures are complex systems of linked behaviors and beliefs. To change one element of a culture is to change others—whether or not these secondary changes are desired or desirable. This reading consists of two parts: a case, "In the Wake of the Wheel," by Wesley L. Bliss, and a list of "Questions for Study," by Edward Spicer. Both writers, who were anthropologists, taught at the University of Arizona. Note that you can use Spicer's "Questions" to guide your thinking about the introduction of any technology, past or present. Wesley Bliss uses several of these questions to examine a past introduction of technology; you will be asked to use them to examine a future introduction of technology.*

In the Wake of the Wheel
Wesley Bliss

1. The Problem

Like other American Indians, the Papagos of southern Arizona knew nothing 1 of the wheel and its uses until the white men came. Relatively isolated in desert country, they did not begin to make much use of wheeled vehicles until shortly before 1900. Their adoption came about partly as the result of a deliberate program of the United States Bureau of Indian Affairs. The program was successful and had far-reaching effects on the simple routine of life in the desert villages.

The Indian agents correctly predicted that the Papagos would find uses for 2 wagons but, so far as is known, no official anticipated the whole train of effects on Papago life. Hence, the introduction of the wagon was not integrated with other plans for the Indians.

What immediate changes in the life of a desert Indian village would you 3 expect from the introduction of a wagon about the year 1900?

2. The Course of Events

1. Spanish missionaries first came into contact with the Papago Indians in 4 1687. The missionaries, and the soldiers and few colonists who followed them, brought metal tools, cattle, horses, wheat and other European seeds, as well as Christianity and some ideas of political and military organization. The horses were used for riding and pack animals; but if wheeled vehicles were introduced, the fact is not recorded.

2.   For almost 200 years following the first intensive contact with the Jesuit 5 missionaries, the Papagos continued to live at the extreme margin of Spanish influence in the New World. The effects of this contact were not at all like those farther south, in Mexico. Spaniards were little interested in the desert country and their influence was felt chiefly along the southern and eastern edges of Papago territory. Here Papagos moved into the villages around the mission churches for longer or shorter periods and learned something of new agricultural techniques and products. In the main, life in the desert villages continued very much as it had for hundreds of years.

3.   About the middle of the nineteenth century, with the coming of Anglo 6 Americans to southern Arizona after the close of the Mexican War, a new era began for the Papagos. They joined as allies with the Americans against their old enemies, the Apaches, and rendered effective service in pacifying the Apache frontier.

4.   The agents of the Bureau of Indian Affairs who first came in contact 7 with the Papagos in the 1860's expressed deep concern for the "poverty-stricken Indians," and efforts were made to help them. Impressed with the Papagos' lack of possessions, the agents undertook as one of their first acts the free distribution of knives, shovels, hoes, and other agricultural implements.

5.   Later, a plan was put into effect for giving a farm-wagon to everyone 8 who would agree to build a house in the Mexican adobe style, in place of the brush types traditional among Papagos. Many families in the village where the Indian agent had settled, at the eastern margin of Papago territory, responded during the next few years and received new farm-wagons.

6.   The majority of Papagos lived far to the west of the agent's village and 9 were not reached by this first program, so that it was only in the eastern villages that wagons came into use.

By the 1890's the program had been changed. A man did not have to build 10 a Mexican-style house; he could obtain a wagon by applying to the agent. Payment could be made at leisure.

7.   Three brothers of the headman of the village of Choulik, 60 miles west 11 of the agent's village, had obtained work at various times as laborers on track construction for the Southern Pacific Railroad. They were thus thrown into rather close contact with Anglo Americans and their vehicles in the towns that had grown up along the railroad route.

8.   When the brothers heard of the Indian agent's offer, they persuaded the 12 headman to ask for a wagon. About a year after the request, the agent sent word that one was ready. The headman rode to the agency and was supplied with a heavy farm-wagon and harness for a team of horses. He drove the wagon back to his home village.

9.   The wagon was put into immediate service and continued in use for several years, until it wore out. It was the beginning of a successful introduction of 13 wagons to all villages in the area neighboring Choulik.

3. Relevant Factors

The Papago pattern of life rested on a combination of hunting and gathering of   14
wild food (cactus fruits and mesquite beans) with very small-scale flood farming
along the intermittent streams. The introduction of cattle by the Spanish added
something to Papago subsistence; the Indians allowed the animals to run wherever they could find forage and then hunted them like wild game. Although relatively few horses and mules were brought into the region, the horses multiplied
through the years. At first they were sometimes used for food but, by 1900,
were commonly employed as pack and riding animals.

Papagos had their own methods of packing. They made saddles of two   15
cylindrical bundles of wheat straw or grass tied together with leather thongs and
slung so that one rested on each side of the horse's back. Goods to be trans-
ported were put in panniers, made of fiber or rawhide nets, which were slung
over the straw-pack saddles. A man always rode a loaded animal. Most villages
in the vicinity of Choudik had, by 1900, at least a small string of horses, usually one or two for each family.

The Indians customarily changed their residence with the season. During   16
the winter months they lived in the mountains, where there were permanent
supplies of water in the form of springs. In the summer they moved down into
the valleys to plant and harvest crops of corn, beans, and wheat. The winter
and summer villages were from 6 or 8 to 15 or 20 miles apart. Often during
the winter in ordinary years, and always in drought years, family groups sought
jobs in the Mexican villages of Sonora, among the Pima Indians on the Gila
River, or among the newly arrived English-speaking migrants, who were establishing mines and cattle ranches in southern Arizona. The village of Choulik was
some 60 miles from the nearest non-Papago settlement and over a hundred
from more thickly populated areas like the Gila Valley to the north or the Alter
Valley to the south.

Trading expeditions were frequently organized by the Papagos for the pur-   17
pose of obtaining seeds to plant. Such trips were usually planned by all the males
of a village, who would decide on types and quantity of seeds and select several men to go out with pack horses to secure them. Buckskin, grass rope, large
baskets, and pottery ollas were the usual trade goods. Papago traders went as
far as 250 miles on such expeditions—reaching Bisbee, Arizona, and Her-
mosillo, Sonora. Families also traveled annually or every other year to Magdal-
ena, Sonora, on religious pilgrimages to visit the famous image of San Francisco.

Papago villages were small, rarely consisting of more than a hundred peo-   18
ple, and were organized as land-using, political units, laying claim to some permanent water supply in the mountains and to an area of arable fields in the
valley. Usually a *charco,* a large dirt-banked reservoir, held the domestic water
supply for a field village during the summer months.

The 7 to 20 families of a village recognized the leadership of a headman.   19
He, working closely with a council of all the adult men, planned and carried out
communal enterprises, such as building water-spreading dams for the fields or
repairing the *charco.* Usually all, or nearly all, of the families in a village were
related in patrilineal system. In village meetings, which might be held as frequently as every night, all males attended and addressed each other during proceedings by kinship terms. The village was consequently a closely knit social
unit, recognizing communal property in fields, water supply, and wild food
resources.

Hardly any surplus was produced in the desert villages, and there was no 20
full-time specialization of labor. All the men, including even the curing and
diagnosing shamans, worked in the fields. They took care of the horses and
managed their packing, and most men could engage in the simple crafts of
leather- and woodworking. Women, besides cooking and performing other
household duties, were part-time specialists in pottery-making and basketry.
The older boys and girls gathered wood from round about the village, armload
by armload, and also carried the water in ollas from the *charcos* or springs to
the houses.

4. The Outcome

The wagon was a desirable and nondisruptive innovation from the Papago 21
point of view. Its use resulted, nevertheless, in a long series of small changes
and new adjustments which affected everyone in the village. Some of these were
of minor importance from any point of view and some were of far-reaching
significance.

The men of Choulik quickly trained their horses to pull the wagon. The 22
rawhide tugs which they had been using in plowing were not transferred to the
wagon. Instead, manufactured harness, introduced simultaneously with the
wagon, was kept in repair, and new harness was bought when the old wore out.
The wagon itself was slightly modified by the addition of a simple wooden frame
to support blankets as a shade for riders.

Within a few months one of the men of the village learned how to work 23
iron by heating and hammering. He became capable of shoeing horses and
keeping the metal parts of the wagon in repair.

The wagon was used intensively from the start, eliminating most of the 24
packing on individual horses. Within a few years the net panniers and pack saddles ceased to be made.

There was also an important effect on another craft. Almost immediately 25
the wagon was turned to use for carrying water from the *charcos* to the households. The only large water containers used up to this time had been the ollas
made by the women, and these were easily broken. Following the example of
white ranchers, wooden barrels were introduced. They were not very practica-
ble, however, in the dry climate of the Arizona desert, since they dried out rapidly and fell apart. The Papagos turned then to metal barrels, which were un-
breakable and unaffected by the dryness. These steadily replaced ollas both for
hauling water and for storing it in the houses. The water supply on hand
increased, and the number of ollas required by a household decreased. The latter were used only for drinking-water, which remained cooler and sweeter in
ollas than in barrels. The making of ollas declined as a craft, with the result that
less time of the women was used.

In order to use the wagon for transportation from the summer to the win- 26
ter village, it became necessary to construct a road. This involved clearing and
grading in order to get the wagon over the extremely rough terrain up the mountain to the winter village site. Some engineering skill was developed and a new
form of group labor was introduced in which all the men participated.

When the question of moving from the summer to the winter village first 27
arose after the wagon was introduced, the village council met and decided
that all seven families of Choulik would use the vehicle in turn. The family that
was prepared first, moved first, and was followed by the others as they were
ready.

Treating the wagon as a common resource of the village was apparent in 28
other ways. Trading journeys, such as those to procure seeds, were now made
by wagon. Since only one or two men, instead of several, were assigned to make
the trips, face-to-face contacts with Mexicans on the southern border of the
Papago country declined.

Uses to which pack horses had not been put developed for the wagon. In 29
addition to the regular hauling of water, it was also employed for carrying large
supplies of firewood. Cutting wood on a large scale by the men of the family,
instead of piecemeal gathering by women and children, became a new pattern.
Soon this practice led to hauling loads of wood for sale to the nearest towns, as
for instance, Tucson. An additional natural resource was thus developed, and
Choulik entered the cash economy of the surrounding society in a new way.
Villagers began also to be interested in raising a little corn and wheat for sale as
the wagon offered an easier means of getting a few sacks to town.

The use of the wagon as a resource of the whole village led to increased 30
cooperation and interaction of the officials of the village government. The management of transportation called for meetings to plan trading expeditions, to
assign the wagon for wood and water hauling, and for all the uses to which it
was put. In addition, the building and maintenance of roads constituted a
new communal activity, which had to be planned and directed by the village
council.

5. Analysis

This summary of the first stage in the introduction of the wagon to pack-animal 31
users suggests the complications of a relatively simple technical innovation even
in a society well prepared for it. The case is only carried to the point where
more than one wagon was acquired by the village. From there on, many other
important innovations arrived, and it is less easy to trace the effects of wagon-
use alone.

Although the effects of the one introduction require several pages to list, 32
the explanation for each consequent change is fairly simple. The connections
between the changes and the primary innovation are clear enough. The point
of emphasis is that such connections must be anticipated in any technological
introduction, if there is to be an attempt to guide the change. Foreseeing at least
some of the interrelations of tools and customs is fundamental.

In the Papago case little or no conscious control of the innovation was exer- 33
cised by the Indian agent. Interest in the wagon on the part of Choulik people
arose from the headman's brothers having seen it used in towns, when they
were working for the railroad. Furthermore, it was accident rather than planning that placed the first wagon in the hands of the headman of Choulik. We
are not able, with the data at hand, to prove that his position in the village influenced the course of events, but it seems reasonable to infer that the development of communal use was related to that fact. If the wagon had come first into
the hands of a person without the status of headman, other results certainly
would have been possible, including disrupting shifts in leadership patterns.

The effects on Choulik technology were considerable. Panniers and pack 34
saddles fell into disuse, those specific articles being replaced, as we should expect, by the wagon. The necessity for repairing the wagon led to the creation
of a new specialty—blacksmithing. A third readily predictable effect was the
introduction of roads and road-building techniques. All of these might have
occurred to anyone who did advance thinking.

Other effects were not so obvious. It would have been difficult to say posi- 35 tively in advance that the time spent in pottery-making by women would be reduced, but it might have appeared as a possibility if the nature of the wagon had been reviewed in detail in relation to all the transportation activities of Papagos. Similarly, the changes in wood-gathering might have been anticipat-ed, together with the consequent shift in the division of labor in household econ-omy, involving increased participation of adult males in activities formerly confined to children and, to some extent, women.

Changes in the total economy that took place were probably of the type 36 the Indian agent desired, although there is no record that he foresaw the spe-cific direction they would take. The growth of needs for manufactured harness, metal wagon parts, and for metal barrels linked Papagos with the general American economy in new ways. Of these, the first, as directly connected with the form of the wagon itself, might have easily been predicted; the second, as an indirect result, might have been foreseen only as a possibility.

The development of firewood as a cash resource might have been foreseen 37 as a result of a detailed review of the growing needs of the new towns at the edges of Papago territory, as might also the stimulus which the wagon gave to production of agricultural surpluses.

Acceptance of the wagon as a resource of the whole village under joint 38 management was surely not a part of the expectation of the Indian agent. He probably thought in terms of individual ownership. What happened was an adjustment to the existing social organization and property concepts of the Papagos. The village headman brought the wagon into the culture as a unique resource, like the land, the use of which must be shared. This sharing led to the new group activity of road-building, in accordance with the same pattern as land improvements. Sharing the wagon as a means of trade led to modifications of the trading customs, with consequent effects on the frequency and mode of contact with outsiders. Through the period that we have discussed, the wagon may be regarded as reinforcing the community ties which already existed. Hence, its effects on the social life of the people were as important as those on the technology.

Thus, we see that the introduction of the wagon, simple as the initial event 39 was, had broad repercussions on the Papago way of life. It not only displaced some parts of the technology and established new techniques and specialties; it also resulted in important shifts in the division of labor, had far-reaching effects on the economy, became for a period a strong factor for greater community sol-idarity, and influenced the relations of Papagos with surrounding peoples.

Questions for Study

Edward Spicer

The first case shows in fairly elementary fashion how different aspects of a cul- 1 ture are linked with one another. It shows how the introduction of one materi-al item—the wagon—brought about changes in the social life of the people, as well as in their stock of tools and ways of making a living. The case suggests that the wise handling of an introduction calls for knowledge of how the differ-ent traditional ways of doing things are linked together and how the new trait may affect this linkage. For example, much could have been foreseen if the Indian agent had asked: "What will the wagon be used for? Who will use it? Will that mean any change in work habits of men and women?" Or more general-ly: "What is the division of labor among the Papagos? Where will a change in transportation affect that division?"

From asking such questions comes the acquisition of information necessary 2 to the intelligent management of change. It is suggested that at this point the student begin to formulate a list of questions. . . .

We present here an example of one such master checklist which might be 3 used for gathering information in a wide variety of situations. It could, of course, be developed further in any number of directions, depending on the needs in a particular problem.

1. What, if anything, will the introduced trait replace?
2. What other tools and techniques are likely to be modified as a result of the introduction?
3. What other tools and techniques will have to be modified if the new trait is accepted?
4. For what new tools and techniques is there likely to be a demand as a result of the introduction?
5. Who in the society will have to abandon or change their occupations, if there is replacement? Who will be likely to modify their occupations and who will be given new occupations?
6. Who within the society will benefit immediately from the introduction? Will the benefits be in terms of economic advantage, increased prestige, or what?
7. Who, if anyone, is likely to suffer immediately? In terms of real or fancied threat to economic security? In terms of social status?
8. Will shifts in occupation affect the division of labor between men and women?
9. What are the formal and informal social organizations in which those affected participate?
10. How are these social organizations likely to be affected? Will their power or social position be enhanced or lowered?
11. Is there a possibility of the introduction opening up new forms of cooper-ation? Of conflict?
12. Do the individuals and group leaders affected understand the nature of the introduction?
13. Who has participated in the planning of the change? Who has not partic-ipated?
14. What customs, other than the technology, are likely to be affected? Food habits? Relations of young and old? Marriage customs? Ceremonials? Religious beliefs? Major values?
15. Does the change reinforce these customs or conflict with them?
16. What are the attitudes toward the innovator (the field worker) as a person? Toward the ethnic group of which he is a member?
17. What is the recent history of the relations between the introducing group and the people?
18. What is the history of similar introductions to this group?

The Many Faces of Technology, the Many Voices of Tradition

Martin Marty

Martin Marty, theologian and philosopher at the University of Chicago, observes that technology in its many manifestations disrupts tradition. Marty's purpose is to investigate and characterize these disruptions, and, most of all, to pursue this question: Is a humane technological order possible? That is, must we expect our rapidly evolving technologies to dehumanize us? If we fear the answer is yes, what can we do to intervene? Marty provides a philosophical framework in which to consider the "mixed blessings" of advancing technologies. This essay was originally prepared as part of the 1986 Andrew R. Cecil Lectures on Moral Values in a Free Society by the University of Texas at Dallas.

Technology wears many faces, one of them being dehumanizing and another being humanizing. 1

Some years ago the donors of a new center of communications assembled 2 a cast of speakers to dedicate it. They, we, were all asked to comment on the role of technology in "the decline of the West." The choice of conference theme represented either an act of courage or of masochism, for the donors made their wealth from communications technology, which critics often score for contributing to the decline of the West.

Speaker after speaker failed to be unambiguously gloomy. They tended to 3 be rather cheerful types, one of whom brightened the conference after he heard some doom-filled prophecies with the comment: "We do not know enough about the future to be absolutely pessimistic."

When some speakers pronounced forthcoming doom because of the bur- 4 geoning computer movement, atop the ever expanding and encroaching system of electronic communications, a sage among us rose to the occasion. A historian, he knew of a similar speech about one hundred years ago. It was given at the Philadelphia Exposition celebrating the United States centennial in 1876. That speech, uttering similar words of doom about dehumanization, was directed against—pause—the telephone! Yet we survived. Of course, many of us hate the technology of the telephone that can interrupt our peace and solitude. But, said the intervener about the other, humanizing, face of technology: think how it helps people make contact if they are in senior citizens' homes, cancer wards, far from their own homes.

Let that incident be a parable for my topic and thesis. While some prophets 5 of hope are Pollyannas who see nothing but promise in electronic technology and others are doom sayers who act as if we could or should get rid of technology if we would, I would pose the issue thus: in the search for the human, for values, for moral values, technology—to use a gambler's term—"raises the stakes on both sides." The question becomes now, "Is a humane technological order possible?" If so, what kind of critique must we make of the present? What might citizens do about various future prospects?

Technology Disrupts Tradition

Let us assume that human nature, whatever that is, does not change; what mat- 6 ters is the human in culture. I know of no evidence to suggest that a first-century person plopped into twentieth-century life would be a better or worse bundle of possibilities than we twentieth-century people. Yet we know that it makes a good deal of difference whether a person gets to live out her possibilities in, say, Albania, Inuit country of Canada, St. Tropez, or Dallas. Culture matters, and technology is a major instrument of culture.

Must we define technology? We cannot, of course, but we know it when we 7
see it. We associate it with practical applications of science in the human world, with "technique" and what accompanies it. We see machines making machines, devices that help transform the natural world. To some it comes with ideology that assaults other ways of life; in the eyes of others, it is "neutral," and serves merely to render more efficient (or less efficient, say some victims of bad technology) processes that would exist in any case. In other words, for them television signals simply do better what smoke signals or messages carried by runners used to do.

For the moment we need only say that whatever technology is and however 8
it does it, when this comes to communications and its corollaries, technology disrupts tradition. One historian speaks of "the world we have lost." The prior less-technological world made it possible for people to live in insulated and isolated cultures. Then came the wheel—and they could leave home. Then came the pump—and women no longer gathered at the well, there to gossip in support of traditional ways and values. Then came the whole industrial revolution—and people moved from town and country to city, where they met strangers and became victims of pluralism and, eventually, of relativizing pluralism.

The process goes on. Technological medicine brought by missionaries disrupts 9
traditional medicine and, while it heals, can also cause people to forget some beneficial agencies and methods or understandings of suffering and well-being. When television came along it was clear to all that it might become pervasive and would disrupt insulated traditions; the television set in the monastery was an example. Fundamentalist colleges whose administrations forbade students from attending good new movies could not prevent them from seeing bad old ones in dormitories, thank to television. Illustrations come easily to mind: Technology disrupts tradition.

• • •

Technology Wears Many Faces, Produces Many Effects

Because of its disruption of tradition, technology appears to many people to be 10
simply destructive. Ivan Illich is well known for showing how it can have negative effects on schooling or medicine or values in the Two-Thirds World. Peter Berger and colleagues write of *The Homeless Mind* dislodged by technology. Jacques Ellul in *The Technological Society* sees only one face to technology, an almost demonically efficient one. He writes that "the power of technique, mysterious though scientific, which covers the whole earth with its methods of waves, wires, and paper, is to the technician the abstract idol which gives him a reason for living and even for joy." How better [to] speak of the role of technology in the field of values than to speak of idolatry, of deepest meanings? (*The Technological Society*, Vintage, 1964, p. 144.)

First, in respect to our approach to the topic, technology and especially 11
communications media are destructive because they bring to us a pluralist world. When American Christians sent missionaries to bad pagan Buddhists and Hindus, all seemed well. When the senders met and came to honor the values of good and spiritually or morally profound Buddhists and Hindus, they created a

new problem. How seriously should we take our source of values if others can do as well or better out of other sources? People turn, or may turn, relativist when radio, cinema, television, cassette, and computer come to their "tribe."

We see illustrations of this, for instance, in portrayals of Amish life, long 12 ago in *Plain and Fancy* or more recently in *Witness* and most often in court cases. The Amish can isolate their children from alien traditions in their elementary schools in rural America. They cannot do so when these children must go to more urban and pluralist consolidated high schools. The pressure of peers shaped by mass media will lure young Amish children to the sinful world of cheerleaders in short skirts, young people who listen to rock music, and the like. We onlookers see something admirable in what is disrupted and inevitably in the disrupting (and possibly liberating) agent. Technology wears more faces than one.

So it is that today we have "textbook" battles over signals that come from 13 a pluralistic culture and violate the tribe of fundamentalism. So we all complain that "our" kind of family is never shown or honored on prime television. The values we nurture are undercut or jostled by others, and that is bad.

Alongside pluralism comes the observation that modern technology of com- 14 munication promotes the secular. This disturbs because moral values for the vast majority of citizens connect with explicitly "sacred" signals, with traditions that connect us with the transcendent, the divine, probably the divine as a particular set of canons and codes and communities describe this. Television does not seem neutral; it comes as a destructive force. This is so—*pace* some critics—not because of a "secular humanist conspiracy" but because of a lack of memory and imagination among communicators and, even more, because of pluralism. What part of what tradition should the media regard as representative and normative? Will non-Mormons permit Mormon values to come into their homes? Will five million Mormons buy deodorant from communicators who provide non- or anti-Mormon spiritual signals? So communicators try to be silent. Yet there is no "ethical vacuum," as philosopher Hans Jonas and many others remind us. Technology must bring some signals from some systems and, by default, this tends to be secular and thus competitive to most peoples' personal and tribal choices.

Thirdly, this means that technology seems or is subversive. This is why 15 so many thoughtful philosophers and counselors in the liberal Western tradition, where the great "advances" are made, have so regularly dealt with one face of technology. It dehumanizes, depersonalizes, creates artificial and illusory cultures and values. Yet we can also hear that the subversion may have positive effects. I choose but one witness, European politician-engineer Egbert Schuurman. For him the spiritual and, indeed, Christian meaning of technology implies "emancipating the body and mind from toil and drudgery, repelling the onslaughts of nature, providing for man's material needs, and conquering disease . . . eliminating unnecessary burdens, freeing time, promoting rest and peace. . . ." (*Reflections on the Technological Society,* Wedge, 1977, p. 21.)

Every reader can take a moment to imagine how Schuurman's positive sce- 16 nario applies in the most threatening/promising sphere, television. Can we not think of moments of profound and delightful entertainment? Has not the picture of ethnic and race relations changed, often positively because the white majority sees affirming images of Asian and African people in serials, broadcasting the news, being in love, caring about human good? Don't we meet saints and heroes on television and don't we confront moral crises there? Think how close South Africa and Nobel prize winners become when the instrument of television invades our living room. We become informed and can make new choices. Indeed, "the stakes are raised on both sides," but that affirmation does include the underused and underviewed possibility that the raising is also on the side of promoting moral values.

• • •

The Situation Today

Today Americans speak of an intensified "values crisis." Under other terms, people have spoken thus since Adam and Eve were fifty years old. Cultural changes brings a threat to traditionalists or custodians of tradition and hence of moral values. They do not often see that change can be for the better as well as for the worse, or do not remember that change for the better can be as inconveniencing as change for the worse. Yet there are good reasons for citizens today to talk about sudden paces of change and a crisis of values. We can survey some of the main areas of concern and trouble.   17

The Family

Technology disrupts it. Some disturbance can come because marriage and sex counselors write on "open marriage." But more comes on more neutral grounds. We might as well blame Big Mac as Dr. Ruth for interruptions of tradition. As both parents work outside the home, as children's school schedules conflict with meal time, as we choose a life with many extra-home commitments, it is easy to "graze" at fast-food outlets which exist because of technology. Without at least one common meal a day on most days—and most families do not have that now—there is little chance for appraising, learning, and transmitting traditions of moral values. So we strike at "secular humanists" who invade our home with televised undercutting signals.   18

Sexuality

The invention of the condom and then the pill, the devising of *in vitro* fertilization and the increase of possibilities for convenient abortion, all connect with technology. They bring changes that may be liberating to some, but strike terror in others. The media, for example cinema and the prime-time serial, constantly glamorize sexual values in conflict with those of traditional culture. So does the world of advertising.   19

Defense

Technology produces ever greater weapons of destruction and the threat to use them. Some "traditionalists" believe that all such weapon systems imaginable should be developed and poised. Others, such as the Roman Catholic bishops, deal with traditions of pacifism and "just war" and find that technological warfare transcends the bounds. What they discuss is brought into the homes of citizens via technologically produced newspapers and television. A values crisis results.   20

The Classroom

The modern textbook reflects and is produced by technology and brings into the second- or third-most intimate zone of community life (at least the family used to be first) a set of signals that jostles those some parents would nurture. In the   21 act of bringing a larger world the text and classroom compete with the chosen and cherished smaller world of fewer signals. Some parents react against "secularism" in the textbooks. We have a values crisis.

• • •

Is a Humane Technological Order Possible?

After all the surveys and case studies we are left with our question. I recall one evening when two Chilean Jesuits were meeting with some of us North American theologians. Two of the theologians were "liberationists" who decried imperial technology and its disruption of Third World cultures. They romanticized the world of the Chilean peasant or slum dweller who was not jarred by television or corrupted by technological healing or advertising. Finally one of the Jesuits said, "No, no, dear colleague: Do not speak for us. We would like our people first to have your problems before they seek your solutions. First give them means and comfort and enjoyment before you see how it might bring bad changes—and *then* work for improvement." Another parable. Technology will not go away; it will advance. How humanize it? 22

It is possible to sketch some outlines. First, technology needs compensatory complementation and supplementation. This means, for instance, that alongside technological medicine there must be a conscious development of "care structures" or, better, the human touch. Alongside electronically propagated Gospels there must be ever richer community life in congregation. As technology comes, there must come buffers, partial insulators, interpreters. 23

Secondly, there have to be ever more strenuous efforts to use persuasion, not coercion, to promote moral values. It is tempting to seek to be Big Brother, to envy those with mass communicative power, to link one's own system with the ballot box and impose values on people where there is no moral consensus. Such efforts overlook the positive values in subcultures and traditions. Thus the notion that all would be well if we would pass laws privileging and favoring "the Judaeo-Christian" tradition would solve little. Whose Judaeo-Christian tradition? Jews'? Christians'? Protestants'? Catholics'? Mormons'? Gentiles'? If Baptists', which Baptists? Such questions point to the fact that we have problems within pluralism apart from technology, and technology of communications brings them close to home but is not the sole agent of confusion. 24

What do we do? 25

1. We seek to interpret technology. To have a handle on what goes on is itself part of counteraction and therapy.

2. Citizens can work to understand the traditions of moral values. Eugene Goodheart says of those who reject what is handed down from, say, Greece and Rome or Jews and Christians: you may not possess the traditions, but the traditions possess you. Our actions are habitual, gestured, reflexive. What are their sources? What in those sources is of value?

3. People can engage in selective retrieval from the many voices of tradition. Much tradition, despite idolizations of it in our nostalgic culture today, was burdening, stultifying, static, enslaving. One must learn to select out of what we inherit what can be of critical value in the present generation—and then project it, perhaps electronically!

4. Concerned folk should rebuild subcommunities. Margaret Mead said twenty years ago that because parents so often had no sense of tradition and no

courage to try theirs out, the children were forced to make a mishmash of all the religions there ever were—and it didn't work and couldn't last. The subcommunities are somehow accessible in the technological world, and they include humane and humanizing elements.

5. In the republic of technology there must be concern for the republic of values. The subcommunities must interact, overlap, support each other. You cannot have a republic of sealed-off moral-values-generating-systems. Mormons and Episcopalians, secularists and Baptists share and must share some values and hopes in the larger culture. Mass media can promote their interaction.

6. There can be stress, if citizens care, on values that come with the larger value systems of our republic. We have shared and do share some common memory, narrative, myth, story, history. The Pilgrims and Einstein and Martin Luther King and war heroes and saints on this soil belong to us all, not just to subcommunities. We share common propositions of moral value ("We hold these truths . . .") and a common legal-constitutional system that implies more. We have common projects, problems, intentions, partial resolutions, and they need communicating and reinforcing. We might even have what Jefferson called "common affection" or a kindred spirit—and technology need not take that away. It may even enhance it, if we intervene and insist that it be supportive.

Tradition, in a republic, has many voices. Technology has many faces. 26 Human agents, many of us would say "under God," are not deprived of all choices in the presence of both. And that is a fairly cheerful or energizing prospect in the face of the doom that would result if we get it, or keep getting it, all wrong.

Three Views on In Vitro Fertilization

Advances made in in vitro fertilization (IVF)—the fertilizing of an egg outside a woman's body and the subsequent implantation of that egg in her uterus—have helped thousands of infertile couples conceive. Recently this same technology has been put to more controversial uses: helping postmenopausal women (that is, women past their natural childbearing age) to bear children; helping couple to have genetically identical twins or triplets years apart; enabling single women—and on some occasions virgins—who do not desire contact with men to give birth. These recent applications of IVF technology have shaken many of our assumptions about family life, about the "right" versus the desire to have children, and about gender stereotypes. Men, for instance, have fathered children well into their sixties and seventies without sparking public debate that they will be elderly—or dead—when their children reach adolescence. If modern medical technology can help women to be reproductively active for as long as men, why not? The very fact that this question has sparked heated debate suggests that we hold deep and unexamined beliefs about the roles and the "fitness requirements" of mothers and fathers. Thus we see that as Mead, Bliss, Spicer, and Marty have argued, new technologies stretch or tear a culture's social fabric.

The three readings that follow explore the social and ethical questions surrounding IVF technology. "In Vitro Outrage" by Richard Scheinin introduces the most controversial applications of the technology, while two editorials—"Menopause for Thought" by Robert Winston, a British scholar of fertility studies, and "Older Women Should Enjoy Access" by the editors of *The Economist* magazine—take strong, and contrasting, positions on these applications. As you read, ask yourself how IVF has changed and will continue to change our views on birth and parenting. More generally, you can approach the topic of in vitro fertilization through Edward Spicer's "Questions for Study."

In Vitro Outrage

Richard Scheinin

For 15 years, Dr. Eldon Schriock has helped infertile couples have babies. 1
Sometimes the women he sees are impregnated through test-tube fertilization of eggs from their ovaries—or from another woman's. Sometimes sperm is sought from another man, in which case the couple are given catalogs from numerous sperm banks to thumb through and select male gametes from a veritable smorgasbord of donors.

"They can pick by height or weight, ethnic heritage or race," Dr. Schriock 2 explains. "That's been standard for as long as I've been practicing, and it's never made headlines. But now women are starting to pick eggs by some of the same criteria, and people are shocked," says a puzzled Dr. Schriock, who directs the ovum donation program at the University of California-San Francisco's in-vitro fertilization clinic.

Ethical debates over the conception of life outside the womb have raged 3 since the first test-tube baby was born in 1978.

In-vitro fertilization has been condemned as "unnatural" and an attempt by 4 doctors to "play God," as has the newer "egg donation" method. But the debate has gotten red hot with the recent media attention to the possibility of pulling eggs from aborted female fetuses, the reality of "designer babies" and postmenopausal pregnancies in women in their 50s and 60s.

Why have the older—really older—moms elicited such outrage? 5

Is it sexism? People often look with admiration upon the siring abilities of 6 elderly men. Why condemn older mothers as irresponsible care-givers who won't live to raise their children? Are there deeper "psycho-social, sexual issues at work" in the response to human fertility issues, as Dr. Schriock suspects? Are men and women fearful of tampering with the female body, viewed as the mysterious source of life for millennia?

Or are people just newly afraid that technological intervention in human 7 reproduction has gone too far—that the magic bottle has been opened too completely?

"I think they are disturbed because this is getting over their heads," says Dr. 8 Francis Polansky, director of the Nova In Vitro Fertilization clinic in Palo Alto, Calif., and co-founder a decade ago of Stanford University's in-vitro fertilization (IVF) program.

(In the IVF method, a woman's eggs are removed from her ovaries, fertil- 9 ized by her partner's sperm in a petri dish, and then implanted in her uterus. In the donation method, eggs from another woman are implanted in the mother, who carries the fetus to term.)

"It seems to be so out of the ordinary, so unreal, that they feel shock and distress over it," Dr. Polansky says. "But it's interesting to see the reaction of our patients—15 percent of the adult population is infertile. Our patients seem to welcome every piece of news that pushes the envelope. To one person it is a great gift, while another person views it as something unnatural that shouldn't have taken place." 10

He says: "Uncertainty, that's what I feel. Do we hold the absolute right to be biological parents? I don't know." 11

Fundamental

The U.S. public is once again asking fundamental questions about the commercialization of the reproductive process and whether the right to procreate is absolute. This discussion is happening against the backdrop of European developments: 12

- A pair of postmenopausal women, ages 59 and 62, are having babies after becoming impregnated with donated eggs that were fertilized with their husbands' sperm in the laboratory.[1] The French government discusses banning such "immoral" pregnancies because 10-year-old children should not have 70-year-old mothers. But what about all those elderly fathers? How come no one talks about banning children? And does anyone want to prevent women who enter menopause prematurely—even in their teens—from becoming pregnant?

- An English researcher announces that it may soon be possible to use eggs from aborted fetuses to produce test-tube babies. Some ethicists say this method of obtaining eggs is "morally superior" to the sometimes painful and risky procedures that women who donate eggs now must endure. But a British doctor talks about the "yuck factor." Disgusted observers wonder whether a market in harvesting eggs from aborted fetuses will develop. And what about the psychological effects on the child who grows from the fetus's egg?

    "What are you going to say when you grow up? 'My mother was a fetus'?" asks Leslie Lafayette, founder of the ChildFree Network, an advocacy group near Sacramento, California for people who choose not to have children.

- Two infertile black women in England and Italy have chosen to be impregnated with eggs donated by white women. As a result, there is troubled discussion of "designer babies" and "genetic engineering." In fact, none of the recent developments involves "genetic engineering"—the substitution of new genetic material into a man's or woman's DNA in order to determine physical characteristics of that person's offspring.

---

[1] A 59-year-old, unmarried and highly successful British businesswoman gave birth to twins on Christmas day, 1993. Mrs. Rosanna della Corte, the oldest known woman to become pregnant, gave birth to a son, Riccardo, on July 18, 1994. Both women were patients of Italian fertility specialist Dr. Severino Antinori. Mrs. della Corte sought out Dr. Antinori after her 17-year-old son, Riccardo, was killed in a motor scooter accident. Dr. Antinori's British patient sought him out after she was denied fertility treatment in Great Britain because of her age.

What Harm?

"Who and what is being harmed?" asks Ruth Macklin, professor of bioethics at 13
the Albert Einstein College of Medicine in New York.

"What ethical principles are being violated? No, nature did not provide for 14
women to bear children after menopause. But did nature arrange for organ
transplantations or Caesarean births or artificial breathing machines? Are they
bad because they are unnatural? If it's human nature to think, create and apply
for the presumed betterment of human beings, why is that unnatural?"

Answers Abby Lippman, chairwoman of the human genetics committee of 15
the Council for Responsible Genetics in Cambridge, Mass.: "It's a desire that
many women have, but I don't think this is a demand that needs to be met by
society. Do I have a right to be taller than I am or shorter than I am because of
what I want? I don't think social resources should be spent providing women
with babies."

Ms. Lafayette of the ChildFree Network, who once considered artificial 16
insemination but didn't go through with it, agrees. She decided that many social
factors—including television sitcoms, advertisements and "baby on board"
signs—were coming together and making her feel inadequate for her inability
to bear a child.

"There's a real attitude of entitlement out there, and I think it's ridiculous. 17
If people want to have a child so badly, there are literally millions of abandoned,
unwanted and abused children in the world who need adoption," she says.

"So what is it with these women?" Ms. Lafayette asks. "They have to give 18
birth? To me it's a very selfish way of approaching the problem. Especially since
the child is not even genetically related to the mother—she's just an incubator.
Will you please explain to me what the point is?"

Very Hard

Lawyer Norma Formanek explains. Married in 1980, she and her husband tried 19
to have children for years. "And wanting to have a child is one of the most fundamental human longings and emotions.

"It's extremely difficult to explain it to family and friends who are having 20
children. It's very, very hard."

Now 39 and living in northern California, Ms. Formanek has gone through 21
four years of medical treatment for her infertility. In-vitro fertilization didn't
work. Egg donation didn't work. She is "pretty much at the end of the line,"
she says, so she and her husband are thinking about adoption. Ms. Formanek,
an only child, remembers her own mother—unable to conceive until age 42.

"When she got pregnant, it was a miracle," Ms. Formanek says. 22

"My father was 55. Everyone mistook my parents for grandparents. My 23
father's health was bad, and he was retired. But the flip side of that was I had
a special relationship with him because he was the one who was home. It was
a very different circumstance from what my little friends had, but it was a wonderful experience. It's just too simple to say this person is too old to have a child
and that person is not."

A widely reported detail in recent news accounts of the 62-year-old Italian 24
woman who is pregnant from a donated egg is her statement that she and her
husband wanted a child after their 17-year-old son was killed in an accident. "I
was taken aback when I read that," says Philip Boyle, associate for medical
ethics at the Hastings Center in Briarcliff Manor, N.Y. "It makes it look like kids
are replacement objects—like fine silverware or a plate that breaks."

And yet fertile couples often have children for such reasons, "and their 25 motives are not normally discussed," says David Pettee of Berkeley, whose wife underwent premature menopause in her 20s yet gave birth to a baby girl two years ago after the couple participated in an egg donation program. "Now you have a small number of older women who want to get involved with egg donation and people are saying: 'You can't do that. Let's check out your motivation and fitness for parenting.' "

Small Numbers

"Do you know how many children have been born in this country through egg 26 donation?" asks Mr. Pettee, a member of the board of directors of Resolve of Northern California, an educational and advocacy group for infertile adults and reproductive issues.

"Between 750 and 1,000, total. The numbers are infinitesimal, and yet 27 there is such outrage. If there was some procedure for 60-year-old men with zero sperm counts to suddenly become potent again, would it be on the front page of every daily in the country?

"It's not as though this is something that's going to become the rage—to 28 become a mother at the age of 60."

Since 1990, Los Angeles physician Mark Sauer and his associates have 29 treated 29 postmenopausal women in their 50s. Eighteen have become pregnant; two miscarried. The women, including two 55-year-olds, have given birth to eight sets of twins. A 51-year-old woman gave birth to triplets in November.

Dr. Sauer's biggest concern is that the health of the women not be jeopardized. They must be screened and monitored to prevent physical or emotional distress. So far, he says, there have been no serious problems.

"If we as a society have allowed men of any age to have children," he 31 argues, "if we've allowed young women with terminal illnesses to have children and grandparents to raise children, then I have trouble seeing the problem. My patients are vital people, and many are married to men who are 10 to 20 years younger.

"These children are being born into loving homes, to active parents who 32 aren't distracted by a career. For the child, that outweighs the detriment of bringing home a friend to see an older face. I will be surprised if any child has regrets about being born. Because that's the alternative—to have never been conceived."

Older Women Should Enjoy Access to Fertility Treatment

The Economist

Art holds the mirror up to nature. Science holds the mirror up to society. And 1 people's worries about scientific novelties reflect the concerns of the age and place in which they live. This is abundantly clear in the latest flap about reproductive technology.

Women impregnated after menopause; black women implanted with white 2 women's eggs; the possibility of eggs from unborn fetuses being used for donation; these play on widespread concerns about age, race and motherhood.

Should this—all of it, some of it—be allowed? It is proper that society should   3
sometimes curtail the new freedoms that technology provides. But only with
good reason.

A good reason to thwart a choice might stem from its adverse effects   4
on those not making it. Sometimes society at large will be adversely affected.
In the present cases the people at risk are the children to be brought into the
world.

How does the use of fetal eggs affect the child that might grow from them?   5
If the technique were perfected, it might allow such children to be created more
promptly, since there is a chronic shortage of eggs for in vitro fertilizations. But
although more eggs might be useful they are not strictly necessary, and their use
could be harmful.

Imagine a stroppy, confused, rebellious teenager—or for that matter, a   6
charming, well-balanced one—trying to work out who she is. For a child to find
out that its real mother was an aborted fetus is likely to be upsetting.

There are other, better, supplies of eggs; from willing live donors, and per-   7
haps soon from willing dead ones. An ovary from a young woman killed in an
accident could provide eggs as readily as one from a fetus. Its donation might
have an uplifting effect on the bereaved, as well as on the recipients.

What if the donor was a white woman, and the mother who received her   8
eggs was black? A black British woman was recently implanted with a white
woman's egg fertilized by the recipient's mixed-race husband, because the wait
for a black donor proved intolerably long.

More controversially, a black woman recently chose a white woman's egg   9
in an Italian clinic because she thought the resulting child would be more likely
to succeed than one that grew from a black woman's egg. Though her country
of origin is unknown, it seems a fair bet that she was right.

If one is to see a wickedness here, it is not that of a mother who wants the   10
best for her child, but that of a society which judges children by color and doles
out opportunities accordingly.

Fetuses are not suitable donors; women of other races are. But what of suit-   11
able recipients? Postmenopausal women are increasingly seeking fertility treatment. The French government is moving swiftly to ban such things. Women too
frail or ill for pregnancy should not be fertilized. But what of the healthy 59-
year-old who gave birth to twins in Britain on Christmas day? What harm has
she done to them, or anyone else?

A child born to people who have led full lives may have a richer upbring-   12
ing than one born to a young couple—or may not, but there is no way of knowing in advance. Worldly wisdom may help parents put up with the vicissitudes
of child rearing.

It is true that such children will face the sorry day on which they lose a par-   13
ent earlier than others. But it is also true that if they have to look after ailing
parents, they will do so in the flush of youth, rather than when middle-aged
themselves. So, from the point of view of the child, older parents are by no
means an obvious disadvantage.

It is true that older people are often barred from adoption, and as embryo   14
implantation is in effect a complex form of adoption, the same criteria should
apply to both procedures. But this is an argument for allowing older people to
adopt, not for stopping them giving birth.

To react to late births with a ban is wrong. But it is right that this issue   15
should exercise society more than the other two, because deferring childbirth
well into middle age could be an option for the fertile, too.

A young woman could have eggs from her healthy ovaries frozen for future 16 use, and be free to have children at a time of her choosing, a freedom that men have enjoyed throughout the ages. A society that opposes such procedures is not holding back an evil science; it is blocking equality between the sexes.

Menopause for Thought

Robert Winston

The report this week that a 58-year-old British woman is expecting twins as the 1 result of IVF treatment in Italy following egg donation has caused widespread concern. On the face of it, what Dr. Severino Antinori in Rome is doing may seem laudable. After all, he has said he is simply helping desperate women to get pregnant and is quoted as saying "they want babies; I give them babies." This reported attitude, which seems to me to be debasing In Vitro Fertilisation (IVF) treatments to the status of trading in a commodity, appears to many to trivialise very serious issues.

First, any pregnancy in a woman in her late fifties or early sixties carries 2 considerable risks to her health. A twin pregnancy, after transfer of several embryos, seems even more fraught. Whilst pregnancy in the forties is now commonplace and easily managed, once a woman gets much beyond the age of 50, virtually all the serious complications of pregnancy are much more likely. High blood pressure, toxaemia of pregnancy, heart disease, diabetes, and thrombosis are all relatively probable and she is less likely to have the strength to care for her newborn in the event of its safe delivery.

Second, there is clearly a very significant chance that she may lose the baby 3 at any time during pregnancy. Pregnancy loss is a shattering event at any stage of a couple's life but this group of older women are particularly vulnerable to suffer extraordinary psychological trauma. The few women who actually seek such treatment in their later years are often desperate people, sometimes quite disturbed emotionally. Clinical experience often shows that they have found themselves unable to come to terms with the cessation of their ability to reproduce. They are, in effect, undergoing a process of bereavement which becomes protracted if they are inappropriately treated. For such a person, getting pregnant and then losing the pregnancy will be a catastrophic blow and the risk of serious depression and greater emotional disturbance very high.

Yet another issue is the question of any child which is born as a result of 4 such misplaced technology. A woman conceiving at 58 will be 70 when her child has not yet reached its teenage years. This seems to start any young person with a serious disadvantage in life, even if his or her parents actually survive until then. Children should reasonably expect that their parents should be young enough to play football in the park with them, or to have energy enough to indulge in the pursuits which are all part of growing up with their family.

While a woman at the age of 58 may well believe that she could cope with 5 a toddler, as she advances in age her physical state is likely to be increasingly less resilient. It is no accident that the British regulatory body, the Human Fertilisation and Embryology Authority, has stated that practitioners of IVF should always bear in mind the welfare of any children who may be brought into existence as a result of conducting fertility treatments.

Moreover, these treatments seem to neglect the rights of those women who 6
most altruistically decide to be donors of eggs. Because a woman of 58 cannot
produce her own eggs, she can only become pregnant as the result of donated
eggs being fertilised by her partner's sperm and then inserted to her uterus. Egg
donors are very remarkable and courageous people. They give eggs, their own
unique genetic material, anonymously, because they sympathise with the plight
of infertile women. In order to give eggs they need a surgical procedure. Before
this they have to undergo long and quite hefty treatments with drugs to induce
ovulation. Administration of these somewhat risky drugs to infertile women who
might themselves benefit from treatment is clearly justified, but it is quite another dimension to undergo complex and demanding treatment from which one
can derive no personal benefit.

I have spoken to hundreds of potential egg donors and all of them say they 7
are horrified at the mere thought that their eggs, their own genetic children,
might be given away to women 20 years older than themselves.

People ask if there should be a cut-off age point, beyond which fertility 8
treatments should not be given. While I believe in a flexible and liberal approach,
I think that it is one consideration to offer treatment to women who have suffered a premature menopause as a result of a pathological event, but it is quite
another to use high technology to subvert a natural, biological event. To do so
seems to me to debase the value of menopause, when our energies and experience may be better spent in more mature activities.

But what chiefly worries me about the activities of Dr. Antinori and the pub- 9
licity which surrounds them, are that they risk bringing a highly valuable and vulnerable technology into public disrepute. Many people have considerable anxieties about the new reproductive treatments which they view with suspicion
because they consider that doctors and scientists are tampering with the very
elements of human life. We practitioners of IVF must always be aware of these
concerns. IVF is already a relatively privileged treatment, heavily rationed by ailing health services throughout the Western world. If we fail to be sensitive to
the worries of ordinary people and our political representatives, we seriously risk
jeopardising the whole funding and future of proper reproductive medicine. It
would be a grave outcome indeed if the accessibility of our complex and expensive technology was limited to even fewer women and men. We have an important responsibility to ensure that many infertile couples continue to have a realistic chance of a healthy baby of their own.

A Guide to the Assignment

This guide is designed to help you through the process of writing your
argumentative essay. Begin with rereading your writing assignment.

Accept for the moment this statement: Within 500 years, technology will
have advanced to the point that our brains can accept plug-in, micro-
chip modules, each of which can provide instant, expert abilities such as
the ability to sight-read music or to think and speak in any language. In
a six- or seven-page argument to be read by your teacher and classmates, explore these questions:

1. If you could choose a plug-in, micro-chip module right now, what instant,
expert ability would you choose? Given this ability, what, if anything,
would change fundamentally about you, about what makes you human?

2. What changes would you expect to see in a culture in which everyone, on demand, could become an instant expert?

3. To what extent would these changes, both personal and cultural, be for the good?

Options

You have three options in writing this essay: the micro-chip module option described above, and these:

Option 2:   Write on the changes and challenges associated with widespread use of "designer" in vitro fertilization (IVF). Assume that at some point in the future infertile *and* fertile couples as well as single women could select eggs and sperm from a bank, according to the specific traits they desire in a child. The child thus selected and born would *not* be genetically related to the parent(s).

Option 3:   Write on the social and ethical questions surrounding any technology that interests you—in which case you can use the articles by Mead, Bliss, Spicer, and Marty in this chapter but will then need to do some additional library research.

Prepare to Write: Explore Your Idea

Discovering Ideas

The activities that follow are designed to promote your thinking about an idea that you want to pursue in your argument. Begin with the writing assignment. Read it and reread it; then write a discovery draft. The following suggestions parallel the questions you have been asked to address in the assignment.

1. Write two pages of a discovery draft in which you describe the plug-in module of your choice. (Recall your options: You can write on the widespread practice of choosing "designer" babies through in vitro fertilization; or you can write on some other technology of your choosing.) Next, describe a day in your life as you are using this advanced technology, and write a few paragraphs of observation about how the technology has changed you. Then describe what life would be like if you suddenly lost all access to the technology. Would any of your human abilities have atrophied?

2. Reread the brief selection by Margaret Mead (pages 457–458) and the questions for study by Edward Spicer (pages 463–464). In a one-page draft, use four or more of Edward Spicer's "Questions for Study" to investigate the cultural changes that you would expect to follow from the widespread use of plug-in modules (or widespread use of "designer" IVF). Recall that Spicer and Mead share the assumption that elements of culture are linked. When one element, such as a key technology, changes, so do other elements.

3. At the top of a new page, write these questions to help identify an idea about which you would be willing to write an argument: "What tensions are here?" ("What debate can I find—and what position would I take in this debate?" (See pages 420–421.) If you are writing on IVF, some of these tensions are made clear in the reading selections.

4. On another page, write: "Are the changes that would come from widespread use of an advanced technology such as plug-in modules (or in vitro fertilization) good and desirable?" Write for ten minutes and discover what you think.

5. Reread what you've written and, with highlight marker or pen in hand, note important sentences and phrases. Then distill your views into a single sentence, an argumentative thesis. This will be the idea, or claim, that you develop and support in your essay. See chapter 2, pages 27–31, on the qualities of an ambitious, interesting claim.

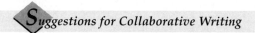

Suggestions for Collaborative Writing

After writing several paragraphs about a day in your life with your new plug-in module or teledildonics system, join a group of several other students from your class. Hand your text to the person on your left; after reading your description, this student should write another paragraph at the end of your description. Meanwhile, you will do the same to the writing you've received from the person on your right. When finished, repeat the process. You may do this as often as you like.

When finished, pass all writings back to the original authors. Read your descriptive commentaries out loud and discuss them. What new ideas have your peers given you? How have your own imaginative insights helped them with their ideas?

Committing Yourself to an Idea

Recall the attitudes of writers whose commitment sparks interest in their readers:

- I write for myself and for my audience.
- I will find some approach to my writing that lets me discover something personally significant.

Before beginning your first draft, take a few moments to respond to these questions. What will be your *personal* connection to this argumentative essay?

Write: Clarify Your Idea and Make It Public

Creating Common Ground with Readers

Creating common ground with readers involves presenting particular details *through which* you develop your ideas. For your essay in progress, this would mean your describing, in detail, your plug-in module (or the process of selecting a baby through "designer" in vitro fertilization). Rather than making abstract statements like "The ability to instantly memorize what I read would liberate me from tedious studying," show readers this tediousness and liberation as you study for a particular exam. Explore interesting questions such as: Is memorization the same as understanding? Respond to this question through the particulars of the case you are developing. When you address the larger question—Is this technology valuable?—once again, develop your response through particulars.

Recall that your readers, your classmates and teacher, need an introduction to your module. (If you choose to write on IVF, do not assume your readers will have read the articles in this chapter. Summarize the pertinent sections of these selections.) Your goal is to create a sense of immediacy in your essay by helping your readers to imagine themselves engaged in this future technology. Whatever idea you want to advance in your argument, address it through particulars.

◆ *Suggestions for Collaborative Writing*

Come up with what you think to be a powerful and convincing claim regarding the value of plug-in modules. Jot down all the reasons and evidence you can think of to support your claim. Also write down as many counterarguments as you can.

In groups of three or four, go around the circle and tell the others what your claim is. Have them write down all the support as well as all the counterclaims they can think of for your claim. Do the same for theirs.

After everyone has finished, compare the results. What types of evidence have others thought of for your claim that you have overlooked? What types of counterclaims have they offered that you missed? Incorporate these ideas into plans for your paper.

Planning a Structure

The idea of your argument will be a response to this question: Is your module (or the creation of babies through "designer" IVF) a good thing? This question suggests an essay of several parts:

- A description of the technology in question.
- An assessment of likely personal and cultural changes brought on by the technology—perhaps in light of Edward Spicer's questions.
- Some clear definition of your values, on the basis of which you will answer the question "Is it good?"

The organization of these parts is yours to choose: You can work inductively, building toward a thesis located at the end of the essay, or you can work deductively, beginning with your thesis.

Understanding Your Logic

Each of the three types of claim you can make in an argument—about fact, value, or policy—is developed according to specific lines of reasoning, which are summarized in table form on page 427. In this table, you see that claims of value can be argued by appealing to the reader's reason; specifically, you can argue from generalization, analogy, and parallel case. You can appeal to authority; you can also appeal to emotion. Consult the Structures and Strategies section of this chapter on how you might pull together these different lines of reasoning into a single, compelling argument.

You might consider devoting one part of your essay to an argument from parallel case: the introduction of the wheel to the Papago Indians, as presented by Wesley Bliss. The logic to this would be as follows: As Margaret Mead has written, culture is an interconnected web of traditions, beliefs, and activities. Change one part of the culture and other parts necessarily change, even when the change is something so apparently simple and inconsequential as the wheel. The next part of the essay would include a summary of the pertinent sections of the article by Wesley Bliss; then you would make a transition back to the technology you are discussing. A transitional statement might look something like this: "If so many unanticipated changes follow from the introduction of a simple technology like the wheel, what can we expect from a technology like _____?" You would complete the sentence with the technology you are presenting.

Realize that any one argument will consist of several parts: one or more appeals to reason; one or more appeals to authority; and, possibly, one or more appeals to emotion. Not every argument will be developed with each of these appeals. As a writer, you must decide which lines of reasoning to present and whether emotional appeals will succeed with a specific audience.

What Ideas Will You Include That Are Contrary to Your Own?

Arguments are believable only when the reader senses that the writer is open to alternate ways of seeing. Create in your argument a challenge to your own position. For instance, if you argue that your plug-in module (or widespread use of IVF) is a good thing, then create the most persuasive case you can that it is *not*. The counter to your argument will probably be based on a system of values that competes with yours. (It was on the basis of your values that you determined that a module was good or bad.) Seriously consider challenges to your position, and let these challenges force you to reexamine your convictions. Raise challenges *before* readers do. For a discussion on making rebuttals, see page 435.

Writing Your First Draft

Writing the first draft of an argument is more a recreation of thinking than an exploration. For the most part, you have already done exploration in your preparations for writing. Although your first draft will help you to refine your essay's idea, you should already have that idea firmly in mind.

Begin your first draft by writing one section of your paper at a sitting. This advice assumes that you know your claim and have sketched lines of reasoning to support it. Each line of reasoning will form its own section of the essay, and each section will likely consist of several paragraphs, at least. A section may take you from a half-hour to several hours (or more) to write. By drafting at least one section of your essay at a sitting, you will see clearly two important sets of relationships: first, of one paragraph to others *within* a section and, second, of whole blocks of paragraphs—of entire sections—to other sections and to your essay's overall idea. Unless your essay is very ambitious and grows very long, you should be able to finish your draft in four or five sittings. For further discussion of what constitutes a "section" of your essay, see pages 493–494. And, generally, see the material on writing a first draft on pages 486–498.

Advance Your Idea with Sources

What facts, opinions, and examples will your argument rely on? Look for support in your source materials. You have read four sources that should have stimulated your thinking about matters related to technology and change. Having written your discovery draft and settled on a claim, turn to your sources for support.

You have already considered the recommendation that Wesley Bliss's discussion of the Papago Indians be used as a parallel case. Related to this case would be Margaret Mead's assumption that elements of a culture are intertwined and that a single change in a culture's technology will have far-reaching effects. The introduction of the wheel to Papago culture is one example. The introduction of the module you are writing about (or the widespread use of IVF) would be another.

In examining the effects of the plug-in module that you chose (or the use of IVF), you might use one or more of Edward Spicer's study questions (pages 463–464). When looking for authoritative opinions to include in your essay, turn to Martin Marty, a distinguished theologian and philosopher who offers much to quote on the ways in which technology disrupts traditions. Notice that all these writers assume that technology disrupts. Perhaps you feel otherwise. Whatever your views, you should find much here to incorporate into your essay and to advance your idea. Consider using your sources for these reasons:

- to clarify the background of your topic
- to support your claim with facts, opinions, and examples
- to locate arguments against your claim
- to respond to arguments against your claim

See chapter 4 for demonstrations of using sources to provide facts, examples, and authoritative opinions and also for specific strategies for introducing sources into an essay. Particularly, see the section on "Sources and Cycles of Development," pages 61–68. Here you will get advice on keeping your essay focused on *your* idea, not on sources; and you will learn how to link sources to create a synthesis.

Suggestions for Writing with a Computer

After writing your draft, go back and identify all the major components of your argument. For example: before every claim, type the word CLAIM in boldface. Wherever you've defined key terms for your readers, type KEY TERMS DEFINED in bold. Wherever you've brought in sources, type EVIDENCE immediately before each new source. Do the same thing for all counterarguments, replies, and resolutions.

By doing this you'll be in a better position to see where, exactly, you've placed all the necessary components of your essay. After labeling the different parts of your essay, consider ways of modifying and enhancing the structure. Where should you add more claims, key terms, or evidence? Have you spent too much time on replies, but not enough on counterarguments? Is the form of your essay unbalanced, with lots of labels in boldface in some sections and few or none in others?

Use these indicators to get a better sense of the shape of your essay. Review accordingly, and then delete these boldface labels when you are finished.

Evaluate and Revise

Your primary challenge in revising your first draft is to make certain that the idea you thought you were writing about turns out, in fact, to be the idea you developed in the draft. The act of writing the draft will virtually always refine your initial idea; on occasion, your writing of the draft will substantially alter that idea, in which case you will have more work to do in revision. For extensive discussion on strategies for revision, see chapters 12–14. For arguments in particular, remember the following critical points.

Critical Points in an Argumentative Essay

- Have you carefully defined for readers key terms in your argument? (See pages 439–440.)
- Have you reasoned logically and fairly, avoiding these errors: faulty generalization, faulty cause and effect, confused causation, faulty analogy, either/or reasoning, begged questions, and personal attacks? (See pages 440–441.)

- Are the facts you cite representative and current? Have you considered negative cases? (See pages 442–443.)
- Are the authorities you quote actually authorities? And are they neutral—do they have an interest in the outcome of an argument? (See page 443.)

Pinpointing the Argument's Idea and Reexamining Its Structure

Reread your first draft to determine, *exactly,* your argument's idea. Expect that your idea will have changed, at least partially. Again, distill this idea into a single statement—a thesis. Once again, think through all the lines of reasoning that you might produce to convince readers that your argument's claim is sound and worth serious consideration. Add, delete, and otherwise refine your essay's sections to ensure their close fit with your claim.

Making Your Personal Commitment Known

Do you see yourself in your essay? Do you see a writer at work who is interested in his or her own ideas? Before releasing this essay to readers, satisfy yourself that your commitment as a writer is coming through: in the claim you have made, in your willingness to develop material patiently, and in your attention to surface-level features such as spelling, grammar, and punctuation.

PART III

Strategies for Writing and Rewriting

CHAPTER **12**

Drafting and Early Revision

There may be as many strategies for planning, developing, and writing a draft as there are writers. Just the same, one principle holds true for all: a writer's thoughts take shape through the very act of writing and rewriting. That is, when you write you are also thinking; and when you revise you are thinking again about your topic and clarifying ideas for yourself—and, in the process, for your readers. Experienced writers produce a first draft and then revise at least once.

The stages of writing unfold more or less in this order: preparing to write (discussed extensively in Part I), writing, and revising. But the stages also blend into each other. In the middle of a first draft, a writer may pause to revise an important sentence or paragraph, deciding to make one part of her document nearly finished while other parts remain rough or not yet written. In a first draft, the writer may discover new approaches to her topic and may stop to write new lists and make new outlines, activities associated with preparing to write. The process of writing is **recursive**: typically, writers loop backward and forward through the stages of writing—several times for any one document.

Writing a Draft

Preparing to Write

The first three chapters in Part I of this text are devoted to preparing to write. For ease of cross-reference, consult this index for guidance on the earliest stages of the writing process:

Several of these concerns are briefly reviewed here, though the majority of what follows will be a discussion of the actual writing and revising of your essays.

Writing a Thesis and Devising a Sketch of Your Paper

A **thesis** is a general statement about a topic, usually in the form of a single sentence that summarizes the controlling idea of an essay. You cannot produce a fully accurate **final thesis** until you have written down a complete draft. When writing a first draft, you will at best have a **working thesis:** a statement that, based on everything you know about your topic, should prove to be a reasonably accurate summary of what you will write.

Devising a Sketch of Your Paper

Look to your working thesis for clues about the ideas you will need to develop in your essay. For an academic paper to succeed, you must develop all directly stated or implied ideas in the thesis. You may want to regard your thesis as a contract. In the final draft, the contract exists between you and your reader; the thesis promises the reader a discussion of certain material, and the paper delivers on that promise. As a tool used in writing a first draft, your working thesis is a provisional contract.

Identifying Significant Parts of Your Thesis

To create a sketch of your first draft, study your working thesis and identify all significant elements, stated directly or indirectly. In your paper, you are obliged to develop each of these elements and to explain how it is related to others. Write the working thesis at the top of a page and circle its significant words. You can then ask development questions of, or make comments about, each circled element. If you are thorough in quizzing your thesis, you will identify most of its significant parts. (You may not discover some parts until you write a first draft.) Having identified these significant parts, briefly sketch the paper you intend to write.

Quizzing Your Thesis

Use the following questions and comments about your thesis to identify the major sections of your paper:

Questions

how does/will it happen?	what has prevented/will prevent it from happening?
how to describe?	
what are some examples?	who is involved?
what are the reasons for?	what are the key features?
what is my view?	what are the reasons against?
compared to what?	how often?
what is the cause?	possible to classify types or parts?
any stories to tell?	what is the effect of this?
how?	which ones?
when?	

Comments

define	review the reasoning
review the facts	explain the contrast or paradox

In writing a thesis, you compress a great deal of information into a single sentence; in writing a paper based on this thesis, you will need to "unpack" and discuss this information. Use the following technique as an aid to unpacking: challenge, or quiz, your thesis with questions. The technique will lead to a sketch of your paper.

Thesis: Though belonging to a group has it benefits, the price of membership is steep: the loss of individual conscience.

Sketching the Paper

Define group identity
Discuss key benefits of belonging to a group
Define individual conscience
Review the process of how an individual sacrifices in order to belong to a group
Explain the paradox: reasons that the strength of a group comes at the expense of an individual's integrity

Thesis: By instituting a curfew and acting on what it believed was the students' behalf, the administration undermined the moral and educational principles it wanted to uphold.

Sketching the Paper

Review the reasoning: in setting a curfew, the administration said it was acting in the best interest of students
Define "students' behalf" from student and administrative perspectives
Define moral issues and educational principles at issue
Explain the paradox: in mandating morality through a curfew, the administration denied students a chance to grapple with moral issues and reach mature decisions on their own. The administration undermined its own educational aims

Devise an action plan: A sketch based on your thesis is an action plan, a paper to be written. Depending on your preference, you can fill in the sketch, converting it to a detailed outline, or you can work with it as a sketch. In either case, this plan—closely connected to your thesis—sets an agenda for the paper to follow.

Option: Preparing a Formal Outline of Your Paper

Many writers feel that a rough sketch is sufficient for beginning the first draft of a paper. Others feel more comfortable with a formal plan of action—an outline with clearly delineated major and minor points. In collaborative writing situations, with different writers responsible for various sections of the project, a formal outline is probably the only way to reach agreement on what each writer will contribute.

Whatever your choice, be aware that before the first draft is written, any form of plan is, at best, *provisional* and subject to change. Outlines are sketches for getting started; they help you unify your paper and avoid discussing any topic not closely related to your thesis. They also help you to develop all significant points of your thesis, and they help you to achieve coherence—to ensure that all parts of the plan will lead logically from one to the next. Typically the parts of an outline are arranged in a logical order: the topic is divided into at least two constituent parts and each part is discussed separately. The order can be *spatial,* in terms of the location of the parts, or *chronological,* in terms of time sequence, or it can be based on some other criterion such as priority of importance to the issue at hand.

Useful as an outline can be, you will still need to discover the important elements of your paper during the process of writing and, necessarily, your outline or sketch will change as the writing takes shape. Here is an example:

Thesis: Establishing colonies on the moon will be possible by the early 21st century.

I. Colonizing the moon
  A. Base
  B. Missions
    1. Science
      a. Astronomy
      b. Geology
    2. Industry
      a. Mining
      b. Crystal growth
  C. Inhabitants
    1. Specialists
    2. Nonspecialists

II. Designing and building the base
  A. Designers
    1. Architects
    2. Psychologists
    3. Engineers
  B. Construction
    1. Materials
    2. Methods
    3. Crews
    4. Dangers

A formal outline establishes the major sections and subsections of your paper. The outline shows how each section is supported by the points you plan to discuss. It also shows how these points are themselves supported. The goal of a formal outline is to make visible the material you plan to use in the paper. Standard outline form is as follows: uppercase roman numerals indicate the most general level of heading in the outline; these headings correspond with major sections of your paper. Uppercase letters mark the major points you will use in developing each heading. Arabic numbers mark the supporting points you will use in developing main points. Lowercase letters mark further subordination—support of supporting points. Note that the entries at each level of heading are grammatically parallel; that each level of heading has at least two entries; and that only the first letter of an entry is capitalized. A formal outline need not show plans for your introduction or conclusion.

Each item of a formal outline can also be written as a sentence, which you may prefer in your efforts to begin writing. The following is one section of the preceding outline, written in sentence form.

B. There will be two broad missions for a Moon Base.
   1. The first mission will be scientific.
      a. By setting up telescopes on the far side of the moon, astronomers will have an unparalleled view of the universe.
      b. Geologists studying samples of lunar soil will be able to learn both about earth's origin and about the origin of the solar system.
   2. The second mission will be industrial.
      a. Mining companies will be able to begin commercial operations almost immediately.
      b. In the light moon gravity, technicians will be able to grow superior crystals.

Exercise 1

Circle significant words or phrases in a thesis you are developing for an essay. Question your thesis, and write comments about your thesis to explore and develop all the ideas within it. Prepare an informal or formal outline of your paper from the stated and implicit ideas of the thesis you have now identified.

Starting the First Draft

Your working thesis and your sketch or outline are essential for giving you the confidence to begin a first draft. Realize, however, that your final paper will not be identical to your original plans, even if they were carefully prepared. Once begun, writing will lead you to discard and revise your original ideas and will lead to new ideas as well. Through writing you will *explore* your subject. As you do, obstacles and opportunities will present themselves: by keeping your eyes open, you will be ready to avoid one and seize the other.

The object of a first draft is to get ideas down on paper, to explore them, and to establish the shape of your paper. Finished, readable documents will come later, through revision. In a first draft, give yourself permission to write in ways that you know will be imperfect but that will nonetheless be an essential step in achieving a final product.

Working Yourself through the Draft

The following strategies are helpful to use when preparing a first draft:

1. Write one section of the paper at a time: write a general statement that supports some part of your thesis, then provide details about the supporting statement. Once you have finished a section, take a break. Then return to write another section, working incrementally in this fashion until you have completed the draft.

- Alternately, write one section of the paper and take a break. Then reread and revise that one section before moving to the next. Continue to work in this fashion, one section at a time, until you complete the draft.

2. Accept two drafts, minimum, as the standard for writing any formal paper. In this way, you give yourself permission to write a first draft that is not perfect.

3. If you have prepared adequately for writing, then trust that you will discover what to write as you write.

4. Save substantial revisions concerning grammar, punctuation, usage, and spelling for later. In your first drafts, focus on content.

Beating Writer's Block

Journalists, novelists, beginning writers, writing teachers, graduate students, business people, students in freshman composition: everybody avoids writing at some point. Be assured that avoidance does not mean you have done things poorly or that you do not "have what it takes" to be a competent writer. Avoidance and the anxiety that causes it are natural parts of the writing process. By no means are they ever-present parts, and if you devote sufficient time to preparing yourself to write, you minimize the danger of writer's block. Still, preparing is not the same as writing a draft, and you inevitably face a moment in which you decide to take a step—or not. Think about the feelings you get when you do not want to write. When you are stuck as a writer, what might you be telling yourself? And how might you get unstuck?

Stuck: I cannot get started. I am afraid of the blank page—or its electronic equivalent, the empty screen: However fully formed ideas for writing may come to me, I can only write one word after the next. And as I do, what I have not written seems so vast that I cannot make a beginning.

Unstuck: Prepare yourself mentally to write one section of the paper, not the entire paper. Three-page papers, just like 500-page books, get written one section at a time. When you sit down to write a draft, identify a section: a grouping of related paragraphs that you can write in a single sitting.

Stuck: I want my writing to be perfect. My early attempts to express anything are messy. I get a sinking feeling when I reread my work and see how much revision is needed. Whenever I cannot think of the right word, I freeze up.

Unstuck: Accept two drafts, minimum, as the standard for writing any formal paper. When you understand that you will rewrite the first draft of all formal papers or letters, you can give yourself permission to write a first draft quickly and at times imprecisely.

Stuck: Why advertise my problems? I worry about grammar, punctuation, and spelling, and I do not want to embarrass myself.

Unstuck: Use a writer's reference tools. Many people are nervous about these errors. The fear is real. As long as you know how to use standard desk references—a dictionary and a handbook—there is no need to memorize rules of grammar, punctuation, and spelling. Of course, knowing the rules does save you time.

Working with Your Sketch or Outline

Following are three strategies for using your sketch or outline as a basis for writing. None of these strategies is correct in the sense that one produces a better draft than the others. All will get you a first draft, and all have advantages and disadvantages. How you choose to use a sketch or outline is a matter of your temperament as a writer.

Adhering Closely to Your Outline

One strategy for writing a draft is to follow closely the sketch or outline you made prior to actual drafting. To make full and frequent use of the detailed outline you have assembled makes a great deal of sense, as long as you are aware that your paper will deviate from the outline.

Advantages

By regularly consulting your outline, you will feel that you are making regular progress toward the completion of your paper.

Disadvantages

A comprehensive outline can so focus your vision that you will not allow yourself to stray and discover the territory of your paper. The paper planned will be the paper written, for better or worse.

Adhering Loosely to Your Outline

Some writers prefer to use a sketch or outline exclusively as a strategy for preparing; in the actual drafting of the paper, they abandon their plan in favor of one that they generate while writing the draft. Examine your outline, studying its first section carefully, and then begin writing. The outline is set aside and, once writing is under way, a new outline for each section of the paper you are about to write is created, based on the material you have just written. As you complete each section, update and adjust your outline.

Advantages

This strategy gives you the best chance of discovering material, since each new section of the paper is based on the writing you have just completed and not on an outline prepared in advance.

Disadvantages

The same freedom that gives you room to be creative can result in paragraphs that do not lead logically from one to the next and whole groupings of paragraphs that drift away from the working thesis.

Combining Strategies

Some writers like to give themselves more freedom than close adherence to a pre-draft outline allows; but at the same time they prefer more structure than the outline-as-you-go approach provides. These writers borrow from both methods. First, they carefully review their pre-draft outline for each section of the paper before writing it; then they write the section without further reference to the outline. At the end of each section, they compare their work against the outline and plan to add or delete material as needed. They also look ahead to the next section and revise the outline, if necessary.

Writing One Section of Your Paper at a Sitting

Unless you are writing an introduction, conclusion, or transition, every paragraph that you write will be situated in a grouping of paragraphs, or a **section** that constitutes part of the larger document. Think of the draft you are writing as a series of sections: typically groupings of three, four, or five related paragraphs. Plan to write *one* section of your paper at a sitting. Then take a break. Sooner than you realize, the pages will add up and you will have finished the draft.

As your draft develops, you will probably find yourself devoting a section to each major point you wish to develop. (Recall that you were able to identify these points, at least most of them, by "quizzing" your working thesis—see page 488.) Every section of your paper should have a dominant, controlling focus—a section thesis that explicitly announces the major point you will address in the grouping of paragraphs to follow. The section thesis will help you to write your draft and, eventually, will help readers to follow your discussion.

How to Write One Section of a Paper

The following sequence will help you write the sections of your paper:

1. **Prepare to write.** Identify purpose and define audience; generate and organize ideas and information; and devise a working thesis.
2. **Identify sections of the paper.** Ask of your thesis: What parts must I develop in order to deliver on the promise of this statement? Your answer of perhaps three or four points will identify the sections you need to write to complete that statement.

3. **Plan to write one section of your paper at a sitting.** If a section is long, divide it into manageable parts and write one part at a sitting.

4. **Write individual paragraphs.** Each paragraph will be related to others in the section. As you begin a second paragraph, clearly relate it to the first; relate the third paragraph to the second, and so on until you finish writing the section. Then take a break.

5. **Write other sections, one at a time.** Continue writing, building one section incrementally on the next, until you complete your first draft.

Exercise 2

Read the following section of a paper on genetically engineered organisms, written by student Josefa Pinto. Analyze Josefa's paragraphs as follows: (1) identify her controlling idea, or section thesis; (2) explain how the paragraphs work together to support this section thesis.

A Student Example by Josefa Pinto

Although these experiments may seem beneficial, there are certain dangers and problems involved with the use and release of genetically engineered organisms into the environment. One such problem is the limited research into and knowledge about these organisms. As Francis Sharples, former member of the Recombinant DNA Advisory Committee, stated, "Knowledge of the biotic and antibiotic interactions of most species in mixed populations in natural ecosystems is extremely limited. Currently the unknowns far outweigh the knowns where the ecological properties of microbes are concerned" (44). Many scientists are concerned with marketing fruits, vegetables, and grains after such a limited amount of research. Ecologists such as Martin Alexander of Cornell feel that more research should be done before genetically altered bacteria are released. Not enough is known to guarantee the safety of these organisms.

There are also potential health hazards that may result from consumer use of these products. Studies have shown that "shuffling" genes has elevated plant toxins. This was the case in the 1960s when scientists bred a new kind of potato that caused human illness. The gene mixing had increased the plant's natural toxins to dangerous levels, thereby forcing the United States Department of Agriculture to recall the poisonous product from the market. Although some scientists argue that illness may be detected within two weeks of consumption, long-term effects are unknown. Other health concerns include potential risks of allergic reactions. Studies have shown that "some microorganisms with potential for extracting metals and oils from the earth such as *Sclerotium Rafi* and various species of *Aureobasidium* have been associated with lung disease and wound infections, respectively" (Office 122).

Perhaps the most dangerous problem associated with genetic engineering is the inability to control organisms or to predict their behavior, once released into the open environment. Some scientists argue that laboratory testing may not be an accurate prediction of an organism's behavior once it is released. According to Francis Sharples, "so many factors interact in the environment to determine where there will be trouble, that predictions of just which species introductions will cause

ecological disruptions is nearly beyond the ability of ecologists and population biologists" (41). There is also the concern for the possibility of
having weeds capture a gene for herbicide resistance to environmentally safe herbicides, thereby forcing scientists to use much harsher and
more dangerous chemicals to control weed growth. As Cornell ecologist
David Pimentel argues, "You can stop using pesticides, but once you put
one of these microbes out there the damn thing will reproduce and grow
and we'll never get rid of it" (16). Past experiences have left ecologists
skeptical: experiments such as the release of the gypsy moth and the
introduction of the Kudzu vine have caused ecological havoc and billions of dollars in damage. What happens if something goes wrong with
an organism once it has been released into the environment? Once it has
been released and found an appropriate habitat, the organism may not
only reproduce and spread but might also evolve in ways that will benefit its existence—not ours (Sharples 40).

Exercise 3

Choose *one* section of any essay in Part II to study in depth. (Define a *section*
as a group of related paragraphs.) Closely read each paragraph in this section,
and prepare an analysis by responding to three points: (1) Identify the controlling idea (the section thesis) of the section. (2) Explain how the paragraphs
work together to support the section thesis. (3) Discuss how the section fits
into the overall structure of the essay.

Identifying and Resolving
Problems in Mid-Draft

It is likely that at some point in the writing process you will find yourself
unable to steam ahead, one section after the next. You will encounter obstacles, which you can recognize as follows: You are aware that your work
in one section of the paper is not as good as it is elsewhere, or you make
several attempts at writing a section and find that you simply cannot do
it. When you are feeling especially frustrated, stop. Step back from your
work and decide how you will get past this obstacle. Ask: Why am I having trouble? Here are several potential obstacles in writing a draft:

1. You do not have enough information to write. You have not gathered the
   information or, if you have, you may not thoroughly understand it.

2. You do not understand the point you planned to make or its relation to the
   rest of your paper.

3. The point you planned to make no longer seems relevant or correct, given
   what you have discovered about your subject while writing.

4. You recognize a gap in the structure of your paper, and you suddenly see
   the need to expand an existing section or to write an entirely new section.

5. The material in the section seems inappropriate for your audience.

6. You have said everything you need to in a page, but the assignment calls
   for six to ten pages.

7. At the moment, you do not have the attention span to write.

Each of these obstacles can frustrate your attempts at writing, and only you can know what is for you a normal and abnormal level of frustration. Whatever your tolerance, develop sensors to let you know when things are not going well. Frustration usually occurs for a good reason, so you should trust the reaction and then act on it. You will come of age as a writer the moment you can realize you are having trouble and can then step away to name your problem and find a solution.

Exercise 4

Using any combination of the strategies discussed in this section, write a rough draft of your paper. Remember, this first draft is rough and imperfect; you may change your original ideas as you explore them.

A Student's First Draft

Following is the first draft of an essay written by student Jim Walker. (Chapters 1 and 2 showed idea generating and thesis development for this paper.) You will see versions of this essay in revision, and you will see a final draft in both this chapter and the next. Comments on the draft were written by Walker's fellow class members and by the instructor.

Draft #1

A lot of people think that our public schools are not safe. You see school violence in all the media. There are newspaper articles about assaults on teachers, magazine articles about students stabbing and shooting other students, T.V. news features showing piles of weapons confiscated from schools. You also see gangbangers protecting their turf or shooting up rivals with Uzis, drug dealers in and around schools armed with a lot more than beepers to protect their business interests. At some school or another you hear about fights over girlfriends or boyfriends, fights over expensive sneakers or designer clothes, fights over someone giving someone else a crazy look, disrespecting them. The perception is that guns and violence are common, everyday occurrences in our public schools. The perception is that students routinely carry weapons and the school itself is an armed camp, filled with roving posses packing guns and looking for an excuse to use them.

Strong introduction

People's reactions to school violence are very difficult. School administrators want more money to put more police in the halls and metal detectors at the doors. They argue about which approach is best to sniff out weapons, the airport-style walk-through detector or the hand-held detectors that allow more random checks, or maybe, if the funds are available, both.

Cut or condense?

Parents and relatives get excited about school violence. They are anxious about the safety of their children. They love to talk about how terrible things are in schools now. They mention the one violent event that made the papers but fail to notice the many good things going on at your school. They think that your school is a combat zone, not the peaceful refuge for study and reflection their high school was.

Teachers and students are more aware of what's really going on in schools, but even some teachers have given up, not expecting too much from students, not pushing them too hard, not knowing which ones might

Means "irrational"?

be (sprung) enough to assault them with words or weapons. These teachers are always talking about the good students they had years ago and about their retirement plans. Not all teachers are that bad. There are plenty of good ones. My point is that students are the ones who really know the truth about school violence. It wasn't that long ago that I was a stu-

Thesis

dent at a big urban high school. I was at the front lines. School violence changes schools and changes the students in them.

People have all kinds of ideas about what schools ought to be. One thing they overlook is that a school is part of a neighborhood, part of a community, part of a national culture. What school is, is a place where all of these outside influences come together. School is a flash point where all kinds of students and teachers, attitudes, ideas and knowledge come together. That is what is exciting about schools and education. Sometimes, however, this mixture is explosive. The problems of the larger society, the

Specific examples?

crime, the violence, the weapons, etc., get acted out in the halls and classrooms of schools. We do a good job of coping with <u>that</u>—and do it at the

Expand. How did you cope with violence?

same time we cope with all the personal stuff that happens as we stop being kids and start becoming adults. We are also doing it at the same time as we prepare for college and life. Even though we know other kids who bring weapons to school we avoid them and stick with our own friends. We learn very quickly how to fit in and fit out. We learn how to survive in a multicultural school.

Good section thesis.

There is a small part of every group in a big, multicultural high school that are bad apples—always talking trash, trying to be bad, walking around with that jaw-clenched, mad-dog stare. These bad apples threaten other students, calling them names like sissy or punk, pushing them to fight so the toughs can add to their reputation as being the baddest. These toughs walk around like actors in a violent movie where the only lines the

What happens?

script gives them are, "I gotta be bad. I gotta be bad." They may have reasons for that (attitude.) But now they are (putting it on everyone.) Fortunately, schools have their own weapons. They are called vice princi-

What reasons? causes? Explanations?

pals and they love to mix it up with that kind of (aggressive attitude.) It's what they get paid for. I was glad to let administrators deal with it because I was in school to get an education. I wasn't there to be a bit player in someone else's psychodrama.

How do other students react, cope?

I didn't identify with that small part of each group who appeared to be without hope in any future, who didn't seem to believe in anything, who

Means irrational?

were not afraid of jail or of dying. These students are (sprung) enough to do anything. You don't know if you do get into a fight with one of them whether they will pull a knife or something on you. Anything you do or say may set them off. Because they may do anything, or nothing, no one really knows for sure. They are truly (dangerous.) They generate a lot of fear

Rewrite section thesis so "rumors" is the focus.

in the school and seem to thrive as their reputation grows.

One sure way to get a reputation is to be the subject of (rumors.) Big high schools are busy places, lots of people, lots of things happening. They have extensive and effective rumor grapevines. A rumor about somebody disrespecting someone else buzzes through the school. Word of mouth, friends talking to friends adds anger to the self-protective fear already present. Another rumor buzzes through the school that someone has a 9mm pistol in his locker. Later you hear it was only a knife, or only a screwdriver, or that it was nothing, just a rumor. Another layer of fear gets added to rising emotions. Student feel uncomfortable passing other people in the hall, uncertain of what they'll do. Students are afraid of getting jumped so they hang out with friends so they are never alone, never vulnerable. Reasonable levels of self-protection slide into paranoia as emotions rise. Students watch what they say more closely, don't look at someone the wrong way and if they do, apologize fast. Then there is a fight, a violent one. Someone is slashed and rolled out on a stretcher. Friends of the victim talk about retaliation as rumors about payback buzz the school. *Summarize this excellent description with a conclusion, summary, or observation.*

Expand this example.

After a fight feelings run higher than ever. Anger and fear raise stress levels. Students become more anxious. Suddenly, even some of the steadiest, best students start carrying boxcutters or X-Acto knives for protection. These are weapons for self-defense. Also, unlike other weapons they can be explained easily. They are still weapons though and now the school

You refer back to the introduction.

Could this help focus a new, more specific thesis?

begins to fit those (media perceptions) we all have. More importantly, there is more potential for violence and emotions are high. Violence feeds on violence. (The cycle of violence) is in place and can only get worse.

You begin with media perceptions of school violence that are good hooks, direct (except for your first sentence), colorful, forceful. You follow with some perceptive but general reactions of various people. I'm interested in more specific examples of changes in individual students, especially you—that's what your working thesis promised!

You discovered at the end of your paper a name for what you've been describing, "the cycle of violence." Quizzing that phrase may help you in your next draft. Another suggestion along that line: some background reading about violence, about that "aggressive attitude" you had to deal with in high school, might fill in some gaps, might help you make some new connections. Again, some in-depth personal examples would balance your paper nicely. And what about a title?

Early Revision

Think of revision as occurring in three stages—early, later, and final:

Early revision: Reread your first draft and rediscover your main idea. What you *intended* to write is not always, or even usually, what you *in fact* have written.

Later revision: Make all significant parts of your document work together in support of your main idea.

Final revision (editing): Correct errors at the sentence level that divert attention from your main point.

As much as a first draft, revision is an act of creation. The difference between your first and second efforts at creating a document is that in a first draft you work to give a document potential: the writing may be incomplete, hurried, or inexact; but you are working toward an important, controlling idea. In your second and subsequent drafts, you work to make an earlier draft's potential *real:* you revise, and through revision—by adding, altering, or deleting sentences and paragraphs—you clarify your main point for yourself and, on the strength of that, for your reader. Accomplished writers expect to revise. They know that good revision reaches deep; that it is not, for the most part, about cosmetic changes (a word scratched out here, another added there) but about fundamental changes and redirections that help you discover meaning. Above all, readers expect *clarity* of ideas in your writing. When you revise, you rethink and you clarify; you will serve your own interests and your reader's by committing yourself to meaningful revision.

Rediscovering Your Main Idea

When writing succeeds, it always works at the largest possible level by clearly communicating a single idea. When writing fails, it is very often because the writer has not understood his or her most important idea well enough to present it to others. A key difference between successful and unsuccessful writing is the commitment a writer makes to revision, since it is the process of revision that helps to clarify the writer's main idea. The important word here is *commitment*, not ability. You can and will learn techniques of revision. What you alone can provide is the commitment to rework drafts until they express your meaning exactly. Early revision involves adding, altering, or deleting entire paragraphs with the sole purpose of clarifying your main idea. Commit yourself to real and meaningful revision, and your writing will be good consistently; back away from this commitment, and your writing will fail to the degree that you back away.

Strategies for Early Revision

Pose three questions to get started on early revision. Your goal is to rediscover and clarify what you have written in a first draft. Here are some tactics to help discover a main idea:

- What I *intended* to write in my first draft may not be what I have *in fact* written. What is the main idea of this first draft?

  Underline one sentence in your draft in answer to this question; if you cannot find such a sentence, write one.

  Choose a title for your second draft. The title will help you to clarify your main idea.

- Does what I have written in this draft satisfy my original purpose for writing?

  Review the assignment or set of instructions that began your writing project. Restate the purpose of that assignment. Reread your draft to determine the extent to which you have met this purpose. To the degree you have not, plan to revise.

- Does my writing communicate clearly to my audience?

  Think of your audience and reread your draft with this audience clearly in mind. If need be, revise your level of language, your choice of illustrations, and your general treatment of the topic in order to help your audience understand.

In addition to posing questions, challenge key elements of your essay:

- **Challenge your thesis:** You began your first draft with a working thesis. The thesis that organized your actual draft may differ from this. Try two strategies for identifying the sentence that will become your final thesis.

   Underline the sentence you intended to be your thesis in the first draft. Ask: "Is this the sentence I wrote about?" For a moment, play a doubting game. Provisionally answer with a *no* and search for a competing thesis. Reread the draft's final paragraphs with special care. If you find no alternate thesis, return to the original.

   Study the sentence you now know to be your thesis and revise repeatedly until it is both precise and concise: make the sentence say what it must in as few words as possible. Base all subsequent revisions of your paper on this new, leaner version of your thesis.

- **Challenge your paper's structure.** What often changes most from first draft to second is the structure of a paper. A first draft is *yours* in the sense that you are writing it, at least partly, to discover what you think about a topic. The second draft is more the *reader's* in the sense that you must consider how others will regard your work and how you might best present it to secure approval and understanding. Rethink the structure of your paper in light of the reader's needs. Challenge the structure of your draft in two ways:

   Consider locating your revised thesis in some different part of the paper. How would this change the order of presentation? Are there advantages to be gained?

   Consider beginning your paper not with your present first paragraph, but with some paragraph from the middle of the draft. How does the paper present itself differently, based on this change? What further changes would be needed to ensure coherence?

Based on your challenges to the paper's thesis and structure, set yourself a "to do" list. A new thesis may require that you write new sections. A revised structure will require careful attention to coherence and at least several new sentences of transition.

Choosing a Revision Strategy That Suits You

There are as many different strategies for revising a paper as there are for writing one, and the strategy you choose will depend on your temperament. Some first-draft writers work on individual paragraphs, revising continually until they achieve their idea for that paragraph before they move on. Others write and revise one section of their paper at a time, revising a grouping of related paragraphs continually until that grouping functions as a single, seamless unit. Still other writers complete an entire first draft and then revise. The approach to revision advocated here is that a writer make several "passes" over a draft and on each pass revise with a different focus. First, revise the largest elements (the sections); on the next pass, revise paragraphs within sections; and on the final pass (or passes), revise individual sentences within paragraphs. Choose a revision strategy that suits your temperament.

Strategies for Clarifying and Developing Your Main Idea

The overall objective of your first revision of a draft, which will be your major revision, is to rediscover your main idea. You began your first draft with a main idea that you wanted to develop. But what you intended to write may not be what you have in fact written. Now is the time to check. On the basis of your evaluation, you will plan a second draft.

Reread your first draft with care, looking for some sentence other than your working thesis that more accurately describes what you have written. Often, such a "competing" thesis appears near the end of the draft, the place where you force yourself to summarize. If you can find no competing thesis and are sure that your original working thesis does not fit the paper you have written, modify the existing working thesis or write a new one. Be prepared to quiz the new thesis as you did before. See page 488 to review techniques for doing this.

Discovering a "Competing" Thesis in a Student Paper

Jim Walker's draft led him to revise the working thesis he used in his rough draft. That thesis was:

> School violence changes schools and changes the students in them.

Rereading his rough draft convinced Jim that what he had written described something more specific. His last paragraph summed up more accurately how he felt about students and violence in schools. Here are the last two sentences of his draft:

> Violence feeds on violence. The cycle of violence is in place and can only get worse.

He liked the phrase "cycle of violence" and had written about the many factors that feed violence and make it worse. He wrote a competing thesis based on what he had discovered in writing his first draft:

> What seems like a random explosion of violence among students is actually the result of many factors that create a cycle of violence and aggressive acts that can spiral out of control. Students can get hurt. Students can also help break the cycle.

Writing a draft enabled Jim Walker to clarify his purpose. In no way did he waste effort by beginning his draft with a thesis he did not, in fact, end up developing. His draft started him on a process of discovery. As a first step in the revision process, reread your draft to see what you have discovered and to determine whether this discovery merits changing your thesis.

Rewriting Based on Your
Newly Clarified Main Idea

You have pinpointed a competing sentence in your first draft, modified your existing thesis, or written an entirely new thesis. Now you have a single, controlling sentence that both fits the paper you wrote (which is not yet complete) and points the way to a revision of that paper. Quiz your new thesis with development questions and comments, exactly as you did the original working thesis. This will lead to a revised outline.

Here is a second draft thesis for Jim Walker's paper:

What seems like a random explosion of violence is actually the result of many factors that create a cycle of violence and aggressive acts that can spiral out of control. Students can get hurt. Students can also help break the cycle.

Quizzing the thesis leads to an outline of the paper's sections:

- Introduction
- Factors of the cycle of violence
- What the aggressive acts are and who commits them
- How students are hurt by violence in schools
- How students can help break the cycle of violence

Plan to write new material and rewrite old material so that you respond to each development question and comment. Depending on how substantially your new thesis differs from the old one, you may have minor work or major work to do. Very likely you have created in your first draft at least a few of the pieces that will fit into the completed puzzle of your final draft. In your second draft you will need to create other pieces of the puzzle. Take heart: you may have some major rewriting to do, but your new draft will be more sharply focused than your original draft. As you are writing, you will have in mind a clear direction that will lead to a successful, completed product.

Incorporate Sections of Your First Draft into Your Revised Outline

Reexamine your first draft to determine how much of it will fit, with or without changes, into your plans for the final paper. Then, using block commands, retrieve your first draft and cut and paste usable sections of this draft onto your final outline. Be sure to reread each sentence of first-draft writing that you move into the second draft. Every sentence must contribute toward developing the meaning of your newly conceived thesis.

In the first-draft paragraph below, student Jim Walker revised material to fit his second-draft outline. Notice that there are two places where Walker has deleted parts not relevant to the new thesis. Also, he moves one sentence and adds new material that reinforces this new thesis.

First Draft

Teachers and students are more aware of what's really going on in schools, but even some teachers have given up, not expecting too much from students, not pushing them too hard, not knowing which ones might be sprung enough to assault them with words or weapons. ~~These teachers are always talking about the good students they had years ago and about their retirement plans. Not all teachers are that bad. There are plenty of good ones.~~ My point is that students are the ones who really know the truth about school violence. It wasn't that long ago that I was a student at a big urban high school. ~~I was at the front lines.~~ School violence changes schools and changes the students in them. → *move this*

Revision

Teachers and students are more aware of what's really going on in schools, but even some teachers have given up, not expecting too much from students, not pushing them too hard, not knowing which ones might be sprung enough to assault them with words or weapons. My point is that students are the ones who really know the truth about school violence **and some ways of dealing with the effects of aggression acted out in schools.** It wasn't that long ago that I was a student at a big urban high school. **What seems like a random explosion of violence is actually the result of many factors that create a cycle of violence and aggressive acts that can spiral out of control. Students can get hurt. Students can also help break the cycle.**

Write New Sections of the Final Outline, as Needed

The preceding step will leave you with a partial paper: a detailed outline, some of the sections of which (imported from your first draft) are close to complete, other sections of which are indicated in the sketchiest possible terms by a phrase in your outline. You will need to write these sections from scratch. Before beginning a new section of your paper, write a section thesis to help focus your efforts (see page 493).

Reconsidering Purpose and Audience

Purpose

At some point early in the process of revision you will want to reconsider your reasons for writing. You may have been asked to explain, describe, argue, compare, analyze, summarize, define, discuss, illustrate, evaluate, or prove. With your purpose firmly in mind, evaluate your first draft to determine the extent to which you have met that purpose. Alter your revision plans, if necessary, to satisfy your reason for writing.

- Identify the key verb in the assignment and define that verb with reference to your topic.
- If you have trouble understanding the purpose, seek out your professor or your professor's assistant. Bring your draft to a conference and explain the direction you've taken.
- Once you identify the parts of a paper that will achieve a stated purpose, incorporate those parts into your plans for a revised draft.

Audience

Revisit your initial audience analysis (see pages 41–42); will your audience be classmates, fellow majors, or a professor? Take whatever conclusions you reached in your analysis and use them as a tool for evaluating your first draft. You may find it useful to pose these questions:

- How will this subject appeal to my readers?
- Is the level of difficulty with which I have treated this subject appropriate for my readers?
- Is my choice of language, in both its tone (see page 50) and its level of difficulty, appropriate for my readers?
- Are my examples appropriate in interest and complexity for my readers?

Make changes to your revision plans according to your analysis of the first draft.

Choosing and Using a Title

Before rewriting your paper, use your revised thesis to devise a title. A title creates a context for your readers; a title alerts readers to your topic and your intentions for treating it. Forcing yourself to devise a title before beginning your major revision will help you to clarify your main idea. A descriptive title directly announces the content of a paper and is appropriate for reports and write-ups of experiments: occasions when you are expected to be direct. An evocative title is a playful, intriguing, or otherwise indirect attempt to pique a reader's interest. Both descriptive and evocative titles should be brief (no longer than ten words).

Jim Walker titled the first draft of his paper "Rough Draft." Not surprisingly, he had only a rough idea about where he was headed in that paper. Writing a draft helped Jim discover a competing thesis that, in turn, prepared for a well-focused second-draft thesis. Here is his second-draft thesis:

> What seems like a random explosion of violence is actually the result of many factors that create a cycle of violence and aggressive acts that can spiral out of control. Students can get hurt. Students can also help break the cycle.

Working with this revised thesis, Jim chose a title that helped him focus on his controlling idea: "Breaking the Cycle of Violence." Jim gave his final draft an evocative title: "When the Trigger Pulls the Finger." That title more accurately matched what he came to understand was his major discovery from writing: weapons can escalate an argument or confrontation into a lethal level of violence with tragic results.

Exercise 5

Following advice offered in this section, revise the first draft of the paper you wrote in response to Exercise 4. Your early revision may be a major one, requiring you to rework your thesis and redefine major sections of the paper.

A Student's Revised Draft

Following is Jim Walker's first major revision of his essay, with additions and deletions noted. Revised and new text appear in bold type.

A lot of people think that our public schools are not safe. You see school violence in all the media. There are newspaper articles about assaults on teachers, magazine articles about students stabbing and shooting other students, T.V. news features showing piles of weapons confiscated from schools. You also see gangbangers protecting their turf or shooting up rivals with Uzis, drug dealers in and around schools armed with a lot more than beepers to protect their business interests. At some school or another you hear about fights over girlfriends or boyfriends, fights over expensive sneakers or designer clothes, fights over someone giving someone else a crazy look, disrespecting them. The perception is that guns and violence are common, everyday occurrences in our public schools. The perception is that students routinely carry weapons and the school itself is an armed camp, filled with roving posses packing guns and looking for an excuse to use them.

~~People's reactions to school violence are very different. School administrators want more money to put more police in the halls and metal detectors at the doors. They argue about which approach is best to sniff out weapons, the airport-style walk-through detector or the hand-held detectors that allow more random checks, or maybe, if the funds are available, both.~~

~~Parents and relatives really get excited about school violence. They are anxious about the safety of their children. They love to talk about how terrible things are in schools now. They mention the one violent event that made the papers but fail to notice the many good things going on at your school. They think that your school is a combat zone, not the peaceful refuge for study and reflection their high school was.~~

Teachers and students are more aware of what's really going on in schools, but even some teachers have given up, not expecting too much from students, not pushing them too hard, not knowing which ones might be sprung enough to assault them with words or weapons. ~~These teachers are always talking about the good students they had years ago and about their retirement plans. Not all teachers are that bad. There are plenty of good ones.~~ My point is that students are the ones who really know the truth about school violence **and some ways of dealing with the tangible and intangible effects of aggression acted out in schools.** It wasn't that long ago that I was a student at a big urban high school. What **seems like a random explosion of violence is actually the result of many factors that come together and create a cycle of violence and aggressive acts that can spiral out of control. People get hurt. People can also stop aggression.**

People have all kinds of ideas about what schools ought to be. One thing they overlook is that a school is part of a neighborhood, part of a community, part of a national culture. What school is, is a place where all of these outside influences come together. School is a flash point where all kinds of students and teachers, attitudes, ideas and knowledge come together. That is what is exciting about schools and education. Sometimes, however, this mixture is explosive. The problems of the larger society, the crime, the violence, the weapons, etc., get acted out in the halls and classrooms of schools. We do a good job of coping with *that*—and do it at the same time we cope with all the personal stuff that happens as we stop being kids and start becoming adults. ~~We are also doing it at the same time as we prepare for college and life. Even though we know other kids who bring weapons to school we avoid them and stick with our own friends.~~ We learn very quickly how to fit in and fit out. We learn how to survive in a multicultural school.

But just avoiding the problem is not enough. We know that aggression is a fact of life. Social psychologists have several theories about what causes it, including aggression-as-instinct, frustration that leads to aggression, aggression learned from the social environment. Whatever the causes, the school is the place where a lot of different people come together and need to learn to get along without resorting to weapons as the first choice in solving conflicts.

There is a small part of every group in a big, multicultural high school that are bad apples—always talking trash, trying to be bad, walking around with that jaw-clenched, mad-dog stare. These bad apples threaten other students, calling them names like sissy or punk, pushing them to fight so the toughs can add to their reputation as being the baddest. These toughs walk around like actors in a violent movie where the only lines the script gives them are, "I gotta be bad. I gotta be bad." They may have reasons for that attitude. But now they are putting it on everyone. Fortunately, schools have their own weapons. They are called vice principals and they love to mix it up with that kind of aggressive attitude. It's what they get paid for. I was glad to let administrators deal with it because I was in school to get an education. I wasn't there to be a bit player in someone else's psychodrama. **But vice principals and plainclothes police can't be everywhere. Students naturally seemed to divert confrontations with a quick apology, or to deflect aggression with humor. This is what social psychologists call reducing levels of aggression with an incompatible response. Further, the school implemented Peer Mediation where if someone felt a physical or emotional threat they could report it. They could talk about it, talk through it, get some help. The important thing was talking, getting two sides together to *talk* rather than using weapons or fists to solve differences. Talking showed students it wasn't worth a visit to the emergency room or legal problems, the flip side of violence that movies or rap videos don't usually show you.**

I didn't identify with that small part of each group who appeared to be without hope in any future, who didn't seem to believe in anything, who were not afraid of jail or of dying. These students are sprung enough to do anything. You don't know if you do get into a fight with one of them whether they will pull a knife or something on you. Anything you do or say may set them off. Because they may do anything, or nothing, no one really knows for sure. They are truly dangerous. They generate a lot of fear in the school and seem to thrive as their reputation grows. **But I felt confident that I had some weapons myself.**

One sure way to get a reputation is to be the subject of rumors. Big high schools are busy places, lots of people, lots of things happening. They have extensive and effective rumor grapevines. A rumor about somebody disrespecting someone else buzzes through the school. Word of mouth, friends talking to friends adds anger to the self-protective fear already present. Another rumor buzzes through the school that someone has a 9mm pistol in his locker. Later you hear it was only a knife, or only a screwdriver, or that it was nothing, just a rumor. Another layer of fear gets added to rising emotions. Students feel uncomfortable passing other people in the hall, uncertain of what they'll do. Students are afraid of getting jumped so they hang out with friends so they are never alone, never vulnerable. Reasonable levels of self-protection slide into paranoia as emotions rise. ~~Students watch what they say more closely, don't look at someone the wrong way and if they do, apologize fast. Then there is a fight, a violent one. Someone is slashed and rolled out on a stretcher. Friends of the victim talk about retaliation as rumors about payback buzz the school.~~

~~After a fight feelings run higher than ever. Anger and fear raises stress levels. Students become more anxious. Suddenly, even some of the steadiest, best students start carrying boxcutters or X-Acto knives for protection. These are weapons for self-defense. Also, unlike other weapons they can be explained easily. They are still weapons though and now the school begins to fit those media perceptions we all have. More importantly, there is more potential for violence and emotions are high. Violence feeds on violence. The cycle of violence is in place and can only get worse.~~

During my junior year in high school, someone got slashed in a fight and that neck wound required 40 stitches. Although it wasn't ever 100% clear, the fight was about disrespecting someone's girlfriend. Rumors flew and finally there was a confrontation with name-calling, punches thrown, a knife was drawn. These were students who thought Peer Mediation was for snitches. They could solve their own problems. An argument became an assault and the circle of victims widened.

Rumors about payback got a lot of students buzzing. Even normally steady, good students got caught up in it—out of loyalty and friendship—and my friend was one of them. It was easy to carry a boxcutter or an X-Acto knife. These were weapons but they could be easily explained if you were caught with one. A boxcutter was especially easy to replace.

Some of us were playing basketball at an outdoor court in our neighborhood. Another game was in progress on the court next to us. Our game was guys from my school, some that I'd played football with that fall, a bunch of scrappy, competitive jocks. The other game was

some older guys from the neighborhood, another bunch of homeboys playing some hoop.

A bad pass sent our ball into their court and my friend ran to get it. He was looking back at us, yelling about who got outs as he chased it down. He wasn't aware that he had disrupted the flow of the other game and collided with one of the other players, knocking him down. That guy got up and he was hot, yelling obscenities at my friend who looked at him, turned his back and coolly walked back toward us. That was too much for the screamer and he threw his ball hard at my friend, slamming it into his back. My friend turned and made a terrible mistake.

He pulled out a boxcutter and flashed it at his new enemy. This is what's called show and tell, showing somebody you've got a weapon and letting him know you have the heart to use it. The other guy reached down and pulled a knife out of a sheath strapped to his leg. Before anybody could say or do anything to break it up or distract them, those two went at it. When it was over, my friend's arm was dangling at his side, tendons and muscles slashed. His enemy's face was slashed, cheek bone showing white and glistening through the blood. This fight was over what? Honor? Respect? Reputation? A basketball that bounced out of bounds? One person was disabled, another disfigured.

My first reaction at the time was as crazy as my friend's but it felt right. I wanted a gun. I thought I could've stopped the whole thing with a gun by raising the ante. Then we all could've just walked away, everything cool again. What I didn't consider until much later was the possibility that one of the other players had a gun too. Then it would have been knives *and* guns in each other's face. Again—for what? More importantly, why? Why is it at the first sign of a conflict that weapons are the first choice to resolve it?

Maybe this situation was ripe for a fight. There was provocation from both sides. It was a short move from one kind of physical confrontation, one-on-one hoop moves ("Show me what you got"), to another, a fist fight. Maybe some kind of line had been crossed, some kind of code broken and a facing up to that had to happen. I am at the heart of aggression right here. Whatever the causes, and there are plenty, it is clear to me now that it was the weapons that pushed this playground scuffle into violence and tragedy. My friend and his new enemy chose the wrong weapons to fight. Neither could escape the violence cycle and apologize or laugh it off or talk it through to another conclusion. I don't defend what he did but I know where he was. A weapon was at hand and the trigger pulled him. Without that weapon to raise the ante, there may have still been a fight. Aggression is a fact of our lives. But it wouldn't have been so lethal.

CHAPTER *13*

Later Revisions: Sections, Paragraphs, and Sentences

Your first major revision of a draft (the revision you achieved if you completed Exercise 5 in chapter 12) requires the courage to look deep into your paper and make fundamental changes in order to present a single idea clearly. Later revisions will not be as dramatic or far-reaching, and will require for the most part that you understand and be able to apply systematically certain principles of organization. Three principles of organization important to a later revision are unity, coherence, and balance.

Bringing Your Main Idea into Focus

As the rewriting process leads you to clarify a main idea and reevaluate sections of the paper, you can put these quizzing techniques to work.

1. Use development questions and comments to quiz your thesis, your section theses, and your topic sentences:

how does it happen?	what will prevent its happening?
what's the cause?	how often?
how? when?	which ones?
define	review the reasoning
review the facts	explain the contrast or similarity

2. Look for unity and coherence in the whole paper:
   - Quiz your thesis.
   - Generate topics, which become sections of the paper.
   - Use topics as a principle of unity at the paper level: each topic becomes a section.
   - Arrange topics to establish paper-level coherence: topics (sections) arranged in logical order.
3. Strive for unity and coherence within sections:
   - Quiz your section thesis.
   - Generate topics, which become paragraphs within sections.
   - Use topics as a principle of unity within the section: each topic becomes one or more paragraphs.
   - Arrange topics to establish section-level coherence: topics (paragraphs) arranged in logical order.
4. Develop unity and coherence within paragraphs:
   - Quiz your topic sentence.
   - Generate topics, which become sentences within paragraphs.
   - Use topics as a principle of unity within the paragraph: each topic becomes one or more sentences.
   - Arrange topics to establish paragraph-level coherence: topics (sentences) arranged in a logically connected sequence.

Revising for Balance and Development

Balance is a principle that guides you in expanding, condensing, and cutting material as you revise. First drafts are typically uneven in the amount of attention given to each section of a paper. In revision, one of your jobs is to review the weight (the extent of development) you have given each of the topics you have discussed and to determine how appropriate that weight is to the importance of that particular point.

Revising for Balance: Expand, Condense, and Cut

At times, you will need to **expand:** to add material, in which case you will need to return to the notes you made in preparing to write. You may need to generate new information by reflecting on your subject, by conducting additional library research, or both. At times, you will need to **condense:** to take a lengthy paragraph, for example, and reduce it to two sentences. At other times you will need to **cut:** to delete sentences because they are off the point or because they give too much attention to a subordinate point.

1. In conjunction with your revision for unity and coherence, reread your paper to determine how evenly you have developed each section.
2. Expand discussions that are underdeveloped.

3. Condense discussions that are overdeveloped.

4. Cut extraneous material or material that gives too much weight to minor points.

Revising for Development

One important element of effective writing is the level of detail you can offer in support of a paragraph's topic sentence. To *develop* a paragraph means to devote a block of sentences to a discussion of its core idea. Sentences that develop will explain or illustrate, and will support with reasons or facts. The various strategies presented here will help you to develop paragraphs that inform and persuade.

Developing Paragraphs: Essential Features

In determining whether a paragraph is well or even adequately developed, you should be able to answer three questions without hesitation:

- **What is the main point of the paragraph?**
- **Why should readers accept this main point?** (That is, what reasons or information have you provided that would convince a reader that your main point is accurate or reasonable?)
- **Why should readers care about the main point of this paragraph?**

When writing the first draft of a paper, you may not stop to think about how you are developing the central idea of every paragraph. There is no need in first-draft writing to be this deliberate. By the second draft, however, you will want to be conscious of developing your paragraphs. The most common technique is **topical development,** that is, announcing your topic in the opening sentence; dividing that topic into two or three parts (in the case of chronological arrangement, into various *times*); and then developing each part within the paragraph.

The various strategies available to you for developing paragraphs have been discussed and illustrated in chapter 3, on creating common ground, and in chapter 7, on writing essays of explanation. This summary/index will refer you to the pertinent discussions:

Focusing the Paper through Unity

A paper is unified when the writer discusses only those elements of the subject implied by its thesis. **Unity** is a principle of logic that applies equally to the whole paper, to sections, and to individual paragraphs. In a unified paper, you discuss only those topics that can be anticipated by someone who reads your thesis. Following is an example of a revised thesis by student Josefa Pinto (whose essay appears in chapter 7). This thesis is followed by the sections of the paper that she generated by quizzing her thesis:

Thesis

Although genetic engineering has been considered the biotechnological breakthrough of the century, there are still many doubts concerning its potential effects on our environment.

Sections Implied by Thesis

Definition of genetic engineering
History, this century
Benefits of genetic engineering
Dangers of genetic engineering
Controversy over genetic engineering

A paper is *not* unified if the writer introduces any topic that strays from the thesis—that is, that strays from the list of topics generated by quizzing the thesis.

A unified section of a paper is a discussion of those topics implied by your section thesis (see page 493). Every topic generated by quizzing the thesis will become a *section* of your final paper. You will devote at least one paragraph to developing each section or subtopic, of the thesis. In a unified paragraph, you discuss only one topic, the one implied by your topic sentence.

Revising to Achieve Paragraph Unity

A unified paragraph will focus on, will develop, and will not stray from a paragraph's central, controlling idea or **topic sentence.** Recall that a *thesis* announces and controls the content of an entire essay, and that a *section thesis* announces and controls the content of a section. Just so, a *topic sentence* announces and controls the content of sentences in a single paragraph. Think of the topic sentence as a paragraph-level *thesis,* and you will see the principle of unity at work at *all* levels of the paper. At each level of the essay, a general statement is used to guide you in assembling specific, supporting parts.

Essay-Level Unity: The thesis (the most general statement in the essay) governs your choice of sections in a paper.

Section-Level Unity: Section theses (the second-most general statements in the essay) govern your choice of paragraphs in a section.

Paragraph-Level Unity: Topic sentences (the third-most general statements in the essay) govern your choice of sentences in a paragraph.

Within a paragraph, a topic sentence can appear anywhere, provided that you recognize it and can lead up to and away from it with some method in mind. Placement options for a paragraph's topic sentence are discussed below.

Placing the Topic Sentence at the Beginning of a Paragraph

Very often, a topic sentence is placed first in a paragraph. You will want to open your paragraphs this way when your purpose is to inform or persuade a reader and you wish to be as direct as possible, as in the following example:

> Factory farm animals need liberation in the most literal sense. Veal calves are kept in stalls five feet by two feet. They are usually slaughtered when about four months old, and have been too big to turn in their stalls for at least a month. Intensive beef herds, kept in stalls only proportionately larger for much longer periods, account for a growing percentage of beef production. Sows are often similarly confined when pregnant, which, because of artificial methods of increasing fertility, can be most of the time. Animals confined in this way do not waste food by exercising, nor do they develop unpalatable muscle.
>
> —PETER SINGER, "Animal Liberation"

Peter Singer begins the paragraph with a direct statement: *Factory farm animals need liberation in the most literal sense.* Every subsequent sentence focuses on and develops this topic sentence.

Placing the Topic Sentence in the Middle of a Paragraph

When you want to present material on two sides of an issue in your paragraph, consider placing the topic sentence in the middle of the paragraph. Lead up to the topic sentence with supporting material concerning its first part; lead away from the topic sentence with material concerning its second part, as in the following example by student Josefa Pinto:

> Those in favor of genetic engineering argue that the exchange of genes taking place during laboratory experiments is merely an imitation of what is done in nature all the time. In other words, genetic engineering is a natural process that is being reproduced by humans. Scientists are confident that strict regulation and principles of agreement between private companies and government agencies will ensure the safety and efficiency of any genetically engineered organism (Hanson 24). Further-

more, American molecular biologists fear that additional road blocks to their research will cause them to fall behind European competitors—and that the United States will lose its lead in yet another area of technology. The dilemmas over genetic engineering are, at their root, based on a struggle between the advancement of knowledge and competition on the one hand and the need for safety on the other. Ecologists who oppose the uses of genetically engineered organisms in the open environment argue that the genetic engineer, today, is a 20th-century sorcerer's-apprentice playing with a technology that is not fully understood (Pimentel 14). Others question the consequences of "playing God." They feel that humans do not know enough about life to manipulate its forms. Nor are they sure who would assume responsibility for any disruption or irreparable damage done to our environment.

Pinto's topic sentence is the pivot on which this paragraph turns: *The dilemmas over genetic engineering are, at their root, based on a struggle between the advancement of knowledge and competition on the one hand and the need for safety on the other.*

Placing the Topic Sentence at the End of a Paragraph

When writing an informative or argumentative paper, you may in specific paragraphs want to postpone the topic sentence until the end. You would do this to ensure that readers would consider all the sentences in a paragraph before coming to your main point. The strategy works especially well when you are arguing, as in the following example:

> The place of history in the world of learning and its relation to the various other fields of study can be argued without end. History is sometimes classed with the humanities, along with literature, the arts, and philosophy, as an aspect of the human achievement over the centuries. However, it differs from all of these subjects in being based on fact rather than on imagination and feeling. More often history is included among the social sciences, together with economics, political science, sociology, anthropology, and some branches of geography and psychology. One may question whether any of these fields deserves to be called a "science" in the sense we associate with the natural or exact sciences, but history is particularly resistant to a strictly scientific approach. It tries to explain by particular description rather than by general analysis and laws; its aim is to depict the significant historical individual or situation in all its living detail. History is defined by its focus on time, but it also has the characteristic of embracing all aspects of human activity as they occurred in the past. History, accordingly, is able to serve as the discipline that integrates the specialized work of the other fields of social science. (32)

> —ROBERT V. DANIELS, *Studying History: How and Why*

If you place the last sentence of this paragraph first, you see that subsequent sentences support and develop the idea that *History . . . is able to serve as the discipline that integrates the specialized work of the other fields of social science.* This statement is debatable, which Daniels acknowledges at the beginning of the paragraph. By delaying his topic sentence, Daniels ensures that his audience will have read his survey of the debate, which is important to accepting Daniels's point.

Omitting the Topic Sentence from a Paragraph

In narrative and descriptive papers, and much less frequently in informative and persuasive papers, writers will occasionally omit the topic sentence from a paragraph. In a narrative paragraph in which you are telling a story, including the topic sentence may be too heavy handed and may ruin an otherwise subtle effect. Descriptive writing may be so obvious that including a topic sentence seems redundant. When you decide to omit a topic sentence from a paragraph, take care to write the paragraph as though a topic sentence were present. With respect to unity, this means that you should focus each sentence on the implied topic and should not include any sentence that strays from that implied topic.

The following is an example of an informative paragraph with an implied, rather than a directly stated, topic sentence:

> Etiquette books used to teach that if a woman had *Mrs.* in front of her name then the husband's name should follow because *Mrs.* is an abbreviated form of *Mistress* and a woman couldn't be a mistress of herself. As with many arguments about "correct" language usage, this isn't very logical because *Miss* is also an abbreviation of *Mistress.* Feminists hoped to simplify matters by introducing *Ms.* as an alternative to both *Mrs.* and *Miss,* but what happened is that *Ms.* largely replaced *Miss* to became a catch-all business title for women. Many married women still prefer the title *Mrs.,* and some resent being addressed with the term *Ms.* As one frustrated newspaper reporter complained, "Before I can write about a woman, I have to know not only her marital status but also her political philosophy." The result of such complications may contribute to the demise of titles which are already being ignored by many computer programmers who find it more efficient to simply use names; for example in a business letter: "Dear Joan Garcia," instead of "Dear Mrs. Joan Garcia," "Dear Ms. Garcia," or "Dear Mrs. Louis Garcia."
>
> —ALLEEN PACE NILSEN, "Sexism in English: A 1990s Update"

The sentence that comes closest to being a topic sentence is the paragraph's long final sentence. But the opening of this sentence, "The result of such complications," assumes another sentence, not written: *There has been a great deal of confusion about the politically correct title of address for women.* Placed at the head of Nilsen's paragraph, this would function adequately as a topic sentence. The paragraph's final sentence is actually built on the validity of this implied topic sentence. Nilsen's choice of every sentence is governed by the implied topic sentence just as if that sentence had actually been included in the paragraph.

Exercise 1

Reread several paragraphs you have recently written for one of your classes. Choose one paragraph to revise for unity: add, delete, or modify sentences as needed.

Exercise 2

Locate the topic sentence in paragraphs 6, 7, 8, and 10 of Josefa Pinto's paper on genetic engineering (pages 176–179). Analyze each paragraph and be prepared to discuss how every sentence contributes to the paragraph's unity.

Focusing the Paper through Coherence

Coherence describes the clarity of the relationship between one unit of meaning and another: between sections of a paper; between paragraphs within sections; and between sentences within paragraphs. Like unity, coherence is a principle of logic that applies equally to the whole paper, to sections, and to individual paragraphs. A whole paper is coherent when its sections (groupings of related paragraphs) follow one another in a sensible order. A section of the paper is coherent when the individual paragraphs that constitute it follow one another in a sensible order. And a paragraph is coherent when individual sentences that comprise it follow one another in a sensible order. At every level of a paper, you establish coherence by building logical bridges, or transitions, between thoughts. A transition may be a word, a sentence, or a paragraph devoted to building a smooth, logical relationship. In all cases, a transition has a double function: to remind readers of what they have just read and then to forecast for them what they are about to read. Transitional expressions include *additionally, likewise, first, second* (and so on), *afterward, for example, of course, accordingly, however, in conclusion,* and *on the whole.*

Transitions serve to highlight relationships that already exist between sections, paragraphs, or sentences that you have placed in a particular order. If you have trouble finding a word or sentence to serve as an effective transition, reexamine the sentences, paragraphs, or sections that you are trying to link. You may not have arranged them coherently in the first place, and may need to rearrange them.

As you revise your paper, pause to analyze its sections *in relation* to each other. Rearrange sections, if need be, in order to improve the logical flow of ideas among the largest units of meaning, the paper's sections. Here is an illustration of a process for coherent arrangement for student Jim Walker's paper on school violence:

Thesis

What seems like a random explosion of violence is actually the result of many factors that create a cycle of violence and aggressive acts that can spiral out of control. Students can get hurt. Students can also help break the cycle.

Sections Implied by Thesis

Explanation of the cycle of violence in schools
Examples of aggressive acts and who commits them in a school setting
Ways students can be hurt
Ways students can break the cycle of violence in schools

Coherent Arrangements

Usually, any of several arrangements of sections will lead to a coherent paper. Choose your arrangement based on your thesis, the evidence you have compiled, and the needs of your audience. Here are alternate arrangements of the sections implied by Jim Walker's thesis:

A. Explanation of the cycle of violence

B. Examples of aggressive acts

C. Ways students can break the cycle

D. Ways students can be hurt (if they don't break the cycle)

A. Examples of aggressive acts

B. Explanation of the cycle of violence

C. Ways students can be hurt (if they don't break the cycle)

D. Ways students can break the cycle

Revising to Achieve Paragraph Coherence

Your job in ensuring the overall coherence of a paragraph is to make clear the logic by which you position sentences in the paragraph. When your paragraphs are coherent, readers will understand the logic by which you move from one sentence to the next, toward or away from your topic sentence. When writing the first draft of a paper, you may not have a plan to ensure paragraph coherence; you may not even have a clear idea of every paragraph's main point. Revision is the time when you sort these matters out, when you can make certain that each paragraph has a clear purpose and a clear, coherent plan for achieving that purpose.

Arranging Sentences to Achieve Coherence

There are standard patterns available to you for arranging paragraphs. The most common are arrangements by space, by time, and by importance. If it occurs to you as you are writing a first draft that one of these patterns lends itself to the particular point you are discussing, then by all means write your paragraph with the pattern in mind. It is not necessary, though, that you map out patterns of coherence ahead of time.

Arrangement by Space

You can help readers visualize what you are describing by arranging a paragraph spatially. Start the reader at a well-defined position with respect to the object being described, and then move him or her from that position to subsequent ones by taking systematic steps, one at a time, until your description is complete. In planning the paragraph, you might divide the object into the parts that you will describe; next, devise a definite plan for arranging these parts. Your description could proceed from front to back, right to left, top to bottom, outside to inside, and so on: the choice is yours. Once you choose a plan for organizing details, stick to the plan and you will help your readers to visualize your topic, as in this paragraph on the Brooklyn Bridge.

> Brooklyn Bridge belongs first to the eye. Viewed from Brooklyn Heights, it seems to frame the irregular lines of Manhattan. But across the river perspective changes: through the narrow streets of lower Manhattan and Chinatown, on Water Street or South Street, the structure looms above drab buildings. Fragments of tower or cable compel the eye. The view changes once again as one mounts the wooden walk of the bridge itself. It is a relief, an open space after dim, crowded streets.
>
> —ALAN TRACHTENBERG, *Brooklyn Bridge: Fact and Symbol*

This description of the bridge is arranged by the various perspectives from which it is viewed: from Brooklyn Heights, the bridge has one appearance; viewed from lower Manhattan, the structure "looms above drab buildings"; viewed from the wooden walkway of the bridge, the view provides a "relief."

Arrangement by Time

You can arrange a paragraph according to a sequence of events. Start the paragraph with a particular event, and move forward or backward in time in some definite order. Give your readers signals in each sentence that emphasize the forward or backward movement. In this example paragraph on the history of genetic engineering, Josefa Pinto moves the reader forward in time with a series of phrases and single words, which are circled.

> The movement of creating genetically engineered organisms began in the (early 1900s) based on the experiments and ideas of the Austrian monk Gregory Mendel. (During the 1800s,) through his cross-breeding experiments, Mendel laid the foundation for future experiments in genetic engineering. (By the 1970s,) American geneticists began developing techniques for isolating and altering genes. They discovered that a soil bacterium known as *Agrobacterium* was nature's own genetic engineer and could exchange pieces of DNA (the raw material of genes) with startling frequency (Carey 18). (On June 30, 1981,) biologists Jack Kemp of the Department of Agriculture and Timothy Hall of the University of Wisconsin first harvested the bacterium's power. The first experiment consisted of using a microbe or microorganism to slip a bean plant gene into a sunflower plant. (Later, in 1982,) bacterially produced insulin became the first recombinant DNA drug approved by the Food and Drug Administration for use by people. (By 1987 and 1988,) genes were being transferred into higher organisms such as plants and animals

(Scherfeas 87). (Presently,) genetic engineers have produced most of the economically important varieties of plants and animals, such as flowers, vegetables, grains, cows, horses, and dogs.

Arrangement by Importance

Just as you discuss different parts of a thesis at different locations in a paper, you will discuss different parts of a topic sentence at different locations in a paragraph. When revising, be aware of a paragraph's component parts so that you can arrange these parts in the most logical, accessible order. Arrangement is largely determined by your positioning of the topic sentence. How will your sentences lead up to and away from the topic sentence? You should be aware of two general patterns: general to specific and specific to general.

General to specific: When the topic sentence begins the paragraph   By far the most common method for arranging sentences in a paragraph is to begin with your topic sentence and follow with specific, supporting details. When beginning a paragraph this way, decide how to order the information that will follow. You might ask: What does this paragraph's topic sentence obligate me to discuss? What are the *parts* of this paragraph and in what order will I discuss them? Arthur C. Clarke discusses three parts of his topic, the portable electronic library—the library's top half, its bottom half, and its overall size—in the following paragraph.

> The great development in your near future is the portable electronic library—a library not only of books, but of films and music. It will be about the size of an average book and will probably open in the same way. One half will be the screen with high-definition, full-color display. The other will be a keyboard, much like one of today's computer consoles, with the full alphabet, digits, basic mathematical functions, and a large number of special keys—perhaps 100 keys in all. It won't be as small as some of today's midget calculators, which have to be operated with toothpicks.
>
> —ARTHUR C. CLARKE, "Electronic Tutors"

Specific to general: When the topic sentence ends the paragraph   When you are writing a description or narration and when you are arguing a point, you may want to delay your topic sentence until the final sentence of a paragraph. Here you reverse the standard arrangement of a paragraph and move from specific details to a general, concluding statement. The goal is to build one sentence on the next so securely that the final sentence strikes the reader as inevitable.

> We drink it, use it to wash, and use it to grow farm products and manufacture goods. We almost take for granted that rain will replenish whatever amount of water we may use up. Water, however, is no longer the infinitely renewable resource that we once thought it was. Consider the giant Ogallala aquifer, which stretches nearly 800 miles under eight states from the Texas panhandle to South Dakota. The aquifer provides

about 30 percent of the total irrigation needs in the United States and serves as the water source for 200,000 wells in 180 counties and for 40 percent of the nation's beef cattle. Water is being drawn from the Ogallala aquifer eight times faster than nature can replenish the supply, creating huge sinkholes in the Texas panhandle. Economists believe that part of the problem is that water has traditionally been underpriced. The law of demand indicates that a higher price of water will reduce the quantity of water used. One solution for the rapidly decreasing water resources, therefore, would be to make it more expensive for consumers to use the water.

—SEMOON CHANG, *Modern Economics*

In this paragraph, Chang makes an argument by moving from specific facts to a general conclusion, or topic sentence. Chang begins with facts concerning water use about which no one could disagree. His second sentence builds on the first by generalizing about attitudes concerning water use: we "almost take for granted" that water is an infinitely renewable resource. The third sentence builds on the second by making another, though debatable, statement of fact that (1) sets up a contrast with the second sentence and (2) is itself supported by several subsequent sentences about the Ogallala aquifer. Chang builds sentence on sentence, leading us to the paragraph's climax in which he applies economic theory to the problem of "decreasing water resources." The solution to this problem is the paragraph's final, topic sentence.

Achieving Coherence with Cues

When sentences are arranged with care, you need only to highlight this arrangement to ensure that readers will move easily through a paragraph. To highlight paragraph coherence, use **cues:** words and phrases that remind readers as they move from sentence to sentence (1) that they continue to read about the same topic and (2) that ideas are unfolding logically. Four types of cues help to highlight sentence-to-sentence connections: pronouns, repetition, parallel structures, and transitions (which will be discussed in the next section). Accomplished writers usually combine techniques in order to highlight paragraph coherence, often not adding cues to a paragraph until the revision stage, when they are better able to discern a paragraph's shape.

Pronouns

The most direct way to remind readers that they continue to examine a certain topic as they move from sentence to sentence is to repeat the most important noun, or the subject, of your topic sentence. To prevent repetition from becoming tiresome, use a pronoun to take the place of this important noun. Every time a pronoun is used, the reader is *cued*, or reminded, about the paragraph's main topic. In the following example, *he* and *his* take the place of the name *Herbert Hoover*. These pronouns are repeated nine times, tying the paragraph together without dulling the reader with repetition.

Herbert Hoover was a perfect symbol of the ideals and hopes of the American business community in the 1920s. He showed that to succeed in the United States and to be elected President you did not have to come from a rich, upper-class family. His life proved that in America character, intelligence, and hard work could make a national leader. Born of Quaker parents on a small farm in Iowa in 1874, he had been orphaned at the age of ten. He worked his way through Stanford University, where he studied engineering. Then he made his fortune as a mining engineer—in Australia, Africa, China, Latin America, and Russia. He was a millionaire by the time he was 40.

—DANIEL BOORSTIN AND BROOKS MATHER KELLEY, *A History of the United States*

Repetition

While unintentional repetition can make sentences awkward, planned repetition can contribute significantly to a paragraph's coherence. The strategy is to repeat identically or to use a substitute phrase to repeat an important word or words in a paragraph. As with pronoun use, repetition cues readers, reminding them of the paragraph's important information. In the next example, concerning the word *meter*, combinations of the following four words are repeated fourteen times: *meter, define/definition, bar, standard.* Skillful use of repetition ties sentences together without boring the reader. Repetition helps to make this paragraph coherent.

The fundamental unit of length in the metric system is the meter. Originally, the meter was defined to be 10^{-7} of the distance from the North Pole to the equator. Later, a platinum-iridium bar was constructed whose length was as close as possible to the original definition. This bar, which became known as the standard meter, is kept at the Bureau of Weights and Measures near Paris. A similar bar was installed at the U.S. Bureau of Standards in Washington, D.C. All rulers, meter sticks, and other length-measuring devices were in the past calibrated by comparison with the standard meter bar. An even more precise standard is currently being used. The meter is now defined to be a length equal to the distance light travels in a vacuum in 1/299,792,458 of a second. The number of digits in this figure shows the great precision with which such measurements can be made.

—PAUL S. COHEN AND MILTON A. ROTHMAN, *Basic Chemistry*

Parallelism

Parallelism involves the use of grammatically equivalent words, phrases, and sentences to achieve coherence and balance in your writing. A sentence whose structure parallels that of an earlier sentence has an echo-like effect, linking the content of the second sentence to the content of the first. As with pronoun use and skillful repetition, parallel structures cue readers by highlighting the paragraph's important information.

Not only have geneticists found beneficial uses of genetically engineered organisms in agriculture, but they have also found useful ways to use these organisms advantageously in the larger environment. According to the Monsanto company, a leader in genetic engineering research, recombinant DNA techniques may provide us with new ways to clean up our environment and with more efficient methods of producing chemicals (Monsanto 24). By using genetically engineered organisms, scientists have been able to produce natural gas. This process will decrease our dependence on the environment and will reduce the rate at which we deplete natural resources. In other processes, genetically engineered bacteria are being used both to extract metals from their geological setting and to speed the breakup of complex petroleum mixtures, which will help to clean oil spills. In addition, firms such as Flow Laboratories are selling genetically engineered microbes to be used in sewage systems for facilitating breakdown and detoxification (Office of Technology Assessment 124).

Josefa Pinto uses parallelism *within* sentences, for the most part.

> Not only have geneticists found . . . but they have also found
> may provide us with new ways . . . and with more efficient methods
> This process will decrease . . . and will reduce
> bacteria are being used both to extract . . . and to speed
> for facilitating breakdown and detoxification

In one case, Josefa uses parallel structures in adjacent sentences.

> This process . . .
> In other processes . . .

Highlighting Coherence with Transitions

Transitions are words that establish logical relationships between sentences, between paragraphs, and between whole sections of an essay. A transition can take the form of a single word, a phrase, a sentence, or an entire paragraph. In each case it functions the same way: first, it either directly summarizes the content of a preceding sentence (or paragraph) or it implies that summary. Having established a summary, transitions then move forward into a new sentence (or paragraph), helping the reader anticipate what is to come. For example, when you read the word *however,* you are immediately aware that the material you are about to read will contrast with the material you have just read. In so brief a transition, the summary of the preceding material is implied—but present. As the reader, *you* do the summarizing.

Transitions *within* Paragraphs

Transitions act as cues by helping readers to anticipate what is coming *before* they read it. Within a paragraph, transitions tend to be single words, as in this example:

> The survival of the robin, (and indeed) of many other species (as well,) seems fatefully linked with the American elm, a tree that is part of the history of thousands of towns from the Atlantic to the Rockies, gracing their streets and their village squares (and) college campuses with majestic archways of green. (Now) the elms are stricken with a disease that afflicts them throughout their range, a disease so serious that many experts believe all efforts to save the elms will in the end be futile. It would be tragic to lose the elms, (but) it would be doubly tragic if, in vain efforts to save them, we plunge vast segments of our bird populations into the night of extinction. (Yet) this is precisely what is threatened.
>
> —RACHEL CARSON, *Silent Spring*

Transitions *between* Paragraphs

Transitions placed between paragraphs help readers move through sections of your paper. If you have done a good job of arranging paragraphs so that the content of one leads logically to the next, then by using a transitional expression you are highlighting a relationship that already exists. By summarizing the previous paragraph and telegraphing something of the content of the paragraph that follows, a transition helps to move the reader through your paper. A transition between paragraphs can be a word or two—*however, for example, similarly*—a phrase, or a sentence. The following is a sentence-length transition used to join two sections of a chapter in a textbook.

> *Just as through* formal religion and civic life the Sumerians at the dawn of recorded history created a new kind of human experience, *so through* writing and figurative art they found a new way to represent that experience. Writing had been invented by the simplifying of pictures into signs, . . .
>
> —*Gardner's Art Through the Ages,* 5th ed.

The first half of this paragraph's lead sentence explicitly summarizes the preceding section of a chapter. The second half of the sentence is the paragraph's topic sentence and points the reader forward to a new discussion on writing and figurative art. If the relationship between sections of a paper is complex, you may want to take some time and write a paragraph-length transition, as in this example.

> So Grant and Lee were in complete contrast, representing two diametrically opposed elements in American life. Grant was the modern man emerging; beyond him, ready to come on the stage, was the great age of steel and machinery, of crowded cities and a restless burgeoning vitality. Lee might have ridden down from the old age of chivalry, lance in hand, silken banner fluttering over his head. Each man was the perfect champion of his cause, drawing both his strengths and his weaknesses from the people he led.
>
> Yet it was not all contrast, after all. Different as they were—in background, in personality, in underlying aspiration—these two great soldiers had much in common. Under everything else, they were marvelous fighters. Furthermore, their fighting qualities were really very much alike.
>
> Each man had, to begin with, the great virtue of utter tenacity and fidelity. Grant fought his way down the Mississippi Valley in spite of acute personal discouragement and profound military handicaps. Lee hung on in the trenches at Petersburg after hope itself had died. In each man there was an indomitable quality . . . the born fighter's refusal to give up as long as he can still remain on his feet and lift his two fists.
>
> —BRUCE CATTON, "Grant and Lee: A Study in Contrasts"

Whatever its length, a transition will establish a clear relationship between sentences, parts of sentences, paragraphs, or entire sections of an essay. Transitions serve to highlight relationships already present by virtue of a writer's having positioned sentences or paragraphs next to one another. Whenever you have trouble finding a word or sentence to serve as an effective transition, reexamine the sentences or paragraphs you are trying to link: it may well be that they are not arranged coherently, and thus are in need of revision. The following list presents the most common transitions, arranged by type of relationship:

To show addition	additionally, again, also, and, as well, besides, equally important, further, furthermore, in addition, moreover, then
To show similarity	also, in the same way, just as . . . so too, likewise, similarly
To show an exception	but, however, in spite of, on the one hand . . . on the other hand, nevertheless, nonetheless, notwithstanding, in contrast, on the contrary, still, yet
To indicate sequence	first, second, third, . . . next, then, finally
To provide an example	for example, for instance, namely, specifically, to illustrate

To show time	after, afterwards, at last, before, currently, during, earlier, immediately, later, meanwhile, now, recently, simultaneously, subsequently, then
To emphasize a point	even, indeed, in fact, of course, truly
To indicate place	above, adjacent, below, beyond, here, in back, in front, nearby, there
To show cause and effect	accordingly, consequently, hence, so, therefore, thus
To conclude or repeat	finally, in a word, in brief, in conclusion, in the end, on the whole, thus, to conclude, to summarize

Combining Techniques to Achieve Coherence

Experienced writers will often combine the four techniques just discussed to establish coherence within a paragraph. A skillful mix of pronouns, repeated words and phrases, parallel structures, and transitions will help to maintain the focus of a paragraph and to provide multiple cues, or signposts, that help readers find their way from one sentence to the next. The following paragraph on the settling of the Kansas frontier in the mid-nineteenth century illustrates the use of all four techniques for establishing paragraph coherence.

Beautiful and bountiful, the land was the great lure of Kansas. Some settlers sought freedom, some yearned for prosperity, some craved adventure, but in the end it was the promise of the land that drew them halfway across a continent. Here they could build their own homes, cultivate their own fields and develop their own communities. Undoubtedly, it took a special kind of fortitude to adjust to this harsh terrain. Yet with hard work, imagination and tenacity, the future was theirs to mold. In this new land, God's own country, they reached to the stars through the wilderness.

—JOANNA STRATTON, *Pioneer Women*

In this paragraph, the word *land* is repeated in six ways. As well, the term for the main actors of the paragraph—the *settlers*—is repeated with six pronouns. In three different sentences, Joanna Stratton makes effective use of parallel structures. Stratton also makes use of transitional expressions: *but, here, undoubtedly,* and *yet.*

Exercise 3

Choose any four example paragraphs in this chapter. For each paragraph, identify the techniques that the author uses to establish coherence. Show the use of pronouns, repetition, parallel structures, and transitions. In addition, identify the use of transitions between paragraphs.

Exercise 4

Reread a paragraph you have recently written, and circle all words that help to establish coherence. If few words suggest themselves to you for circling, this may be a sign that your paragraph lacks coherence. Photocopy your paragraph and then revise it for coherence, using the techniques discussed previously: arrange sentences according to a pattern and then highlight that arrangement with pronouns, repeated words, parallel structures, and transitions. When you are done revising, write a clean copy of the paragraph and make photocopies of both the original and the revision for classmates to use in a small-group discussion. Prepare a brief presentation in which you discuss the changes you have made.

Paragraphs of Introduction and Conclusion

The introduction and conclusion to a paper can be understood as a type of transition. Transitions provide logical bridges in a paper: they help readers to move from one sentence to another, one paragraph to another, and one section to another. At the beginning of a paper, the introduction serves as a transition by moving the reader from the world outside of your paper to the world within. At the end of the paper, the conclusion works in the opposite direction by moving readers from the world of your paper back to their own world—with, you hope, something useful gained by their effort.

Introductions

Writing an introduction is often easier once you know what you are introducing; for this reason many writers choose not to work seriously on an introduction until they have finished a draft and can see the overall shape and content of a paper. Other writers need to begin with a carefully written introduction. If this is your preference, remember not to demand perfection of a first draft, especially since the material you will be introducing has yet to be written. Once it is written, your introduction may well need to change.

Strategies for Writing Introductions

1. Announce your topic, using vocabulary that hints at the perspective from which you will be writing. On completing your introduction, readers should be able to anticipate the type of language, evidence, and logic you will use in your paper.

2. If readers lack the background needed to understand your paper, provide this background. In a paragraph or two, choose and develop a strategy that will both orient readers to your subject and interest them in it:

> define terms
> present a brief history
> review a controversy

3. If readers know something of your subject, then devote less (or no) time to developing background information and more time to stimulating interest. In a paragraph or two, choose and develop a strategy that will gain the reader's attention:

> raise a question
> quote a source familiar to the reader
> tell a story
> begin directly with a statement of the thesis

4. Once you have provided background information and gained the reader's attention with an opening strategy, gradually turn that attention toward your thesis, which you will position as the last sentence of the introductory paragraph(s).

The Introduction as a Frame of Reference

Introductions establish frames of reference. On completing an introduction, readers know the general topic of your paper; they know the disciplinary perspective from which you will discuss this topic; and they know the standards they will use in evaluating your work. Readers quickly learn from an introduction if you are a laboratory researcher, a field researcher, a theorist, an essayist, a reporter, a student with a general interest, and so on. Each of these possible identities implies for readers different standards of evidence and reasoning by which they will evaluate your work. Consider the paragraph that follows, which introduces a paper that you will find in chapter 10. The introduction, explicitly in the thesis and implicitly in the writer's choice of vocabulary, establishes a frame of reference that alerts readers to the type of language, evidence, and logic that will be used in the subsequent paper. Thus situated, readers are better able to anticipate and evaluate what they will read.

Language of literary analysis (circled)

Evidence: based on close reading of a story

Logic: generalization

Drinking and church going related to a need for power

Also comparison/contrast

(James Joyce's) "Counterparts" (tells the story) of a man, Farrington, who is abused by his boss for not doing his job right. Farrington spends a long time drinking after work; and when he finally arrives home, he in turn abuses—he beats—his son Tom. In eleven pages, Joyce tells much more than a story of yet another alcoholic (venting failures and frustrations) on family members. *In "Counterparts," Farrington turns to drink in order to gain power—in much the same way his wife and children turn to the Church.*

By comparison, read the following introduction to a paper written from a sociological perspective:

Language of sociology
(circled)

Evidence: based on
review of sociological
literature

Logic: cause and effect.
Will show how denial
complicates diagnosis
and treatment.

Currently in the United States there are at least two million women alcoholics (Unterberger, 1989, p. 1150). Americans are largely unaware of the extent of this debilitating disease among women and the problems it presents. Numerous women dependent on alcohol remain invisible largely because friends, family, coworkers and the women themselves refuse to acknowledge the problem. *This denial amounts to a virtual conspiracy of silence and greatly complicates the process of diagnosis and treatment.*

The Introduction as an Invitation to Continue Reading

Aside from establishing a frame of reference and set of expectations about language, evidence, and logic, an introduction should also establish in your reader a desire to *continue* reading. A complete introduction provides background information needed to understand a paper. An especially effective introduction gains the reader's attention and gradually turns that attention toward the writer's thesis and the rest of the paper. Writers typically adopt specialized strategies for introducing their work. In the discussion that follows you will learn several of these strategies, all of which can be developed in one or two paragraphs, at the end of which you will place your thesis. These examples by no means exhaust the possible strategies available to you for opening your papers. Here is a student example by Daniel Burke on "Defense of Fraternities":

> A revolutionary event took place at Raleigh Tavern in 1776, an event that has added an important dimension to my life at college. In fact, nearly all American undergraduates are affected in some way by the actions of several students from the College of William and Mary on December 5, 1776. The formation of the first Greek-letter fraternity, Phi Beta Kappa, started the American college fraternity-sorority tradition that today can be an important addition to your undergraduate education.

In this example, student writer Daniel Burke provides pertinent historical information that sets a context for the paper. By linking a "revolutionary event" in 1776 to his own life over two hundred years later, Burke captures the reader's interest.

The following example begins with a question, the response to which leads to the author's thesis. (The reference to "Valenti" is to Jack Valenti, head of the Motion Picture Production Association when Stephen Farber wrote his book.)

> How are [movie] ratings actually determined? Official brochures on the rating system provide only very brief general definitions of the four categories, and I do not believe the categories can or should be defined much more specifically. It is impossible to set hard-and-fast rules; every film is different from every other film, and no precise definition could possibly cover all films made. Valenti has frequently toyed with the idea of more detailed definitions, though any rigid demarcations between the categories inevitably seem hopelessly arbitrary.
>
> —STEPHEN FARBER, *The Movie Rating Game*

Conclusions

One important job in writing a paper is to explain to readers what you have accomplished and why your ideas are significant. Minimally, a conclusion will summarize your work, but often you will want to do more than write a summary. Provided you have written carefully and believe in what you have written, you have earned the right to expand on your paper's thesis in a conclusion: to point the reader back to the larger world and to suggest the significance of your ideas in that world. This is exactly what student Josefa Pinto does in the conclusion of her paper.

> Having weighed the pros and cons of the debate, I feel that nature is too precious to be gambled with. We may be tempted to use the opportunities presented by the revolution in genetic engineering, but we should always exercise caution. As Albert Einstein once advised, "Concern for man himself and his fate must always form the chief interest of all technical endeavors, in order that the creations of our minds, and I would add, our laboratories, shall be a blessing and not a curse" (qtd. in Wickelgren 124). I hope that man's search for perfection will not blind him to the consequences and dangers that the search may bring.

A conclusion gives you an opportunity to answer a challenge that all readers raise—*So what? Why does this paper matter to me?* A well-written conclusion will answer these questions and will leave readers with a trace of your thinking as they turn away from your paper and back to their own business.

The example conclusions that follow do not exhaust the strategies for closing your papers; these examples should, however, give you a taste for the variety of techniques available. Here is a paragraph that presents the simplest possible conclusion: a summary.

> One can see by the number of steps involved in the legislative process that the odds are very great against an average bill becoming law. At almost every turn a bill may be killed. Hundreds of bills may start out, but only a few survive to become law.
>
> —Kevin Costello, "Long Odds: How a Bill Becomes Law"

A more ambitious conclusion will move beyond a summary and call for involvement on the reader's part. For instance, you might ask the reader to address a puzzling or troubling question, to speculate on the future, or to reflect on the past. In this next example, the reader is asked to help resolve a problem plaguing college sports. This concludes a student paper by Jenafer Trahar, "Athletes and Education," which you will find in chapter 9.

> We don't need to eliminate college sports. We probably couldn't anyway, what with all the money being made. Eliminating sports would do more harm than good, taking away both a source of pride in college life and an important source of revenue. Changing the admissions process to deny marginally prepared student-athletes would not be fair, since for many of these kids sports is their only avenue of exposure to college life and the possibility of a higher education. To eliminate the chance to

attend college for marginal student-athletes would be heartless, because it places on them a burden they did not make, a burden that should and can be lifted with the proper approach. That's why a plan that modifies the present system, not destroys it, makes the most sense. Let's take advantage of all the money that college sports generates and use that money to *really* educate the student-athlete. The proposals I have made not only would allow student-athletes to gain access to college but also would increase the chances of their actually receiving an education.

Two additional strategies for concluding a paper are discussed next: using a quotation and telling a story.

The Opening and Closing Frame

You might consider creating an introductory and concluding frame for your papers. The strategy is to use the same story, quotation, question—any device that comes to mind—as an occasion both to introduce your subject and, when the time is right, to conclude emphatically. Provided the body of a paper is unified, coherent, and well developed, an opening and closing frame will give the paper a pleasing symmetry. In the following example, Rachel L. Jones works with a quotation.

Introduction

William Labov, a noted linguist, once said about the use of black English, "It is the goal of most black Americans to acquire full control of the standard language without giving up their own culture." He also suggested that there are certain advantages to having two ways to express one's feelings. I wonder if the good doctor might also consider the goals of those black Americans who have full control of standard English but who are every now and then troubled by that colorful, grammar-to-the-winds patois that is black English. Case in point—me.

Conclusion

I would have to disagree with Labov in one respect. My goal is not so much to acquire full control of both standard and black English, but to one day see more black people less dependent on a dialect that excludes them from full participation in the world we live in. I don't think I talk white; I think I talk right.

—RACHEL L. JONES, "What's Wrong with Black English"

Exercise 5

Locate a collection of essays and or articles: any textbook that is an edited collection of readings will work. Read three articles and examine the strategies the authors use to introduce and conclude their work. Choose one article to analyze more closely. Examine the strategies for beginning and ending the selection and relate these strategies to the selection itself. Why has the writer chosen these *particular* strategies? Be prepared to discuss your findings in a small group.

Exercise 6

In connection with a paper you are writing, draft *two* opening and *two* closing paragraphs, using different strategies. Set your work aside for a day or two and then choose which paragraphs appeal to you the most. Be prepared to discuss your choices in a small group.

Determining Paragraph Length

Paragraphs vary greatly in length. As long as the governing idea of a paragraph remains clear, all sentences are unified, and the paragraph is coherent, then in theory a paragraph can be one sentence, five sentences, or twenty. This said, you should realize that readers will tire of a paper whose paragraphs are consistently one typewritten page or longer. If for no other reason than to give readers visual relief, keep paragraphs moderate in length. *Moderate* is a variable and personal term. Perhaps you decide that visually your paragraphs should average one-third to two-thirds of a typewritten page. If your sentences tend to be brief, then your average number of sentences per paragraph may be ten or twelve; if your sentences tend to be long, then the average of sentences per paragraph may drop to six.

Devote your energies to the content of your paragraphs first. Turn to paragraph length in the later stages of revision when you are relatively satisfied with your work. Then think of your reader and the way your paragraphs appear on the page. Visually, does the length of your paragraphs invite the reader into your paper? Consistently short paragraphs may send the signal that your ideas are not well developed. Consistently long paragraphs may give the impression that your writing is dense or that your ideas are not well differentiated. You should freely divide a long paragraph for reasons of length alone. A new paragraph created because of length does not need its own topic sentence, provided this paragraph is a clear continuation of the one preceding it.

Brief paragraphs of one, two, or three sentences can be useful for establishing transitions between sections of a paper and, as illustrated in this next example, for creating emphasis.

A coyote also eats avocados, oranges, melons, berries, chickens, small dogs, livestock and fowl with relish. The rare but rising number of attacks on small children indicates that once certain coyotes overcome their inherent fear of man, very young human specimens also look like food. And if his own offspring or mate is killed, he might well snack off the carcass. A meal's a meal.

To Brother Coyote, it's truly a dog-eat-dog world.

Coyotes, it was discovered, are so intelligent they can learn from their own mistakes and the mistakes of fellow coyotes. Remarkably, they also teach their young to avoid those mistakes.

—MICHELLE HUNEVEN, "The Urban Coyote"

If in revising a first draft you find that your paragraphs are consistently two or three sentences, consider ways in which you can further develop each paragraph's topic sentence. Unless you are writing in a journalism class or in some other context where consistently brief paragraphs are valued, once again the advice is to maintain a moderate length and only rarely—for clear reasons—use very brief or very long paragraphs.

Exercise 7

Reread your draft and examine paragraph length. Make adjustments as needed, based on the preceding discussion.

Final Revision

Editing

Editing is revision at the sentence level: the level at which you attend to style, grammar, punctuation, and word choice. Depending on their preferences, writers will edit (just as they revise) throughout the writing process, from the first draft through to the last. It would be misleading to state flatly that the process of sentence-level rewriting should wait until all issues of unity and coherence are resolved. Still, to the extent that you *can* hold off, save editing until the later drafts, once you are relatively confident that your paper has a final thesis and that the major sections of the paper are in order. In any event, don't allow sentence-level concerns to block your writing process early on—especially since the sentence you are fretting over may not even make it to the final draft.

Matters of precision are not so easily held off, however. Precise wording means precise thinking; and no doubt your ability to think clearly at any point in the draft will affect your subsequent writing. Use your judgment. If you find yourself struggling with the wording of an especially important sentence, take the time to edit and get it right. But if you are groping for a word in a sentence that is not central to your thinking, hold off your editing. Later in the writing process you will have time enough to settle questions of style, grammar, punctuation, usage, and spelling. By no means must you memorize rules concerning these matters as long as you can recognize problems and seek help in a handbook and a dictionary.

A Checklist for Writing Effective Sentences

The following checklist will assist you in writing effective sentences.

1. Have you been precise at every opportunity, stating your *exact* meaning?
2. Have you been concise, eliminating *all* words, phrases, and sentences that do not add directly to your meaning? Have you made sentences brief when possible?

3. Have you used parallel structures to add balance and emphasis to your writing?

4. Have you varied sentence openings in order to create rhythmically pleasing paragraphs?

5. Have you used vivid and concrete language to create immediacy in your writing?

6. Have you correctly subordinated and coordinated sentence parts?

7. Have you used strong verbs that keep your sentences lively and direct?

8. Have you used the passive voice sparingly, and for good reason?

9. Have you avoided sexist language or pronoun use?

10. Have you maintained a consistent tone, appropriate to the occasion for writing?

The final version of Jim Walker's paper went through many stages of sentence-level revision that led to a final draft. Following is an early version of a paragraph and the revisions that were necessary to bring it to final form. Each paragraph in Jim's paper underwent similar revisions:

Some people ~~think of schools as this separate place, detached from society, where students go to learn and teachers go to teach~~ *have all kinds of ideas about what schools ought to be.* What they don't ~~realize~~ is that a school is part of a neighborhood, part of a community, ~~eventually~~ part of a national culture. ~~School is more than just detached from the world.~~ School is where all these outside influences come together. ~~It is the flash point where people and ideas come together every day.~~ That is ~~the~~ exciting ~~thing~~ about education. Sometimes, this mixture is ~~volatile~~. The ~~tensions~~ of the larger society, the crime, the violence, the guns, etc. get acted out in the halls and classrooms of the schools. ~~Most~~ students do a good job coping with *that*—and do it at the same time ~~they~~ cope with all the personal stuff that happens as we stop being kids and start ~~trying~~ adult ~~attitudes~~. ~~Even though we know other kids who bring weapons to school we avoid them and stick with our own friends.~~ **We learn very quickly how to fit in and fit out. We learn how to survive in a multicultural school by avoiding confrontations.**

A Checklist for Avoiding Common Sentence and Grammar Errors

The following checklist will assist you in avoiding common errors.

1. Have you identified and corrected fragments?

2. Have you identified and corrected comma splices and fused sentences?

3. Have you corrected misplaced or dangling modifiers? Watch especially in sentences beginning with an *-ing* phrase that you follow with the noun being modified.
4. Have you avoided shifts in person, number, tense, and tone?
5. Have you avoided mixed constructions and incomplete sentences?
6. Have you checked tense endings? Have you used tenses consistently?
7. Have you maintained agreement between subjects and verbs and between pronouns and antecedents?
8. Have you used correct pronoun cases? Have you reviewed each use of a pronoun and clarified its reference?
9. Have you distinguished properly between adjectives and adverbs? Have you positioned them correctly?

Proofreading

Before you call a paper finished, check for minor errors that may annoy readers and embarrass you. Reread your paper to identify and correct misspelled words; words (often prepositions) omitted from sentences; words that have been doubled; punctuation that you tend to forget; and homonyms (writing *there* instead of *their*). If you have trouble spotting these minor errors in your writing, find a way to disrupt your usual pattern of reading so that the errors will become visible to you. One technique is to photocopy your work and have a friend read it aloud. You read along and make corrections. Another technique is to read each line of your paper in reverse order, from the last word on the line to the first. This approach forces you to focus on one word at a time. Besides checking for minor errors, review your occasion for writing one last time to make sure you have prepared your manuscript in an appropriate form.

A Checklist for Punctuation

The following checklist will assist you in checking your use of punctuation.

1. Have you used a period, a question mark, or (rarely) an exclamation point—but *not* a comma—to end sentences?
2. Have you placed a comma after introductory elements in your sentences?
3. Have you remembered to use a *second* comma to mark the end of a nonessential word, phrase, or clause appearing in the middle of a sentence?
4. Have you checked for consistent and correct use of the apostrophe and quotation marks?
5. Have you used a colon after a complete sentence?
6. Have you used semicolons to separate grammatically equal elements?
7. Have you used hyphens correctly?
8. Have you used elements of mechanics correctly: capitals, abbreviations, numbers, and italics?

Determining When a Final
Draft Is *Final*

At some point you must determine that your paper is finished. In the age of word processing, this is not always an easy decision since you can make that one last correction and have the computer print a new page with relative ease. If you work with a typewriter and not a computer, then the decision about your final draft is more clear cut. At some point you will refuse to retype another page if the change you are making does not seem worth the effort.

When changes seem not to improve the product, then you have reached an end to revision and editing. To consider a draft final, you should be satisfied that your paper has met these standards:

- The paper has a clearly stated main point to communicate.
- It has met all requirements of unity and coherence at the levels of the paper, section, and paragraph.
- It is punctuated correctly and is free of errors in grammar and usage.

Stylistically, you could edit your papers *ad infinitum.* For especially important papers, take extra time to ensure that your writing is crisp and direct and that your sentence rhythms are pleasing. But once you have met your obligations in the final draft, any changes you make will amount to refinements of an already competent work. To be sure, stylistic editing can mean the difference between a good work and an excellent one. Eventually, however, you will reach a point at which changes do not improve the quality of your paper. When you reach this point, stop.

Exercise 8

Edit the draft of the paper you have revised for purpose, coherence, and balance. Realize that you may need to make several passes at your draft to put it into final form. Now proofread your final draft.

Student Paper: Final Draft

Jim Walker wrote three drafts of his paper, developing a successively more ambitious thesis in each. In early revisions, he settled large-scale matters of unity and coherence. Then, in a final effort he corrected errors in grammar, punctuation, and usage. As you will see, Walker spent time refining his sentences so that they would read effortlessly. You will find in his essay the paradox evident in all good writing: When sentences are clear and easy to read, they mask the considerable effort that went into their making. Good writing looks to a reader as though it took no work at all; but of course the writer knows otherwise.

Changes that Walker made in his third draft of this paper are indicated by boldface type. Lines of the paper set in regular type are more or less original to his first draft. The boldface type shows that in his final effort, Jim Walker generalized the focus of his paper: he used his experiences to discuss the larger question of the relationships between escalating violence and availability of weapons.

STUDENT PAPER

Final Draft, "When the Trigger Pulls the Finger"

There is a constant barrage of media images that reinforce the common belief that our public schools are not safe. There are newspaper articles about assaults on teachers, magazine articles about students stabbing and shooting other students, T.V. news features showing piles of weapons confiscated from schools. You see gangbangers protecting their turf or shooting up rivals with Uzis, and drug dealers in and around schools armed with a lot more than beepers to protect their business interests. At some school or another, **or maybe your own,** you hear about fights over girlfriends or boyfriends, fights over expensive sneakers or designer clothes, fights over someone giving someone else a crazy look, disrespecting them. The perception is that guns and violence are common, everyday occurrences in our public schools. The perception is that students routinely carry weapons and the school itself is an armed camp, filled with roving posses packing guns and looking for an excuse to use them.

Even though the overwhelming majority of actual students do not share this exaggerated media perception and feel safe at school, many do not. It *is* **true that there are more weapons in schools now and that weapons can raise aggression to lethal levels.** My point is that students are the ones who really know the truth about violence in schools. Students are at the front lines. **Students can confront the violence in themselves, can refuse to arm themselves, and can actively implement some ways of dealing with aggression** ~~that help~~ break the cycle of violence.

My experiences at a big urban high school **made me aware of all kinds of aggressiveness—arguments, confrontations, fights—all of it fueled by rumors.** What seems like a random explosion is actually the result of many factors that come together and create a cycle of violence and aggressive acts that can spiral out of control. Students can get hurt. Students can also help break the cycle.

People have all kinds of ideas about what schools ought to be. One thing they overlook is that a school is part of a neighborhood, part of a community, part of a national culture. What school is, is a place where all of these outside influences come together. School is a flash point where all kinds of students and teachers, attitudes, ideas and knowledge come together. That is what is exciting about schools and education. Sometimes, however, this mixture is explosive. The problems of the larger society, the crime, the violence, the weapons, etc., get acted out in the halls and classrooms of schools. We usually do a good job of coping with *that*—and do it at the same time we cope with all the personal stuff that happens as we stop being kids and start becoming adults. We learn very quickly how to fit in and fit out. We learn how to survive in a multicultural school by **avoiding confrontations.**

But just avoiding **confrontations** is not enough. **The problem of aggressive acts is real and can be lethal as more students bring weapons to school.** We know that aggression is a fact of life. Social psychologists have several theories about what causes it, including aggression-as-instinct, frustration that leads to aggression, aggression learned from the social environment. Whatever the causes, the school is the place where a lot of different people come together and need to learn to get along **and resolve conflicts** without resorting to weapons.

There is a small part of every group in a big, multicultural high school that are bad apples—always talking trash, trying to be bad, walking around with that jaw-clenched, mad-dog stare. These bad apples threaten other students, calling them names like sissy or punk, pushing them to fight so the toughs can add to their reputation as being the baddest. They may have reasons for their attitude. But now they are putting it on everyone. Fortunately, schools have their own weapons. They are called vice principals and they love to mix it up with that kind of aggressive attitude. But vice principals and plainclothes police can't be everywhere. Students **need some tools of their own to help reduce levels of aggression, protect themselves from bad apples, and just as importantly, decide to stop feeding the cycle of violence by arming themselves.**

Better communication and social skills can help. All students need to be aware of what some students know naturally, **that they can** divert **or reduce aggression** with a quick apology, or with humor. This is what social psychologists call reducing levels of arousal **by introducing** an incompatible response. **Also,** the school can implement Peer Mediation where if someone **feels** a physical or emotional threat they **can** report it and discuss it with other students. They **can** talk about it, talk through it, get some help. The important thing **is** talking, getting two sides together to talk rather than using weapons or fists to solve differences. Talking **can also show** students it **isn't** worth a visit to the emergency room or **worth the legal problems or medical bills**—the consequences of violence **that** movies or rap videos don't usually show you. **If more students would have used these simple measures at my high school, I'm convinced that it would have made a difference during those few but dangerous times when emotions were running high.**

~~I didn't identify with that small part of each group who appeared to~~ be without hope in any future, who didn't seem to believe in anything, who were not afraid of jail or of dying. These students are sprung enough ~~to do anything. You don't know if you do get into a fight with one of them~~

whether they will pull a knife or something on you. Anything you do or say may set them off. Because they may do anything, or nothing, no one really knows for sure. They are truly dangerous. They generate a lot of fear in a school and seem to thrive as their reputation grows. But I **tried to never worry if someone was going to hurt me. I felt I had some workable alternatives to violence as a way to settle differences. I wanted my reputation to be that of someone who was fearless and tough enough to protect himself if absolutely necessary—but not violent.**

Rumors can feed the cycle of violence by increasing fear and anger levels among students. Big high schools are busy places. There **are** extensive and effective rumor grapevines. A rumor about somebody disrespecting someone else **sometimes** buzzes through the school. Word-of-mouth **chatter,** friends talking to friends, **can** add anger to the self-protective fear already present. Another rumor buzzes through school that someone has a 9mm pistol in his locker. Later you hear it was only a knife, or only a screwdriver, or that it was nothing, just a rumor. Another layer of fear gets added to rising emotions. Students feel uncomfortable passing other people in the hall, uncertain of that they'll do. Students are afraid of getting jumped so they hang out with friends so they are never alone, never vulnerable. Reasonable levels of self-protection slide into paranoia as emotions rise. **Reasonable students can make stupid choices. This is when anti-aggression techniques need to be talked about and used. This is when students need to talk to friends, teachers, counselors, social workers, somebody. Whenever students feel any sense of physical or emotional threat is when mediation is needed. If students don't take charge, things can get out of hand.**

During my junior year in high school, someone got slashed in a fight and that neck wound required 40 stitches. Although it wasn't 100% clear, the fight was about disrespecting someone's girlfriend. Rumors flew and finally there was a confrontation with name-calling, punches thrown, a knife was drawn. These were students who thought **talking about problems** was for snitches. They could solve their own problems. An argument **that might have been mediated** became an assault and the circle of victims widened.

Rumors about payback got a lot of students buzzing. Even normally steady, good students got caught up in it—out of loyalty **or** friendship—and my friend was one of them. **If you were afraid and had no other alternatives** it was easy to carry a boxcutter or an X-Acto knife. These were weapons but they could be easily explained if you were caught with one.

Some of us were playing basketball at an outdoor court in our neighborhood. Another game was in progress on the court next to us. Our game was guys from my school, some that I'd played football with that fall, a bunch of scrappy, competitive jocks. The other game was some older guys from the neighborhood, another bunch of homeboys playing some hoop.

A bad pass sent our ball into their court and my friend ran to get it. He was looking back at us, yelling about who got outs as he chased it down. He wasn't aware that he had disrupted the flow of the other game and **he** collided with one of the other players, knocking him down. That guy got up and he was hot, yelling obscenities at my friend. **My friend** looked at him, turned his back and coolly walked back toward us. That was too much for the screamer and he threw his ball hard at my friend, slamming it into his back. My friend turned and made a terrible mistake, **compounding an earlier stupid choice to arm himself.**

He pulled out a boxcutter and flashed it at his new enemy. This is what's called show and tell, showing somebody you've got a weapon and letting him know you have the heart to use it. The other guy reached down and pulled a knife out of a sheath strapped to his leg. Before anybody could say or do anything to break it up or distract them, these two went at it. When it was over, my friend's arm was dangling at his side, tendons and muscles slashed. His enemy's face was slashed, cheek bone showing white and glistening through the blood. This fight was over what? Honor? Respect? Reputation? A basketball that bounced out of bounds? One person was disabled, another disfigured **because the first and only choice to settle a conflict was a weapon.**

My first reaction at the time was as crazy as my friend's but it felt right **in the heat of the moment.** I wanted a gun. I thought I could've stopped the whole thing with a gun by **simply** raising the ante, **waving my gun to checkmate their knives.** Then we all could've just walked away, everything cool again. What I didn't consider until later was the possibility that one of the other players had a gun too. Then it would have been knives and guns in each other's face. Again—for what? More importantly, why? **Why can't the choice be to deflect or divert violence by any means available?** Why is it the first sign of a conflict that weapons are the first **and only** choice to resolve it? **I understand all the theories, the reasons, the provocations for aggressive acts. I realize my friend had not committed to breaking the cycle of violence. He chose to feed into it. I would've been a casualty myself if I had been armed, a casualty for nothing because nothing would've changed except the victim count. I am bitter at the lack of a coherent counterattack by individuals against the pervasive violence in our society that puts each of us at risk. This is where schools can be valuable in teaching alternatives to using weapons to solve conflicts.**

Maybe this situation was ripe for a fight. There was provocation from both sides. It was short move from one kind of physical confrontation, one-on-one hoop moves ("Show me what you got"), to another, a fist fight. Maybe some kind of line had been crossed, some kind of code broken and a facing up to *that* had to happen. I am at the heart of aggression right here, **the place where the choices are made.** Whatever the causes, and there are plenty, it is clear to me now that it was the weapons that pushed this playground scuffle into violence and tragedy. My friend and his new enemy chose weapons **and everyone lost.** Neither could escape the violence cycle and apologize or laugh it off or talk it through to **some** other conclusion. I don't defend what he did but I know why **he did it.** A weapon was at hand and the trigger pulled him. Without that weapon to raise the ante, there may have still been a fight. **High levels of** aggression are everywhere we look. But it wouldn't have been so lethal **and it wouldn't have continued to feed the cycle of violence that has been a fact of life in our society and our schools.**

It will be in schools that students learn effective social and communication skills that will help reduce the levels of aggression and divert the damage that rumors, confrontations and fights cause. Talking about differences, talking through differences and deflecting aggressive acts by apologizing and by our sense of humor will show by example that we have the heart to live together, have the courage and good sense to get along. We can break the cycle of violence by seeing weapons as part of the problem, not the solution to the lethal levels of violence in our society.

14

Writing and Rewriting in Groups[1]

No published writer works in a vacuum. In fact, practically all professional writing is, to some degree, a collaborative enterprise. While an author remains the primary composer of his or her text, by the time an essay or book reaches print it has been looked at, commented on, and often revised by a host of readers: reading committees, agents, editors, publishers, and copyeditors. Even before this point, a great many published authors share drafts with friends and colleagues in order to receive constructive feedback. Although the image of the solitary writer working in self-imposed isolation may be appropriate for certain moments of the composing process, it is hardly representative of how much professional writing gets done, both in academia and in the business world. Consequently, students who write papers all on their own, never sharing them with outside readers for critical peer review, approach the task unrealistically.

The primary goal of peer review and peer editing is to gather a variety of outside perspectives so that they may enhance your work. No matter how good we are at approaching our work from an objective distance, nothing compares to hearing the comments of a concerned, critical peer editor who has taken the time to carefully read our work. And no matter

---

[1]This chapter was written by Derek Owens, of Saint John's University.

how experienced we are as writers, we never stop learning from hearing what others have to say about our prose, or from presenting our own insights into the work of others.

Students who shy away from sharing their texts with others typically do so for one of two reasons: either they think that by working with other readers they risk plagiarism or they're too insecure about their own work. But sharing your work with a peer editor who gives you suggestions that may later find their way into your paper is not plagiarism so long as you remain the only writer of the paper and make a concentrated effort to put any such ideas into your own words. And as for being embarrassed about your writing, realize that this is simply the sign of a concerned writer. If you care enough to be nervous about showing your prose to another person, that's a good indication that you're taking your work seriously. Just keep in mind that almost *all* writers, no matter how experienced, are terribly self-conscious about everything they commit to paper. There's a story about how the poet Allen Ginsberg used to be so nervous before public readings that he would often get physically ill; yet when someone attempted to teach him relaxation techniques to prevent these attacks of nerves, he refused, claiming his agitated state actually enhanced his performance. While you certainly should not be throwing up at the prospect of sharing your work with other students, you should be aware that it is perfectly natural to feel hesitant, even downright reluctant, about showing your words to other readers.

There's another reason why working with other writers is essential. Even though most, if not all, of the writing you create in school will ultimately be for an audience of one—your teacher—it is crucial that you envision yourself writing for a hypothetical audience of unlimited readers. Truly successful writing will appear so to multiple readers, not just one professor. Thus, it is increasingly important that you receive a variety of feedback that allows you to hear a range of reactions that a single reader, even a teacher, can never offer. And since different readers will very often give you conflicting advice, you will have to make decisions on your own rather than simply adhering to the advice of a single instructor.

Giving and Receiving Editorial Advice

Some writing courses feature workshops in which you can give and receive suggestions about the writing you and your peers create. Even if workshops do not play a central role in your class, you can still keep this collaborative spirit alive in various forms of peer review, whether in small groups, over a computer network, or simply by passing your writing back and forth so that another may read it, write a letter of response, and hand it back to you. Whatever your situation, peer review involves receiving commentaries from outside readers and presenting those readers with your insights about their work. Such exchanges help foster an environment conducive to the cross-fertilization of ideas, thereby creating a communal relationship that can enhance your prose significantly. It can also be a lot more fun to have such conversations with your peers than to always make compositional decisions by yourself.

How to Give Advice

There are some general guidelines you need to consider before giving and receiving suggestions. First, when reading the work of another person, avoid the tendency to zero in on the most obvious mistakes: typos, grammatical errors, glitches in syntax. It is very common for students to start out their peer review as if they were a proofreader or copyeditor, while paying little attention to larger, more substantive concerns. This is because we learn from our predecessors: many of our teachers in the past adopted a similar stance when evaluating our work, marking all the mistakes in red pen while avoiding lengthy discussions about the bigger ideas struggling to make themselves heard within a text. It's up to you to avoid falling into this trap.

This is not to say drawing attention to such mistakes is unimportant. But you can do so simply by circling any errors you find. If the writer is serious about her or his work, she or he will look closely at these circled areas and try to identify the problems. If the writer is not interested in checking these circled sections, then it is certainly not your job to comment on them further.

What should you do instead, then? There are at least four main ingredients to good peer responses. First, you must attempt to envision the work from an "aerial perspective." In other words, pull yourself away from the text and think about how it works as a whole. Start out by seeking the big picture, so to speak, and address the larger issues: What is the paper's main idea? How does the organization help or hinder this idea? How has evidence been used? Are there sufficient counterarguments? How have outside sources been woven into the text?

Second, you must be specific and direct. If you offer generalizations ("I like the paper a lot"; "I could relate to it"; "Your argument is a good one"; "I like your examples"; "You explain things well"; "I get lost near the end . . . "), they will not be useful at all unless you immediately follow them up with specific examples. For example, don't just tell the author her argument is a good one; show her exactly where the argument seems to be working, and explain why. Pinpoint those pieces of evidence that bring home a point, as well as any evidence that isn't working for you, explaining your reactions. If you begin to get lost in places, show the author exactly where and then offer a suggestion or two as to how this problem might be resolved. The more detailed your response, the better.

Third, you must not only be honest and considerate, but responsible as well. Peer review and workshops do not give you a license to "tear apart" someone else's paper (even if some of your teachers don't necessarily follow this advice). Unfortunately, suggestions can come across as overly critical or too demeaning if you are not careful to speak in a respectful and conscientious manner. Realize the power of your criticism. Many people feel fragile about their writing, so when you must criticize, be respectful. Most writing has something good in it. If possible, couple your criticisms with compliments. Say, for instance, "These later sentences aren't nearly as powerful as the prose in your introduction, and here's why. . . . " Be aware that criticizing another writer's work carries with it a certain degree of responsibility: for every weakness or problem you point out, you should offer an example or suggestion of how this problem might be tackled. Your job is not merely to point out what does and doesn't work; the crucial part of your response lies in how well you give suggestions that the writer can use in revising the draft. Anyone can find fault with any piece of writing; the true sign of intellectual ability is how well you can come up with good ideas about how such weak areas might be made stronger. In other words, always give the writer ideas that she or he can take home and use.

Finally, you must allow the writer his or her topic and interest in it. Understand that this is not your paper that you are commenting on. Disinvest your ego from the job so that you do not attempt in your comments to make the paper yours. Do not criticize a paper because the topic does not interest you; if you are bored with the work, then you are probably not working hard enough to make it interesting. Also, do not attack an essay simply because the author's opinion is opposite from your own; your job is not to make the person come around to your way of thinking, but to help him or her create a stronger essay. (Imagine how insulted you would be if your teachers made it their mission to convert you to their beliefs, rather than to help you better articulate your own stances.) If you choose to play the role of devil's advocate, go right ahead, but maintain a respectful and honest demeanor.

How to Receive Advice

Without question, it is difficult and sometimes painful to be told by an instructor or fellow student that your paper needs major reworking. As the writer of an effort that does not yet succeed, you should be aware that as long as they come from a responsible source, critical comments are directed at your work and not at you. After all, your peers and your instructor probably don't even know you well enough to be able to make any valid judgments about your character or personality; usually all they have to go on are your written words. Try to understand that it is your *writing* that is being criticized; do your best to disengage your ego from the editorial review and respond not according to your hurt feelings but to the substance of the comments directed at your paper.

Chances are good that you will be receiving feedback to your writing periodically in group workshops. This is a crucial time for you as a writer; you may very well gain more insight about your work during these moments than at any other time in the class. Sometimes these groups will be small, perhaps four or five people, and other times the entire class might be responding to your writing. In either case, it is essential that you follow closely the comments of your peers and respond to them in ways that will benefit you as a writer. Your instructor may have the class follow a certain workshop format. For example, all readers first get to comment on your writing; then, you are permitted to respond with your own questions and rejoinders. Whatever the case, use whatever time you are given to speak up and ask your readers lots of questions, pressing them to be as specific as they can.

To be honest, this is not easy. It's hard to be assertive in a friendly way with students you may not know that well. Many times a writer will politely listen to all peer review comments, thank reviewers when they're finished, and move on to workshop another student's paper. But this is too passive, and chances are that if you do this, you won't retain significant information that will be valuable to you three nights later when it's time to revise the paper. During the peer review it is your responsibility to ask your readers to clarify the points they make. You must constantly encourage them to give detailed examples instead of generalities. If readers are getting caught up with nitpicky things like typos or minor grammatical errors, it's up to you to steer them down a path that is more beneficial to you; encourage them to talk about the main idea(s) in the essay and its overall organization. For example, ask: "Why, exactly, does my introduction seem too generic?" or "Can you show me where, exactly, you would suggest introducing some of the counterarguments I seem to have missed?"

Remember that when listening to student responses, you should be doing just what you do when reading assigned readings: write all of these insights down immediately. Use your journal if you wish, and make a list of all the comments they give you; later on, you can determine which ones you'll use and which can be disregarded. If you have time, make comments and changes right in your own draft as they describe for you what they considered to be the strengths and weaknesses of your paper.

Remember that you have the absolute prerogative to accept, to accept partially, or to reject editorial advice. Of course you will also bear the burden of rejecting potentially good advice. But if you truly disagree with your editor or even your instructor who will at some point be grading you, then you should hold your ground and thoughtfully explain what you were trying to do in the paper, what you would like to do, and why you cannot accept a particular suggestion for revision. If you are determined not to use your instructor's advice, you may owe it to the instructor to give persuasive opinions as to why such advice is not right for you at this time, and also what alternative ideas you are going to use. Whatever the case, it's essential that you be thoughtful and tactful when rejecting advice. First, give your editor the benefit of any doubt and assume that the advice offered is well founded. If the advice seems wrong, say: "I don't understand . . . Could you explain again. . . . " If you understand but continue to disagree, say so, and give your reasons. But remember that all suggestions you receive deserve an honest hearing.

Finally, don't make decisions based on all of the comments you hear right away. Wait a day or two before revising your work, letting the many suggestions you've heard ferment in your mind. This is especially helpful if you've received conflicting advice, or if you've gotten a healthy dose of particularly critical advice. Many times your initial reaction might be one of anger or frustration if your writing has not met with the kind of praise you had hoped for. This is quite common for both beginning and experienced writers. Keep in mind that you should probably allow a little time for these initial emotional responses to fade before attempting to incorporate any of the peer response suggestions. (How often have you been disgruntled at hearing advice you didn't want to hear, only to realize later on that such advice made perfect sense?) Often this might mean not doing anything to your paper on the day you receive such criticism and waiting for a day or two to pass so that you can approach all those comments from a clearer perspective.

Peer Review Checklists

A Checklist for Writers

You have just finished your draft and are eager to show it to another reader or share it with a workshop at your next class. But before passing copies of your work around to other readers or sending copies to them electronically via your computer, reserve some time to consider the questions below and answer them in a brief "cover letter" that should precede your essay. In this manner you can guide readers by making them aware of questions and concerns you have about your paper. The more assistance you can give your readers, the more focused and relevant their feedback will be.

In your cover letter, respond to the following questions as succinctly as you can:

1. What is my main idea in this draft? What is my primary goal in writing this? And what do I want readers to get out of this piece of writing?

2. What was the original assignment, and how well have I met the instructor's expectations?

3. What parts of the paper am I pleased with? (Be very specific about what seems to have worked: the organization, a particular description, the opening, use of outside sources, etc.)

4. When I think about this draft, what am I still not satisfied with? Are there things I've left undeveloped? If so, what are they?

Finally, ask your readers any additional questions; for example, is there anything specific they can answer for you or comment on that will help you as you revise and expand on this draft? Remember, the more focused your initial questions, the more focused their feedback will be.

Exercise 1

Before submitting your paper for peer review, it might help to imagine yourself as an outside reader. Take a draft you have written and reread it as if you were someone else, such as the editor of a magazine that might want to print your essay. As you read over your essay from this outside perspective, ask yourself the following questions:

- Does the author have a consistent idea running throughout his or her entire essay? If so, what is it (summed up in just a few sentences)?
- Does the essay sound as if the author is investigating something he or she is generally interested in, or does the prose read as if it is just a response to an arbitrary assignment?
- Does the essay seem as if the author wrote it solely for him- or herself, or could it be appreciated by a number of other readers? What does this person want the readers to get out of this piece of writing—what's in it for them?
- How much of the essay consists of examples and details that stand out and present a vivid picture for the reader? How much of the essay consists of language that does not offer crisp, imaginative details?

After asking yourself these questions, write a letter to yourself from the imaginary editor in which you offer suggestions and comments about your prose. Rewrite your draft accordingly, and then submit it for peer review. Compare the reactions of your peer editors with those of your "imaginary editor."

A Checklist for Reviewers

Freewriting and Preliminary Exercises

Teachers will often assign preliminary exercises in an attempt to get you to contemplate memories, anecdotes, ideas, and themes in the hope that such freewriting and brainstorming will help get you started before the actual writing of a first draft. Even though such writings are created very early in the composing process, long before a first draft is even started, and as such are often "raw" and unfinished, it is still tremendously helpful to give and receive feedback for such early assignments. In fact, the feedback you receive during these early stages may be extremely useful. Here is a checklist to help guide your comments when responding to a peer's preliminary exercise.

1. What are some of the things that stand out to you in this piece of writing? A particular image? A phrase? A term? The opening? The ending? The author's vocabulary? Underline specific examples, and explain why, exactly, they catch your attention.

2. Are there places in the writing where you would like to have additional information? Do you have any specific questions you want answered?

3. Are there places where the writer has told you what has happened, but hasn't really shown you by using a vivid description? If so, do you have any suggestions as to how he or she might make the presentation of information more exciting?

4. Can you separate those passages that seem to be narrative—that is, that tell a story or relate information—from those selections that are more reflective, where the author has attempted to put this information into perspective in order to say something about it? If the author has not spent much time reflecting, where exactly might such passages be added to the writing?

5. If this exercise were the opening of an essay, what do you think that essay might be about? What potential themes are lurking within this piece of writing? What suggestions do you have for the writer as to what he or she might do now? How might this develop into a larger piece of writing? List all the possible directions you can think of in which this piece of writing could go.

Exercise 2

Take a piece of freewriting or an early exercise and give a copy of it on floppy disk to one or more readers. Or, send readers your preliminary text over a computer network. Ask readers to respond to any of the questions above and add several more questions of your own related more specifically to the assignment at hand. In return, answer the questions your readers pose about some piece of their early writing.

Keep in mind what the ultimate assignment is going to be, and offer your comments with an eye to the eventual assignment. When finished, consider the comments of your readers. Notice all of the places where they picked up on something that you took for granted during the initial writing of the exercise; compare the ways in which they were reading your prose with the way you read your own work. Also, compare the manner in which they gave you feedback with the way you offered feedback to them.

We often think that once a final draft has been completed, proofread, and evaluated, the work is truly finished. This is especially the case if you submit a piece of writing and it receives a good grade. But this is, of course, never the case; it is highly unlikely that you will write sentences and paragraphs that are so "perfect" that they could not be improved.

Find a final draft that you feel good about, something that has been workshopped. Or, find a paper that received what you consider to be a good grade. Exchange this final piece of writing with at least two other students, and select three paragraphs from their papers to revise significantly. Do everything you can to those sentences to make them more interesting, varied, colorful, and imaginative. Alter vocabulary; combine some sentences into more complex ones, while shortening others to make them more succinct; introduce semicolons, dashes, and colons if the author has not made use of such punctuation, and so forth. Make two changes per line, at the very least.

When finished, compare your changes with those of the other student. What do such changes say about our writing? Can a writer ever be completely finished with an essay? How extensively should you revise your own work on such a microscopic level before turning it in?

Common Problems with Peer Review and Group Workshops

Peer review and workshops are some of the most difficult parts of any writing course. It takes time for students to become comfortable enough with each other to offer substantive feedback. It takes practice to see things from an aerial perspective and not get preoccupied with insignificant details. It's also tough for many students to sustain the workshop experience. After just five minutes of discussion, everyone might suddenly fall silent and the group may interpret this as a sign that nothing more needs to be said. In reality, this is just the beginning. You must not give in to the temptation to stop talking about your writing after a few minutes of conversation. And you must not allow the discussion to wander off track and away from your writing. If, after a while, you realize that everyone is talking about a movie they saw last night instead of discussing your paper, it's your responsibility to pipe up and say, "That's nice, but can we get back to my paper? I've got some questions that still need answering, namely . . . "

Workshops and peer review take practice, but once you become more familiar with the art of giving and receiving feedback, the benefits can be immense. You begin to learn ways of always saying something else about a piece of writing, which is a sign of an intelligent, critical reader. You develop more focus and discipline in discussing your writing and that of others, traits that can help you immeasurably when writing on your own outside of class. Finally, you gain practice in speaking with other students in an academic context; and since in today's schools there's often less emphasis on public speaking, this is a valuable skill useful beyond the writing classroom.

When a Group Is Asked to Create a Single Text

In assigning a writing project, your professor may require you to be part of a group whose task is to create a single research project or essay. The great advantage of creating a document collaboratively is that you can put the power of several minds to work on a task that one person might find overwhelming. On the other hand, working with others in this fashion requires good communication skills and the ability to cooperate and compromise. Both in content and in presentation, however, your group's work should read as though *one* person wrote it even if several people have been involved in the actual writing. Consider the following when working in conjunction with others on a single writing project:

- To minimize rewriting, meet with group members before any writing takes place. Decide on a structure and an outline for the overall document and then assign parts to individual members. Agree on a consistent point of view for the paper. At this first meeting determine a schedule of periodic deadlines, so that all members will know when their portions are due.

- At a second meeting after writing and research has begun, ask each group member to outline his or her section and to discuss its structure. As a group, think specifically of the ways in which one section will build from and lead to another. Also, raise and address any problems encountered thus far in the writing.

- At the completion of a first draft, distribute the assembled document to the entire group and have each member revise for content and consistency of perspective. You might even workshop each section, referring to the peer editing checklists above.

- Incorporate all revisions in a single version of the document. Assign one member of the group to rewrite the paper for continuity of style and voice, adding and modifying the necessary transitions. Make sure that your Works Cited page, if there is one, adheres to the proper style expected by your teacher.

Computers and Collaboration

Writing with a computer facilitates the author/editor relationship in major ways. If you are working with a group on a single project you can easily swap drafts by exchanging disks, thereby saving considerable time during the revision process. Or, if you're working on your own paper, you can still send your drafts to others over a network within seconds; then they can respond rapidly with feedback. In fact, with a network, you can reach readers virtually all over the world.

Disk Swapping Techniques

Once you have a complete draft of your paper, consider giving a hard copy of it as well as an electronic copy on floppy disk to a friend for peer review; this will then allow him or her to either make annotated comments on the hard copy, or to make detailed revisions directly on the disk. The speed of the computer allows your reader to make more revisions than might otherwise be possible, and you can keep or modify those suggestions that make sense to you while disregarding the others. (Some word processing programs have a feature that allows an editor to suggest deletions and additions without destroying any of your text. When your editor returns the document, the suggestions will show up on your screen either shaded or underlined.) Note: Make sure that, prior to giving anyone a copy of your work, you have made a second copy of your original draft on another disk in your possession. That way, you can compare your version of the draft with that of your peers, and also have a backup copy in case your reader loses or damages your disk. It is a good idea to have anyone who is going to alter your text place the modified draft into a separate file with the date of the changes. This way, if there are several of you rewriting the same draft over a period of time, you will have a dated record of every version of the paper. This can be a tremendous service should you wish to review the progress of a paper, and also if your instructor ever asks to see earlier versions of the assignment.

Using Networks

If you have a "computer account" at your school, then you are able to send memos and texts to other computer users with "e-mail" (electronic mail) addresses. This means that within seconds, you can electronically deposit a draft of your paper into another reader's "mailbox," even if that reader is at another school across the country. Using a computer network like Internet or Bitnet can bring you into contact with many readers, and can also bring their comments to you in an extremely rapid fashion. Familiarize yourself with the academic computing center at your school, set up your own computer account, and learn how to take advantage of the network. Not only is learning how to get on the network relatively easy, but it can also be fun to suddenly find yourself able to contact so many people through a computer. Note, though, that there are usually fees involved for accessing these networks.

There are software programs available now that allow multiple writers to work simultaneously on a single text, whether they are all congregated at linked terminals in a computer lab or working at remote sites and connected via telephone lines. Such software typically works like this: As you write a sentence or paragraph, those words will appear almost simultaneously on everyone else's screen, just as their words will be materializing on your screen. With such software you can have everyone write separate paragraphs and thus work on separate sections of the text, or you can all work simultaneously within the same paragraph. And, rather than waiting a period of time in order to get feedback before revising a text, editing decisions can be made during the same session in which a first draft is created: that is, all writers are free to return to any part of the text and change it. Usually the procedure for doing this is to use small dialogue boxes off to one side of the screen, where you can converse with the other writers about any editorial changes prior to making them, thereby avoiding stepping on the toes of other writers and ensuring that your collaborative writing session does not degenerate into chaos. This can be a fascinating way to work with other writers, for you get to see not only what other people write in response to your words, but you also get to watch the idiosyncrasies of their writing processes as the words "magically" appear and undergo changes on your screen.

Chances are good that sooner or later you'll be in a situation where you can benefit greatly from collaborating with another writer via a computer, whether your career takes you into business, medicine, law, education, the arts, or any other area. Consequently, it will be to your advantage to get a taste of what computer collaboration might entail now, so that transitions to future technologies will be easier.

PART IV

The Research Paper

15

The Research Process

Defining the Scope of Your Paper

Determining the Research Assignment

What you write about in your research paper—the subjects you pursue—is determined primarily by the discipline in which you are working. A paper on the incidence of alcoholism among student-athletes would be suitable for a sociology course, but not for a literature or business course; a paper on the genetic factor in crack cocaine addiction would be suitable for a biology course, but not for a sociology course.

Formulating a Research Question

In preparing to write a paper on the general subject of police stress, consider the range of questions you might ask. If you were writing a paper in the *social sciences*, you might ask: Are stressed-out police officers a danger to the community? What kinds of stress counseling should be available to police officers? A *humanities* major, however, might ask: How has the problem of police stress been presented in movies? Do prevailing cultural images of police officers help to create stress? A paper from a *science* major might ask: Are the physiological effects of stress on female officers different from those on males? What effect does stress have on an officer's day-to-day performance? A *business* major would pursue yet another track and might ask: How much does stress contribute to employee absenteeism or resignation? Will new stress-management programs help police departments cut health-care costs?

Most of these questions are too broad as they now stand; you would have to narrow them down considerably to make them suitable for a paper of ten to twenty-five pages. In looking at the question of stress in police officers, you could collect information on the reality of police life from news accounts or directly from officers; you could distinguish physical from mental effects of stress; or you could research whether certain personality types seem to be more seriously affected by stress.

Before you narrow the focus too sharply, however, it would be wise to do some preliminary research on the subject. Otherwise, you may overlook aspects that you would have found particularly interesting. This preliminary research could involve reading an encyclopedia or magazine article, a section of a textbook, or possibly even a short book on the subject. Such reading may raise particular questions in your mind—"burning" questions that you feel compelled to pursue. Afterward, you will be in a better position to narrow your focus—and you will do this primarily by searching your sources to discover the answer to one primary *research question.* This research question may be one of the questions posed here, or it may be another question that was raised in the course of your preliminary reading. The advantage of a question, as opposed to a thesis, at this point, is that you are acknowledging that you still have to discover the answer(s), rather than just to find evidence to support a prematurely established conclusion.

Generating Ideas for the Research Paper

Perhaps you have selected a broad subject, which you may have already begun to narrow down. Or you may have started with a "burning question" and have begun to follow it up with further questions. Here, we will consider ways of further narrowing your focus and of searching for information sources about your topic. Specifically, we will consider (1) how to keep a research log of your ongoing ideas; (2) how to develop a search strategy for preliminary reading; and (3) how to develop a search strategy for more focused reading, leading toward the development of your working thesis.

Keep a Research Log

Many students find it valuable to keep track of their ideas in a research log. They write down their initial questions in this log and update it as often as possible. The log becomes a running record of all their inspirations, false starts, dead ends, second thoughts, breakthroughs, self-criticisms, and plans.

One technique that is particularly useful at the outset of a project is called *nonstop writing.* Nonstop writing (sometimes called *brainstorming* or *freewriting*) requires you to put pen to paper, consider your topic, and write down anything that occurs to you. Do not stop to revise, fix punctuation or spelling, or cross out bad ideas. Do not even stop to think what to say next—just write. The goal is to generate as many ideas as you possibly can within a limited period of time—say, ten or fifteen minutes. At the end of a session of nonstop writing, you may (or may not) have some useful ideas that you want to pursue.

Here, for example, are some initial ideas generated by nonstop writing sessions about police stress. Note the difference in personal styles: the first is a stream-of-consciousness entry; the second is a list; the third is a rough plan for designing a questionnaire.

1. criminals, creeps, never know who's around the corner, behind the door. heartburn, heart disease, ulcers, alcoholism, people yelling at you—public, other officers, sergeant, mayor, citizens groups—spouse? kids? always in coffee shops or chasing criminals, serious heartburn. divorce rate might be high, maybe suicide, killing someone must be hard to deal with unless you're crazy, compare to other jobs

2. guns—police shoot people
   people shoot police
   people don't like cops, "I pay your salary"
   dregs of society
   politics—mayor, commissioner, ACLU
   bad food, antacid commercials, coffee, ulcers, high blood pressure, bars
   danger—all kinds
   bored then BOOM
   family life—divorce? kids? what did you do at work today?

3. There must be many things in a police officer's life that help to create stress and stress must cause some kind of damage. I think I can get information from the library, but to make things really new and interesting I'll contact the police department to see what they do to help manage stress. I'll try to set up some interviews with police officers. Maybe I should distribute a questionnaire or a survey. I'll have to get help on that right away. Then I think I'll try to talk to a doctor about the physical problems that stress causes. And I'll need to find out what other problems it creates. Maybe the police union has some good information on stress or stress reduction programs, or the mayor's office, or . . .

Even though these ideas are in crude form, you can see a paper beginning to take shape here. As you proceed with your research, keep your log updated. You will want to do this not just to preserve a record of your research (often valuable in itself), but also to allow you to return to initially discarded ideas that may assume new relevance or importance at a later stage in the paper.

Researchers use a log for other purposes, as well.

1. To jot down *sources* and possible sources—not only library sources, but also names and phone numbers of people to interview.
2. To freewrite their *reactions* to the material they are reading and to the people they are interviewing; these reactions may later find their way into the finished paper.

3. To jot down *questions* that occur to them in the process of research, which they intend to pursue later.

4. To try out and revise ideas for *theses,* as their research progresses.

Do not use your log for actually taking notes on your sources; it is best to do this on note cards.

Work toward a Thesis

You have now focused on a particular research question; you have done some preliminary reading and perhaps have talked to one or two authorities on the subject; and you have begun generating some written ideas and have given some thought to your purpose and audience. At this point—having begun to formulate some informed opinions on the subject—you may be ready to venture a thesis. For detailed discussion on writing a thesis, see chapter 2, pages 27–31, and chapter 12, pages 487–490. Remember that having selected a tentative thesis, you are under no obligation to zealously guard it against all changes. Quite possibly, you will need to adjust your focus, and therefore your thesis, as your research and your thinking on a subject develop.

Library Research: Preliminary Reading

Research logs and other strategies can be useful for getting down on paper ideas and information that you already have. Conferences with your professor can help get you thinking about a subject. Obviously, though, there are numerous aspects of that subject of which you are not yet aware, and one of these aspects may interest you enough to become your final topic. The best way to discover some of the possibilities is to use a systematic library search strategy.

Develop a Preliminary Search Strategy

A good search strategy begins with the most general reference sources: encyclopedias, bibliographic listings, biographical works, and dictionaries. The diagram at the top of page 558 shows a skeleton view of such a library search strategy. By consulting such sources at the outset, you will be able to narrow your subject to a manageable scope—that is, to one that you can cover in adequate depth within the length specified.

Having narrowed your subject, you can then locate additional information, from both (1) periodicals and newspapers, which you locate through indexes and abstracts and/or computer search; and (2) books, which you locate through the card catalog and/or computer search. During this part of your search, you may further narrow your topic, and you can consult additional books and articles as necessary, along with additional reference sources such as biographical dictionaries, specialized dictionaries, and book reviews.

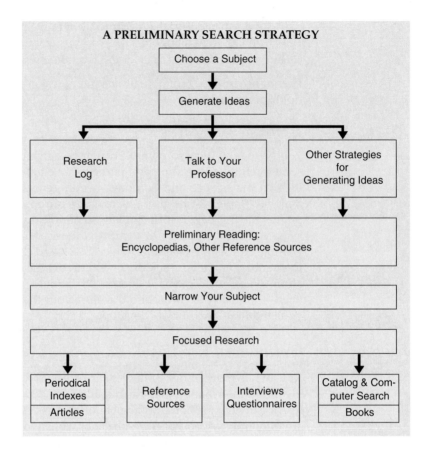

The following diagram illustrates how the narrowing down process might proceed.

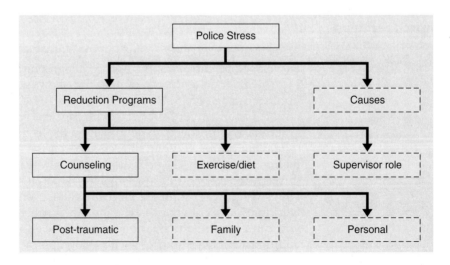

This diagram illustrates the process of narrowing the topic of police stress. After some idea-generating strategies, the student decides to focus her paper on stress-reduction programs. Since this subject is obviously still too broad for a relatively short paper, she does some preliminary reading and considers whether to focus on psychological counseling, exercise, and diet workshops, or on the role of supervisory personnel. After some additional reading, she decides to concentrate on counseling programs available to officers. But finding that even this narrowed-down topic is too broad, she finally decides on a paper dealing with the counseling available to police officers after traumatic incidents.

You should recognize that any diagram of the search strategy or of the narrowing-down procedure makes these processes look neater than they generally are. In practice, they are often considerably less systematic. What is crucial is to keep in mind the kinds of resources and procedures that are available to you, and—given the constraints on your time—to use as many as you can.

As you proceed, you will discover that research is to some extent a self-generating process. That is, one source will lead you—through references in the text, citations, and bibliographic entries—to others. Authors will refer to other studies on the subject; and frequently, they will indicate which ones they believe are the most important, and why. At some point you will realize that you have already looked at most of the key research on the subject. This is the point at which you can be reasonably assured that the research stage of your paper is nearing its end.

Use Librarians as a Resource

We list "librarians" as a primary source, because they are a *major* resource too frequently overlooked both by harassed students *and* by professors. Frequently, the key to getting the information you need is simply knowing where to look. The next section will provide some assistance in this area. Your reference librarian will be able not only to supplement our list of sources, but also to tell you which ones are best for your purposes.

Look into the General Sources

General sources, such as general encyclopedias and biographical dictionaries, are designed for people who want to familiarize themselves relatively quickly with basic information about a particular subject. Authors of general sources assume that their readers have little or no prior knowledge of the subjects covered and of the specialized terminology used in the field. Thus, if they use specialized terminology, they are careful to define it. General sources are also comprehensive in their coverage.

On the other hand, general sources tend to lack depth. They typically cover a subject in less detail than does a specialized source, such as an encyclopedia of music or a business periodical index. They also cover fewer subjects in a given field.

Encyclopedias

A general encyclopedia is a comprehensive, often multivolume work that covers events, subjects, people, and places across the spectrum of human knowledge. The articles, usually written by specialists, offer a broad overview of the subjects covered. From an encyclopedia you may be able to discover a particular aspect of the subject that interests you and to see how that aspect relates to the subject in general. Encyclopedia entries on major subjects frequently include bibliographies.

Keep in mind that encyclopedias—particularly general encyclopedias—are frequently not considered legitimate sources of information for college-level papers. Thus, while you may want to use an encyclopedia article to familiarize yourself with the subject matter of the field and to locate specific topics within that field, you probably should not use it as a major source, or indeed, for anything other than background information.

Biographical Sources

Frequently you may have to look up information on particular people. Note that some biographical sources are classified according to whether the person is living or dead.

Dictionaries and Other Sources

Dictionaries enable you to look up the meaning of particular terms. As with encyclopedias, dictionaries may be either general or specialized in scope. In addition to encyclopedias, biographical sources, and dictionaries, you may find the following sources useful:

- Guides to the literature enable you to locate and use reference sources within particular disciplines.
- Handbooks provide facts and lists of data for particular disciplines.
- Almanacs also provide facts and lists of data, but are generally issued annually.
- Yearbooks, also issued annually, update data already published in encyclopedias and other reference sources.
- Atlases and gazetteers provide maps and other geographical data.
- Citation indexes indicate when and where a given work has been cited *after* its initial publication; these are useful for tracing the influence of a particular work.
- Book review indexes provide access to book reviews; these are very useful for evaluating the scope, quality, and reliability of a particular source.
- Government publications are numerous and frequently offer recent and authoritative information in a particular field.

Consult your librarian for information on guides to the literature, almanacs, and other reference guides relevant to your subject.

Bibliographic Index

The *Bibliographic Index* is an excellent research tool both for browsing through some of the subtopics of a subject and for directing you to additional sources. The *Bibliographic Index* is an annual bibliography of bibliographies (that is, a bibliography that lists other bibliographies), arranged by subject. Here, for example, is part of the listing under "stress" in the 1993 *Bibliographic Index*.

Each of these listings represents a bibliography that appears in another source—a book, a pamphlet, or an article. In most cases, the bibliography appears as a source of additional readings at the conclusion of the book, the chapter, or the article. In some cases, however, the bibliography stands by itself as an independent publication. If you browse through a few successive years of listings on a subject, you will probably discover some topics that interest you, as well as a source of readings on that topic.

Stress (Psychology)
 See also
 Anxiety
 Burn out (Psychology)
 Job stress
 Life change events
 Post-traumatic stress disorder
 Type A behavior
Aspinwall, L. G. and Taylor, S. E. Modeling cognitive adaptation: a longitudinal investigation of the impact of individual differences and coping on college adjustment and performance. *J Pers Soc Psychol* 63:1001-3 D '92
Avison, W. R. and McAlpine, D. D. Gender differences in symptoms of depression among adolescents. *J Health Soc Behav* 33:93-6 Je '92
Cook, Marshall. Slow down—and get more done. Betterway Bks. 1993 p175-81 annot
Edwards, J. R. A cybernetic theory of stress, coping, and well-being in organizations. *Acad Manage Rev* 17:265-74 Ap '92
Eysenck, H. J. Prediction of cancer and coronary heart disease mortality by means of a personality inventory: results of a 15-year follow-up study. *Psychol Rep* 72:514-16 Ap '93
Fox, M. L. and others. Effects of stressful job demands and control on physiological and attitudinal outcomes in a hospital setting. *Acad Manage J* 36:315-17 Ap '93
Friedland, N. and others. Controlling the uncontrollable: effects of stress on illusory perceptions of controllability. *J Pers Soc Psychol* 63:930-1 D '92

Devising a Working Thesis

During your preliminary reading you began to focus on a *research question*. As you continue to read about your subject—including arguments on both sides of an issue and anecdotal and statistical information about the experiences of certain individuals—you should begin to develop your own ideas about your subject. Such observations and reflections on your part should eventually come into focus as a *working thesis*. This thesis is, of course, subject to change as you come across new material and as your thinking about the subject develops further. For now, however, this working thesis is the main idea that shapes your thinking. The working thesis will also influence the focused reading of your subsequent research since, by defining relevant areas and eliminating irrelevant ones, it narrows the scope of your search for supporting evidence.

For the sake of example, let's consider four working theses. First, we will consider the narrower topics developed from the main subject:

> For a paper in the *social sciences,* the topic is kinds of stress counseling available to police officers.
> For a paper in the *humanities,* the subject is whether prevailing cultural images of police officers help to create stress.
> For a paper in *science,* the subject is the physiological effects of stress on male and female officers.
> For a paper in *business,* the issue is the connection between stress and absenteeism or resignation.

So far, these are only *topics*—not theses. To develop a working thesis from each of these topics, you will need to make a *statement* about the topic (after surveying a good deal of source material). Here are four statements that can be used as working theses:

> *Social Science:* There are many good programs all over the country that deal with police stress, though most officers don't have access to them.
> *Humanities:* Some officers feel stress because they find it hard to live up to the image of the good and benevolent neighborhood protector that they grew up with.
> *Science:* Police stress programs must deal with the physiological effects common in male and female officers since the problems range from daily irritations to terminal illness.
> *Business:* Departments should invest in stress-management programs since the cost of such programs will be offset by reduced rates of absenteeism and savings on insurance premiums.

Doing Focused Reading

If you have looked through a number of general sources, you have some basic knowledge about your subject and some tentative ideas about it. But you need more specific information to pursue your thesis.

Finding What You Need in Focused Sources

An overview of available sources will help you focus on the ones that best address your thesis. This overview will start with articles in order to emphasize the fact that periodical indexes are often preferable to the card catalog as a first step in conducting focused research.

General Periodical Indexes: Magazines

Periodicals are magazines and newspapers published at regular intervals—quarterly, monthly, daily. Periodical articles often contain information available from no other source and are generally more up-to-date than books published during the same period. You are probably familiar with the *Readers' Guide to Periodical Literature* as a means of locating magazine articles, but there are numerous other periodical reference guides.

For example, consider *Ulrich's International Periodicals Directory.* This is not a periodical index, but rather a subject guide to periodicals; that is, it directs you to periodicals on a given subject. To find out more about the nature or scope of a particular magazine, check *Katz's Magazines for Libraries.* This reference tool lists the most commonly used magazines and offers basic descriptive and evaluative information about each.

Like encyclopedias, periodical indexes are of two types: *general* and *specialized.* The most commonly used general periodical index is, of course, the *Readers' Guide to Periodical Literature,* which indexes magazines of general interest such as *Time, Newsweek, U.S. News and World Report, The New Republic, Sports Illustrated, Commonweal.* Here, for example, is a recent *Readers' Guide* entry for Stress.

STRESS

See also
Anxiety
Crisis management (Psychology)
Job stress
Oxidative stress
Post-traumatic stress disorder
Time pressure

21 ways to cope with stress [excerpt from The stress solution; ed. by Larry Rothstein]. L. H. Miller and A. D. Smith. il *Ladies' Home Journal* v110 p80+ Ap '93
25 ways to unwind. J. Csatari. il *Men's Health* v8 p68-71 My '93
Blown away [taking balloon ride to counter effects of stress] R. Lipsyte. il *American Health* v12 p20+ Ja/F '93
Don't let stress become distress. *USA Today (Periodical)* v121 p6 D '92
Ending the silence of the heart [link between stress and silent myocardial ischemia; research by Peter Kaufmann] il *Psychology Today* v26 p8-9 Jl/Ag '93
Hidden stress: is it harming your health? D. Kotz. il *McCall's* v120 p52+ Je '93
The holidays don't have to be stressful [views of Theresa Farrow] il *USA Today (Periodical)* v121 p12 D '92
The humor doctor—prescribes a dose of laughter [S. Sobel] P. Grout. por *Career World* v21 p25 Ja '93
Lampenfieber [stress-induced fever in rats; research by Matthew Kluger] *Discover* v14 p26+ S '93
The male stress syndrome. R. Laliberte. il *Men's Health* v8 p46-9 Ja/F '93
Outsmarting stress. D. Sobel. il *Working Woman* v18 p83-4+ My '93
Overstressed kids. K. Levine. il *Parents* v68 p246+ D '93
Psychological stress linked to cancer [study by Joseph G. Courtney] K. Fackelmann and J. Raloff. *Science News* v144 p196 S 25 '93
Stress and distress [men's anxieties about their children] il *Harvard Business Review* v71 p9 Jl/Ag '93
"Stress is ruining our marriage". S. J. Longshore. il *Ladies' Home Journal* v110 p16+ F '93
Support, stress and sugar [effects of stress and social support on glucose regulation in diabetics; research by Linda Griffith] il *Prevention (Emmaus, Pa.)* v45 p11-12 Mr '93
A toll on the tummy [stress produces excessive cortisol and increases fat deposition on the abdomen; research by Mareille Rebuffe-Scrive and Judith Rodin] il *Psychology Today* v26 p9 Jl/Ag '93

Another useful general periodical index is the *Essay and General Literature Index,* which indexes (by subject, author, and sometimes by title) articles and essays that have been collected into books. The index is especially useful since it gives you access to material that might not otherwise have surfaced in your search. These articles and essays generally would be classified under the humanities, but some deal with social science issues as well.

General Periodical Indexes: Newspapers

Most libraries have back issues of important newspapers on microfilm. The *New York Times Index* may be used to retrieve articles in the *Times* as far back as 1913. There are also indexes for the *San Francisco Chronicle*, the *Los Angeles Times*, and the *Wall Street Journal* (an important source of business news). The *Newspaper Index* lists articles from the *Chicago Tribune*, the *New Orleans Times-Picayune*, the *Los Angeles Times*, and the *Washington Post*. You can print out "hard copies" (from microfilm) of articles you need. If you're looking for articles in newspapers other than these, check dates of stories in the *New York Times Index*, or see whether the newspaper has a search service.

Here is part of a sample entry on "Stress" from a recent *Times-Picayune Index:*

STRESS
James Gill, a Jesuit priest and psychiatrist, was one of about a dozen speakers at the Louisiana Convention of Priests in New Orleans. Gill related secrets on dealing with vocational stress. (M) Ap 29 - B, 4:4

As fun as family reunions can be, they can be a source of anxiety. Therapist and clinical social worker Lucia Milling knows the psychological perils of family reunions. Expectations, low or high, can cause a lot of stress before a reunion. (M) My 9 - OTT, 1:2

Louisiana's River Parishes Hospital sponsored a Women's Day in LaPlace that featured several professionals who gave talks and offered tips on dealing with the stress frequently experienced by women; photo. (M) Je 20 - OTR, 1:5

Carol Wolfram says that the Christmas season can be a time of cheer and of stress. Marian D'Antonio, a Slidell LA social worker, offers suggestions for dealing with the stress. (M) D 9 - OTS, 1:1

Computerized Databases

During the past decade or so, library research has been revolutionized by the development of computerized databases—electronic indexes to vast numbers of articles, reports, and books. These electronic indexes, which may also provide abstracts (and in some cases the complete texts) of relevant sources, can make your research much more efficient and comprehensive than it would be if you were to rely exclusively on print indexes. An additional advantage of computerized databases is that they are much more current than print indexes, since they are updated every week, or even more frequently. You may read information from databases directly from the screen, or you may prefer to obtain printouts.

Computerized databases are generally of two types: *on-line* and *CD-ROM*. On-line databases originate from off-campus commercial information services (or "vendors"). The largest such service is DIALOG, which provides access to more than 100 million items in over 300 separate databases in the humanities, the social sciences, the natural sciences, and business. Among these specialized databases are PsycINFO, which references items in psychological journals; ERIC, which references items in educational journals; and Arts and Humanities Search. Another important information service is WILSONLINE, which provides electronic access to the printed indexes published by the H. W. Wilson Co., including *Readers' Guide, Education Index,* and *Social Science Index.*

To use these databases, you must type in (or supply the librarian with) *key words* or *descriptors*—that is, subject headings—that focus your search on a particular area. Key words are terms or phrases that appear in the title of the item or that are used to categorize items in the database. (Many databases include a *thesaurus* or *dictionary* of key words.) The computer will search for all occurrences of the word *in a given database,* with no regard for word or connotation. It is important that your key words be sufficiently narrow to make your search manageable. If you chose the National Criminal Justice Reference System database and typed in "police," you'd find 34,901 entries; for "stress" you'd find 2,979 entries listed. The two words together result in total entries of 1,140 which is better but still too large. You will need to continue to narrow your search by adding more key words to get a manageable number of entries (25–50 perhaps). Some words/phrases to add might include *U.S.* (there are police all over the world, after all), *organizational* stress, *post-traumatic* stress, and so on. The following is one of the titles you would uncover in such a search:

```
1/5/3
140494
TITLE: Beating Burnout: Don't Let the Stress Get You Down
AUTHOR(S): Albrecht, S
JOURNAL NAME: Texas Police Journal, V 40, N 11 (December 1992), P
   1-3 1992 3 p
COUNTRY OF PUBLICATION: United States
DOCUMENT TYPE(S): article
INTELLECTUAL CONTENT: Surveys
LANGUAGE(S): English
ABSTRACT: The key to being a successful police officer, according to
this author, is balancing the desire to be an officer with the needs
of a personal life.
   Comparing modern police officers to the Perfect Scholar-Divine
Warriors of early feudal Japan, he urges law enforcement officers to
master and control their "warrior" side, while simultaneously nur-
```

turing and developing their "scholarly" side. Unlike obsessed officers, who often suffer from failed marriages, alcohol and drug abuse,
and strained relations with family and friends, the warrior officer
will be able to achieve moderation in all pursuits. Some veteran
officers have a ritual they follow when leaving their station every
day; the ritual helps them to relax and to make the transition into
their personal lives. They make a conscious effort to reduce their
stress and to leave their work behind when off duty. The warrior
officer, unlike the obsessive officer, is able to assess his weaknesses, strengths, partners, and limits, and most important, to accept his own mortality.
DESCRIPTORS: Burnout syndrome; Police work attitudes; Police occu-
    pational stress
DESCRIPTOR CODES: 08337; 08674; 05387

One caution about on-line database searching: since libraries have to
pay for the use of such services, they frequently pass on the cost of an individual search to the user. You may pay by the item or by the amount of
time on-line. Since these charges often range from $30 to $40 an hour or
even higher, on-line searches are not always practical for the undergraduate researcher.

CD-ROM databases, as the name implies, are on compact disk (read-
only memory), and are more likely than on-line databases to be provided
free to the user. Most periodical indexes available in print (*Readers' Guide,
Humanities Index,* etc.) are also available on CD-ROM. Since one CD can
store several years' worth of indexes, a CD-ROM search takes less time
and effort than a search through bound volumes of printed indexes.

One important compact disk index is InfoTrac, which provides access
to articles in over 1,000 business, technological, and general-interest periodicals, as well as the *New York Times* and the *Wall Street Journal.*

A limitation of both on-line and CD-ROM databases is that they generally catalog material that is only five or ten years old. If you needed
sources published before that—contemporary material, for example, on
the Watergate scandal of the early 1970s—you would need to rely on the
print indexes for that period.

The Card Catalog

Most libraries have now computerized their card catalogs; if this process
is not yet complete, some of the older books may be accessible only
through the traditional 3 x 5 card files. But whether on-line or on cards, a
given item in the catalog will be classified in three ways—by *author,* by
title, and by *subject.* Browsing through some of the subject cards is a good
way to locate books on your topic; but before you do this, you should have
at least begun to narrow your subject. Otherwise, you could be overwhelmed with the sheer number of books available. (There may be several hundred books on various aspects of post-traumatic stress.)

Notice the call number in the upper left-hand corner of the cards. One
or more letters preceding the number indicates that the book has been

cataloged according to the Library of Congress System, the most common cataloging system for larger libraries. Smaller libraries use the Dewey Decimal System, which always begins with a number. If, for example, you are doing literary research in a library that uses the Library of Congress System, most of the books you will need will have call numbers beginning with "PR" (English literature) or "PS" (American Literature); if you are working on a political science paper, you will probably be looking in the "E" section. In a library using the Dewey Decimal System, literary books are in the 800 series and political science books are in the 300 series. Check the reference desk at your library for a key to the cataloging system. The reference desk should also have a library map or shelving guide that will enable you to locate the books or bound periodicals that you need. Be certain that you accurately copy down the call numbers; a missing or incorrect letter or number may send you to the wrong section.

Shown below and continuing on page 568 are four catalog entries for *Stress and the Police Officer* by Katherine W. Ellison and John L. Genz: printed subject, author, and title cards, and an electronic display for author. One advantage of using the computerized catalog, besides ease and speed of search, is that the displayed items may provide circulation information: You can see whether the book is on the shelf or checked out, and if so, when it is due back.

The miracle of electronic catalog searching should not blind you to the old-fashioned advantages and pleasures of going into the stacks and browsing along the shelves in your area of interest. Browsing is not an efficient or comprehensive substitute for catalog searching (some important books may be checked out; others may be shelved in another area). But pulling out promising titles and examining the contents may reveal valuable sources that you might otherwise have overlooked.

SUBJECT CARD

```
POLICE—UNITED STATES—JOB STRESS.

HV7936
J63          Ellison, Katherine W.
E4              Stress and the police officer / by
1983         Katherine W. Ellison and John L. Genz.
             —Springfield, Ill., U.S.A. : C.C.
             Thomas, c1983.
                xi, 209 p. : forms ; 24 cm.
                ISBN 0-398-04829-0

                1. Police—United States—Job stress.

   MBNU            NEDDuc                      83-441
```

AUTHOR CARD

```
HV7936
J63          Ellison, Katherine W.
E4               Stress and the police officer / by
1983         Katherine W. Ellison and John L. Genz.
             —Springfield, Ill., U.S.A. : C.C.
             Thomas, c1983.
                 xi, 209 p. : forms ; 24 cm.
                 Bibliography: p. 185-200.
                 Includes indexes.
                 ISBN 0-398-04829-0

                 1. Police—United States—Job stress.
             I. Genz, John L. II. Title

MBNU         11 JUN 85       9217079        NEDDuc        83-441
```

TITLE CARD

```
                              Stress and the police officer
HV7936
J63          Ellison, Katherine W.
E4               Stress and the police officer / by
1983         Katherine W. Ellison and John L. Genz.
             —Springfield, Ill., U.S.A. : C.C.
             Thomas, c1983.
                 xi, 209 p. : forms ; 24 cm.
                 ISBN 0-398-04829-0

                 1. Police—United States—Job stress.

MBNU                          NEDDuc                      83-441
```

AUTHOR CARD—COMPUTER DISPLAY

```
AUTHOR(s):      Ellison, Katherine W.
TITLE(s):       Stress and the police officer / by  Katherine
                    W. Ellison and John L. Genz.

                Springfield, Ill., U.S.A. : C.C. Thomas. c1983.
                xi, 209 p. : forms : 24 cm.
                Includes indexes.
                Bibliography: p. 185-200.

OTHER ENTRIES:  Police United States Job stress. Genz, John L.
LOCN:  SNELL STACKS       STATUS:  Checked out —
CALL #:  HV 7936.J63E4 1983
```

Library of Congress Subject Headings

If you have not narrowed down your subject by the time you begin your catalog search, you should probably check the *Library of Congress Subject Headings.* This is a set of volumes that indicates how the subjects listed according to the Library of Congress System are broken down. For example, drug abuse is broken down into such subtopics as "religious aspects," "social aspects," and "treatment." You can use the *Library of Congress Subject Headings* as you used the encyclopedia entries or the *Bibliographic Index.* First, you can survey the main aspects of that subject. Second, you can select a particular aspect that interests you. Third, you can focus your subject search (in both the book and periodical indexes) on the particular aspect or subtopic that interests you, since these subtopics indicate which headings to look under in these indexes.

Book Review Digest

An invaluable source for determining the quality of books is the *Book Review Digest.* This publication, collected into annual volumes, indexes many of the most important books published during a given year by author, title, and subject. More important, it provides lists of reviews of those books, as well as brief excerpts from some of the reviews. Thus, you can use the *Book Review Digest* to quickly determine not only the scope of a given book (each entry leads off with an objective summary) but also how well that book has been received by reviewers. If the reviews are almost uniformly good, that book will be a good source of information. If they are almost uniformly bad, stay away. If the reviews are mixed, proceed with caution.

Trade Bibliographies and Bibliographies of Books

For books too recent to have been acquired by your library or that the library does not have, you may wish to consult *Books in Print* and *Paperbound Books in Print.* These volumes, organized by author, title, and subject, are available in some libraries and in most bookstores. For books that your library does not have, but that may be in other libraries, consult the *Cumulative Book Index* and the *National Union Catalog.*

Conducting Interviews and Surveys

Although you will probably conduct most of your research in the college library, remember that professional researchers do most of their work *outside* the library—in the field, in labs, in courthouses, and in government and private archives. Consider the possibilities of conducting original research for your own paper by interviewing knowledgeable people and devising and sending out questionnaires. Many subjects have been extensively discussed by experts on television news programs, talk shows, and documentaries. It may be possible to borrow videocassettes or to obtain printed transcripts of such programs.

Interviews

Interviews allow you to conduct primary research and to acquire valuable information unavailable in print sources. By recounting the experiences, ideas, and quotations of people who have direct knowledge of a particular subject, you add considerable authority and immediacy to your paper. Those you select to interview may include business people, government officials, doctors, professors, community activists, or your own grandparent. If you would like to talk to a business executive or a government official but do not have a particular individual in mind, call the public relations office (in a business) or the public information office (in a government agency) and ask for the names of possible interviewees. Then, call the individual and try to schedule an appointment. Even busy people can usually find some time to give an interview; many will be glad to talk to someone about their experiences. But if you are turned down, as sometimes happens, try someone else.

A Checklist for Interviews

The following list will assist you in preparing for an interview.

- Determine what kind of information you need from the person, based on the requirements of your paper and its thesis.
- Make an appointment, telling the person what your paper is about and how long the interview will take.
- Become knowledgeable about the subject so that you can ask informed questions. If the person has written a relevant article or book, read it.
- Prepare most of your questions in advance.
- Take pen, pencil, and a hardback notebook to the interview. If you take a tape recorder, ask the person's permission to record the interview. Even if you do record the conversation, take notes on especially important comments.
- At the end of the interview, thank the person for his or her time. Promise to send a copy of the finished paper. Soon afterward, send a follow-up thank you note.

It is important to prepare adequately for your interview. Devise most of your questions in advance; you can improvise with other questions during the interview, according to the turns it takes. Avoid *leading* questions that presume certain conclusions or answers:

> Why do you think that American workers are lazier today than they were a generation ago?
> What do you think of the fact that the present administration wants to burden small businesses with added health-care costs?

Ask *neutral* questions that allow the interviewee to express his or her own observations:

> What changes, if any, have you noticed in the work habits of your present employees from those who worked here in the 1960s?

To what extent has government funding of genetic research changed during the present administration?

Also avoid *dead-end* questions that require yes/no answers or *forced choice* questions that impose a simplistic choice on the interviewee:

Do you think that this was an important experiment? (dead end)
What should take priority, in your view: jobs or the environment? (forced choice)

Instead, ask *open-ended* questions that allow the interviewee to develop her or his thoughts at some length:

In what way was this an important experiment for you?

Throughout the interview show your interest in what your respondent is saying. On the other hand, keep in mind that your own reactions may unintentionally create cues that affect your subject's responses.

Surveys

Surveys are useful when you want to measure behavior or attitudes of a fairly large, identifiable group of people—provided that both the group and the measurements are carefully specified. An identifiable group could be freshmen on your campus, Democrats in town, Asian Americans in a three-block area, or auto workers in two factories; measuring attitudes or behavior could mean obtaining records and comparing the frequency of responses made to specific and carefully worded questions. On the basis of measured comparisons among the responses to questions, a researcher might venture some broad claims about patterns of response as indicators of attitudes or behaviors within the population measured (it is not safe to generalize beyond the group actually measured without rigorous statistical procedures). Such generalizations are usually made in quantitative terms: "Fewer than two-thirds of the respondents said they feel threatened by the possibility of contracting AIDS."

To get honest answers to your questions, it is essential to guarantee your respondents' anonymity. Most frequently, questions and answers to surveys are written, though occasionally they may be oral (as when, for example, you ask students entering the library for their attitudes on mandatory national service). When devising questions for a survey, some of the same considerations apply as for interviews. For example, do not ask *loaded* questions that lead the respondent toward a particular answer ("Do you think that the money the university is spending to upgrade the president's residence would be better spent to reduce class size?"). For surveys, short-answer questions are better than open-ended questions, which are difficult to compare precisely or to quantify. It is relatively easy to quantify yes/no responses or responses on a five-point scale ("How concerned do you feel about the threat of AIDS? 5—extremely concerned; 4—very concerned; 3—moderately concerned; 2—somewhat concerned; 1—unconcerned").

16

Using Sources

Your ability to write a research paper depends on your ability to use sources. And your ability to use sources, the subject of this chapter, depends *entirely* on your ability to read well. Chapters 1 and 4 of this text are devoted to reading sources with care and to advancing an essay's idea with sources. Refer to those discussions, in tandem with the discussion here, for advice on using sources.

Examining Sources

Classifying Sources: Primary and Secondary

When attempting to determine the value and quality of a source, keep in mind the distinction between *primary* and *secondary* sources. Primary sources are written by people who have *direct* knowledge of the events or issues under discussion: they were participants in or observers of those events. Examples of primary sources are letters, diaries, autobiographies, oral histories, and historical documents. Authors of secondary sources have only *indirect* knowledge; they rely on primary or other secondary sources for their information. Examples of secondary sources include biographies, textbooks, historical surveys, and literary criticism.

For example, the following statements by Premier Nikita Khruschev of the Soviet Union and President John F. Kennedy serve as primary sources on the Cuban missile crisis of 1962:

> It was during my visit to Bulgaria that I had the idea of installing missiles with nuclear warheads in Cuba without letting the United States find out they were there until it was too late to do anything about them. (Khruschev)

This urgent transformation of Cuba into an important strategic base—by the presence of these large, long-range, and clearly offensive weapons of sudden mass destruction—constitutes an explicit threat to the peace and security of all the Americas. (Kennedy)

The following statement by historian Louise FitzSimons, who was not a participant in the crisis, is a secondary source:

> President Kennedy was moved to act because of his history of preoccupation with Cuba as an issue; because he feared that his prestige would suffer, that Khruschev would think him weak; because he permitted vestiges of cold war thinking to freeze his policy and prevent any flexibility in dealing with the Soviet Union; and because of his fear that the American public would respond to the missiles by removing his party or even himself from office.

A single source may be used either as a primary or as a secondary source, depending on what is being studied. A written piece that reacts to or interprets some previous event is a secondary source for anyone studying the original event or situation; however, for anyone studying typical ways of reacting to or thinking about that event, the same piece could be primary material. An editorial written during the Cuban missile crisis would be a secondary source for students seeking information on Soviet response to American actions, but it could be a primary source for students of contemporary popular reactions, images, or interpretations of the crisis.

Primary sources are not necessarily superior (or inferior) to secondary sources, but it is good to recognize the strengths and limitations of each. Primary sources provide facts and viewpoints that are generally not available from other sources; they often have immediacy and drama. On the other hand, primary sources may be colored by the bias of authors who want to inflate their own importance, justify questionable decisions, or willfully misrepresent the facts.

Authors of secondary sources, by contrast, often have the opportunity to write from a different and broader perspective on the original events, to use hindsight and more varied information, or to be less affected by intense passions than those who experienced the original events. In spite of those opportunities, authors of secondary sources can always be biased by their own agendas or be narrow-minded or unperceptive, while some primary writers close to original events might be quite reliable and unbiased. You will need to make your own determination of the reliability and credibility of every source, whether primary or secondary.

Critically Reading Sources

Consider how the strategies described in chapter 5 for the critical reading of any text might work when applied to potential sources for your research paper. Suppose you are working on a paper on the progress of the Equal Rights Amendment, which was approved by Congress in 1972 but defeated by the deadline of 1982 when it fell three states short of ratification. If your *research question* asked why the amendment was defeated, your *thesis* would provide a summary answer to this question. Your reading would be conducted at four levels or stages:

1. **Reading to understand.** Your main goal during this stage is to familiarize yourself with your sources and to determine their *relevance.*

2. **Reading to respond.** During this stage, your main goal is to read your source carefully enough to *react* and to *ask questions.* Check the credentials of the author and the critical reception of his or her work. Does the author's background or professional affiliation suggest to you the point of view he or she will take? (For example, can you predict the likely viewpoint of an officer of the National Rifle Association on handgun control?) Identify the author's stance on the subject: Is she or he pro, con, or neutral? Relatively detached or passionately involved (or something in-between)? Is the tone angry, cynical, witty, solemn, or earnest? Does the author have a personal stake in the issue under discussion? If so, how might this affect your acceptance of her or his arguments?

Highlight important questions, particularly those most directly relevant to your research question; make marginal notations; take notes; look for important quotations you may be able to use in your paper.

Finally, be alert to *differences* between sources: for example, what Ann Scott (an official of the National Organization for Women) said of the ERA, and what Phyllis Schlafly (head of the conservative Eagle Forum) said about it. After critical reading and additional research, you will probably want to discuss such differences.

3. **Reading to evaluate.** During this stage, your goals are to determine the *reliability* of your sources. This involves attempting to separate fact from opinion in the source; identifying and assessing the author's assumptions; and evaluating both the evidence offered by the author in support of his or her argument and the logic by which the conclusions are reached.

Reading to evaluate also involves considering the source of publication for an article or book. Was the article published in a popular magazine (intended for a general audience) or an academic or professional journal (intended for a specialized audience)? Articles in journals will probably be more difficult to read, but will tend to have more authority and credibility. Was the book or pamphlet published by a commercial or academic publisher, or by a publisher with a special interest?

4. **Reading to synthesize.** During this stage, your main goal is to determine how the evidence from one source is related to evidence from other sources. You must compare what you find in your sources, evaluate the information and assumptions in each, and form your own ideas about the most important relationships among them.

Creating a Working Bibliography

Your **working bibliography** is a list of all of the sources you locate in preparing your paper. This includes books, articles, entries from biographical sources, handbooks, almanacs, and the various other kinds of sources cited in chapter 15. The bibliography should also include sources you locate in indexes that you intend to check later. Your working bibliography differs from your **final bibliography** in that it is more comprehensive: The final bibliography consists only of those sources that you actually use in writing the paper.

It is absolutely essential that you prepare your working bibliography *at the same time* that you are compiling and consulting your sources. That way you can be sure to have accurate and complete information when the time comes to return to your sources to obtain more information or to double-check information, and to compile your final bibliography.

I recommend that you compile a working bibliography on 3" × 5" index cards. A card file allows you to easily alphabetize entries or to arrange them in any other order (such as by topic and subtopic order, or by sources you have already examined and ones you have not) that is most useful to you during the research and writing process. As you consult each new source, carefully record key information:

1. full name of author (last name first)
2. title (and subtitle)
3. publication information:
   a. place of publication
   b. name of publisher
   c. date of publication
4. inclusive page numbers

In case you have to relocate the source later, indicate the library call number (in the upper right-hand corner) and the name and date of the index where you located the source (at the bottom). It is also a good idea to include (either below the publication information or on the back of the card) a brief annotation, in which you describe the contents of that source or the author's main idea, and indicate your reaction to the source and how you might use it in your paper. Finally, you should assign a code number to each bibliographic entry. Then, when you are taking notes on the source (perhaps on 4" × 6" note cards), you can simply put that code number in the upper right-hand corner of the note card, which saves you from having to recopy your complete bibliographic information.

When the time comes to prepare your final bibliography, you can simply arrange the cards for the sources you used in alphabetical order and type up the pertinent information as a list. Here's a sample bibliography card for a book:

> (4)   Ellison, Katherine W., and John L. Genz.
>   *Stress and the Police Officer.* Springfield, IL: HV 7936
>   Charles C. Thomas, 1983.   J63 E4
>   1983
>
> *Discusses what stress is, how to recognize it, how it relates specifically to police, and techniques to combat it both by an individual and within an organization.*

Here's a sample card for an article:

> (18)   *Lord, Vivian B., Denis O. Gray, and Samuel*   *HV6000*
> *B. Pond, III "The Police Stress Inventory: Does*
> *It Measure Stress?" Journal of Criminal Justice*
> *19 (1991): 139–149.*
>
> *Evaluates Police Stress Inventory test and other measurements of police to*
> *determine whether empirical evidence supports claims of high job stress. Finds*
> *that job satisfaction is most important in controlling levels of stress and that*
> *PSI and other such tests must be prepared and administered more carefully*
> *so they can contribute fairly to policy decisions.*

Taking Notes

Use 4" × 6" cards for taking notes. You could use other materials, of course, but you will have difficulty sorting through and rearranging individual entries. Notecards solve this problem and allow you to add or drop entries with ease.

Researchers use various formats for notecards, but the following elements are most important:

1. a *code number* (corresponding to the code number on your bibliography card) or the bibliographic reference;
2. a *topic* or *subtopic* label (these enable you to easily arrange and rearrange the cards in topical order);
3. the *note* itself;
4. a *page reference*.

Do not attempt to include too much information on a single notecard. For example, do not summarize an entire article or chapter on one card, particularly if you are likely to use information from a single card in different places in your paper. By limiting each card to a single point or illustration, you make it easier to arrange your cards according to your outline, and to rearrange them later if your outline changes. A sample notecard follows for *Stress and the Police Officer*. For comparison, it is placed directly after the bibliography card for the same source.

> (4)   *Ellison, Katherine W., and John L. Genz.*   *HV 7936*
> *Stress and the Police Officer. Springfield, IL:*   *J63 E4*
> *Charles C. Thomas, 1983.*   *1983*
>
> *Discusses what stress is, how to recognize it, how it relates specifically to*
> *police, and techniques to combat it both by an individual and within an orga-*
> *nization.*

Stress Definition

Researchers tend to mean three things when they talk about stress:

(1) things that happen outside of a person (p. 4)

(2) things inside a person (various emotions) (p. 4)

(3) "observable response to an external (or internal) stimulus or situation" (p. 5)

When to Summarize, Paraphrase, or Quote a Source

There are three methods of notetaking: *summarizing, paraphrasing,* and *quoting.* These methods can be used singly or in combination. *Summarizing* is used when there is a relatively long passage of text from which you need to extract one or two main points; these points would probably be used as background information for your own paper. *Paraphrasing* is used with a relatively brief passage of important material that is central to your discussion or argument. *Quoting* is used if the person being quoted has made a point in a particularly dramatic or incisive way, or if the reputation of this person would enhance the credibility of your presentation. The preceding notecard on stress used a combination of quotation and summary.

The basic situations suited to each method are:

Summarize

- to present the main points from a relatively long passage
- to condense information essential to your discussion

Paraphrase

- to clarify complex ideas in a short passage
- to clarify difficult language in a short passage

Quote

- when the language of the source is particularly important or effective
- when you want to enhance your credibility by drawing on the words of an authority on the subject

To illustrate how each of these methods of notetaking would show up in the final paper, we will use as an example one section of a chapter entitled "Police Officers Must Make Snap Decisions" in Robert Coulson's book, *Police Under Pressure: Resolving Disputes,* 1991, p. 21:

Judgment in the Use of Weapons

Cops carry guns, and department rules are intended to insure that these weapons are not abused. For example, police officers in New Jersey are not allowed to fire weapons unless their life is being threatened. In one case, several New Jersey cops shot up a car that had been borrowed by some teenagers. They were disciplined, correctly so.

From time to time, these sorts of incidents are publicized, and the subject of police brutality gains media attention. For example, the heavily publicized Rodney King incident in Los Angeles in 1991 attracted nationwide attention, and, when the police officers were acquitted, set off violent riots there and elsewhere around the country.

An officer who ends up injuring someone by accident may be accused of using excessive force, and a complaint filed by the injured person may result in a disciplinary hearing, and, ultimately, a hearing before an arbitrator.

Cops have to be allowed to protect themselves, and they must be able to control their prisoners, but they should not abuse their authority. Police officers are not above the law.

It can be difficult for a police officer to judge how much force is necessary to make an arrest, and at times, an officer has to subdue a dangerous person. Society expects officers to use appropriate force, but how much force is appropriate?

Here is how the information in that passage might turn up in the final paper. Brackets indicate those sections summarized, paraphrased, and quoted from the original.

Summary — There are rules that control when an officer uses her/his gun, and officers should be corrected or punished when they use a gun improperly. Whenever an officer uses force there is a chance of claims of excessive force as in the Rodney King case and there are procedures to be followed.

Paraphrase — The purpose of the gun is to protect innocent parties and to control trouble-makers, but police must not use the gun to become trouble-makers.

Quote — "Society expects officers to use appropriate force, but how much force is appropriate?"

Summarizing Sources

A *summary* is a relatively brief, objective account, in your own words, of the main ideas in a source passage. As mentioned previously, you would summarize a passage when you wanted to extract the main ideas and use them as background material in your own paper. For details on the process of writing summaries, see pages 85–87.

Suppose you were preparing this paper dealing with stress management. You have already looked up material in several criminal justice indexes and in some medical reference books, but you decide you need a brief survey of the history of stress-management programs and look for various points of view about such programs. You shift your research efforts to the behavioral science area and locate a book titled *Stress: The Nature and History of Engineered Grief* by Robert Kugelmann (Westport, CT: Praeger, 1992). You locate the following section titled "The Monster in the Shadow of Stress Management."

The Monster in the Shadow of Stress Management

Stress management intends a good end—the easing of human suffering and pain, and it has not been without success. Yet trailing the good intentions, like a shadow, is a sinister presence that undoes the good and compounds the suffering by miring us deeper in stress. Stress management attempts to construct a rational, powerful, creative, calm being whose body is an animated corpse. For this being, suffering, grief, illness, and even death are not inevitable. The changes to which it adapts include medical advances that sustain its life for an increasing time and creature comforts that eliminate physical work and the discomforts of nature. The price that this being pays for these benefits, however, is enormous: a craving to become the very source of energy that preserves the formless, abstract, bodiless realm of stress. It entails, most fundamentally, not living through the work of grief, never resolving the conflict of grief, but accepting an endless series of hammer blows of loss as the condition for receiving the benefits of stress. When we adopt the metaphor of stress to describe our sufferings and to manage our lives, we become monstrous beings who feed on our own suffering and that of others.

Here is a sample summary from this source.

While the intentions of stress management are good and it can work, there is a dark underside since it can create a being who is only the shell of a human. The external comfort is paid for by internal, emotional emptiness. When a person recognizes she/he is under stress, management encourages the person to gain energy by dealing with the stress itself, rather than with the sources of stress.

Paraphrasing Sources

A *paraphrase* is a restatement, in your own words, of a passage of text. Its structure reflects the structure of the source passage. Paraphrases are sometimes the same length as the source passage, sometimes shorter. In certain cases—particularly if the source passage is written in densely constructed or jargon-laden prose—the paraphrase may be even longer than the original. You would paraphrase a passage when you want to preserve all of the points in the original, both major and minor, and when—perhaps for the sake of clarity—you want to communicate the ideas in your own words. Keep in mind that only an *occasional* word (but not whole phrases) from the original source appears in the paraphrase, and that a paraphrase's sentence structure does not reflect that of the source. The following is a paraphrase of the previous passage from "The Monster in the Shadow of Stress Management":

Stress management tries to help people live better lives and sometimes it works. But it has another side that in the long run is worse because it causes more stress. Stress management teaches people to accept problems and difficult times and to cope with the stress they produce. Even when dealing with sadness or grief from whatever cause, a person emphasizes the stress caused, not the events or the emotions themselves. People learn to "deal" with all of these painful parts of life, to stay rational in the face of events that *aren't* rational. Stress management tells them not to fight it, but to take the punches and convert them to energy. People learn to call negative events *stress* rather than what they truly are, and so to deal with them only as stress. We use the unhappiness of our lives as fuel.

Quoting Sources

You may decide to quote from a passage when the author's language is particularly well chosen, lively, dramatic, or incisive, and when you think you could not possibly express the same idea so effectively. Or you may decide to quote when you want to bolster the credibility of your argument with the reputation of your source. By the same token, you may occasionally decide to discredit an idea by quoting a discredited or notorious source.

Avoiding Overquoting

Knowing how much to quote is an art in itself. If you underquote, your paper may come across as dry and secondhand. If you overquote, your paper may come across as an anthology of other people's statements ("a scissors-and-paste job"), rather than an original work. Some professors have developed rules of thumb on quoting. One such rule is that for a ten-page paper, there should be no more than two extended quotations (i.e., indented quotations of more than 100 words); and each page should contain no more than two short quotations. If this rule of thumb makes sense to you (or your professor), adopt it; otherwise, modify it to the extent you think reasonable.

How to Quote

Suppose you are working on a paper on the relationship between stress and absenteeism or other business costs. Here are several paragraphs from an article entitled "Employers Recognizing What Stress Costs Them, U.N. Report Suggests," by Frank Swoboda, that appeared in the *Washington Post* on March 28, 1993:

> In the United States alone, the ILO estimates job stress costs employers approximately $200 billion a year in absenteeism, lower productivity, rising health insurance costs and other medical expenses.
>
> And in Great Britain the agency estimates the annual cost may be equal to 10 percent of that nation's economic output.
>
> Absenteeism, high turnover, increased on-the-job accidents and "burnout" are all products of job stress, according to the ILO report. One consequence in the United States, the report said, may be reflected in the large increase in worker compensation claims.
>
> In 1980, the report said, stress-related claims amounted to 50 percent of all worker compensation claims. By the end of the decade, stress claims amounted to 15 percent of all worker compensation claims.

> In California, which has become the cradle of trends in the United States in recent years, stress-related worker compensation claims increased sevenfold during the 1980s.
>
> Perhaps more important, the ILO said, 90 percent of the legal claims in that state were successful.

The following note contains one useful quotation.

Increasing Employer Costs

"In 1980, the report said, stress-related claims amounted to 5 percent of all worker compensation claims. By the end of the decade, stress claims amounted to 15 percent of all worker compensation claims." (p. H2)

Another note might include another useful quotation.

"In California, . . . stress-related worker compensation claims increased sevenfold during the 1980s." (p. H2)

Sometimes you may wish to quote a passage that has itself been quoted by your source author. For example, in researching the rising costs of stress on the job, you locate an interesting Associated Press piece that discusses rising stress at work. Entitled "Odd Jobs," it accompanies the article referred to above. Here are some paragraphs that might be helpful to your discussion.

> The factory workweek grew by 24 minutes in the last five months and by 12 minutes in February alone. The [Bureau of Labor Statistics] does not measure overtime hours in the non-factory work force but does estimate that the workweek is expanding in many fields.
>
> "If we could go back to the amount of overtime worked in 1982, we would create 3 million new jobs without increasing the federal deficit," said John Zalusky, an economist at the AFL-CIO. He said many workers are putting in extra hours for extra pay against their wishes.

If you are interested in what the expert says, but not so interested in the reporter's words, you might create a notecard that looks like this:

Increasing Job Stress

Calculation of John Zalusky, AFL-CIO economist:
"If we could go back to the amount of overtime worked in 1982, we would create 3 million new jobs without increasing the federal deficit."

Note that these are the *exact* words from the original. The student has added nothing, omitted nothing, and changed nothing.

Using Brackets and Ellipses in Quotations

Sometimes for the sake of clarity, conciseness, or smoothness of sentence structure, you will need to make additions, omissions, or changes to quotations. For example, suppose you wanted to quote a passage beginning with the following sentence: "In 1979, one week after receiving a 13.3% pay raise, she was called on the carpet." To clarify the pronoun *she*, you would need to replace it with the name of the person in question enclosed in a pair of brackets: "In 1979, one week after receiving a 13.3% pay raise, [Virginia Rulon-Miller] was called on the carpet."

Suppose you also decided that the 13.3% pay raise was irrelevant for your purpose in quoting the material. You could omit this phrase, and indicate the omission by means of an *ellipsis*—three spaced dots: "In 1979 ... [Virginia Rulon-Miller] was called on the carpet." Note that when using brackets, you do not need to use the ellipsis to indicate that the pronoun (*she*) has been omitted; brackets surrounding proper nouns imply that one word (or set of words) has replaced another.

Sometimes you need to change a capital letter to a lowercase one in order to smoothly integrate the quotation into your own sentence. For example, suppose you want to quote the following sentence: "Privacy today matters to employees at all levels, from shop-floor workers to presidents." You could smoothly integrate this quotation into your own sentence by altering the capitalization, as follows.

> The new reality, as John Hoerr points out, is that "[p]rivacy today matters to employees at all levels, from shop-floor workers to presidents."

Smoothly Integrating Quotations into Your Text

Whether or not you alter quotations by means of ellipses or brackets, you should strive to smoothly integrate them into your own text. Suppose, for example, you decide to use the following sentences from *Stress: The Nature and History of Engineered Grief* by Robert Kugelmann.

> In the United States, the Vietnam War has come to symbolize stress in its pure form. With that war stress came to imply a trauma so intense that psychologists surrendered their once rock-solid belief in childhood experience as the primary cause of psychopathological symptoms (Praeger Press, 1992).

You could integrate this quotation in any of several ways.

1. Kugelmann points to the Vietnam War as the event that taught us to think of stress "in its pure form" as traumatic (25).
2. Scientists once had a "rock-solid belief" that psychopathology originated in childhood, but the Vietnam War showed that it could come from stress (Kugelmann 25).
3. According to Kugelmann, stress can produce "psychopathological symptoms" in adults who might have had normal childhoods (25).
4. Kugelmann argues that the Vietnam War taught us that stress is not just trauma, but "intense" trauma that can lead to "psychopathological symptoms" (25).
5. Kugelmann puts it bluntly: "[T]he Vietnam War has come to symbolize stress in its pure form" (25).

Using Attributive Phrases with Quotations

Note that single, quoted sentences should never stand by themselves, without an attributive phrase like "According to Kugelmann, ..." For example, you would not write:

Kugelmann sees the Vietnam War as a milestone in our understanding of stress. "With that war stress came to imply a trauma so intense that psychologists surrendered their once rock-solid belief in childhood experience as the primary cause of psychopathological symptoms" (25).

Even though it ends with a citation, the quotation needs to be integrated with the previous material. You could do this by substituting a *colon* for the period after "our understanding of stress," or by inserting a phrase like "As he points out," before the quotation.

Phrases that help you attribute quotations use present-tense verbs. To vary attributive phrases, you might consider verbs such as these:

adds	denies	rejects
agrees	derides	relates
argues	disagrees	reports
asks	disputes	responds
asserts	emphasizes	reveals
believes	explains	says
claims	finds	sees
comments	holds	shows
compares	illustrates	speculates
concedes	implies	states
concludes	insists	suggests
condemns	maintains	thinks
considers	notes	warns
contends	observes	writes
declares	points out	
defends	refuses	

Again, note that all of the attributive verbs in the box are in the *present* tense. Even though your source has already been written (and so technically, the author has already declar*ed* or stat*ed* or conclud*ed*), when quoting sources you should use the present tense (declares, states, concludes). This applies even if you are discussing a literary work; thus you would say that Hamlet ponders: "To be or not to be. . . ." The only exception to the use of the present tense would be if you were reporting the historical progress of some development or debate and you wished to emphasize that certain things were said at a particular point in time. ("The Senator assert*ed*: 'I do not intend to dignify these scurrilous charges by responding to them.' ")

Block quotations.   You should integrate most quotations into your own text, using quotation marks. If a quotation runs longer than four lines, however, you should set it apart from the text by indenting it ten spaces from the left margin. Quotation marks are not required around block quotations. Block quotations should be double spaced, like the rest of the text.

Eliminating Plagiarism

Plagiarism is an unpleasant subject, but one that must be confronted in any discussion of research papers. In its most blatant form, **plagiarism** is an act of conscious deception: an attempt to pass off the ideas or the words of another as your own. To take an extreme example, a student who buys a research paper from a commercial "paper mill" and turns it in for academic credit is guilty of the worst kind of plagiarism. Only slightly less guilty is the student who copies into his paper passages of text from his sources without giving credit or using quotation marks.

The penalties for plagiarism can be severe—including a failing grade in the course or even a suspension from school. Graduate students guilty of plagiarism have been dropped from advanced degree programs. Even professionals no longer in school can see their reputations damaged or destroyed by charges of plagiarism. During the 1988 presidential campaign, a Democratic candidate was forced to drop out of the race when it was revealed that some of the material in his campaign speeches was copied from a speech by a prominent British politician.

Much plagiarism is unintentional. Students may not intend to pass off as their own the work of others; but either through ignorance of the conventions of quotation, attribution, and citation, or simply through carelessness, they may fail to distinguish adequately between their own ideas and words and those of their sources.

Here are two general rules to help you avoid unintentional plagiarism:

1. Whenever you *quote* the exact words of others, place these words within quotation marks and properly cite the source.
2. Whenever you *paraphrase* or *summarize* the ideas of others, do not use whole phrases, or many of the same words, or sentence structures similar to the original. You must identify the source of the paraphrased or summarized material: do not assume that you are under no obligation to credit your source if you simply change the wording of the original statement or alter the sentence structure.

Determining What Is Common Knowledge

The only exception to the second rule just stated is if the information summarized or paraphrased is considered common knowledge. For example, you need not cite the source of the information that General Lee commanded the Confederate forces during the Civil War, or the fact that Mars is the fourth planet from the sun, or the fact that Ernest Hemingway wrote *The Sun Also Rises.* If, on the other hand, you are summarizing one particular theory of why Lee's forces faced almost certain defeat, or the geological composition of the Martian surface, or how the critical assessment of Hemingway's *The Sun Also Rises* has shifted over the years, then you are obliged to cite the sources of your information or ideas, whether or not you quote them directly.

Admittedly, it is not always easy for a nonspecialist to determine whether a particular fact or idea is considered common knowledge. The course of Hemingway's shifting reputation is common knowledge among American literature professors, though not among most freshmen (or physics professors). And even the fact that Hemingway wrote *The Sun Also Rises* (or when it was first published) is unlikely to be common knowledge to the general population. It might be helpful to ask yourself whether the average, college-educated person is likely to be familiar with this particular fact or idea, or whether it would be readily available in any number of easily accessible sources, such as a textbook or a one-volume encyclopedia. If the same fact is available in several sources, it is probably common knowledge. As you progress in your research, and later in your major field, you will gradually learn what is considered common knowledge in a subject area and what is not. In the meantime, if you are unsure about the status of a particular idea or fact, the safest course is to cite it.

Identifying Blatant Plagiarism of a Source

The sample passage below will illustrate what can happen when source ideas undergo several possible levels of intentional or unintentional plagiarism in the student examples that follow. The passage is from Steven F. Bloom's "Empty Bottles, Empty Dreams: O'Neill's Use of Drinking and Alcoholism in *Long Day's Journey into Night*," which appears in *Critical Essays on Eugene O'Neill*, edited by James J. Martine (Boston: G.K. Hall, 1984):

> In *Long Day's Journey into Night*, O'Neill captures his vision of the human condition in the figure of the alcoholic who is constantly and repeatedly faced with the disappointment of his hopes to escape or transcend present reality. As the effects of heavy drinking and alcoholism increase, the alcoholic, in his attempt to attain euphoric forgetfulness, is repeatedly confronted with the painful realities of dissipation, despondency, self-destruction, and ultimately, death. This is the life of an alcoholic, and for O'Neill, this is the life of modern man.

Here is a plagiarized student version of this passage:

> *Long Day's Journey into Night* shows O'Neill's vision of the human condition in the figure of the alcoholic who is constantly faced with the disappointment of his hopes to escape. As the effects of heavy drinking and alcoholism increase, the alcoholic, in his attempt to attain forgetfulness, is repeatedly confronted with the painful realities of dissipation, self-destruction, and, ultimately, death. This is the life of an alcoholic, and for O'Neill, this is the life of modern man.

This is the most blatant form that plagiarism can take. The student has copied the passage almost word for word and has made no attempt to identify the source of either the words or the ideas. Even if the author *were* credited, the student's failure to use quotation marks around quoted material would render this version unacceptable.

Avoiding Unintentional Plagiarism of a Source

Here is another version of the same passage.

> The figure of the disappointed alcoholic who hopes to escape reality represents the human condition in *Long Day's Journey into Night*. Trying to forget his problems, the alcoholic, while drinking more and more, is confronted with the realities of his self-destructive condition, and, ultimately, with death. For Eugene O'Neill, the life of the alcoholic represents the life of modern man.

In this version, the writer has attempted (for the most part) to put the ideas in his own words; but the result still so closely resembles the original in sentence structure, in the sequence of ideas, and in the use of key phrases ("confronted with the realities") that it is also unacceptable. Note that this would hold true even if the author *were* credited; that is, had the first sentence begun, "According to Steven F. Bloom, . . ." The student may not have intended to plagiarize—he may, in fact, believe this to be an acceptable rendition—but it would still be considered plagiarism.

Making Legitimate Use of a Source

Here is another version:

> According to Steven F. Bloom, alcoholism in *Long Day's Journey into Night* is a metaphor for the human condition. The alcoholic drinks to forget his disappointments and to escape reality, but the more he drinks, the more he is faced with his own mortality. "This is the life of an alcoholic," asserts Bloom, "and for O'Neill, this is the life of modern man" (177).

This version is entirely acceptable because the student has carefully attributed both the paraphrased idea (in the first part of the passage) and the quotation (in the second part) to the source author, Steven Bloom. The student has also taken special care to phrase the idea in her own language.

It is crucial that you give your readers no cause to believe that you are guilty either of intentional or unintentional plagiarism. When you are summarizing or paraphrasing a particular passage, you must do more than change a few words. You must fully and accurately cite your source, by means of parenthetical citations or by means of attributive phrases, such as "According to Bloom, . . ."

Quoting Accurately

When you do quote material directly, be certain that you quote it accurately. For example, consider a student quotation of the preceding passage (which follows the student's introduction).

> *Long Day's Journey into Night* is O'Neill's "vision of the human condition," according to Steven F. Bloom:
>> As the effects of his heavy drinking and alcoholism increase, the alcoholic, attempting to achieve forgetfulness, is repeatedly confronted with

all the painful realities of dissipation, self-destruction, and death. This is the life of an alcoholic for O'Neill and it is also the life of modern man.

At first glance, this quotation may seem to be accurate. But it is not. The student has *omitted* some words that were in the source passage (in the first sentence, "euphoric" and "despondency"; in the second sentence, "and"); has *changed* other words (in the first sentence, "attempting to achieve," instead of "in his attempt to attain"; in the second, "it," instead of "this"); has *added* some words that were not in the original (in the first sentence, "all"; in the second sentence, "also"); and has also omitted punctuation (in the second sentence, the comma after "O'Neill").

These changes may seem trivial and may not seem to essentially change the meaning of the passage, but once you place a passage within quotation marks, you are obligated to copy it *exactly.* Deleted material should be indicated by an ellipsis (. . .); your own insertions should be indicated by brackets ([ ]). Otherwise, the material within your quotation marks must be word for word, punctuation mark for punctuation mark, *identical* to the original.

CHAPTER

17

A Research Paper

As you complete your research and prepare to write a paper, you probably will have more information than you can possibly absorb. How will you get from those stacks of 4″ × 6″ notecards to a finished paper?

Evolving a Writing Plan from a Research Thesis

To help show the stages of writing a research paper, we will assume that your reading has prompted you to attempt a preliminary working thesis, perhaps for a social science course:

There are many good programs all over the country that deal with police stress, though most officers don't have access to them.

As you progress in your notetaking, perhaps you discover studies showing that employees in a wide range of professions experience as much or more stress than do police officers. Such a discovery would encourage you to consider whether all the attention paid to police stress is really warranted. Or suppose you decide to focus on those programs set up to help officers deal with traumatic incidents (you can deal with the standard programs in one or two paragraphs in the introduction), and then discover that there isn't really much help available and officers rarely seek it anyway. You could consequently adjust your thesis to read as follows:

Good programs to help police officers deal with traumatic events must be expanded, and police officers must be required to use them in order to assure that the incident and its accompanying stress are dealt with effectively.

Or consider the working thesis of a student taking a science course: "Police stress programs must deal with the physiological effects common in male and female officers since the problems range from daily irritations to terminal illness." Suppose that several readings on the physiological effects of stress convince you that women experience some of the same effects as men, but also several different ones that are usually left out of stress-management programs focused primarily on male officers. You would want to adjust your thesis accordingly.

After you have considered how your sources can help establish common ground with readers (chapter 3) and how they can help you advance your main idea (chapter 4), you need to organize your sources. Your main task is to review the notes you have taken and to consolidate them into categories that will help you to refine your thesis and support it. If you have been conscientiously applying headings to each of your notecards, your task will be considerably easier. Stack the cards into piles according to their headings. For example, you may have devised this heading: "Psychological Effects—Men," referring to all cards that summarize, paraphrase, or quote material that provides information only on psychological effects of stress in men. You may have another heading, "Ineffective Programs," to collect examples of programs that don't work and look for reasons why they don't work.

If you have not already written headings on your cards, write them as you review your notes. There are two ways to do this. Either you can draft a provisional outline and then write the appropriate headings and subheadings on the notecards, or you can write headings on the individual cards and then draft an outline based on groupings of cards.

Outlines and sketches for a paper come in all shapes and sizes (see chapter 12). Informal outlines generally have only two levels: one level for topics and another for subtopics. For example:

Police Stress Programs
 —organizational
 —individual
 —family

Formal outlines have several levels. The most common type employs a combination of Roman and Arabic numerals and letters.

   I. Major topic: *Police Stress Programs*
      A. Subtopic: *Police organizational programs*
         1. Minor subtopic: *Content of the programs*
            a. sub-subtopic (or illustration)
               (a) illustration, example, explanation
               (b) illustration, example, explanation
         2. Minor subtopic: *Purposes—to restore morale*
      B. Subtopic: *Police programs for individuals and families*
  II. Major topic: *Response to stress programs*

For more information on how to write outlines and to generate a working plan from a thesis, see chapter 4, "Advancing Your Idea with Sources." For a discussion on how to work from outlines as you write a first draft, see chapter 12.

Conveying Your Ideas through Sources

To avoid overreliance on sources, as well as to clarify the main lines of a paper's argument, some researchers write their first draft referring only to their outlines—and not to their notecards. As they write, they note the places where source material (in summarized, paraphrased, or quoted form) will later be inserted. Drafts written in such a manner are simply scaffolds, of course. But by examining the scaffold, you can easily see whether your logic stands up. Does the argument make sense to you? Does one part logically follow from another? It should, even without the material on your notecards. The evidence, after all, is for your readers' benefit, not yours.

At some point in the drafting process, however, you will need to turn to your notecards. Arrange them in the order in which you intend to use them; but do not simply transcribe your notes onto your rough draft. Keep your mind on your purpose and on your audience: tell them—as if you were in conversation with them—what they should know about the subject and why you believe as you do.

To avoid having to transcribe lengthy quotations from the notecards onto your draft, you may want to consider taping or stapling these notecards (or photocopies of the quotations) directly onto the appropriate spots on the draft. When you do incorporate your quotations, summaries, and paraphrases, remember to transfer your bibliographic codes and page numbers as well, so that later you can enter the correct citations.

When you begin to revise your paper, get as much feedback as possible from others (see chapter 14 for more on peer editing and peer review). It is difficult even for professional writers to get perspective on what they have written immediately after they have written it. You are likely to be too close to the subject, too committed to your outline or to the particular words you have written, to be very objective at this point. Show your draft to a friend or classmate whose judgment you trust and to your instructor. Obtain reactions on everything from the essay as a whole to the details of word choice.

Determining Your Voice

As an author, how do you want to come across to your readers? As an authority, lecturing to the uninitiated? As an old friend, casually discussing your observations on a subject? As serious? cynical? excited? warm? distant? The option you select determines the *voice* as well as the *tone* and *register* that comes across in the paper.

Consider, for example, the voice of the following passage written by Theresa Martelli, L. K. Waters, and Josephine Martelli for an article that appeared in *Psychological Reports* (1989) *64*, 267–273.

> Early research, although not empirically based, has allowed for some insight into the nature of law enforcement work and has been useful in the identification of facts associated with stress among police. Symonds

(1970) posited one of the first useful and parsimonious models of sources of stress in police work. The first category reflected the nature of police work. Stressors that represented this category included exposure to danger, facing the unknown, unpredictable situations, and confronting hostility. A second category of stress reflected the nature of the police organization. These stressors stem from the structure of police organizations and include such stressors as rules, regulations, disagreeable job assignments, and limited promotional opportunities.

The voice of this passage is serious, somewhat dry, impersonal, and scientific. The authors make little attempt to engage their readers and certainly none to entertain them. But these are social scientists speaking to psychology professionals who need to know what causes stress in police officers. Though it may be dry, the writing in this passage is to the point.

Now consider the following passage, by Teresa Watanabe, which appeared in the *Los Angeles Times* on January 14, 1992 (H6).

Sakae Iwata was just 23 years old when she suddenly died of an acute asthma attack triggered, her parents say, by extreme overwork as a window clerk in the securities division of a major bank. As overtime demands intensified in October, 1988, keeping her at work until 10 every night, Iwata lost weight, had increasing trouble breathing, complained that stress was going to kill her.

The difference in voice between the two passages could hardly be greater. Watanabe is personal, ironic, and appeals to us as a storyteller; she also sets out to shock us rather than merely present information. Clearly the purpose of each piece is different, though each addresses an audience interested in the issue of job stress and how much is too much. Each author, however, chose a voice suitable for her own audience.

Using Documentation to Give Credit and Assist Readers

Why go to the trouble to document your sources? Perhaps the first reason is to avoid charges of plagiarism. You certainly do not want to give your readers the impression that you are claiming credit for ideas or words that are not yours. The second reason is to allow your readers to gauge the accuracy and reliability of your work. Any research paper will stand or fall according to how well (how resourcefully, perceptively, accurately, or selectively) you use sources. The third reason turns on the word *credit* itself—that is, you should give credit where it is merited. Your sources have done a great deal of work for you; by acknowledging them, you acknowledge the value of their work. The fourth reason for giving credit is to allow the reader who is interested in a particular point in your paper, or in a particular source that you have employed, to return to the original document.

Placing Documentation
References

Documentation is provided in two places: (1) *in the text,* and (2) *following the text.* With an identifying signal leading to further documentation, the in-text citation provides an exact location for where credit is needed. In the form of a list of references at the end of the text, bibliographic information lets readers pursue sources in more detail.

It is important that *all* information and ideas be documented—not simply the sources that you quote directly. Summaries or paraphrases also require source acknowledgment. The only exception to this rule is that *common knowledge* need not be documented. For the particular documentation form in the discipline areas, see chapter 18.

A Sample Paper: "Better Ways to Deal with Police Stress"

The following research paper demonstrates the process of research and writing discussed in these chapters. The student writer, Janey O'Reilly, chose the topic of "Better Ways to Deal with Police Stress" because, as a Criminal Justice major, she worked over the summer in a police station and was concerned about some of the discussions she heard on the subject of police stress. In talking with some of the officers she had worked with, Janey discovered a "burning question": Are police departments doing enough to combat the effects of stress on police officers? Janey's paper conforms to Modern Language Association (MLA) documentation style.

Better Ways to Deal with Police Stress

by

Janey O'Reilly

English 160, Section 8

Professor Harper

April 3, 1994

Outline

<u>Thesis Statement</u>: In order to maintain a well-trained, well-adjusted and healthy police force, it is vital that post-traumatic stress counseling be made available and mandatory.

I. Definition of stress: It can be both helpful and harmful, and people tend to mean many different things when they use the word.

   A. Typically refers to external events that cause anxiety; internal anxious reaction to external events; or the physical symptoms of anxiety.

   B. Ellison and Genz combine the various levels and suggest dealing with the entire package, especially good when dealing with police.

II. Outline the causes of stress for police officers.

   A. Dr. Bernie Patterson's nine causes, which range from the danger that is part of the job, to organizational and political causes that are changeable.

   B. Pendergrass and Ostrove, Ellison and Genz lists of causes reported by police officers, all relating to the dangers of the job.

   C. Underlying feelings of officers often not considered.

III. Effects of the post-traumatic stress identified above as the primary contributor to officers' feelings of stress.

   A. Little effect on one-third, moderate effect on one-third, severe effect on one-third.

   B. High rates of divorce, alcoholism, and suicide.

   C. Seventy percent of severely affected will resign within seven years.

O'Reilly iii

IV. Overview of the programs or approaches available
to combat high levels of police officer stress:
    A. There are no programs in most departments,
       only in large cities or crime areas.
       Elsewhere, department psychologists are often
       relied on, but they are not necessarily spe-
       cialized, confidential, or mandatory.
    B. Macho attitudes make it difficult to admit
       need for help. Training at the academy, for
       supervisors, and peer counseling can help, but
       don't overcome these prevailing attitudes.
    C. Positive personal coping mechanisms include
       exercise programs, but these are most effec-
       tive for typical, daily stress, not post-trau-
       matic.
    D. Examples of Critical Incident Stress
       Debriefing teams.
       1. Atlanta
       2. New Jersey
V. Conclusion. There is a great deal of stress in
   an officer's life, both from external events and
   from internal reaction to events which, if unat-
   tended to, leads to problems at home, alcoholism,
   divorce, suicide, early retirement, etc.
    A. Individual responses are fine, but insuffi-
       cient.
    B. Debriefing teams are good and need to be
       established everywhere.
       1. Must be mandatory, at least initially.
       2. Must be confidential and distinct from
          departmental personnel.

Janey O'Reilly

Professor Harper

English 160, Section 8

April 3, 1994

Better Ways to Deal with Police Stress

People in many lines of work talk often about   A
stress and its effects on their health and well-being.
Advertisements set up their products as antidotes to
stress, whether the product is flavored tea or coffee,
alcohol or tobacco, a bubble bath, a vacation spot, or
a health club. Health organizations and adult education programs offer classes in how to reduce stress.
So the presence of stress is almost a given in our
society. Many people claim that police officers experience more stress than people in other occupations,
resulting in higher rates of divorce, suicide, and
substance abuse. Though some social scientists challenge the evidence of greater stress (Ellison and
Genz; Lord, Gray and Pond), we can all look at any
number of cases such as the Rodney King beating and
wonder if stress contributed to the actions of those
officers. For the past 20 years or so police stress
has received so much attention that a bibliography on
the subject was compiled in 1990 (Miletich). Discussions have ranged from the special stresses of female
officers in a macho environment or other minorities in
a field previously dominated by white males, to the
effects of strict hierarchy, political maneuvering,
shift work, and on and on. Yet one area that often
receives less attention is post-traumatic stress
intervention, also called critical incident

First-Page Format: This is the first-page format for a paper *without* a cover page. Provide double-spaced information, flush with the left margin, as shown. Skip two lines and center your title. Skip four lines and begin your paper. Number the page, *with* your name in the upper-right corner.

For a paper *with* a cover page, skip two lines between your title and first paragraph. Number the first page at the upper-right corner, *without* a name. Your last name *and* page number appear beginning with page 2.

For a paper *with* a cover page, outlines are optional. Place the outline immediately after the cover page. Number the outline, with your name, in the upper-right corner with lowercase roman numerals, beginning with *i*.

Paragraph A (Textual source of information: Ellison and Genz, p. 40)

A growing body of literature emphasizes the emotional hazards of police work. A government-sponsored bibliography on police stress (Duncan, Brenner, and Kravitz, 1979) lists 133 articles and 33 training films on the subject. A journal has been devoted to it. Somodevilla and his colleagues (1978) have called policing "the most emotionally hazardous job of all," and Hans Selye himself (1978) said that "police work . . . ranks as one of the most hazardous professions, even exceeding the formidable stresses and strains of air traffic control."

While much has been claimed, little has been demonstrated conclusively. The first problem comes in deciding how to measure the relative stressfulness of different jobs.

Paragraph A (Textual source of information: Lord, Gray, and Pond, pp. 139–140)

Although conclusions about the association between law enforcement work and stress seem reasonable, widely accepted empirical support for the prevalence of stress, as well as the effects of stress on law enforcement personnel and organizations and related issues, is difficult to find. A number of studies have supported the high prevalence of stress among law enforcement personnel (Fennell, 1981; Maslach and Jackson, 1981), and some studies have examined its effects (French, 1975; Martin, 1980). However, many investigators question the quality of this research and consequently the conclusions based on it (Bayley and Mendelsohn, 1969; Malloy and Mays, 1984; Niederhoffer and Niederhoffer, 1978; Terry, 1981).

Paragraph A (Paraphrase and common knowledge): The suggestion that "police officers experience more stress than people in other occupations" is not quoted or attributed to any source (though it is available in the two passages listed above) since it is common knowledge and is widely available in a variety of sources. The same is true for the claim of "macho" attitudes in police forces. The references to Ellison and Genz and Lord, Gray, and Pond are paraphrases of longer discussions that form the very basis for each of those works.

stress. Officers who experience trauma on the job
often don't get any counseling because they feel too
"macho" to ask for help, or they worry about confidentiality or the reaction of their peers. In order to
maintain a well-trained, well-adjusted and healthy
police force, it is vital that post-traumatic stress
counseling be made available and mandatory.

What exactly is stress? A standard dictionary   B
(<u>Webster's Unabridged,</u> 2nd ed.) defines stress with
such negative words as <u>strain, pressure, urgency,</u>
<u>tension, distress</u> but also more positive words like
<u>importance, significance.</u> Among authorities in the
field, there is actually some disagreement (Ellison
and Genz 3-5). How social scientists use the word
reflects their approach to dealing with it, and
Ellison and Genz point to three ways that the word
is typically used, to describe: (1) "the event or
situation outside the person"; (2) "the inner state
of the individual" that can only "be inferred from
behavior"; and (3) the "observable response to an
external (or internal) stimulus or situation" (4-5).
Each of these approaches would lead to a different
discussion on what (if anything) needs to be done and
on what level (personal or institutional). Ellison and
Genz seek to combine all these uses in their own definition, worrying less about whether the cause was
external or internal, and more about whether it leads
to "negative consequences" (5). This definition allows
for intervention on as many levels as necessary, but
does not require it when not necessary. As Dufford
points out, sometimes too much attention can be paid
to stress:

Paragraph B (Quotation—attributed and run in with text): Janey wanted to use the many words listed in the dictionary under "stress" but chose to distinguish them with italics rather than quotation marks so that the sentence is more readable. She summarized a longer passage from Ellison and Genz by setting it up as a numbered list and using their exact words. Here is her textual source:

> A first area of disagreement in stress research is over how the term stress should be used (Dohrenwend and Dohrenwend, 1974; van Dijkuizen, 1980). Some researchers use it to mean the event or situation outside the person, such as extremes of temperature, crowding, physical isolation, loud noise, a new job, shift work, a death in the family, or a reprimand from a superior. Others use it for the inner state of the individual, a state that cannot be measured directly but can be inferred from behavior, such as clenched teeth or expressions of distress, or from some other measurable state, such as the level of certain chemicals in the blood. Anxiety, anger, joy, frustration, sadness fit into this category. (Indeed, Cofer and Appley [1964] point out rather irritably that "it has all but preempted a field previously shared by a number of other concepts," [p. 441] including frustration, conflict, and anxiety. They and others seem to feel that such a broad scope so dilutes the meaning of the term as to make it almost meaningless, and certainly makes it virtually impossible to study with any scientific rigor.)
>
> A third common use of the term stress is in referring to an observable response to an external (or internal) stimulus or situation, a response such as sweating palms, pounding heart, yelling and cursing, increased adrenaline flow, and the like. To attempt to clear up some of this confusion, some researchers suggest the use of the terms stressors, or stressful events, for the stimulus and strain for the response.

Paragraph B (Paraphrase and quotation—attributed and run in with text): Janey made a notecard as she read Ellison and Genz and quoted their definition of stress, knowing that she would have to define stress in her paper. In writing her draft, she originally quoted this definition, but decided later that the quotation from their work earlier in her paragraph was sufficient to set up the concept behind their definition. She thus chose to paraphrase their point and avoided excessive quotation by including only "negative consequences" as one phrase that was best left in its original form. Here is her notecard:

---

(4)

"The psychologist Richard Lazarus (1966) points out that while both the environmental stimulus and the reacting individual are vital elements, it is the nature of the interaction--the relationship between the two--that is crucial. He defines stress as 'a very broad class of problems differentiated from other problem areas because it deals with any demands which tax the system, ... and the response of that system.' The present authors find this broad definition the most useful one.

"According to the definition, any demand placed on the person or any event that is experienced by the individual as change (and the individual's definition of the situation is very important) is stressful to some degree; however, not all change, or even all change perceived as harmful, necessarily leads to negative consequences" (p. 5)

O'Reilly 3

Stress has a bad reputation. We are bombarded
with information about stress. There is distress (bad), eustress (good); mild and
extreme stress; big and important or small
and annoying stress. We are instructed how to
cope, avoid, manage, use, tolerate, and
reduce stress. We are stressed being told we
are stressed. (56)

So where does this leave police officers? Anyone
who watches the evening news is familiar with brutal
and senseless murders, rapes, assaults. We see small
children shot by gangs, households torn apart by
domestic violence, and officers dying in the line of
duty. Yet as we sit in our homes watching TV, we may
not really think about the personal effects of circumstances such as these. Dr. Bernie Patterson identified
nine causes of stress: "danger, decision making, personal support from supervisors and employers, technical support such as manpower and equipment, ineffec-
tiveness of the criminal justice system, racial pressures in agencies and communities, political pressures, and pay and work schedules" (qtd. in "Expert").
Pendergrass and Ostrove produced lists of events that
cause stress which, while slightly different for male
and female officers, have the same top three: (1)
"Fellow officer killed in the line of duty" (#1 for
men, #2 for women); (2) "Killing someone in the line
of duty" (#2 for men, #1 for women); and (3) "Exposure
to dead or battered children" (qtd. in Ellison and
Genz 5). There are undoubtedly many things that cause
stress in police officers, but the most stressful are
events that most of the rest of us never have to deal
with. Though this is part of the job, and something

Paragraph B (Janey's voice): While the last section of Janey's paragraph is based on the passage above, her own commentary is critical in tying it into her own discussion; it also provides her own viewpoint. This viewpoint allows Janey to deal with the various types of stress as a whole, rather than forcing her to deal with causes, effects, and solutions to any one kind of stress (internal, external, physical expressions). She thus puts the quote to her own purpose and ensures that her voice, not the voices of her sources, predominates in the paper.

Paragraph B (Block quotation—attributed): The quotation at the end of paragraph B was chosen for the point it makes so effectively. Because of its length, Janey chose to reproduce the whole thing. Notice that it is introduced with a colon and indented; there are no quotation marks needed since it is offset on the text; the page reference comes in parentheses after the ending period.

Paragraph C (Quotations quoted from sources): Janey found some interesting discussions of studies that she had not found in her own research, but which her sources had read and used in their analyses (Dr. Bernie Patterson's study and the one by Pendergrass and Ostrove). Janey chose to quote the quote, and did so by attributing the ideas to the original source and then citing the source from which she borrowed the words and ideas by using "qtd. in" before a standard citation.

Paragraph C (Paraphrase and quotations quoted from sources): Janey also wanted as much information as she could find from police officers. Since the topic wasn't something that many officers she knew wanted to be interviewed about, she relied on newspaper articles on the subject and their quotations of officers. Here are the sources for the references at the end of this paragraph:

> The call came on the night of Nov. 9, 1991. A man with a gun was assaulting a woman in a restaurant parking lot. Officer Rafael Garcia of the Elizabeth Police Department responded, pursuing the man into a parking lot where the man raised his gun in what Officer Garcia believed was a threatening manner.
>
> "That's when I shot him in the chest," the 24-year-old officer recalled recently. "He tried to grab his gun again, and that's when I shot him in the stomach."
>
> The man died four days later at University Hospital in Newark. And Officer Garcia has not got over it.
>
> The night after the shooting, he suffered heart palpitations and cold sweats. For the first eight months, he said, it was all he could think about, his sleeping pattern was disrupted and he had feelings of guilt and depression. "Even now it always comes back," he said. "You think about it on every job you go to, a feeling of knowing it could happen like it did that time." (Dauler)

officers can anticipate ahead of time, they still
often react very strongly to such events. Officer
Rafael Garcia suffered "heart palpitations and cold
sweats" after shooting and killing a man who shot at
him first. For eight months "it was all he could think
about; his sleeping pattern was disrupted, and he had
feelings of guilt and depression" (Dauler). Officer
Dianne Yociss claims that "[t]he public thinks we're
hardened and that everything's a big joke" but that
the falseness of that belief is evidenced by "everything from sleeplessness to sexual dysfunction" (qtd.
in Hagans J5). Retired officers of the New York Police
Department have organizations in several areas of the
country because of the memories that "still haunt
them" (Wong).

   The effects of post-traumatic stress are varied,
and Sewell, et al. estimate that one-third of police
officers involved in a critical incident have "minimal, if any, problems; one-third have moderate problems; and another one-third have severe difficulty"
(96) which affects both the officer and his/her family, and we might logically conclude that it can also
affect people on the force or citizens with whom the
officer comes into contact. According to Joe
Vanderhoff, a retired NYPD patrolman, "It's no secret
that this kind of mental stress can be devastating--
the occupational hazard of just being a cop. . . . Our
kind of job has resulted in one of the highest
divorce, alcoholism and suicide rates of any field"
(qtd. in Wong). The problems for an estimated 70 percent of the severely affected also result in resignation from the department (Sewell et al. 96; Dauler).
Ellison and Genz quote a study showing "a very high

It was only two days before Christmas, but Gwinnett police Officer Sandra Pryor was having a hard time feeling festive.

There was little holiday spirit in the home of the family she tried to console after their newborn baby died in its crib of sudden infant death syndrome.

Although the public often buys into what psychologists call the "superman syndrome," police officers, firefighters, and paramedics have feelings, too.

• • •

"The public thinks we're hardened and that everything's a big joke," said Officer Dianne Yociss, who coordinates the CISD team.

Not so, said Officer Yociss, who has seen officers react to stress with everything from sleeplessness to sexual dysfunction. (Hagans)

"Living out here [southern California] is like paradise, a Shangri-La," said Murphy, 51, who served 22 years as a NYPD patrolman. "You know what? Every morning, I face Sacramento and kiss the ground."

Despite his offhanded, jovial comment, Murphy, like the others, knows also that the memories of their days on the force can still haunt them—3,000 miles away. (Wong)

Revising the Paper

In revision, the following three rough-draft paragraphs were combined to yield the final paragraph (D):

If we really stop to think of having to deal with so many of the things officers might have to deal with, we might suspect that officers must be seriously affected by traumatic incidents. This isn't necessarily true. **The effects of post-traumatic stress are varied. *and* Sewell, et al. estimate that one-third of police officers involved in a critical incident have "minimal, if any, problems; one-third have moderate problems; and another one-third have severe difficulty" (96) which affects both the officer and his/her family—and people like Rodney King.** But who is severely affected and who isn't? No one seems to be studying this, although a good answer might be helpful in hiring the best kinds of officers or in making work assignments once officers are hired.

, and we might logically conclude that it can also affect people on the force or citizens with whom the officer comes into contact.

According to Joe Vanderhoff, a retired NYPD patrolman, "It's no secret that this kind of mental stress can be devastating—the occupational hazard of just being a cop. . . . Our kind of job has resulted in one of the highest divorce, alcoholism and suicide rates of any field" (qtd. in Wong). One question that we might ask is, if it's no secret, why are people so surprised? Are they bad cops anyway? **The problems for an esti-**

proportion of officers involved in fatal shootings
ultimately leave their departments because of 'stress
disability'" (56). So we see a job that includes the
risk of traumatic incident, and a large number of the
people so involved could end up divorced, alcoholic,
or dead by suicide, and chances are good they will
leave the force even if they are good cops. Even
though we appreciate that traumatic events strike a
heavy blow, why do such events become so devastating?
Michael Galenski says that "[t]he problem is the
F-word, . . . In the police profession, feelings have
to be squelched" (qtd. in Matchan). Yet how can a person avoid feelings in light of traumatic incidents?
This is where the need for post-traumatic stress management programs becomes obvious.

    With all the discussion about police stress and
its many causes and manifestations, what is most surprising is that there are fewer programs actually
offered to combat the stress than one might expect. In
Massachusetts, in 1991, only the largest forces in
large metropolitan areas had any stress management programs (Matchan). In many departments the programs that
do exist deal only with alcoholism and substance abuse.
Articles about innovative programs are interesting, but
the programs often exist only in one lucky department.
Many police departments have a psychologist on staff,
but the objection is repeatedly made that officers will
not go to her/him if it is optional due to concerns
about confidentiality that might affect job status or
worries about how other officers will respond to them
seeking such help. According to Sgt. Thomas Fleming,
"There is a feeling that if you go for help, you're
not fit for the job" (qtd. in Matchan).

E

mated 70 percent of the severely affected also result in resignation from the department (Sewell, et al. 96; Dauler). ~~Maybe these people shouldn't be cops anyway.~~ Ellison and Genz quote a study showing "a very high proportion of officers involved in fatal shootings ultimately leave their departments because of 'stress disability' " (56). ~~This is, of course, very expensive, so if we could weed out these people beforehand, we could save this expense.~~

So we are confronted with a job that includes the risk of traumatic incident, and a large number of people so involved could end up divorced, alcoholic, or dead by suicide, and ~~they might leave the force~~ *chances are good they will leave the force even if they are good cops. Even though we appreciate that traumatic events strike a heavy blow, why do such events become so devastating?* ~~even if they are good cops. What we don't know is how these different events relate to each other. Maybe the alcoholism is not related to the job, but leads to divorce or resignation. Maybe the suicide comes as a result of the divorce? Maybe they resign because they hate other elements of the job, or just want to collect a pension.~~ Michael Galenski says that "[t]he problem is the F-word, . . . In the police profession, feelings have to be squelched" (qtd. in Matchan). ~~Since to some extent this is necessarily true in police work, how much can the department be expected to really do with people's lives?~~

Yet how can a person avoid feelings in light of traumatic events? This is where the need for post-traumatic stress management programs becomes obvious.

Paragraph E (Paraphrase, common knowledge, and quotation): Janey had trouble finding good numbers on the types of programs available in all of the many police departments across the country, so she chose to paraphrase some specific evidence and combine it with the common knowledge that was frequently expressed in her sources and by police officers she spoke with. But when she came to the suggestion that officers are not comfortable going for help, she wanted a quote to serve as a direct testimonial of prevailing attitudes.

The most logical place to begin is at the police
academy, yet there is much evidence that little or no
training occurs at most academies. A survey made by
the Fraternal Order of Police showed that "of the 750
respondents, 'three-quarters of them' . . . felt the
training academy was not adequate in training them"
and more than 70 percent say "their ongoing in-service
training is inadequate" (qtd. in Gaines-Carter).
Academy training can be different from state to state,
and even from force to force, so that improvements
must be made all over the country.

F

There are accounts of better training for supervisors in recognizing stress in patrolmen (Sewell, et
al.; Norvell and Belles), but few forces seem willing
to pay the cost. According to social worker James
Hart, "Police departments will put more money into a
damaged car than a damaged cop" (qtd. in Matchan), and
these still don't address the problems of the discre-
tionary use of a department psychologist or the perceived threat to job status. Still, supervisors
trained to recognize changes in personality, physical
change, or changes in work patterns (Ellison and Genz
77-79) could be very helpful to officers in crisis.

G

The police are often identified as a very close
group, and one response to post-traumatic stress is
informal peer discussion. But here there can be a
problem for minority or female officers who don't feel
as free to associate with or open up to other officers
(Ellison and Genz 67-69). In some cases, peer counseling units have been established on a more formal basis
as well. Yet it becomes clear that the macho image
police hold of themselves even makes discussion of
such a program touchy; people associated with a pro-

H

Paragraph G (Paraphrase and attributed quotation): Janey wanted to make a point about programs for supervisors, but felt that going into any detail was not necessary to her purpose since one small program in one of thousands of departments didn't seem relevant except in passing, and general calls for better programs were only worth discussing at length if that is what one really sought. She chose simply to refer her readers to the articles where she had read more extensive recommendations for change.

gram in Boston were reluctant to talk about it or
admit its existence.

Some officers establish their own coping mecha-
nisms, such as working out regularly in a gym, and
many discussions focus on "Individual Stress Management" (Ellison and Genz), though these programs might
be best for handling the typical stresses, not the
atypical critical incident stress.   I

Dr. Jeffrey Mitchell, president of the Inter-   J
national Critical Incident Stress Foundation, says "87
percent of emergency workers will at one time or
another experience critical incident stress reactions"
and repeats that 70 percent will leave that job within
seven years (Dauler)—a huge personnel drain. Georgia
has established a program that might serve as a model
for departments around the country, Critical Incident
Stress Debriefing (CISD) teams which step in as an
"emotional Band-aid" to help "officers relieve the
stress and pressure that come with the job" (Hagans).
Dauler describes a program that New Jersey has established, the Critical Incident Stress Debriefing
Network, which has seven 20-member teams of volunteers
representing the clergy, emergency-service workers,
and psychologists. Important components of this program are the fact that at least one session is mandatory after a traumatic incident, and all discussions
are confidential and do not include employees of the
department (9). This is one time when a police officer
is encouraged to recognize and discuss her/his feelings, according to volunteer Steven Crimando (Dauler
9). Officer Garcia, who was referred to above, testi-
fied to the effectiveness of the program, saying that
although he didn't want to participate at first,

Paragraph J (Paraphrase and attributed quotation): Janey summarizes two descriptions of Critical Incident Stress Debriefing teams but makes a blanket attribution to the article so that particular page references are made only when specific facts or quotes are incorporated into her text.

it did help him (Dauler 9). Col. Justin J. Dintino,
Superintendent of the New Jersey State Police, also
believes that the program is both good and worthwhile
(Dauler 9).

We can see, then, that there is a great deal of   K
stress in a police officer's life, both the stress
that comes from the external events surrounding
her/him, and the stress that comes from internal
beliefs and attitudes. It is clear that the better a
police force deals with stress from both causes, the
more healthy and happy their officers will be, and the
more likely they will be to keep good men and women on
the force. Especially important is the provision of
special support for the traumatic incidents that are
inherent to a police officer's job. These events are
the hardest to deal with individually and are also the
most difficult for people outside of the force to
understand. One of the best approaches to post-traumatic stress is the debriefing teams being established
in some states. There is a great need for teams such
as these to be established everywhere. The most pressing argument for more debriefing programs around the
country is made by Jeffrey T. Mitchell at the
University of Maryland:

> If you have wet concrete, while it's wet, you
> can shape it and mold it and even wash it
> away. . . . But if you let it dry, you have to
> chip it away, and it's a lot more difficult
> and it takes a lot longer. You have to avert
> people from withdrawing. That seems to be a
> fairly natural way to react, but it's not the
> right way. You have to get them to talk, and
> get them to talk immediately. ("Program")

Paragraph K (Summary of points made, reiteration of thesis, final argument for change): In paragraph K, Janey summarizes the conclusions reached in her early discussion areas, repeats her thesis, and uses the analogy offered by one of her sources to make a final plea for the need and value of expanding CISD programs around the country.

O'Reilly 9

Works Cited

Dauler, Karla. "When Officers Kill in the Line of
    Duty." 1993: <u>New York Times</u> 17 Jan. 1993: NJ1+.

Dufford, Priss. <u>Police Personal Behavior and Human</u>
    <u>Relations</u>. Springfield, IL: Charles C. Thomas, 1986.

Ellison, Katherine W., and John L. Genz. <u>Stress and the</u>
    <u>Police Officer</u>. Springfield, IL: Charles C. Thomas,
    1983.

"Expert: Main Stress For Police Doesn't Come From
    Danger." <u>Atlanta Constitution</u> (Associated Press) 31
    July 1989: A11.

Gaines-Carter, Patrice. "D.C. Police Union Links Poor
    Training to Brutality." <u>Washington Post</u> 25 Mar.
    1991: A8.

Hagans, Gail. "Public Safety Officers Meet Grief in Line
    of Duty." <u>Atlanta Constitution</u> 27 Jan. 1993: XJ1+.

Lord, Vivian B., Denis O. Gray, and Samuel B. Pond,
    III. "The Police Stress Inventory: Does It Measure
    Stress?" <u>Journal of Criminal Justice</u> 19 (1991):
    139–49.

Matchan, Linda. "Fighting the Police Taboo of Stress."
    <u>Boston Globe</u> 30 Oct. 1991: 16.

Miletich, John J. *Police,* <u>Firefighter, and Paramedic</u>
    <u>Stress: An Annotated Bibliography</u>. New York:
    Greenwood Press, 1990.

Norvell, Nancy, and Dale Belles. "A Stress Management
    Curriculum for Law Enforcement Personnel
    Supervisors." <u>The Police Chief</u> Aug. 1987: 57–59.

"Program Offers Quick Comfort to Trauma Victims." <u>New</u>
    <u>York Times</u> 29 Nov. 1991: A25.

Sewell, James D., Katherine W. Ellison, and Joseph J.
    Hurrell. "Stress Management in Law Enforcement:
    Where Do We Go From Here?" <u>The Police Chief</u> Oct.
    1988: 94–98.

Wong, Herman. "New York's Finest Answer a New Call."
    <u>Los Angeles Times</u> 28 Aug. 1990: E1+.

18

Documenting Research

There are basically two ways for a writer to show a "paper trail" to sources. The format most used today is the parenthetical reference, also called an *in-text citation.* This is a telegraphic, shorthand approach to identifying the source of a statement or quotation. It assumes that a complete list of references appears at the end of the paper. Each entry in the list of references includes three essential elements: authorship, full title of the work, and publication information. In the references, entries are arranged, punctuated, and typed to conform to the bibliographic style requirements of the particular discipline or of the instructor. With this list in place, the writer is able to supply the briefest of references—a page number or an author's name—in parentheses right in the text, knowing that the reader will be able to locate the rest of the reference information easily in the list of references. The second method for showing a paper trail is the footnote style—which is less often used today than the parenthetical system.

For more detailed information on the conventions of style in the humanities, social sciences, business disciplines, and sciences, refer to the style manuals listed below.

- Gibaldi, Joseph, and Walter S. Achtert. *MLA Handbook for Writers of Research Papers.* 3rd ed. New York: MLA, 1988.
- *Publication Manual* (of the American Psychological Association). 4th ed. Washington, DC: APA, 1994.
- *Chicago Manual of Style.* 14th ed. Chicago: University of Chicago Press, 1993.
- *CBE Style Manual.* 6th ed. Chicago: CBE, 1992.

Using the MLA System of Documentation

The Modern Language Association (MLA) publishes a style guide that is widely used for citations and references in the humanities. This section gives detailed examples of how the MLA system of parenthetical references provides in-text citation. In a research paper, these source citation are followed at the end by a list of references. In the MLA system, the list of references is called "Works Cited." Keep in mind that the complete information provided in the list of references will be the basis of your in-text citations. The parenthetical form provides minimal information and sends the reader to the list of references to find the rest.

Making In-Text Citations in the MLA Format

When you make a parenthetical in-text citation, you assume that your reader will look to the Works Cited list for complete references. The list of references at the end of your paper will provide three essential pieces of information for each of your sources: author, title, and facts of publication. Within your paper, a parenthetical citation may serve either of two purposes: to point to a source considered as a whole, or to point to a specific page location in a source. Here is an example of an MLA in-text citation referring to a story as a whole.

```
In "Escapes," the title story of one contemporary author's book
of short stories, the narrator's alcoholic mother makes a pub-
lic spectacle of herself (Williams).
```

The next example refers to a specific page in the story. In the MLA system, no punctuation is placed between a writer's last name and a page reference.

```
In "Escapes," a story about an alcoholic household, a key moment
occurs when the child sees her mother suddenly appear on stage
at the magic show (Williams 11).
```

Here is how the references to the Williams story would appear as described in the list of references or "Works Cited."

```
Williams, Joy. "Escapes." Escapes: Stories. New York: Vintage,
    1990. 1-14.
```

Deciding when to insert a source citation and what information to include is often a judgment call. Use common sense. Where feasible, incorporate citations smoothly into the text. Introduce the parenthetical reference smoothly at a pause in your sentence, at the end if possible. Place it as close to the documented point as possible, making sure that the reader can tell exactly which point is being documented. When the in-text reference is incorporated into a sentence of your own, always place the parenthetical reference *before* any enclosing or end punctuation.

> In Central Africa in the 1930s, a young girl who comes to town drinks beer with her date because that's what everyone does (Lessing 105).

> In a realistic portrayal of Central African city life in the 1930s (Lessing), young people gather daily to drink.

When a quotation from a work is incorporated into a sentence of your own, the parenthetical reference *follows* the quotation marks, yet precedes the enclosing or end punctuation.

> At the popular Sports Club, Lessing's heroine finds the "ubiquitous glass mugs of golden beer" (135).

Exception: When your quotation ends with a question mark or exclamation point, keep these punctuation marks inside the end quotation marks, then give the parenthetical reference, and end with a period.

> Martha's new attempts at sophistication in town prompted her to retort, "Children are a nuisance, aren't they?" (Lessing 115).

Naming an Author in the Text

When you want to emphasize the author of a source you are citing, incorporate that author's name into your sentence. Unless you are referring to a particular place in that source, no parenthetical reference is necessary in the text.

> Biographer Paul Mariani understands Berryman's alcoholism as one form of his drive toward self-destruction.

Naming an Author in the Parenthetical Reference

When you want to emphasize information in a source but not especially the author, omit the author's name in the sentence and place it in the parenthetical reference.

> Biographers have documented alcohol-related upheavals in John Berryman's life. Aware, for example, that Dylan Thomas was in an alcohol-induced coma, dying, Berryman himself drank to escape his pain (Mariani 273).

When you are referring to a particular place in your source and have already incorporated the author's name into your sentence, place only the page number in parentheses.

> Biographer Paul Mariani describes how Berryman, knowing that his friend Dylan Thomas was dying in an alcohol-induced coma, himself began drinking to escape his pain (273).

Documenting a Block Quotation

For block quotations, set the parenthetical reference—with or without an author's name—*outside* of the end punctuation mark.

The story graphically portrays the behavior of Central African
young people gathering daily to drink:

> Perry sat stiffly in a shallow chair which looked as
> if it would splay out under the weight of his big
> body . . . while from time to time—at those moments
> when laughter was jerked out of him by Stella—he
> threw back his head with a sudden dismayed movement,
> and flung half a glass of liquor down his throat.
> (Lessing 163)

A Work by Two or Three Authors

If your source has two or three authors, name them all, either in your text
or in a parenthetical reference. Use last names, in the order they are given
in the source, connected by *and*.

> Critics have addressed the question of whether literary artists
> discover new truths (Wellek and Warren 33-36).

> One theory claims that the alcoholic wants to "drink his envi-
> ronment in" (Perls, Hefferline, and Goodman 193-194).

Reference to Two or More Sources with the Same Authorship

When you are referring to one or two or more sources written by the same
author, include in your in-text citation a shortened form of each title so
that references to each text will be clear. The following example discusses
how author Joy Williams portrays the drinking scene in her fiction. Note
that a comma appears between the author's name and the shortened title.

> She shows drinking at parties as a way of life in such stories
> as "Escapes" and "White Like Midnight." Thus it is matter of
> course that Joan pours herself a drink while people talk about
> whether or not they want to survive nuclear war (Williams,
> "White" 129).

Two or More Sources in a Single Reference

Particularly in an introductory summary, you may want to group together a number of works that cover one or more aspects of your research
topic. Separate one source from another by a semicolon.

> Studies that confront the alcoholism of literary figures direct-
> ly are on the increase (Mariani; Dardis; Gilmore).

A Literary Work

Well-known literary works, particularly older ones now in the public do-
main, may appear in numerous editions. When referring to such a work or
a part of one, give information for the work itself rather than for the particular edition you are using, unless you are highlighting a special feature
or contribution of the edition.

For a play, supply act, scene, and line number in Arabic numerals, unless your instructor specifies using Roman numerals for act and scene (II. iv. 118–19). In the following example, the title of the literary work includes numerals referring to the first of two plays that Shakespeare wrote about Henry IV, known as parts 1 and 2.

```
Shakespeare's Falstaff bellows, "Give me a cup of sack, rogue.
Is there no virtue extant?" (1 Henry IV 2.4.118-19).
```

To cite a modern editor's contribution to the publication of a literary work, adjust the emphasis of your reference. The abbreviation *n.* stands for *note.*

```
Without the editor's footnote in the Riverside Shakespeare ex-
plaining that lime was sometimes used as an additive to make
wine sparkle, modern readers would be unlikely to understand
Falstaff's ranting: "[Y]et a coward is worse than a cup of sack
with lime in it. A villainous coward!" (1 Henry IV 2.4.125-26n.).
```

Preparing a List of References in the MLA Format

In research papers following MLA format, the list of references is called "Works Cited" when it includes those sources you have referred to in your paper. Be aware that some instructors request a more comprehensive list of references—one that includes every source you consulted in preparing the paper. That list would be titled "Bibliography."

The examples in this section show how entries in the "Works Cited" list consist of three elements essential for a list of references: authorship, full title of the work, and publication information. The basic format for each entry requires the first line to start at the left margin, with each subsequent line to be indented five typed spaces from the left margin.

Not every possible variation is represented here. In formatting a complicated entry for your own list, you may need to combine features from two or more of the examples. The MLA "Works Cited" list begins on a new page, after the last page of your paper, and continues the pagination of your paper. Entries in the list are alphabetized by the author's last name. An anonymous work is alphabetized by the first word in its title (but disregard *A, An,* and *The*).

Listing Books in the MLA "Works Cited" Format

The MLA "Works Cited" list presents book references in the following order:

1. *Author's name:* Put the last name first, followed by a comma and the first name (and middle name or initial) and a period. Omit the author's titles and degrees, whether one that precedes a name (Dr.) or one that follows (Ph.D.). Leave two typed spaces after the period.

2. *Title of the book:* Underline or italicize the complete title. If there is a subtitle, separate it from the main title by a colon and one typed space. Capitalize all important words, including the first word of any subtitle. The complete title is followed by a period and two typed spaces.

3. *Publication information:* Name the city of publication, followed by a colon and one typed space; the name of the publisher followed by a comma; the date of publication followed by a period. This information appears on the title page of the book and the copyright page, on the reverse side of the title page.

If the city of publication is not well known, add the name of the state, abbreviated as in the zip code system. Shorten the name of the publisher in a way that is recognizable. "G. P. Putnam's Sons" is shortened to "Putnam's." For university presses use "UP" as in the example "U of Georgia P." Many large publishing companies issue books under imprints that represent particular groups of books. Give the imprint name first, followed by a hyphen and the name of the publisher: Bullseye-Knopf.

Any additional information about the book goes between author and title or between title and publication data. In the examples that follow, you will notice the kinds of information that can be added to an entry. Observe details of how to organize, abbreviate, and punctuate this information.

A Book with One Author
The basic format for a single-author book is as follows:

    Mariani, Paul. Dream Song: The Life of John Berryman. New York:
        Morrow, 1990.

A Book with Two or Three Authors
For a book with two or three authors, follow the order of the names on the title page. Notice that first and last name are reversed only for the lead author. Notice also the use of a comma after the first author.

    Roebuck, Julian B., and Raymond G. Kessler. The Etiology of Alco-
        holism: Constitutional, Psychological and Sociological Ap-
        proaches. Springfield: Thomas, 1972.

A Book with Four or More Authors
As in the example under in-text citations, you may choose to name all the authors or to use the abbreviated format with "et al."

    Stein, Norman, Mindy Lubber, Stuart L. Koman, and Kathy Kelly.
        Family Therapy: A Systems Approach. Boston: Allyn, 1990.
    Stein, Norman, et al. Family Therapy: A Systems Approach.
        Boston: Allyn, 1990.

A Selection from an Edited Book or Anthology
For a selection from an edited work, name the author of the selection and enclose the selection title in quotation marks. Underline or italicize the title of the book containing the selection, and name its editor(s). Give the page numbers for the selection at the end of your entry.

    Davies, Phil. "Does Treatment Work? A Sociological Perspec-
        tive." The Misuse of Alcohol. Ed. Nick Heather, et al. New
        York: New York UP, 1985. 158-77.

When a selection has been reprinted from another source, include that information too, as in the following example. State the facts of original publication first, then describe the book in which it has been reprinted.

> Bendiner, Emil. "The Bowery Man on the Couch." <u>The Bowery Man</u>.
> New York: Nelson, 1961. Rpt. in <u>Man Alone: Alienation in</u>
> <u>Modern Society</u>. Ed. Eric Josephson and Mary Josephson. New
> York: Dell, 1962. 401-10.

Two or More Works by the Same Author(s)

When you cite two or more works by the same author(s), you should write the author's full name only once, at first mention, in the reference list. In subsequent entries immediately following, substitute three hyphens and a period in place of the author's name.

> Heilbroner, Robert L. <u>The Future as History</u>. New York: Harper
> Torchbooks-Harper, 1960.
> ---. <u>An Inquiry into the Human Prospect</u>. New York: Norton, 1974.

Listing Periodicals in the MLA "Works Cited" Format

A *periodical* is any publication that appears regularly over time. A periodical can be a daily or weekly newspaper, a magazine, or a scholarly or professional journal. As with listings for books, a bibliographical listing for a periodical article includes information about authorship, title, and facts of publication. Authorship is treated just as for books, with the author's first and last names reversed. Citation of a title differs in that the title of an article is always enclosed in quotation marks rather than underlined or italicized; the title of the periodical in which it appears is always underlined or italicized. Notice that the articles *a, an,* and *the,* which often begin the name of a periodical, are omitted from the bibliographical listing.

The facts of publication are the trickiest of the three elements because of the wide variation in how periodicals are dated, paginated, and published. For journals, for example, the publication information generally consists of journal title, the volume number, the year of publication, and the page numbering for the article cited. For newspapers, the listing includes name of the newspaper, full date of publication, and full page numbering by both section and page number(s) if necessary. The following examples show details of how to list different types of periodicals. With the exception of May, June, and July, you should abbreviate the names of months in each "Works Cited" entry.

A Journal with Continuous Pagination through the Annual Volume

A continuously paginated journal is one that numbers pages consecutively throughout all the issues in a volume instead of beginning with page 1 in each issue. After the author's name (reversed and followed by a period and two typed spaces), give the name of the article in quotation marks.

Give the title of the journal, underlined or italicized and followed by two typed spaces. Give the volume number, in Arabic numerals. After a typed space, give the year, in parentheses, followed by a colon. After one more space, give the page number(s) for the article, including the first and last pages on which it appears.

> Kling, William. "Measurement of Ethanol Consumed in Distilled Spirits." <u>Journal of Studies on Alcohol</u> 50 (1989): 456-60.

In a continuously paginated journal, the issue number within the volume and the month of publication are not included in the bibliographical listing.

A Journal Paginated by Issue

> Latessa, Edward J., and Susan Goodman. "Alcoholic Offenders: Intensive Probation Program Shows Promise." <u>Corrections Today</u> 51.3 (1989): 38-39+.

This journal numbers the pages in each issue separately, so it is important to identify which issue in volume 51 has this article beginning on page 38. The plus sign following a page number indicates that the article continues after the last-named page, but after intervening pages.

A Monthly Magazine

This kind of periodical is identified by month and year of issue. Even if the magazine indicates a volume number, omit it from your listing.

> Waggoner, Glen. "Gin as Tonic." <u>Esquire</u> Feb. 1990: 30.

Some magazines vary in their publication schedule. *Restaurant Business* publishes once a month or bimonthly. Include the full date of publication in your listing. Give the day first, followed by an abbreviation for the month.

> Whelan, Elizabeth M. "Alcohol and Health." <u>Restaurant Business</u> 20 Mar. 1989: 66+.

A Daily Newspaper

In the following examples, you see that the name of the newspaper is italicized. Any introductory article (*a, an,* and *the*) is omitted. The complete date of publication is given—day, month (abbreviated), year. Specify the edition if one appears on the masthead, since even in one day an article may be located differently in different editions. Precede the page number(s) by a colon and one typed space. If the paper has sections designated by letter (A, B, C), include the section before the page number.

If the article is unsigned, begin your entry with the title, as in the second example ("Alcohol Can Worsen . . . ").

> Welch, Patrick. "Kids and Booze: It's 10 O'Clock—Do You Know How Drunk Your Kids Are?" <u>Washington Post</u> 31 Dec. 1989: C1.

The following entry illustrates the importance of including the particular edition of a newspaper.

```
"Alcohol Can Worsen Ills of Aging, Study Says." New York Times
     13 June 1989, natl. ed.: 89.
"Alcohol Can Worsen Ills of Aging, Study Says." New York Times
     13 June 1989, late ed.: C5.
```

A Weekly Magazine or Newspaper

An unsigned article listing would include title, name of the publication, complete date, and page number(s). Even if you know a volume or issue number, omit it.

```
"A Direct Approach to Alcoholism." Science News 9 Jan. 1988: 25.
```

Listing Other Sources in the MLA "Works Cited" Format

A Film or Videotape

Underline or italicize the title, and then name the medium, the distributor, and the year. Supply any information that you think is useful about the performers, director, producer, or physical characteristics of the film or tape.

```
Alcoholism: The Pit of Despair. Videocassette. Gordon Jump. AIMS
     Media, 1983. VHS and Beta. 20 min.
```

A Television or Radio Program

If the program you are citing is a single episode with its own title, supply the title in quotation marks. State the name and role of the foremost participant(s). Underline or italicize the title of the program, identify who produced it, and list the station on which it first appeared, the city, and the date.

```
"The Broken Cord." Interview with Louise Erdrich and Michael
     Dorris. Dir. and prod. Catherine Tatge. A World of Ideas
     with Bill Moyers. Exec. prod. Judith Davidson Moyers and
     Bill Moyers. Public Affairs TV. WNET, New York. 27 May 1990.
```

Using the APA System of Documentation

The American Psychological Association's *Publication Manual* has set documentation style for psychologists. APA documentation is similar to the MLA system in coupling a brief in-text citation, given in parentheses, with a complete listing of information about the source at the end of the paper. In the APA system this list of references is called "References." In the in-text citation itself, APA style differs by including the date of the work cited. The publication date is often important for a reader to have immediately at hand in psychology and related fields, where researchers may publish frequently, often modifying conclusions reached in prior publications.

Making In-Text Citations in the APA Format

For every fact, opinion, or idea from another source that you quote, summarize, or otherwise use, you must give credit. You must also give just enough information that your reader can locate the source. Whether in the text itself or in a parenthetical note, APA documentation calls for you to name the author and give the date of publication for every work you refer to. When you have quoted from a work, you must also give the page or page numbers (preceded by *p.* or *pp.,* in APA format). When you summarize or paraphrase, as well, it is often helpful to supply exact location of the source material by page number as part of the parenthetical reference. Supply the page number(s) immediately following a quotation or paraphrase, even if the sentence is not at a pause point.

In the sample paragraphs that follow, you will find variations on using APA in-text citation. Notice that, wherever possible, reference information is incorporated directly into the text and parentheses are used as a supplement to information in the text. Supply the parenthetical date of publication immediately after an author's name in the text. If you refer to a source a second time within a paragraph, you need not repeat the information if the reference is clear. If there is any confusion about which work is being cited, however, supply the clarifying information. If in your entire paper you are citing only one work by a particular author, you need give the date only in the first reference. If the page number for a subsequent reference differs from the earlier page number, supply the number. Separate items within a parenthetical reference by commas.

> Dardis's study (1989) examines four twentieth-century American writers—three of them Nobel Prize winners—who were alcoholics. Dardis acknowledged (p. 3) that American painters too include a high percentage of addicted drinkers. Among poets, he concludes (p. 5) that the percentage is not so high as among prose writers.
>
> However, even a casual reading of a recent biography of poet John Berryman (Mariani, 1990) reveals a creative and personal life dominated by alcohol. Indeed, "so regular had [Berryman's] hospital stays [for alcoholism] become . . . that no one came to visit him anymore" (Mariani, p. 413). Berryman himself had no illusions about the destructive power of alcohol. About his friend Dylan Thomas he could write, "Dylan murdered himself w. liquor, tho it took years" (qtd. in Mariani, p. 274). Robert Lowell and Edna St. Vincent Millay were also prominent American poets who had problems with alcohol (Dardis, p. 3).

A Work by Two Authors

To join the names of two authors of a work, use *and* in text but use the ampersand (&) in a parenthetical reference. Notice how the parenthetical information immediately follows the point to which it applies.

> Roebuck and Kessler (1972) summarized the earlier research (pp. 21–41).

```
A summary of prior research on the genetic basis of alcoholism
(Roebuck & Kessler, 1972, pp. 21-41) is our starting point.
```

Two or More Works by the Same Author

If the work of the same author has appeared in different years, distinguish references to each separate work by year of publication. If, however, you refer to two or more works published by the same author(s) within a single year, you must list the works in alphabetical order by title in the list of references, and assign each one an order by lowercase letter. Thus,

```
(Holden, 1989a)
```

could represent Caroline Holden's article "Alcohol and Creativity," while

```
(Holden, 1989b)
```

would refer to the same author's "Creativity and Craving," published in the same year.

Distinguishing Two Authors with the Same Last Name

Distinguish authors with the same last name by including first and middle initials in each citation.

```
(J. Williams, 1990)
```

```
(C. K. Williams, 1991)
```

Two or More Sources in a Single Reference

Separate multiple sources in one citation by a semicolon. List authors alphabetically within the parentheses.

```
We need to view the alcoholic in twentieth-century America from
many perspectives (Bendiner, 1962; Dardis, 1989; Waggoner, 1990)
in order to understand how people with ordinary lives as well
as people with vast creative talent can appear to behave iden-
tically.
```

Preparing a List of References in the APA Format

In research papers following the APA system, the list of references (which is alphabetized) is called "References." Within an entry, the date is separated from the other facts of publication. The APA list of references includes only those works referred to in your paper.

Listing Books in the APA Format

Leave two typed spaces to separate items in an entry. Double-space the list throughout. Start each entry at the left margin; if the entry runs beyond one line, indent subsequent lines three typewriter spaces. The following order of presentation is used:

1. Author's name(s): Put the last name first, followed by a comma. Use first and middle initial, instead of spelling out a first or middle name.
2. Date: Give the year of publication in parentheses followed by a period. If your list includes more than one title by an author in any one year, distinguish those titles by adding a lowercase letter (a, b, etc.) to the year of publication (as in 1989a and 1989b).
3. Title of the book: Underline or italicize the complete book title. Capitalize only the first word in a title or subtitle, in addition to proper names.
4. Publication information: Name the city of publication, followed by a colon. Give the full name of the publisher, but without the "Co." or other business designation.

```
Dardis, T. (1989). The thirsty muse: Alcohol and the American
    writer. New York: Ticknor & Fields.
```

A Book with Two Authors

Invert both names; separate them by a comma. Use the ampersand (&).

```
Roebuck, J. B., & Kessler, R. G. (1972). The etiology of alco-
    holism: Constitutional, psychological and sociological ap-
    proaches. Springfield, IL: Charles C. Thomas.
```

A Book with Three or More Authors

List *all* authors, treating each author's name as in the case of two authors. Use the ampersand before naming the last. (This book was first published in 1951, then reissued without change.)

```
Perls, R., Hefferline, R. F., & Goodman, P. (1965). Gestalt psy-
    chology: Excitement and growth in the human personality. New
    York: Delta-Dell. (Originally published 1951)
```

Listing Periodicals in the APA Format

A Journal with Continuous Pagination through the Annual Volume

The entry for a journal begins with the author's last name and initial(s), inverted, followed by the year of publication in parentheses. The title of the article has neither quotation marks nor underline. Only the first word of the title and subtitle are capitalized, along with proper nouns. The volume number, which follows the underlined or italicized title of the journal, is also underlined or italicized. Use the abbreviation *p.* or *pp.* when referring to page numbers in a magazine or newspaper. Use no abbreviations when referring to the page numbers of a journal.

```
Kling, W. (1989). Measurement of ethanol consumed in distilled
    spirits. Journal of Studies on Alcohol, 50, 456-460.
```

A Journal Paginated by Issue

In this example, the issue number within volume 51 is given in parentheses. Give all page numbers when the article is not printed continuously.

Latessa, E. J., & Goodman, S. (1989). Alcoholic offenders: Intensive probation program shows promise. <u>Corrections Today</u>, 51(3), 38-39, 45.

A Monthly Magazine

Invert the year and month of a monthly magazine. Write the name of the month in full. (For newspapers and magazines use the abbreviations *p.* and *pp.*)

Waggoner, G. (1990, February). Gin as tonic. <u>Esquire</u>, p. 30.

A Weekly Magazine

If the article is signed, begin with the author's name. Otherwise, begin with the article's title. (You would alphabetize the following entry under *d*.)

A direct approach to alcoholism. (1988, January 9). <u>Science News</u>, p. 25.

A Daily Newspaper

Welch, P. (1989, December 31). Kids and booze: It's 10 o'clock—Do you know how drunk your kids are? <u>Washington Post</u>, p. C1.

Listing Other Sources in the APA Format

A Film or Videotape

For nonprint media, identify the medium in brackets just after the title.

Jump, G. (1983). <u>Alcoholism: The pit of despair</u> [Videocassette, VHS and Beta]. New York: AIMS Media.

A Television or Radio Program

Erdrich, L., & Dorris, M. (1990, May 27). The broken cord [Interview]. <u>A world of ideas with Bill Moyers</u> [Television program]. New York: Public Affairs TV. WNET.

Using the CBE Systems of Documentation

The Council of Biology Editors (CBE) systems of documentation are standard for the biological sciences and, with minor or minimal adaptations, are also used in many of the other sciences. You will find many similarities between the CBE styles of documentation and the APA style, which was derived from the conventions used in scientific writing. As in APA and MLA styles, any in-text references to a source are provided in shortened form in parentheses. For complete bibliographic information, readers expect to consult the list of references at the end of the document.

Making In-Text Citations in the CBE Formats

The CBE Style Manual presents three formats for citing a source in the text of an article. Your choice of format will depend on the discipline in which you are writing. Whatever format you choose, remain consistent within any one document.

The Name-and-Year System

The CBE convention that most closely resembles the APA conventions is the name-and-year system. In this system a writer provides in parentheses the name of an author and the year in which that author's work was published. Note that, in contrast to the APA system, no comma appears between the author's name and the year of publication.

```
Slicing and aeration of quiescent storage tissues induces a
rapid metabolic activation and a development of the membrane
systems in the wounded tissue (Kahl 1974).
```

If an author's name is mentioned in a sentence, only the year of publication is set in parentheses.

```
Jacobsen et al. found that a marked transition in respiratory
substrate occurs in sliced potato tissue that exhibits the phe-
nomenon of wound respiration (1974).
```

If your paper cites two or more works published by the same author in the same year, assign a letter designation (a, b, etc.) to inform the reader of precisely which piece you have cited. This form of citation applies both to journal articles and to books.

```
Chen and Amsel (1980a) obtained intermittent reinforcement
effects in rats as young as eleven days of age. Under the same
conditions, they observed that the effects of intermittent rein-
forcement on perseverance are long lived (Chen and Amsel 1980b).
```

When citing a work by an organization or government agency with no author named, use the corporate or organizational name in place of a reference to an individual author. Provide the year of publication following the name as indicated previously.

```
Style guides in the sciences caution that the "use of nouns
formed from verbs and ending in -tion produces unnecessarily
long sentences and dull prose" (CBE Style Manual Committee
1983).
```

The Number Systems

The briefest form of parenthetical citation is the number system, a convention in which only an Arabic numeral appears in parentheses to identify a source of information. There are two variations on the number system. With references *in order of first mention,* you assign a reference number to a source in the order of its appearance in your paper. With references *in alphabetized order,* you assign each source a reference number that identifies it in the alphabetized list of references at the end of the paper.

Citation for a Reference List in Order of First Mention

```
According to Kahl et al., slicing and aeration of quiescent
storage tissues induces a rapid metabolic activation and a
development of the membrane systems in the wounded tissue (1).
Jacobsen et al. found that a marked transition in respiratory
substrate occurs in sliced potato tissue that exhibits the phe-
nomenon of wound respiration (2).
```

Citation for a Reference List in Alphabetized Order

```
According to Kahl et al., slicing and aeration of quiescent
storage tissues induces a rapid metabolic activation and a
development of the membrane systems in the wounded tissue (2).
Jacobson et al. found that a marked transition in respiratory
substrate occurs in sliced potato tissue that exhibits the phe-
nomenon of wound respiration (1).
```

These numbered text citations are linked to corresponding entries in a list of references. The reference list may be numbered either in the order of first mention or alphabetically.

Preparing a List of References Using CBE Systems

In the sciences the list of references appearing at the end of the paper is often called "Literature Cited." If you adopt the name-and-year system for in-text citation, the entries in your list of references are alphabetized, much as with the APA system, rather than numbered. Like the list of references in the APA system, the "Literature Cited" list is double-spaced; each entry starts at the left margin and the second or subsequent lines are indented three typewriter spaces.

If you adopt one of the numbered systems for in-text citation, you will either number entries alphabetically or in order of appearance in the paper. A numbered entry, beginning with the numeral, starts at the left margin. Place a period after the number, skip two spaces, and list the author's last name followed by the rest of the entry. For the spacing of the second or subsequent lines of a numbered entry, there are two conventions: either align the second line directly beneath the first letter of the author's last name, or indent the second and subsequent lines five spaces from the left margin. Select a convention depending on the preference of your professor. The following are some of the basic formats for listing sources in the CBE systems.

Listing Books in the CBE Format

In preparing a list of references in the CBE format, leave two typed spaces between each item in an entry. Sequence the items in an entry as follows:

- *Number:* Assign a number to the entry if you are following a numbered system.
- *Author's name:* Put the last name first, followed by a comma and the initials of the first and middle names.

- *Title of the book:* Do not use underlining or italics. Capitalize the first letter of the first word only. End the title with a period. If the work is a revised edition, abbreviate the edition as 2d, 3d, 4th, etc.
- *Publication information:* Name the city of publication (and state, if needed to clarify). Place a colon and give the full name of the publisher. Place a semicolon, and give the year of publication followed by a period.

If you refer to more than one work published by the same author(s) in the same year, list the works in alphabetical order by title in the list of references, and assign each one a lowercase letter according to its order.

Books by Individual or Multiple Authors

For a book with one author follow the conventions immediately above. For a book with multiple authors, place a semicolon after each coauthor.

```
1. Beevers, H.  Respiratory metabolism in plants.  Evanston, IL:
   Row, Peterson and Company; 1961.
2. Goodwin, T. W.; Mercer, E. I.  Introduction to plant bio-
   chemistry.  Elmsford, NY: Pergamon Press; 1972.
```

Listing Periodicals in the CBE Format

Leave two typed spaces between each item in an entry. Sequence the items as follows:

- *Number:* Assign a number to the entry if you are using a numbered system.
- *Author's name:* Put the last name, followed by a comma and the initials of the first and middle names. If there are multiple authors, see the convention for books above.
- *Title of the article:* Do not use underlining or quotation marks. Capitalize the first letter of the first word only.
- *Journal name:* Abbreviate the name, unless it is a single word, without underlining or italics. For example, The Journal of Molecular Evolution would be abbreviated as J. Mol. Evol.
- *Publication information:* Put the volume number, followed by a colon, followed by page numbers (use no abbreviations), followed by a semicolon and the year of publication.

Articles by Individual and Multiple Authors

```
6. Kling, W.  Measurement of ethanol consumed in distilled spir-
   its.  J. Stud. Alcohol.  50:456-460; 1989.
7. Coleman, R. A.; Pratt, L. H.  Phytochrome: immunological as-
   say of synthesis and destruction in plants.  Planta 119:221-
   231; 1974.
```

Newspaper Articles

```
8. Welch, P.  Kids and booze: it's 10 o'clock—do you know how
   drunk your kids are?  Washington Post. 1989 Dec. 21:C1.
```

PART V

Special Formats and Occasions

19

Writing with a Computer[1]

Computers play such an integral role in our lives that it is difficult to imagine being without them. These machines are everywhere—in our cars, stereos, televisions, video games, telephones, microwaves, watches, coffee makers, toys, even our toothbrushes. In fact, it will not be long before computers will be as prevalent as telephones, and things like hypertext, virtual reality, the "Net," electronic bulletin boards, and e-mail will be part of our everyday vocabularies. Today's children are amazingly computer literate, a result not only of considerable video game playing, but also of a heavy emphasis on computers in grade school.

Despite the number of new computer technologies appearing every day, many writers are still unfamiliar with how computers (specifically, word processing programs) can greatly enhance the writing process—an ironic fact, considering that the majority of people are more comfortable before a television screen or video display terminal (VDT) than they are facing a blank piece of paper.

With a little patience you can learn simple word processing techniques that will eradicate difficulties that used to plague writers. Whether you own a computer, a word processor, or simply have access to a computer at school or work, this tool exists to make life easier for you at every stage of the writing process. It makes sense to take advantage of it.

---

[1]This material was prepared by Derek Owens of Saint John's University.

What a Computer Can Do That a Typewriter Can't

The most obvious edge a computer's word processing software has over a typewriter is that it eliminates the tedium of retyping an entire page or document for the sake of a small correction like a spelling error. Only a few keystrokes are needed to enter changes and command a printer to print a new page, where in the past writers had to retype an entire page, or even an entire essay, for the sake of a few minor changes. Even if this were the only thing computers enabled us to do, it would provide enormous benefit. Fortunately for us, computers perform a great many tasks for the writer, removing busywork and allowing that much more time for composing.

Advantages

Cutting and Pasting

This technique allows you to rearrange your text in significant ways, as often as you like. You might wish to move your third and seventh paragraphs to the very beginning of the paper; or, you might want to copy the first four pages of the paper and put them into a separate file, where you can experiment with them separately. Shuffling like this can be done in seconds, whereas if a writer had just finished typing a ten-page paper on a typewriter, she or he would have to begin typing the entire text again from scratch in order to accomplish the same ends.

Find

Perhaps you are worried about overusing a certain phrase or word in your writing. Using the Find command, the computer will instantly highlight every place in the text where you've used this phrase. If, for example, your teacher has suggested you cut back on the number of times you use the first person, you could go back to your essay and see, within seconds, the number of times this happened.

Search and Replace

This feature is like the Find function, only it goes one step further. Imagine you've just completed a fifteen-page term paper for your psychology class, only to discover you've spelled the word "unconscious" wrong every single time. The Search and Replace feature can substitute the correct word for every misspelled word within minutes. Or, if you are writing a paper and you need to continually use a long term or phrase ("post–World War II," for example), rather than type it out every time it appears you could type an abbreviation instead (say, "pww2"). Then, right before printing the final draft, you can simply tell the computer to substitute the correct term for the abbreviation throughout the text, a command the computer would execute in minutes.

Spell-Checkers

With its dictionary of 200,000 words or more, a spell-checker compares every word of your paper against the words in its memory. When no match can be found, the computer flags the word and prompts you to make a decision regarding possible replacements. In this way it will call your attention to overlooked typos ("auhtority" instead of "authority") as well as any words the computer doesn't recognize (say, "Frieda Kahlo"). The drawback to a spell-checker is that it will not call attention to mistakes that also happen to be correctly spelled words. If you write "their" when you should have written "there," the computer won't catch the mistake. Consequently, spell-checkers are not a replacement for solid proofreading.

Thesauri and Grammar-Checkers

Like the spell-checker, the computer's thesaurus can give you alternatives for overused words. (It can even tell you how many times a word appears in your paper.) Grammar-checkers attempt to show you places in your text where there may be a problem with your grammar; style-checkers can identify patterns within your prose that you might want to enhance or eliminate. As with any such tools, you must always determine whether the computer's suggestions are valid; after all, tools like these, while beneficial, are only screening devices. Sometimes their suggestions may make sense, other times not; either way, you must always monitor the computer when using them.

Endnote and Footnote Formats

Word processors can automatically create footnotes for you, wherever you want them. You no longer have to worry about leaving just the right amount of room at the bottom of the page, as the computer will take care of this automatically for you. This can also be done in Endnote format. (Some software exists that will even write your Bibliography for you in the correct style; all you need to do is punch in the relevant information, in any order, and the computer will rearrange your Works Cited page all on its own, and in accordance with numerous style formats.)

Page Numbers and Headers

The computer will not only automatically number all of your pages for you, wherever you want the number to be, it will also insert a small header at the top or "footer" at the bottom of each page. For example, you could have your name and the date written in a smaller font in the upper right corner of each page.

Incorporating Graphs and Images

Suppose you want to neatly insert a photograph into the middle of a page, where it would be surrounded by text. Using a scanner, you could reproduce that photograph into your computer's memory, and then use certain software to retrieve it and reproduce it at the correct spot. This can also be done with graphs, charts, and diagrams. Be sure to get permission to use any art or photos that are not your own.

Desktop Publishing

It used to be that if you wanted your words published, you had to rely on some outside publisher. Because computers and printers have become so sophisticated, it's possible to produce texts that look as professional as any published text.

On-Line Communication

One of the most exciting things about knowing how to use a computer is the ability to hook up via Internet with literally thousands of other writers, as well as discussion lists, listservs, and library catalogs via electronic mail ("e-mail"). Not only will you have access to sources of information unavailable anywhere else, but you will be able to send memos, notes, drafts, and even entire essays to friends, peers, and professors within seconds. To get an e-mail account and an e-mail user ID, you will need to contact your academic computing department.

Drawbacks

Initial Frustration for the Novice

It's no secret that computers have a reputation for being inaccessible, difficult, and hard to master. Chances are you or someone you know cringes at the thought of using one, perhaps because of several bad experiences. And the truth is, if you've never worked with a computer before and you're what some people would call "computer phobic," your first few attempts might be less than enjoyable. In fact, you might well need several sittings before you come to fully appreciate all the benefits of this technology. This can be the case with learning any new, complex machine. The good news is that all of the popular word processing programs have built-in tutorials that will take you by the hand and painlessly show you how to use the software. Chances are good you'll even have fun—so long as you don't forget that the computer is just a plastic box stuffed with chips and wires.

Size of Display

Most computers only give you a partial glimpse into any text. Only the largest monitors will show you an entire page, and even these can't let you see an entire essay all at once. In order to compensate for the keyhole effect, you will have to "scroll" up and down throughout the text repeatedly, as well as print out various "hard copies" as you revise.

Cost and Size

Computers obviously are larger and more expensive than dimestore notebooks. On the other hand, many portable laptop computers are considerably smaller and lighter than the average typewriter. And while computers aren't cheap, better and less expensive models appear on the market every season, making a lot of equipment surprisingly affordable.

Verbosity

Because of the numerous ways computers make writing more efficient, many writers discover that they can now fill up pages of text in a short time. While this can be exciting and liberating for the writer who used to sit and stare at a blank page for hours, it also presents a new risk: rambling on and adopting an overly chatty prose style. This is not so much a problem as long as you are aware of the risk. Before turning in any final text, always print a hard copy first and subject it to some ruthless editing. Then return to the computer and make the necessary alterations.

False Sense of Security

Although your computer has various screening devices, many writers make the mistake of thinking such safeguards will render their prose error free. Not so. For example, when inserting text you must make sure you delete any prior words that no longer belong. Consider this sentence: "Emily Dickinson's questioning of obsession with death is everywhere throughout her poetry." Here the writer, after rethinking his sentence, has chosen to replace the words "questioning of" with the words "obsession with." The problem is, he has forgotten to delete the old phrase after adding the substitute, thereby making a classic word-processing mistake. (Also, you can easily insert corrected text into the wrong place, simply because the cursor is not in exactly the right spot.) Also, be wary of grammar-checkers. These can be valuable in identifying patterns in your grammar and syntax you might not otherwise have noticed. But a computer's grammar-checker will not "fix" your grammar; there may be times when rhetorically you ought to resist the advice of such a tool. The message behind all of these examples is: don't take anything for granted, and always take final responsibility for your work.

Crashes

Even the best computers occasionally "crash." This can happen due to power surges, the introduction of some "virus" into the hard drive, or any number of reasons. Therefore, always make backup disks for all your work, and never insert someone else's disk into your computer without first checking it for bugs and viruses that could damage your system.

New Aches and Pains

Remember when you used to get writer's cramp after clutching your pencil for a long time? Well, you might not get writer's cramp at a keyboard, but you can easily acquire a host of newer health problems: eye fatigue from staring at a VDT, back and neck strain, and even carpal tunnel syndrome (CTS), a serious ailment affecting the wrists due to improper position of the hands and repeated hand motions with a limited range of movement. If you're going to spend a lot of time at a computer, it's essential that your posture and position be correct. (See the diagram on the facing page.)

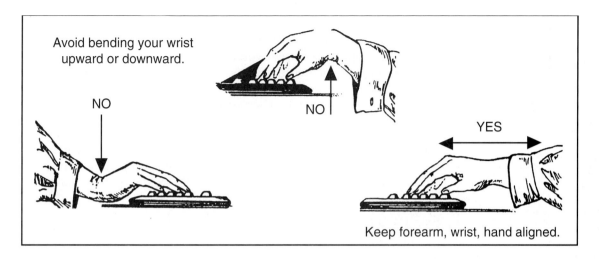

Avoid bending your wrist upward or downward.

NO

NO

YES

Keep forearm, wrist, hand aligned.

Some Basic Terminology

Making Files

In the old days we started writing by opening our notebooks or by putting a piece of paper into the typewriter, and that document was our "file." Obviously with the computer there's no paper involved until you go to print, so a file is created electronically. Your word processor will have specific commands that will tell you how to "open" a file—which means a specially designated blank screen where you can put down your words—and then how to "save" your file when finished. If you don't save your file, it might get erased automatically the moment you "exit" your word processing program. (**Note:** It's vitally important that you save your work frequently, about every fifteen minutes, and not just at the end of a session! This way, if you accidentally exit the program, or if there's a power surge, you'll still have most of your work saved.)

You'll also have to title your file. The computer will usually ask you to do this the first time you save your text. The purpose of a file name is to enable you to differentiate among many different texts located in the same "directory"—that is, on the same disk or on the same hard drive. Consequently, make sure your title is specific enough that you'll be able to recognize it when you open up the directory. As you write, you'll create more and more files, and you don't want to get them confused with one another. Let's say you've completed the first draft for an art history paper on Jackson Pollock. You wouldn't want to title your file "DRAFT," since this will be too general. Rather, you could type "POLLOCK.1" or "Pollock Essay, Version 1" (depending on whether you're working with an IBM-compatible machine, which allows only for shorter titles, or a Macintosh, which permits longer titles).

Entering text

This is a simple process: just start typing. Your text will appear wherever the cursor happens to be, and you can move that cursor by using either the arrow keys or the mouse. There's an automatic wraparound feature in all word processing programs, so you won't have to hit a carriage return at the end of each line, only when you wish to begin a new paragraph.

Changing Text

With a typewriter, errors, deletions, or changes have to be made with white-out or erasable ribbon; with a computer, all you need do is position your cursor immediately following the part you want to erase, and hit the backspace key.

Working with Blocks of Text

By "blocking" off parts of your text, either with the arrow keys or the mouse, you can select large portions of your text to work with. This is one of the most valuable features of any word processing program.

When you block text—say an entire paragraph—and "cut" it, it disappears, but it is saved in what is sometimes called a "clipboard." Sometimes you'll just want to leave things that way. But if you want to insert that paragraph somewhere else in your paper, you move the cursor to the new spot and hit "paste." The excerpted paragraph will instantly reappear at that point as it is retrieved from the clipboard.

At other times you might want to "copy" a portion of the text, perhaps so that an extra copy of it may be kept in another file. In this case you would simply hit "copy" instead of "cut," and your computer would save a copy of that excerpted passage until you told it where to put it.

Finally, blocking text allows you to reformat that text. You can block an entire essay, for example, and then tell the computer to change the font size or typeface. Or, you can block a word or sentence and have it changed to boldface or italics.

Printing

Once you decide to see a "hard copy" of your text, you tell the computer to print a copy. Before doing so you can also "reformat" your paper, which means changing the margin size, repositioning the page number, making the text single or double spaced, and so on. Depending on the word-processing program you have, you might be able to "preview" your work, in which case you will be shown a miniature version of what a page from your paper might look like in its entirety.

Computers and the Writing Process

Preparing to Write

Once you've familiarized yourself with the basics of your word-processing software, you're ready to use the computer for a specific assignment.

But before you begin, you need to focus. As you sit down, ask yourself these key questions: What is the assignment asking me to do? What will the audience expect? What do I know about this topic? What do I want to say to my audience?

A good way to begin is to jot down notes in a preliminary file. Whether you consider this "prewriting" or "freewriting," the task is the same: to clear your mind by putting down any thoughts, questions, insights, and ideas that come to you. Don't worry about spelling or grammar at this point; the goal here is to gather raw material that might later lead you down more specific paths. If at this time you wander off on tangents, fine; remember, this is not a first draft but an assemblage of early impressions. It's okay if things are sloppy; at this point you are generating a quantity of information. Make sure you save this file, perhaps under a name like "Rawnotes.Ex1."

Organizing Your Notes

You've now spent one or more sessions at the computer, compiling preliminary thoughts and ideas. Now it's time to put this information into some sort of order. Reread your jumble of ideas and seek patterns within the entries. Ask yourself questions: What do some of these entries have in common? Where do they differ? Once you've located several themes or threads within this information, use the block move or cut/paste commands to rearrange this material into sections with a subtitle for each one. (For example, different thoughts might be gathered under subheadings such as "Introductory Comments," "Ideas for Counterarguments," "Historical Background," "Research Data," "Descriptive Anecdotes," "Concluding Ideas," "Misc. Fragments," and so forth.)

Once you've grouped every thought or question under some heading, go back and review these sections. Which material do you think might belong at the beginning of your paper? Which at the end? How might you arrange the material in the middle? Again, using the cut/paste command, rearrange these entire sections so that they proceed in what looks like a sensible order.

Keep in mind that at this point nothing is set in stone. There's no reason to worry if what you've put in one section really belongs there or not. Your paper will go through a variety of revisions, and there will be time enough to make changes later. For now, your main goal is to inject some semblance of organization into your notes. The sooner you can see things in sections and categories rather than as a big lump of words, the better.

The advantage to organizing your thoughts in this manner is that the computer can help free you from any inclination to think that only one plan for a paper exists. A paper can be structured in numerous ways. The more flexible you are in experimenting with different outlines, the more likely it is that you'll create a design indicating a strong, creative synthesis of possible approaches.

Using Computers in Your Research

If you are writing a research paper, take a printout of your initial jottings and questions with you to the library as you begin the general search process. If your computer is hooked into a network, you might not even need to travel to the library to check its holdings since you might have access to the library's on-line catalog via phone lines. Some colleges will even have general references on a mainframe computer, and you will be able to peruse these references and do your initial reading while seated at your own computer.

If you belong to certain related discussion lists or "listservs" on the network, you can send general inquiries across that network, soliciting information from any subscribers to that list. You might introduce readers to the nature of your research and ask them if they know any related books or articles that would be worth exploring.

You can take notes at the computer, too, by creating files that divide your research topic into important categories. If categories get too large or ill defined, you can split them into separate files. And if you have a laptop computer, you can take your computer with you to the library, where you can research and write all in one session.

Writing a First Draft

At this point you should have a detailed, working outline full of thoughts and impressions that could feasibly be built on and turned into entire paragraphs. Print out this document and reread it, annotating it if you wish. You're now in a good position to begin writing a first draft.

Some people need the physical connection of hand to pen to paper when writing. If this is the case for you, go ahead and write your first draft by hand and write successive drafts at the keyboard. But keep in mind that writing out a draft longhand has two disadvantages compared with composing at the computer: even if you're a poor typist, a computer keyboard encourages speed, something that can come in handy if you're a student with a busy schedule. And secondly, later on when you work from a rough handwritten copy at the computer, you may be tempted to simply retype that same hard copy, rather than composing and revising it anew, a process that not only is inefficient but does not teach you how to dramatically revise your work. Yes, it does take time to sensitize yourself to the medium and cultivate an approach in which you're typing rough drafts directly into the computer, but in the long run this may not only save you valuable time, it may enhance your ability to revise.

Revising

Whether you're going to write only one first draft or (ideally) a series of intermittent drafts, there's one thing you ought to do after each one: print out a hard copy, read it, and make changes on that copy. Once you're satisfied with your changes, transfer them into your latest draft along with any other major and minor revisions.

There are several reasons to periodically print out and read hard copies of your work. For one, your eye will catch mistakes on paper that it will miss on the screen. (Incidentally, it's a great idea to read your work out loud as well, so that your ear will catch errors your eye might not see.) Also, there's a definite advantage to seeing the entire text on a piece of paper as opposed to visualizing your paper only through the keyhole of the computer screen. After all, chances are your final text will be presented to an audience in hard copy format, so it would be wise to familiarize yourself with what such a printout looks like at various phases throughout the revising process.

Fine-Tuning Your Final Draft

During the final stages of your revision, when you have assured yourself that the content of your paper is solid and organized to your liking, it is important to address smaller but equally vital concerns—namely, the style of your prose.

Throughout your revisions you will have stopped to revise particular sentences and clauses, but you will not have devoted systematic, document-wide attention to the construction of your sentences. A word processor encourages you to be a wordsmith—to quibble with word choices and to experiment with alternate phrasings. Ultimately the goal is to achieve a consistent style that allows you to communicate your main ideas as clearly, succinctly, and artfully as you can.

Your word processor provides an opportunity to rework your grammar, usage, and punctuation. At this late stage in your writing you ought not take anything for granted; that is, let no mark on your paper go unexamined. Are there passages where your language is markedly different from other sections? Will such unexpected rhetorical transitions enhance your prose or distract the reader? Have you overused certain words or phrases? Does every comma belong where you've put it? Might your text benefit from the inclusion of more (or fewer) semicolons, dashes, and colons? Are your paragraphs relatively consistent in length (or, conversely, could your text benefit from having a greater variety of paragraph lengths)?

Finally, run your final draft through the spell-checker. After all, you've worked too hard on your paper to let trivial errors of spelling, doubled words, or inadvertently used homonyms mar the end product. And even after you've run it through the spell-checker, it's essential to proofread the final draft one last time before turning it in, to catch the types of glitches the spell-checker cannot find.

This may seem like a lot of revisions, and it is. But good writers take pride in their work and are careful not to turn in anything unless they are sure it meets their own standard of excellence.

Printing

When you have proofread your document, print two final copies: one for you and one for your instructor. Make sure the format—in the line spacing, font, and margins—meets the requirements of your audience. It may be necessary to print out several copies before all of these final details are in order.

You should save at least some of the various drafts you've worked on prior to this point; in some cases an instructor might wish to see them to gauge your progress as a writer. While it's not always necessary to print your final paper out on a laser printer, which in some computer labs might require a fee, at least make sure that your text is dark and readable. Dot matrix printouts are sometimes hard to read, which is why some instructors don't permit them. Finally, remember to recycle any unnecessary copies you may have printed out.

Looking to the Future

So far we have discussed just one very important, albeit small feature of computers: the word-processing software. But for a writer, technological advancements in computer science and artificial intelligence offer exciting tools for the construction of ideas, and with them new ways of thought. "Hypertext" offers us alternative ways of creating prose in a nonlinear, linked format where the reader chooses the order in which the prose is to be read. Soon, when hypermedia becomes more accessible to general users, written texts will be accompanied by sound, three-dimensional graphics, and video on a regular basis. As more and more writers join networked discussion lists and international listservs, the possibilities for collaborative writing will increase considerably. And in the case of virtual reality, where users put on goggles, gloves, and body suits and "enter" virtual worlds, the possibilities for writers will undergo profound changes.

While it may be some time before such innovative technologies replace the traditional two-dimensional college research paper, such advancements are nevertheless available right now, and every day become a more vivid part of our surroundings. Whether you are excited or skeptical about such shifts, we have reached a point in history where a writer can be at a significant disadvantage if he or she remains computer illiterate, especially now that very young children are learning how to use computers in their classrooms. Learning how to write with a word processor will not only help you create better writing, but it might offer you a limited initiation into the technological environments rapidly altering our daily landscape.

Writing under Pressure: Essay Exams

Increasingly, professors across the curriculum are using essay exams to test student mastery of important concepts and relationships. A carefully conceived exam will challenge you not only to recall and organize what you know of a subject but also to extend and apply your knowledge. Essay exams will require numerous responses; but the one response to *avoid* is the so-called information dump in which at first glimpse of a topic you begin pouring onto the page *everything* you have ever read or heard about it. A good answer to an essay exam question requires that you be selective in choosing the information you discuss. What you say about that information and what relationships you make with it are critical. As is often the case with good writing, less tends to be more—provided that you adopt and follow a strategy.

A Strategy for Taking Essay Exams

Prepare

Ideally, you will have read your textbooks and assigned articles with care *as* they were assigned during the period prior to the exam. If you have read closely, or "critically," your preparation for an exam will amount to a *review* of material you have already thought carefully about. Skim assigned materials and pay close attention to notes you have made in the margins or have recorded in a reading log. Take new notes based on your original notes: highlight important concepts from each assignment. Then reorganize your notes according to key ideas that you think serve as themes or focus points for your course. List each idea separately, and beneath each, list any reading that in some way comments on or provides information about that idea. In an American literature course this idea might be "nature as a character" or "innocence lost." In a sociology course the idea might be "social constructions of identity." Turn next to your class notes (you may want to do this *before* reviewing your reading assignments), and add information and comments to your lists of key ideas. Study these lists. Develop statements about each idea that you could, if asked, support with references to specific information. Try to anticipate your professor's questions.

Read the Entire Exam before Beginning to Write

Allot yourself a certain number of minutes to answer each essay question, allowing extra time for the more complex questions. As you write, monitor your use of time.

Adopt a Discipline-Appropriate Perspective

Essay exams are designed in part to see how well you understand particular ways of thinking in a discipline. If you are writing a mid-term exam in chemistry, for instance, appreciate that your professor will expect you to discuss material from a chemist's perspective. That is, you will need to demonstrate not only that you know your information but also that you can *do* things with it: namely, think and reach conclusions in discipline-appropriate ways.

Adapt the Writing Process According to the Time Allotted for a Question

Assuming that you have thirty minutes to answer an essay question, spend at least five minutes of this allotted time in plotting an answer.

- Locate the assignment's key verb and identify your specific tasks in writing. (See the list that follows.)
- Given these tasks, list information you can draw on in developing your answer.
- Examine the information you have listed and develop a thesis, a statement that directly answers the question and that demonstrates your understanding and application of some key concept associated with the essay topic.
- Sketch an outline of your answer. In taking an essay exam, you have little or no time for writing to discover. Know before you write what major points you will develop in support of your thesis and in what order.

Spend twenty minutes of your allotted time on writing your answer. When you begin writing, be conscious of making clear, logical connections between sentences and paragraphs. Well-chosen transitions not only will help your professor follow your discussion but also will help you to project your ideas forward and to continue writing. As you do in formal papers, develop your essay in sections, with each section organized by a section thesis. Develop each section of your essay by discussing *specific* information.

Save five minutes to reread your work and ensure that its logic is clear and that you address the exam question from a discipline-appropriate point of view. Given the time constraints of the essay exam format, professors understand that you will not submit a polished draft. Nevertheless, they will expect writing that faces the question and that is coherent, unified, and grammatical. Again, avoid an information dump. Select information with care and write with a strategy.

The Importance of Verbs in an Essay Question

In reading an essay assignment, you will need to identify a specific topic and purpose for writing. Often, you can identify exactly what a professor expects by locating a key verb in the assignment such as *illustrate, discuss,* or *compare.* The words that follow are frequently used in essay examinations:[1]

summarize	sum up; give the main points briefly. *Summarize the ways in which food can be preserved.*
evaluate	give the good points and the bad ones; appraise; give an opinion regarding the value of; talk over the advantages and limitations. *Evaluate the contributions of teaching machines.*
contrast	bring out the points of difference. *Contrast the novels of Jane Austen and William Makepeace Thackeray.*
explain	make clear; interpret; make plain; tell "how" to do; tell the meaning of. *Explain how man can, at times, trigger a full-scale rainstorm.*
describe	give an account of; tell about; give a word picture of. *Describe the Pyramids of Giza.*
define	give the meaning of a word or concept; place it in the class to which it belongs and set it off from other items in the same class. *Define the term "archetype."*
compare	bring out points of similarity and points of difference. *Compare the legislative branches of the state government and the national government.*

[1]Source: Andrew Moss and Carol Holder, *Improving Student Writing: A Guide for Faculty in All Disciplines* (Dubuque, IA: Kendall/Hunt, 1988) 17–18.

discuss   talk over; consider from various points of view; present the different sides of. *Discuss the use of pesticides in controlling mosquitoes.*

criticize   state your opinion of the correctness or merits of an item or issue; criticism may approve or disapprove. *Criticize the increasing use of alcohol.*

justify   show good reasons for; give your evidence; present facts to support your position. *Justify the American entry into World War II.*

trace   follow the course of; follow the trail of; give a description of progress. *Trace the development of television in school instruction.*

interpret   make plain, give the meaning of; give your thinking about; translate. *Interpret the poetic line, "The sound of a cobweb snapping is the noise of my life."*

prove   establish the truth of something by giving factual evidence or logical reasons. *Prove that in a full-employment economy, a society can get more of one product only by giving up another product.*

illustrate   use a word picture, a diagram, a chart, or a concrete example to clarify a point. *Illustrate the use of catapults in the amphibious warfare of Alexander.*

PART VI

Handbook

"Spot Checking" for Common Errors

The following pages provide you with a system for spot-checking your writing—troubleshooting and locating the kinds of grammar and usage errors that cause over 90 percent of the most common problems in writing. A nine-section chart on pages 648–650 encapsulates common errors in basic recognition patterns and sentences. Look in these chart sections for sentence patterns and word forms close to what you have written. If any of these examples or explanations leads you to suspect an error in your work, follow the references to the "Spotlight" units that follow.

The nine "Spotlight" units should help narrow the search for sentences or situations that may resemble a questionable sentence you have written. These sections provide very basic revision guidance with a minimum of grammatical terminology. Look at the errors and revisions suggested. Do you suspect a possible error? If so, *note* the reference given to sections in the Reference Handbook where the revisions are explained.

Finally, in the Reference Handbook, locate a usage guideline and example that describes the possible error in your work. If your sentence resembles the situation described in the Handbook, then make a decision about revising your sentence.

SPOTLIGHT ON COMMON ERRORS

I. NOUN AND PRONOUN FORMS

Apostrophes can show possession or contraction. Never use an apostrophe with a possessive pronoun. (See page 651.)

FAULTY FORMS	REVISED
The scarf is *Chris*. It is *her's*.	The scarf is *Chris's*. It is *hers*.
Give the dog *it's* collar.	Give the dog *its* collar.
Its a difficult thing.	*It's* [it is] a difficult thing.

Choose a pronoun's form depending on its use. For pronouns connected by *and*, or with forms of the verb *be* (*is/are/was/were*), decide which forms to use (*I/he/she/they* OR *me/him/her/them*).

FAULTY FORMS	REVISED
This is *him*. It was *me*. Is that *her?*	This is *he*. It was *I*. Is that *she?*
The ball landed between *she* and *I*.	The ball landed between *her* and *me*.
Her and *me* practice daily.	*She* and *I* practice daily.

II. VERBS

Keep verb tenses consistent when describing two closely connected events. (See page 653.)

INCONSISTENT	REVISED
She *liked* the work. Still, she *keeps* to herself.	She *likes* the work. Still, she *keeps* to herself.

(a) Choose the right verb forms with an *if* clause expressing an unreal or hypothetical condition.
(b) Decide on which of these verb forms to use: *sit* or *set*, *lie* or *lay*, *rise* or *raise*.

FAULTY VERB FORM	REVISED
(a) If it *would be* any colder, the pipes *would* freeze.	If it *were* any colder, the pipes *would* freeze.
(b) *Lie* the books here. Then *lay* down.	*Lay* the books here. Then *lie* down.

III. AGREEMENT

Match subjects with verbs. Make sure both are either singular or plural. (See page 655.)

NOT IN AGREEMENT	REVISED
The *reason* she wins *are* her friends.	The *reason* she wins *is* her friends.

Match pronouns with the words they refer to. (a) Words joined by *and* require a plural pronoun and verb. (b) For words joined by *or/nor*, match the pronoun and verb to the nearer word.

NOT IN AGREEMENT	REVISED
(a) My friends **and** Sue *likes* *her* pizza hot.	My friends **and** Sue *like their* pizza hot.
(b) Neither her friends **nor** Sue *like their* pizza cold.	Neither her friends **nor** Sue *likes her* pizza cold.

IV. SENTENCE CONSTRUCTION AND FRAGMENTS
Recognize sentence boundaries. Mark where sentences should end, usually with a period (or sometimes with a semicolon). Avoid a FRAGMENT—a word group that will not stand alone with a full subject and predicate. (See page 656.)

FAULTY	REVISED
If our cousins arrive today. [Fragment]	Our cousins may arrive today.

V. SENTENCE CONSTRUCTION AND SENTENCE BOUNDARIES
Recognize boundaries. (a) Avoid a FUSED SENTENCE: two sentences with no connecting word or punctuation. (b) Avoid a COMMA SPLICE: two sentences with only a comma between them. (See page 657.)

FAULTY	REVISED
(a) He's here now later he'll go to Iowa. [Fused]	He's here now. Later he'll go to Iowa.
(b) He's here now, later he'll go to Iowa. [Splice]	He's here now; later he'll go to Iowa.

VI. PRONOUN REFERENCE
Make a pronoun refer to a SPECIFIC word. For clarity, avoid long phrases that separate a pronoun and the word it refers to. (See page 658.)

UNCLEAR REFERENCE	REVISED
If Amy and Mae arrive by noon, *she* will call. [Who?]	If Amy and Mae arrive by noon, *Mae* will call.

(a) Write specific references to avoid a vague *it*, *this*, or *that*. (b) Write consistent references to avoid shifts among *I/we*, *you*, or *s/he/it/they*.

VAGUE/INCONSISTENT REFERENCE	REVISED
(a) His late arrival caused delays. *This* couldn't be avoided. [Which? Late arrival, or delays?]	His late arrival couln't be avoided. His lateness caused delays.
(b) Transfer *students* must take care. The transfer may cost *you* credits. [Who is *you?*]	Transfer *students* must take care. The transfer may cost *them* credits.

VII. MODIFIERS
Keep a modifier close to the word it describes. Position a modifier so that it refers clearly to a specific word in the sentence. (See page 660.)

WORD MODIFIED UNCLEAR	REVISED
The car was made for a demanding driver *with a wide body.* [Which body is described?]	The car *with a wide body* was made for a demanding driver.
Those who walked *quickly* reached home.	Those who walked **reached** home *quickly.*
Being from the country, the skyscrapers looked threatening. [Who is from the country?]	Being from the country, *I thought* the skyscrapers looked threatening.

VIII. PARALLELISM

Sentences often make direct or indirect comparisons and contrasts. Compared or contrasted elements—often grouped with *and/but/or/nor,* or in lists—must be expressed with similar (or parallel) constructions. (See page 661.)

FAULTY	REVISED
He could speak **both** *with passion* **and** *could be coldly calculating.*	He could speak **both** *with passion* **and** *with cold calculation.*
Wash **all these:** *the* floor, *the* window, and *clean up my* sink.	Wash *all these: the* floor, *the* window and *the* sink.

IX. COMMA USE

Use a comma (a) before *and, but, or, for* and *so* to join sentences. Use a comma (b) to set off an introductory expression, and (c) to separate a series of three or more parts. Typically, a two-part series or a word grouping that ends a sentence is NOT separated with a comma. (See page 662.)

FAULTY	REVISED
(a) Jen needed cash so Amy loaned her some.	Jen needed cash, so Amy loaned her some.
(b) Incidentally I'll arrive, after sunset.	Incidentally, I'll arrive after sunset.
(c) Tim, and I collect bugs fish and rocks.	Tim and I collect bugs, fish, and rocks.

(d) Use a pair of commas in a sentence to set off *nonessential* **information. (e) Do NOT set off information that is** *essential* **to clarifying the meaning of a key word.**

FAULTY	REVISED
(d) My oldest brother George is 28.	My oldest brother, George, is 28. [Nonessential]
(e) The leader, whom I admire most, is Lincoln.	The leader whom I admire most is Lincoln. [Essential for establishing *which* leader]

I. SPOTLIGHT ON COMMON ERRORS—NOUN AND PRONOUN FORMS

These are the errors most commonly associated with a pronoun's case. For full explanations and suggested revisions, follow the cross-references.

CASE FORM ERRORS occur when writers misunderstand a pronoun's function in a sentence as a subject, object, or indicator of possession. These common situations lead to errors.

■ When a noun or an indefinite pronoun (such as *one, anyone, somebody*) shows possession, use an apostrophe (see section 15).

FAULTY	REVISED
This is Alberts signature.	This is Albert**'s** signature.
Rondas team is impressive.	Ronda**'s** team is impressive.
The families decision was final.	The family**'s** decision was final.
Somebodies book is here.	Somebody**'s** book is here.
This is nobodies business.	This is nobody**'s** business.

■ A personal pronoun that shows possession (such as *his, her, mine, ours*) uses NO apostrophe (see sections 15 and 5a).

FAULTY	REVISED
This coat is her's.	This coat is her**s** (This is her coat.)
Give the cat it's food.	Give the cat it**s** food.
These coats are their's.	These coats are their**s** (These are their coats.)
Your's are the first hands to touch this.	Your**s** are the first hands to touch this. (Your hands are the first hands to touch this.)

■ After a form of the verb *be (is, are, was, were)*, use a pronoun's subjective form (*I, you, he, she, we, they*) or its possessive form (*mine, yours, his, hers, theirs, ours*) with *no* apostrophe (see section 5a).

FAULTY	REVISED
This is her. This is him.	This is **she.** This is **he.**
Is that her? It is me.	Is that **she?** It is **I.**
This is our's. That is her's.	This is **ours.** That is **hers.**

■ When a personal pronoun (such as *I, me, you, he, she, it*) follows the word *and*, choose the pronoun's form as if the pronoun were alone in the sentence (see section 5d).

FAULTY	REVISED
Sally and me went to the movies.	Sally and **I** went to the movies. [TEST: I went to the movies alone.]
She and me went.	She and **I** went.
Her and me went.	[TEST: She went. I went.]
Tom went with Sally and I.	Tom went with Sally and **me.** [TEST: Tom went with me.]

It's a secret between you and I.

It's a secret between you and **me.**
[TEST: It's a secret between me and a friend.]

That's between he and Sally.

That's between **him** and Sally.
[TEST: That's between him and a friend.]

■ Use *its* to show possession; use *it's* ONLY for a contraction of *it is* (see section 15).

FAULTY

A dog hates it's fleas
Its raining.

REVISED

A dog hates **its** fleas.
It's raining. (It is raining.)

■ For a contraction with the verb *be (is, are)*, use an apostrophe (see section 15).

FAULTY

Its a difficult position.

Their coming home.

There coming home.

Shes home.
Your home.
Whos there?

REVISED

It**'s** a difficult position.
   (It is a difficult position.)

They**'re** coming home.
   (They are coming home.)

They**'re** coming home.
   (They are coming home.)

She**'s** home. (She is home.)
You**'re** home. (You are home.)
Who**'s** there? (Who is there?)

II. SPOTLIGHT ON COMMON ERRORS—VERBS

These are errors commonly associated with verb use. For full explanations and suggested revisions, follow the cross-references.

TENSE ERRORS occur when the time relationships among two or more verbs in closely linked clauses or sentences are not kept clear.

■ If you refer to *past events occurring at roughly the same time,* use past-tense verbs (see section 4f):

FAULTY

Tom *had traveled* where jobs *presented* themselves. [past perfect/past]
Tom *traveled* where jobs *had presented* themselves. [past/past perfect]
[The different tenses wrongly suggest that the events happened at different times.]

REVISED

     past event   past event
Tom *traveled* where jobs *presented* themselves. [past/past].
[The sentence refers to events that occurred at the same time.]

■ If you refer to *past events occurring one before the other,* use the past tense for the more recent event and the past perfect for the earlier event.

FAULTY

I remembered Mrs. Smith, who showed me kindness. [past/past]
[The tenses wrongly suggest that actions occurred at the same time.]

REVISED

     later event   earlier event
I *remembered* Mrs. Smith, who *had shown* me kindness. [past/past perfect]
[Mrs. Smith's "showing" occurred before the remembering.]

BUT if a key word (such as *before* or *after*) establishes a clear time relation, then the past perfect form of the verb is not used.

          earlier event   later event
I *was* unable to follow current events, *before* Mrs. Smith *showed* me how to read. [past/past]

■ Avoid abrupt tense shifts between closely linked sentences (see section 4f).

FAULTY TENSE SHIFT

The problem started when Fred forgot his appointment. Today he comes in late again.

REVISED

The problem started when Fred forgot his appointment. Today he came in late again.
[All action is in the past tense.]

ERRORS OF VERB FORM occur when writers confuse regular verbs with irregular verbs; the moods of verbs; and transitive verbs like *lay* with intransitive verbs like *lie* (see sections 4a and 4c).

- Regular/irregular: Know whether a verb is regular or irregular (see section 4a).

FAULTY	REVISED
I begun the story.	I began the story.
I had drank three full glasses.	I had drunk three full glasses.

- Mood: When writing about an event that is unreal or hypothetical, use a verb's subjunctive forms. Expressions such as *recommend, suggest,* and *it is important* signal an unreal or hypothetical event (see sections 22b and 4b).

FAULTY	REVISED
I recommend that Sarah builds a playhouse.	I recommend that Sarah *build* a playhouse.

In sentences expressing unreal conditions and beginning with *if*, use *were* in the first part of the sentence and *would* as a helping verb in the second part (see 4g).

FAULTY	REVISED
If it was any colder, the pipes will freeze.	*If it were* any colder, the pipes *would freeze.*

- Transitive/intransitive: Use a transitive verb (*set, lay, raise*) to show an action transferred from an actor to an object. Use an intransitive verb (*sit, lie, rise*) to limit action to the subject (see section 4c).

FAULTY	REVISED
Sit the books on the table.	*Set* the books on the table. [Transitive]
It hurts only when I set.	It hurts only when I *sit*. [Intransitive]
I think I'll lay down.	I think I'll *lie* down [Intransitive]
Lie the blanket in the corner.	*Lay* the blanket . . . [Transitive]

The forms of *lie* and *lay* are particularly tricky. (see section 4c.)

FAULTY	REVISED
Yesterday, I laid down to rest.	Yesterday, I *lay* down to rest.
I had lain the book on the table.	I had *laid* the book on the table.

III. SPOTLIGHT ON COMMON ERRORS—AGREEMENT

These are the errors most commonly associated with agreement between subject and verb or pronoun and antecedent. For full explanations and suggested revisions, follow the cross-references.

AGREEMENT ERRORS occur when the writer loses sight of the close link between the paired subjects and verbs, or between pronouns and the words they refer to (antecedents). Paired items should both be singular (referring to *one* person, place, or thing) or both be plural (referring to *more than one* person, place, or thing).

- A subject and its verb should both be singular or both be plural (they should agree), whether or not they are interrupted by a word or word group (see section 3a). Match subject and verb. Disregard interrupting words.

FAULTY	REVISED
Some people, when not paying attention, easily *forgets* names.	Some **people,** when not paying attention, easily *forget* names.

- A sentence with a singular subject needs a singular form of the verb *be (am, is, was);* a sentence with a plural subject needs a plural form of the verb *be (are, were)* (see section 3a). To ensure agreement in sentences beginning with the subject, ignore words following the verb *be.*

FAULTY	REVISED
The reason for her success *are* her friends.	The **reason** for her success *is* her friends.

When the subject comes after the verb in sentences beginning with *it* or *there*, verb and subject must still agree. Ignore the word *it* or *there.*

FAULTY	REVISED
There *is* seven hills in Rome.	There **are seven hills** in Rome. [The subject, *hills,* needs a plural verb.]

- When *and* joins words to create a two-part subject or a two-part pronoun referent, the sense is usually plural and so the matching verb or pronoun is plural (see sections 3a and 6b). When *or/nor* creates a two-part subject or pronoun referent, the nearer word determines whether the matching verb or pronoun is singular or plural (see sections 3a and 6b).

FAULTY	REVISED
A cat and a dog often *shares* **its** food.	A cat and a dog often **share their** food. [Here, *cat and dog* serve as a two-part subject and as a two-part referent.]

FAULTY	REVISED
Neither the rats nor the dog *chase* **their** tail.	Neither the rats nor the dog **chases** *its* tail. [The verb and pronoun match the nearer singular subject, *dog.*]

IV. SPOTLIGHT ON COMMON ERRORS—SENTENCE CONSTRUCTION AND FRAGMENTS

These are the errors most commonly associated with sentence construction and fragments. For full explanations and suggested revisions, follow the cross-references.

FRAGMENT ERRORS arise when writers incorrectly mark a group of words as a sentence. Apply a three-part test to confirm that a grouping of words can stand alone as a sentence (see section 1).

Test 1: Locate a verb: A sentence must have a verb.

Churchill *was* a leader.	**A leader of great distinction.**	**When he *became* Prime Minister.**
[Verb—*was*]	[No verb—this grouping of words cannot be a sentence; it is a FRAGMENT.]	[Verb—*became*—BUT this word grouping fails Test 3 below, so it is still a FRAGMENT.]

REVISED Churchill was *a leader of great distinction.*

NOTE: Be sure the word selected as a verb is not a verbal, which looks like a verb but actually serves as a subject, object, or modifier (see "Sentence Completeness" and section 1.)

After *serving* his country in the first World War.

[Verbal: *serving* looks like a verb but is actually an object in the prepositional phrase beginning with *after*. This grouping of words is therefore a FRAGMENT.]

REVISED   **After serving his country in the first World War,** he became Prime Minister.

Test 2: Locate the verb's subject: A sentence must have a subject.

Churchill was a leader	***When* he became prime minister.**
[Subject—*Churchill*]	[Subject—*he*—BUT this word grouping fails Test 3 so it is still a FRAGMENT.]

Test 3: Be sure that words such as *when, while, because* or *who, which, that* do not prevent the word group from being a sentence (see subordinating conjunctions and relative pronouns, section 9b).

SENTENCE   Churchill *was* a leader.

[No words prevent the grouping from being a sentence.]

FRAGMENTS	***When* he became Prime Minister.**	***Who* became Prime Minister.**

[*When* (a subordinating conjunction) and *who* (a relative pronoun) prevent these word groups from standing alone as sentences.]

REVISED   **He became Prime Minister.**

See section 1 for ways to correct fragments once you have identified them.

V. SPOTLIGHT ON COMMON ERRORS—SENTENCE CONSTRUCTION AND SENTENCE BOUNDARIES

These are the errors most commonly associated with sentence construction and sentence boundaries. For full explanations and suggested revisions, follow the cross-references.

SENTENCE BOUNDARIES are usually marked with a period. Not marking the end clearly will result in a FRAGMENT (see section 1), a FUSED SENTENCE (see section 2), or a COMMA SPLICE (see section 2).

CORRECT: Winston Churchill became a leader. He served his country in the first World War. Churchill was a leader of distinction.

FUSED SENTENCES: Winston Churchill became a leader he served his country in the first World War Churchill was a leader of distinction.

COMMA SPLICES: Winston Churchill became a leader, he served his country in the first World War, Churchill was a leader of distinction.

ERRORS OF SENTENCE CONSTRUCTION can be revised by recognizing sentence boundaries (see sections 1 and 2). Link sentences with these strategies:

- Link by combining parts of two sentences into one.

Winston Churchill became a leader. Churchill was a leader **of distinction.**

Winston Churchill became a leader of distinction.

- Link by using a comma plus one of these conjunctions—*and, but, or, nor* (see coordinating conjunctions, sections 9a, 13a).

Winston Churchill served his country in the first World War, ***and*** he became a leader of distinction.

- Link by using a semicolon (see sections 2 and 12).

Winston Churchill served his country in the first World War; he became a leader of distinction.

- Link by using a semicolon (or period) and a word like *however, consequently,* or *therefore* (see conjunctive adverbs, sections 2 and 9a).

Winston Churchill served his country in the first World War; **subsequently,** he became a leader of distinction.

- Link by using a word like *when, while,* or *because* (see subordinating conjunctions, section 9b).

After he served his country in the first World War, Winston Churchill became a leader of distinction.

VI. SPOTLIGHT ON COMMON ERRORS—PRONOUN REFERENCE

These are the errors most commonly associated with pronoun reference. For full explanations and suggested revisions, follow the cross-references.

PRONOUN REFERENCE ERRORS arise when a sentence leaves readers unable to link a pronoun with an *antecedent*—a specific noun that the pronoun refers to and renames (see section 6). If the identity of this antecedent is unclear, readers may miss the reference and become confused. Four error patterns lead to problems with pronoun reference.

- A pronoun should refer clearly to a single noun. When the pronoun can refer to either of two (or more) nouns within a sentence or between sentences, revise sentence for clarity (see section 6a).

Within a sentence

FAULTY	REVISED
When Mark and Jay return home, *he* will call. [To whom does *he* refer?]	When Mark and Jay return home, *Mark* will call.

Between sentences

FAULTY	REVISED
The conversation between Clara and Nancy lasted two hours. At the end, *she* was exhausted. [Which one is *she?*]	The conversation between Clara and Nancy lasted two hours. At the end, *Clara* was exhausted.

- A pronoun should be located close to the noun it renames. When a pronoun is too far from its antecedent, revise the sentence to narrow the distance and clarify meaning (see section 6a).

Within a sentence

FAULTY	REVISED
The statement that Dr. Parker made about a city water fountain and that she issued as a formal warning infuriated the mayor, who knew *it* would alarm the public. [Does *it* clearly refer to the faraway *statement* and not to something else?]	Issued as a formal warning, Dr. Parker's *statement* about a city water fountain alarmed the public, and *it* infuriated the mayor. [Less distance between the pronoun and antecedent makes the reference clear.]

Between sentences

FAULTY	REVISED
Major oil spills have fouled coastlines in Alaska, France, and England and have caused severe ecological damage. *Some* could almost certainly be avoided. [Does *some* refer to faraway *spills* or *coastlines?*]	Major oil spills have fouled coastlines in Alaska, France, and England and have caused severe ecological damage. *Some spills* could almost certainly be avoided. [*Spills* is added to clear up the reference.]

- The pronouns *this* and *that* should refer to specific words. When either is used as a one-word summary of a preceding sentence, revise to clarify the reference between sentences by adding an additional word or phrase of summary (see section 6a).

FAULTY

The purpose of the conference was to explore the links between lung cancer and second-hand smoke. *This* was firmly established. [What was established?]

REVISED

The purpose of the conference was to explore the links between lung cancer and second-hand smoke. *This connection* was firmly established. [A summary word added makes the reference clear.]

- Once you establish a pattern of first-person (*I*/*we*), second-person (*you*), or third-person pronouns (*he*/*she*/*it*/*they*) in a sentence or paragraph (see section 6b), keep references to your subject consistent. Prevent confusion by avoiding shifts and revising sentences for consistency (see section 8).

Within a sentence

FAULTY

Students generally fare better when *you* are given instruction on taking lecture notes. [Confusion arises between third-person *students* and second-person *you*. Who is the subject?]

REVISED

Students generally fare better when *they* are given instruction on taking lecture notes. [Consistent third person]
OR
As a student *you* will generally fare better when *you* are given instruction on taking lecture notes.

Between sentences

FAULTY

Students fare better when given *instruction on basic skills.* You can improve *your* note taking after getting help with the techniques. [Have *students* suddenly become *you?*]

REVISED

*Students fare better when given in-*struction on basic skills. *They* can improve *their* note taking after getting help with the techniques.

VII. SPOTLIGHT ON COMMON ERRORS—MODIFIERS

These are the errors most commonly associated with modifiers. For full explanations and suggested revisions, follow the cross-references.

MODIFIER ERRORS arise under two conditions: when the word being modified is too far from the modifier (a misplaced modifier); and when the word being modified is implied but does not appear in the sentence (a dangling modifier). Both errors will confuse readers.

- Position a modifier near the word it modifies (see section 7).

FAULTY	REVISED
A truck rumbled down the street, gray with dirt. [What is gray and dirty?]	A **dirty, gray** truck rumbled down the street. A truck rumbled down the **gray, dirty** street.

- Make a modifier refer clearly to one word (see section 7c).

FAULTY	REVISED
The supervisor who was conducting the interview thoughtfully posed a question. [Was this a thoughtful interview or thoughtful question?]	The supervisor who was conducting the interview posed a final, **thoughtful question.** The supervisor, who was conducting a **thoughtful interview,** posed a final question.

- Reposition a modifier that splits sentence elements (see section 7).

FAULTY	REVISED
Vigorous exercise—complemented by a varied diet that includes nuts, grains, vegetables, and fruits—is one key to fitness. [The "key to fitness" is unclear.]	Vigorous exercise, one key to fitness, should be complemented by a varied diet that includes nuts, grains, vegetables, and fruits.
The agent signed, with her client seated beside her, the contract. [What is "signed" is unclear.]	With her client seated beside her, the agent **signed the contract.**

- Make introductory phrases refer clearly to a *specific* word in the independent clause (see 7a).

FAULTY	REVISED
After considering his difficulty in the interview, the application was withdrawn. [Who withdrew the applications?]	After considering his difficulty in the interview, **the candidate withdrew** his application.

VIII. SPOTLIGHT ON COMMON ERRORS—PARALLELISM

These are the errors most commonly associated with parallelism. For full explanations and suggested revisions, follow the cross-references.

FAULTY PARALLELISM occurs when writers compare or contrast sentence parts without using similarly constructed wordings. In the examples that follow, parallel structures are highlighted.

- Conjunctions suggest comparisons and require parallel structures. Conjunctions such as *and* and *but* require parallel structures (see coordinating conjunctions, sections 8a, 8c).

FAULTY	REVISED
The candidate was a visionary but insisting on realism. [The verb forms *was a visionary* and *insisting* are not parallel.]	The candidate was visionary but realistic. [Similarly worded adjectives are linked by the conjunction *but*.]
The candidate attended meetings, spoke at rallies, and she shook thousands of hands. [The candidate's three activities are not parallel.]	The candidate attended meetings, spoke at rallies, and shook thousands of hands. [The candidate's three activities are similarly worded.]

Paired conjunctions such as *either/or* and *both/and* require parallel structures (see correlative conjunctions, section 9a).

FAULTY	REVISED
Explorers can be both afraid of the unknown and, when they encounter something new, they want to understand it. [The verb forms *can be afraid* and *encounter* are not parallel.]	Explorers can be both **afraid of the unknown** and **curious about it.** [Similarly worded adjectives and phrases are joined by the conjunction *both/and*.]

- Direct comparisons and contrasts require parallel structures (see section 8b).

FAULTY	REVISED
The staff approved the first request for funding, not the second presenter requesting funds. [The objects *request* and *presenter* are not parallel.]	The staff approved **the first request for funding,** not **the second.** [Two types of *request* are being compared and share similar wording.]

IX. SPOTLIGHT ON COMMON ERRORS—COMMA USE

These are clues to the errors most commonly associated with comma use. For full explanations and suggested revisions, follow the cross-references.

COMMA ERRORS arise when the use—or absence—of commas leaves readers unable to differentiate between a main sentence and the parts being set off. Five error patterns account for most of the difficulty with comma use.

- Use a comma to set off introductory words or word groupings from the main part of the sentence (see section 13b).

FAULTY	REVISED
Yesterday the faucet stopped working.	Yesterday, the faucet stopped working.

FAULTY	REVISED
Once the weather turned cold the faucet stopped working.	Once the weather turned cold, the faucet stopped working.

- Do *not* use a comma to set off concluding words or word groupings from a main sentence (see section 13b).

FAULTY	REVISED
The faucet stopped working, yesterday.	The faucet stopped working yesterday.

FAULTY	REVISED
The faucet stopped working, once the weather turned cold.	The faucet stopped working once the weather turned cold.

- Place a comma before the word *and, but, or, for,* or *so* when it joins two sentences (see section 13a).

FAULTY	REVISED
The faucet stopped working *and* the sink leaks.	The faucent stopped working, *and* the sink leaks.

FAULTY	REVISED
I'll fix them myself *and* I'll save money.	I'll fix them myself, *and* I'll save money.

BUT use no comma if one key word, usually the subject, keeps the second grouping of words from being considered a sentence.

FAULTY	REVISED
I'll fix them myself, and save money.	I'll fix them myself and save money.

- Use a comma to separate three or more items in a series (see section 13a).

FAULTY

I'll need a washer a valve and a wrench.

REVISED

I'll need a washer, a valve, and a wrench.

or I'll need a washer, a valve and a wrench.

- Use a *pair* of commas to set off from a sentence any word or word group that adds nonessential information (see section 13c).

FAULTY

Ahorn Hardware which is just around the corner will have the materials I need.

REVISED

Ahorn Hardware, which is just around the corner, will have the materials I need.

[Since a specific hardware store is named and its identity is clear, the added information is nonessential and is set off with a pair of commas.]

BUT use *no* commas if a word or word group adds essential information needed for identifying some other word in the sentence.

FAULTY

The hardware store, which is just around the corner, will have the materials I need.

REVISED

The hardware store which is just around the corner will have the materials I need.

[Since the added information is essential for identifying *which* hardware store (perhaps there is more than one store in the area), no commas are used.]

A Brief Reference Handbook

Sentence Completeness

Sentences make complete statements by using three basic structures. A **simple sentence** contains a single independent clause with a core subject and verb, often with various modifiers.

> **Simple:**   Jazz forms [*subject*] evolved [*verb*] with the players.

A **compound sentence** contains two or more independent clauses connected by a coordinating conjunction such as *and, but, nor.*

> **Compound:**   Jazz forms evolved with the players, *but* many listeners today aren't aware of different forms.

A **complex sentence** contains an independent clause and at least one dependent clause, with a connecting word such as *which, whom, that, after, although.*

> **Complex:**   The jazz forms that evolved with the players included be-bop and progressive jazz.

In addition to these basics, a **compound/complex** sentence is a combination structure involving both a compound sentence (with two or more independent clauses) and a complex sentence (with at least one dependent clause).

> **Compound/Complex:**   Jazz forms, which evolved with the players, included be-bop and progressive jazz, but many listeners today aren't aware of these different forms.

Sentences may also contain **verbal phrases** as components. These include **infinitive phrases** serving as nouns and using a base verb form frequently preceded by an infinitive marker, *to;* **gerundive phrases** serving as nouns and using the verb form plus an *-ing* ending; and **participial phrases** serving as adjective modifiers and using the verb form plus an *-ing* ending.

> **Infinitive Phrase:**   Some jazz forms are hard *to distinguish.*
> **Gerundive Phrase:**   *Distinguishing jazz forms* can be difficult.
> **Participial Phrase:**   The jazz forms *evolving with the players* are interesting.

These verb-form constructions, commonly used as nouns or modifiers within sentences, cause problems if they are left by themselves without a main verb; they cannot stand alone as complete statements or sentences.

A complete sentence must have both a subject and a verb. A word grouping that lacks a subject, a verb, or both is considered a fragment.

> **Incomplete:**   At the beginning of the meeting. [There is no verb.]
> **Revised:**   At the beginning of the meeting, the treasurer reported on recent news.
> **Incomplete:**   The fact that this is an emergency meeting. [The use of *that* leaves the statement incomplete, without a verb.]
> **Revised:**   This is an emergency meeting of the board.

A sentence must have a *logically compatible* subject and verb. A sentence in which a subject is paired with a logically incompatible verb is sure to confuse readers.

Incompatible: The meeting room is sweating. [A room does not normally sweat.]

Revised: Those gathered in the meeting room are sweating.

A sentence must have a subject and verb that *agree in number.* A subject and verb must both be singular or plural. The conventions for ensuring consistency are found in the next section.

Inconsistent: The treasurer are a dynamic speaker. [The plural verb does not match the singular subject.]

Revised: The treasurer is a dynamic speaker.

A sentence must have a subject close enough to the verb to ensure clarity. Meaning in a sentence can be confused if the subject/verb pairing is interrupted with a lengthy modifier. See below for a discussion of misplaced modifiers ("Sentence Structure").

Interrupted: We because of our dire financial situation and our interests in maintaining employee welfare have called this meeting.

Revised: We have called this meeting because of our dire financial situation and our interests in maintaining employee welfare.

1   Avoiding Fragments

To avoid writing an incomplete thought punctuated as if it were a sentence, check sentences to be sure they are complete.

1. Find a main verb, expressing action or status. *Disqualify verbals* and verbal phrases like those shown above for infinitives, gerundives, or participials.

2. Locate a subject for the verb: a noun, a pronoun, or any verbal phrase serving as a noun.

3. Look for connecting words (e.g., *which, whom, that, after, although*) that may create a dependent clause that is not properly linked to a simple or compound sentence (see above, *Complex sentences.*)

If you find a fragment:

1. **Revise any dependent clause set off as a sentence.**
   Convert the dependent clause to an independent clause:

Fragment: Although computers may be revolutionizing the world.
Revised: ~~Although~~ Computers may be revolutionizing the world.

Join the dependent clause to a new sentence.

Fragment: Although computers may be revolutionizing the world.
Revised: Although computers may be revolutionizing the world, *relatively few people understand how they function.*

2. **Revise any phrase set off as a sentence.**
There are various kinds of phrases: verbal, prepositional, absolute, and appositive. None can stand alone as a sentence.

Fragment: After years of drought.
Revised: After Years of drought *can devastate a national economy.*
Revised: After years of drought, *a nation's economy can be devastated.*

3. **Revise repeating structures or compound predicates set off as sentences.**
Repeating elements and compound predicates cannot stand alone. Incorporate such structures into an existing sentence or add words to construct a new sentence.

Fragment: College sports has long been conducted as a business. A profitable business. [The repeating element is a fragment.]
Revised: College sports has long been conducted as a business—*a* profitable business. [The repeating element has been incorporated into an existing sentence.]
Fragment: Some coaches achieve legendary status on campus. And are paid legendary salaries. [The second element is part of a compound verb.]
Revised: Some coaches achieve legendary status on campus *and* are paid legendary salaries. [The second verb and its associated words are incorporated into an existing sentence.]

Exercise 1

Correct each sentence fragment either by joining it with an independent clause or by rewriting it as an independent clause.

Example: When the influential scholar Ulrich B. Phillips declared in 1918 that slavery in the Old South had impressed upon African savages the glorious stamp of civilization. He set the stage for a long and passionate debate. [The first unit is a dependent clause.]

When the influential scholar Ulrich B. Phillips declared in 1918 that slavery in the Old South had impressed upon African savages the glorious stamp of civilization, he set the stage for a long and passionate debate. [The dependent clause is connected to the sentence that follows it.]

1. As the decades passed and the debate raged on. One historian after another confidently professed to have deciphered the real meaning of slavery. That "peculiar institution."
2. The special situation of the female slave remained unexamined. Amidst all this scholarly activity.
3. Because the ceaseless arguments about her "sexual promiscuity" or her "matriarchal" proclivities obscured the condition of Black women during slavery.
4. If and when a historian sets the record straight on the experiences of enslaved Black women. She (or he) will have performed an inestimable service.

2   Eliminating Comma Splices and Fused Sentences

Sentences of explanation with expanded examples, or sentences with a transitional word such as *therefore, consequently, so,* or *for example,* may signal a risk for a **comma splice**—two sentences insufficiently connected with a simple comma—or a **fused sentence**—two sentences with no boundary between them.

Fused Sentence: Jazz forms can be hard to distinguish so many listeners today can't tell one form from another.

Comma Splice: Jazz forms may be hard to distinguish, therefore many listeners today can't tell one form from another.

There are several ways to correct this error.

1. Make two sentences.

   Jazz forms may be hard to distinguish. Therefore many listeners today can't tell one form from another.

2. Use a semicolon to separate the clauses.

   Jazz forms may be hard to distinguish; therefore many listeners today can't tell one form from another.

3. Separate clauses with a comma and coordinating conjunction.

   Jazz forms may be hard to distinguish, and that's why many listeners today can't tell one form from another.

4. Make one clause dependent to create a complex sentence.

   Jazz forms may be so hard to distinguish that many listeners can't tell one form from another.

2a   Four Ways to Avoid Comma Splices

Use these strategies to avoid comma splices:

1. Separate the two clauses with a period.

   Christopher Columbus is considered a master navigator today. He died in neglect.

2. Join the two clauses with a coordinating conjunction and a comma.

   Christopher Columbus is considered a master navigator today, but he died in neglect.

3. Join the two clauses with a conjunctive adverb and the appropriate punctuation.

   Christopher Columbus is considered a master navigator today; nevertheless, he died in neglect.

4. Join the two clauses by making one subordinate to the other.

   Although Christopher Columbus is considered a master navigator today, he died in neglect.

2b **Five Ways to Mark the Boundary between Sentences**

Use these strategies to mark the boundary between sentences:

Mark a sentence boundary with punctuation.

1. Use a period: He laughed. He danced. He sang.
2. Use a semicolon: He laughed; he danced and sang.

Mark a sentence boundary with a conjunction and punctuation.

3. Use a coordinating conjunction: He laughed, and he danced.
4. Use a subordinating conjunction: While he laughed, he danced.
5. Use a conjunctive adverb: He laughed; moreover, he danced.

Exercise 2

Correct the fused sentences and comma splices in the following paragraphs, making use of all five strategies discussed in this chapter. One consideration governing your choice of corrections should be sentence variety. Vary methods for correcting fused and spliced clauses to avoid repeating sentence structures in consecutive sentences.

> We primates are very social animals watch a troop of baboons crossing the African savanna, or a group of gorillas preparing their overnight bivouac, and the importance of communal living soon becomes apparent. Human behavior centers on the social group, too, the profusion of modern and extinct societies offers a bewildering variety of ways and means of ordering social relations. These have spawned an anthropological jargon that tries to divide and place other cultures into neat groupings.

Sentence Parts

3 **Subject–Verb Agreement**

A predicate verb must agree in number and person with its subject; both must be either singular or plural. This normal pattern is a problem only in certain confusing situations where extra caution and remedial action are required.

3a **Make a Third-Person Subject Agree in Number with Its Verb**

The suffix *-s* or *-es*, affixed to a present-tense verb, indicates an assertion about a singular third-person subject (A frog do*es* this.); the suffix *-s* or *-es*, affixed to most nouns or third-person pronouns, indicates a plural (Frogs do this.).

A Subject Agrees with Its Verb Regardless of Whether Any Phrase or Clause Separates Them

Often a subject may be followed by a lengthy phrase or clause that comes between it and the verb, confusing the basic pattern of agreement. To clarify the matching of the subject with the verb, mentally strike out or ignore phrases or clauses separating them.

The *purpose of* practicing daily for several hours <u>is</u> to excel.

A Compound Subject Linked by the Conjunction *and* Is in Most Cases Plural

When a compound subject linked by *and* refers to two or more people, places, or things, it is usually considered plural.

UPS and Federal Express <u>compete</u> with the U.S. postal system.

When Parts of a Compound Subject Are Linked by the Conjunction *or* or *nor,* the Verb Should Agree in Number with the Nearer Part of the Subject

When all parts of the compound subject are the same number, agreement with the verb is fairly straightforward.

Either John or *Maria* <u>sings</u> today.

Either the Smiths or the *Taylors* <u>sing</u> today.

When one part of the compound subject is singular and another plural there can be confusion; the subject nearest the verb determines the number of the verb. If the nearest subject is singular, the verb is singular.

Neither the crew members nor the *captain* <u>speaks</u> Arabic.

A Linking Verb Agrees in Number with Its Subject, Not with the Subject Complement

In a sentence with a linking verb (*be, seem, become,* etc.), identify the singular or plural subject when deciding the number of the verb. Disregard any distracting phrase or clause that interrupts the subject and verb; also disregard the subject complement *following* the linking verb.

One *reason* for his success <u>is</u> his friends.

His *friends* <u>are</u> one reason for his success.

In Sentences with Inverted Word Order, a Verb Should Agree in Number with Its Subject

The subject of an English sentence is normally placed before a verb. When this order is rearranged, the subject and verb continue to agree in number. Most errors with rearranged sentences occur with the verb be.

Here *is* Michael.   Here *are* Janice and Michael.   There *is* a strategy.

The Verb of a Dependent Clause Introduced by the Pronoun *Which, That, Who,* or *Whom* Should Agree in Number with the Pronoun's Antecedent

In such a dependent clause, both the pronoun subject (*which, that,* etc.) and verb are dependent for their number on an antecedent in the main clause.

The *books, which* <u>are</u> old, <u>are</u> falling apart.   *Which book* <u>is</u> mine?

Phrases and Clauses That Function as Subjects Are Treated as Singular and Take Singular Verbs

Often a noun clause, or a phrase with a gerund or infinitive, will act as the subject of a sentence. Such a construction is always regarded as a singular element in the sentence.

To swim well <u>is</u> the first prerequisite for scuba diving.

That the child is able to cough <u>is</u> a good sign.

3b   **Most Group Nouns or Pronouns Are Singular and Agree with Singular Verbs**

Most Indefinite Pronouns Have a Singular Sense and Take a Singular Verb

Indefinite pronouns (such as *any* and *each*) do not have specific antecedents—they rename no particular person, place, or thing and thus raise questions about subject–verb agreement.

Virtually *everybody* in developed countries <u>travels</u> by bus.

Many who live elsewhere <u>have</u> no choice but to walk.

Collective Nouns Have a Plural or a Singular Sense, Depending on the Meaning of a Sentence

When a collective noun, such as *audience, band, bunch, crew, crowd, faculty, family, group, staff, team,* and *tribe,* refers to a single unit, the sense of the noun is singular and the noun takes a singular verb. The context of a sentence will give you clues about the number of its subject.

At this school, the *faculty* <u>meets</u> as a group with the President.

Nouns Plural in Form But Singular in Sense Take Singular Verbs

The nouns *athletics, economics, mathematics, news, physics,* and *politics* all end with the letter *-s,* but they nonetheless denote a single activity. **Note:** *Politics* can be considered plural, depending on the sense of a sentence.

Economics <u>depends</u> heavily on mathematics.

Exercise 3

In the following sentences, determine whether a subject is singular or plural. Choose the correct form in parentheses and be able to explain your choice.

> *Example:* How (do/does) we get other people to agree with us?
>
> > How *do* we get other people to agree with us? [The subject of the sentence is the plural pronoun, *we*. Even though the auxiliary part of the verb, *do*, is placed before the subject to form a question, the full verb (including the auxiliary) and the subject must agree in number.]

1. One reason for making a purchase (is/are) a buyer's emotional needs.
2. There (is/are) no single method that (assure/assures) success in persuading others; still, several methods (seem/seems) helpful.
3. One effective way of getting a "yes" from other people (is/are) to get them to like us.
4. Flattery, an extremely common tactic for gaining compliance, (has/have) a long history.
5. Both flattering people and getting them to talk about themselves (work/works) in surprisingly consistent ways.

---

4   Verb Forms

All verbs other than *be* have two basic forms and three principal parts; these five forms and parts are the foundation for all the varied uses of verbs. A full dictionary entry may present these forms and parts: base form, *-s* form, past tense, past participle, and present participle.

The **base** (or infinitive) **form** of a verb—often called its **dictionary form**—is the base from which all changes are made. Use the base form of a verb with *no* ending for occasions when the action of a verb is present for plural nouns or for the personal pronouns *I, we, you,* or *they*.

4a   The Principal Parts of Regular Verbs

Base Form	Present Tense (-s Form)	Past Tense	Past Participle	Present Participle
share	shares	shared	shared	sharing
start	starts	started	started	starting
climb	climbs	climbed	climbed	climbing

Most verbs are regular in that they form the past tense and past participle with the suffixes *-ed* or *-d*. An irregular verb will form its past tense and past participle by altering the spelling of the base verb, as in *build/built* or *bring/brought*. A dictionary entry for an irregular verb shows the principal parts and basic forms of a verb as the first information in the entry. This will show you when a verb is irregular—when it does not take an *-ed* ending in its past tense and past participle forms. Because irregular verbs are some of the most commonly used words in the language, most speakers and readers are accustomed to, and expect, them. You should take care to use correct irregular forms. Memorize troublesome forms or look them up as necessary.

4b Kinds of Verbs

Transitive verbs transfer action from an actor—the subject of the sentence—to a person, place, or thing receiving that action.

> *buy, build, kick, kiss, write*
> Wanda *built* a snowman.

Intransitive verbs show action; yet no person, place, or thing is acted on.

> *fall, laugh, sing, smile*
> Stock prices *fell.*

Linking verbs allow the word or words following the verb to complete the meaning of a subject.

> *be (am, is, are, was, were, has/have been), look, remain, sound, seem, taste*
> Harold *seems* happy.

Helping or **auxiliary verbs** help to show the tense and mood of a verb.

> *be (am, is, are, was, were) has, have, had, do, did, will*
> I *am* going. I *will* go. I *have* gone. I *did* go.

Modal auxiliaries such as *might, would, could,* and *must* help a verb to express urgency, obligation, and likelihood.

> I *should* go. I *might* go. I *could* go.

The **mood** of a verb indicates the writer's judgment as to whether a statement is a fact, a command, or an unreal or hypothetical condition contrary to fact. In the **indicative mood,** a writer states a fact, opinion, or question. Most of our writing and speech is in the indicative mood.

> The mayor has held office for eight years. [fact]
>
> The mayor is not especially responsive. [opinion]
>
> Did you vote for the mayor? [question]

In the **imperative mood,** a writer gives a command, the subject of which is "you," the person being addressed. In this book, for example, the imperative addresses readers with specific guidelines for writing or making revisions. An imperative uses the verb in its base form. Often, the subject of a command is omitted, but occasionally it is expressed directly.

> Follow me!
>
> Do not touch that switch.
>
> Don't you touch that switch!

By using the **subjunctive mood,** a writer shows that he or she believes an action or situation is unreal or hypothetical. With a subjunctive verb, a writer can also make a recommendation or express a wish or requirement, usually preceded by such a verb construction as *recommend, suggest, insist, it is necessary,* or *it is important.* The **present subjunctive** uses the base form (infinitive) of the verb, for all subjects.

> I recommend that he *develop* his math skills before applying.
> I recommend that they *develop* their skills.

The **past subjunctive** uses the past-tense form of the verb—or, in the case of *be*—the form *were.*

> If management *assumed* traveling costs, the team would be happier.
> He wished he *were* four inches taller.

> See 22b for descriptions of situations involving subjunctive verbs in conditional sentences.

4c   Verbs Frequently Confused: Transitive and Intransitive Forms

Some verbs with similar sounds and related meaning are commonly confused and given incorrect roles in a sentence. A **transitive verb** takes a direct object.

> *The city editor* [subject] <u>sets</u> [transitive verb] *standards* [object].

An **intransitive verb** takes no action on any object.

> *At last the city editor* [subject] <u>sits</u> [intransitive verb with no object].

The transitive verb *set* is incorrect in such a sentence.

Similarly the transitive verb *lay* takes an object (*A reporter lays groundwork.*), but the intransitive verb *lie* takes no object (*Here the story lies.*); in the latter sentence the transitive verb *lay* is incorrect.

The transitive verb *raise* takes an object (*Legislators raise taxes.*), but the intransitive verb *rise* takes no object (*Taxes rise.*); in the latter sentence the transitive verb *raise* is incorrect.

4d   The Split Infinitive

The infinitive—the base verb form—is frequently preceded by an infinitive marker *to.* Some readers are disturbed by any verbal modifier that "splits" the marker (*to*) from the base form (*challenge*).

> **Split:** The editor's job is *to* rigorously and promptly *challenge* the facts.

However, the split formation may often prevent more awkward phrasing in a sentence full of complex modifiers. (See "Modifiers" below.)

Exercise 4

Choose the appropriate form of *sit/set, lie/lay,* or *rise/raise* in these sentences.

> *Example:* A squirrel was (*sit/set*) _____ on a picnic table.
> A squirrel was *sitting* on a picnic table.

1. A man walked by and (*sit/set*) _____ a newspaper on a nearby table.
2. He then (*sit/set*) _____ down and unfolded the paper.
3. From one pocket he produced a tomato, which he (*lie/lay*) _____ on the paper.
4. From another pocket came a salt shaker, which he (*rise/raise*) _____ ceremoniously.
5. The squirrel (*rise/raise*) _____ at the scent of food.

4e Verbs in the Active and Passive Voice

Verbs in the **active voice** name the subject of the clause as actor or protagonist of the act or assertion that the verb expresses. When the verb is transitive, anything acted on becomes the object of the verb.

> **Active:** The *reporter* [subject] <u>found</u> [active verb] *talkative sources* [object].

The active voice is the clearest and simplest mode for making direct statements, and it is preferable for most general exposition.

Verbs in the **passive voice** are useful to emphasize the object acted on, and also to avoid the active voice's emphasis on the actor. Passive verbs are formed with the past participle verb form and a form of *be,* with the original subject relegated to a *by* phrase.

> **Passive**: Several talkative sources *were found* by the reporter.

If the *by* phrase is dropped, the object of the verb receives even more emphasis and the actor is eliminated from view.

> **Passive**: Several talkative sources *were found.*

Because the passive voice leaves the actor less specific and is sometimes wordy, many readers strongly object to its frequent use. Passive voice is sometimes used deliberately to avoid responsibility for a statement or to give a false impression of objectivity.

Exercise 5

Change the passive-voice sentences that follow to the active voice and change the active-voice sentences to passive. If need be, invent a subject for the active-voice sentences.

Example: Stocks and securities are bought by an arbitrageur and then quickly sold for a profit. [The passive voice involves two verbs: *"are bought . . . and . . . sold."*]

An arbitrageur buys stocks and securities and then quickly sells them for a profit. [changed to active voice]

1. In the 1980s, an increase in the number of stock broker arbitrageurs was seen.
2. Originally, companies were invested in by arbitrageurs after a merger was announced.
3. Investments were based on the relationship between the stock prices of the two firms involved and the probabilities that the two firms would merge.
4. In the mid-1980s, investments were made in firms that *might* be candidates for mergers.
5. Arbitrageurs hoped to make a profit on the price increases at the time of the merger announcement.

4f **Verb Tenses in Sequence**

A verb's tense indicates when an action has occurred or when a subject exists in a given state. There are three basic tenses in English: *past, present,* and *future.* Each has a **perfect** form, which indicates a completed action; each has a **progressive** form, which indicates ongoing action; and each has a **perfect progressive** form, which indicates ongoing action that will be completed at some definite time.

When two closely related events are described in adjoining sentences or with subordinate clauses, the sequence of tenses needs attention.

- **To establish a relationship between two events, both of which occur in the past:** Use the simple past tense for one past event and any of the four past tenses for the other event.

  Jones *attacked* Representative Kaye, who *had proposed* the amendment.
  Jones *has spent* months preparing for the trial that *will begin* next week.

- **To establish a relationship between a past event and a future event:** Use the simple past tense for the past event and the simple future or the future progressive for the future event.

  We *reserved* tickets for the play that *will open* on Saturday. [The reservations were made in the past for a play that opens in the future.]

- **To establish a relationship between a past event and an acknowledged fact or condition:** Use the simple past tense for the main clause and the simple present tense in the dependent clause.

  The study *concluded* that few people *trust* strangers. [The study has been completed and has reached a conclusion about human nature.]

Use the past perfect tenses for the past event and the simple present tense for the acknowledged fact or condition.

  Smith *had argued* that everyone *needs* basic services. [The argument occurred in the past concerning an ongoing need.]

5   Forms of Nouns and Pronouns

Nouns and pronouns have the following functions in sentences:

Subject: a noun, pronoun, or noun-like word group that produces the main action of the sentence or is described by the sentence.

Subject	verb
We	*look.*

Direct Object: a noun, or group of words substituting for a noun, that receives the action of a transitive verb (tr.). A direct object answers the question *What or who is acted upon?*

Subject	verb (tr.) direct object
Stories	*excite the imagination.*

Indirect Object: a noun, or group of words substituting for a noun, that is indirectly affected by the action of a verb. Indirect objects typically follow transitive verbs such as *buy, bring, do, give, offer, teach, tell, play,* or *write.* The indirect object answers the question *To whom or for whom has the main action of this sentence occurred?*

Subject	verb (tr.) indirect object direct object
Stories	*offer us relief.*

Object Complement: an adjective or noun that completes the meaning of a direct object by renaming or describing it. Typically, object complements follow verbs such as *appoint, call, choose, consider, declare, elect, find, make, select,* or *show.*

Subject	verb (tr.) direct object object complement
They	*make us tense.*

Subject Complement: a noun or adjective that completes the meaning of a subject by renaming or by describing it. Subject complements follow linking verbs such as *appear, feel, seem, remain,* as well as all forms of *be.*

Subject	verb (linking) subject complement
We	*are readers.*

A noun or pronoun may change in form, depending on its function in a sentence. Nouns do not change their form when their function changes from subject to object. Especially when revising, you may change a pronoun's function—say, from object to subject. By understanding how a pronoun's function changes, you will be prepared to make a corresponding change to the pronoun's form. There are eight classes of pronouns. Most troublesome are the **personal pronouns,** which refer to people and things, and these will be the focus of discussion here.

5a   **Pronouns Used as Subjects**

These are the forms of pronouns used as subjects or subject complements:

	Singular	*Plural*
1st person	I	we
2nd person	you	you
3rd person	he, she, it	they

Use the Subjective Case When a Pronoun Functions as a Subject, as a Subject Complement, or as an Appositive That Renames a Subject

She speaks forcefully. The speaker is *she.*
The executive officers—and only *they*—can meet here.

Use the Subjective Case for Pronouns with the Linking Verb *Be*

The linking verb *be* in a sentence serves as a grammatical "equals" sign; it links the subject of the sentence to a completing or "complement" word that is made identical to the subject. When pronouns are involved in this equation, they too are made identical to the subject and are also used in the subjective form.

The speaker is *she.*   These are *they.*   It is *I.*

5b   **Pronouns Used as Objects**

These are the forms of pronouns used as objects or object complements:

	Singular	*Plural*
1st person	me	us
2nd person	you	you
3rd person	him, her, it	them

Use the Objective Forms for Pronouns Functioning as Objects

The governor handed *her* the report. The job appealed to *me.*
We enjoyed taking *them* to dinner.

Use the Objective Form for Pronouns Functioning as the Subject of an Infinitive

When a pronoun appears between a verb and an infinitive, the pronoun takes the objective form. In this position, the pronoun is called the subject of the infinitive.

Study enabled *us* to reach the goal.

5c   **Possessive Forms of Pronouns**

These are the possessive pronoun forms:

	Singular	*Plural*
1st person	my, mine	our, ours
2nd person	your, yours	your, yours
3rd person	his, her, hers, its	their, theirs

Certain Possessive Pronouns Are Used as Subjects or Subject Complements to Indicate Possession

> *Yours* are the first hands to touch this.
> These are *theirs*.

The possessive pronouns *mine, ours, yours, his, hers, theirs* are used in place of a noun as subjects or subject complements.

> *Ours* is a country of opportunity for both men and women, Eleanor Roosevelt argued. This opportunity is *ours*. (*mine, yours, his, hers, theirs*)

Use a Possessive Noun or Pronoun before a Gerund to Indicate Possession

> The group argued for *her* getting the new position.

5d   ### Pronouns in Expanded Sentences and Questions

In a **compound construction,** use pronouns in the objective or subjective form according to their function in the sentence. The coordinating conjunction *and* can create a compound construction—a doubled subject or object. These can sometimes mask how a pronoun functions in a sentence. When you have difficulty choosing between a subjective or objective pronoun in a compound construction, try this test: *Create a simplified sentence by dropping out the compound;* then *try choosing the pronoun.* With the compound gone in the simpler construction, you should be able to tell whether the pronoun operates as a subject or an object.

> Sally and *I* went to the movies. Tom went with Sally and *me*.

In a question, choose a subjective, objective, or possessive form of *who(m)* or *who(m)ever* according to the pronoun's function.

> *Who* is going? To *whom* are you writing? *Whose* birthday is it?

To test the correct choice for these pronouns at the beginning of a question, mentally *answer* the question, substituting the personal pronouns *I/me, we/us, he/him,* or *she/her* for *the relative pronoun.* Your choice of the subjective or objective form in the answer sentence will likely be quite clear, and it will be the same choice to make for the form of *who(m)* or *who(m)ever.*

In a dependent clause, choose the subjective, objective, or possessive form of *who(m)* or *who(m)ever* according to the pronoun's function within the clause. To choose the correct case for a relative pronoun in a dependent clause, eliminate the main clause temporarily; consider the pronoun's function *only* in the dependent clause.

> Henry Taylor, *who* writes poems, lives in Virginia. Taylor, *whom* critics have praised, has a new book. The poet, *whose* book won a prize, lives quietly.

In a clause, the relative pronouns *who* and *whom* take the place of nouns (or pronouns) that function as subjects or objects. Choosing the correct relative pronoun requires that you see that pronoun in relation to the words immediately following. You must examine the broader context of the clause in which the pronoun is located. Two questions should help you to choose correctly between *who* and *whom.*

- Is the relative pronoun followed by a verb?

—"Yes": choose the subjective-case *who* or *whoever.*

A relative pronoun followed by a verb indicates the pronoun occupies the subject position of the clause. To confirm this choice, substitute *I, we, you, he,* or *she* for the pronoun.

> Clinton, *who* won by a landslide in the electoral college, did not win as convincingly in the popular vote. [*Who* is followed by a verb, and when it is converted to *he* yields a sentence: "*He* won by a landslide. . . ."]

—"No": choose the objective-case *whom* or *whomever.* See the next test.

- Is the relative pronoun followed by a noun or by any of these pronouns: *I, we, you, he, she, few, some, many, most, it* or *they?*

—"Yes": choose the objective-case *whom* or *whomever.*

A relative pronoun followed by a noun or one of the listed pronouns indicates that the normal order of the clause (subject-verb-object) has been rearranged, suggesting the need for a pronoun in its objective form. To confirm your choice of *whom* or *whomever,* consider the pronoun and the words immediately following. Rearrange these words and substitute *him, her,* or *them* for the relative pronoun.

> Clinton, *whom* most analysts counted out of the presidential race, surprised supporters and detractors alike. [*Whom* is followed by *most,* and when it is converted to *him* yields a sentence: "Most analysts counted *him* out."]

Exercise 6

In the following sentences, correct the usage of the italicized pronouns. If a pronoun choice is correct, circle the pronoun.

> *Example:* Anne told me it was Simon's fault; but between you and *I,* she's as much to blame as *him.*
>
> Anne told me it was Simon's fault; but between you and *me,* she's as much to blame as *he.* [Pronouns that follow a preposition must be objective case: thus, <u>between you and me.</u> The second part of the comparison requires a subjective-case pronoun: <u>She is to blame as much as he is to blame.</u>]

1. It was *me* who asked Helen to go to the museum.
2. It was not *him* who called.
3. "*Whom* may I ask is calling? Yes, this is *her.*"
4. "To *Who* It May Concern" is not an especially effective opening for a business letter.
5. He gave the present to both *you* and *she.*
6. *You* and *she* have been friends for many years.

7. A group that can't afford cutbacks in health care is *us* salaried employees.
8. *Whomever* the people elect is the person *who* we depend upon.
9. Richard Nixon, *who* was elected, resigned from office.
10. *Him* resigning was the first presidential abdication in *our* history.

5e   Gender in Nouns and Pronouns

Pronouns in the third-person singular show gender forms as *he, she, it*. These forms involve decisions about gender references and are treated in the next section.

Nouns that signal gender stereotypes can be offensive and should be replaced with gender-neutral nouns whenever possible.

Avoid: stewardess (and generally nouns ending with *-ess*)
Use: flight attendant

Avoid: workmen; manpower
Use: workers; work force; personnel

Avoid: chairman
Use: chair or chairperson

Avoid: the girl in the office
Use: the woman; the manager; the secretary

Avoid: woman driver; male nurse
Use: woman who was driving; driver; nurse; man on the nursing station

Avoid: mothering
Use: parenting, nurturing

Avoid: mankind
Use: people; humanity; humankind

6   Pronouns and Antecedents: Reference and Agreement

A pronoun renames and refers to a noun or indefinite pronoun located somewhere nearby in the same or a neighboring sentence; every pronoun needs an **antecedent** to which it refers clearly in order to get a specific meaning.

6a   Pronoun Reference

To make the reference clear, observe these rules:

Keep Pronouns Close to Their Antecedents

Too many nouns between a pronoun and its antecedent can be confusing (e.g., News reporters or city editors when dealing with angry readers or troubled sources must keep *their* [whose?] tempers cool.). Rewriting to close the gap will help (e.g., News reporters or city editors must keep *their* tempers cool when . . .).

Be Sure Pronouns Refer to Specific Things or Persons

Avoid using vague pronoun constructions such as *you know, they say, it figures*, and be sure to make *this, that, which*, or *it* refer to specific nouns.

Check for sentences with vague or implied antecedents (e.g., In a thunderstorm *it* [?] creates a lightning discharge); rewrite them to make a specific antecedent (e.g., If an electric *charge* builds during a thunderstorm, *it* creates lightning.).

6b   Pronoun Agreement

To make an accurate reference, a pronoun must agree with the number, person, and gender of its antecedent. Some sentence situations may make this agreement unclear and may require some corrective action. Here are some of these situations:

Agreement When There Is a Compound Antecedent

When two or more antecedent nouns are joined by certain conjunctions, the pronoun should be plural if the connecting conjunction is *and;* the pronoun should be singular if the connecting conjunction is either *or* or *nor.*

Singular: Either the news reporter or the city editor, whoever *is* willing to assume responsibility, should handle the situation.

Plural: Both the reporter and the city editor, who *are* responsible for the situation, should be involved in the decision.

Agreement When the Antecedent Is a Common Indefinite Pronoun

The pronoun should be singular when referring to the following indefinite antecedents:

each	anyone	everyone
either	anybody	everybody
neither	someone	no one
one	somebody	person

6c   Pronouns and Gender Inclusiveness

Choosing the appropriate gender for the personal pronoun referring to one of the antecedents listed above is no problem when the antecedent is intentionally limited to a all-male or all-female group (e.g., the nuns took turns singing; *each* took *her* turn singing). However, in most other cases these singular indefinite antecedents create a dilemma for the nonsexist writer, who must either use the somewhat awkward *he or she* construction or rewrite the sentence. Rewriting strategies commonly used include:

- *Plural construction*

  They *all* took *their* turns singing prayers.

- *Passive voice, de-emphasizing the actors*

  Prayers were sung in turn.

Understand the Gender Messages Implied by Your Pronouns

Gender-specific pronoun use can be inaccurate and offensive. Be aware, when choosing a pronoun, of the larger social setting in which you work. To avoid unintentional sexism, use five techniques, either alone or in combination.

1. **Use the construction** *he or she, his or her,* **and** *him or her* **in referring to an indefinite pronoun or noun.** Choose this option when the antecedent of a pronoun must have a singular sense. Realize, however, that some readers object to the *he or she* device as cumbersome. The variants *(s)he* and *he/she* are considered equally cumbersome. The *he or she* device can work, provided it is not overused in any one sentence or paragraph.

   Awkward: To some extent, *a biologist* must decide for <u>him or herself</u> which system of classification <u>he or she</u> will use.

   Revised: To some extent, *a biologist* must decide which system of classification <u>he or she</u> will use.

   Revised: To some extent, *a biologist* must decide which system of classification to use. [The infinitive *to use* avoids the *he or she* difficulty.]

2. **Make a pronoun's antecedent plural.** If the accuracy of a sentence will permit a plural antecedent, use this device to avoid unintentional sexism in pronoun selection.

   Plural: To some extent, *biologists* must decide for <u>themselves</u> which system of classification *they* will use. [Note the possible shift in meaning: *biologists* may imply a group discussion.]

3. **Use the passive voice to avoid gender-specific pronouns—but only if it is appropriate to de-emphasize a subject.** Note, however, that using the passive voice creates its own problems of vague reference.

   Neutral: It is every biologist's responsibility to specify which system of classification *is being used.*

4. **Reconstruct the entire statement and avoid the problem.** Often it is easier to rewrite sentences to avoid pronouns altogether.

   Neutral: When choosing among competing systems of classification, the biologist makes a choice that greatly affects later work both in the field and in the lab. [*Later work* is left without a limiting, gender-specific modifier.]

5. **Link gender assignments to specific indefinite antecedents.** Some writers will arbitrarily assign a masculine identity to one indefinite antecedent and a feminine identity to another. The gender assignments are then maintained throughout a document.

   Alternate Gender Assignments: A *biologist* must decide which system of classification *she* will use. An *anthropologist* must also choose when selecting the formal, stylistic, and technological attributes <u>he</u> will use in distinguishing ancient objects from one another.

Exercise 7

Revise the following sentences so that pronouns refer clearly to their antecedents. Place a check beside the sentences that need no revision.

> *Example:* Manic-depressive illness is a disorder characterized by extreme changes in mood between low (or depressed) and high (or manic). They usually are affected by the illness in the third or fourth decade of life.
>
> Manic-depressive illness is a disorder characterized by extreme changes in mood between low (or depressed) and high (or manic). *Manic-depressives* usually are affected by the illness in the third or fourth decade of life.

1. In recent years, the disorder has been called "bipolar affective disorder," because of the two opposite affects—or moods—involved. They say the illness differs from depression, which is termed a "unipolar" illness.
2. The "blue moods" of manic-depressives are characterized by feelings of discouragement, low energy level, and loss of interest in activities usually enjoyed. They tend to think slowly and often have difficulty concentrating.
3. Characteristically, there are other distressing symptoms, such as insomnia, sleeping too much, restless sleep, poor appetite, and often a pervasive anxiety and tension. This usually lasts for weeks or months.
4. The opposite mood is the elated, euphoric, or manic mood, which gives one an abundance of energy and a diminished need for sleep.
5. They say you can recognize a person's manic phase by listening to his or her speech, that is usually fast and pressured in an effort to keep pace with the rapid and shifting flow of ideas.

Sentence Structure

7   Modifiers: Placement and Misplacement

In general, **modifiers** refer most clearly when they are placed *immediately before or after the word they modify.* However, their placement must also avoid breaking up the basic integrity of the sentence. In certain situations, especially with lengthy modifiers, placement must be done with care to prevent confusion.

Reposition a lengthy modifier that splits a subject and its verb, or that splits a verb and its object or complement. Usually a lengthy modifying phrase or clause will be less disruptive if it is moved to the beginning or end of the main statement.

Confusing:	Judges are, because of their habitual and healthy skepticism, often hesitant to declare an opinion.
Repositioned:	Because of their habitual and healthy skepticism, judges are often hesitant to declare an opinion.

7a Use Care with Limiting Modifiers

Limiting modifiers—*only, almost, nearly, even, simply*—can change meaning significantly, and they must be placed with special care. Notice the different meanings:

> *Nearly* all of our 40,000 miners are on strike.
>
> All of our *nearly* 40,000 miners are on strike.

Reposition modifiers that describe two elements simultaneously. In certain phrasings a modifier's placement between two elements can create ambiguity.

> People who voiced objections *quietly* spoke of their regrets. Repositioning the modifier will clarify meanings, either as "People who *quietly* voiced . . ." or ". . . spoke *quietly* of their regrets."

7b Correct "Dangling" Modifiers

A modifier may "dangle" when the word it modifies is not clearly visible in the sentence. This will happen *either* when a long introductory phrase or clause is not followed by a word it can modify, *or* when a sentence with a passive-voice verb (see above) provides no mention of the performer of the action. Correct the problem by rewriting sentences to provide a word that can be clearly modified.

> **Dangling:** After talking to the witnesses, a story was filed.
>
> **Corrected:** After talking to the witnesses, he filed a story.

7c Challenge Your Placement of Modifiers

Modifiers provide much of the interest in a sentence; but when misused, they undermine communication by forcing readers to stop and figure out your meaning. In every case, you should know precisely *which* word in a sentence you are modifying. Posing three questions should help you to be clear.

1. What modifiers am I using in this sentence? To use modifiers effectively and correctly, you should be able to recognize modifiers when you write them. Single words, phrases, and clauses can function as modifiers.

Modifying Word

> **Adjective:** The artist made a *deliberate* effort.
>
> **Adverb:**   The artist succeeded *brilliantly*.

Modifying Phrase

> **Adjective:** The painting, *displayed on a dark wall*, glowed.
>
> **Adverb:**   Patrons responded *with an unusual mix of excitement and nervousness*.

Modifying Clause

Adjective: Many attended the opening, *which had become a much-antici-pated event.*

Adverb: *After the gallery closed that evening,* the staff celebrated.

2. What word is being modified?

The artist made a *deliberate* effort. [the noun *effort* is being modified.]

The artist succeeded *brilliantly.* [The verb *succeeded* is being modified.]

Several patrons who returned repeatedly called the young artist "a wonder." [Confusing: The single-word modifier *repeatedly* seems to modify two words, *returned* and *called.*]

Having made a commitment of time and money, it was gratifying to see a successful show. [Confusing: The phrase *having made a commitment of time and money* does not modify any specific word.]

3. Does the modifying word, phrase, or clause clearly refer to this word?

On returning, several patrons repeatedly *called* the young artist "a wonder." [The modifier *repeatedly* now clearly modifies the verb *called.*]

Having made a commitment of time and money, *the manager* was gratified to see a successful show. [The modifying phrase now clearly modifies the noun *manager.*]

8   Parallelism

Words, phrases, and clauses that are paired or compared must share an equivalent or parallel grammatical form to achieve sentence clarity and consistency. This principle operates within sentences whenever coordinating or correlative conjunctions are used, or whenever comparisons or contrasts are made.

8a   Use Parallel Words, Phrases, and Clauses with Coordinating and Correlative Conjunctions

When elements are joined or paired by coordinating conjunctions—*and, but, for, or, nor, so, yet*—or when they are contrasted with correlative conjunctions—*either/or, neither/nor, both/and, not only/but also*—then the linked elements must be the same kind of grammatical unit.

Parallel Adjectives

Not Parallel: A city editor must be both a tyrant and accommodating.

Parallel: A city editor must be both tyrannical and accommodating.

Parallel Phrases

Not Parallel: Reporters need split-second timing yet to work carefully.

Parallel: Reporters need to work quickly yet carefully.

8b   **Use Parallel Structures with Compared and Contrasted Elements**

Elements are contrasted or compared using expressions such as *rather than, on the other hand, like, unlike,* or *just as/so too.* The compared elements must share an equivalent grammatical form.

> **Not Parallel:**   News editors describe the work as progressively debilitating rather than as a threat to health.
>
> **Parallel:**   News editors describe the work as progressively debilitating rather than as threatening to health.

8c   **Match Parallel Content with Parallel Phrasing**

Words and word groups that refer to comparable content should show comparisons with parallel phrasing. The only indication of *faulty parallelism* may be that a sentence sounds "off" or illogical. Learn to recognize situations that call for parallel structures and to correct sentences with parallelism.

Recognizing Situations That Call for Parallel Structures

Any time you use a coordinating conjunction (*and, but, or,* or *nor*), you are combining elements from two or more elements into a single sentence.

> The children are fond of   The children are fond of
> ice cream.   salty pretzels.

Combined elements are logically comparable, and they should share a single grammatical form; otherwise, they are not parallel.

> **Parallel:**   The children are fond of ice cream and salty pretzels.
>
>   The children are fond of eating ice cream and salty pretzels.
>
> **Not Parallel:**   The children are fond of ice cream and eating salty pretzels.

Correct Faulty Parallelism

1. *Recognize a sentence that is not parallel.*

> **Not Parallel:**   Before they had horses, Indians hunted buffalo by chasing them over blind cliffs, up box canyons, or *when they went* into steep-sided sand dunes.

To revise a sentence with faulty parallelism, *determine which elements should be parallel* (that is, logically comparable), and then *revise the sentence so that these elements share an equivalent grammatical form.* Think of parallel elements as word groupings that complete slots in a sentence. The same grammatical form that you use to complete any one slot in a parallel structure must be used to complete all remaining slots.

H
A
N
D
B
O
O
K

2. *Determine the parallel elements.*

　　by chasing them ___Slot 1___ , ___Slot 2___ , and ___Slot 3___ .

　　by chasing them *over blind cliffs* , ___Slot 2___ , and ___Slot 3___ .

Because Slot 1 is completed with a prepositional phrase (*over blind cliffs*), Slots 2 and 3 should be filled with prepositional phrases. The series *over blind cliffs, up box canyons, or* <u>when they went</u> *into steep-sided sand dunes* lacks parallel structure because the third element in the series introduces a *when* clause, which is not consistent with the grammatical form of Slot 1.

3. *Revise so that parallel elements have equivalent grammatical form.*

Parallel: Before they had horses, Indians hunted buffalo by chasing them *over blind cliffs, up box canyons,* or *into steep-sided sand dunes.*

8d　**Use Parallel Grammatical Forms for Entries in a List or Outline**

To emphasize the logical connections among items in outlines and lists, make sure the elements are of equivalent grammatical form.

Not Parallel: Items needing attention:
　　　　　　　—lack of cooperation　　—to find witnesses
　　　　　　　—making contacts　　　　—how to get the real story

Parallel:　　Items needing attention:
　　　　　　　—promoting cooperation　—finding witnesses
　　　　　　　—making contacts　　　　—getting the real story

Exercise 8

The following sentences contain coordinating or correlative conjunctions, or elements of comparison and contrast. Revise each to correct the faulty parallel structure.

Example: Native Americans have one of the highest unemployment rates in the nation, the lowest educational attainment of any U.S. minority group, and they fare worst in the area of health.

Native Americans have one of the highest unemployment rates in the nation, the lowest educational attainment of any U.S. minority group, and *the worst record of health care.* [Each slot in the series now begins with an adjective in its superlative form: *highest, lowest, worst.* Each adjective is followed by a noun and each noun by a prepositional phrase.]

1. Designating Asian Americans as the "model minority" is problematic not only because the term obscures the diversity of the group but they are represented in only a small percentage of top-ranking positions in the U.S.
2. Some sociologists say that racism is rooted in a preference for one's "own kind" rather than social causes.

3. Conflict theorists feel that racism results from competition for scarce resources and an unequal distribution of power and racial tension increases during periods of economic decline.
4. Corporate managers do not tend to wield the political power of professionals such as lawyers and doctors, nor workers whom they supervise.
5. Either the percentage of the elderly living below the poverty line has decreased or to underestimate the number of elderly living in poverty is prevalent.

---

9 Coordination and Subordination

Writers combine phrases and clauses to establish two basic relationships: coordination or subordination. Elements can have a **coordinate** connection, emphasizing a balance or equality between elements. Otherwise, elements can have a **subordinate** or **dependent** connection, emphasizing that the elements are unequal, with one having a dependent link to another.

Phrases and clauses are often logically linked with connecting words, **conjunctions** and **conjunctive adverbs,** that require students to consider carefully the kind of connection they wish to establish.

9a Choose the Right Connection for Coordinate Structures

Connecting words for a coordinate, or balanced relationship include **coordinating conjunctions** (*and, but, or, nor, so, for, yet*), **correlative conjunctions** (*either/neither, neither/nor, both/and, not only/but, whether/or, not only/ but also*) and many **conjunctive adverbs** (*however, nevertheless, accordingly, also, besides, afterward, then, indeed, otherwise,* etc.). These words show relationships of contrast, consequence, sequence, and emphasis.

Coordinating Conjunctions and the Relationships They Establish

To show addition: *and*	**To show contrast:** *but, yet*
To show choice: *or, nor*	**To show cause:** *for*
To show consequences: *so*	

Use coordinating conjunctions with punctuation in this pattern:

Independent clause   **,**   CONJUNCTION   independent clause

Fused Sentence:	Newton developed calculus he discovered laws of gravity.
Comma Splice:	Newton developed calculus, he discovered laws of gravity.
Revised:	Newton developed calculus, and he discovered laws of gravity.

Conjunctive Adverbs and the Relationships They Establish

To show contrast: *however, nevertheless, nonetheless,* and *still*
To show cause and effect: *accordingly, consequently, thus,* and *therefore*

To show addition: *also, besides, furthermore,* and *moreover*
To show time: *afterward, subsequently,* and *then*
To show emphasis: *indeed*
To show condition: *otherwise*

Use conjunctive adverbs with punctuation in these patterns:

Independent clause   ;   CONJUNCTION   ,   independent clause

Independent clause   .   CONJUNCTION   ,   independent clause

Revised: Newton developed calculus; moreover, he discovered laws of
gravity.

Revised: Newton developed calculus. Moreover, he discovered laws of
gravity.

After deciding on the desired relationship among sentence parts, select
a *single set of connecting words* and avoid a mixture of words that may can-
cel out the meaning.

Mixed: They were *both* competitive, *but however* they were well
matched. [The mixed connecting words show similarity and
contrast at the same time.]

Balanced: They were *both* competitive, *and* they were well matched.
They were competitive; *however,* they were well matched.

9b   Choose a Subordinating Conjunction for a Dependent Relationship

Following is an array of subordinating conjunctions that establish different relationships. These include conditional relationships, or relationships
of contrast, cause and effect, time and place, or purpose and outcome.

**Subordinating Conjunctions and the Relationships
They Establish**

To show condition: *if, even it, unless,* and *provided that*
To show contrast: *though, although, even though,* and *as if*
To show cause: *because* and *since*
To show time: *when, whenever, while, as, before, after, since, once,* and *until*
To show place: *where* and *wherever*
To show purpose: *so that, in order that,* and *that*

Use subordinating conjunctions with punctuation in these patterns:

CONJUNCTION clause   ,   independent clause

Independent clause   CONJUNCTION   clause

Revised: After Newton developed calculus, he discovered laws of
gravity.

Revised: Newton discovered laws of gravity after he developed calculus.

Choose a single subordinating conjunction, and avoid combinations that
are contradictory or confusing.

> **Mixed:** *Because* she was sick, *so* she went to the clinic. [A relation of cause and effect is confusingly combined with one of purpose or outcome.]
>
> **Clear:** *Because* she was sick, she went to the clinic. [cause/effect]

Exercise 9

Repair the dangling modifiers that follow by restoring the word modified to each sentence. (You will find this word in parentheses.) Place a check in front of any sentence in which modifiers are used correctly.

> *Example:* Having conquered an area stretching from the southern border of Colombia to central Chile, civilian and military rule was maintained for two hundred years before the Spanish discovery of America. (the Incas)
>
> Having conquered an area stretching from the southern border of Colombia to central Chile, *the Incas* maintained civilian and military rule for two hundred years before the Spanish discovery of America.

1. Centering on the city of Cuzco in the Peruvian Andes, the coastal and mountain regions of Ecuador, Peru, and Bolivia were included. (the empire)
2. As the only true empire existing in the New World at the time of Columbus, wealth both in precious metals and in astronomical information had been assembled. (the Inca empire)
3. Knitting together the two disparate areas of Peru, mountain and desert, an economic and social synthesis was achieved. (the Incas)
4. Growing and weaving cotton and planting such domesticated crops as corn, squash, and beans, Peru had been settled dating from before 3000 B.C. (the Incas)

10   Clear, Direct, and Concise Sentences

When you are revising a first draft, search out wordiness and eliminate it. Try to avoid saying things two different ways or with two words when one will do. Eliminating extra words is a reliable way to give your message direct impact.

Combine Sentences That Repeat Material

When writing a first-draft paragraph you are apt to string together sentences that repeat material. When revising your work, combine sentences to eliminate wordiness and to sharpen focus.

Eliminate Wordiness from Clauses and Phrases

Eliminate wordiness by eliminating relative pronouns and by reducing adjective clauses to phrases or single words.

Complex: Josephine Baker, *who was* the first black woman to become an international star, was born poor in St. Louis in 1906. [The clause creates some interruption in this complex sentence.]

Concise: Josephine Baker, the first black woman to become an international star, was born poor in St. Louis in 1906.

Wordiness can be eliminated by shortening phrases. When possible, reduce a phrase to a one-word modifier.

Wordy: *Recent revivals* of Baker's French films have included *re-releases of subtitled versions of* "Zou-Zou" and "Princess Tam-Tam."

Concise: *Recently* Baker's French films "Zou-Zou" and "Princess Tam-Tam" have been *re-released with subtitles*. [The phrases are reduced to simpler modifiers.]

Revise Sentences That Begin with Expletives

Expletive constructions (*it is, there is, there are, there were*) fill blanks in a sentence when a writer inverts normal word order. Expletives are almost always unnecessary, and should be replaced with direct, active verbs, whenever possible.

Eliminate Buzzwords

Buzzwords are vague, often abstract expressions that sound as if they mean something but are only "buzzing" or adding noise to your sentence, without contributing anything of substance. Buzzwords can be nouns: *area, aspect, case, character, element, factor, field, kind, sort, type, thing, nature, scope, situation, quality.* Buzzwords can be adjectives, especially those with broad meanings: *nice, good, interesting, bad, important, fine, weird, significant, central, major.* Buzzwords can be adverbs: *basically, really, quite, very, definitely, actually, completely, literally, absolutely.* Eliminate buzzwords. When appropriate, replace them with more precise expressions.

Eliminate Redundancy

Occasional, intentional repetition can be a powerful technique for achieving emphasis. Writers may not realize they are repeating themselves, and the result for readers is usually a tedious sentence. When you spot unintended repetition in your own writing, eliminate it.

Redundant: In *Cinderella*, feminine, lady-like actions and behavior are praised and rewarded.

Revised: In *Cinderella*, feminine behavior is rewarded.

Eliminate Long-Winded Phrases

Long-winded phrases such as *at this point in time* do not enhance the meaning or elegance of a sentence.

Wordy	*Direct*
at this moment (point) in time	now, today
at the present time	now, today

Wordy	*Direct*
due to the fact that	because
in order to utilize	to use
in view of the fact that	because

Using such phrases muddies your sentences, making them sound either pretentious or like the work of an inexperienced writer. Eliminate these phrases and strive for simple, clear, direct expression.

Give Preference to Verbs in the Active Voice

Unless a writer intends to focus on the object of the action, leaving the actor secondary or unnamed, the active voice is the strongest way to make a direct statement. When the actor needs to be named, a passive-voice sentence is wordier and thus weaker than an active-voice sentence.

> **Passive:** The accused *were known as* "pinkos" while the prosecutors *were identified as* "red baiters." [The passive voice here conceals who promoted these labels.]

> **Active:** Pro-Committee partisans identified the accused as "pinkos" while defenders of *the accused* identified the prosecutors as "red baiters."

Use Forms of *Be* and *Have* as Main Verbs Only When No Alternatives Exist

The verbs *have* or *be* can function as an auxiliary in forming other tenses. These verbs tend to make a weak and indirect statement when used alone as the main verb of a sentence. Replace forms of *have* or *be* with strong, active-voice verbs.

> **Weak:** The blacklist *had the effect of getting* people to inform on their friends and families. [The verb produces a vague statement.]

> **Stronger:** The blacklist *pushed* people to inform on their friends and families. [Replacement with another verb produces a definite statement.]

Revise Nouns Derived from Verbs

A noun can be formed from a verb by adding a suffix: dismiss/dismiss*al*, repent/repent*ance*, devote/devo*tion*, develop/develop*ment*. Often these constructions result in a weak, wordy sentence, since the noun form replaces what was originally an active verb and requires the presence of a second verb. When possible, restore the original verb form of a noun derived from a verb.

> **Wordy:** Many people *found that cooperation* with HUAC *was necessary for survival*. [The noun form, the dependent clause, and the *be* verb make a weak, redundant sentence.]

> **Direct:** Many people eventually *cooperated* with HUAC *to survive*. [The noun form is changed to a verb, producing a stronger statement.]

Exercise 10

Revise these sentences to eliminate wordiness by combining repeated material, reducing phrases and adjective clauses, and avoiding expletives.

> *Example:* What type of consumer do you want to advertise to? Specifying the target or consumer that you want to reach with your product is the main step in advertising.
>
> Effective advertising targets specific consumers.

1. When defining the purpose of advertising some experts admit that it is a manipulation of the public while others insist that advertising promotes the general well-being of its audience.
2. Advertising is one of the most eye-catching methods of selling a product. This is because advertising is a medium of information.
3. There are many consumers who are drawn to a product because the advertising campaign has been effectively utilized.
4. There are many qualities which an advertisement must have to lure the public to buy its product. The advertisement must be believable, convincing, informative, and persuasive. With these qualities in the ads, they will be the first ones to sell.
5. Like I mentioned before, it is not only women who are being portrayed sexually. Men are used in many advertisements also.

Sentence Punctuation

11   End Punctuation

11a   Periods

Periods are used to mark the end of a sentence. A period is always placed inside quotation marks that end a sentence. A period is placed inside a parenthesis only if the parenthetical remark is a complete sentence. Periods are used with most standard abbreviations: *Mr., Mrs., Ave., Dr.,* and also with *Ms.* (even though it is not an abbreviation). A period is *not* used with acronymns or acronym abbreviations: *CIA, NATO, NPR, FDIC.*

11b   Question marks

A direct question is marked with an end question mark. After a quoted question, the question mark appears within quotation marks. However, an indirect question (such as "He asked why we should do it.") uses no question mark.

11c   Exclamation marks

Exclamation marks would not normally be used as part of informative academic writing except after a direct exclamatory quotation within marks. Overuse of exclamation marks often conveys a breathless, somewhat frivolous tone to a statement.

12   Semicolons

12a   Use a Semicolon, Not a Comma, to Link Independent Clauses

Semicolons can link clauses that are intended to be closely related; commas cannot do this without creating the comma splice error (see above, "Sentence Completeness"). The choice between separating clauses into sentences using a period and linking clauses with a semicolon depends on your intention about their relationship and your tone and timing if the two clauses are spoken. Thus in the following examples, you might hear a difference in relationships of parts:

> You should mix oil and cheese with basil. They blend perfectly.

> You should mix oil and cheese with basil; they blend perfectly.

Similarly, independent clauses can be linked by semicolons immediately before the following conjunctions and conjunctive expressions: *however, therefore, moreover, nevertheless, furthermore, instead, consequently, accordingly, of course, for example.*

> You should mix cheese with basil; of course they blend perfectly.

12b   Use a Semicolon to Join a Series of Clauses or Phrases That Require Commas within Them

> The flags of the United States, Poland, and Italy respectively contain the colors red, white, and blue; red and white; and red, white, and green.

Semicolons are placed outside of end quotation marks.

> The flag of the United States is often called "Old Glory"; its colors are red, white, and blue.

13   Commas

Commas can clarify sentences by setting off or separating words, phrases, or clauses. When commas are incorrectly used to join totally independent sentences, they create a comma splice error. (See above, "Sentence Completeness.") The following situations illustrate the correct use of commas.

13a   Use Commas to Separate Words, Phrases, and Clauses

- **Use a comma before a coordinating conjunction to join two independent clauses.** One of the principal ways to join two independent clauses is to link them with a comma and a coordinating conjunction: *and, but, or, nor.*

  > The faucet stopped working, and the sink leaks.

  > We can fix the problems ourselves, or we can call a plumber.

Options: You have several options for linking independent clauses: (1) you can separate the clauses and form two distinct sentences (see "End Punctuation" above); (2) you can use a semicolon to link the clauses within one sentence (see "Semicolons" above); (3) you can make one clause subordinate to another (see "Sentence Structure" below).

- **Use commas between items in a series.** One major function of the comma is to signal a brief pause that separates items in a series—a string of related elements. Commas are used to separate three or more items in a series.

    We'll need a washer, a valve, and a wrench.

Some writers prefer to omit the final comma in a series—the comma placed before the coordinating conjunction and. The choice is yours. Whatever your preference, be consistent.

Option: Exercise appears *to reduce the desire to smoke, to lessen any tendency toward obesity and to help in managing stress.*

A series of adjectives will often appear as a parallel sequence: the *playful, amusing* poet; an *intelligent, engaging* speaker. When the order of the adjectives can be reversed without affecting the meaning of the noun being modified, the adjectives are called **coordinate adjectives.** Coordinate adjectives can be linked by a comma or by a coordinating conjunction.

Place a comma between two or more coordinate adjectives in a series if no coordinating conjunction joins them.

    Getting under the sink can be a tricky, messy job.

13b Use Commas to Set Off Introductory or Transitional Units

Use commas with introductory and concluding expressions in these situations:

- Place a comma after a modifying phrase or clause that begins a sentence.

    Yesterday, the faucet stopped working.

    Once the weather turned cold, the faucet stopped working.

- Place a comma after a transitional word, phrase, or clause that begins a sentence.

    Actually, we've had this problem for years.

- Use a comma (or commas) to set off a modifying element that ends or interrupts a sentence *if* the modifier establishes a qualification, contrast, or exception.

    The ships return to port at all hours, often at night.

    The storm warning was broadcast on the A channel, not the B channel.

13c   **Use Commas to Set Off Nonessential or Interrupting Units**

Commas are often used to set apart clauses or phrases that are **nonessential,** that is, not limiting to a basic sentence's meaning. Such units (also called *nonrestrictive*) do not restrict meaning but merely add more information. Commas should not be used with any essential (restrictive) clause or phrase that limits and thereby clarifies meaning with an important modifier.

Essential Modifier—No Commas

> The reports *that were written yesterday* contained no misinformation. [The modifying clause means we're limiting discussion to yesterday's reports; any reports written before or after yesterday are not under discussion.]

Nonessential—Set Off with Commas

> The reports, *which were written yesterday,* contained no misinformation. [Here we're discussing all aspects of the reports, which incidentally were written yesterday.]

Because the nonessential additional information is seen as an interruption to the basic statement, it is set off or surrounded by commas. However, if on rereading you decide that such information is essential and should set a limiting restriction on the meaning intended, you should signal this by eliminating any commas around the clause or phrase.

Exercise 11

Correct the misuse of commas in the following paragraph. In making your corrections, you may need to add or delete words. You should feel free to combine sentences.

> *Example:* The Arlmart Market which has been in operation for seventy years closed its doors last month.
>
> The Arlmart Market, which has been in operation for seventy yearas, closed its doors last month.

Neighbors and politicians wanted to know how an institution which many affectionately called their "temple of gossip" could close. Mayor Judith Flynn said "We should have supported them more" and she vowed to organize both formal and informal efforts to reopen the store. For those who are old enough to remember the store opened between the two world wars, "Pa" Lettelier handpainted the signs and served as butcher baker and stock manager. "Ma" Lettelier who kept books and arranged credit for mostly anyone in need could usually take a few minutes away from her desk to engage in neighborly talk. Their only son Frank says "They worked 18 hours most days." Frank Lettelier took over twenty years ago, he worked just as hard as his parents and he flourished until the large food chains opened stores in town. "They are interested in money not service" people often heard him complain. Customers even friends eventually abandoned the market, they felt guilty doing so but they had their own finances to worry about, the Arlmart Market couldn't compete. "I'm not bitter" Frank Lettelier says "only saddened."

---

14   Colons and Dashes

14a   Colons

Colons are used after a complete sentence to announce a list (or another statement) that appears separate from the announcing sentence.

> Ingredients to make pesto include the following: high quality olive oil, grated parmesan cheese, and fresh-picked basil.

> You can use three basic ingredients to make pesto sauce: in a blender you can mix high quality olive oil, grated parmesan cheese, and fresh-picked basil.

A colon should follow a complete sentence, *not* a fragment that lacks critical parts.

> **Incorrect:** The colors are: red, white, and green.

Correct this error by completing the sentence before the colon.

> **Correct:** These are the colors: red, white, and green.

14b   Dashes

Dashes, which are used in more informal situations than colons, are used to announce a list (or another statement) that appears separate from or as an interruption to an opening statement. Dashes are also used to set off and emphasize a statement added to a complete sentence. The added statement is usually itself a complete sentence, but it may be a phrase or clause.

> We came home—we had driven all night—and collapsed.

Emphatic interruptions with dashes should be used sparingly in most academic writing. A dash is indicated on a typewriter or computer by a double hyphen.

Punctuation for Word Forms and Quotations

15   Apostrophes

Apostrophes are used to show possession, to show omission of letters in contractions, and to mark certain plural forms.

Apostrophes and Personal Pronouns

Apostrophes should *never* be used to show possession with personal pronouns, which have their own form in the possessive case (see section 5):

your, yours, (e.g., your book; the book is yours), *its, whose, our, ours,* etc. These forms must be systematically distinguished from nonpossessive pronouns, which use apostrophes in contractions with *be* verbs: *it's* (it is), *who's* (who is), *you're* (you are).

Apostrophes for Contractions

While formal academic writing has traditionally refrained from using contraction forms (*can't, won't, it's*), much everyday writing and journalism uses a contraction style. When in doubt, check writing similar in tone that is addressed to audiences like those for whom you're writing.

Possession with Multiple Nouns

When a pair or cluster of words functions as a single unit, or when joint possession is indicated, add an *'s* to the last word: *John and Susan's car; brother-in-law's car.* If possession is individual to each person named, each gets an *'s: Both John's and Susan's songs are melodious.*

With Certain Plurals

An *'s* is used to pluralize named letters, numerals, or words identified as words: *dot your i's, three 2's, two and's. Never* use apostrophes to form regular plurals of nouns.

16   Punctuation for Quotations

16a   Quotation Marks

Use double quotation marks (" ") to set off a short direct quotation from the rest of a sentence. Short quotations, which span four or fewer lines of your manuscript, can be incorporated into your sentences as part of your normal paragraphing. When quoting a source, reproduce *exactly* the wording and punctuation of the quoted material.

- Use commas to enclose explanatory remarks that lie outside a quotation. Place periods and commas inside the end quotation mark.

    According to Stuart Koman, "Current solutions for in-patient hospital care are too expensive."

    "Current solutions for in-patient hospital care are too expensive," according to Stuart Koman.

- Place colons, semicolons, footnotes, and parenthetical citations outside the end quotation mark.

    Koman believes in a "balanced care system": an individualized program that combines in-patient and out-patient services.

    Koman believes in a "balanced care system" (14).

    Koman believes in a "balanced care system."[2]

- Place question marks and exclamation points inside or outside end quotation marks, depending on meaning.

Place the mark *inside* when it applies to the quoted material only.

> Jarred posed a thoughtful question: "Can we make them play by our rules?"

Place the mark *inside* when it applies to both the quoted material and the entire sentence.

> Was it Jarred who asked, "Can we make them play by our rules?"

Place the mark *outside* when it applies to the entire sentence but *not* to the quotation.

> How dare you say "It's only a game"!

> Was it Jarred who said, "It's only a game"?

16b   Display Quotations and Titles

- **Display—that is, set off from text—lengthy quotations.** Quotation marks are *not* used to enclose a displayed quotation. Quotations of five or more lines are too long to run in with sentences in a paragraph. Instead they are displayed in a block format in a narrower indentation, without being enclosed by quotation marks.

> In his remarks, Bill Bradley spoke on the impressive economic growth of East Asia:
>
> > East Asia is quickly becoming the richest, most populous, most dynamic area on earth. Over the last quarter century, the East Asian economies grew at an average real growth rate of 6 percent annually while the economies of the United States and the countries of the European Community grew at 3 percent.

- **Use single quotation marks (' ') to set off quoted material or titles of short works within a quotation enclosed by double quotation marks (" ").** Consider these passages to be quoted:

> Piecing through the ruins of our culture, anthropologists in the year 3000 will refer to our span of the twentieth century as the "mall era."

> Read Lukow's "Quest for Supremacy," an essay in this month's *Politics as Usual.*

Quotations

> Anthropologist Richard Marks believes that his colleagues 1000 years from now "will refer to our span of the twentieth century as the 'mall era.' "

> "Read Lukow's 'Quest for Supremacy,' " said professor Lapidus.

- **Run in brief quotations of poetry with your sentences. Indicate line breaks in the poem with a slash (/). Quote longer passages in displayed form.** A full quotation of or a lengthy quotation from a poem is normally made in displayed form:

The Black Riders
42

I walked in a desert.
and I cried:
"Ah, God, take me from this place!"
A voice said: "It is no desert."
I cried, "Well, but—
The sand, the heat, the vacant horizon."
A voice said: "It is no desert."

—Stephen Crane

When quoting a brief extract—four lines or fewer—you can run the lines into the sentences of a paragraph, using the guidelines for quoting prose; however, line divisions are shown with a slash (/) with one space before and one space after.

> Stephen Crane's bleak view of the human condition is expressed in lyric 42 of his series "The Black Riders." Walking in a desert, his narrator cries: " 'Ah, God, take me from this place!' / A voice said: 'It is no desert.' "

■ **Indicate the titles of brief works with quotation marks: chapters of books, short stories, poems, songs, sections from newspapers, essays, etc.[1]**

> I read the "Focus Section" of the *Boston Sunday Globe* every week.

> "The Dead" is, perhaps, Joyce's most famous short story.

> "Coulomb's law" is the first chapter in volume two of Gartenhaus's text, *Physics: Basic Principles*.

17 Parentheses, Brackets, Ellipses, and Slashes

17a Parentheses

■ Use parentheses to set off nonessential information: examples, comments, appositives.

Examples

> The new computer will be useful for memory-intensive applications (for example, graphics packages).

Comments

> Domesticated animals (especially pigs) can quickly turn wild if returned to a forest setting.

---

[1]The title of longer works—books, newspapers, magazines, long poems—are underlined in typewritten text and italicized in typeset text.

H
A
N
D
B
O
O
K

Appositives

> The information content of a slice of pizza (advertising, legal expenses, and so on) accounts for a large percentage of its cost.

■ Use parentheses to set off dates, translations of non-English words, and acronyms.

Dates

> Thomas Aquinas (b. 1225 or 1226, d. 1274) is regarded as the greatest of scholastic philosophers.

Translations

> The look on the faces of the Efe tribesmen made it clear that they could think of nothing worse than to have a *muzungu* (foreigner) living with them for even a day.

Acronyms

> Lucy Suchman, staff anthropologist of Xerox's Palo Alto Research Center (better known as PARC), watches workers in airline operations.

■ Use parentheses to set off numbers or letters that mark items in a series, when the series is run in with a sentence.

> Chip designers use increased packing density of transistors in one of two ways: (1) they increase the complexity of the computers they can fabricate, or (2) they keep the complexity of the computer at the same level and pack the whole computer into fewer chips.

When the series appears in list form, parentheses are omitted.

> Chip designers use increased packing density of transistors in one of two ways:
>
> 1. They increase the complexity of the computers they can fabricate.
> 2. They keep the complexity of the computer at the same level and pack the whole computer into fewer chips.

17b   Brackets

Use brackets [ ] to clarify or insert comments into quoted material. Throughout this section the following passage will be altered to demonstrate the various uses of brackets.

> Elephant sounds include barks, snorts, trumpets, roars, growls, and rumbles. The rumbles are the key to our story, for although elephants can hear them well, human beings cannot. Many are below our range of hearing, in what is known as infrasound.
>
> The universe is full of infrasound: It is generated by earthquakes, wind, thunder, volcanoes, and ocean storms—massive movements of earth, air, fire, and water. But very low frequency sound has not been thought to play much of a role in animals' lives. Intense infrasonic calls have been recorded from finback whales, but whether the calls are used in communication is not known.

Why would elephants use infrasound? It turns out that sound at the lowest frequency of elephant rumbles (14 to 35 hertz) has remarkable properties—it is little affected by passage through forests and grasslands. Does infrasound, then, let elephants communicate over long distances?

- **Use brackets to insert your own words into quoted material.** When you alter the wording of a quotation either by adding or deleting words, you must indicate as much to your reader with appropriate use of punctuation.

Brackets to Clarify a Reference

According to Katherine Payne, "Many [elephant rumbles] are below our range of hearing, in what is known as infrasound."

Brackets to Weave Quoted Language into Your Sentences

The human ear can discern a wide band of sounds, but there are animals we can't hear without special equipment. Elephants emit inaudible (that is, to humans), very low-frequency rumbles called infrasound. At frequencies of 14 to 35 hertz, elephant rumbles have "remarkable properties—[they are] little affected by passage through forests and grasslands" (Payne 67).

The bracketed verb and pronoun have been changed from their original singular form to plural in order to agree in number with the plural *elephant rumbles*.

Brackets to Show Your Awareness of an Error in the Quoted Passage

When you quote a sentence that contains an obvious error, you are still obliged to reproduce exactly the wording of the original source. To show your awareness of the error and to show readers that the error is the quoted author's, not yours, place the bracketed word *sic* (Latin, meaning "thus") after the error.

"Intense infrasonic calls have been recorded from finback whales, but weather [sic] the calls are used in communication is not known."

- **Use brackets to distinguish parentheses inserted within parentheses.**

Katherine Payne reports that "sound at the lowest frequencies of elephant rumbles (14 to 35 hertz [cycles per second]) has remarkable properties—it is little affected by passage through forests and grasslands."

17c | Ellipses

Using an Ellipsis to Indicate a Break in Continuity

An **ellipsis,** noted as three spaced periods (. . .), shows that you have deleted either words or entire sentences from a passage you are quoting. Throughout this section the following passage will be altered to demonstrate the various uses of ellipses.

First, for Americans, the human cost of the Civil War was by far the most devastating in our history. The 620,000 Union and Confederate soldiers who lost their lives almost equaled the 680,000 American soldiers who died in all the other wars this country has fought combined. When we add the unknown but probably substantial number of civilian deaths—from disease, malnutrition, exposure, or injury—among the hundreds of thousands of refugees in the Confederacy, the toll of the Civil War may exceed war deaths in all the rest of American history.

- **Know when *not* to use an ellipsis.** Do *not* use an ellipsis to note words omitted from the beginning of a sentence. In the following example, three words are deleted.

    Faulty: James McPherson observes that "... the human cost of the Civil War was by far the most devastating in our history."

    Revised: James McPherson observes that "the human cost of the Civil War was by far the most devastating in our history."

    Do *not* use an ellipsis if the passage you quote ends with a period and ends your sentence as well.

    Faulty: James McPherson believes that "the toll of the Civil War may exceed war deaths in all the rest of American history. ..."

    Revised: James McPherson believes that "the toll of the Civil War may exceed war deaths in all the rest of American history."

- **Use an ellipsis to indicate words deleted from the middle of a sentence.**

    "[T]he human cost of the Civil War was ... the most devastating in our history," writes James McPherson.

- **Use an ellipsis to indicate words deleted from the end of a sentence.** You may want to end your sentence with a quotation that does not end a sentence in the original. If so, whatever mark of punctuation (if any) follows the last quoted word in the original should be deleted. Then add a period and an ellipsis, following one of two conventions. If you *do not* conclude your sentence with a citation, place the sentence period after the final letter of the quotation; place the ellipsis; and conclude with the end quotation mark.

    Official mortality figures for the Civil War do not include the "probably substantial number of civilian deaths—from disease, malnutrition, exposure, or injury. ..."

    If you *do* conclude your sentence with a citation, skip one space after the final letter of the quotation; place the ellipsis and follow with an end quotation mark; skip one space and place the citation; and then place the sentence period.

    Official mortality figures for the Civil War do not include the "probably substantial number of civilian deaths—from disease, malnutrition, exposure, or injury ..." (McPherson 42).

17d   **The Slash**

- **Use slashes to separate the lines of poetry run in with the text of a sentence.** Retain all punctuation when quoting poetry. Leave a space before and after the slash when indicating line breaks, as shown in section 16b.

- **Use slashes to show choice.** Use slashes, occasionally, to show alternatives, as with the expressions *and/or* and *either/or*. With this use, do not leave spaces before or after the slash.

    Either/Or is the title of a philosophical work by Kierkegaard.

    As a prank, friends entered the Joneses as a husband/wife team in the *Supermarket Sweepstakes.*

- Use a slash in writing fractions or formulas to note division.

    The February 1988 index of job opportunities (as measured by the number of help wanted advertisements) would be as follows:

    $(47,230/38,510) \times 100 = 122.6$

    1/2   5/8   20 1/4

Mechanics

18   **Italics**

Italics are rendered in slanted type in typography, or with an underline on most typewriters or word processors. In general, italics may be used to call specific attention to a word or letter. On special occasions a few words in a sentence may need specific emphasis to clarify meaning.

> While commas are useful, they may *not* be used alone to join independent clauses.

Overuse of italics devalues such emphasis and makes writing appear overexcited and unconvincing. Most writing for technical communities makes very sparing use of italics for emphasis.

Mechanical Uses

Italics have three main mechanical uses.

1. Italics identify key technical terms or numerals that will be defined or referred to as words or numerals:

The term *consonant* will be further labeled as types *1* and *2*.

2. Italics identify foreign words or expressions not yet assimilated into English, as in the Latin expression *post hoc* (after the fact). Note that many foreign terms have been assimilated into English and no longer use italics, as in the Latin expression "alter ego" (someone's stand-in). For any given word, your dictionary or the style sheet for your discourse community is the final arbiter.

3. Italics are key elements in bibliographical conventions. Both in text and in a reference listing, italics designate titles for the following:

books, long poems, plays
movies, broadcast shows, works of art, or long musical works
individually named transport craft: ships, trains, aircraft
newspapers, magazines, and periodicals

When citing newspapers it is conventional not to italicize the word *the,* even if it is part of the paper's title (as in the *New York Times*). With academic journals of all kinds, it is best to consult a bibliography from your discipline to determine how titles are presented.

19   Abbreviations and Acronymns

Be extremely careful that the readers in your discipline know what the abbreviations you are citing stand for, especially when using acronyms or when designating the names of academic or news journals. In formal academic writing, use as few abbreviations as possible.

An **acronym** is the uppercase, pronounceable abbreviation of a proper noun—a person, organization, government agency, or country. Periods are not used with acronyms. If there is any chance that a reader might not be familiar with an acronym or abbreviation, spell it out on first mention, showing the acronym in parentheses.

19a   Abbreviating Titles and Times

- The following titles of address are usually abbreviated before a proper name.

    Mr.   Mrs.   Ms.   Dr.

Though not an abbreviation, *Ms.* is usually followed by a period.

The following abbreviated titles or designations of honor are placed *after* a formal address or listing of a person's full name.

    B.A.   M.A.   M.S.   Ph.D.   C.P.A.
    Jr.   Sr.   M.D.   Esq.

Place a comma after the surname, then follow with the abbreviation. If more than one abbreviation is used, place a comma between abbreviations.

- **Clock time,** indicated as prior to noon or after, uses abbreviations in capitals or in lowercase.

    5:44 P.M. (or p.m.)

    5:44 A.M. (or a.m.)

When typeset, A.M./P.M. often appear in a smaller type size as capital letters: 5:44 P.M.

- When **numbers** are referred to as specific items (such as numbers in arithmetic operations or as units of currency or measure), they are used with standard abbreviations.

    No. 23 or no. 23 $2 + 3 = 5$

    $23.01   99 bbl. [barrels]

    54%

- Abbreviations for time, numbers, units, or money should be used only with reference to specific dates or amounts. Numerical concepts must be fully written out as part of a sentence, not given shortened treatment with abbreviations, unless they are attached to specific years, times, currencies, units, or items.

    Faulty: We'll see you in the A.M.

    Revised: We'll see you in the morning.

19b   **Conventions in References**

From Latin, the traditional language of international scholarship, we have inherited conventional expressions used in research to make brief references or explanations. These are conventionally used in footnotes, documentation, and sometimes in parenthetical comments. All of these Latin expressions should be replaced in a main sentence by their English equivalents.

e.g. (*exempli gratia*)	for example
et al. (*et alii*)	and others
i.e. (*id est*)	that is
N.B. (*nota bene*)	note well
viz. (*videlicet*)	namely
cf. (*confer*)	compare
c. or ca. (*circa*)	about
etc. (*et cetera*)	and such things; and so on

The extremely vague abbreviation *etc.* should be avoided unless a specific and obvious sequence is being indicated, as in: *They proceeded by even numbers (2, 4, 6, 8, etc.).*

20   **Capital Letters and Numbers**

20a   **Capitalization**

In addition to designating the beginning of each sentence, capital letters are used in titles for words of significance. The first letter of the first and last words of a title are capitalized, even if these words are articles. Capital letters are also used for prepositions of five letters or more; short prepositions and the articles *a, an, the* are otherwise *not* capitalized in titles.

Proper Noun Capitalization

Capital letters are conventionally used for any noun that refers to a *particular* person, place, or object that has been given an individual (proper) name or title. This includes the following:

1. Names of people or groups of people.
2. Religions, religious titles, and nationalities.
3. Languages, places (including those in addresses), and regions. Capitalize *the South* (a region) but *not* a compass heading as in *we headed south*.
4. Adjectives formed from proper nouns (French perfume) and titles of distinction that are part of proper nouns.
5. Names of days, months, holidays, historical events, periods.
6. Particular objects (*Hope Diamond*) and brand-name products.
7. Abbreviations for words that are themselves capitalized.
8. Acronyms for companies, agencies, established abbreviations.

20b   Numbers

Numbers that begin sentences or numbers that can be expressed in one or two words (seventy-six, three-fourths) are normally written out. When time is expressed with the term *o'clock* the number is written out (ten o'clock *but* 10 A.M.). As you proofread, it's important to be sure that short numbers have been treated consistently throughout the document.

Treatment of numbers and abbreviations must conform to the standards set by academic journals you refer to regularly.

An ESL Reference Guide

21   Using English Nouns, Pronouns, and Articles

21a   Using the Different Classes of English Nouns

Identifying and Using Count Nouns

In English, **count nouns** name things or people that are considered countable. They identify one of many possible individuals or things in the category named. Count nouns have three important characteristics.

- Singular count nouns can be preceded by *one*, or by *a/an*—the indefinite articles that convey the meaning "one (of many)."

  one car   a rowboat   a truck   an ambulance

  Singular count nouns can also be preceded by demonstrative pronouns (*this, that*), by possessive pronouns (*my, your, their*), and often by the definite article (*the*).

- Plural count nouns can be preceded by expressions of quantity (*two, three, some, many, a few*) and can use a plural form.

  two cars   some rowboats   many trucks   a few ambulances

- A count noun used as a singular or plural subject must agree with a singular or plural verb form.

Identifying and Using Noncount (Mass) Nouns

In English, **noncount (mass) nouns** name things that are being considered as a whole, undivided group or category that is not being counted. Noncount (mass) nouns name various kinds of individuals or things that are considered as group categories in English.

Objects considered too numerous or shapeless to count are often treated as noncount nouns, as with the word *rock* in this sentence.

We mined dense *rock* in this mountain.

As such objects become individually identifiable, the same word may be used as a count noun.

Four *rocks* fell across the road.

Some nouns name things that can be considered either countable or noncountable in English, depending on whether they name something specific or something generic.

Countable (and Specific):	A *chicken* or two ran off.
	A *straw* or two flew up.
Noncountable (and Generic):	*Chicken* needs a lot of cooking.
	Straw can be very dry.

Using Expressions of Quantity with Count and Noncount Nouns

Expressions of quantity—such as *many, few, much, little, some,* and *plenty*—are typically used to modify nouns. Some expressions are used to quantify count nouns; some are used with noncount nouns; and others are used with both kinds of nouns.

Count Nouns	*Noncount Nouns*	*Both Count and Noncount Nouns*
many potatoes	*much* rice	*lots of* potatoes and rice
few potatoes	*little* rice	*plenty of* potatoes and rice
		some, any potatoes and rice

When the context is very clear, these expressions can also be used alone as pronouns.

Do you have *any* potatoes or rice?
I have *plenty* if you need *some.*

Distinguishing Pronouns in Specific and Indefinite or Generic Uses

Most pronouns, including personal pronouns, rename and refer to a noun located elsewhere that names a specific individual or thing. However, indefinite pronouns, such as *some, any, one, someone,* or *anyone,* may refer to a noun in an indefinite or generic sense.

Personal Pronoun:	Where are my pencils? I need *them.* [Meaning: I need specific pencils that are mine.]
Indefinite Pronoun:	Where are my pencils? I need *some.* [Meaning: I need generic, indefinable pencils; I will use any I can find.]

21b   Using Articles with Nouns

Nouns Sometimes Take the Indefinite Articles *a* and *an*

The indefinite articles *a* and *an* are grammatically the same: They are singular indefinite articles that mean "one (of many)," and they are used only with singular count nouns.

A is sometimes used with the quantifiers *little* and *few.* Note the differences in the following examples.

Example	*Meaning*
a few onions; a little oil	a small amount of something
few onions; little oil	a less-than-expected amount of something

Nouns Sometimes Take the Definite Article *the*

Use *the* with specific singular and plural count nouns and with noncount nouns.

Specific Nouns

I need *the tool* and *the rivets.* [one singular and one plural noun]

I need *the equipment.* [a noncount noun]

I need *the tool* on *the top shelf.*

[Note the modifiers, clauses, and phrases that make the nouns specific.]

Generic Nouns

I need tools for that work. [In this case, no article is used.]

Use *the* in a context where a noun has previously been mentioned, or where the writer and the reader both know the particular thing or person being referred to.

I saw a giraffe at the zoo. *The giraffe* was eating leaves from a tree.

Other Uses of the Definite Article

- Use *the* with items that are to be designated as one of a kind (*the* sun, *the* moon, *the* first, *the* second, *the* last).
- Use *the* with official names of countries when it is needed to give specific meaning to nouns like *union, kingdom, state(s), republic, duchy,* etc.

- Use *the* when a noun identifies institutions or generic activities *other than sports,* and in certain usages for generic groups.

   > Sergei plays *the* piano, *the* flute, and *the* guitar.
   >
   > *The* whales are migratory animals. *The* birds have feathers.

   Without an Article: Nadia plays basketball, hockey, and volleyball.

- Use *the* with names of oceans, seas, rivers, and deserts.

   the Pacific   *the* Amazon   *the* Himalayas   *the* Sahara

   Without an Article: Lake Michigan   Mt. Fuji

- Use *the* to give specific meaning to expressions using the noun *language,* but not for the proper name of a language by itself.

   > He studied the Sanskrit language, not the Urdu language.

   Without an Article: He studied Sanskrit, not Urdu.

- Use *the* with names of colleges and universities containing *of.*

   > He studied at *the* University *of* Michigan.

   Without an Article (Typically): He studied at Michigan State University.

Nouns Sometimes Take No Article

Typically no article is needed with names of unique individuals, as they do not need to be made specific and they are not usually counted as one among many. In addition, nouns naming generalized persons or things in a generic usage commonly use no article: *Managers often work long hours. Whales are migratory animals.*

Some situations in which no article is used are shown above. Here are some others.

- Use no article with proper names of continents, states, cities, and streets, and with religious place names.

   Europe   Alaska   New York   Main Street   heaven   hell

- Use no article with titles of officials when accompanied by personal names; the title effectively becomes part of the proper noun.

   President Truman   King Juan Carlos   Emperor Napoleon

- Use no article with fields of study.

   Ali studied literature.
   Juan studied engineering.

- Use no article with names of diseases.

   He has cancer.
   AIDS is a very serious disease.

- Use no article with names of magazines and periodicals, unless the article is part of the formal title.

   Life   Popular Science   Sports Illustrated
   BUT: *The New Yorker* [The article is part of the proper name.]

22   Using English Verbs

22a   Distinguishing Different Types of Verbs and Verb Constructions

Linking Verbs Are Used in Distinctive Patterns

Linking verbs, the most common example of which is *be,* serve in sentences as "equals signs" to link a subject with an equivalent noun or adjective. Some other linking verbs are *appear, become,* and *seem.*

Expletives. Linking verbs also serve in a distinctive English construction that uses changed word order with an **expletive** word, *there* or *it.* Expletives are used only with linking verbs, as in these sentences.

It *is* important to leave now.

There *seems* to be a problem.

There or *it* form "dummy subjects" or filler words that occupy the position of the subject in a normal sentence; the true subject is elsewhere in the sentence, and the verb agrees with the true subject.

Expletive in Subject Position	*True Subject*
There is a cat in that tree.	*A cat* is in that tree.

The expletive *it* also has a unique role in expressing length of time with *take* followed by an infinitive.

It takes an hour to get home by car.

It took us forever.

22b   Changing Verb Forms

Verb forms express *tense,* an indication of when an action or state of being occurs. The three basic tenses in English are the past, the present, and the future.

Not All Verbs Use Progressive Tense Forms

Each of the three basic tenses has a progressive form, made up of *be* and the present participle (the *-ing* form of the verb). The progressive tense emphasizes the *process* of doing whatever action the verb asserts. The tense is indicated by a form of *be:* present progressive (I *am going*), past progressive (I *was going*), past perfect progressive (I *had been going*), future progressive (I *will be going*).

Certain verbs are generally *not* used in the progressive form; others have a progressive use only for process-oriented or ongoing meanings of the verb.

Words That Are Rarely Seen in a Progressive Form

Think (in the sense of "believe"): "I think not."
Believe, understand, recognize, realize, remember: "You believe it."
Belong, possess, own, want, need: "We want some." "We once owned it."
Have: "You have what you need."

Be, exist, seem: "This seems acceptable."
Smell, sound, and **taste** as intransitive verbs, as in "It smells good"; "it sounds funny"; "it tastes bad."
Appear in the sense of "seem": "It appeared to be the right time."
See: "I can never see why you do it."
Surprise, hate, love, like: "It surprises me"; "I absolutely hate it."

Using the Perfect Forms

The perfect tense is made up of *have* and the past participle (the *-ed* form of the verb). The form of *have* indicates the tense: present perfect (*has* worked), past perfect (*had* worked), and future perfect (*will have* worked).

Sometimes students confuse the use of the simple past with the use of the present perfect. The present perfect is used when an action or state of being that began in the past continues to the present; it is also used to express an action or state of being that happened at an indefinite time in the past.

> **Present Perfect:** Linda has worked in Mexico since 1987.

> **Present Perfect:** Ann has worked in Mexico. [The time is unspecified.]

By contrast, the simple past is used when an action or state of being began *and ended* in the past.

> **Simple Past:** Linda worked in Mexico last year. [She no longer works there.]

Using *Since* or *For* with Perfect Tenses in Prepositional Phrases of Time

A phrase with *since* requires using the present perfect (*has worked*) or past perfect tenses (*had worked*); it indicates action beginning at *a single point in time* and still continuing at the time shown by the verb tense.

> She [has/had worked] *since* noon
>
> > *since* 1991
> >
> > *since* the baby was born

A time phrase with *since* cannot have a noun object that shows plural time; *since* phrases must indicate a single point in time.

> **Faulty:**   He lived here since three months.
>   I am here since May.

> **Revised:**   He has lived here *for* three months.
>   I have been here since May.

Also, a time phrase with *since* cannot modify a simple past tense or any present tense.

> **Faulty:**   He lived here since three months.
>   I am here since May.

> **Revised:**   He *had lived* here since February.
>   I *have been* here since May.

A modifying phrase with *for* indicates action *through a duration of time.*

> He [has/had worked] *for* three hours
> > *for* a month and a half
> > *for* two years
> > *for* a few weeks

When a phrase uses a plural noun, thus showing duration of time, this signals that the preposition in the modifier must be *for,* not *since.*

Faulty: I had worked on it since many years.

Revised: I had worked on it for many years.

Using the Varied Forms of English Future Tenses

The following list shows different ways of expressing the future.

Verb Form	*Explanation*
She *will call* us soon. She *is going* to call us soon.	These examples have the same meaning.
The movie *arrives* in town tomorrow. The next bus *leaves* in five minutes. The bus *is leaving* very soon.	The simple present and the present progressive are used to express definite future plans, as from a schedule.
Your flight *is taking off* at 6:55. The doctor *is operating* at once. I *am calling* them right now.	The present progressive is sometimes used to make strong statements about the future.
Hurry! The movie *is about* to begin. Finish up! The bell *is about* to ring.	The "near" future is expressed by some form of *be* plus *about to* and a verb.
It's cold. *I'm going to* get a sweater. It's cold. *I'll lend* you a sweater.	This suggests a plan. This suggests a willingness.

Verbs expressing thoughts about future actions, such as *intend* and *hope,* are not used in any future tense, and the verb *plan* uses a future tense only in the idiomatic *plan on* (to make or follow a plan).

Using Verb Tenses in Sentences with a Sequence of Actions

In complex sentences that have more than one verb, it is important to adjust the sequence of verb tenses to avoid confusion. See the discussion on verb tense combinations in 4f.

Verb tenses with reported speech. Reported speech, or indirect discourse, is very different from directly quoted speech, which gives the exact verb tense of the original.

Direct Speech: Ellie said, "He is taking a picture of my boat."

Indirectly quoted speech may occasionally be reported immediately.

Reported Speech: Ellie just said [that] he is taking a picture of her boat.

Some kinds of reported speech can be summarized with verbs like *tell, ask, remind,* or *urge,* followed by an infinitive:

Reported Speech: Ellie asked him to take a picture of her boat.

Most often, however, reported speech has occurred sometime before the time of the main verb reporting it. In English, the indirect quotation then requires changes in verb tense and pronouns.

Reported Speech: She said [that] he had taken a picture of her boat.

In this situation, the reported speech itself takes the form of a *that* noun clause (although the word *that* is often omitted); its verb tense shifts to past tense.

The following table shows a few patterns for changing verb tenses, verb forms, and modal auxiliaries in reported speech or indirect discourse.

Direct Speech		*Reported Speech*
Tenses:		
present	→	**past**
Ellie said, "I like horses."		Ellie said [that] she liked horses.
past	→	**past perfect**
Ellie said, "I rode the horse."		Ellie said [that] she had ridden the horse.
present progressive	→	**past progressive**
Ellie said, "I'm going riding."		Ellie said [that] she was going riding.
present perfect	→	**past perfect**
Ellie said, "I have ridden there."		Ellie said [that] she had ridden there.

Using Verb Tenses in Conditional and Subjunctive Sentences

Conditional sentences talk about situations that are either possible in the future or else unreal or hypothetical (contrary to fact) in the present or past. Conditional sentences typically contain the conjunction *if* or a related conditional term (*unless, provided that, only if, (only) after, (only) when,* etc.). The following are guidelines for using verb forms in conditional sentences.

Possible or real statements about the future. Use the present tense to express the condition in possible statements about the future; in the same sentence, use the future to express the result of that condition.

	conditional + present	future (*will* + base form)
Real Statement:	*If I have* enough money,	*I will go* next week.
	When I get enough money,	*I will go.* [**Meaning:**
	The speaker may have enough money.]	

Hypothetical or unreal statements about the future. Use the past subjunctive form (which looks like a past tense) with sentences that make "unreal" or hypothetical statements about the future; in the same sentence, use the past form of a modal auxiliary (usually *would, could,* or *might*) to express an unreal result of that stated condition.

<table>
<tr><td></td><td>*If + past*</td><td>*past form of modal (would)*</td></tr>
</table>

Unreal Statement: *If you found* the money,   *you would go* next week.
[**Meaning:** The speaker now is fairly sure you will not have the money.]

Hypothetical or unreal statements about the past. Use the subjunctive with appropriate perfect tense verb forms with sentences that make hypothetical or unreal statements about the past. Use the past perfect tense for the unreal statement about the past. In the same sentence, use the past form of the modal auxiliary plus the present perfect to express the unreal result.

<table>
<tr><td>*If + past perfect*
(had made)</td><td>*past modal + present perfect*
(would) *(have gone)*</td></tr>
</table>

Unreal Statement: *If I had made* money,   *I would have gone* last week.
[**Meaning:** At that time the speaker did not have the money.]

Expressing a Wish or Suggestion for a Hypothetical Event

In stating a wish in the present that might hypothetically occur, use the **past subjunctive** (which looks like the past tense) in the clause expressing the wish. (The object of the wish takes the form of a *that* clause, although the word *that* is often omitted.)

present	[that]	past subjunctive (like past tense)
He *wishes*	[that]	she *had* a holiday.
I *wish*	[that]	I *were* on vacation.

The auxiliaries *would* or *could* (which have the same form in the present and past tenses) are often used to express the object of a wish.

present	[that]	*would/could + base form*
I *wish*	[that]	she *would stay.*
We *wish*	that	we *could take* a vacation day.

Expressing a Recommendation, Suggestion, or Urgent Request

In stating a recommendation, suggestion, or urgent request, use the **present subjunctive**—the base form of the verb (*be, do*)—in the *that* clause.

present	[that]	present subjunctive = base form
We *suggest*	that	he *find* the money.
We *advise*	[that]	you *be* there on time.

22c Changing Word Order with Verbs

Invert the Subject and All or Part of the Verb to Form Questions

The subject and verb are inverted from normal order to form questions. The following patterns are used with the verb *be*, with modal auxiliaries, with progressive forms, and with perfect forms.

	Normal Statement Form	*Question Form*
Be	He *is* sick today.	*Is he* sick today?
Modals	She *can* help us.	*Can she* help us?
Progressive	They *are* studying here.	*Are they* studying here?
Perfect	It *has* made this sound before.	*Has it* made this sound before?

Questions (and Negatives) with the Auxiliary *Do/Does*

Verbs other than those shown above use the auxiliary verbs *do/does* to form questions, and also to form negatives with *not*. In this form, when the auxiliary verbs *do/does* are added, the verb changes to the base form (the dictionary form). Use this pattern for the simple present and simple past.

Question Form/Negative Form: Do + Base Form

Statement:	He *gets on* this bus.
Question:	*Does* he *get on* this bus?
Negative:	He *does not get on* this bus.
Avoid:	Does he *gets on* this bus? [Needs a base form.]
Statement:	She *finishes* at noon.
Question:	*Does* she *finish* at noon?
Negative:	She *does not finish*.
Avoid:	Does she *finishes* at noon? [Needs a base form.]

Use Modal Auxiliaries for a Wide Range of Meanings

Modal auxiliaries include *can, could, may, might, should, would,* and *must,* as well as the four modals that always appear with the particle *to: ought to, have to, able to,* and *have got to.* The base form of the verb (the dictionary form) is always used with a modal auxiliary, whether the time reference is to the future, present, or past. For a past time reference, use the modal plus the past perfect (*have* + the past participle).

Meaning Expressed	*Present Time or Past Time*	*Modal + Past Perfect*
ability and permission	She can drive. She could drive.	She could have driven.
possibility	She may drive. She might drive.	She might have driven.
advisability	She should drive. She ought to drive. She had better drive.	She should have driven. She ought to have driven.
necessity	She must drive. She has to drive.	She had to drive.
negative necessity versus prohibition*	She does not have to drive. [she need not] She must not drive. [she is not allowed]	

*Note that the two negatives above have very different meanings.

22d   **Choosing Gerunds and Infinitives with Verbs**

There are three types of verbals: infinitives, gerunds, and participles.

Learning Idiomatic Uses of Verb/Verbal Sequences

Sometimes it is difficult to determine which verbs are followed by a gerund, which are followed by an infinitive, and which can be followed by either verbal. This usage is idiomatic and must be memorized; there are no rules to govern these forms. Note in the following examples that verb tense does not affect a verbal.

Verb + Gerund	*Verb + Infinitive*	*Verb + Either Verbal*
enjoy	**want**	**begin**
I enjoy swimming.	I want to swim now.	Today I begin swimming.
		Today I begin to swim.
go	**agree**	**continue**
I went swimming.	I agreed to swim.	I continued swimming.
I continued to swim.		
enjoy + gerund	want + infinitive	begin + either verbal
go + gerund	agree + infinitive	continue + either verbal
finish + gerund	decide + infinitive	like + either verbal
recommend + gerund	need + infinitive	prefer + either verbal
risk + gerund	plan + infinitive	start + either verbal
suggest + gerund	seem + infinitive	love + either verbal
consider + gerund	expect + infinitive	hate + either verbal
postpone + gerund	fall + infinitive	can't bear + either verbal
practice + gerund	pretend + infinitive	can't stand + either verbal

Note: There is no difference in meaning between *I begin to swim* and *I begin swimming.* However, sentences with other verbs differ in meaning depending on whether a gerund or an infinitive follows the verb. This difference in meaning is a function of certain verbs. See the following examples.

Example	*Meaning*
I always remember *to lock* the car.	I always remember to do this.
I remember *locking* the car.	I remember that I did this.
They stop *to drink* some water.	They stopped in order to drink.
They stopped *drinking* water.	They didn't drink anymore.

Information on idiomatic usage is provided in ESL dictionaries such as the *Longman Dictionary of American English: A Dictionary for Learners of English,* 1983.

22e   **Using Two- and Three-Word Verbs with Particles**

Phrasal verbs consist of a verb and a **particle.** Note that a particle can be one or more prepositions (*off, up, with*) or an adverb (*away, back*). English has many phrasal verbs, often built on verbs that have one basic meaning in their simple one-word form, but different meanings when particles are added.

The coach *called off* the game because of the storm.

He *left out* some important details.

The meaning of a phrasal verb is idiomatic; that is, the words as a group have a different meaning from each of the words separately. Most of these varied meanings are found in a standard English dictionary.

Some Phrasal Verbs Are Separable

With separable phrasal verbs, a noun object either can separate a verb and particle or follow the particle.

noun object   noun object

Correct: I *made out* <u>a check</u> to the IRS.   I *made* <u>a check</u> *out* to the IRS.

However, a pronoun object always separates the verb and the particle. A pronoun never follows the particle.

pronoun object

Faulty: I *made out* <u>it</u> to the IRS.

Revised: I *made* <u>it</u> *out* to the IRS.

Other separable phrasal verbs include the following:

call off	find out	hand out
check out	fit in	leave in, out
divide up	give back, up	look up [research]
fill in	hang out, up	pick up
	[suspend: trans.]	

Some Phrasal Verbs Are Nonseparable

With nonseparable phrasal verbs, a noun or pronoun object always follows the particle. For these verbs it is not possible to separate the verb and its particle with a noun or pronoun object.

noun object   pronoun object

Faulty: I ran Mary into.   **Faulty:**   I ran her into.

Revised: I ran into Mary   **Revised:** I ran into her.

Other nonseparable phrasal verbs include the following:

bump into	call on	do without
get into	get over	get through

Some Phrasal Verbs Can Be Either Separable or Nonseparable

The meaning of a phrasal verb will change, depending on whether or not the phrase is separated by an object. Note the difference in meaning that appears with the placement of the object in the similar verbs below.

Examples	*Meaning*
I *saw through* it. [nonsep.]	I found it transparent.
I *saw* it *through.* [sep.]	I persisted.
She *looked over* the wall. [nonsep.]	She looked over the top of it.
She *looked* the wall *over.* [sep.]	She examined or studied it.

23   Using Modifiers in English Sentences

23a   Using Adjectival Modifiers with Linking Verbs and Prepositions

Adjectives and past participle adjectives are often followed by a modifying prepositional phrase.

> We are *ready*. We are *ready for* the next phase of training.
>
> Jenny seems an *involved* person. She is *involved with* a boyfriend.

The preposition to be used in such phrases is determined by the adjective or participle adjective. With each such adjective, the choice of preposition is idiomatic, not logical; therefore, adjective/preposition combinations must be memorized. Sometimes the same adjective will change its meaning with different prepositions, as in this example.

> Jenny was *involved in* planning from the start. Meanwhile, she was *involved with* a new boyfriend.

Past-participle adjective examples include the following:

excited about	acquainted with	divorced from
composed of	opposed to	scared of/by

Single-word adjective examples include the following:

absent from	afraid of	mad at
bad for	clear to	sure of
crazy about	familiar with	cruel to

Note: Standard dictionaries may not indicate which preposition is typically used with a given adjective. However, this information is provided in ESL dictionaries such as the *Longman Dictionary of American English: A Dictionary for Learners of English,* 1983.

23b   Positioning Adverbial Modifiers

Adverbs have typical or standard locations in English sentences, although these patterns can be varied for special emphasis. Adverbs are typically located immediately before a transitive or intransitive verb.

> **Faulty:**   She finishes always her homework.
>
> **Revised:**   She always finishes her homework.
>
> **Emphatic:** She finishes her homework—always!

Adverbs are typically placed after the verb *be* and helping verbs in normal sentences.

> He was frequently at the gym on Fridays.
>
> She may often discuss politics.

However, when sentences are inverted for questions or negatives, the adverb is usually placed before the helping verb.

Faulty: They don't frequently talk. It doesn't sometimes matter.

Revised: They frequently don't talk. It sometimes doesn't matter.

23c **Using Phrases and Clauses to Modify Nouns and Pronouns**

Positioning Adjective Phrases and Clauses

Unlike single-word adjective modifiers (which are placed before a noun and after a linking verb), a phrase or clause functioning as an adjective must immediately *follow* the noun or pronoun it modifies in order to avoid confusion with adverbial modifiers in the sentence.

Faulty: I brought the tire to the garage *with the puncture.*
I brought the tire to the garage *which had a puncture.*
[The modifier next to *garage* is very confusing.]

Revised: I brought the tire *with the puncture* to the garage.
I brought the tire, *which had a puncture,* to the garage.

If two or more adjective phrases or clauses modify the same noun, typical patterns of sequence operate, as shown below.

Avoid Adding Unnecessary Pronouns after Adjective Clauses

The subject in an English sentence can be stated only once; pronouns in the sentence refer to the subject (or to other nouns) but they do not repeat it. When a lengthy adjective clause follows the subject as a modifier, it is important not to repeat the subject with an unnecessary pronoun before the verb.

Faulty: The *person* who works in office #382 *she* decides. [The subject is repeated with an unnecessary pronoun.]

Revised: The person who works in office #382 decides.

This error is likely to occur because of a failure to observe the steps in forming a dependent clause. Here is the process for forming an adjective clause, using *who, which,* or *that* to replace the noun or pronoun of the dependent clause:

Two Sentences: The person decides. *She* works in office #382.

Transform to a Clause: [*she = who*] *who* works in office #382

Place the Clause: The person <u>who</u> *works in office #382* decides.

Use the Relative Pronoun *Whose* for a Clause Showing Possession

An adjective clause is often constructed with the relative pronoun *whose* to show possession by the person or thing modified. Students sometimes omit a step in transforming a separate possessive statement into an adjective clause with *whose.*

Faulty: The person whom her office was locked called security.

Revised: The person whose office was locked called security.

When transforming a sentence showing possession to a relative clause showing possession, use *whose* to replace the possessive noun or pronoun.

23d   Observing Typical Order of Cumulative Adjectives

Single-word adjective modifiers are placed close to a noun, immediately before a noun, or after a linking verb.

Cumulative adjectives are groups of adjectives that modify the same noun. There is a typical order of modifiers and cumulative adjectives in an English sentence. A major disruption of typical order can be confusing.

Faulty: a beach French gorgeous tent   red light my small bulb

Revised: a gorgeous French beach tent   my small red light bulb

Although some stylistic variations from typical order in the location of cumulative adjectives are possible for emphasis, typical locations in an English sentence provide a very strong normal pattern. Here are some guidelines.

Possessives precede numbers. Ordinal numbers follow cardinal numbers.

Jill's first car   my first nine drafts

The typical order of descriptive adjectives is shown below:

(1) Opinion	(2) Size	(3) Shape	(4) Condition	(5) Age	(6) Color	(7) Origin	(8) Noun
ugly		round			green		fenders
	huge		muddy				spots
lovely				old	red	Turkish	slippers
comfortable			sunny				room

A Brief Glossary of Usage

This glossary is intended to provide definitions and descriptions of selected word usages current in formal academic writing. In consulting this kind of glossary, writers should be prepared to make informed decisions about the meaning and the level of diction that is most appropriate to their writing project.

a, an   Use *a* when the article precedes a noun beginning with a consonant. For example, *At last we found a hotel.* Use *an* when the article precedes a word beginning with a vowel or an unpronounced *h. It was an honor to receive an invitation.*

accept, except   Use *accept* when your meaning is "to receive." Use *except* when you mean an exception, as in *He invited everyone except Thuan.* You can also use *except* as a verb that means "to leave out," as in *The report excepted the two episodes of misconduct.*

affect, effect   If your sentence requires a verb meaning "to have an influence on," use *affect.* If your sentence requires a noun meaning "result," use *effect. Effect* can also be a verb, however. Use *effect* as a verb when you mean "to make happen," as in *He was able to effect a change in how the city council viewed the benefits of recycling.*

all ready, already   Use *all ready* when you mean "prepared" as in *He was all ready for an expedition to Antarctica.* Use *already* when you mean "by this time," as in *The ushers at Symphony Hall will not seat you if the concert has already started.*

all together, altogether   Use *all together* when you mean "as a group" or "in unison," as in *Once we got the family all together, we could discuss the estate.* Use *altogether* when you mean "entirely," as in *Some of the stories about Poe's addictions and personal habits are not altogether correct.*

allude, elude   Use *allude* when you mean "to refer indirectly to." Use *elude* when you mean "to avoid or escape."

allusion, illusion   Use *allusion* when you mean "an indirect reference," as in *The children did not understand the allusion to Roman mythology.* Use *illusion* when you mean "false or misleading belief or appearance," as in *Smith labored under the illusion that he was a great artist.*

a lot   Do not use *a lot* in formal writing. Use a more specific modifier instead. When you use *a lot* in other contexts, remember that it is always two words.

among, between   Use *between* when you are expressing a relationship involving two people or things, as in *There was general agreement between Robb and Jackson on that issue.* Use *among* when you are expressing a relationship involving three or more separable people or things, as in *He failed to detect a link among the blood cho-lesterol levels, the red blood cell counts, and the T-cell production rates.*

as, like   Use *as* either as a preposition or as a conjunction, but use *like* as a preposition only. If your sentence requires a preposition, use *as* when you are making an exact equivalence, as in *Edison was known as the wizard of Menlo Park.* Use *like* when you are referring to likeness, resemblance, or similarity, as in *Like Roosevelt, Reagan was able to make his constituency feel optimism.*

as, than   When you are making a comparison, you can follow both *as* and *than* with a subjective- or objective-case pronoun, depending on meaning. For example, *We trusted O'Keeffe more than him [we trusted Smith]* and *We trusted O'Keeffe more than he [Jones trusted O'Keeffe]. O'Keeffe was as talented as he [was talented]* and *We found O'Keeffe as trustworthy as [we found] him.*

assure, ensure, insure   Use *assure* when you mean "to promise" as in *He assured his mother that he would return early.* Use *ensure* when you mean "to make certain," as in *Taking a prep course does not ensure success in the SATs.* Use *insure* when you mean "to make certain" in a legal or financial sense, as in *He insured his boat against theft and vandalism.*

bad, badly   Use *bad* as an adjective, as in *Bad pitching changed the complexion of the game.* Use *badly* as an adverb, as in *The refugees badly needed food and shelter.* Use *bad* to follow linking verbs that involve appearance or feeling, as in *She felt bad about missing the party.*

complement, compliment   Use *complement* when you mean "something that completes," as in *The wine was the perfect complement for the elegant meal.* Use *compliment* when you mean "praise," as in *The administrator savored the compliment on her organizational skills.*

could of, would of, should of, might of, may of, must of   In formal writing, avoid combining modal auxiliaries (*could, would, should, might, may,* and *must*) with *of.* Instead, write *could have, would have, should have, might have, may have,* and *must have.*

couple, couple of   Do not use *couple* or *couple of* to mean "a few" in formal writing. Instead, write *a few.*

criteria   Use *criteria* when you want a plural word referring to more than one standard of judgment. Use *criterion* when you are referring to only one standard of judgment.

different from, different than   Use *different from* when an object or phrase follows, as in *Braque's style is different from Picasso's.* Use *different than* when a clause follows, as in *Smith's position on the deficit was* <u>different</u> *when he was seeking the presidency* <u>than</u> *it was when he was president.*

differ from, differ with   Use *differ from* when you are referring to unlike things, as in *Subsequent results of experiments in cold fusion differed radically from results first obtained in Utah.* Use *differ with* to mean "disagree," as in *One expert might differ with another on a point of usage.*

discreet, discrete   Use *discreet* to mean "respectfully reserved," as in *He was always discreet when he entered the synagogue.* Use *discrete* to mean "separate" or "distinct," as in *The essay was a discrete part of the examination and could be answered as a take-home assignment.*

disinterested, uninterested   Use *disinterested* to mean *"impartial,"* as in *An umpire should always be disinterested in which team wins.* Use *uninterested* to mean "bored" or "not interested."

elicit, illicit   Use *elicit* to mean "to draw out," as in *The social worker finally elicited a response from the child.* Use *illicit* to mean "illegal," as in *Illicit transactions on the black market fuel an underground Soviet economy.*

explicit, implicit   Use *explicit* when you mean "stated outright," as in *The Supreme Court rules on issues that are not explicit in the Constitution.* Use *implicit* when you mean "implied," as in *Her respect for the constitution was implicit in her remarks.*

farther, further   Use *farther* when you are referring to distance, as in *He was able to run farther after eating carbohydrates.* Use *further* when you are referring to something that cannot be measured, such as *Further negotiations are needed between the central government and the people of Azerbaijan.*

fewer, less   Use *fewer* when you are referring to items that can be counted, as in *There are fewer savings accounts at the branch office this year.* Use *less* when you are referring to things that cannot be counted, as in *The East German people have less confidence in the concept of unification than they had one year ago.*

good, well   Use *good* as an adjective, as in *Astaire gave a good performance, but not one of his best.* Use *well* as an adverb, as in *He danced well.* You can also use well as an adjective when you refer to good health, as in *She felt well* or *She is well today.*

he, she; he/she; his, her; his/her; him, her; him/her   When you are using a pronoun to refer back to a noun that could be either masculine or feminine, you might use *he or she* in order to avoid language that is now considered sexist. For example, instead of writing *A doctor must be constantly alert; he cannot make a single mistake* to refer generally to doctors, you could write *A doctor must be constantly alert; he or she cannot make a single mistake.* Or you could recast the sentence in the plural to avoid this problem: *Doctors must be constantly alert; they cannot make a single mistake.*

herself, himself, myself, yourself   Use pronouns ending in *-self* when the pronouns refer to a noun that they intensify, as in *The teacher himself could not pass the test.* Do not use pronouns ending in *-self* to take the place of subjective- or objective-case pronouns. Instead of writing, for example, *Joan and myself are good friends,* write *Joan and I are good friends.*

impact   Use *impact* when you are referring to a forceful collision, as in *The impact of the cars was so great that one was flattened.* Do not use *impact* as a verb meaning "to have an effect on." Instead of writing *Each of us can positively impact waste reduction efforts,* write *Each of us can reduce waste.*

implicit, explicit   See *explicit, implicit.*

imply, infer   Use *imply* when you mean "to suggest without directly stating," as in *The doctor implied that being overweight was the main cause of my problem.* Use *infer* when you mean "to find the meaning of something," as in *I inferred from her lecture that drinking more than two cups of coffee a day was a health risk.*

in regards to   Do not use *in regards to* in formal writing. Generally, you can substitute *about* for *in regards to.*

incredible, incredulous   Use *incredible* to mean "unbelievable," as in *Some of Houdini's exploits seem incredible to those who did not witness them.* Use *incredulous* to mean "unbelieving," as in *Many islanders were incredulous when they heard tales of white people capturing men, women, and children who lived on the coast.*

irregardless, regardless   Do not use *irregardless*. Use *regardless* instead.

is when, is where   Do not use *is when* and *is where* when you are defining something. Instead of writing *Dinner time is when my family relaxes*, write *At dinner time, my family relaxes.*

its, it's   Use *its* when your sentence requires a possessive pronoun, as in *Its leaves are actually long, slender blades.* Use *it's* only when you mean "it is."

lay, lie   Use *lay* when you mean "to put" or "to place," as in *She lays the present on the table.* Use *lie* when you mean "recline," as in *She lies awake at night* or when you mean "is situated," as in *The city lies between a desert and a mountain range.* Also, remember that *lay* is a transitive verb that takes a direct object.

man, mankind   Do not use *man* and *mankind* to refer to all people in general. Instead, consider using *people, men and women, humans,* or *humankind.*

principal, principle   Use *principal* when you refer to a school administrator or an amount of money. Use *principle* when you are referring to a law, conviction, or fundamental truth. You can also use *principal* as an adjective meaning "major" or "most important," as in *The principal players in the decision were Sue Marks and Tom Cohen.*

quotation, quote   Use *quotation* when your sentence requires a noun, as in *The quotation from Nobel laureate Joseph Goldstein was used to lend credence to the theory.* Use *quote* when your sentence requires a verb, as in *She asked Goldstein whether she could quote him.*

raise, rise   Use *raise* when you mean "to lift." Use *rise* when you mean "to get up." Remember that *raise* is transitive and takes a direct object; *rise* is intransitive.

set, sit   Use *set* when you mean "to place." *Set* is a transitive verb that requires an object, as in *I set the book on the table.* Do not use *set* to mean "to sit" in formal writing.

sit, set   See *set, sit.*

so   Do not use *so* in formal writing to mean "very" or "extremely," as in *He is so entertaining.* Use *very, extremely,* or, preferably, a more specific intensifier instead. Or follow *so* with an explanation preceded by *that,* as in *The reaction to the Freedom Riders was* <u>so violent that</u> *Robert F. Kennedy ordered a military escort.*

than, then   Use *than* when you mean "as compared with," as in *The violin is smaller than the cello.* Use *then* when you are stating a sequence of events, as in *First, he learned how to play the violin. Then he learned to play the cello.* Also use *then* when you mean "at that time" or "therefore."

that, which   Use *that* or *which* in an essential (or restrictive) clause, or a clause that is necessary to the meaning of the sentence, as in *This is the book that explains Locke's philosophy.* Use *which* in a nonessential (nonrestrictive) clause, or one that is not necessary to the meaning of the sentence, as in *My library just acquired Smith's book on Locke, which is not always easy to find.*

their, there, they're   Use *their* as a possessive pronoun, as in *Their father prevented William and Henry James from being under the control of any one teacher for more than a year.* Use *there* to refer to a place, as the opposite of *here.* Use *they're* to mean "they are."

use, utilize   When you need a word that means "use," prefer *use*. *Utilize* is a less direct choice with the same meaning.

very   Avoid using *very* as an intensifier. Sometimes you will want to replace more than one word in order to eliminate *very*. For example, in the sentence *It was a very nice painting*, you could substitute more precise language, such as *It was a colorful [or provocative or highly abstract] painting*.

which, who   Use *which* when you are referring to things. Use *who* when you are referring to people.

who's, whose   Do not use *who's* in formal writing. Use *who is* instead. Use *whose* to show possession, as in *Whose computer did you use?*

who, whom   Use *who* when a sentence requires a subject pronoun, as in *Who can answer this question?* Use *whom* when a sentence requires an object pronoun, as in *Whom did you invite?*

Author/Title Index

Asterisk (*) indicates a student author.

Subject Index

Action plan, for writing, 488–489
  generation of, 17
Advertisment, analyzing,
    256–264
  examples, 257–262
  group response to, 262–263
  individual response to, 262
  projecting an essay on,
    263–264
Almanacs, 560
Analogy
  argument from, 308, 427, 430
    faulty, 441
  to create common ground,
    49–50
  definition of, 427, 430
Analysis (analytical writing),
    231–280
  analytical tools for. *See also*
    Definition(s); Principle
  matching to topic, 275
  sources for identifying,
    257–262
  argument in, 246–248
  collaborative writing for, 276
  commitment to ideas for, 245,
    276
  creating common ground in,
    245–246, 276
  critical points in, 254–255, 280
  deductive arrangement,
    277–278
  definition of, 231
  directing questions to object
    under analysis, 279–280
  discovering ideas for, 244,
    275–276
  evaluation, 253–255, 279–280
  examples of, 232–243

  in explanatory writing,
    190–191
  first draft of, 278
  inductive arrangement,
    277–278
  logic for
    developing, paragraph by
      paragraph, 249–251
    understanding, 248–251,
      277–278
  preparing to write, 243–245,
    275–276
  revision, 253–255, 279–280
  significance of, 255
  structure for, planning,
    246–248, 277
  versus summary, 254
  systematic, 254
  tone for, 246
  topics for, 256. *See also*
    Advertisment,
    analyzing; Television
    shows, analyzing
    content of
  using sources in, 257
  writing, 245–251, 256–278
    with computer, 277
Analyze, definition of, 31
Anecdotes. *See also* Narration
  to advance an idea, 130–131
APA system of documentation,
    621–625
  for in-text citations, 622–623
    distinguishing two authors
      with same last name
      and, 623
    two or more sources in
      single reference and,
      623

    two or more works by
      same author and, 623
    works by two authors and,
      622–623
  for reference lists, 623–625
    books in, 623–624
    other sources in, 625
    periodicals in, 624–625
Argue, definition of, 32
Argument, 403–484. *See also*
    Debate; Rebuttal(s)
  advancing ideas using sources
    in, 435–438, 482–483
  from analogy, 308, 427, 430
    faulty, 441
  in analysis, 246–248
  by appeal to authority, 308,
    427, 431–433
  by appeal to emotion, 427,
    433–434
  by appeal to reason, 427–431
  begged question in, 442
  from causation, 308, 406–407,
    427–429
    confusion with correlation,
      441
    faulty, 440
  challenges to, 481
  claims, 404–407
    answering questions with,
      404–405
    defining terms in, 405,
      439–440
    of fact, supporting, 427
    of policy, supporting, 427
    presenting reasons for,
      406–407
    supporting, 405–407
    of value, supporting, 427

Handbook Index